Silver Burdett

MATHEMATICS

AUTHORS

SENIOR SERIES AUTHORS
Lucy J. Orfan • Bruce R. Vogeli

SENIOR PROBLEM SOLVING AUTHORS
Stephen Krulik • Jesse A. Rudnick

Sadie C. Bragg • Ruth I. Champagne • Gerald A. Goldin • Edith E. Grimsley
Deborah B. Gustafson • John F. LeBlanc • William D. McKillip • Fernand J. Prevost

SILVER BURDETT COMPANY
MORRISTOWN, NJ

Atlanta, GA • Cincinnati, OH • Dallas, TX • Northfield, IL • San Carlos, CA • Agincourt, Ontario

Table of Contents

1 Adding and Subtracting Whole Numbers

1

2 Multiplying and Dividing Whole Numbers

29

3 Adding and Subtracting Decimals

63

Theme: Mountains

Place Value

How big is a trillion?

Trillions			Billions			Millions			Thousands			Ones		
h	t	o	h	t	o	h	t	o	h	t	o	h	t	o
				1,	0	0	0,	0	0	0,	0	0	0	
					5,	3	4	0,	0	0	6,	0	0	0

5 billion

3 hundred million   4 ten million

6 thousand

A stack of one trillion dollar bills is twice as high as Mt. Everest.

The decimal numeration system is a place-value system. Each place has a value ten times the value of the place to its right. The value of a digit depends on its place in the number. Commas separate numbers into periods.

standard form   5,340,006,000

- read   5 billion, 340 million, 6 thousand
- write in words   five billion, three hundred forty million, six thousand

You can show the value of each digit by writing a number in expanded form. Here are two ways to write **5,340,006,000**.

5,000,000,000 + 300,000,000 + 40,000,000 + 6,000

(5 × 1,000,000,000) + (3 × 100,000,000) + (4 × 10,000,000) + (6 × 1,000)

Another Example

standard form   8,024,005,000

- read   8 billion, 24 million, 5 thousand
- write in words   eight billion, twenty-four million, five thousand
- expanded form   8,000,000,000 + 20,000,000 + 4,000,000 + 5,000
   or (8 × 1,000,000,000) + (2 × 10,000,000) + (4 × 1,000,000) + (5 × 1,000)

CLASSWORK

Give the value of the digit 3 for each number. Then write the expanded form in two ways.

1. 350,600   **2.** 48,600,397   **3.** 18,306,489,512

PRACTICE

For the number 8,347,506,129, write the digit that is in the place named.

1. hundred millions
2. ten thousands
3. thousands
4. billions
5. hundreds
6. ten millions

Write the word name for each.

7. 5,126,384
8. 492,578,160
9. 7,354,871,002
10. 725,490,162,300

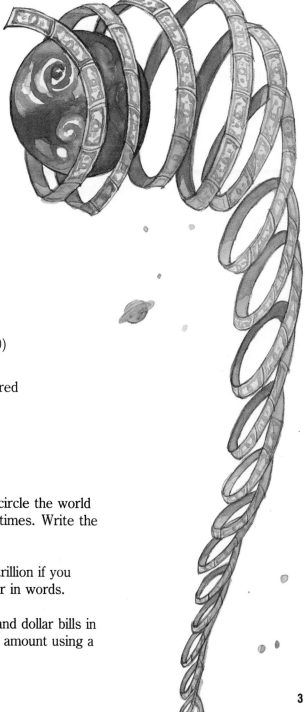

Write the expanded form in two ways.

11. 7,348
12. 109,653
13. 3,000,513
14. 2,000,400,890

Write the standard form for each.

15. 7 million, 618 thousand
16. 43 billion, 5 million, 6 hundred
17. 800,000 + 7,000 + 9
18. 4,000,000 + 90,000 + 6,000
19. seven million, one hundred eighty-seven thousand, three hundred
20. (40 × 1,000,000,000) + (2 × 1,000,000) + (80 × 1,000) + (9 × 1)
21. thirty-seven trillion, six billion, three hundred million, seven thousand, forty-four

APPLICATION

22. A trillion dollar bills set end to end would circle the world three thousand, eight hundred eighty-two times. Write the number in standard form.

23. It would take 31,688 years to count to a trillion if you counted 24 hours a day. Write this number in words.

★ 24. By 1976 there were about 375 ten-thousand dollar bills in circulation in the United States. Write this amount using a number in standard form.

Comparing and Ordering Whole Numbers

About 126,500 people have climbed the Matterhorn, including an 11-year-old girl and a 76-year-old man. About 159,800 people have climbed Mt. Rainier. Have more people climbed Mt. Rainier or the Matterhorn?

Compare 159,800 and 126,500.

Start at the left and compare digits in the same place.

159,800 = 126,500

Find the first place where the digits are different.

159,800 = 126,500

5 > 2

Since 5 > 2, 159,800 > 126,500.

More people climbed Mt. Rainier than the Matterhorn.

List the numbers below in order from least to greatest.

73,138; 72,645; 73,442; 170,382

▶To order numbers from least to greatest, find the least number. Then find the greatest number. Compare the remaining numbers.

7 3 ,138

7 2 ,645 ←——— the least number

7 3 ,442

17 0 ,382 ←——— the whole number with most digits is greatest

Compare 73,138   73,442

1 < 4   so 73,138 < 73,442

The numbers in order are   72,645; 73,138; 73,442; 170,382.

CLASSWORK

Compare. Use >, <, or = for each ●.

1. 79,853 ● 798,524   **2.** 378,692 ● 358,450   **3.** 1,642,692 ● 1,642,450

List in order from least to greatest.

4. 34,896; 34,968; 34,986; 34,698   **5.** 63,701; 65,701; 6,371; 63,507

4

Compare. Use >, <, or = for each ●.

1. 3,212 ● 3,112   >   **2.** 6,341 ● 6,314   **3.** 63,181 ● 63,181

4. 179,684 ● 179,864 <   **5.** 41,457,364 ● 1,453,463   **6.** 7,861,364 ● 7,861,643

7. 875,198 ● 875,189 >   **8.** 60,000 ● 60,100   **9.** 6,483,122 ● 6,483,122

10. 5,436,009 ● 5,346,900   **11.** 7,609,234 ● 76,009,234

12. 96,000,000 ● 9,600,000   **13.** 52,000,780 ● 520,007,806

14. 80,000,000 ● 79,411,282   **15.** 300,468,124 ● 300,648,124

16. 3,002,175,842 ● 301,175,841   **17.** 94,126,754 ● 94,126,754

List in order from least to greatest.

18. 706; 670; 760

19. 8,419; 7,981; 8,149; 8,491

20. 43,926; 34,926; 58,124; 54,385

21. 600,000; 588,732; 598,984; 589,456

List in order from greatest to least.

22. 92,783; 93,738; 92,873

23. 877,873,548; 876,428,374; 877,863,542

★ **24.** 543,821; 534,821; 534,218; 544,821; 535,281

Find the least digit that will make each statement true.

25. 3,1█4,897 > 3,128,675   **26.** 58,624 < 58,█42   **27.** 1█8,917 < 148,894

28. 163,4█5 = 163,485   **29.** 428,█56 > 428,364   **30.** 18,█33,485 = 18,933,485

★ **31.** How many three-digit numbers can be written using each
of the digits 5, 6, and 7 only once in each number? List
the numbers in order from least to greatest.

APPLICATION

32. Does Mt. Whitney or Mt. Rainier offer a
mountain climber the farther climb?

33. Which mountain is the highest?

34. Which mountains are lower than Mt.
Rainier?

★ **35.** List the heights of the mountains in order
from greatest to least.

U.S. MOUNTAINS	
Name	**Height in Feet**
Mt. Whitney	14,495
Mt. McKinley	20,320
Mt. Hood	11,245
Mt. Rainier	14,410
Pikes Peak	14,110

Rounding Whole Numbers

An archeologist is raising money for an expedition to the Andes. She budgeted the cost to be $168,745. To the nearest hundred thousand, about how much money will she need to raise?

Round $168,745 to the nearest hundred thousand.

Step 1   Find the rounding place.   1**6**8,000
↓

Step 2   Look at the digit to the right.   16**8**,000

If it is less than 5, leave the digit in the rounding place unchanged.

If it is 5 or more, increase the digit in the rounding place by 1.   6 > 5
2__,___

Step 3   Change each digit to the right of the rounding place to zero.   200,000

The archeologist will need to raise about $200,000.

More Examples

a. Round to the nearest million.   8,507,263   rounds to   9,000,000

b. Round to the nearest dollar. $239.24   rounds to $239

c. Round to the nearest ten dollars. $197   rounds to $200

CLASSWORK

Round 977,561,079 to the place named.

1. nearest thousand   **2.** nearest hundred thousand   **3.** nearest million

Round to the nearest dollar and the nearest ten dollars.

4. $289.36   **5.** $143.45   **6.** $176.75

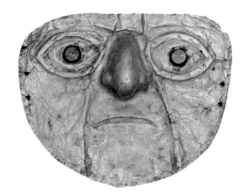

PRACTICE

Round each number to the place named.

nearest thousand	**1.** 4,399	**2.** 14,812	**3.** 347,196
nearest ten thousand	**4.** 16,941	**5.** 37,464	**6.** 354,726
nearest hundred thousand	**7.** 156,000	**8.** 421,200	**9.** 951,000
nearest million	**10.** 4,385,622	**11.** 8,760,025	**12.** 6,195,835
nearest dollar	**13.** $35.16	**14.** $57.65	**15.** $72.50
nearest ten dollars	**16.** $67.18	**17.** $95.15	**18.** $73.95

Write the rounding place for each.

19. 74 → 70

20. 479 → 500

21. 7,861 → 8,000

22. 244,505 → 200,000

23. $261.95 → $262

24. $349.50 → $300

Find the least and the greatest possible original numbers.

	Rounding Place	Rounded Number	Least Number	Greatest Number
	Hundreds	200	150	249
★ **25.**	Thousands	7,000		
★ **26.**	Hundred Thousands	400,000		

★ **27.** How many numbers can be rounded to 40 when rounding to the nearest 10?

★ **28.** How many numbers can be rounded to 400 when rounding to the nearest 100?

APPLICATION

29. Round each number in the table to the nearest ten thousand dollars.

30. Round each number in the table to the nearest hundred thousand dollars.

Expedition	Cost
Lake Titicaca	$165,000
Machu Picchu	$256,000
Arica	$115,000

Problem Solving

FACTS FROM PICTURES AND TEXT

The College Hiking Club is on a rock-climbing trip. Robert is taking the Middle Route up the mountain. He climbed 485 meters (m), then stopped on a ledge for a short rest. He then climbed another 360 m to the next ledge. How much farther does he have to go to reach the top?

Many kinds of problem-solving situations occur in school, at home, at work, or at play. In order to become a good problem-solver, you must have a plan to follow. Here is a four-step plan for solving this and other problems.

THINK   **What is the question?**

How much farther does Robert have to go to reach the top?

What are the facts?

Sometimes you must gather facts from the text and also from the picture. The story says that Robert has taken the Middle Route and climbed distances of 485 m and 360 m. The picture shows that the Middle Route is 1,675 m long.

PLAN   **How can the answer be found?**

Add the distances Robert has already climbed. Subtract that sum from the total distance of the Middle Route.

SOLVE   **Carry out the plan. Do the work and find the answer.**

$$
\begin{array}{ll}
485 \text{ m} & 1{,}675 \text{ m} \text{ (total distance)} \\
\underline{+\ 360 \text{ m}} & \underline{-\ \ \ 845 \text{ m}} \text{ (distance climbed)} \\
845 \text{ m} & \ \ 830 \text{ m}
\end{array}
$$

Robert has to climb 830 m more to get to the top.

LOOK   **Has the question been answered? Is your arithmetic**
BACK   **correct? Does your answer make sense?**

$$
\begin{array}{r}
\text{Add to check the answer.} \quad 845 \\
\underline{+\ 830} \\
1{,}675
\end{array}
$$

The answer is correct.

Use the picture on page 8 to answer the questions.

1. How much longer is the Middle Route than the Short Scramble?

2. How much shorter is the Short Scramble than Climbers' Folly?

3. Susan climbed 1,885 meters up Climbers' Folly. How much farther does she have to ascend to reach the top?

4. Betty climbed the Middle Route to the top. The last time she climbed the mountain, she took the Short Scramble. How many meters did she climb in all on both routes?

5. David climbed 550 m, rested on a ledge, and then climbed another 600 m up the Short Scramble. How much farther must he climb to reach the top?

6. Luis has 650 m left to climb on Climbers' Folly. Greta has 150 m left to climb on the Middle Route. Who has climbed farther? How much farther?

Use the information on the poster at the right to solve the following.

7. Where is the concert being held?

8. If Bruno arrives at 7:30 P.M., will he see the whole concert?

9. What group is playing?

10. If Kathy has $12.00, can she buy two tickets at the door?

★ 11. Jesse has $42.00. What is the maximum number of tickets he can buy on Friday? If he waits until the concert on Saturday, how many tickets can he buy?

★ 12. Frank bought two tickets in advance and two at the door. He spent $4.00 on refreshments. How much did he spend altogether?

☆ Country Music Concert ☆
SILVER MOUNTAIN ARENA
Saturday, June 27
7:00 PM – 11:00 PM

Starring The Mountaineers ☆

Admission $5.50 advance purchase
$7.50 at the door

═══ CREATE YOUR OWN PROBLEM ═══

The picture shows three mountains and their heights. Create a problem that uses both addition and subtraction.

Mt. Washington   Mt. Mitchell   Mt McKinley
1,917 m   2,057 m   6,194 m

Properties of Addition

How many beginner and intermediate runs does Pine Hill have?

$$11 + 16 = 27$$

How many ski runs does Pine Hill have?

$$(11 + 16) + 13 = 40$$

Pine Hill has 27 beginner and intermediate runs. It has 40 ski runs in all.

▶ Use the properties of addition to help find the sums.

Commutative Property	The order of the addends does not change the sum.

$$a + b = b + a$$
$$11 + 16 = 16 + 11$$

Associative Property	The way that addends are grouped does not change the sum.

$$(a + b) + c = a + (b + c)$$
$$(11 + 16) + 13 = 11 + (16 + 13)$$
Work inside the parentheses first.

Identity Property	Any number plus zero is that number.

$$a + 0 = a \qquad 0 + a = a$$
$$27 + 0 = 27 \qquad 0 + 40 = 40$$

You can use the properties to add quickly and easily.

$$27 + 34 + 3 \qquad\qquad (16 + 17) + 13$$

$$27 + 3 = 30 \qquad\qquad 16 + (17 + 13)$$
$$30 + 34 = 64 \qquad\qquad 16 + \quad 30 \quad = 46$$

CLASSWORK

Find each missing addend. Name the properties you used.

1. $23 + 0 = \square$

2. $(76 + 30) + 14 = 76 + (30 + \square)$

3. $14 + 62 = \square + 14$

4. $(28 + 17) + 12 = 28 + (\square + 17)$

PRACTICE

Name the properties that are used.

1. $(7 + 8) + 2 = 7 + (8 + 2)$ 2. $3 + 9 = 9 + 3$ 3. $14 + 0 = 14$
4. $4 + (7 + 6) = 4 + (6 + 7)$ 5. $(5 + 3) + 7 = 5 + (3 + 7)$ 6. $(5 + 1) + 2 = 5 + (2 + 1)$

Find each missing addend. Name the properties you used.

7. $(12 + 3) + 5 = \square + (3 + 5)$ 8. $27 + \square = 27$
9. $(32 + \square) + 8 = 32 + (8 + 7)$ 10. $35 + 0 + \square = 35 + 9 + 0$
11. $(4 + \square) + 16 = 4 + (16 + 12)$ 12. $(2 + 19) + \square = (2 + 8) + 19$

Use the properties to complete each sentence.

13. $24 + 12 + 6 = \square$ 14. $0 + 45 + 7 = \square$ 15. $33 + 10 + 7 = \square$
16. $65 + 20 + 115 = \square$ 17. $479 + 0 = \square$ 18. $238 + 72 = \square$
19. $0 + 574 = \square$ 20. $127 + 54 + 13 = \square$ 21. $113 + 17 + 54 = \square$
22. $536 + 57 + 94 = \square$ 23. $702 + 34 + 98 = \square$ 24. $621 + 63 + 19 = \square$
25. $1{,}613 + 47 + 0 = \square$ 26. $327 + 22 + 81 = \square$ ★27. $2{,}201 + 19 + 523 = \square$

APPLICATION

28. The sum of the number of chair lifts and tows is 12. There are 4 chair lifts. How many tows are there?

29. There are 2 more T-bars than chair lifts. What is the total number of T-bars and chair lifts?

30. What is the sum of the number of T-bars and tows?

★31. Arrange the digits 1, 2, 3, 4, 5, 6, 7, 8, and 9 in the circles on the triangle to the right so that the sum along each side is 17.

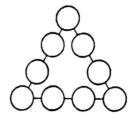

11

Estimating Sums and Differences

The Lee family is vacationing in the Rocky Mountains. Their travel record and the map show part of their route.

Estimate the total number of miles they traveled for the days shown.

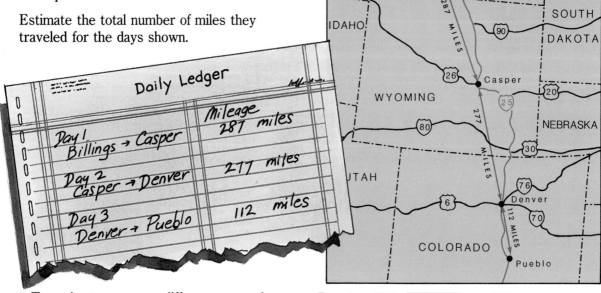

Daily Ledger

Mileage	
Day 1 Billings → Casper	287 miles
Day 2 Casper → Denver	277 miles
Day 3 Denver → Pueblo	112 miles

▶To estimate a sum or difference, round each number to the greatest place of the greatest number. Then add or subtract.

They traveled about 700 miles.

Day 1	287	rounds to	300
Day 2	277	rounds to	300
Day 3	112	rounds to	+ 100
			700

To get a closer estimate, round to one more place to the right.

a. Estimate 8,115 − 475.

Round to nearest thousand.

$$\begin{array}{r} 8,000 \\ -\quad\ 0 \\ \hline 8,000 \end{array}$$ Estimate too large

Round to nearest hundred.

$$\begin{array}{r} 8,100 \\ -\quad 500 \\ \hline 7,600 \end{array}$$ Closer estimate

b. Estimate $225.67 + $19.75.

Round to nearest hundred.

$$\begin{array}{r} \$200 \\ +\quad\ 0 \\ \hline \$200 \end{array}$$ Estimate too small

Round to nearest ten.

$$\begin{array}{r} \$230 \\ +\quad 20 \\ \hline \$250 \end{array}$$ Closer estimate

CLASSWORK

Give the estimate and the closer estimate.

1. $\begin{array}{r} 293 \\ + 482 \end{array}$

2. $\begin{array}{r} \$821 \\ -\ 385 \end{array}$

3. $\begin{array}{r} 4,129 \\ -\ 792 \end{array}$

4. $\begin{array}{r} 6,821 \\ + 5,333 \end{array}$

5. $\begin{array}{r} 8,215 \\ - 1,748 \end{array}$

6. $4,315 − $295   7. 17,462 + 4,657   8. 1,552 + 2,485 + 3,068   9. 715,609 − 47,380

Give the estimate and the closer estimate.

1. 5,621
    − 1,243

2. 4,962
    + 2,318

3. 25,148
    − 17,809

4. $6,314
    − 1,867

5. 10,490
    − 5,675

6. 1,206
    + 8,520

7. 54,321
    + 6,856

8. 72,560
    − 1,720

9. $65,920
    + 8,156

10. 37,595
    − 16,578

11. $4,014
    8,627
    + 2,133

12. $2,809
    362
    + 458

13. 693,418
    − 64,107

14. 978,147
    − 231,915

15. $394,128
    854,796
    + 12,511

16. 9,816 − 3,562

17. $7,841 − $2,109

18. 9,075 + 2,314 + 5,921

19. 68,215 − 48,600

20. $26,215 + $48,911

21. 89,108 + 12,164 + 24,571

22. 76,013 − 9,215

23. $72,146 + $8,259

24. $5,289 + $36,111

25. 520,781 − 58,123

26. 189,701 − 132,623

27. 350,901 + 201,631

★ 28. (19,542 + 4,852) − 9,711

★ 29. (51,076 − 11,756) + 8,339

APPLICATION

30. The expenses for the Lees' trip were $884.68 for hotels, $63.42 for souvenirs, and $354.88 for meals. Estimate the total amount.

31. The Lees visited three national parks. Which park is largest? About how much larger is the largest park than the other two combined?

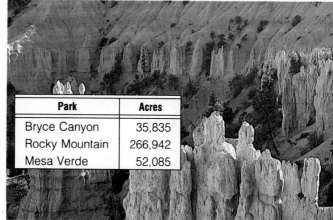

Park	Acres
Bryce Canyon	35,835
Rocky Mountain	266,942
Mesa Verde	52,085

MENTAL ARITHMETIC

Add mentally by keeping partial sums in your head.

Think

Example   14 { 14

17 { +10 = 24
      + 7 = 31

26 { +20 = 51
      + 6 = 57

+ 18 { +10 = 67
        + 8 = 75

75

1. 12
    19
    23
    + 15

2. 75
    24
    16
    + 13

3. 11
    64
    34
    45
    + 51

4. 54
    42
    63
    85
    + 22

Adding

Jeff's family traveled 1,975 miles north through the Canadian Rockies last summer. They drove 2,464 miles on the return trip. How many miles did they travel in all?

Add to find the total miles.
Regroup if necessary.

Step 1	Step 2
Add ones.	Add tens.

$$\begin{array}{r} 1{,}975 \\ +\,2{,}464 \\ \hline 9 \end{array} \qquad \begin{array}{r} \overset{1}{1}{,}975 \\ +\,2{,}464 \\ \hline 39 \end{array}$$

Step 3	Step 4
Add hundreds.	Add thousands.

$$\begin{array}{r} \overset{1\,1}{1}{,}975 \\ +\,2{,}464 \\ \hline 439 \end{array} \qquad \begin{array}{r} \overset{1\,1}{1}{,}975 \\ +\,2{,}464 \\ \hline 4{,}439 \end{array}$$

Jeff's family traveled 4,439 miles.

Estimate to be sure the answer makes sense or add in reverse order to check.

Estimate.   Add.

1,975	rounds to	2,000	1,975 ↑
+ 2,464	rounds to	+ 2,000	+ 2,464
		4,000	4,439

More Examples

a.
$$\begin{array}{r} \overset{1}{\$}59.21 \\ +\,14.07 \\ \hline \$73.28 \end{array}$$

b.
$$\begin{array}{r} \overset{1\ 1}{2}14{,}381 \\ +\,16{,}584 \\ \hline 230{,}965 \end{array}$$

c.
$$\begin{array}{r} \overset{1}{5}7{,}009 \\ +\,16{,}340 \\ \hline 73{,}349 \end{array}$$

d.
$$\begin{array}{r} \$\ \overset{11\ 1}{2}4.34 \\ +\,89.96 \\ \hline \$114.30 \end{array}$$

CLASSWORK

Add. Estimate to be sure each answer makes sense.

1.
$$\begin{array}{r} 1{,}657 \\ +\ 918 \\ \hline \end{array}$$

2.
$$\begin{array}{r} 21{,}486 \\ +\ 9{,}314 \\ \hline \end{array}$$

3.
$$\begin{array}{r} \$449.50 \\ +\ 116.13 \\ \hline \end{array}$$

4.
$$\begin{array}{r} \$674.05 \\ +\ 72.59 \\ \hline \end{array}$$

5.
$$\begin{array}{r} 19{,}009 \\ +\ 6{,}131 \\ \hline \end{array}$$

6. 15,655 + 3,836 + 25,944

7. 367,302 + 424,878

14

PRACTICE

Find each sum. Add in reverse order to check.

1. 643
    + 281

2. 825
    + 719

3. $469.27
    + 134.08

Add. Estimate to be sure each answer makes sense.

4. 618
    73
    + 164

5. 24,869
    13,527
    +   634

6. 232,606
    604,007
    + 116,845

7. $293.00 + $94.70 + $5.86

8. $482.15 + $189.60 + $74.09 + $219.12

Use properties to make each sentence true. Compute each sum to check.

9. 37 + 12 = ☐ + 37

10. 87 + (75 + 42) = (87 + ☐) + 42

★11. 66 + 0 + 344 + ☐ = 344 + ☐ + 66 + 0

Complete. Add 6 to the input and double.

	Input	Output
	7	26
12.	9	
13.		36
14.	18	

	Input	Output
	5	22
15.		44
16.		70
17.	41	

	Input	Output
	14	40
18.	21	
19.		68
20.	35	

	Input	Output
	31	74
21.		88
22.	45	
23.		118

APPLICATION

24. Jeff bought a compass for $7.50, a flashlight for $18.25, and hiking boots for $27.50. Estimate the total cost. Then find the actual cost.

25. Estimate the cost of three backpacks. Then find the actual cost.

$18.50 Tax $1.20

Mixed Practice

1. 72 + 49

2. 648 + 75

3. $28.09
    + 15.38

4. 197
    638
    + 425

5. 86
    − 49

6. 125 − 37

7. $7.21
    − 6.98

8. $1,203.05
    548.28
    +   97.83

9. 0 + 89 + 123

10. 70 − 19

11. 1,575
     + 293

Round to the nearest thousand.

12. 5,673

13. 10,099

14. 16,582

15. 29,850

16. 172,779

15

Subtracting

Jenny hiked the Appalachian Trail from Maine to Georgia. How much higher was the climb up Mt. Katahdin than the climb up Springer Mountain?

Subtract to find the difference.

Regroup if necessary.

Step 1	Step 2	Step 3	Step 4
Subtract ones.	Subtract tens.	Subtract hundreds.	Subtract thousands.

Step 1
$$\begin{array}{r} 5,267 \\ -\ 3,782 \\ \hline 5 \end{array}$$

Step 2
$$\begin{array}{r} 5,2\overset{1\ 16}{\cancel{6}}7 \\ -\ 3,782 \\ \hline 85 \end{array}$$

Step 3
$$\begin{array}{r} \overset{4}{\cancel{5}},\overset{\overset{11}{\cancel{1}}\ 16}{\cancel{2}\cancel{6}}7 \\ -\ 3,782 \\ \hline 485 \end{array}$$

Step 4
$$\begin{array}{r} \overset{4}{\cancel{5}},\overset{\overset{11}{\cancel{1}}\ 16}{\cancel{2}\cancel{6}}7 \\ -\ 3,782 \\ \hline 1,485 \end{array}$$

Mt. Katahdin is 1,485 feet higher than Springer Mountain.

Estimate to be sure the answer makes sense, or add to check.

Estimate.

5,267	rounds to	5,000
−3,782	rounds to	−4,000
1,485		1,000

Add.

$$\begin{array}{r} 5,267 \\ -3,782 \\ \hline 1,485 \end{array} \qquad \begin{array}{r} 3,782 \\ +\ 1,485 \\ \hline 5,267 \end{array}$$

More Examples

a.
$$\begin{array}{r} \overset{7}{\cancel{8}},\overset{\overset{1213}{\cancel{2}\cancel{3}}16}{\cancel{4}\cancel{6}} \\ -\ \ \ \ 747 \\ \hline 7,599 \end{array}$$

b.
$$\begin{array}{r} 5\overset{4}{\cancel{5}},\overset{11\ 0\ 15}{\cancel{1}\cancel{1}\cancel{5}} \\ -\ 12,306 \\ \hline 42,809 \end{array}$$

c.
$$\begin{array}{r} \$1\overset{6\ 10}{\cancel{7}\cancel{0}}.\overset{8\ 10}{\cancel{9}\cancel{0}} \\ -\ \ 151.15 \\ \hline \$\ \ 19.75 \end{array}$$

d.
$$\begin{array}{r} \overset{2\ 11}{\cancel{3}\cancel{1}},\overset{0\ 17}{4\cancel{1}\cancel{7}} \\ -\ 14,008 \\ \hline 17,409 \end{array}$$

CLASSWORK

Subtract. Estimate to be sure each answer makes sense.

1.
$$\begin{array}{r} \$29.46 \\ -\ 18.75 \end{array}$$

2.
$$\begin{array}{r} 15,923 \\ -\ 6,487 \end{array}$$

3.
$$\begin{array}{r} 150,020 \\ -\ 28,431 \end{array}$$

4.
$$\begin{array}{r} \$81.09 \\ -\ 12.24 \end{array}$$

5.
$$\begin{array}{r} \$51.15 \\ -\ 17.25 \end{array}$$

6. $38,921 - 17,843$ 7. $407,535 - 253,061$ 8. $\$6,728.92 - \$956.08$

Subtract. Add to check.

1. 782 − 467	**2.** 946 − 875	**3.** 423 − 201	**4.** $84.91 − 63.99	**5.** 8,346 − 747
6. 23,065 − 1,890	**7.** 652,706 − 29,070	**8.** $483.47 − 65.08	**9.** 2,627,331 − 1,418,425	**10.** 1,759,607 − 1,631,213

Subtract. Estimate to be sure each answer makes sense.

11. 65,030 − 43,092	**12.** 80,019 − 38,520	**13.** 18,127 − 6,198	**14.** $950.34 − 616.85	**15.** $6,624.62 − 4,916.07

16. 367,405 − 147,117 **17.** 8,467,624 − 2,109,669

18. 5,161,519 − 2,879,321 **19.** $3,507.17 − $2,879.05

Compare. Use >, <, or = for each ⬤.

20. 416 − 201 ⬤ 521 − 427 **21.** 1,739 − 1,003 ⬤ 941 − 109

22. $264.15 − $118.00 ⬤ $294.75 − $148.60 **23.** 1,879 − 613 ⬤ 1,688 − 513

Find each missing digit.

24. 9 2 1 − 4 ▮ 8 ▮ 8	**★25.** 7, 6 2 0 − 2 ▮ 8 7, ▮ 4 ▮	**★26.** $1 7 ▮ . 9 6 − 6 3 . ▮ 5 $▮ ▮ 5 . 5 ▮	**★27.** 5, 4 6 ▮ − 8 7 4 4, ▮ ▮ 8	**★28.** 7 ▮ , 1 ▮ 6 − 7 4, ▮ 8 0 7 4 6

APPLICATION

Daniel Boone	Born	Crossed the Appalachians	Died
	1734	1767	1820

29. How many years did Daniel Boone live?

30. Daniel Boone discovered Kentucky. How old was he when he first crossed the Appalachian Mountains?

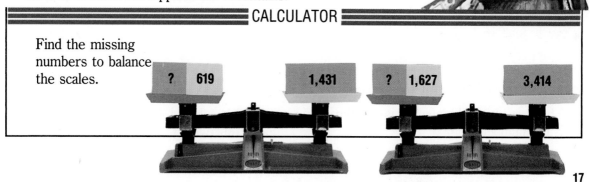

CALCULATOR

Find the missing
numbers to balance
the scales.

? 619   1,431   ? 1,627   3,414

Equations

Sancho Panza's donkey would not start up the mountain trail until his packs were perfectly balanced. How many pounds should Sancho add to the left pack to make the sides equal?

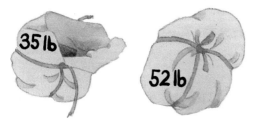

35 pounds plus some more equals 52 pounds.

Write $35 + n = 52$.

n is a variable. A variable stands for a number that makes the sentence true. $35 + n = 52$ is a number sentence, or **equation**.

To solve $35 + n = 52$, write a related equation.

$35 + n = 52$ **Think** Addition and subtraction
$n = 52 - 35$ are inverse operations.

So $\quad n = 17$ **Check** $35 + 17 = 52$
Replace n with 17.

Sancho must add 17 pounds to the pack.

▶Solve an addition equation by using a related subtraction equation.

$a + 5 = 11$
$\quad a = 11 - 5$
$\quad a = 6$ **Check** $6 + 5 = 11$

▶Solve a subtraction equation by using a related addition equation.

$b - 6 = 4$
$\quad b = 4 + 6$
$\quad b = 10$ **Check** $10 - 6 = 4$

CLASSWORK

Write a related equation to solve each.

1. $8 + a = 13$ **2.** $b - 7 = 12$ **3.** $c - 9 = 7$ **4.** $d + 6 = 11$ **5.** $v + 3 = 17$

6. $37 = e - 19$ **7.** $12 + f = 41$ **8.** $g + 16 = 30$ **9.** $7 = h - 21$ **10.** $47 = h + 31$

Write an equation for each problem. Then write a related equation to solve. Use r for the variable.

11. The sum of 8 and a number is 37. What is the number?

12. If 25 is subtracted from a number, the difference is 11. What is the number?

PRACTICE

Write a related equation for each. Then solve.

1. $a + 52 = 91$
2. $t + 65 = 87$
3. $n + 14 = 19$
4. $d - 9 = 18$
5. $x - 19 = 35$
6. $b + 39 = 79$
7. $17 + n = 32$
8. $63 = 48 + r$

Use a related equation to solve each.

9. $63 = a + 25$
10. $a + 8 = 31$
11. $b - 12 = 4$
12. $16 + c = 19$
13. $y + 14 = 29$
14. $x + 19 = 35$
15. $5 = m + 2$
16. $n - 15 = 13$
17. $23 + c = 51$
18. $h + 39 = 83$
19. $29 = 13 + s$
20. $45 = n + 22$
21. $58 = g + 35$
22. $m - 17 = 39$
23. $g + 46 = 92$
24. $16 + r = 24$
25. $24 + t = 38$
26. $18 + a = 71$
27. $31 + w = 63$
28. $17 + s = 85$
★29. $y - 350 = 350$
★30. $16 + 5 + n = 24$
★31. $10 - 4 + t = 14$
★32. $7 - 5 = m - 8$

APPLICATION

Write an equation for each problem. Then write a related equation to solve. Use n for the variable.

33. A number plus 124 equals 148. What is the number?

34. 220 is subtracted from a number. The difference is 120. Find the number.

35. Sancho Panza and his donkey set out on a 45-mile trip. They stopped to rest after 18 miles. How many miles were left to travel?

36. Sancho unpacked 29 pounds from the saddlebag. The saddlebag then weighed 56 pounds. How many pounds did it weigh before unpacking?

MATH HISTORY

The mathematician Leonardo Fibonacci (1170–1250) discovered this sequence of numbers. 1, 1, 2, 3, 5, 8, 13, . . .

The three dots mean the numbers continue in the same pattern. Each new number is found by adding the two previous numbers.

$0 + 1 = 1; 1 + 1 = 2; 1 + 2 = 3; 2 + 3 = 5 . . .$

Find the next 10 numbers in the Fibonacci sequence.

Problem Solving

SKILLS AND STRATEGIES REVIEW Camping

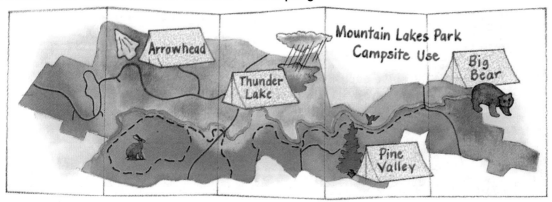

Ranger Perkins is studying the use of campsites in Mountain Lakes Park. The chart shows how many campsites were used during two months in different parts of the park.

Use the map to answer the questions.

1. How many campers did Thunder Lake have in July?

2. How many campers did Arrowhead have in June?

3. Which site had the fewest campers in July?

4. Which site had the most campers in June?

5. How many more people used the Pine Valley site than used the Big Bear site in June?

6. What was the increase in attendance at Thunder Lake from June to July?

7. Was the increase in attendance from June to July greater at Arrowhead or Big Bear? How much greater?

8. What was the total attendance at the campsites for June and July?

9. Any campsite that has had over 5,000 campers by the end of July holds a special party. Which sites had parties?

10. How many more people would have had to come to Pine Valley in July in order for the site to show an increase in attendance?

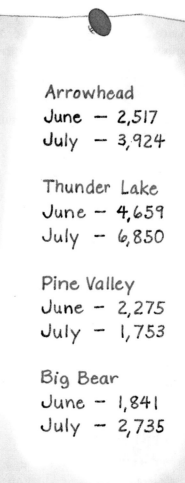

Arrowhead
June — 2,517
July — 3,924

Thunder Lake
June — 4,659
July — 6,850

Pine Valley
June — 2,275
July — 1,753

Big Bear
June — 1,841
July — 2,735

Problem Solving

WHAT IF. . . ?

So far 1,875,643 people have taken the SCENIC GONDOLA RIDE

THE SCENIC GONDOLA RIDE
of Mountain Lakes Park

1½ hours of breathtaking views

Adults	$ 12.50
Youths (ages 8-15)	$ 10.50
Children (ages 3-7)	$ 8.50

Look at the picture. Then answer the questions.

1. What would be the total cost of tickets for Mr. and Mrs. Jacoby and their nine-year-old son, Steve?

2. Mrs. West used a $50 bill to pay for herself and her two children, ages 7 and 12. How much change will she receive?

3. Mr. and Mrs. Marens and their sons Tony, age 12, and Ralph, age 6, want to go on the gondola ride. They have $35.00. Can they go?

★ 4. The Warrens take the noon ride. Their home is an hour's ride away. About what time will they arrive home if they leave right after the ride?

What if Mr. and Mrs. Sloane go on the ride and afterward spend $6.00 for souvenirs and $4.50 for refreshments?

5. How much will they spend in all?

6. How much will they have left from $45?

7. Can they take their daughter Susan, age 5, on the ride too?

8. How much will they have left from $45 if they take Susan on the ride?

What if children can take the ride for half price after 5:00 P.M.?

9. How much will it cost Mr. and Mrs. Fong and their two children, ages 13 and 7, to go on the ride at 6:00 P.M.?

10. How much would a family of 2 adults and 3 children, ages 4, 6, and 9, save by waiting until 5:30 P.M. to take the ride?

What if 29,372 people take the ride in June and 38,596 people take the ride in July?

11. How many visitors will the sign list at the end of July?

12. How many visitors will be needed in August to bring the number of visitors up to 2,000,000?

★ 13. Before the summer season, the Mountain Lakes Tourist Bureau estimated that 26,575 people would take the gondola ride in June and 43,650 people would take the ride in July. How close was the estimate to the actual number of visitors?

★ 14. The Mountain Lakes Tourist Bureau is planning an advertising campaign to attract visitors during the month of August. They hope to have 18,250 more riders on the gondola in August than in July. What will be the number of visitors to date at the end of August?

CHAPTER REVIEW

Write the standard form for each. pages 2–3

1. 45 million, 6 hundred

2. 57 billion, 24 thousand, 8

3. 7,000,000,000,000 + 30,000,000,000 + 4,000,000,000 + 70,000,000 + 5,000,000 + 100,000 + 6,000 + 200

For the number 635,617,105,006 write the digit that is in the place named. pages 2–3

4. ten millions

5. hundred billions

6. ten thousands

Compare. Use > or < for ⬤. pages 4–5

7. 571,604 ⬤ 517,406

8. 237,941 ⬤ 239,741

Round each number to the place named. pages 6–7

9. nearest hundred thousand 95,671,034

10. nearest million 617,504,312

Write the property that is used for each. pages 10–11

11. (24 + 11) + 3 = 24 + (11 + 3)

12. 75 + 0 = 75

13. 95 + 8 = 8 + 95

Choose the estimated sum or difference that is closer to the actual sum or difference. pages 12–13

14.
```
  728,263    a. 700,000
-  59,306    b. 670,000
```

15.
```
  $348    a. $600
   273    b. $650
+   26
```

16.
```
  667,419    a. 600,000
-  74,815    b. 700,000
```

Add or subtract. pages 14–17

17. 52 + 39

18. 115,176 + 18,492

19. $367,419 − $74,815

20.
```
  $593.57
- 159.35
```

21.
```
    342
  1,262
+ 1,538
```

22.
```
  $5,614.42
    882.60
     23.17
+    47.01
```

23.
```
  513,000
- 58,716
```

Write a related equation for each. Then solve. pages 18–19

24. $p - 79 = 81$

25. $68 + s = 235$

26. $m + 312 = 540$

Solve. pages 8–9, 20–21

27. The Alpine Club has 5,467 members. The Highland Hiking Club has 2,682 members. How many more members does the Alpine Club have?

28. Estimate the total cost of the camping equipment. Then find the actual cost.

$27.00

$67.42

$83.90

CHAPTER TEST

Write the expanded form in two ways.

1. 307,050   **2.** 21,000,500   **3.** 8,250,000,000

List in order from least to greatest.

4. 56,821; 568,210; 568,120   **5.** 786,500,250; 78,650,250; 785,600,250

Round each number to the place named.

6. nearest dollar $647.56   **7.** nearest million   481,986,305

Choose the estimated sum or difference that is closer to the actual sum or difference.

8. 529,290   **a.** 500,000   **9.** $437   **a.** $840   **10.** 546,094   **a.** 540,000
   − 78,349   **b.** 450,000   361   **b.** $800   − 14,185   **b.** 500,000
                  + 39

Add or subtract.

11. 83 − 67   **12.** 147,329 + 321,943   **13.** $246,378 − $47,928

14. $692,401   **15.**   24,880   **16.** $4,382.71   **17.**   25,825
    − 593,732   7,649   397.27   − 17,726
               + 19,749   11.92
                            + 560.24

Write the property that is used for each.

18. (16 + 4) + 7 = 16 + (4 + 7)   **19.** 25 + 0 = 25   **20.** 17 + 4 = 4 + 17

Write a related equation for each. Then solve.

21. $n − 114 = 62$ **22.** $47 + d = 153$ **23.** $r + 216 = 412$

Solve.

24. Find the difference in the heights of the two mountains.

25. A trip's expenses were $18.50; $79.00; $87.50; and $375.40. Give an estimate and then find the total expenses.

HIKE IN COLORADO

Mount Elbert 14,433 feet   Mount Columbia 14,073 feet

Find this 3-digit number. The sum of its digits is 14. The hundreds digit is 2 less than the ones digit. The tens digit is twice the hundreds digit.

EGYPTIAN CODE

The ancient Egyptians used a numeration system based on grouping by tens. The table below shows the symbols that they used.

SYMBOL		DECIMAL-SYSTEM VALUE	SYMBOL		DECIMAL-SYSTEM VALUE
│	staff	1	∬	pointing finger	10,000
∩	heel bone	10	⌒	tadpole	100,000
9	scroll	100	⅄	astonished man	1,000,000
∮	lotus flower	1,000			

The Egyptian system of numeration was not a place-value system. The value of a number did not change as the position of a symbol changed. Combinations of the symbols were used to name numbers.

9∩∩∩│ = 100 + 10 + 10 + 10 + 1 = 131

⅄⌒ = 1,000,000 + 100,000 = 1,100,000

∮ ∮∩ = 1,000 + 1,000 + 10 = 2,010

∬ 9││││ = 10,000 + 100 + 4 = 10,104

99∩∩∩│││ could name the same number as 9∩9∩∩│││

Break the Code!

**Translate each Egyptian number into a standard number.
Then find the matching letter for each in the code box below
to read the message.**

99│││ ∩∩│││││ │││││∩∩ ∮   │││∩∩ ∮   ∮ 9│││ ∩∩│││││

│∩∩ 999││││ ∬9│ ∩∩│││ ││99 │∩∩∩ ∩∩∮ │999

A	B	C	D	E	F	G	H	I	J	K	L	M
23	302	111	1,020	24	30	11	103	31	12	10,110	1,200	203

N	O	P	Q	R	S	T	U	V	W	X	Y	Z
310	10	21	13	10,101	301	1,000	403	37	1,001	42	304	40

Make up your own coded message using the Egyptian symbols. Challenge a friend to decode it.

LOGIC: VENN DIAGRAMS

A Venn diagram is a drawing that can be useful in solving problems.

The Venn diagram at the right represents two groups of numbers—the whole numbers from 1 to 8 and the odd numbers from 1 to 15. The **intersection** of the circles contains all the numbers common to both groups—1, 3, 5, and 7.

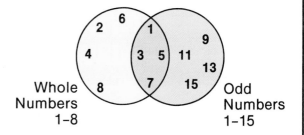

Fifty students in New Hampshire were asked to choose among three ski areas—Canon Mountain, Loon Mountain, and Waterville Valley—for a class trip. Some students indicated more than one choice. Their choices are shown in the Venn diagram below.

How many students preferred each of the following?

1. Only Loon

2. Both Loon and Canon

3. Loon

4. Both Loon and Waterville, but not Canon

5. Only Waterville

6. Only Canon

7. Both Waterville and Canon

8. Both Loon and Waterville

9. Both Loon and Canon, but not Waterville

10. Both Waterville and Canon, but not Loon

11. Waterville, Canon, and Loon

12. Waterville, Canon, or Loon

13. None of the three locations

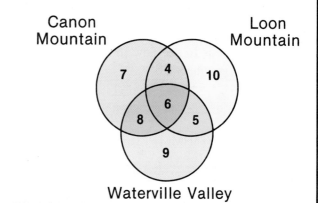

INTRODUCING THE CALCULATOR

The keyboard of a calculator has 3 kinds of keys.

Control keys   C CE = M+ CM RM

Number entry keys   0 1 2 3 4 5

                              6 7 8 9 .

Function keys   + − × ÷ %

Compare the keys on your calculator with the keys shown above.

Some pocket calculators have memory keys.   M+ CM RM
A calculator with memory can store a number
for use at a later time.

Follow the steps to learn how to use the memory keys.

press 2 4 6

press M+ ⟶ `246.M` ⟵ This means that the number is
                                               in the calculator's memory.

press C to clear the display. ⟶ `0.M` ⟵ The M remains to remind you
                                               that you have a number stored.

press RM to recall the number. ⟶ `246.M`

press CM to clear the memory. ⟶ `246.`

Follow the steps to see how the calculator's memory can be
used in this example. $48 \times 54 - 96 + 54$

press 5 4 ⟶ `54.`

press M+ ⟶ `54.M`

press 4 8 × RM − 9 6 + RM = ⟶ `2550.M`

WITH A CALCULATOR

Store 16,754 in memory. Add it to each number.

1. 45,287   **2.** 219,318   **3.** 415,875   **4.** 990,394

Store 5,096 in memory. Subtract it from each number.

5. 19,285   **6.** 28,000   **7.** 394,287   **8.** 60,057

Store 583 in memory. Calculate.

9. $(15{,}741 \div 583) + 583 + 583$ **10.** $583 \times 583 + 583$ **11.** $24 \times 583 + 583 - 583$

Use memory to calculate.

12. $(24 \times 37) + (52 \times 17)$ **13.** $(72 \times 19) + (972 \div 27)$

INTRODUCING THE COMPUTER

A computer system is made up of **hardware** and **software**. Hardware is the machinery that makes up the system. Software consists of computer programs. Compare this to a cassette player and tapes. The cassette player is the hardware and the tapes are the software. Computer hardware includes:

- an **input** device, such as a keyboard, for entering information into the computer

- a **central processing unit (CPU)** where all calculations are performed

- **memory** which stores all information and instructions to be used by the CPU when needed

- an **output** device, such as a screen or printer, for getting information out of the computer

A **program** is a set of instructions that tells the CPU what to do. A computer can switch from one job to another as different programs are entered. There are many languages available for programming. Some of these are FORTRAN, Pascal, and Logo. Most home computers use a language called BASIC. Here are the BASIC translations for some mathematics symbols.

Mathematics Symbol	BASIC Symbol	Example
+	+	15 + 24
−	−	23 − 14
×	*	4 * 5
÷	/	18/9

A **PRINT** statement is used to tell a computer to output words or numbers.

input	PRINT 4 * 6	input	PRINT "18/3"
output	24	output	18/3

input   PRINT "3 + 5 = "; 3 + 5 ⟵——— When quotation marks are used, the computer
output 3 + 5 = 8   outputs exactly what is in the quotation marks.

AT THE COMPUTER

Input the commands. Write each output.

1. PRINT 34 + 98

2. PRINT 9 * 8

3. PRINT 45/5

4. PRINT 112 - 78

5. PRINT "112 - 78"

6. PRINT "START"

7. PRINT "7 + 4 = "; 7 + 4

8. PRINT "10/2 = "; 10/2

9. PRINT "3 * N"

MAINTAINING SKILLS

Choose the correct answers. Write A, B, C, or D.

1. What is the value of 2 in 215,073?

- **A** 2 hundred thousand **C** 2 thousand
- **B** 20 thousand   **D** 2 billion

2. In what place is the digit 4 in 3,642,792,106?

- **A** ten thousands   **C** ten millions
- **B** millions   **D** not given

3. Compare. 1,073,215 ⬤ 1,049,915

- **A** >   **C** <
- **B** =   **D** not given

4. Order from least to greatest.
3,907; 3,069; 3,079

- **A** 3,079; 3,069; 3,907   **C** 3,907; 3,079; 3,069
- **B** 3,069; 3,907; 3,079   **D** not given

5. Round 7,771,369 to the nearest hundred.

- **A** 7,771,370   **C** 7,771,300
- **B** 7,771,400   **D** not given

6. Round 7,771,369 to the nearest million.

- **A** 8,000,000   **C** 7,800,000
- **B** 7,000,000   **D** not given

7. What addition property is used?
(2 + 11) + 6 = 2 + (11 + 6)

- **A** associative   **C** commutative
- **B** identity   **D** not given

8. Estimate. 3,960 − 892

- **A** 2,000   **C** 4,000
- **B** 3,000   **D** not given

9. Estimate. 1,133 + 6,881

- **A** 8,000   **C** 9,000
- **B** 6,000   **D** not given

10. 24,103 + 58,911

- **A** 83,013   **C** 83,014
- **B** 82,014   **D** not given

11. 378,915 − 184,723

- **A** 194,212   **C** 194,192
- **B** 194,292   **D** not given

12. What is the related equation for $n + 13 = 72$?

- **A** $n = 72 + 13$ **C** $n - 13 = 72$
- **B** $n = 72 - 13$ **D** not given

13. What is the related equation for $d - 11 = 20$?

- **A** $d = 20 - 11$ **C** $d + 11 = 20$
- **B** $d = 20 + 11$ **D** not given

Use the picture for 14 and 15.

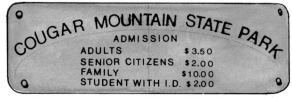

COUGAR MOUNTAIN STATE PARK

ADMISSION

ADULTS	$3.50
SENIOR CITIZENS	$2.00
FAMILY	$10.00
STUDENT WITH I.D.	$2.00

14. How much would 23 families pay for admission?

- **A** $64   **C** $80.50
- **B** $230   **D** not given

15. How much would 6 adults and 9 senior citizens pay?

- **A** $39   **C** $30
- **B** $43.50   **D** not given

Multiplying and Dividing Whole Numbers 2

Theme: Aerospace

Properties of Multiplication

During the 12-week filming of a television series, stunt pilot Gina Mitchell flew a 1929 airplane twice a week. How many times did she perform?

Multiply to find how many times she performed.

$$12 \times 2 = 24$$
$$\uparrow \quad \uparrow \qquad \uparrow$$
factors   product

Gina Mitchell performed 24 times.

Use these properties of multiplication to find products.

Commutative Property

The order of the factors does not change the product.

$$a \times b = b \times a$$
$$5 \times 4 = 4 \times 5$$
$$20 = 20$$

Associative Property

The way that factors are grouped does not change the product.

$$a \times (b \times c) = (a \times b) \times c$$
$$2 \times (8 \times 10) = (2 \times 8) \times 10$$
$$2 \times 80 = 16 \times 10$$
$$160 = 160$$

Identity Property

The product of any number and one is that number.

$$a \times 1 = a \quad 1 \times a = a$$
$$32 \times 1 = 32 \quad 1 \times 32 = 32$$

Zero Property

The product of any number and zero is 0.

$$a \times 0 = 0 \quad 0 \times a = 0$$
$$4 \times 0 = 0 \quad 0 \times 4 = 0$$

Distributive Property of Multiplication over Addition

If one factor is a sum, multiplying before adding does not change the product.

$$a \times (b + c) = (a \times b) + (a \times c)$$
$$6 \times (4 + 5) = (6 \times 4) + (6 \times 5)$$
$$6 \times 9 = 24 + 30$$
$$54 = 54$$

CLASSWORK

Name the property of multiplication illustrated.

1. $3{,}456 \times 0 = 0$

2. $8 \times 15 = 15 \times 8$

3. $17 \times 1 = 17$

4. $(7 \times 3) \times 6 = 7 \times (3 \times 6)$

5. $3 \times (4 + 1) = (3 \times 4) + (3 \times 1)$

Name the property of multiplication illustrated.

1. $76 \times 0 = 0$ **2.** $6 \times (5 + 4) = (6 \times 5) + (6 \times 4)$ **3.** $54 \times 1 = 54$

4. $(3 \times 5) \times 6 = 3 \times (5 \times 6)$ **5.** $9 \times 12 = 12 \times 9$ **6.** $1 \times 0 = 0$

Write *true* or *false*. If true, name the property of multiplication illustrated.

7. $3 \times 0 = 3$ **8.** $0 \times 5 = 0$ **9.** $1 \times 7 = 7$

10. $6 \times 5 = 5 \times 6$ **11.** $(8 \times 3) \times 2 = 8 \times (3 \times 2)$ **12.** $7 \times 5 \times 0 = 0$

13. $(3 \times 4) + (4 \times 5) = (3 + 4) \times 5$ **14.** $(8 + 2) \times 3 = (8 \times 3) + (2 \times 3)$

15. $4 \times 1 \times 3 \times 1 = 4 \times 3$ **16.** $7 \times (4 + 2) = 7 \times 4 + 2$

17. $7 \times 82 = (7 \times 80) + (7 \times 2)$ **18.** $10 \times 96 = 90 \times 10 + 6$

19. $5 \times (9 \times 2) = 5 \times (2 \times 9)$ **20.** $5 \times (2 \times 6) \times 5 = (5 \times 2) \times (6 \times 5)$

Suggest a name for the property of multiplication illustrated.

★ **21.** $6 \times (8 - 5) = (6 \times 8) - (6 \times 5)$

APPLICATION

Name and illustrate the property you use.

22. The Old Rhinebeck Aerodrome Museum in New York State gives 2 shows each weekend for 24 weeks from May through October. How many shows are given?

★ **23.** At the museum the Coopers took 2 exciting rides in early-model planes. Each flight circled the area in one direction for 7 minutes and circled in the other direction for 8 minutes. For how long did the Coopers fly?

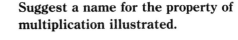

=== MENTAL ARITHMETIC ===

Use the distributive property to find each product quickly in your head.

Example: $6 \times 23 = (6 \times 20) + (6 \times 3) = 120 + 18 = 138$

1. 5×43 **2.** 8×35 **3.** $5 \times \$48$ **4.** 9×63

5. 6×72 **6.** 20×101 **7.** 5×142 **8.** 6×212

Multiplication Patterns

In 1903 the Wright brothers' plane flew at 30 miles per hour. In 1931 the *Supermarine SB6* flew at least 10 times as fast. In 1967 the rocket-driven *X-15A-2* could fly at least 100 times as fast. In 1972 the *Pioneer 10* flew at least 1,000 times as fast. How fast could each craft fly?

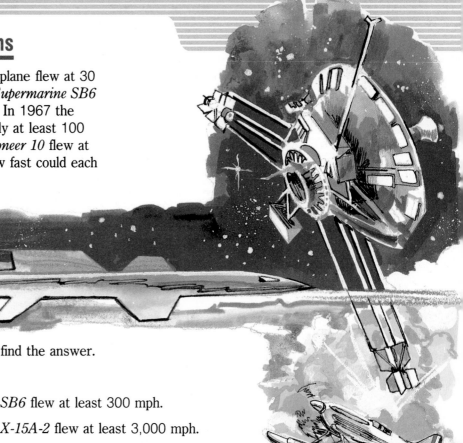

Use multiplication patterns to find the answer.

$1 \times 30 = 30$

$10 \times 30 = 300$ The *SB6* flew at least 300 mph.

$100 \times 30 = 3,000$ The *X-15A-2* flew at least 3,000 mph.

$1,000 \times 30 = 30,000$ The *Pioneer 10* flew at least 30,000 mph.

Look for the patterns below.

$60 \times 4 = 240$	$25 \times 5 = 125$
$600 \times 4 = 2,400$	$25 \times 50 = 1,250$
$6,000 \times 4 = 24,000$	$25 \times 500 = 12,500$
$60 \times 40 = 2,400$	$250 \times 500 = 125,000$
$60 \times 400 = 24,000$	$250 \times 5,000 = 1,250,000$

CLASSWORK

Use a pattern to find each product.

1. 10×12
100×12
$1,000 \times 12$

2. 20×3
200×3
$2,000 \times 3$

3. 32×20
32×200
320×200

4. 78×100

5. $9 \times 4,000$

6. 6×500

7. 20×50

8. $50 \times 2,000$

9. 200×500

PRACTICE

Use a pattern to find each product.

1. 10 × 15
2. 100 × 15
3. 1,000 × 15
4. 5 × 40
5. 5 × 400
6. 5 × 4,000
7. 20 × 21
8. 200 × 210
9. 30 × 210
10. 100 × 42
11. 1,000 × 42
12. 1,000 × 420
13. 10 × 83
14. 100 × 830
15. 1,000 × 83
16. 33 × 30
17. 33 × 300
18. 33 × 3,000
19. 24 × 100
20. 24 × 200
21. 240 × 2,000
22. 100 × 86
23. 10 × 860
24. 1,000 × 860
25. 1,000 × 75
26. 100 × 750
27. 2,000 × 750
28. 10 × 250
29. 400 × 250
30. 4,000 × 250
★31. 50 × 400 × 30
★32. 6 × 1,000 × 40
★33. 32 × 1,000 × 20

Compare. Use >, <, or = for each ⬤.

34. 40 × 900 ⬤ 400 × 9
35. 450 × 20 ⬤ 450 × 200
36. 36 × 1,000 ⬤ 360 × 100
37. 50 × 60 ⬤ 5 × 10 × 6 × 10
38. 24 × 200 ⬤ 2,400 × 20
39. 800 × 40 ⬤ 80 × 4,000

Find each missing factor.

40. 50 × □ = 15,000
41. 200 × □ = 100,000
42. 40 × 300 = 400 × □
43. 6,000 × 500 = 60 × □

APPLICATION

44. The smallest plane ever flown was the *Stits Sky Baby*, which weighed 452 lb. The *Boeing B-52H Strato* weighs 1,000 times as much. What is the weight of the *Boeing B-52H*?

45. At a country fair air show, a hot-air balloon travels a distance of 25 ft for every foot it rises into the air. How far from its original starting point will the balloon be when it is 1,000 ft above the ground?

★46. There are 300 passengers on Transpolar Airlines flight 34 from San Francisco to Tokyo. If the average weight for each passenger is 150 lb, what is the total passenger weight for this flight?

Estimating Products

Steve operates a crane helicopter that has a lifting capacity of 20,000 lb. He needs to lift 15 concrete slabs to workers at the top of the skyscraper. Each slab weighs 1,859 lb. Can he lift all the slabs in one trip?

Estimate the product and compare it to the helicopter's lifting capacity.

▶ To estimate a product, round each factor to its greatest place. Then multiply the rounded factors.

$$
\begin{array}{rcr}
1{,}859 & \text{rounds to} & 2{,}000 \\
\times \quad 15 & \text{rounds to} & \times \quad 20 \\
\hline
 & & 40{,}000 \\
\end{array}
$$

Since 40,000 > 20,000, Steve cannot lift the slabs in one trip.

More Examples

a. Estimate 52 × $17.43.

$$
\begin{array}{rcr}
\$17.43 & \text{rounds to} & \$20 \\
\times \quad 52 & \text{rounds to} & \times \quad 50 \\
\hline
 & & \$1{,}000 \\
\end{array}
$$

b. Estimate 68 × 340.

$$
\begin{array}{rcr}
340 & \text{rounds to} & 300 \\
\times \quad 68 & \text{rounds to} & \times \quad 70 \\
\hline
 & & 21{,}000 \\
\end{array}
$$

CLASSWORK

Estimate.

1. 32 × 57	**2.** 49 × 19	**3.** 291 × 43	**4.** $4.30 × 12	**5.** 786 × 427

6. 19 × $19.88   **7.** 78 × 61   **8.** 12 × $103.50   **9.** 27 × 753

PRACTICE

Estimate.

1.	57 × 13	**2.**	93 × 47	**3.**	52 × 19
4.	$232 × 12	**5.**	210 × 36	**6.**	$671 × 23
7.	423 × 87	**8.**	504 × 49	**9.**	$719 × 215
10.	1,971 × 406	**11.**	5,097 × 983	**12.**	3,115 × 481

13. 368 × 6,238

14. $8,321 × 3,627

15. 64 × 16,208

16. 2,350 × 1,767

Estimate. Use the properties of multiplication to make estimation easier.

17. 83 × 58 × 49

18. 36 × 92 × 53

19. 41 × 56 × 53

20. 196 × 684 × 513

For each pair tell which estimated product is closer to the exact product. Explain why.

★**21.** 96 × 703
75 × 753

★**22.** 111 × 111
98 × 389

APPLICATION

23. Bill Marcus works as a pilot on a helicopter air-taxi service. The service carries 178 passengers a week from one airport to another. About how many passengers does it carry in a year? (52 weeks in 1 year.)

★**24.** The record time for a helicopter trip around the world is 699 hours 8 minutes 32 seconds at an average speed of just over 32 miles per hour. Estimate the distance flown around the world.

Mixed Practice

1.	1,572 + 829
2.	32,496 + 8,657
3.	2,396 953 + 8,719

4. 718 + 56

5. 5,237 + 694

6.	863 − 487
7.	12,396 − 5,958
8.	$6,357.15 − 929.49

9. 1,239 − 897

10. 6,532 − 2,956

11. 182,490 − 6,889

Compare. Use >, <, or = for each ●.

12. 4,211 ● 4,112

13. 9,314 ● 9,314

14. 310,123 ● 309,989

15. 1,121,113 ● 1,112,113

16. 17,089 ● 17,121

17. 212,108 ● 212,099

35

Multiplying

In the movie *Brewster McCloud,* Brewster built wings that he hoped would let him fly like an eagle. If he worked 128 hours a month for 8 months, how many hours did he spend building his wings?

Multiply to find the product.

Step 1

Multiply ones.

$$\begin{array}{r} \overset{6}{1}28 \\ \times\quad 8 \\ \hline 4 \end{array}$$

Step 2

Multiply tens.

$$\begin{array}{r} \overset{26}{1}28 \\ \times\quad 8 \\ \hline 24 \end{array}$$

Step 3

Multiply hundreds.

$$\begin{array}{r} \overset{26}{1}28 \\ \times\quad 8 \\ \hline 1,024 \end{array}$$

Estimate to be sure the answer makes sense.

128	rounds to	100
× 8	rounds to	× 10
		1,000

The product makes sense.

Brewster McCloud spent 1,024 hours building his wings.

▶To multiply by a 2-digit number, follow these steps.

Step 1

Multiply by ones.

$$\begin{array}{r} \overset{25\ 7}{\$23.69} \\ \times\quad 28 \\ \hline 189\ 52 \end{array}$$

Step 2

Multiply by tens.

$$\begin{array}{r} \overset{1\ 1}{\overset{25\ 7}{\$23.69}} \\ \times\quad 28 \\ \hline 189\ 52 \\ 473\ 80 \end{array}$$

Step 3

Add.

$$\begin{array}{r} \overset{1\ 1}{\overset{25\ 7}{\$23.69}} \\ \times\quad 28 \\ \hline 189\ 52 \\ 473\ 80 \\ \hline \$663.32 \end{array}$$

Place dollar sign and decimal point ←in the product

CLASSWORK

Multiply. Estimate to be sure each answer makes sense.

1. $\begin{array}{r} 79 \\ \times\ 4 \\ \hline \end{array}$

2. $\begin{array}{r} 516 \\ \times\ 8 \\ \hline \end{array}$

3. $\begin{array}{r} 386 \\ \times\ 5 \\ \hline \end{array}$

4. $\begin{array}{r} 6,408 \\ \times\ 6 \\ \hline \end{array}$

5. $\begin{array}{r} \$54.62 \\ \times\ 18 \\ \hline \end{array}$

6. 62 × 3,800

7. 28 × 1,572

8. 6 × 38,390

9. 21 × 45,123

Multiply. Estimate to be sure each answer makes sense.

1. 315 × 9	**2.** 147 × 8	**3.** 306 × 5	**4.** $924 × 6	**5.** 6,257 × 8
6. 8,367 × 3	**7.** $27.98 × 4	**8.** 13,197 × 6	**9.** 56,192 × 8	**10.** $105.19 × 7
11. 521 × 16	**12.** 608 × 35	**13.** $15.25 × 72	**14.** 3,709 × 26	**15.** 4,582 × 56
16. 21,860 × 34	**17.** 36,540 × 96	**18.** 18,491 × 63	**19.** 50,294 × 70	**20.** 46,418 × 87

21. 57 × 6,342   **22.** 18 × $15.97   **23.** 6 × 15,006   **24.** 18 × 237

25. 35 × 1,805   **26.** 66 × $4,372   **27.** 19 × 98,103   **28.** 37 × 12,084

Find each missing digit.

★**29.**
```
  1 3 2
×     ■
  ■ 9 2
```

★**30.**
```
    5 2 6
×    ■ ■
  1 0 ■ 2
2 1 ■ 4 ○
2 2 , ■ ■ 2
```

★**31.**
```
    ■ ■ 6
×   ■ 5
  2 4 3 ■
■ ■ 0 ■ ○
3 6 , 4 5 0
```

★**32.**
```
    ■ 2 ■
×   ■ 4
  1 3 ■ ■
■ ■ 3 5 ○
■ ■ , ■ ■ 8
```

APPLICATION

33. The wingspan of a Boeing 747 jumbo jet is about 27 times as long as the wingspan of an eagle. About how long is the wingspan of a Boeing 747?

34. Suppose you can travel on your bike at a speed of 25 miles per hour. How far can you travel in 12 hours of total biking time?

35. Alana, a student pilot, flew an average of 135 miles each week of last year. How many miles did she fly last year? (1 year = 52 weeks)

★**36.** A hummingbird flaps its wings 62 times per second. How many times does it flap its wings in one hour?

7 ft

Multiplying Greater Numbers

The space shuttle can travel at a speed of
27,400 kilometers per hour. How far can it
travel in 6 days? (6 days = 144 hours)

Multiply 144 × 27,400.

Step 1

Multiply by ones.
```
  27,400
×    144
 109 600
```

Step 2

Multiply by tens.
```
  27,400
×    144
 109 600
1096 00
```

Step 3

Multiply by hundreds.
```
  27,400
×    144
 109 600
1096 00
2740 0
```

Step 4

Add.
```
   27,400
×     144
  109 600
1 096 00
2 740 0
3,945,600
```

Estimate to be sure the answer makes sense.

144 × 27,400 **rounds to** 100 × 30,000, or 3,000,000.

The product makes sense.

The space shuttle can travel 3,945,600 kilometers in 6 days.

More Examples

a.
```
    394
  × 507
  2 758
  0 00   ← 0 × 394
197 0
199,758
```

Shortcut
```
    394
  × 507
  2 758  ← 7 × 394
197 0    ← 500 × 394
199,758
```

b.
```
   $3.68
  ×  235
   18 40
  110 4
  736
 $864.80
```

CLASSWORK

Multiply. Estimate to be sure each answer makes sense.

1.
```
  322
× 125
```

2.
```
  426
× 570
```

3.
```
 $2.74
×  300
```

4.
```
 1,609
×  273
```

5.
```
 $10,502
×     450
```

6. 486 × 903

7. 255 × 3,070

8. 442 × $68.74

9. 647 × 85,090

PRACTICE

Multiply. Estimate to be sure each answer makes sense.

1.	2.	3.	4.	5.
418 × 124	$783 × 243	504 × 490	870 × 493	$5.79 × 601

6.	7.	8.	9.	10.
3,217 × 290	6,815 × 702	$4,109 × 366	$84.90 × 500	5,027 × 327

11.	12.	13.	14.	15.
56,890 × 309	$214.12 × 653	$20,203 × 360	42,009 × 772	57,921 × 527

16. 555 × 216   17. 604 × $7.98   18. 127 × 8,564   19. 238 × $79.07

20. 470 × 1,087   21. 2,642 × 1,740   22. 811 × $624.30   23. $37.75 × 2,081

Estimate to choose the correct product for each.

24. 174 × 425   a. 70,100   b. 73,950   c. 92,000

25. 483 × 206   a. 99,498   b. 88,098   c. 120,908

★ 26. 118 × 27 × 509   a. 1,821,674   b. 2,421,674   c. 1,621,674

★ 27. 115 × 56 × 36 × 210   a. 48,686,400   b. 50,863,200   c. 55,863,200

APPLICATION

28. The *Voyager 2* space probe took pictures of Mercury. One complete day on Mercury lasts for 176 Earth days because it rotates so slowly. How many Earth days do 365 Mercury days equal?

★ 29. Jupiter rotates once every 9 hours 55 minutes. How many minutes would 376 rotations take?

CALCULATOR

Place the multiplication sign so that the product in each example is correct.

Example 1 2 3 4 5 6 = 41,472
         1 2×3 4 5 6 = 41,472

1. 1 2 3 4 5 6 = 56,088   2. 1 3 5 7 9 0 = 122,130

3. 3 3 3 3 3 3 = 109,989   4. 7 8 9 3 4 5 6 = 4,736,070

Exponents

Michele is writing a report about comets. She learned that the tail of a comet is a vapor trail about 10,000 miles long.

You can use exponents to write large numbers.

$$10,000 = 10 \times 10 \times 10 \times 10$$
factors

10 is used as a factor 4 times.

$$10,000 = 10^4 \leftarrow \text{exponent}$$
base

$$10,000 = 10^4$$
Read   ten to the fourth power

An **exponent** tells how many times the **base** is used as a factor.

The vapor trail of a comet is 10^4 miles long.

More Examples

Exponent	Read	Factors	Standard Form
6^2	six to the second power or **six squared**	6×6	36
5^3	five to the third power or **five cubed**	$5 \times 5 \times 5$	125
4^1	four to the first power	4	4
7^5	seven to the fifth power	$7 \times 7 \times 7 \times 7 \times 7$	16,807

CLASSWORK

Write each using exponents.

1. $6 \times 6 \times 6 \times 6 \times 6$ **2.** $1 \times 1 \times 1 \times 1$ **3.** 9×9 **4.** $10 \times 10 \times 10 \times 10 \times 10$

Write as a product of factors. Then write each in standard form.

5. 4^2 **6.** 10^4 **7.** 6^3 **8.** 7^1 **9.** 5^4 **10.** 3^2

PRACTICE

Write each using exponents.

1. $7 \times 7 \times 7 \times 7$ **2.** 12×12 **3.** $1 \times 1 \times 1 \times 1 \times 1 \times 1$ **4.** $8 \times 8 \times 8$

5. $4 \times 4 \times 4$ **6.** $2 \times 2 \times 2 \times 2 \times 2$ **7.** $9 \times 9 \times 9 \times 9 \times 9$ **8.** 15×15

Write each as a product of factors.

9. 5^3 **10.** 4^2 **11.** 10^2 **12.** 3^5 **13.** 2^7 **14.** 6^4

15. 6^1 **16.** 12^3 **17.** 8^3 **18.** 9^2 **19.** 1^6 **20.** 4^4

Write each in standard form.

21. 3^4 **22.** 9^2 **23.** 7^2 **24.** 1^5 **25.** 5^3 **26.** 11^2

27. 4^3 **28.** 7^1 **29.** 3^1 **30.** 9^4 **31.** 14^2 **32.** 2^5

33. 3^5 **34.** 3^6 **35.** 8^3 **36.** 5^1 **37.** 6^2 **38.** 6^4

Write the square and cube of each number.

39. 8   **40.** 10   **41.** 4   **42.** 5   **43.** 12   **44.** 3

Make each sentence true.

★ **45.** $14^\square = 196$ ★ **46.** $5^\square = 125$ ★ **47.** $\square^3 = 1{,}000$ ★ **48.** $2^\square = 128$

APPLICATION

49. A comet is a large ball of glowing gases, dust, and ice. A comet can be more than 10^6 miles wide. Write the width in standard form.

★ **50.** Halley's Comet was photographed in August 1909 when it was 3×10^8 miles from the sun. In October of 1982, astronomers photographed Halley's Comet when it was 10^9 miles from the sun. On which date was it closer to the sun? Write these two distances in standard form to check your answer.

LOGICAL THINKING

Guess the number.

1. The number is 4 more than 5^2. What is the number?

2. The number is greater than 2^4 and less than 2^5. It is a power of 5. What is the number?

3. The number can be written as a power of 2, 4, or 8. It is greater than 3^3. What is the number?

Problem Solving

TOO MUCH OR TOO LITTLE INFORMATION

THINK
PLAN
SOLVE
LOOK
BACK

You must look for important facts in problem solving. Is there more information than you need? Is there enough information to solve the problem? You must decide what facts are needed.

The astronauts completed 3 missions in space. During each mission, they spent 12 hours eating, 48 hours sleeping, and 62 hours performing experiments. How many hours were spent performing experiments on the 3 missions?

THINK   **What is the question?**

How many hours were spent performing experiments on the 3 missions?

What are the facts?

Activity	Hours per mission
Eating	12
Sleeping	48
Performing Experiments	62

Is there too much information?

Yes; the time spent eating and sleeping is not needed.

Is any information missing? No.

PLAN   **How can the answer be found?**

Multiply the hours spent performing experiments on each mission by the number of missions.

$$3 \times 62 = n$$

SOLVE   **Carry out the plan. Then answer the questions.**

$$\begin{array}{r} 62 \\ \times\ 3 \\ \hline 186 \end{array}$$ The astronauts spent 186 hours performing experiments.

LOOK BACK   **Have you answered the question? Does your answer make sense?**

Estimate.   62 rounds to   60
$$\begin{array}{r} \times\ 3 \end{array}$$ $$\begin{array}{r} \times\ 3 \\ \hline 180 \end{array}$$

180 is close to 186. The answer makes sense.

PRACTICE

Decide whether there is enough information to solve each problem. If there are missing facts, tell what facts are needed. If there are extra facts, tell what is not needed. Solve each problem, if possible.

1. Richard is part of a 5-member team of astronauts scheduled for a space shuttle flight. In order to complete his experiments, Richard will work 8 hours each day of the flight. How many hours will he spend working on experiments during the flight?

2. Lee is performing an agricultural experiment at the space station. She planted 60 Type A seeds and 30 Type B seeds. 40 of the Type A seeds sprouted and 24 of the Type B seeds sprouted. How many Type A seeds did not sprout?

3. Lee works 6 hours on Monday, 8 hours on Tuesday, and 8 hours on Wednesday, performing different experiments in the space station. Does she work more than 40 hours per week performing experiments in the space station?

4. Type B seedlings grow 1 cm per day on Earth. How much do Type B seedlings grow in 3 days in space?

5. Juan is one of 5 scientists in a rocket program. He works 42 hours per week. How many hours over 1,000 does he work in 26 weeks?

6. Rocket I has a mass of 18,500 kg. The flight lasted for 105 days. Rocket II has a mass of 338 kg less than Rocket I. What is the mass of Rocket II?

7. The length of the flight of Rocket III was 27 days longer than the flight of Rocket IV. What was the length of the flight of Rocket III?

8. The higher the orbit of a satellite, the lower is the speed it needs to stay in orbit. A communications satellite orbiting Earth at a height of 320 km must travel at 24,400 km per hour to stay in orbit. What is the distance traveled by the satellite in 24 hours?

9. Three astronauts completed 158 orbits around Earth. They traveled 45,680 km per orbit. They took 15,000 photographs. How many kilometers did they travel in their orbits?

CREATE YOUR OWN PROBLEM

This table lists three large objects and the weight of each. Create two problems that use some or all of this data. One problem should have too much information, and one should not have enough information. Have a classmate identify each type and solve the one that can be solved.

Object	Weight
	45,000 kg
	3,000 kg
	120,000 kg

Averages

Whose model rocket came closest to the average time for the test flight of the six rockets?

To find the average, first find the sum of all the numbers and then divide the sum by the number of addends.

MODEL ROCKET TEST FLIGHTS		
Name	Time in Seconds	Distance in Yards
Jeff	35	182
Tim	23	95
Sonia	31	150
Valerie	30	161
Mike	18	63
Rafael	25	87

Step 1		Step 2

Find the sum.

Divide by the number of addends.

```
  35
  23              27 ← quotient
  31   divisor → 6)162 ← dividend
  30              12
  18              42
+ 25              42
 162               0
```

The average time is 27 seconds. Rafael's rocket flight of 25 seconds came closest to the average time.

▶ The short form of division is useful for dividing by 1-digit numbers.

Find the average of $2.56, $3.75, $2.96.

Add.

```
 $2.56
  3.75
+ 2.96
 $9.27
```

Divide.

Long form

```
   $3.09
3)$9.27
   9
   0 2
     0
    27
    27
     0
```

Short form

Step 1	Step 2	Step 3

Step 1
```
     $3.
      0
3)$9.27
```
$3 \times 3 = 9$
$9 - 9 = 0$

Step 2
```
     $3.0
      0 2
3)$9.2 7
```
$0 \times 3 = 0$
$2 - 0 = 2$

Step 3
```
     $3.0 9
      0 2
3)$9.2 7
```
$9 \times 3 = 27$

CLASSWORK

Find each average.

1. 8, 6, 6, 10, 5

2. 12¢, 20¢, 22¢

3. 26, 35, 32, 19, 21, 17

4. 57, 210, 84, 125

5. $1.98, $3.57, $2.43

6. 330, 156, 200, 112, 222

Find each average.

1. 12, 18, 20, 14

2. 6, 7, 8, 8, 11

3. 26, 25, 27

4. $4.20, $4.60, $3.80

5. 86, 88, 88, 93, 100

6. 17, 27, 35, 22, 34

7. 85, 93, 78, 96, 83

8. 63¢, 32¢, 37¢

9. $5.83, $4.25, $2.16

10. 28, 50, 46, 20, 30, 30

11. $120, $125, $132, $127

12. 100, 250, 120, 260, 100

13. $28.75, $32.15, $51.60, $47.50

14. 188, 210, 209, 176, 257

15. $240, $250, $240, $280, $240, $250

Find the missing number in each group. The average is given.

⋆**16.** 87, 93, 72, ☐

Average is 85.

⋆**17.** 119, 213, ☐

Average is 163.

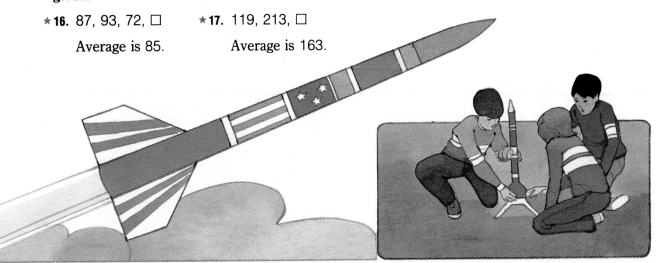

APPLICATION

Solve each problem. If there is not enough information, tell what is missing.

18. Whose model rocket test flight came closest to the average distance of the six rockets? Use the table at the top of the previous page.

19. Jackie and Phil spent a total of $16.84 on model rocket equipment. Their friends spent a total of $27.32. What was the average spent per person?

20. Find the average flight distance of the model rockets if Jessica joins the club. Her rocket went 158 yards.

21. In eight separate test flights, Rafael's rocket flew a total of 768 yards. What was the average distance for these flights?

⋆**22.** Tim tested a new rocket he built. The first two flights each lasted 21 seconds. The next three flights each lasted 26 seconds. What is the average flight time for Tim's new rocket?

⋆**23.** Jessica's rocket can remain in the air longer than the others. Including her rocket, the club's average time is increased to 29 seconds. How long does Jessica's rocket remain in the air?

Estimating Quotients

Mr. Ramirez is planning to take flying lessons. About how much will each lesson cost?

Estimate to find the answer.

Step 1

If the divisor has more than one digit, round it to its greatest place.

$$26)\overline{\$1,250} \quad \text{rounds to} \quad 30)\overline{\$1,250}$$

Step 2

Find the first digit of the quotient. Write zeros for the other places.

$$
\begin{array}{r}
\$40 \\
30)\overline{\$1,250} \\
\underline{1\,20} \\
5
\end{array}
$$

Think $\quad 30)\overline{125} \quad 3)\overline{12}$

Each lesson will cost about $40.

-LEARN TO FLY-
Join now:
Private lessons at
Sussex Air
26 lessons for $1,250

More Examples

a. Estimate $245.91 ÷ 22.

$$22)\overline{\$245.91} \quad \text{rounds to} \quad 20)\overline{\$245.91} \quad \$\,10.00$$

Think $\quad 20)\overline{24} \quad 2)\overline{2}$

b. Estimate 238,674 ÷ 67.

$$67)\overline{238,674} \quad \text{rounds to} \quad 70)\overline{238,674} \quad 3,000$$

Think $\quad 70)\overline{238} \quad 7)\overline{23}$

CLASSWORK

Estimate.

1. $72)\overline{5,248}$ **2.** $55)\overline{1,272}$ **3.** $58)\overline{\$3,715}$ **4.** $73)\overline{50,375}$ **5.** $14)\overline{175,809}$

6. 1,984 ÷ 22   **7.** 2,079 ÷ 15   **8.** $167.01 ÷ 39   **9.** 85,007 ÷ 81   **10.** 751,980 ÷ 62

PRACTICE

Estimate.

1. $81\overline{)6{,}718}$
2. $62\overline{)3{,}673}$
3. $49\overline{)\$3{,}592}$

4. $83\overline{)7{,}009}$
5. $65\overline{)6{,}703}$
6. $89\overline{)\$99.85}$

7. $82\overline{)48{,}698}$
8. $37\overline{)\$252.20}$
9. $67\overline{)64{,}116}$

10. $59\overline{)137{,}846}$
11. $73\overline{)286{,}421}$
12. $17\overline{)\$606{,}007}$

13. $3{,}162 \div 74$
14. $\$1{,}723 \div 29$
15. $83{,}714 \div 67$

16. $601{,}237 \div 25$
17. $254{,}710 \div 23$
18. $904{,}785 \div 44$

Choose the appropriate division for each estimate.

★19. Estimate is 70.

   a. $26\overline{)1{,}439}$

   b. $23\overline{)1{,}439}$

   c. $23\overline{)14{,}390}$

★20. Estimate is 400.

   a. $48{,}007 \div 13$

   b. $48{,}007 \div 15$

   c. $4{,}800 \div 13$

★21. Estimate is 2,000.

   a. $68\overline{)15{,}278}$

   b. $68\overline{)132{,}783}$

   c. $68\overline{)152{,}783}$

APPLICATION

22. Sussex Air received 2,487 requests for information in one year. About how many requests did they receive per month?

23. The school pays its 18 instructors a total of $420,000 per year. Estimate the average yearly salary of a flight instructor.

★24. Joe Collins is an instructor at Sussex Air School. He flew 948 hours last year and twice that many hours this year. Estimate the average number of hours he flew each month.

Mixed Practice

1. $\begin{array}{r} 2{,}046 \\ + 1{,}399 \end{array}$

2. $\begin{array}{r} 156{,}809 \\ 76{,}597 \\ + 273{,}008 \end{array}$

3. $\begin{array}{r} 213 \\ - 175 \end{array}$

4. $\begin{array}{r} 1{,}248 \\ 629 \\ + \quad 355 \end{array}$

5. $\begin{array}{r} \$130.06 \\ 29.45 \\ + \quad 281.04 \end{array}$

6. $2{,}870 - 2{,}096$

7. $\$24.97 + \$8.03$

8. $\$123.75 - \$67.89$

9. $496{,}000 - 387{,}954$

10. $n + 17 = 89$

11. $n - 46 = 23$

12. $n = 29 + 57$

13. $19 + n = 74$

14. $10 = n - 5$

Round to the nearest ten thousand.

15. $10{,}873$

16. $67{,}409$

17. $557{,}564$

18. $802{,}987$

19. $1{,}735{,}575$

47

Dividing

Janine collected 512 stamps showing achievements in aerospace. She wants to put an equal number of stamps on each page in her album. The album has 32 pages. How many stamps should be on each page?

Divide 512 by 32 to find how many stamps on each page.

Step 1

Decide where to place the first digit in the quotient.

32)5̆12 **Think** Not enough hundreds. Divide tens.

Step 2

Round the divisor and estimate the quotient digit.

30
32)5̆12 **Think** 30)51
3)5
Try 1.

Step 3

Multiply.

```
    1
32)512
  32
```

Check 32 × 16 = 512

Step 4

Subtract and compare.

```
    1
32)512
  32
  19  ← 19 < 32
```
The difference *must* be less than the divisor.

Step 5

Bring down the next digit. Repeat the steps.

```
30    16
 32)512
    32
   192   Think   30)192
   192           3)19
     0           Try 6.
```

Janine should place 16 stamps on each page.

More Examples

Check

a.
```
30       423 R14
 58)24,548
    23 2
     1 34
     1 16
       188
       174
        14 ← Place remainder in quotient.
```
```
      423
   ×   58
    3 384
   21 15
   24 534
 +    14  ← Remainder
   24,548
```

b.
```
30      $ 14.25
  63)$897.75
     63
     267
     252
      15 7
      12 6
       3 15
       3 15
          0
```
Check
```
   $14.25
 ×     63
   42 75
  855 0
 $897.75
```

CLASSWORK

Divide. Multiply to check.

1. 30)780
2. 21)966
3. 19)866
4. 38)17,260
5. 62)45,942

6. 1,032 ÷ 43
7. 12,470 ÷ 28
8. $158.13 ÷ 21
9. 377,572 ÷ 53

Divide. Multiply to check.

1. $31\overline{)992}$ 2. $61\overline{)2,318}$ 3. $23\overline{)9,485}$ 4. $70\overline{)3,220}$ 5. $42\overline{)3,654}$

6. $23\overline{)8,123}$ 7. $81\overline{)2,187}$ 8. $39\overline{)\$8,619}$ 9. $94\overline{)1,316}$ 10. $41\overline{)\$252.15}$

11. $87\overline{)49,359}$ 12. $32\overline{)\$1,684.80}$ 13. $48\overline{)39,668}$ 14. $29\overline{)21,564}$ 15. $81\overline{)38,240}$

16. $12\overline{)25,689}$ 17. $19\overline{)830,241}$ 18. $52\overline{)387,625}$ 19. $59\overline{)316,340}$ 20. $68\overline{)291,425}$

21. $824 \div 30$ 22. $502 \div 18$ 23. $2,684 \div 33$ 24. $4,256 \div 81$

25. $42,134 \div 58$ 26. $\$905.96 \div 22$ 27. $191,642 \div 31$ 28. $213,812 \div 37$

Write *true* or *false*.

★ 29. $750 \div 50 = (1,000 \div 50) - (250 \div 50)$
★ 30. $(50 - 5) \div 5 = (50 \div 5) - (5 \div 5)$

Follow the rule to find each missing number.

Rule: Divide the input by 12.

	Input	Output
	384	32
31.	852	
32.	2,568	

Rule: Divide the input by 23; then multiply by 10.

	Input	Output
	598	260
33.	782	
34.	9,798	

Rule: Divide the input by 32.

	Input	Output
★ **35.**	480	
★ **36.**		9
★ **37.**		26

APPLICATION

38. In all, Janine has collected 1,674 stamps from 62 countries. What is her average number of stamps from each country?

★ 39. In a cooperative project, students at Wilcox High School collected stamps from various countries depicting achievements in space. The students collected 546 stamps from Africa, 935 from Europe, and 847 from North and South America. If a stamp album can hold 24 stamps per page, how many pages will the collected stamps fill?

Changing Quotient Estimates

In Madeleine L'Engle's *A Wrinkle in Time,* Meg, Charles, and Calvin saw identical gray houses on the dark planet Camazotz. If there were 4,366 houses on square blocks with each block containing 74 houses, how many blocks did they see?

Divide 4,366 by 74 to find how many blocks.

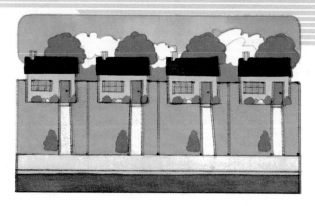

Step 1

Decide where to place the first digit of the quotient.

$$74\overline{)4{,}366}$$

Think
Not enough thousands or hundreds. Divide tens.

Step 2

Round the divisor and estimate the quotient digit.

$$74\overline{)4{,}366}$$ *(70)*

Think $70\overline{)436}$
$7\overline{)43}$
Try 6.

Step 3

Divide. Sometimes it is necessary to change the estimate.

$$\begin{array}{r} 6 \\ 74\overline{)4{,}366} \\ 4\ 44 \end{array}$$

444 > 436
6 is too large.
Try 5.

$$\begin{array}{r} 5 \\ 74\overline{)4{,}366} \\ 3\ 70 \\ \hline 66 \end{array}$$

$$\begin{array}{r} 59 \\ 74\overline{)4{,}366} \\ 3\ 70 \\ \hline 666 \\ 666 \\ \hline 0 \end{array}$$ *(70)*

Think $70\overline{)666}$
$7\overline{)66}$
Try 9.

Check 74 × 59 = 4,366

Meg, Charles, and Calvin saw 59 identical blocks.

Another Example

$$86\overline{)6{,}198}$$ *(90)*

Think $90\overline{)619} \rightarrow 86\overline{)6{,}198}$
$9\overline{)61}$
Try 6.

$$\begin{array}{r} 6 \\ 86\overline{)6{,}198} \\ 5\ 16 \\ \hline 1\ 03 \end{array}$$

103 > 86
6 is too small.
Try 7.

$$\begin{array}{r} 72\ \text{R6} \\ 86\overline{)6{,}198} \\ 6\ 02 \\ \hline 178 \\ 172 \\ \hline 6 \end{array}$$ *(90)*

$$\begin{array}{r} 86 \\ \times\ 72 \\ \hline 172 \\ 6\ 02 \\ \hline 6{,}192 \\ +\quad\ 6 \leftarrow \text{remainder} \\ \hline 6{,}198 \end{array}$$

CLASSWORK

Divide. Multiply to check.

1. $34\overline{)2{,}584}$ **2.** $75\overline{)3{,}850}$ **3.** $53\overline{)7{,}851}$ **4.** $46\overline{)31{,}464}$ **5.** $84\overline{)\$8{,}286.60}$

6. 6,863 ÷ 27   **7.** 30,854 ÷ 36   **8.** $3,805.20 ÷ 45   **9.** 36,360 ÷ 64

PRACTICE

Divide. Multiply to check.

1. 16)4,992   **2.** 87)7,154   **3.** 56)2,296   **4.** 26)7,956   **5.** 24)8,252

6. 65)56,615   **7.** 76)47,430   **8.** 44)$332.64   **9.** 67)$546.05   **10.** 35)19,884

11. 66)27,766   **12.** 67)54,605   **13.** 56)28,120   **14.** 87)436,192   **15.** 16)78,320

16. 34)91,338   **17.** 38)22,856   **18.** 48)310,200   **19.** 56)227,640   **20.** 47)328,225

21. 6,221 ÷ 26   **22.** $642.60 ÷ 84   **23.** 34,587 ÷ 63   **24.** 41,830 ÷ 27

25. $24,366 ÷ 62   **26.** 36,998 ÷ 54   **27.** 239,470 ÷ 35   **28.** 168,292 ÷ 26

Find each missing dividend or divisor.

29. 64)▮▮,▮▮▮ *(158)*   ★ **30.** ▮▮)4,902 *(86)*   ★ **31.** 32)▮▮,▮▮▮ *(568 R17)*   ★ **32.** ▮▮)3,184 *(67 R35)*

APPLICATION

33. If 4,116 flowers lined the front paths of 98 identical houses on Camazotz, how many flowers lined each path?

34. Each day on Camazotz, 75 route boys deliver 10,200 papers. If each boy delivers an equal number, how many papers does each boy deliver?

★ **35.** If the same number of people live on each block of Camazotz, and there are 10,360 people on 35 blocks, how many people would be living on 18 blocks?

★ **36.** Of all the children on Camazotz, 2,400 children are bouncing balls in unison, 5,200 are jumping rope, 1,700 are swinging on swings, and 1,600 are playing hopscotch. The children attend 25 identical schools. There are the same number of children in each school. How many children are there in each school?

Dividing Greater Numbers

One football team saved money by chartering flights to games. A charter flight cost $9,944 for 113 passengers. How much was the cost per person?

Find $9,944 ÷ 113.

Step 1

Decide where to place the first digit in the quotient.

```
        ⊔
113)$9,944
```

Think
Not enough thousands or hundreds. Divide tens.

Step 2

Round the divisor and estimate the quotient digit.

```
  100        ⊔
       113)$9,944
```

Think
```
    100)994
      1)9    Try 9.
         9
    113)994
      1017  1017 > 994
9 is too large.
Try 8.
```

Step 3

Multiply.

```
       $   8
113)$9,944
     9 04
```

Step 4

Subtract and compare.

```
       $   8
113)$9,944
     9 04
        90   90 < 113
```

Step 5

Bring down. Repeat the steps.

```
100    $   88
     113)$9,944
          9 04
           904      Think   100)904
           904      Adjust the estimate.     9
             0
```

Check $88 × 113 = $9,944

The flight cost $88 per person.

More Examples

a.
```
  400        125 R250
    393)49,375
        39 3
        10 07
         7 86
         2 215
         1 965
           250  250 < 393
```

b.
```
  800      $    63.24
    811)$51,287.64
        48 66
         2 627
         2 433
           194 6
           162 2
            32 44
            32 44
                0
```

c.
```
  400        180 R406
    409)74,026
        40 9
        33 12
        32 72
           406  406 < 409
```

CLASSWORK

Divide. Multiply to check.

1. 204)71,810   **2.** 672)$88,704   **3.** 712)886,450   **4.** 376)320,352

52

PRACTICE

Divide. Multiply to check.

1. $400\overline{)26{,}384}$ **2.** $196\overline{)93{,}688}$ **3.** $234\overline{)95{,}480}$ **4.** $127\overline{)66{,}200}$

5. $314\overline{)178{,}352}$ **6.** $708\overline{)\$39{,}853.32}$ **7.** $492\overline{)445{,}270}$ **8.** $523\overline{)463{,}378}$

9. $212\overline{)128{,}900}$ **10.** $629\overline{)345{,}950}$ **11.** $118\overline{)237{,}534}$ **12.** $399\overline{)618{,}151}$

13. $409\overline{)\$88{,}474.88}$ **14.** $234\overline{)586{,}424}$ **15.** $618\overline{)335{,}676}$ **16.** $312\overline{)626{,}898}$

17. $\$76{,}700 \div 118$ **18.** $224{,}950 \div 279$ **19.** $807{,}700 \div 394$

20. $298{,}811 \div 611$ **21.** $671{,}823 \div 319$ **22.** $881{,}984 \div 288$

Estimate to choose the exact quotient for each.

23. $28\overline{)69{,}300}$
  a. 2,475
  b. 3,475
  c. 2,975

24. $32\overline{)60{,}960}$
  a. 1,095
  b. 1,905
  c. 19,005

25. $318\overline{)159{,}636}$
  a. 5,002
  b. 492
  c. 502

★**26.** $4{,}075\overline{)1{,}731{,}875}$
  a. 4,025
  b. 425
  c. 525

APPLICATION

27. A charter flight for 350 passengers on a jumbo jet cost $62,650. How much is that per passenger?

★**28.** The regular air fare from New York to Miami would total $79,475 for 275 passengers. At this rate, what would be the total for 300 passengers?

VISUAL THINKING

Match all parts that together will form a circle.

1   2   3   4

5   6   7   8

Equations

During a shuttle launch the countdown was stopped a total of 48 minutes for minor repairs. The average time of each repair was 6 minutes. How many times was the countdown stopped?

$$n \times 6 = 48$$

To find the missing factor, write a related division equation.

$n \times 6 = 48$ **Think** Multiplication
$n = 48 \div 6$ and division are inverse operations.

So $n = 8$ **Check** $8 \times 6 = 48$

The countdown was stopped 8 times.

▶ Solve a multiplication equation by using a related division equation.

$a \times 5 = 35$
$a = 35 \div 5$
$a = 7$

Check $5 \times 7 = 35$

▶ Solve a division equation by using a related multiplication equation.

$b \div 3 = 4$
$b = 4 \times 3$
$b = 12$

Check $12 \div 3 = 4$

More Examples

a. $40 = 4 \times y$
$40 \div 4 = y$
$10 = y$

Check $40 = 4 \times 10$

b. $\frac{x}{6} = 5 \leftarrow \frac{x}{6}$ means $x \div 6$

$x = 5 \times 6$
$x = 30$

Check $\frac{30}{6} = 5$

CLASSWORK

Find each missing factor.

1. $4 \times n = 28$ **2.** $12 \div n = 3$ **3.** $30 = 5 \times c$ **4.** $7 \times n = 42$ **5.** $72 \div b = 8$

Write a related equation to solve each.

6. $7 \times a = 56$ **7.** $n \div 7 = 10$ **8.** $\frac{x}{8} = 4$ **9.** $150 = 5 \times q$ **10.** $12 = c \div 12$

Find each missing factor.

1. $3 \times c = 27$ **2.** $20 \div n = 4$ **3.** $60 = 6 \times p$ **4.** $y \times 9 = 9$ **5.** $44 \div x = 4$

Choose the related equation that will solve each.

6. $n \div 8 = 56$

  a. $n = 56 \div 8$
  b. $n \div 56 = 8$
  c. $n = 56 \times 8$

7. $r \times 9 = 63$

  a. $r \times 63 = 9$
  b. $r = 63 \div 9$
  c. $9 \times 63 = r$

8. $75 = 15 \times y$

  a. $75 \div 15 = y$
  b. $y = 15 \div 75$
  c. $y = 15 \times 75$

9. $b + 19 = 31$

  a. $b = 31 + 19$
  b. $b = 31 - 19$
  c. $b + 31 = 19$

10. $a - 16 = 21$

  a. $a + 16 = 21$
  b. $a = 21 - 16$
  c. $a = 21 + 16$

11. $\frac{j}{12} = 9$

  a. $j = 12 \times 9$
  b. $\frac{9}{j} = 12$
  c. $9 \times j = 12$

Write a related equation and solve.

12. $5 \times m = 25$ **13.** $c \times 11 = 66$ **14.** $a \div 6 = 4$ **15.** $n \times 4 = 56$

16. $10 \times r = 270$ **17.** $p \div 18 = 9$ **18.** $276 = p \times 23$ **19.** $950 = 38 \times b$

20. $y \div 50 = 7$ **21.** $1 = d \div 24$ **22.** $10 = r \div 18$ **23.** $18 = t \times 18$

24. $29 \times d = 377$ **25.** $\frac{m}{8} = 12$ **26.** $0 = \frac{n}{8}$ **27.** $180 = 45 \times t$

28. $47 = n \div 18$ **29.** $s \times 15 = 210$ **30.** $19 = \frac{c}{12}$ **31.** $3{,}140 = 314 \times p$

★**32.** $21 = (5 + 2) \times j$ ★**33.** $t \times (6 + 15) = 399$ ★**34.** $4 = h \div (9 - 5)$

APPLICATION

Choose the appropriate equation for each.

35. The product of 9 and a number is 234.

  a. $n \times 234 = 9$
  b. $n \div 9 = 234$
  c. $9 \times n = 234$

36. A number divided by 8 has a quotient of 40.

  a. $q \times 8 = 40$
  b. $q \div 8 = 40$
  c. $8 \div q = 40$

37. Space Shuttle 3 orbited the earth 129 times in 8 days. How many orbits was this per day?

  a. $a \div 8 = 129$
  b. $a \times 8 = 129$
  c. $a = 129 \times 8$

★**38.** The average age of 2 astronauts on Space Shuttle 1 was 46. If one of them was 43 years old, how old was the other?

  a. $(x + 43) \div 2 = 46$
  b. $(x + 46) \div 2 = 43$
  c. $x = (46 + 43) \div 2$

Problem Solving

SKILLS AND STRATEGIES REVIEW   Life on Planet Lemma

Gila is a city on Lemma, a planet in another solar system. Gila has a population of 875,000. Some of the inhabitants have one head with two antennas. They are called biants. Others have two heads but no antennas. They are called bicranes.

Solve each problem that has enough information. If there is not enough information, tell what facts are needed.

1. What is the name of the city?

2. How far from Earth is Lemma?

3. How many inhabitants are in Gila?

4. How many biants are in Gila?

What if there are 448,000 bicranes in Gila?

5. How many biants are there?

6. How many hats would be needed if each head in Gila is to have one hat?

7. How many of these hats must have holes for two antennas?

The distances between cities are measured in mylters on Lemma. This roadmap shows the number of mylters between various major cities.

8. What is the distance between Kura and Siva?

9. The distance between Kura and Siva is about how many times greater than the distance between Gila and Kura? Estimate the answer.

10. If a biant travels on the road from Gila through Kura to Siva, how many mylters does it travel?

11. Which is greater, the distance from Kura through Gila to Vita or the distance from Kura through Siva to Vita? How much greater?

56

Problem Solving

WHAT IF . . . ?

**Solve each problem if there is enough information. If there
is not enough information, tell what facts are needed.**

1. Imagine that it is the year 2001, and you have completed your education. You are an engineer at a space center. What is your age?

2. You have been put in charge of a small project. You earn $45,624 per year, and you work 5 days per week. How much money do you earn per month?

3. What are the federal taxes on your salary?

4. What is your weekly salary?

What if you have three assistants. Their hourly earnings are shown in the table at the right.

Use the information to answer 5–12.

Person	Hourly wage
Luanne	$21
Mack	$18
Vince	$16

5. How much does Mack earn per week if each assistant works 35 hours per week?

6. How much more than $30,000 does Mack earn per year?

7. How much more does Luanne earn per week than Vince?

8. How much more does Luanne earn per year than Mack?

What if the assistants worked 39 hours per week?

9. How much would Mack earn in 4 weeks?

10. How much would Vince earn per week?

11. How many weeks would it take Mack to work 1,560 hours?

★ 12. About how many weeks would it take Luanne to earn $40,000?

What if a new pay scale and work schedule are put into effect? Suppose each assistant receives a $2 increase in hourly wages and works according to the following schedule: 7 hours per day on Monday through Thursday, and 4 hours per day on Friday and Saturday.

13. How many hours will each person work in 4 weeks?

14. How many hours will each person have off during 4 weeks?

15. About how many weeks will it take each person to work 1,000 hours? Estimate the answer. Write the answer as a whole number.

16. Each assistant receives a $2-an-hour increase after working 2,520 hours. How many weeks of work is that?

CHAPTER REVIEW

Name the property of multiplication illustrated in each example. pages 30–31

1. $8 \times 5 = 5 \times 8$

2. $9 \times (4 + 7) = (9 \times 4) + (9 \times 7)$

3. $0 \times 12 = 0$

4. $(3 \times 6) \times 2 = 3 \times (6 \times 2)$

5. $32 \times 1 = 32$

6. $9 \times (10 + 4) = (9 \times 10) + (9 \times 4)$

Estimate each product. pages 34–35

7.	**8.**	**9.**	**10.**	**11.**
76	$33	1,280	5,465	8,603
$\times\ 24$	$\times\ 88$	$\times\ \ \ 19$	$\times\ \ \ 237$	$\times\ 2,099$

Multiply. pages 36–39

12.	**13.**	**14.**	**15.**	**16.**
67	434	2,405	$67.49	32,500
$\times\ \ 8$	$\times\ \ 7$	$\times\ \ \ 12$	$\times\ \ \ 205$	$\times\ \ 1,482$

Find the missing exponent or product. pages 40–41

17. $6^{\square} = 216$ **18.** $4^5 = \square$ **19.** $16^{\square} = 256$ **20.** $9^{\square} = 9$ **21.** $3^4 = \square$ **22.** $2^7 = \square$

Find each average. pages 44–45

23. 17, 24, 34

24. 39¢, 49¢, 57¢, 63¢, 57¢

25. 748, 659, 723, 698

Choose the estimate closer to the actual quotient. pages 46–47, 50–51

26. $25\overline{)3,287}$
   a. 200
   b. 100

27. $83\overline{)82,709}$
   a. 900
   b. 1,000

28. $17\overline{)670,083}$
   a. 30,000
   b. 3,000

Divide. pages 48–49, 52–53

29. $2,352 \div 42$

30. $29,743 \div 36$

31. $62,089 \div 300$

32. $401,952 \div 158$

Write a related equation for each and solve. pages 54–55

33. $3 \times n = 147$

34. $\frac{s}{9} = 5$

35. $360 = 10 \times a$

36. $q \div 12 = 8$

Solve. pages 42–43, 56–57

37. Brooke is flying from New York to Paris. The trip takes about 7 hours. The plane leaves at 1:00 P.M. and flies at an average speed of 520 miles per hour. Estimate the distance between New York and Paris.

38. The Galaxy 1 cable television satellite orbits the earth once every 1,440 minutes. How many hours does one orbit take?

Name the property of multiplication illustrated in each example.

1. $8 \times (4 \times 9) = (8 \times 4) \times 9$

2. $10 \times 5 = 5 \times 10$

3. $0 \times 11 = 0$

Estimate each product or quotient.

4. 79×43

5. $27\overline{)1,304}$

6. $239 \times 1,903$

7. $43,704 \div 44$

Multiply.

8. $\begin{array}{r} 2,408 \\ \times\quad 9 \\ \hline \end{array}$

9. $\begin{array}{r} 835 \\ \times\quad 28 \\ \hline \end{array}$

10. $\begin{array}{r} \$10.67 \\ \times\quad 205 \\ \hline \end{array}$

11. $\begin{array}{r} 37,490 \\ \times\quad 1,687 \\ \hline \end{array}$

Find the missing exponent or product.

12. $2^{\square} = 32$

13. $5^3 = \square$

14. $7^2 = \square$

15. $3^{\square} = 729$

Divide.

16. $9\overline{)358}$

17. $36\overline{)1,944}$

18. $29\overline{)2,048}$

19. $402\overline{)130,650}$

Write a related equation for each and solve.

20. $6 \times b = 216$

21. $p \div 8 = 7$

22. $432 = 9 \times a$

23. $47 = 47 \times n$

Solve.

24. A certain airline will allow up to 55 pounds of luggage per passenger. What is the maximum weight of the luggage on an airplane carrying 134 passengers?

25. An airplane covered the following distances in 3 trips: 1,300 miles, 972 miles, and 1,580 miles. The average speed of the plane was 550 miles per hour. What was the average distance covered in the 3 trips?

Start with a number. Divide it by 25. Multiply that quotient by 16. The result is 64. What is the starting number?

HEARTBEATS

The *Skylab* astronauts exercised regularly to keep their hearts strong during the long period of weightlessness. Their heartbeats were carefully monitored in space and on their return to earth.

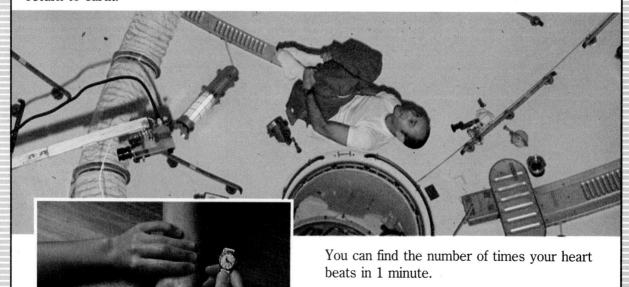

You can find the number of times your heart beats in 1 minute.

- Work with a partner.
- Use a watch with a second hand.
- Take your pulse.

1. Take a pulse count for 15 seconds. Repeat. Then take a third count. Record the results.

2. Find the average of the 3 counts. Round your answer to the nearest whole number.

3. Multiply the average by 4 to find the number of times your heart beats in 1 minute.

Use a calculator to find about how many times your heart beats.

4. in 1 math period   **5.** in 6 hours   **6.** in 1 day

About how many times will your heart beat?

7. in 1 year   **8.** in 5 years   **9.** in 12 years

Find each to the nearest whole number.

10. the number of days it takes your heart to beat 1 million times

11. the number of years it takes your heart to beat 1 billion times

GEOMETRIC SEQUENCES

Gary was offered an unusual job that paid 1¢
on the first day, 2¢ on the second day, 4¢ on
the third day, 8¢ on the fourth day, and so
on. How much money would Gary earn on the
tenth day?

The numbers 1, 2, 4, 8, . . . form a
geometric sequence. A sequence is a
list of numbers. The numbers in a
sequence are called **terms.** In a
geometric sequence, each term is the result
of multiplying the previous term by a given
number.

The rule for the sequence in the problem
above is to multiply each term by 2. Using
this rule, you can continue the sequence to
find the tenth term.

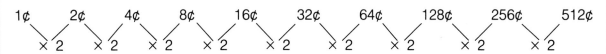

On the tenth day, Gary would earn 512¢, or $5.12.

Would you take the job?

Continue the geometric sequence.
How much money would you earn on each day?

1. the 15th day   **2.** the 20th day   **3.** the 25th day

Write the rule for each sequence. Then find the next three terms.

4. 1, 3, 9, 27, . . .   **5.** 2, 8, 32, 128, . . .   **6.** 4, 20, 100, 500, . . .

7. 1, 10, 100, 1,000, . . .   **8.** 5^1, 5^2, 5^3, 5^4, . . .   **9.** 2^1, 2^3, 2^5, 2^7, . . .

Find the missing term in each sequence.

10. 2, 6, n, 54, . . .   **11.** n, 4, 16, 64, . . .   **12.** n, 5, 25, 125, . . .

13. 12, 24, 48, n, . . .   **14.** 8, 24, n, 216, . . .   **15.** 1, n, 81, 729, . . .

16. 7, 35, n, 875, . . .   **17.** 111, 333, 999, n, . . .   **18.** 10, 40, n, 640, . . .

19. 10^1, 10^2, n, 10^4, . . .   **20.** 2^2, 2^4, n, 2^8, . . .   **21.** 3^1, 3^4, 3^7, n, . . .

MAINTAINING SKILLS

Choose the correct answers. Write A, B, C, or D.

1. What is the value of 8 in 1,086,493?

  A 80 billion   C 8 million

  B 80 thousand   D 8 billion

2. Compare. 7,399 ⬭ 7,408

  A >   C =

  B <   D not given

3. Round 24,896 to the nearest thousand.

  A 24,000   C 30,000

  B 25,000   D not given

4. What addition property is used?
$97 + 0 = 97$

  A commutative   C identity

  B associative   D not given

5. Order from least to greatest.
43,009; 43,090; 43,089

  A 43,090; 43,089;   C 43,009; 43,089;
  43,009   43,090

  B 43,089; 43,009;   D not given
  43,090

6. $374.86 + $91.17

  A $465.93   C $466.03

  B $376.03   D not given

7. $219.42
  − 164.07

  A $55.35   C $155.45

  B $55.49   D not given

8. Estimate. 34,493 − 19,103

  A 10,000   C 30,000

  B 20,000   D not given

9. What is the related equation for
$42 = x + 35$?

  A $x = 42 + 35$ C $x = 42 - 35$

  B $x = 42 \times 35$ D not given

10. 216 × 446

  A 96,306   C 86,336

  B 96,336   D not given

11. Estimate. 9,062 ÷ 33

  A 30   C 300

  B 200   D not given

12. $22\overline{)\$91.30}$

  A $4.25   C $4.11

  B $4.15   D not given

13. What is the related equation for $\frac{b}{7} = 14$?

  A $b \times 7 = 14$ C $b = 14 - 7$

  B $b = 14 \div 7$ D not given

**Use the information given below to solve
14 and 15.**

Washington Middle School has an enrollment of
847 sixth-graders, 909 seventh-graders, and
878 eighth-graders.

14. How many more students are in the
seventh grade than in the sixth grade?

  A 162   C 31

  B 62   D not given

15. Last year, the school had an enrollment of
2,597 students. By how many students
has enrollment increased this year?

  A 37   C 47

  B 48   D 137

Decimals

Sandy Strong is a biologist who studies the life forms in rivers and streams. She found tiny flatworms, called planarians, under the rocks of a flowing stream.

Planarians are seldom longer than 3 centimeters. This one is 2.86 centimeters long.

The number 2.86 is a decimal. It is shown here as a model and on the place-value table below.

1			1		$\frac{8}{10}$ or 0.8	$\frac{6}{100}$ or 0.06
	two wholes				eight tenths	six hundredths

hundreds	tens	ones	tenths	hundredths	thousandths	
100	10	1	0.1	0.01	0.001	
100	10	1	$\frac{1}{10}$	$\frac{1}{100}$	$\frac{1}{1,000}$	
		2.	8	6		← read 2 *and* 86 hundredths
	3	5.	1	4	9	← read 35 *and* 149 thousandths

The value of a digit depends on its place in the number. Each place in the decimal is ten times the value of the place to its right. Look at the place-value table. What is the value of the digit 9 in the number 35.149?

$$35.149$$

0.009, or 9 thousandths write nine thousandths

CLASSWORK

Write each as a decimal.

1.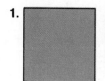

2.

3.

4. $\frac{5}{10}$

5. $\frac{3}{100}$

6. $\frac{34}{1,000}$

7. $1\frac{4}{10}$

8. $6\frac{103}{1,000}$

9. $10\frac{10}{1,000}$

Write each decimal in words. Give the value of the digit 7 in each.

10. 0.7

11. 0.27

12. 1.371

13. 2.047

14. 16.705

PRACTICE

Write each as a decimal.

1. 　　**2.** 　　**3.**

4. $\frac{3}{10}$　　**5.** $\frac{9}{100}$　　**6.** $3\frac{23}{100}$　　**7.** $\frac{157}{1,000}$　　**8.** $5\frac{46}{1,000}$　　**9.** $\frac{5}{1,000}$

10. five and six tenths

11. one and twenty-four thousandths

12. eight and seventy-one hundredths

13. three hundred nine thousandths

14. two and four hundredths

15. two and four thousandths

Write each decimal in words. Give the value of the digit 5 in each.

16. 2.5　　**17.** 6.05　　**18.** 0.507　　**19.** 5.123　　**20.** 1.025

21. 52.63　　**22.** 321.95　　**23.** 6.152　　**24.** 513.6　　**25.** 0.145

Match.

26. sixty-eight hundredths　　　　　　　　**a.** 6.8

27. sixty and eight thousandths　　　　　　**b.** 0.068

28. six and eight tenths　　　　　　　　　**c.** 0.68

29. sixty-eight and eight thousandths　　　**d.** 0.680

30. sixty-eight thousandths　　　　　　　**e.** 6.08

31. sixty-eight and sixty-eight hundredths　**f.** 60.008

32. six and eight hundredths　　　　　　　**g.** 68.008

33. six hundred eighty thousandths　　　　**h.** 68.68

APPLICATION

34. Sandy found a planarian that is two and nine hundredths centimeters long. Write its length as a decimal.

★ **35.** Sandy collected a sample of 1,000 planarians. She recorded their lengths. Only 18 of them were longer than 3 cm. Write the decimal that represents the part of the sample with planarians longer than 3 cm. Write the decimal for the part of the sample with planarians *not* longer than 3 cm.

Decimals to Millionths

While working in the Philippine Islands, Niki Lee, a biologist, found a dwarf goby fish that weighed 0.000156 ounce. The dwarf goby is the smallest known fish in the world.

To help read a decimal number like 0.000156, the place-value table is extended to the millionths place.

hundreds	tens	ones	tenths	hundredths	thousandths	ten-thousandths	hundred-thousandths	millionths	
100	10	1	0.1	0.01	0.001	0.0001	0.00001	0.000001	
100	10	1	$\frac{1}{10}$	$\frac{1}{100}$	$\frac{1}{1,000}$	$\frac{1}{10,000}$	$\frac{1}{100,000}$	$\frac{1}{1,000,000}$	
		0.	0	0	0	1	5	6	← read 156 millionths
	3	6.	0	0	2	4	7		← 36 *and* 247 hundred-thousandths

You can use the place-value table to find the value of each digit. The value of the digit 5 in 0.000156 is

$5 \times 0.00001 = 0.00005$ ← read 5 hundred-thousandths

You can write a decimal in expanded form to show the value of each digit.

0.000156 = 0.0001 + 0.00005 + 0.000006
    or   (1 × 0.0001) + (5 × 0.00001) + (6 × 0.000001)

36.00247 = 30 + 6 + 0.002 + 0.0004 + 0.00007
    or   (3 × 10) + (6 × 1) + (2 × 0.001) + (4 × 0.0001) + (7 × 0.00001)

CLASSWORK

Write each as a decimal.

1. 125 hundred-thousandths

2. 3 and 18 millionths

3. (5 × 1) + (6 × 0.0001) + (7 × 0.00001)

4. 3 + 0.9 + 0.008 + 0.000004

Give the value of each underlined digit.

5. 4.0967

6. 31.863159

7. 0.0408

8. 0.000452

PRACTICE

Write each as a decimal.

1. 6 and 19 hundredths
2. 215 thousandths
3. 3,125 ten-thousandths
4. 5 and 42 millionths
5. 2 and 36 thousandths
6. 86 hundred-thousandths
7. 6 + 0.2 + 0.005 + 0.0009
8. 90 + 7 + 0.04 + 0.00005
9. (5 × 0.1) + (6 × 0.01) + (3 × 0.001)
10. (4 × 1) + (8 × 0.001) + (7 × 0.0001)
11. (6 × 0.1) + (9 × 0.001) + (4 × 0.00001)
12. (4 × 100) + (6 × 1) + (3 × 0.000001)

Give the value of each underlined digit.

13. 15.16$\underline{7}$3
14. 0.000$\underline{9}$1
15. 3.19765$\underline{2}$
16. 0.008$\underline{5}$23
17. 0.00005$\underline{6}$
18. 7$\underline{2}$.0145
19. 6.0004$\underline{5}$9
20. 0.9$\underline{8}$0051

Write each in expanded form in two ways.

21. 6.083
22. 3.2054
23. 0.010073
24. 23.000045

Copy and complete each pattern.

★ 25. 0.27, 0.28, 0.29, □, □, □
★ 26. 0.012, 0.017, 0.022, □, □, □

APPLICATION

27. Niki Lee found a dwarf goby fish that measures 0.2904 in. long. Write the word name for this length.

★ 28. Niki Lee found another tiny fish. It weighs 4 thousandths of an ounce more than the dwarf goby. The dwarf goby weighs 0.000156 ounce. What is the weight of the other fish?

CALCULATOR

Enter [2] [·] [3] [4] [5] [6]. Next enter [−] [·] [0] [4] [=].

Your calculator will display $\boxed{2.3056}$ because you subtracted 4 hundredths.

Begin with $\boxed{2.3456}$ each time. What will you enter to get each display?

1. $\boxed{2.3406}$
2. $\boxed{2.0456}$
3. $\boxed{2.345}$
4. $\boxed{2.3006}$
5. $\boxed{2.0056}$
6. $\boxed{0.3456}$

Comparing and Ordering Decimals

The members of the White Water Club held a kayak race on the Kennebec River. Who finished the race in the least time?

To compare two decimals, start at the left and compare digits in the same places. Find the first place where the decimals differ.

Racer	Minutes	Time Seconds
Bill	4	9.835
Devin	4	9.752
Arlene	4	9.843
Nita	4	9.755

9.835 ⬤ 9.752   9.835 ⬤ 9.843   9.752 ⬤ 9.755
└─ 8 > 7 ─┘   └─ 3 < 4 ─┘   └─ 2 < 5 ─┘

9.835 > 9.752   9.835 < 9.843   9.752 < 9.755

In order from least to greatest, the times in the kayak race are as follows.

9.752 < 9.755 < 9.835 < 9.843

Devin finished the race in the least time.

▶ Decimals that name the same number are called **equivalent decimals.** Annexing zeros does not change the value of a decimal.

0.3 = 0.30 = 0.300 = 0.3000

4.8 = 4.80 = 4.800 = 4.8000

6 = 6.0 = 6.00 = 6.000

▶ When the number of decimal places in two decimals are different, annex zeros to compare.

6.3142 ⬤ 6.314

6.3142 ⬤ 6.314   6.314 = 6.3140
    └─ 2 > 0 ─┘

6.3142 > 6.314

CLASSWORK

Compare. Use >, <, or = for each ⬤.

1. 6.72 ⬤ 6.48

2. 0.08 ⬤ 0.083

3. 2.080 ⬤ 2.08

4. 1.5535 ⬤ 1.5530

5. 0.52 ⬤ 0.520

6. 0.0153 ⬤ 0.0162

Write in order from least to greatest.

7. 4.869, 4.871, 4.853, 4.792

8. 3.6, 3.642, 3.648, 3.644

PRACTICE

Compare. Use >, <, or = for each ⬤.

1. 8.723 ⬤ 8.713
2. 0.07 ⬤ 0.72
3. 3.42 ⬤ 3.420
4. 13.5 ⬤ 13.7
5. 7.03 ⬤ 7.30
6. 35.6 ⬤ 3.56
7. 0.654 ⬤ 0.645
8. 0.006 ⬤ 0.0006
9. 7.314 ⬤ 7.31
10. 0.703 ⬤ 0.7030
11. 5.81 ⬤ 5.18
12. 54.61 ⬤ 546.1
13. 7.14 ⬤ 71.48
14. 16.65 ⬤ 1.665
15. 3.6004 ⬤ 3.604

Write in order from least to greatest.

16. 0.3546; 0.3846; 0.3536
17. 0.623; 0.627; 0.614
18. 35.62; 3.562; 356.2
19. 7.030; 7.0310; 7.029
20. 3.2003; 3.20301; 3.20013; 3.2
21. 7.405; 7.045; 7.540; 7.054
22. 0.314; 0.31; 0.3; 0.3145; 0.3154
23. 2.84; 2.8; 2.48; 2.81; 2.4

Write the greater decimal in standard form.

24. nine hundred ten-thousandths or nine hundred four thousandths

25. two and forty-one hundredths or two and three hundred ninety thousandths

26. forty and thirty-one thousandths or forty and thirty-one hundredths

27. one thousand one ten-thousandths or one thousand one millionths

Write three decimals that are between each pair.

★28. 2.57 and 2.58
★29. 3.681 and 3.682
★30. 18.53 and 18.54

APPLICATION

31. Who finished the second race in the least time?

32. In what order did the racers finish the second race?

★33. Peter missed tying the club's record for this race by 3 hundredths of a second. What is the club's record time?

KAYAK RACE #2

Racer	Time	
	Minutes	Seconds
Thalia	6	0.953
Marc	6	1.09
Peter	6	0.95
Kate	6	1.125

Rounding Decimals

The St. Lawrence Seaway is the final link in the busy waterway from Duluth, Minnesota, to the Atlantic Ocean. Canals and locks enable ships to avoid rapids and falls in the St. Lawrence River.

What distance does this lock raise ships? Round to the nearest tenth.

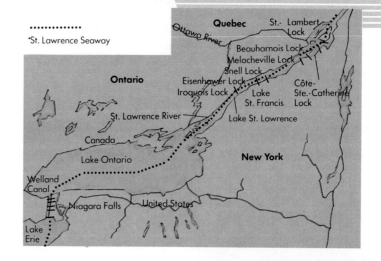

Step 1 Find the rounding place.

12.87

Step 2 Look at the digit to the right.

If it is less than 5, leave the digit in the rounding place unchanged.

If it is 5 or more, increase the digit in the rounding place by 1.

12.87

7 > 5

12.9

Step 3 Remove all digits to the right of the rounding place.

12.9

The lock raises ships about 12.9 m.

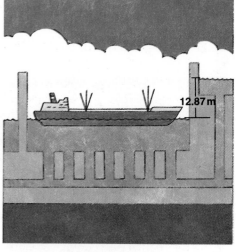

More Examples

a. Round to the nearest dollar.

$57.54 rounds to $58

5 = 5

b. Round to the nearest hundredth.

0.1947 rounds to 0.19

4 < 5

c. Round to the nearest thousandth.

4.0008 rounds to 4.001

8 > 5

d. Round to the nearest ten-thousandth.

3.96196 rounds to 3.9620

6 > 5

CLASSWORK

Round to the place named.

1. $3.18 to the nearest ten cents

2. 0.14879 to the nearest ten-thousandth

3. 0.4 to the nearest one

4. 7.6143 to the nearest thousandth

5. 8.604 to the nearest hundredth

6. 9.954 to the nearest tenth

Round to the place named.

nearest
hundredth

1. 3.1617 **2.** 19.316 **3.** 0.7168

nearest
thousandth

4. 0.0161 **5.** 98.1604 **6.** 18.3097

7. 0.2763 **8.** 54.0967 **9.** 0.9996

nearest
ten-thousandth

10. 8.23603 **11.** 18.140658 **12.** 139.62183

13. 1.48007 **14.** 13.90909 ★ **15.** 5.18995

nearest dollar

16. $1.11 **17.** $19.75 **18.** $15.99

nearest ten cents

19. $5.19 **20.** $18.25 ★ **21.** $12.95

nearest cent

22. $17.133 **23.** $2.0574 ★ **24.** $1.896

nearest
hundred-thousandth

★ **25.** 0.050057 ★ **26.** 0.0160995 ★ **27.** 99.999997

APPLICATION

28. To the nearest hundredth, what part of the tonnage shipped on the seaway is bulk commodities?

29. To the nearest hundredth, what part of the tonnage shipped on the seaway is manufactured products? What part is other products?

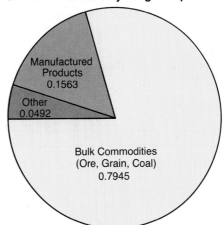

St. Lawrence Seaway Cargo Shipments

Manufactured Products 0.1563

Other 0.0492

Bulk Commodities (Ore, Grain, Coal) 0.7945

LOGICAL THINKING

Write each number. Use the digits 0, 1, 2, 3, 4, and 5 once in each number.

1. the smallest number less than 1

2. the largest number less than 1

3. the smallest number between 1 and 2

4. the largest number between 1 and 2

5. the smallest number between 4 and 5

6. the largest number between 4 and 5

Problem Solving

SIMULATION

Some problems are solved by actually doing an experiment or gathering and analyzing data. When it is not practical to do the experiment or to gather data, you can make a **model** that represents the action. This is called a **simulation** of the problem.

Two boats leave a river dock and travel in opposite directions. Boat A travels 6 km east, where its passengers disembark. Boat B travels 5 km west, where its cargo is unloaded. By noon, Boat A has traveled 2 km west, to its next stopping place, and Boat B has traveled 3 km west of its first stop. How far apart are the boats at noon?

THINK **What is the question?**

How far apart are the boats?

What are the facts?

Boat A traveled 6 km east, then 2 km west. Boat B traveled 5 km west, then 3 km west.

PLAN **How can the answer be found?**

The action of this problem cannot actually be carried out. Simulate the action with a drawing instead. Then solve the problem by computing or measuring.

SOLVE **Carry out the plan. Then answer the question.**

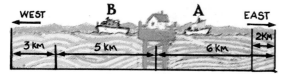

The drawing makes the situation clear.

The distance between boats is:
3 + 5 + 6 − 2 = 12 km
The two boats are 12 km apart.

LOOK BACK **Have you answered the question? Does your answer make sense?**

Boat A is 6 − 2, or 4 km east of the original dock.

Boat B is 5 + 3, or 8 km west of the original dock.

4 + 8 = 12; so the two boats are 12 km apart. The answer is correct.

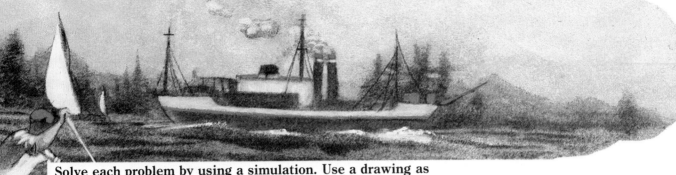

Solve each problem by using a simulation. Use a drawing as a model, or use objects when it's more convenient.

1. Randi paddles her canoe 3 km east, then 2 km north. After that she paddles 6 km west, then 2 km south. How far is she from her starting point?

2. Mario paddles his canoe 2 km east, then 5 km west. He then paddles 4 km east. How far is Mario from his original starting point?

3. A section of the river is roped off because of dangerous rocks. The section is a square, 32 meters on each side. Marker buoys are placed every 4 meters. How many buoys are there?

4. There are 4 boats on the river. The yellow boat is in front of the red boat. The blue boat is behind the green boat. The yellow boat is behind the blue boat. What is the order of the boats?

5. Boat X and Boat Y leave a dock and travel in opposite directions. Boat X travels 6 km east to drop off its passengers. Boat Y travels 8 km west, where its passengers disembark. Then Boat X travels 3 km east, and Boat Y travels 8 km east. How far apart are the boats?

6. Dennis has 4 uncles who have offices on different floors in the Harbor Office Building. One day, Dennis visits his uncles. First, he goes up to the 12th floor, then down 5 floors. Later, he goes up 3 floors and down 7 floors. What floor is he on when he visits the last uncle?

★ 7. A rubber ball is dropped from a height of 12 meters. It bounces up 9 meters on the first bounce. It bounces back up 5 meters on the second bounce. What is the total distance the ball has traveled when it hits the ground the third time?

★ 8. Inez places 20 pennies in a row on her desk. She replaces every third coin with a nickel. Next, she replaces every fourth coin with a dime. Finally, she replaces every fifth coin with a quarter. What is the value of the 20 coins now in a row?

CREATE YOUR OWN PROBLEM

This table gives the distances that Pierre sails his boat on Monday through Friday. Assume that the pattern continues for the next two days. Create two problems using his sailing data from Monday through Sunday. Solve each problem.

Day	Distance in km
Monday	7
Tuesday	5
Wednesday	8
Thursday	6
Friday	9

Estimating Sums and Differences

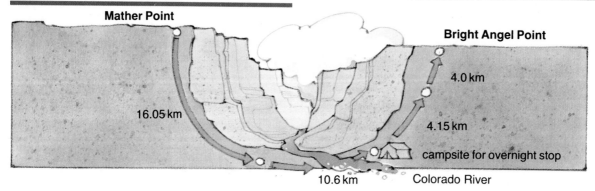

Mather Point

Bright Angel Point

16.05 km

4.0 km

4.15 km

campsite for overnight stop

10.6 km   Colorado River

Eric and John went hiking in the Grand Canyon. They hiked from Mather Point and crossed the Colorado River the first day. On the second day they climbed to Bright Angel Point. About how many kilometers did they hike on the trip?

Estimate to find the answer.

To estimate a sum or a difference, round each number to the greatest nonzero place of the greatest number. Then add or subtract.

Round to tens.

16.05	→	20
4.0	→	0
10.6	→	10
+ 4.15	→	+ 0
		30

They hiked about 30 kilometers.

▶ To get a closer estimate, round each number one more place to the right.

a. Estimate $10 − $4.34.

Round to nearest ten.	Round to nearest one.
$10 Estimate	$10 Closer
− 0 too large	− 4 estimate
$10 ←	6 ←

b. Estimate 2.403 + 0.48.

Round to nearest one.	Round to nearest tenth.
2 Estimate	2.4 Closer
+ 0 too small	+ 0.5 estimate
2 ←	2.9 ←

CLASSWORK

Estimate.

1. 51.176
      + 42.479

2. $9.87
      − 1.40

3. 9.16
      + 8.178

4. 8.99
      − 7.21

5. 77.1486
      − 54.87

Give the estimate and the closer estimate.

6. 76.512
      − 9.21

7. $20.00
      − 16.79

8. $19.23
      + 8.75

9. 0.48
      + 1.39

10. 321.98
      + 48.67

PRACTICE

Estimate.

1. $19.25
   + 36.15

2. $154.19
   − 76.20

3. 7.063
   − 0.745

4. 19.2
   − 8.9

5. 8.22
   + 3.06

6. 30.57
   − 18.93

7. $24.16
   5.12
   + .38

8. 17.416
   9.38
   + 15.63

9. 396.45
   78.21
   + 516.30

Give the estimate and the closer estimate.

10. $59.29
    − 3.13

11. 21.59
    + 3.06

12. 5,480.16
    + 375.014

13. 78.918 − 4.6219

14. $1,720.40 − $412.90

15. 834.61 + 32.9

16. 3.21 + 0.487

 Estimate to find how much change. Use a calculator to tell if the actual change is more or less than the estimate.

	Sum of Purchases	Paid with	Estimated Change
17.	$7.35	$10 bill	
18.	$38.95	$50 bill	
19.	$79.95	$100 bill	
20.	$15.10	$20 bill	
★ 21.	$519.10	$1,000 bill	

APPLICATION

22. Estimate the distance Eric and John hiked each day.

23. On which day did they hike farther? About how much farther did they hike that day?

24. Five other hikers, who had hiked 15.5 km, bought snacks at Bright Angel Point. Estimate how much the group spent in all if the purchases were $1.85, $2.40, $1.20, $2.65, and $1.70.

Mixed Practice

1. 654
   93
   + 852

2. 1,025
   − 796

3. 327 + 58 = n

4. 8,034 − 859 = n

5. 125 × 30 = n

6. 7)634

7. 6)485

8. 2,008
   × 24

9. 8,742
   × 396

10. 23)1,803

11. 32,545 ÷ 45

12. 82)33,292

13. 16,084
    × 27

Solve.

14. y − 15 = 32

15. 4t = 52

16. $\frac{r}{7} = 21$

17. n + 11 = 24

18. n ÷ 3 = 8

75

Adding Decimals

Louisiana Lou runs a fleet of fishing boats in the great salt marshes and waters off Louisiana's coast.

How many thousand kilograms of shrimp did Louisiana Lou catch in three years?

Add to find the total.

Louisiana Lou's Fish and Shrimp Company

Yearly catch in thousands of kilograms

	Menhaden (Herring)	Shrimp
1982	4.203	3.834
1983	5.024	1.972
1984	3.97	2.05

Step 1	Step 2

Step 1

Align the decimal points. Use zeros to hold places.

```
  3.834
  1.972
+ 2.050
```

Step 2

Add as with whole numbers. Place the decimal point in the sum.

```
  1 1
  3.834
  1.972
+ 2.050
  7.856
```

Lou caught 7.856 thousand kilograms of shrimp in three years.

Estimate to be sure your answer makes sense or add in reverse order to check.

Estimate.

```
  3.834   rounds to      4
  1.972   rounds to      2
+ 2.050   rounds to    + 2
                         8
```

Add.

```
  1 1
  3.834
  1.972
+ 2.050
  7.856
```

More Examples

a.
```
  16.2
+ 55.0
  71.2
```

b.
```
     1
 $32.72
+ 41.40
 $74.12
```

c.
```
  1 1
  26.534
   9.700
+ 33.650
  69.884
```

d.
```
      1
  220.0317
  161.3500
+   8.0750
  389.4567
```

CLASSWORK

Add. Estimate to be sure each answer makes sense.

1.
```
  17.64
+ 9.081
```

2.
```
   6.003
+ 12.0825
```

3.
```
  15.4569
+  4.918
```

4.
```
  17.1564
   8.1091
+  5.4832
```

5.
```
   5.250
  11.375
+  8.872
```

6. 7.45 + 0.9 + 2.031

7. 12 + 1.2 + 3.45 + 2.069

PRACTICE

Add. Estimate to be sure each answer makes sense.

1. $\begin{array}{r} 2.2 \\ +\ 0.7 \end{array}$	**2.** $\begin{array}{r} 4.8 \\ +\ 9.7 \end{array}$	**3.** $\begin{array}{r} 128.4 \\ +\ \ 94.9 \end{array}$	**4.** $\begin{array}{r} \$47.48 \\ +\ \ \ \ 8.53 \end{array}$	**5.** $\begin{array}{r} 214.96 \\ +\ \ \ 38.23 \end{array}$
6. $\begin{array}{r} 3.71 \\ +\ 0.95 \end{array}$	**7.** $\begin{array}{r} 315.93 \\ +\ \ \ 17.65 \end{array}$	**8.** $\begin{array}{r} 84.161 \\ +\ 29.74 \end{array}$	**9.** $\begin{array}{r} 4.073 \\ +\ 0.906 \end{array}$	**10.** $\begin{array}{r} 75.164 \\ +\ 93.756 \end{array}$
11. $\begin{array}{r} 84.24 \\ 6.314 \\ +\ 19.31 \end{array}$	**12.** $\begin{array}{r} 45.63 \\ 8.145 \\ +\ 93.27 \end{array}$	**13.** $\begin{array}{r} 18.145 \\ 26.38 \\ +\ \ 7.416 \end{array}$	**14.** $\begin{array}{r} 46.1542 \\ 8.175 \\ +\ 32.3164 \end{array}$	**15.** $\begin{array}{r} 54.163 \\ 8.9174 \\ +\ 33.819 \end{array}$

16. $15.29 + $28.50

17. 3.647 + 5.49

18. 2.4 + 5 + 17.13

19. 13.45 + 1.345 + 134.5

20. 74.12 + 7,412 + 741.2 + 7.412

Rewrite each problem. Use decimal points in the addends or the sum to make each answer correct.

21. $\begin{array}{r} 1.255 \\ +\ 4.78 \\ \hline 6035 \end{array}$	**22.** $\begin{array}{r} 31495 \\ +\ 9.1672 \\ \hline 12.3167 \end{array}$	**23.** $\begin{array}{r} 18.914 \\ +\ 38149 \\ \hline 22.7289 \end{array}$	**★ 24.** $\begin{array}{r} 891473 \\ +\ \ \ 5468 \\ \hline 9.46153 \end{array}$	**★ 25.** $\begin{array}{r} 567781 \\ +\ 293814 \\ \hline 597.1624 \end{array}$

APPLICATION

26. Did Louisiana Lou make a better total catch in 1983 or 1984?

27. What was Lou's total catch for the three years?

28. In which of the three years shown on his record sheet did Louisiana Lou make his best catch?

29. One day Lou and his crew made 3 catches of shrimp. First they stopped 2.5 km south of the dock. For the next two catches, they traveled south 1.7 km and 4 km. How far was their trip back to the dock?

MENTAL ARITHMETIC

1. 22 + 10	**2.** 35 + 20	**3.** 0.4 + 0.1	**4.** 0.44 + 0.1
0.22 + 0.10	0.35 + 0.20	0.4 + 0.01	0.44 + 0.01
0.022 + 0.010	0.45 + 0.30	0.4 + 0.001	0.44 + 0.001

Subtracting Decimals

With his old-fashioned skates, Hans Brinker's time in the race was probably about 15.5 minutes. With modern skates he could have finished in 7.36 minutes. How much faster could he have raced with modern skates?

Find $15.5 - 7.36$.

Step 1

Align the decimal points. Use zeros to hold places.

$$
\begin{array}{r}
15.50 \\
-\ 7.36 \\
\end{array}
$$

Step 2

Subtract as with whole numbers. Place the decimal point in the difference.

$$
\begin{array}{r}
^{4\ 10}\\
15.\cancel{5}0 \\
-\ 7.36 \\
\hline
8.14 \\
\end{array}
$$

Hans could have raced 8.14 minutes faster.

Estimate to be sure the answer makes sense or add to check.

Estimate.

$$
\begin{array}{rl}
15.50 & \text{rounds to} \quad 16 \\
-\ 7.36 & \text{rounds to} \quad -\ 7 \\
\hline
8.14 & \qquad\qquad 9 \\
\end{array}
$$

Add.

$$
\begin{array}{r}
8.14 \\
+\ 7.36 \\
\hline
15.50 \\
\end{array}
$$

More Examples

a.
$$
\begin{array}{r}
^{4\ \ 10\ 12}\\
\$2\cancel{5}.\cancel{1}\cancel{2} \\
-\ \ \ \ 9.86 \\
\hline
\$15.26 \\
\end{array}
$$

b.
$$
\begin{array}{r}
^{7\ 11\ \ 9\ 9\ 10}\\
\cancel{8}\cancel{2}.\cancel{0}\cancel{0}\cancel{0} \\
-13.671 \\
\hline
68.329 \\
\end{array}
$$

c.
$$
\begin{array}{r}
^{0\ 13}\\
6.\cancel{1}\cancel{3}468 \\
-6.07250 \\
\hline
0.06218 \\
\end{array}
$$

CLASSWORK

Subtract. Estimate to be sure each answer makes sense.

1.
$$
\begin{array}{r}
2.7 \\
-\ 1.8 \\
\end{array}
$$

2.
$$
\begin{array}{r}
\$45.73 \\
-\ 30.64 \\
\end{array}
$$

3.
$$
\begin{array}{r}
7.04 \\
-\ 7.017 \\
\end{array}
$$

4.
$$
\begin{array}{r}
63.744 \\
-\ 12.51 \\
\end{array}
$$

5.
$$
\begin{array}{r}
\$89.41 \\
-\ 7.13 \\
\end{array}
$$

6. $18.45 - 9.362$

7. $26.3021 - 7.3596$

8. $5.0696 - 2.0994$

Subtract. Add to check.

1. 27.8 − 18.4	**2.** 216.5 − 98.8	**3.** $15.00 − 7.98	**4.** 4,324.1 − 856.6	**5.** 7.56 − 3.48
6. $500.00 − 496.58	**7.** 15.4 − 6.38	**8.** $246.03 − 59.75	**9.** 810.03 − 376.575	**10.** 6.54 − 6.453
11. 19.601 − 5.074	**12.** 137.128 − 75.204	**13.** 75 − 6.314	**14.** 12.004 − 10.6055	**15.** 7.15325 − 3.2819

16. 635.1 − 82.4

17. 0.60 − 0.53

18. 23 − 15.6

19. 8.174 − 0.04

20. 654 − 32.178

21. 411.603 − 79.71

22. 0.859 − 0.684

23. 14.153 − 8.1529

24. 1.2035 − 0.962

Complete. To find the output, subtract 1.5 from the input.

	Input	Output
	14.3	12.8
25.	11.8	
26.		7.9
27.	6.7	

	Input	Output
	10.09	8.59
28.		16.13
29.	14.25	
30.		8.58

	Input	Output
	19.01	17.51
31.		1.508
32.	14.19	
33.		7.74

Add or subtract. Do the work inside parentheses first.

34. (86.5 − 32.3) − 41.8 = n

35. (98.45 − 53.9) − 27.36 = n

★ **36.** 76.05 + (32.9 − 14.01) = n

★ **37.** (38.96 + 63.25) − (57.5 + 32.9) = n

APPLICATION

38. Skater Jeen van der Berg completed a 200-km course down Dutch canals in 455 min. Nikolai Dougan rowed the same distance in 409.68 min. How much slower was the skater?

★ **39.** A four-man relay team skated the 200-km course in 435.57 min. A second team covered the first 3 legs of the race in 329.29 min. What must the fourth skater's time be for his team to beat the first team?

Problem Solving

SKILLS AND STRATEGIES REVIEW   Mathematics on the Job

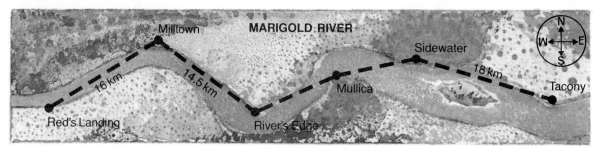

Imagine that you work for your state. You are responsible for safety on Marigold River. From a helicopter you keep track of the positions of all the canoes using the river.

Make a copy of the map. Mark unknown distances as you compute them to answer the questions. Place marks on the map to show where each group camps each night.

1. The river distance between Red's Landing and Tacony is 70.5 km. How far is it from River's Edge to Sidewater?

2. If Mullica is the same distance from River's Edge as it is from Sidewater, how far is Mullica from Sidewater?

3. The Star Canoe Club left Red's Landing at the same time that the White Water Canoe Club left Tacony. They will meet along the river in a few days. The Star Club camped 3 km past Milltown the first night. How far did the Star Club travel that first day?

4. When the White Water Club finally set up camp the first night, they found that they had traveled down the river a total of 21 km. Where did the White Water Club camp the first night?

5. How far apart were the Star Club and the White Water Club at the end of the first day's travel?

6. The Star Club traveled only 4.5 km the second day. The White Water Club traveled 17 km. Where did each group camp the second night?

7. How far apart were the two groups at the end of the second day?

8. The next day the two groups met after traveling an equal distance. Where did they meet?

9. What was the total distance that the White Water Club traveled?

10. Which club traveled the greater total distance? how much greater?

Luis Marin has been working at a weather station near a mountain lake for six months. The table on the right shows the actual rainfall he measured for each of the six months. It also shows the average rain that fell each of those months over the past ten years.

MONTHLY RAINFALL IN CENTIMETERS		
Month	Actual	Ten-year Average
January	12.29	13.47
February	12.42	14.61
March	15.98	17.82
April	17.53	19.95
May	9.86	10.04
June	8.78	9.03

Use the table to answer 11-15.

11. For which month is the average rainfall the greatest? Was the actual rainfall during that month also the greatest?

12. What is the difference between the average rainfall and the actual rainfall for January?

13. For which month is the difference between the average rainfall and the actual rainfall the least?

14. Which period had the greater amount of actual rainfall: January through March, or April through June? how much greater?

15. What is the total amount of actual rainfall for the six months?

Angela Marin is a salesperson for a boat company. The log on the right shows the number of kilometers she drove during her first three years on the job.

First Year	66,892 km
Second Year	67,256 km
Third Year	72,000 km

Use the log to answer 16-21.

16. What is the average distance she drove per year?

17. How many kilometers per liter of gas did Angela average during her second year?

18. One month Angela spent $152.39 for gas, $54.96 for car repairs, and $136.52 for auto insurance. To the nearest dollar, how much did she spend on her car that month?

19. About how many more kilometers did Angela drive during the third year than during the first year? Estimate the answer.

20. Angela used an average of 463 liters of gas per month during her first year as a salesperson. Estimate the number of kilometers per liter of gas she averaged.

★ **21.** Angela drove an average of 6,050 km per month during her fourth year. By how much does this increase her average yearly distance?

Write each as a decimal. pages 64–67

1. three tenths
2. one and sixteen hundredths
3. seventy-nine thousandths
4. five and eighty-one ten-thousandths
5. two hundred thirty-one millionths

Write each decimal in words. pages 64–67

6. 0.83
7. 4.009
8. 0.0013
9. 1.09073
10. 0.000107

Write each in expanded form in two ways. pages 66–67

11. 4.014
12. 2.3907
13. 0.090038

Compare. Use >, <, or = for each ⬤. pages 68–69

14. 9.0 ⬤ 0.90
15. 14.070 ⬤ 14.07
16. 0.737010 ⬤ 0.73710

Write in order from least to greatest. pages 68–69

17. 0.63, 0.603, 0.632
18. 10.17, 1.17, 101.7, 1.1
19. 9.099, 0.099, 9.99, 9.909

Round to the place named. pages 70–71

nearest hundredth

20. 0.095
21. 5.3856
22. 0.154
23. 1.996
24. 10.3379

nearest thousandth

25. 0.3652
26. 0.4866
27. 12.12369
28. 4.0097
29. 1.9998

Estimate. pages 74–75

30. $33.56
    + 47.38

31. 672.833
    + 27.94

32. 132.85
    − 35.15

33. 32.88
    − 18.01

Add or subtract. pages 76–79

34. 63.095 + 145.36
35. 821.671 − 50.99
36. 500 − 301.93
37. 98.0014 + 61.84 + 190.5 + 0.832
38. 73.201 + 200.001 + 0.732 + 3.9

Solve. pages 72–73, 80–81

39. Nell hiked 0.42 km north from her cabin. Then she traveled 0.72 km east, 0.42 km south, and 0.28 km west before stopping to rest. How far was her resting place from the cabin?

40. Estimate the total cost of hiking equipment bought by four hikers if the purchases were $37.75, $53.03, $69.82, and $46.98.

Write each as a decimal.

1. twenty and six hundredths

2. thirteen thousandths

3. eighty and three ten-thousandths

4. two thousand fifteen millionths

Write each decimal in words.

5. 0.00439

6. 22.0903

Round each to the nearest hundredth and the nearest thousandth.

7. 0.1374

8. 13.0965

9. 0.00895

Write each in expanded form in either of two ways.

10. 0.902

11. 12.03004

Compare. Use >, <, or = for each ⬤.

12. 10.08 ⬤ 10.8

13. 10.88 ⬤ 10.880

14. 0.19563 ⬤ 0.19559

Write in order from least to greatest.

15. 2.17, 2.173, 2.169, 2.106

16. 5.35, 53.5, 5.305, 53.55

Estimate.

17.
$$\begin{array}{r} 125.62 \\ -\ \ 29.21 \end{array}$$

18.
$$\begin{array}{r} 19.83 \\ +\ 26.08 \end{array}$$

19.
$$\begin{array}{r} \$275.08 \\ -\ \ 96.47 \end{array}$$

Add or subtract.

20.
$$\begin{array}{r} 137.59 \\ +\ \ 36.807 \end{array}$$

21.
$$\begin{array}{r} 15.3 \\ -\ 6.39 \end{array}$$

22.
$$\begin{array}{r} 31.291 \\ 146.05 \\ +\ \ \ 7.8 \end{array}$$

23. 10.05 + 1.5 + 13.055 + 0.005

Solve.

24. Estimate the total time of a three-man skating team if their individual times were 16.3 min, 17.37 min, and 12.9 min.

25. Jim water skied 1.8 km east from the dock and then 3.5 km west, where he lost his balance and splashed into the lake. How far from the dock was he when he fell?

If the decimal portion of the tonnage of bulk commodities shipped on the St. Lawrence Seaway is 0.7864, what decimal portion of the tonnage is not bulk commodities?

THE DEWEY DECIMAL SYSTEM

The Dewey decimal system is the most widely used method of classifying books by subject. Your school and city libraries probably use this method.

The system is named for Melvil Dewey, who developed it in 1876.

The table gives the 10 main classifications in the Dewey decimal system.

000–099	Generalities (encyclopedias, periodicals, etc.)	500–599	Pure sciences (mathematics, physics, etc.)
100–199	Philosophy and related disciplines	600–699	Technology (applied sciences)
200–299	Religion	700–799	Arts
300–399	Social sciences	800–899	Literature
400–499	Language (dictionaries, grammar, foreign languages)	900–999	General geography and history

Each classification is divided into 10 divisions and each division into 10 sections. The sections are even further divided, as shown at the right.

700–799	Arts and recreation
790–799	Games and recreation
796	Sports
796.323	Basketball

1. Write a report on the Dewey decimal system. A librarian in your town or school library may help you find more information. Your report might include

   a. why it is called a **decimal** system

   b. identification of the major divisions in a main classification (Choose a subject area that interests you.)

   c. where to find books on mathematics in the library

2. Find the Dewey decimal number for a book on each of the following subjects.

   a. chess
   c. mountaineering

   b. magic
   d. track and field

3. Identify the sections in the mathematics division: 510–519. How many are represented in the library?

BASE TWO

WOULD YOU LIKE TO LEARN A LITTLE BIT ABOUT A COMPUTER?

ITS PROCESSING CHIPS IDENTIFY AND RECORD DATA WITH ON AND OFF ELECTRICAL SWITCHES.

0 MEANS "OFF" AND 1 MEANS "ON." THESE ARE THE ONLY TWO DIGITS A COMPUTER UNDERSTANDS.

THE PLACE-VALUE TABLE ON THIS PAGE SHOWS HOW TO WRITE STANDARD NUMBERS AS NUMBERS IN BASE TWO, OR IN THE BINARY SYSTEM.

STUDY THE CHART, THEN DO THE EXERCISES.

HOPE YOU GET 1100100! IF YOU UNDERSTAND THE BINARY SYSTEM, YOU'LL KNOW WHAT THAT MEANS.

The binary system uses the number two as its base. As you move left, each place has a value two times the value of the place to its right.

sixty-fours	thirty-twos	sixteens	eights	fours	twos	ones	means	number in standard form	number in base two
				1	1	0	1 four + 1 two + 0 ones 4 + 2	6	110_{two}
		1	1	0	1	1	16 + 8 + 2 + 1	27	11011_{two}
	1	0	1	0	1	1	32 + 8 + 2 + 1	43	101011_{two}
1	1	1	0	0	0	0	64 + 32 + 16	112	1110000_{two}

Write each as a number in standard form.

1. 10_{two} **2.** 1101_{two} **3.** 10111_{two} **4.** 100111_{two}

5. 100100_{two} **6.** 1010011_{two} **7.** 1100101_{two} **8.** 1111001_{two}

Write each as a base-two number.

9. 7 **10.** 14 **11.** 29 **12.** 42 **13.** 60 **14.** 65

15. 73 **16.** 103 **17.** 117 **18.** 125 **19.** 128 **20.** 261

FLOWCHARTS

The step-by-step procedure used to solve a problem is called an **algorithm.** A diagram that shows the steps of an algorithm is a **flowchart.** A computer programmer often makes a flowchart before writing a program.

Each symbol in the step of a flowchart has a meaning.

⬭ is used for start or stop.

▱ is used for input or output.

▭ is used for operations and directions.

◇ is used for a decision.

This flowchart shows the steps for rounding a whole number. Follow the arrows to round 5,643 to the nearest hundred and 3,726 to the nearest ten.

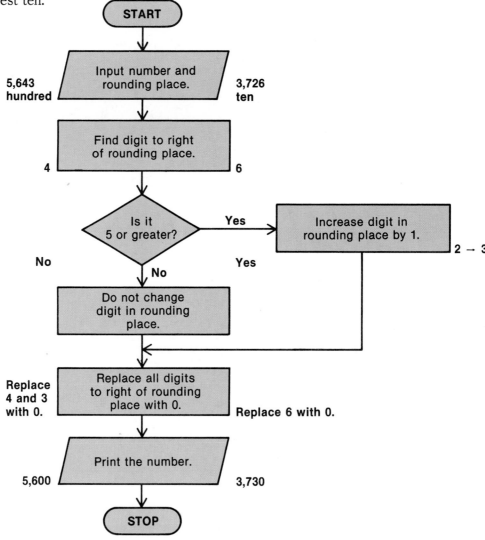

Write each step in the correct flowchart symbol.

1. Divide *n* by 2.

2. Print "HELLO".

3. Is *n* even?

4. STOP

5. Print the number.

6. Is the temperature below freezing?

Show the work for the steps of each flowchart.

7.

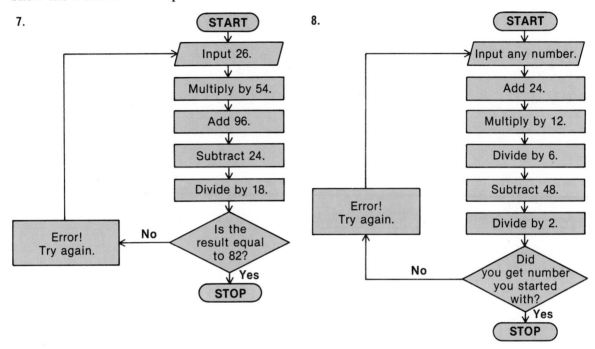

8.

Enlarge each flowchart. Write each step in the correct place.

9. How to dial a phone number

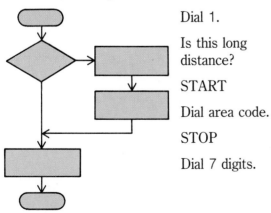

Dial 1.

Is this long distance?

START

Dial area code.

STOP

Dial 7 digits.

10. How to eat cereal

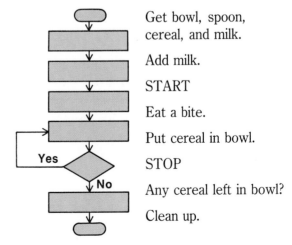

Get bowl, spoon, cereal, and milk.

Add milk.

START

Eat a bite.

Put cereal in bowl.

STOP

Any cereal left in bowl?

Clean up.

Make a flowchart for each.

11. How to find the average of 3 numbers

12. How to round any number to any place

MAINTAINING SKILLS

Choose the correct answers. Write A, B, C, or D.

1. 61,916
  + 35,706

 A 97,612 **C** 96,212

 B 96,612 **D** not given

2. 11,007 − 4,612

 A 7,619 **C** 7,615

 B 6,395 **D** not given

3. $31.48
  ×   6

 A $188.88 **C** $188.48

 B $18.88 **D** not given

4. 621 × 103

 A 63,963 **C** 80,730

 B 8,073 **D** not given

5. Write 12 × 12 × 12 × 12 using exponents.

 A 12^3 **C** 12^4

 B 4^{12} **D** not given

6. What is 9^3 in standard form?

 A 27 **C** 243

 B 729 **D** not given

7. What is the average of 15, 9, 18, 11, 10, 21?

 A 18 **C** 14

 B 13 **D** not given

8. 17,575 ÷ 25

 A 73 **C** 730

 B 703 **D** not given

9. Compare. 6.47 ⬤ 6.37

 A > **C** =

 B < **D** not given

10. Round 0.967 to the nearest tenth.

 A 0.9 **C** 0.1

 B 1.0 **D** not given

11. 365.21
  + 58.063

 A 423.273 **C** 423.84

 B 423.27 **D** not given

12. 12 − 0.67

 A 12.33 **C** 11.33

 B 11.67 **D** not given

Solve each problem, if possible. If there is not enough information, choose the fact that is needed.

13. On the earth, Walter weighs 84 kg and can jump 61 cm. On the moon, he could jump 6 times as high. How high could he jump on the moon?

 A 504 cm **C** 366 cm

 B need weight on the moon **D** not given

14. Seven astronauts have been on the space station for 12 days. How many more days will they need to complete their mission?

 A 12 days **C** 5 days

 B need total mission length **D** not given

Theme: Energy

Estimating Products

The Jameson-Merlin, a very powerful 6-wheeled car, has a gas tank that can hold 72 gallons of fuel. About how much will this driver pay for 71.3 gallons?

Estimate to find the answer.

▶To estimate a product, round each factor to its greatest nonzero place. Then multiply.

$1.60	rounds to	$ 2
× 71.3	rounds to	× 70
		$140

The driver will pay about $140 for the fuel.

More Examples

a.	0.96	rounds to	1
	× 4.5	rounds to	× 5
			5

b.	105.018	rounds to	100
	× 4.37	rounds to	× 4
			400

CLASSWORK

Estimate.

1.	2.6	2.	4.86	3.	0.957	4.	7.107	5.	$419.63
	× 1.2		× 7.2		× 39.6		× 6.7		× 11.8

6.	3.08	7.	$15.97	8.	87.5	9.	123.64	10.	11.609
	× 5.9		× 20.5		× 2.69		× 33.7		× 10.47

11. 4.86 × 89.65   **12.** 3.2 × $8.96   **13.** 6.7 × 0.85   **14.** 1.63 × 238.9

PRACTICE

Estimate.

1. $\begin{array}{r} 5.95 \\ \times\ 3.61 \end{array}$	**2.** $\begin{array}{r} 48.9 \\ \times\ 1.7 \end{array}$	**3.** $\begin{array}{r} \$2.37 \\ \times\ 2.6 \end{array}$	**4.** $\begin{array}{r} 28.5 \\ \times\ 5.03 \end{array}$	**5.** $\begin{array}{r} 3.86 \\ \times\ 2.9 \end{array}$
6. $\begin{array}{r} 12.6 \\ \times\ 1.59 \end{array}$	**7.** $\begin{array}{r} 18.2 \\ \times\ 3.94 \end{array}$	**8.** $\begin{array}{r} 1.798 \\ \times\ 3.2 \end{array}$	**9.** $\begin{array}{r} 0.962 \\ \times\ 14.3 \end{array}$	**10.** $\begin{array}{r} 1.141 \\ \times\ 9.5 \end{array}$
11. $\begin{array}{r} 5.378 \\ \times\ 7.39 \end{array}$	**12.** $\begin{array}{r} \$190.84 \\ \times\ 10.931 \end{array}$	**13.** $\begin{array}{r} 3.497 \\ \times\ 47.5 \end{array}$	**14.** $\begin{array}{r} \$27.60 \\ \times\ 1.24 \end{array}$	**15.** $\begin{array}{r} 596.5 \\ \times\ 0.93 \end{array}$

16. 3.25×100.96

17. 2.5×34.65

18. 3.32×41.068

19. 162.4×109.41

20. $3.9063 \times 3,906.3$

21. $907.3 \times 8,135.4$

★ **22.** $3.18 \times 43.26 \times 631.9$

★ **23.** $8.47 \times 91.6 \times 0.9584$

★ **24.** $74.6 \times 8.41 \times 31.674$

Estimate to choose the correct product.

25. $25 \times \$1.36$
 a. $34
 b. $3.40
 c. $.34
 d. $340

26. 5.7×17.5
 a. 9,975
 b. 99.75
 c. 0.9975
 d. 997.5

27. 0.98×2.67
 a. 26,166
 b. 261.66
 c. 2.6166
 d. 2,616.6

28. 6.5×8.45
 a. 5.4925
 b. 54,925
 c. 549.25
 d. 54.925

APPLICATION

29. Anna and Bob began their test driving at the same point. Anna drove 10.2 mi north, 2.5 mi east, and then 8.7 mi north again. Bob drove 6.9 mi east and 18.9 mi north. How far apart were they?

30. The Jameson-Merlin can go as fast as 185 miles per hour! At this speed, about how many miles would the car travel during a test drive that lasts 1.25 hours?

★ **31.** Another very powerful car is the jet-engined Thrust 2, which can go as fast as 633.468 miles per hour. About how many more miles than the Jameson-Merlin would the Thrust 2 travel in 2.25 hours?

Multiplying Decimals

A woman burns up 7.3 calories of food energy per minute while running. If Joan Benoit runs the first mile of a marathon in 5.23 minutes, how many calories does she use?

$7.3 \times 5.23 = n$

Step 1

Multiply as with whole numbers.

```
   5.23
 × 7.3
   1569
  3661
  38179
```

Step 2

Place the decimal point in the product by counting the total number of decimal places in the factors.

```
    5.2 3  ←— 2 decimal places
  ×  7.3   ←— 1 decimal place
    1 5 6 9
  3 6 6 1
  3 8.1 7 9  ←— 3 decimal places
```

Estimate to be sure the answer makes sense.

7.3×5.23　rounds to　$7 \times 5 = 35$

Joan Benoit uses 38.179 calories in 5.23 minutes of running.

More Examples

a.
```
   3.6  ←— 1 place
 × 4    ←— 0 places
  14.4  ←— 1 place
```

b.
```
   3.5 8   ←— 2 places
 × 0.4 8   ←— 2 places
   2 8 6 4
 1 4 3 2
 1.7 1 8 4  ←— 4 places
```

c.
```
    5.6 2 3 7   ←— 4 places
 ×      6.2 5   ←— 2 places
    2 8 1 1 8 5
  1 1 2 4 7 4
  3 3 7 4 2 2
  3 5.1 4 8 1 2 5  ←— 6 places
```

CLASSWORK

Place the decimal point correctly in each product.

1.	2.	3.	4.	5.
7.3	3.54	10.007	8.014	0.2615
× 0.18	× 8	× 2.4	× 6.7	× 6.3
1314	2832	240168	536938	164745

Multiply. Estimate to be sure each answer makes sense.

6.	7.	8.	9.	10.
3.148	0.36	8.94	1.6231	3.482
× 0.13	× 2.9	× 0.3	× 5.9	× 5.26

92

PRACTICE

Place the decimal point correctly in each product.

1. 4.6
   × 5.5
   2530

2. 3.8
   × 6.3
   2394

3. 6.04
   × 0.59
   35636

4. 5.538
   × 23.2
   1284816

5. 1.907
   × 3.27
   623589

Multiply. Estimate to be sure each answer makes sense.

6. 5.76
   × 0.5

7. 3.4
   × 0.7

8. 13.7
   × 0.9

9. 3.47
   × 0.8

10. 26.84
    × 0.58

11. 1.82
    × 0.25

12. 62.7
    × 1.25

13. $3.20
    × 4.6

14. 5.94
    × 2.36

15. 32.15
    × 6.4

16. 2.401
    × 9.08

17. 3.65
    × 8.71

18. $5.20
    × 3.05

19. 24.8
    × 24.8

20. 8.008
    × 30.03

21. 0.94 × 5.806

22. 8.14 × 12.48

23. 2.002 × 24.801

★ 24. 0.6 × 5.2 × 7

★ 25. 1.85 × 0.2 × 6.32

★ 26. 6.01 × 5.8 × 0.324

★ 27. (9.1483 − 6.342) × 0.9

★ 28. (1.43 + 7.89) × (8.46 − 2.3)

Choose the missing factor for each.

29. $0.5 \times n = 0.25$
    a. 5
    b. 0.5
    c. 0.05

30. $0.6 \times n = 1.8$
    a. 3
    b. 0.3
    c. 30

31. $0.2 \times n = 4$
    a. 20
    b. 2
    c. 0.2

32. $0.8 \times n = 0.32$
    a. 40
    b. 4
    c. 0.4

APPLICATION

33. While sitting in class, Ellen uses 1.33 calories per minute. How many calories does she use during a 45-minute math class?

★ 34. While Gary is sleeping he uses 0.92 calories per minute. How many calories did he use last night if he slept 7.5 hours?

LOGICAL THINKING

Place decimal points in the factors so that each multiplication is different and each product is equal to 31.62. You may annex zeros to the beginning or to the end of a number where needed.

1. 51
   × 62

2. 51
   × 62

3. 51
   × 62

4. 51
   × 62

5. 51
   × 62

Zeros in the Product

Water generates 0.14 of all the electricity produced in the United States. The Pacific Northwest region produces 0.48 of that amount. What part of the electricity produced in the United States is water-generated in the Pacific Northwest?

ELECTRICITY PRODUCED IN THE UNITED STATES

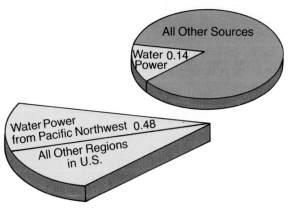

$0.48 \times 0.14 = n$

Step 1	**Step 2**	**Step 3**
Multiply as with whole numbers.	Find the number of decimal places in the product.	Write zeros in the product to place the decimal point correctly.

Step 1:
```
  0.14
× 0.48
  112
  56
  672
```

Step 2:
```
  0.14  ←— 2 places
× 0.48  ←— 2 places
  112
  56
  672  ←— 4 places
```

Step 3:
```
  0.14
× 0.48
  112
  56
  0.0672
```

In the United States 0.0672 of the electricity produced is water-generated in the Pacific Northwest.

More Examples

a.
```
    0.046  ←— 3 places
×    0.04  ←— 2 places
  0.00184  ←— 5 places
```

b.
```
   0.003  ←— 3 places
×      4  ←— 0 places
   0.012  ←— 3 places
```

c.
```
    0.006  ←— 3 places
×    0.03  ←— 2 places
  0.00018  ←— 5 places
```

CLASSWORK

Multiply.

1.
```
  0.07
× 0.8
```

2.
```
  0.05
× 0.03
```

3.
```
  0.125
× 0.04
```

4.
```
  0.003
× 0.002
```

5.
```
  0.976
× 0.04
```

6. 0.06×7

7. 0.05×0.463

8. 0.037×0.59

9. 1.07×0.008

Multiply.

1.	0.148 × 0.07	**2.**	0.0472 × 0.3	**3.**	0.0056 × 0.4	**4.**	0.093 × 0.07	**5.**	0.35 × 0.006

6.	0.16 × 0.09	**7.**	0.031 × 0.05	**8.**	0.012 × 0.008	**9.**	0.034 × 0.002	**10.**	0.0015 × 0.19

11.	0.088 × 0.8	**12.**	0.845 × 0.005	**13.**	0.083 × 0.24	**14.**	0.0007 × 0.09	**15.**	0.0098 × 3.6

16. 0.02×0.09 **17.** 0.08×0.549 **18.** 1.2×0.0075 **19.** 0.006×0.097

20. 0.04×0.05 **21.** 0.6×0.018 **22.** 0.03×0.0012 **23.** 0.005×0.011

24. 0.3×0.015 **25.** 0.11×0.032 **26.** 2.3×0.006 **27.** 3.1×0.0014

Use zeros and a decimal point to make each product correct.

28.	0.147 × 0.07 1029	**29.**	0.31 × 0.06 186	**30.**	0.36 × 0.07 252	**31.**	0.74 × 0.08 592	**32.**	0.008 × 0.031 248

Find the pattern in each sequence to complete the next three decimals.

★ **33.** 7, 0.7, 0.07, 0.007, □, □, □   ★ **34.** 1, 0.5, 0.25, 0.125, □, □, □

★ **35.** 0.9, 0.18, 0.036, 0.0072, □, □, □

APPLICATION

36. In 1978 about 0.73 of the world's energy came from oil and coal. Oil alone accounted for 0.63 of this amount. What amount of the world's energy came from oil at that time?

★ **37.** In 1978 what amount of the world's energy came from coal?

MENTAL ARITHMETIC

Use the distributive property to compute each product quickly.

Example $5 \times 2.3 = 5 \times (2 + 0.3) = (5 \times 2) + (5 \times 0.3)$
$$= 10 + 1.5 = 11.5$$

1. 6×2.4 **2.** 3×4.2 **3.** 7×6.2 **4.** 5×4.8
5. 40×2.6 **6.** 3×4.05 **7.** 30×2.5 **8.** 4×2.05

Problem Solving

WORKING BACKWARDS

Most problems ask you to find the end result of an action. Sometimes, however, you are given the end result and asked to supply information about the beginning. To do these problems, you *work backwards*.

A crew loads coal on a railroad car to be taken to the top of the mine. At the end of each day, a scale shows how much coal was mined since the beginning of the month. On Monday, July 15th, the crew mined 34.3 tons of coal. On Tuesday, they mined twice as much as on Monday. On Wednesday, they mined 48 tons. On Thursday, they mined 0.6 as much as on Wednesday. On Friday, they mined 50 tons. At the end of Friday's shift, the scale showed 688 tons. What was the scale reading at the beginning of their shift on Monday, July 15th?

What is the question?

What did the scale read at the beginning of the shift on Monday?

What are the facts?

Final reading	688 tons		Wednesday	48 tons
Monday	34.3 tons		Thursday	0.6 × 48 tons
Tuesday	2 × 34.3 tons		Friday	50 tons

How can the answer be found?

Do the computation to find the amounts for Tuesday and Thursday. Find the total tons mined for the week by adding. Now work backwards to find the reading of the scale on Monday morning.

Tuesday	**Thursday**
$2 \times 34.3 = 68.6$	$0.6 \times 48 = 28.8$

$34.3 + 68.6 + 48 + 28.8 + 50 = 229.7$

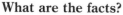
$688 - 229.7 = 458.3$

The scale read 458.3 tons when the shift began on Monday.

How can the answer be checked?

Add each day's production to 458.3 tons. Does the answer come out to be 688? It does.

Solve.

1. Ava Mongillo works a 5-day week at the Commonwealth Power Company. Each week she buys a loaf of bread for her lunches. One week she ate $1\frac{1}{2}$ sandwiches each day that she took her lunch to work. One day she bought a hot lunch. At the end of the week there were 6 slices of bread left. How many slices did the loaf have when she bought it?

2. The Commonwealth Power Company has an exercise program for its employees. The members of the jogging club ran 9.65 miles in one week. On Monday they ran 1.7 miles. On Tuesday they ran 1.5 times as far. On Wednesday, Thursday, and Friday, they ran equal distances. How far did they run each day?

3. The Commonwealth Power Company sponsors a radio quiz show called *Multiply Your Money.* In the first round a contestant must answer four questions. Each question after the first one is worth twice as much as the previous question. The fourth question is worth $32. How much is the first question worth?

4. In the second round of *Multiply Your Money,* each question is worth three times as much as the previous question. The fourth question is worth $405. What is the first question worth?

The Simian Research Institute is conducting an experiment involving apes and elevators. Each ape has been taught to press an elevator button and to wait until the elevator stops before pressing another button. Below are the records for three apes on a given day. Find the floor on which each ape started its elevator journey.

5. *Sampson*
   went up 3 floors
   went up 4 floors
   went down 6 floors
   finished on floor 8

6. *Griselda*
   went down 4 floors
   went up 3 floors
   went down 6 floors
   went up 2 floors
   finished on floor 4

7. *Hercules*
   went down 3 floors
   went up 4 floors
   went up 5 floors
   went down 6 floors
   went up 3 floors
   finished on floor 6

CREATE YOUR OWN PROBLEM

Keep track of the money you spend doing various activities during a typical week. Then write a problem that can best be solved by working backwards. Ask a classmate to solve it.

Multiplying and Dividing by Powers of Ten

If the energy from sound waves could be converted into electricity, it would take the energy of 100,000 mosquito buzzes to light a flashlight.

$100{,}000 = 10 \times 10 \times 10 \times 10 \times 10$

100,000 is a **power of 10.**

▶ To multiply by a power of 10, move the decimal point to the right. The number of zeros in the power of ten tells how many places.

4.16×10	$= 41.6$	1 place
4.16×100	$= 416$	2 places
$4.16 \times 1{,}000$	$= 4160$	3 places ←——— Sometimes it is necessary to write zeros in the product.
$4.16 \times 10{,}000$	$= 41{,}600$	4 places

▶ To divide by a power of 10, move the decimal point to the left. The number of zeros in the power of 10 tells how many places.

$84.2 \div 10$	$= 8.42$	1 place
$84.2 \div 100$	$= 0.842$	2 places ←——— Sometimes it is necessary to write zeros in the quotient.
$84.2 \div 1{,}000$	$= 0.0842$	3 places
$84.2 \div 10{,}000$	$= 0.00842$	4 places

You can use exponents to write powers of 10.

$100{,}000 = 10 \times 10 \times 10 \times 10 \times 10 = 10^5$ ←——— 10 used as a factor 5 times

$10^1 = 10$	$10^2 = 100$	$10^3 = 1{,}000$	$10^4 = 10{,}000$	$10^5 = 100{,}000$
↑ 1 zero	↑ 2 zeros	↑ 3 zeros	↑ 4 zeros	↑ 5 zeros

CLASSWORK

Multiply or divide.

1. 3.845×100

2. $0.0481 \times 1{,}000$

3. $64.9 \times 10{,}000$

4. $64.94 \div 10$

5. $479.2 \div 10{,}000$

6. $0.4 \div 100$

7. $0.5 \div 10^2$

8. 3.2×10^3

9. $56 \div 10^2$

PRACTICE

Multiply or divide.

1. 1.94×10
2. $0.063 \times 1,000$
3. 23.5×100
4. $8.9 \times 10,000$
5. $16 \div 10,000$
6. $65.3 \div 100$
7. $1.96 \div 10$
8. $75.8 \div 1,000$
9. 36.42×10
10. $264 \times 10,000$
11. 0.37×100
12. $7.4 \times 1,000,000$
13. $0.876 \div 10$
14. $0.07 \div 10^2$
15. $85.4 \div 100,000$
16. $135.3 \times 10,000$
17. 0.00036×10^3
18. $6.48 \times 100,000$
19. $6,040.7 \div 10,000$
20. $193 \div 1,000,000$

Write each power of 10 using exponents.

21. $100,000$
22. $10,000,000$
23. 100
24. 10

Complete. Follow the rule to find each missing number.

Rule: Multiply the input by 100.

	Input	Output
25.	87.5	
26.	0.09	
27.	0.6	
28.	1.0073	

Rule: Divide the input by 1,000.

	Input	Output
29.	423	
30.	32.5	
31.		0.1
32.		3.62

Find the missing factor for each.

★ 33. $14.6 \times n = 146$
★ 34. $0.631 \times n = 63.1$
★ 35. $52.9 \div n = 5.29$
★ 36. $123 \div n = 0.0123$
★ 37. $972 \div n = 0.00972$
★ 38. $0.0865 \times n = 86,500$

APPLICATION

39. The energy consumed in the United States in one day is enough to send a car around the world 3.6×10^4 times. Write the number in standard form.

★ 40. A lighthouse on the coast of France gives out a light equal to that of 6,250,000 flashlights. Write this number as 6.25 times a power of 10.

Mixed Practice

1. 1.085
    $+ 2.679$

2. 3.69
    $- 0.758$

3. $4.27 + 15.3$

4. $15.379 - 4.8$

5. $70 - 42.6$

6. 23
    $\times 75$

7. 80×500

8. $150 \div 25$

9. $456 \div 30$

10. $342\overline{)19,836}$

11. $58\overline{)116,464}$

12. $n \div 3 = 18$

13. $n + 13 = 75$

14. $n - 18 = 103$

15. $10n = 150$

Estimate.

16. 67×19

17. $458 \div 46$

18. $1.5 + 2.3$

19. $16.9 - 7.6$

99

Dividing Decimals by Whole Numbers

This is a copy of Jan's electric bill for a period of 31 days. What is the average amount of electricity used each day?

Divide the amount of electricity used by the number of days in the service period.

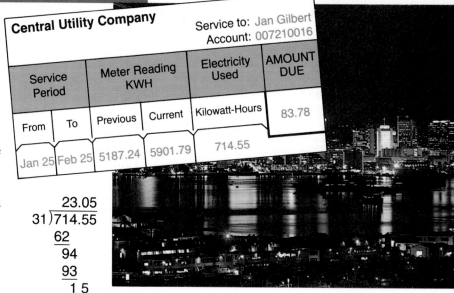

Central Utility Company				Service to: Jan Gilbert Account: 007210016	
Service Period		Meter Reading KWH		Electricity Used	AMOUNT DUE
From	To	Previous	Current	Kilowatt-Hours	83.78
Jan 25	Feb 25	5187.24	5901.79	714.55	

▶ Divide with decimals as you do with whole numbers. Place the decimal point in the quotient directly above the decimal point in the dividend.

Jan used an average of 23.05 kilowatt-hours (kwh) of electricity each day.

```
      23.05
31)714.55
    62
    94
    93
    1 5
      0
    1 55
    1 55
       0
```

Think 31 > 15
Place a zero in the quotient to hold the place.

Estimate to be sure the answer makes sense.

Step 1

Round the divisor.

```
  30
31)714.55
```

Step 2

Place the decimal point in the quotient.

```
  30     .
31)714.55
```

Step 3

Find the first digit of the quotient.

```
  30    2 .
31)714.55
```

Step 4

Write zeros for all other quotient digits.

```
  30    20.00
31)714.55
```

The answer 23.05 is reasonable since it is close to 20.

▶ Sometimes you may need to annex zeros to the dividend to complete the division.

```
   0.62
8)5.02
  4 8
   22
   16
    6
```

```
   0.6275
8)5.0200  ← Annex zeros
  4 8        to continue.
   22
   16
   60
   56
   40
   40
    0
```

CLASSWORK

Divide until the remainder is zero. Estimate to be sure each answer makes sense.

1. 8)2.88   2. 7)21.623   3. 25)100.15   4. 18)0.0468   5. 12)3.75

PRACTICE

Divide until each remainder is zero. Estimate to be sure
each answer makes sense.

1. $6\overline{)0.618}$

2. $7\overline{)7.056}$

3. $8\overline{)\$9.12}$

4. $6\overline{)28.95}$

5. $15\overline{)594}$

6. $12\overline{)83.4}$

7. $16\overline{)0.41008}$

8. $24\overline{)147.6}$

9. $32\overline{)\$402.88}$

10. $36\overline{)126.882}$

11. $35\overline{)1,401.75}$

12. $44\overline{)68.2}$

13. $5.2 \div 8$

14. $3.0 \div 8$

15. $5.0 \div 16$

16. $6.2 \div 5$

Find each missing dividend or divisor.

★ 17. $5\overline{)\blacksquare\blacksquare\blacksquare\blacksquare}$ $\overset{21.86}{}$

★ 18. $\blacksquare\blacksquare\overline{)10.8}$ $\overset{1\ 2}{}$

★ 19. $6\overline{)\blacksquare\blacksquare\blacksquare\blacksquare}$ $\overset{0.974}{}$

★ 20. $\blacksquare\blacksquare\overline{)37.5}$ $\overset{1.5}{}$

 Follow the rule to find each missing number.

Rule: Divide the input
by 32.

	Input	Output
	17.92	0.56
21.	14.4416	
22.	117.1872	

Rule: Divide the
input by 19.

	Input	Output
23.	16.15	
24.		0.325
25.		4.675

Rule: Divide the
input by 0.8.

	Input	Output
★ 26.		19.3125
★ 27.		0.44
★ 28.		3.0625

APPLICATION

29. The Gilberts want to buy an energy-efficient refrigerator.
They found out the number of kilowatt-hours of electricity
that several brands were expected to use each year under
normal use. Complete the chart by finding the average
monthly kilowatt-hours used by each brand.

Refrigerator Model	Kilowatt-hours per Year	Kilowatt-hours per Month
Maxi Space 410	122.4	
Maxi Space 510	160.8	
Deep Freeze II	149.4	

★ 30. If the electric rate in the area where the Gilberts live is
7.5¢ per kilowatt-hour, how much can they expect to save
each month by purchasing the Maxi Space 410 rather than
the Deep Freeze II? Round to the nearest cent.

Dividing Decimals

Robots usually run on batteries. This robot, which is used to deliver mail, has to be recharged every 9.75 hours. If it covers a mail route in 1.5 hours, how many routes can it complete before it has to be recharged?

$9.75 \div 1.5 = n$

Use this rule to divide by a decimal.

▶Multiplying divisor and dividend by the same power of 10 does not change the value of the quotient.

Step 1

Multiply the divisor by a power of 10 to make it a whole number.

$$1.5\overline{)9.75}$$

$1.5 \times 10 = 15$

Multiply to check.

```
   1.5
 × 6.5
   7 5
 9 0
 9.7 5
```

Step 2

Multiply the dividend by the same power of 10. Place the decimal point in the quotient.

$$1.5\overline{)9.75}$$

$9.75 \times 10 = 97.5$

Step 3

Divide.

```
      6.5
1.5)9.7 5
    9 0
    7 5
    7 5
      0
```

The robot can complete 6.5 routes.

More Examples

a. Find $2.59 \div 0.14$.

```
            18.5          Check
× 100 0.14)2.59 0 × 100   18.5
           1 4          × 0.14
           1 19           740
           1 12           185
             7 0         2.590
             7 0
               0
```

b. Find $0.9 \div 0.006$.

```
              150.          Check
× 1000 0.006)0.900 × 1000    150
             6             × 0.006
             30             0.900
             30
             00
              0
              0
```

CLASSWORK

Place the decimal point in each quotient.

1. $0.4\overline{)1.28}$ quotient 32

2. $0.86\overline{)2.15}$ quotient 25

3. $0.125\overline{)6.775}$ quotient 542

4. $4.8\overline{)5.76}$ quotient 12

Divide. Multiply to check.

5. $0.9\overline{)0.333}$

6. $2.5\overline{)0.38}$

7. $0.004\overline{)3.68}$

8. $0.09\overline{)0.459}$

PRACTICE

Place the decimal point in each quotient.

1. $\overset{72}{0.6\overline{)4.32}}$

2. $\overset{6\ 15}{2.3\ \overline{)141.45}}$

3. $\overset{39975}{0.08\overline{)3.198}}$

4. $\overset{548}{0.012\overline{)0.6576}}$

Divide. Multiply to check.

5. $0.8\overline{)1.064}$

6. $0.02\overline{)4.6}$

7. $0.08\overline{)9.04}$

8. $0.9\overline{)0.432}$

9. $0.02\overline{)7.1}$

10. $0.05\overline{)25}$

11. $0.7\overline{)4.354}$

12. $0.13\overline{)0.364}$

13. $0.004\overline{)0.6}$

14. $0.34\overline{)0.884}$

15. $1.6\overline{)1.36}$

16. $0.073\overline{)0.1387}$

17. $13.5 \div 0.75$

18. $1.281 \div 0.021$

19. $132 \div 0.06$

20. $7.50 \div 0.025$

21. $1.328 \div 8.3$

22. $0.0481 \div 0.037$

23. $39.48 \div 4.8$

24. $53.95 \div 2.6$

Estimate to choose the correct quotient.

25. $0.92\overline{)6.256}$
   a. 0.68
   b. 68
   c. 6.8

26. $5.02\overline{)417.162}$
   a. 8.31
   b. 83.1
   c. 830

27. $16.7\overline{)868.4}$
   a. 520
   b. 52
   c. 5.2

28. $3.92\overline{)490}$
   a. 125
   b. 12.5
   c. 1.25

Compare. Use >, <, or = for each ⬤.

★ 29. $192.4 \div 3.7$ ⬤ $192.4 \div .37$

★ 30. $0.091 \div 0.035$ ⬤ $0.0702 \div 0.027$

APPLICATION

31. A robot does 6 jobs and takes the following number of minutes to complete them: 1.4, 6.5, 3.0, 0.2, 1.4, and 2.8. What is the robot's average time for each job?

★ 32. A robot arrived at Mark's office at 3:30 P.M. It had made 10 mail deliveries. Each delivery had taken 8 minutes. When did the robot start from the mailroom?

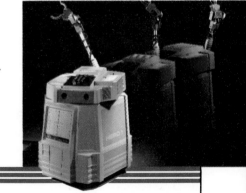

MENTAL ARITHMETIC

Use patterns to find each quotient.

1. $347.2 \div 56 = 6.2$
   $34.72 \div 56 = \square$
   $3.472 \div 56 = \square$
   $0.3472 \div 56 = \square$

2. $280 \div 35 = 8$
   $28.0 \div 35 = \square$
   $2.80 \div 35 = \square$
   $0.280 \div 35 = \square$

3. $24.6 \div 0.024 = 1{,}025$
   $24.6 \div 0.24 = \square$
   $24.6 \div 2.4 = \square$
   $24.6 \div 24 = \square$

Rounding Quotients

The Garcias received an oil delivery last Monday. The delivery person forgot to enter the price charged per gallon. Using the information on the bill, find the price charged for each gallon.

Round the answer to the nearest cent.

$113.75 \div 96.4 = n$

To round a quotient, follow these steps.

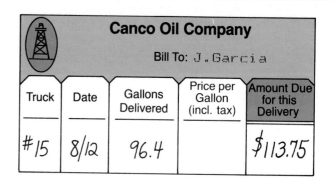

Canco Oil Company

Bill To: J. Garcia

Truck	Date	Gallons Delivered	Price per Gallon (incl. tax)	Amount Due for this Delivery
#15	8/12	96.4		$113.75

Step 1

Divide. Annex zeros to the dividend when necessary.

```
            $1.1 7
96.4 )$ 1 1 3.7 5 0
       9 6 4
       1 7 3 5
         9 6 4
         7 7 1 0
         6 7 4 8
           9 6 2
```

The price per gallon was $1.18.

Step 2

Divide to one more place than the place to which you are rounding.

```
            $1.1 7 9
96.4 )$ 1 1 3.7 5 0 0
       9 6 4
       1 7 3 5
         9 6 4
         7 7 1 0
         6 7 4 8
           9 6 2 0  ← To round to hundredths,
           8 6 7 6     divide to thousandths.
             9 4 4
```

Step 3

Round the quotient.

$1.1 7 9   **rounds to** $1.18

More Examples

a. Find $3 \div 11$ to the nearest hundredth.

```
      0.272      rounds to   0.27
11)3.000
   2 2
    80
    77
     30  ← To round to hundredths,
     22     divide to thousandths.
      8
```

b. Find $52.48 \div 13$ to the nearest thousandth.

```
       4.0369     rounds to   4.037
13)52.4800
   52
    4
    0
    48
    39
    90
    78
   120  ← To round to thousandths,
   117     divide to ten-thousandths.
     3
```

CLASSWORK

Divide. Round each quotient to the place named.

1. $83.24 \div 4$
   nearest tenth

2. $6.17 \div 8.4$
   nearest hundredth

3. $0.07 \div 0.3$
   nearest thousandth

4. $75.67 \div 11$
   nearest cent

Divide. Round each quotient to the place named.

nearest tenth

1. $9\overline{)4.32}$ **2.** $1.1\overline{)23.94}$ **3.** $0.19\overline{)0.459}$

4. $4.67 \div 0.2$ **5.** $1.252 \div 0.003$ **6.** $12 \div 14$

nearest hundredth

7. $8\overline{)37.65}$ **8.** $1.2\overline{)39.39}$ **9.** $0.15\overline{)1.376}$

10. $15.1 \div 6$ **11.** $5.42 \div 0.7$ **12.** $4 \div 9$

nearest thousandth

13. $3.6\overline{)4.615}$ **14.** $0.37\overline{)0.6516}$ **15.** $74\overline{)22.65}$

16. $3.057 \div 63$ **17.** $1 \div 6$ **18.** $130.6 \div 0.87$

nearest cent

19. $2\overline{)\$7.89}$ **20.** $8\overline{)\$129.02}$ **21.** $0.15\overline{)\$71.80}$

22. $\$9 \div 8$ **23.** $\$2.43 \div 0.29$ **24.** $\$215 \div 19$

Which division results in the given quotient? Each quotient has been rounded to the nearest hundredth.

★ **25.** quotient: 7.82

    a. $9.4\overline{)73.5684}$

    b. $6\overline{)46.917}$

    c. $0.23\overline{)1.65186}$

★ **26.** quotient: 0.56

    a. $64\overline{)37.6}$

    b. $50\overline{)2.81}$

    c. $0.9\overline{)0.5022}$

★ **27.** quotient: 2.88

    a. $12\overline{)26.166}$

    b. $18\overline{)51.843}$

    c. $0.5\overline{)1.392}$

★ **28.** quotient: 12.32

    a. $5.8\overline{)71.459}$

    b. $6.2\overline{)76.818}$

    c. $0.7\overline{)8.421}$

APPLICATION

29. Bob's last delivery from Canco Oil Company cost $125.32. A total of 80.5 gallons was delivered. What was the price per gallon to the nearest cent?

★ **30.** Michelle's bill from Concord Electric Company was $32.59 last month. What was the rate charged by the company if Michelle used 643 kilowatt-hours of electricity? Electric rates are given as hundred-thousandths of a dollar.

=== CALCULATOR ===

Divide to find the unit price of each item.
Then round each unit price to the nearest cent.

Detergent
64 oz for $7.89
Price per ounce
_____

Soup
3 cans for $2.00
Price per can
_____

Chopped Meat
$7.95 for
4 lb pack
Price per pound
_____

Pencils
15 for $1.00
Price per pencil
_____

Scientific Notation

It is difficult to imagine the tremendous energy produced by the sun. Much of it is lost on its way to the earth. Even so, in an average second, 22,000,000,000 (22 billion) kilowatt-hours of power reach the earth's surface.

22,000,000,000 can be written in scientific notation.

number in standard form   scientific notation

$$22{,}000{,}000{,}000 = 2.2 \times 10^{10}$$

         ↑   ↑
    a number   a power
  from 1 to 10 × of 10

▶To express a number in scientific notation, write it as a product of two factors.
(a number from 1 to 10) × (a power of 10)

Divide by a power of 10 to name a number between 1 and 10.

$2{,}500{,}000. = 2.5 \times 10^6$

6 places   **Think** $2{,}500{,}000 \div 10^6$
Move the decimal point 6 places to the left.

$186{,}000. = 1.86 \times 10^5$

5 places

$40{,}300{,}000. = 4.03 \times 10^7$

7 places

$7{,}000. = 7 \times 10^3$

3 places

▶Multiply by a power of 10 to change a number from scientific notation to standard form.

$3.6 \times 10^4 = 36{,}000.$

4 places **Think** 3.6×10^4
Move the decimal point 4 places to the right.

$2.8615 \times 10^9 = 2{,}861{,}500{,}000.$

9 places

CLASSWORK

Write each missing exponent.

1. $37{,}000 = 3.7 \times 10^{\square}$

2. $700{,}000 = 7 \times 10^{\square}$

Write each in scientific notation.

3. 8,500

4. 2,853,000,000

5. 154,000,000

Write each in standard form.

6. 3.9×10^3

7. 2.76×10^5

8. 8.123×10^7

PRACTICE

Write each missing exponent.

1. $6,300 = 6.3 \times 10^{\square}$

2. $2,850,000 = 2.85 \times 10^{\square}$

3. $43,920,000 = 4.392 \times 10^{\square}$

4. $518,000,000 = 5.18 \times 10^{\square}$

Write each in scientific notation.

5. 2,300

6. 9,510

7. 44,000

8. 67,800

9. 160,000

10. 374,100

11. 7,900,000,000

12. 99,000,000,000

13. 4,513,000,000

★14. 31 million

★15. 2 billion, 500 million

★16. 5 million, 621 thousand

Write each in standard form.

17. 8.1×10^2

18. 7.5×10^4

19. 6.66×10^6

20. 1.98×10^8

21. 5.731×10^5

22. 1.11×10^9

23. 4.52×10^5

24. 6.145×10^7

APPLICATION

Write each number in scientific notation.

25. The diameter of the sun is 1,392,000 kilometers.

26. An atomic reaction inside the sun changes 596,000,000 metric tons of hydrogen into 592,000,000 metric tons of helium.

27. In this atomic reaction, 3,600,000 metric tons of matter is changed into solar energy.

★28. Scientists think the sun will supply energy for the next 15 billion years.

=== CALCULATOR ===

Too many digits in a product cause a calculator to overflow and show an error message.

$615,000 \times 27,290 =$ ⌈ 167.83350^E ⌉ ← means error

Avoid overflow by dropping terminal zeros in factors. Then add the zeros to the answer you get.

Enter $615 \times 2729 = 1678335$

16,783,350,000 ←— Replace 4 terminal zeros.
or
1.678335×10^{10} ←— Write scientific notation.

Write each answer in standard form and in scientific notation.

1. $92,000 \times 467,000$

2. $345,600 \times 95,000$

3. $86,780 \times 105,000$

Problem Solving

SKILLS AND STRATEGIES REVIEW Energy

Read each problem and solve if there is enough information.

1. Hilton School held an Energy Sources Fair. Darlene did a project on solar energy. She spent $26.70 on materials and had $4.30 left in her project budget. How much had she budgeted for materials?

2. Sven's project used 3 batteries and 2.55 m of wire. After making his project he had 5 extra batteries and 3.5 m of wire left. He also had 0.25 m of wire scraps. How much material had Sven bought originally?

3. The Hurleyville Boosters Club held a special track meet to raise money to buy solar heating panels. Avi ran the 200-meter race in 23.3 seconds. What was his speed per second? Give your answer to the nearest 0.1 meter.

4. Each solar heating panel that the Hurleyville Boosters Club wants to buy costs $265. How many panels can the club buy with the money they earned at the special track meet?

5. Ken can average 6.4 m per second in a short race. How far can he run in 15 seconds?

6. Bob averages 7.2 m per second in a short race. How many fewer than 100 m does he run in 9.5 seconds?

Lisa ran the 3,000-meter run in 10 minutes 32.7 seconds. This was 12.8 seconds faster than Beth ran in the same race. Use a calculator to solve 7–10.

7. What was Lisa's speed per second? Give your answer to the nearest 0.1 meter.

8. What was Beth's speed per second? Give your answer to the nearest 0.1 meter.

★ 9. Mario ran the 3,000-meter run. He averaged 6.6 m per second the first 4.5 minutes. He averaged 5.4 m per second the next 3.5 minutes. How many meters had he run after 8.0 minutes?

★ 10. What was his average speed per minute during the total 8.0 minutes that he ran? Give your answer to the nearest 0.1 meter.

Problem Solving

WHAT WOULD YOU DO . . . ?

You just bought some expensive tropical fish. They need a constant water temperature to live. In order to keep the tank at a constant temperature, a series of light bulbs must generate exactly 350 watts of energy. Bulbs come in 40-watt, 60-watt, and 75-watt sizes.

Think about the situation and answer the questions to help you decide what to do.

1. Can bulbs all having the same wattage be used to generate the required heat?

2. Make a chart to show all the possible combinations of bulbs that could be used.

3. Can the 350 watts be generated by more than 1 combination of bulbs?

4. What is the least number of bulbs that could be used?

Bulbs sell for different prices, depending on wattage. Each 40-watt bulb costs 60¢; each 60-watt bulb costs 80¢; each 75-watt bulb costs $1. You have to buy the bulbs with your allowance. You want to spend as little as possible. What would you do?

You are installing a home heating system. The table shows costs for three different systems. The home will use heat only 6 months a year.

5. What would the cost be to purchase, install, and run each system for six months?

6. Which system would cost the least for the first year?

7. The cost of the heater and its installation is paid only once. To heat the house for 2 years, which would be the least expensive system?

8. You expect to heat the house for at least 17 years. It is important to keep costs at a minimum. What would you do?

HOME HEATING COSTS			
Item	Solar	Oil	Gas
Equipment	$2,000	$1,200	$1,700
Installation	$500	$300	$300
Montly cost	$10	$75	$100

CHAPTER REVIEW

Estimate each product. pages 90–91

1. $\;\;$ 4.16 $\times\;$ 1.9	2. $\;\;$ 98.4 $\times$ 6.83	3. $\;\;$ 1.845 $\times\;$ 2.39	4. $\;\;$ 49.67 $\times$ 22.67	5. $\;\;$ 516.32 $\times\;\;\;$ 2.91

Multiply. pages 92–95

6. $\;\;$ 82.9 $\times$ 4.68	7. $\;\;$ 61.78 $\times\;$ 2.67	8. $\;\;$ 42.53 $\times\;\;$ 56.8	9. $\;\;$ \$100.15 $\times\;\;\;\;\;\;$ 24	10. $\;\;$ 7.005 $\times$ 0.914
11. $\;\;$ 0.008 $\times\;$ 0.04	12. $\;\;$ 0.015 $\times\;\;\;$ 0.6	13. $\;\;$ 0.03 $\times$ 0.04	14. $\;\;$ 0.12 $\times\;$ 0.6	15. $\;\;$ 1.3 $\times$ 0.02

16. $28 \times \$56.30 = n$

17. $0.02 \times 0.0025 = n$

18. $3.24 \times 73.61 = n$

Multiply or divide. pages 98–99

19. 2.35×100

20. $78.9 \div 10$

21. $0.899 \times 1{,}000$

22. 4.25×10^2

23. 8.6×10^5

24. $16.98 \div 10^2$

25. $3.2 \div 1{,}000$

26. $0.4 \div 100$

Divide. pages 100–103

27. $4\overline{)8.98}$

28. $33\overline{)\$282.15}$

29. $5\overline{)24.12}$

30. $11\overline{)0.638}$

31. $0.3\overline{)8.34}$

32. $2.4\overline{)0.222}$

33. $0.34\overline{)95.2}$

34. $1.2\overline{)0.03}$

Divide. Round each quotient to the place named. pages 104–105

35. nearest cent

$3\overline{)\$45.65}$

36. nearest tenth

$44\overline{)98.3}$

37. nearest thousandth

$0.7\overline{)6.60}$

Write each in standard form. pages 106–107

38. 1.23×10^4

39. 4.6×10^5

40. 1.2×10^6

41. 7.23×10^8

Solve. pages 96–97, 108–109

42. Melanie starts work at the power plant at 8:30 A.M. From her house she has a 5-minute walk to the bus stop, a 20-minute bus ride, and a 10-minute walk to the plant. When must she leave home?

43. Janice estimated that she used 1,083 kilowatt-hours of electricity for lighting last year. On the average, how many kilowatt-hours per month is this? Find the answer to the nearest hundredth.

Estimate each product.

1.   9.2
       × 1.2

2.   98.04
       × 22.3

3.   1.763
       ×   1.8

Multiply.

4.   90.45
       × 1.272

5.   3.55
       × 12.4

6.   1.8
       × 0.004

7. $11.99
       ×   62

Divide.

8. $9\overline{)56.25}$

9. $4\overline{)0.088}$

10. $3.2\overline{)\$87.68}$

11. $0.4\overline{)0.022}$

Divide. Round each quotient to the place named.

12. nearest cent

$6\overline{)\$7.16}$

13. nearest tenth

$0.8\overline{)0.29}$

14. nearest thousandth

$1.1\overline{)91.11}$

Multiply or divide.

15. $8.9 \times 1{,}000$

16. $4.56 \div 10$

17. 0.098×100

18. 2.24×10^2

19. $234 \div 10^3$

20. 98.6×10^4

Write each in scientific notation.

21. 14,900

22. 4,500,000

23. 61,500,000,000

Solve.

24. The Johnsons' color TV used an average of 26.12 kilowatt-hours each month. How many kilowatt-hours is this for the year?

25. A robot programmed to tighten bolts on machines can complete one job in 1.5 minutes. It was able to complete 60 jobs by 11:30 A.M. When did it start?

Jim jogged 4 days this week. He took his usual 3.2-mile jogging route on each of 2 days. On the third day he took a longer 4.6-mile route. Find the length of his route on the fourth day if his average daily mileage for the week is 4.05 miles.

ENERGY USAGE

A **watt** is a unit used for measuring electric power. A **kilowatt** is equal to 1,000 watts. Monthly electric bills report the total number of kilowatt-hours used. A **kilowatt-hour (kwh)** indicates the amount of power that a one-kilowatt appliance would use in one hour.

A lamp using a 100-watt bulb consumes 1 kilowatt-hour in 10 hours of use.

100 watts × 10 hours = 1,000 watt-hours = 1 kilowatt-hour

100 watts = 0.1 kilowatt

↑
means
1,000 watts

0.1 kw × 10 h = 1 kwh

Answer these questions about energy usage.

1. Most hair dryers use between 1,000 and 1,400 watts of power. Suppose you use a 1,200-watt dryer. If it takes 12 minutes to dry your hair, how many kilowatt-hours of energy do you use?
   (Express 1,200 watts as kilowatts.   12 minutes = 0.2 hour)

2. If you use your hair dryer for a total of one hour per week and the average cost of electricity is $.08 per kwh, about how much does it cost to run your dryer for a year?

3. A small portable television uses 415 watts. How many kilowatts does it use in 6 hours?

4. Compare the cost of using one 100-watt bulb with the cost of using two 60-watt bulbs. (Use $.08 as the cost of electricity per kwh and assume 10 hours of use.) About how much could you save by using a single lamp with a 100-watt bulb rather than two lamps with 60-watt bulbs?

5. Find out what the cost of electricity is in your city or town. Time yourself when you use a hair dryer, a television, or other electrical appliance. Then complete the chart. Most appliances have a label stating the watt usage.

Appliance _____	Watts _____	
	Per Day	Per Year
Time used		
Cost		

MULTIPLICATION AND SCIENTIFIC NOTATION

Look at the following relationship.

$100 \times 10{,}000 = 1{,}000{,}000$
$10^2 \times 10^4 \quad = \quad 10^6$

▶To multiply powers of 10, add the exponents.

$10^a \times 10^b = 10^{a+b}$

Use this fact and scientific notation to multiply large numbers.
To find $4{,}200{,}000 \times 350{,}000$, follow these steps.

- Write each factor in scientific notation.
  $4.2 \times 10^6 \times 3.5 \times 10^5$

- Using the Commutative Property of Multiplication, rearrange factors.
  $4.2 \times 3.5 \times 10^6 \times 10^5$

- Multiply the decimals. Then multiply the powers of 10.
  14.7×10^{11}

- To write the answer in scientific notation, rewrite the product so that the first factor is a number from 1 to 10.
  $14.7 = 1.47 \times 10^1$
  $14.7 \times 10^{11} = 1.47 \times 10^1 \times 10^{11}$
  $\qquad\qquad\quad = 1.47 \times 10^{12}$

Multiply. Write each product in scientific notation.

1. $(2.3 \times 10^4) \times (3.7 \times 10^2)$

2. $(6.5 \times 10^5) \times (1.7 \times 10^6)$

3. $(4.6 \times 10^6) \times (3.8 \times 10^6)$

4. $(5 \times 10^3) \times (4.1 \times 10^7)$

5. $48{,}000 \times 1{,}400$

6. $93{,}000{,}000 \times 600$

7. $7{,}200 \times 18{,}000$

8. $150{,}000{,}000 \times 4{,}000$

9. $140{,}000 \times 12{,}400{,}000$

10. $1{,}300{,}000 \times 15{,}500{,}000$

11. $3{,}200{,}000 \times 52{,}000$

12. $51{,}000{,}000{,}000 \times 800{,}000$

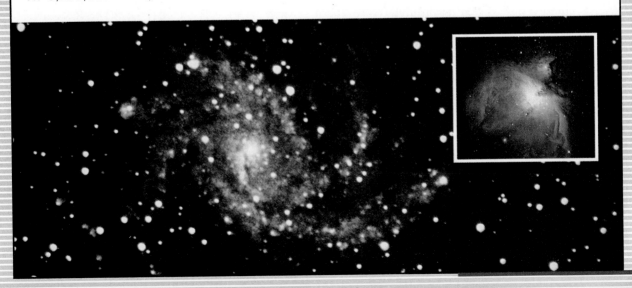

Choose the correct answers. Write A, B, C, or D.

1. Round 5,816,393 to the nearest ten thousand.

    A 5,800,000   **C** 5,820,000

    B 5,810,000   **D** not given

2. Round 5,816,393 to the nearest million.

    A 6,000,000   **C** 5,800,000

    B 5,000,000   **D** not given

3. 37,109 + 3,904 + 390 + 6,724

    A 48,127   **C** 48,117

    B 38,127   **D** not given

4.   20,685
   − 18,391

    A 2,314   **C** 2,394

    B 2,294   **D** not given

5. $31.46 − $7.71

    A $23.75   **C** $24.75

    B $24.35   **D** not given

6. What multiplication property is used?
$3 \times (9 + 4) = (3 \times 9) + (3 \times 4)$

    A identity   **C** associative

    B distributive   **D** not given

7. Estimate. 311×49

    A 12,000   **C** 15,000

    B 14,000   **D** not given

8. Estimate. $8,130 \div 21$

    A 4,000   **C** 300

    B 400   **D** not given

9. What multiplication property is used?
$1 \times 6 = 6$

    A zero   **C** identity

    B commutative   **D** not given

10. $27.39 × 203

    A $5,560.17   **C** $629.97

    B $556.01   **D** not given

11. $95,431 \div 43$

    A 2,219   **C** 2,218 R57

    B 2,219 R14   **D** not given

12. What is the average? 90, 100, 90, ⁻60, 80

    A 70   **C** 80

    B 90   **D** not given

13. What is the standard form for 3^5?

    A 15   **C** 125

    B 81   **D** not given

14. What is the related equation for $n \times 3 = 30$?

    A $n = 30 \div 3$ **C** $n \times 30 = 3$

    B $n = 30 \times 3$ **D** not given

15. What is the decimal for $\frac{71}{1,000}$?

    A 7.1   **C** 0.071

    B 0.71   **D** not given

16. What is the decimal for 21 millionths?

    A 0.21   **C** 0.00021

    B 21,000,000   **D** not given

Choose the correct answers. Write A, B, C, or D.

17. Compare. 9.90760 ⬤ 9.9076

   A >   **C** =

   B <   **D** not given

18. Round 4.79013 to the nearest hundredth.

   A 4.79   **C** 4.789

   B 4.80   **D** not given

19. Estimate. 42.235
           + 58.603

   A 90   **C** 110

   B 100   **D** not given

20. 7.16 + 8.062

   A 15.222   **C** 1.512

   B 15.122   **D** not given

21. Estimate. $9.53
           − .75

   A $10.00   **C** $9.00

   B $8.00   **D** not given

22. 21.641 − 8.704

   A 12.937   **C** 12.837

   B 12.947   **D** not given

23. Estimate. 6.5 × 1.3

   A 14   **C** 7

   B 12   **D** not given

24.   34.11
     × 0.36

   A 12.28   **C** 12.2796

   B 122.796   **D** not given

25. 0.003 × 0.7

   A 0.21   **C** 0.0021

   B 2.1   **D** not given

26. 2.601×10^3

   A 2,601   **C** 26,010

   B 260.1   **D** not given

27. $7.5 \div 10^4$

   A 0.00075   **C** 7,500

   B 0.75   **D** not given

28. 7)6.3

   A 9   **C** 0.9

   B 90   **D** not given

29. 0.6)4.8

   A 0.08   **C** 80

   B 0.8   **D** not given

30. 1.344 ÷ 0.21

   A 0.64   **C** 64

   B 6.4   **D** not given

31. What is the quotient to the nearest cent?
     $119.96 ÷ 34

   A $3.52   **C** $3.60

   B $3.53   **D** not given

32. What is the missing exponent?
     $5{,}796{,}000 = 5.796 \times 10^{\square}$

   A 3   **C** 6

   B 5   **D** not given

Choose the correct answers. Write A, B, C, or D.

Use the picture for 33 and 34.

Aug. - 3,876
Sept. - 1,316

Mountain Lakes Park
Campsite Use

Aug. - 3,166
Sept. - 1,994

Arrowhead

Big Bear

Thunder Lake

Aug. - 5,167
Sept. - 3,805

Pine Valley

Aug. - 2,916
Sept. - 2,194

33. What was the total attendance at Pine Valley for August and September?

A 5,192　　C 722

B 5,110　　D not given

34. By how much did the attendance decrease at Big Bear from August to September?

A 5,160　　C 1,172

B 1,994　　D not given

Solve.

35. Larry earns $4.50 per hour. He worked 7 hours on Monday, 5 hours on Tuesday, and 8 hours on Wednesday. How much more did he earn on Monday than on Tuesday?

A $9.00　　C $31.50

B $22.50　　D not given

36. A rocket with a weight of 2,100 kg completed 510 orbits around the earth. It completed 39,170 km per orbit. How far did it travel in total?

A 1,071,000 km　　C 82,257,000 km

B 19,976,700 km　　D not given

Solve. You can use a drawing as a model.

37. Judy, Ken, Lou, and May are water skiing. May sees two skiers in front of her. Judy is between Lou and May. Ken is behind May. What is the order of the skiers? (Use students' initials.)

A L, K, M, J　　C L, J, M, K

B M, J, L, K　　D not given

38. Nina rows 1.2 km south, then 6.4 km east. She then rows 0.8 km north, then 6.4 km west. How far is she from her starting point?

A 2 km　　C 0.4 km

B 5.2 km　　D not given

Solve.

39. For his science experiments, Jeremy used 4 L of water and 4 empty beakers. He poured 0.6 L into the first beaker and twice that amount into the second. He used 0.4 L less water for the third beaker than for the second. How much water did Jeremy pour into the fourth beaker?

A 2.6 L　　C 1.4 L

B 2.4 L　　D not given

40. If Jeremy had filled the third beaker with 0.6 L, how much more water would he pour into the fourth beaker?

A 1.6 L　　C 2.4 L

B 0.2 L　　D not given

41. Jeremy combined the water from the last two beakers. He then added more water to total 2.5 L. How much water did he add?

A 0.3 L　　C 1.7 L

B 0.7 L　　D not given

Theme: Traveling in Canada

Units of Length

▶ The **meter (m)** is a unit of length in the metric system.

Pat's bike is about 1 m high.

▶ The **kilometer (km)** is used to measure long distances.

1 km = 1,000 m

The distance from Mount St. Elias in the Yukon to Cape Spear in Newfoundland is 5,187 km.

▶ The **centimeter (cm)** is used to measure short lengths.

1 cm = 0.01 m

The Canadian ten-cent coin is slightly less than 2 cm wide.

▶ The **millimeter (mm)** is used to measure very short lengths.

1 mm = 0.001 m

The ten-cent coin is about 1 mm thick.

10 mm = 1 cm	**1,000 mm = 1 m**
100 cm = 1 m	**1,000 m = 1 km**

Pat, ready to begin her bike trip in Canada

CLASSWORK

Choose kilometer (km), meter (m), centimeter (cm), or millimeter (mm) to measure each.

1. the length of a shoelace

2. the length of the Yukon River

3. the size of a pinhead

4. the length of a clothesline

1 mm 2 cm

Estimate each length. Then measure to the nearest centimeter and nearest millimeter.

5.

6.

Complete.

7. 6 km = _____ m

8. 5 cm = _____ mm

9. 40 m = _____ cm

118

PRACTICE

Choose kilometer (km), meter (m), centimeter (cm), or millimeter (mm) to measure each.

1. height of the chalkboard

2. distance from Montreal to Toronto

3. length of your thumb

4. thickness of a piece of cardboard

Choose the best estimate.

5. height of your classroom   **a.** 4 mm   **b.** 4 cm   **c.** 4 m

6. distance of a cross-country race   **a.** 10 m   **b.** 10 km   **c.** 1,000 km

7. length of a postcard   **a.** 12 cm   **b.** 1.2 m   **c.** 12 m

Estimate each length. Then measure to the nearest centimeter and millimeter.

8. |——————————————————————|

9. |————————|

10. length of your pen

11. thickness of your math book

Complete.

12. 6 m = ___ cm

13. 4 km = ___ m

14. 5,000 mm = ___ m

15. 70 cm = ___ mm

16. 31 m = ___ cm

17. 18,000 m = ___ km

★**18.** 36 mm = ___ cm ___ mm

★**19.** 450 cm = ___ m ___ cm

★**20.** 5,300 m = ___ km ___ m

APPLICATION

21. In lacrosse, a popular game in Canada, the goal is about 180 cm high. How many millimeters is this?

22. The Yukon River is 3,220 kilometers long. How many meters is this?

★**23.** Anna is 157 cm tall. Is this more or less than 2 meters? How much more or less?

★**24.** One morning Pat rode 63.8 kilometers on her bike. That afternoon she rode 52,000 meters. Which was the greater distance? how much greater?

=== VISUAL THINKING ===

16 sticks are arranged to form 8 small triangles. Remove 4 of the sticks to leave 4 small triangles.

Relating Units Of Length

The millimeter, centimeter, meter, and kilometer are the most commonly used metric units of length. Other units that are used less often are the **decimeter (dm),** the **dekameter (dam),** and the **hectometer (hm).**

The table below shows the meaning of each prefix.

Prefix	Symbol	Meaning	Unit of Length
kilo-	k	1,000	1 km = 1,000 m
hecto-	h	100	1 hm = 100 m
deka-	da	10	1 dam = 10 m
deci-	d	0.1	1 dm = 0.1 m
centi-	c	0.01	1 cm = 0.01 m
milli-	m	0.001	1 mm = 0.001 m

To convert metric units, multiply or divide by a power of 10. Use this table.

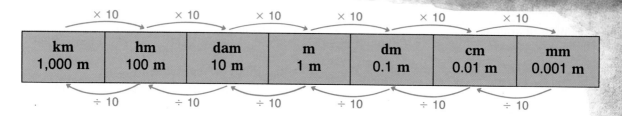

▶ To change from a larger unit to a smaller unit, multiply. There will be more smaller units.

12 m = ___ cm

12 × 100 = 1,200   **Think** Multiplying by 100 moves the decimal point 2 places to the right.

12 m = 1,200 cm

▶ To change from a smaller unit to a larger unit, divide. There will be fewer larger units.

50 cm = ___ dam

50 ÷ 1,000 = 0.05   **Think** Dividing by 1,000 moves the decimal point 3 places to the left.

50 cm = 0.05 dam

More Examples

a. 7.2 km = ___ hm   **Think** larger unit to smaller— multiply

7.2 × 10 = 72

7.2 km = 72 hm

b. 35 mm = ___ dm   **Think** smaller unit to larger— divide

35 ÷ 100 = 0.35

35 mm = 0.35 dm

CLASSWORK

Complete.

1. 13 m = ___ dm

2. 24 dam = ___ dm

3. 1.6 dam = ___ hm

4. ___ cm = 7 mm

5. 5.2 km = 5,200 ___

6. 72 cm = ___ dam

PRACTICE

Complete.

1. 4 km = ___ m
2. 600 cm = ___
3. 9 m = ___ cm
4. 8 dm = ___ cm
5. 6 km = ___ hm
6. 3,000 m = ___ km
7. 2,500 mm = ___ m
8. 40 cm = ___ mm
9. 15,000 m = 15 ___
10. ___ m = 6 km
11. 200 mm = ___ dm
12. ___ m = 1.2 km
13. ___ mm = 8.3 cm
14. 240 ___ = 0.24 km
15. 15 cm = 150 ___
16. 1.4 hm = ___ cm
17. 0.3 m = ___ km
18. 0.3 dam = ___ dm

Compare. Use >, <, or = for each 〇.

19. 1 m 〇 1 hm
20. 5 m 〇 50 mm
21. 200 cm 〇 20 dm
22. 200 dm 〇 2 hm
23. 0.21 m 〇 2.1 cm
24. 600 cm 〇 0.06 km

APPLICATION

25. Mount Logan, the highest peak in Canada, is 6,050 meters high. How much more than 6 kilometers is this?

26. The woodland caribou, which inhabits Canada's eastern provinces, may have antlers up to 120 cm wide. How many decimeters is this?

★ 27. Marie took a bus trip of 224 km from Quebec City to Montreal. The next day she rode 160 km from Montreal to Ottawa. How many hectometers did she travel in all?

★ 28. At the Vancouver Zoo, Pierre saw a pelican with a wingspan of 221 cm and a swan with a wingspan of 28.4 dm. Which bird had the greater wingspan? how much greater?

≡ MENTAL ARITHMETIC ≡

Compute each product or quotient mentally.

1. 3.4 × 1,000
2. 9.1 ÷ 10
3. 852 ÷ 100
4. 9.2 × 1,000
5. 35,000 ÷ 10,000
6. 8.123 × 10,000
7. 0.816 × 100
8. 81 ÷ 1,000
9. 43.15 × 1,000
10. 386 ÷ 100,000
11. 0.012 ÷ 10
12. 43 × 1,000,000

Gram and Kilogram

▶The **gram (g)** is a unit of mass in the metric system.

It is common outside the field of science to use weight to mean the same as mass.

A berry weighs about 1 g.

▶The **milligram (mg)** is used to measure very light objects.
1 mg = 0.001 g

A few grains of soil weigh 1 mg.

▶The **kilogram (kg)** is used to measure heavier objects.

1 kg = 1,000 g

The fish weighs about 1 kg.
The Siamese cat weighs about 5 kg.

▶The **metric ton (t)** is used to measure very heavy objects.

A small car weighs about 1 t.

1,000 mg = 1 g	1,000 g = 1 kg	1,000 kg = 1 t

CLASSWORK

Estimate each weight. Measure to nearest gram or kilogram to check your estimates.

1. an orange
2. a notebook
3. a piece of chalk
4. a math book
5. a baseball bat
6. a 13-year-old boy

Complete.

7. 6 kg = ___ g
8. 15,000 kg = ___ t
9. 21 g = ___ mg
10. ___ mg = 12 g
11. 2,000 mg = 2 ___
12. 8 kg = 8,000 ___

PRACTICE

Choose milligram (mg), gram (g), kilogram (kg), or metric ton (t) to measure each.

1. a pebble
2. a slice of bread
3. a bowling ball
4. a grain of sand
5. a maple leaf
★6. 10 hockey players

Choose the best estimate for each.

7. a tennis ball
  a. 60 mg
  b. 60 g
  c. 60 kg

8. a whale
  a. 90 g
  b. 90 t
  c. 90 kg

9. a vitamin C tablet
  a. 160 mg
  b. 60 g
  c. 60 kg

10. a bar of soap
  a. 100 mg
  b. 100 g
  c. 100 kg

Complete.

11. 3 g = ___ mg
12. 7 kg = ___ g
13. 15,000 kg = ___
14. ___ t = 9,000 kg
15. 5,000 g = ___ kg
16. 2,000 mg = ___ g
17. ___ g = 15 kg
18. ___ g = 12,000 mg
19. 27 t = ___ kg
20. ___ mg = 18 g
21. ___ kg = 6,000 g
★22. 10 g = ___ kg
★23. 1,000,000 g = ___ t
★24. 6 kg = ___ mg

APPLICATION

25. The retriever carried a stick weighing 1 kg. Later it carried a 600-g bone. Which was lighter? how much lighter?

26. The bull terrier met a bear that weighed 680 kg. How much less than 1 t is this?

★27. Two paperback books weigh 330 g and 410 g. How many kilograms do both books weigh together?

Mixed Practice

1. 72,957 + 8,652

2. 8,008 − 989

3.   156,174
  − 29,897

4. 816 × 72

5.   92,385
  ×   37

6. 64)‾56,132

7. 29)‾117,479

8. 42.6 + 1.095

9. 73 + 6.7 + 0.8

10. 52.17 − 6.3

11. 81 − 5.23

12.   86.31
  ×   18

13. 0.4 × 0.02

14. 6)‾94.8

15. 0.4)‾3.8

16. 1.2)‾0.768

17. 5.6×10^3

18. $320 \div 10^5$

19. 0.251×10^4

20. 14.8 ÷ 100

21. 6.31 × 10,000

Milliliter and Liter

▶ The **liter (L)** is a unit of capacity in the metric system.

A container that measures 10 cm long, 10 cm wide, and 10 cm high has a capacity of 1 L.

▶ The **milliliter (mL)** is used to measure very small capacities.

1 mL = 0.001 L

A container that measures 1 cm long, 1 cm wide, and 1 cm high has a capacity of 1 mL.

A glass of milk holds about 250 mL.

10 cm

10 cm

10 cm

1 cm

1 cm

1 cm

▶ The **kiloliter (kL)** is used to measure large capacities.

A container that measures 1 m long, 1 m wide, and 1 m high has a capacity of 1 kL.

A swimming pool holds about 100 kL.

| **1,000 mL = 1 L** | **1,000 L = 1 kL** |

More Examples

a. The bottle holds about 1 L of juice.

b. The cup holds about 180 mL of juice.

c. The lake holds about 450,000 kL of water.

CLASSWORK

Complete. Choose liter (L) or milliliter (mL).

1. A bucket holds 20 ___.

2. A soup bowl holds 375 ___.

3. An eyedropper holds 1 ___.

Complete.

4. 2,000 mL = ___ L

5. 5 L = ___ mL

6. 2 kL = ___ L

Complete. Choose liter (L) or milliliter (mL).

1. The bottle contains 360 ___ of shampoo.

2. Jake used 110 ___ of water to wash his car.

3. The orange contained about 30 ___ of juice.

4. Karen made 8 ___ of punch for the party.

5. The salad has 5 ___ of dressing on it.

6. A child's pool holds 50 ___ of water.

Choose the best estimate for each.

7. a glass of juice
   a. 240 mL
   b. 24 L
   c. 240 L

8. a bottle of eye drops
   a. 0.5 mL
   b. 50 mL
   c. 50 L

9. water in a tropical fish tank
   a. 20 mL
   b. 2 L
   c. 20 L

10. a teaspoon of tea
    a. 5 mL
    b. 5 L
    c. 50 mL

11. water in a lake
    a. 5,000 mL
    b. 5,000 L
    c. 500,000 kL

12. soup in a large pot
    a. 6 mL
    b. 6 L
    c. 600 L

Complete.

13. 4 L = ___ mL

14. 6,000 mL = ___ L

15. ___ L = 9,000 mL

16. 8 kL = ___ L

17. ___ L = 9 kL

18. ___ L = 12,000 mL

19. 5,500 mL = ___ L

20. 250 mL = ___ L

21. ___ kL = 7,100 L

★ 22. 1 kL = ___ mL

★ 23. 3,250 mL = ___ L ___ mL

★ 24. 2 L 100 mL = ___ mL

APPLICATION

Environmentalists in Canada and the United States are interested in water conservation. The answers to these questions will suggest ways to conserve water.

25. How many liters of water can be saved by taking a shower instead of a bath?

26. How much total water is used by washing a load of dishes and a load of clothing by machine?

★ 27. Which requires more water: washing dishes by hand 3 times a day or using the dishwasher once? how much more?

★ 28. How many milliliters of water do you use brushing your teeth 3 times a day for 1 week?

AVERAGE AMOUNT OF WATER USED	
Showering for 5 minutes	150 L
Taking a bath	250 L
Brushing teeth	1 L
Washing hands or face	3 L
Washing clothes in washing machine	150 L
Washing dishes by hand	30 L
Washing dishes in dishwasher	50 L

Relating Units

The Calgary Stampede is held every July in the province of Alberta. In the barrel racing event, Sue Ellen rode 240 meters in a path around three barrels. Cathy's path was 0.25 kilometers. Whose path was shorter?

Convert 0.25 kilometers to meters to compare.

To convert metric units, multiply or divide by a power of ten.

▶To change a larger unit to a smaller unit, multiply.

> 0.25 km = ___ m
>
> 0.25 × 1,000 = 250
>
> 0.25 km = 250 m

Think To change km to m, multiply by 1,000. Move the decimal point 3 places to the right.

Sue Ellen's path was shorter than Cathy's because 240 m < 250 m.

▶To change a smaller unit to a larger unit, divide.

> 5 L = ___ hL
>
> 5 ÷ 100 = 0.05
>
> 5 L = 0.05 hL

Think To change L to hL, divide by 100. Move the decimal point 2 places to the left.

Use the metric prefixes in the table below with meter, gram, and liter to name other units of measure.

kilo- (k) 1,000	hecto- (h) 100	deka- (da) 10	unit 1	deci- (d) 0.1	centi- (c) 0.01	milli- (m) 0.001

1 kiloliter (kL) = 1,000 L
1 hectometer (hm) = 100 m
1 dekagram (dag) = 10 g

1 deciliter (dL) = 0.1 L
1 centimeter (cm) = 0.01 m
1 milligram (mg) = 0.001 g

CLASSWORK

Complete.

1. 2.1 hm = ___ dam

2. 6 mg = ___ dg

3. 0.5 daL = ___ cL

4. 1.4 kg = ___ g

5. 250 mL = ___ L

6. 245 g = ___ kg

7. 92 kL = 92,000 ___

8. 150 mm = 15 ___

9. ___ hL = 125 L

Complete.

1. 720 g = ___ kg

2. 17 dL = ___ L

3. 1 mm = ___ m

4. 10 cm = ___ dm

5. 20 dg = ___ g

6. 7.2 m = ___ cm

7. 34 dag = ___ g

8. 6.4 m = 6,400 ___

9. 300 dL = ___ hL

10. 0.056 km = ___ dm

11. 63.1 cm = 0.631 ___

12. 1 hL = 100 ___

★**13.** 0.7 kL = ___ cL

★**14.** 1,200 mg = 0.0012 ___

★**15.** 0.03 mL = ___ L

Compare. Use >, <, or = for each ●.

16. 1 kL ● 100 daL

17. 15 cm ● 0.15 m

18. 450 g ● 45 kg

19. 5 L ● 500 mL

20. 5.2 km ● 520 m

21. 75 cL ● 7.5 L

Complete. In each chart the input is equal to the output.

	Input	Output
	31 g	31,000 mg
22.	4.5 g	mg
23.	g	500 mg

	Input	Output
24.	1.7 kg	g
25.	3.18 kg	g
26.	kg	750 g

	Input	Output
27.	800 kg	t
28.	kg	0.45 t
29.	9,250 kg	t

APPLICATION

30. In the rope throwing event, Sue Ellen used a rope that weighed 1.3 kg. Nina's rope weighed 1,250 g. Whose rope was heavier?

★**31.** Before one event, Raoul's horse had to be weighed. The saddle was already in place and weighed 123 hg. The horse and saddle together weighed 712.3 kg. How much did the horse weigh?

LOGICAL THINKING

Glenda has these three jars of nuts to mix for a party after the rodeo.

If she uses only cashews and peanuts, there will be 1,000 grams of nuts. If she uses only pecans and peanuts, there will be 700 grams of nuts. If she combines all three, there will be 1,300 grams of nuts. How many grams of each kind of nut are there?

Problem Solving

DIVIDE AND CONQUER

When a problem is complex, a good strategy is to try to divide the problem into parts. Do each part separately, then put the parts back together for the final solution.

A weight-lifting contest was held at Olympic Stadium in Montreal. There were three rounds. The bar graph shows the results for the two top contestants. How much greater was the winner's average?

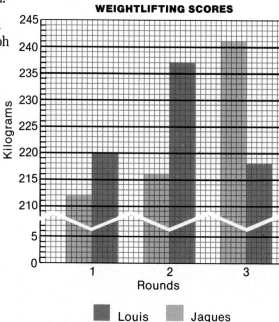

WEIGHTLIFTING SCORES

■ Louis   ■ Jaques

What is the question?

How much greater was the winner's average?

What are the facts?

Read the scores from the bar graph.
Louis lifted 212 kg, 216 kg, and 241 kg.
Jacques lifted 220 kg, 237 kg, and 218 kg.

How can the answer be found?

Find the average weight that each person lifted. Then subtract the lesser average from the greater one.

Louis: 212 kg
        216 kg
      + 241 kg
        669 kg   669 kg ÷ 3 = 223 kg

Jacques: 220 kg
          237 kg
        + 218 kg
          675 kg   675 kg ÷ 3 = 225 kg

225 kg − 223 kg = 2 kg

Jacques' average was 2 kg greater.

Is your arithemetic correct?

Add in reverse order to check.

241 kg   218 kg
216 kg   237 kg
+ 212 kg   + 220 kg
669 kg   675 kg

Multiply to check the division.

223 kg   225 kg
×   3   ×   3
669 kg   675 kg

Does your answer make sense?

2 kg + 223 kg = 225 kg   The answer is correct.

PRACTICE

The Wilson School Athletic Club toured Canada last week. The bar graph shows how far they traveled each day. Use the graph to solve problems **1–4**.

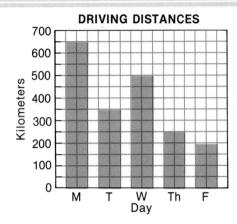

DRIVING DISTANCES

1. What was the average distance in kilometers traveled per day?

2. How much farther did the club travel on Monday than on Friday?

3. Joan joined the club on Wednesday. How many kilometers less than the other members did she travel?

4. The members wanted to drive 2,000 km. Did they reach their goal? How many kilometers more or less did they drive?

5. Janet bought a camera for $425. She could have bought it for $135 down and $30 per month for 12 months. How much did she save by paying for the camera all at once?

6. Janet used 4 rolls of film. Each roll cost $6.97. It cost $4.25 to have each roll developed. How much did she spend in all for her pictures?

7. Olympic Stadium in Montreal needed new turf for the 900-square meter surface of the infield. Artificial turf costs $15 per square meter. Regular turf costs $12 per square meter. How much more would it cost to cover the infield with artificial turf?

8. The relay team ran the four legs of a 5-kilometer race in 16 minutes. Jack ran the first 1,250 meters in 4 minutes. Li ran the next leg in 4 minutes 8 seconds. Lucy ran the leg in 3 minutes 57 seconds. What was Randy's time for the last leg?

9. Phil buys and sells antique game boards. While in New Brunswick, he bought an 1837 game board for $325 and then sold it for $450. Later he bought it back for $575 and resold it for $650. How much did Phil gain or lose on these transactions?

★ 10. The P.T.A. fair will raise money to buy uniforms for the 36 members of the Athletic Club. Running shoes cost $38.50, jerseys cost $18.75, and pants cost $21.50. The profit from each person who attends is $7.50. How many people must attend to cover the cost of the uniforms?

CREATE YOUR OWN PROBLEM

The Mercer family stayed in a hotel in Quebec City for two nights. The parents' room cost $47.50 per night. The three boys stayed in a room for $54.50 per night. The family spent a total of $71.98 in the restaurant of the hotel. Use this information to make up a problem that can be solved by dividing it into parts.

Units of Time

Jackie's cross-country ski team raced in Canada's Elk Island National Park. In the 40-km relay, her team completed the course in 150 minutes. How many hours did it take them?

150 min = ___ h

60 seconds (s) = 1 minute (min)	
60 minutes = 1 hour (h)	
24 hours = 1 day (d)	
7 days = 1 week (wk)	
52 weeks = 1 year (yr)	
12 months (mo) = 1 year	
365 days = 1 year	
100 years = 1 century (c)	

▶To change from a smaller unit to a larger unit, divide.

Think
1 h = 60 min
Divide 150 by 60.

$$\begin{array}{r} 2.5 \\ 60\overline{)150.0} \\ \underline{120} \\ 30\ 0 \\ \underline{30\ 0} \\ 0 \end{array}$$

150 min = 2.5 h

The team completed the course in 2.5 h.

▶To change from a larger unit to a smaller unit, multiply.

2 yr 5 wk = ___ wk

Think
1 yr = 52 wk
Multiply 2 × 52.

2 yr = 2 × 52 wk = 104 wk

2 yr 5 wk = 104 wk + 5 wk = 109 wk

▶To add or subtract units of time, you may need to regroup.

a.
$$\begin{array}{r} 6\ d\quad 14\ h \\ +\ 5\ d\quad 12\ h \\ \hline 11\ d\quad 26\ h \end{array}$$

Think
26 h = 24 h + 2h
= 1 d 2 h

b.
$$\begin{array}{r} \overset{5}{\cancel{6}}\ h\quad \overset{70}{\cancel{10}}\ min \\ -\ 2\ h\quad 40\ min \\ \hline 3\ h\quad 30\ min \end{array}$$

Think
Regroup 6 h 10 min as 5 h 70 min.

11 d 26 h = 12 d 2 h

CLASSWORK

Complete.

1. 8 wk = ___ d

2. 200 min = ___ h ___ min

3. 27 mo = ___ yr

Add or subtract.

4.
$$\begin{array}{r} 3\ wk\quad 5\ d \\ +\ 1\ wk\quad 4\ d \end{array}$$

5.
$$\begin{array}{r} 2\ yr\quad 3\ mo \\ +\ 1\ yr\quad 9\ mo \end{array}$$

6.
$$\begin{array}{r} 3\ h\quad 15\ min \\ -\ 1\ h\quad 24\ min \end{array}$$

7.
$$\begin{array}{r} 5\ d\quad 18\ h \\ -\ 2\ d\quad 18\ h \end{array}$$

PRACTICE

Complete.

1. 4 yr = ___ mo
2. 9 d = ___ h
3. ___ min = 6 h
4. 85 s = ___ min ___ s
5. 5 h 42 min = ___ min
6. 38 mo = ___ yr ___ mo
7. 3 wk 4 d = ___ d
8. 7 yr 3 mo = ___ mo
9. 114 wk = ___ yr ___ wk
10. ___ min = 8 h 10 min
11. 10 yr 6 mo = ___ mo
12. 7 d 7 h = ___ h
13. 1 h = ___ s
14. 1 d = ___ min
15. 1 wk = ___ h
★16. 1 yr = ___ h
★17. 2 yr 5 wk = ___ d
★18. 3 h 20 s = ___ s

Add or subtract.

19. 12 yr 5 mo
   + 2 yr 6 mo

20. 17 h 45 min
   − 5 h 16 min

21. 12 yr 5 wk
   − 5 yr 17 wk

22. 35 wk 3 d
   + 17 wk 4 d

23. 13 d 16 h
   + 7 d 15 h

24. 1 c 35 yr
   + 2 c 85 yr

25. 15 min 17 s
   − 14 min 20 s

26. 54 yr 7 mo
   − 46 yr 8 mo

★27. 7 h 36 min 40 s
   + 3 h 40 min 50 s

★28. 13 wk 7 d 17 h
   − 9 wk 7 d 20 h

★29. 22 h 58 min 2 s
   + 1 h 1 min 58 s

APPLICATION

30. Inga completed the first round of a ski contest in 3 min 21 s. The second round took her 2 min 47 s. How long did both rounds take?

★31. In a practice run for a cross-country ski relay, Steve's team completed the course in 2 h 30 min. The team's time for the actual relay was 135 min 42 s. Did they do better in practice or in the actual relay? how much better?

CALCULATOR

How much air do you breathe? Your lungs take in about 0.47 liter of air in each breath.

Find the number of breaths you take in 1 minute. Then use a calculator to find how much air you breathe in 1 day.

Press ☐ ✕ · ④ ⑦ ✕ ⑥ ⓪ ✕ ② ④ ⚌ ___ .

↑
number of breaths per minute

Find how much air you will breathe.

1. in 1 week
2. in 1 year
3. in 5 years
4. if you live to be 100 (Watch for error message.)

Elapsed Time

Caroline biked from Toronto to the Shakespeare Festival in Stratford, Ontario. She left Toronto at 8:20 A.M. and reached Stratford at 12:10 P.M. How long did the ride take?

The time that passed between 8:20 A.M. and 12:10 P.M. is called elapsed time.

▶Use a clock to count the time that elapses between the A.M. and P.M. hours.

Count the complete hours. Then count the remaining minutes.

3 h elapsed between 8:20 A.M. and 11:20 A.M.

50 min elapsed between 11:20 A.M. and 12:10 P.M.

Caroline's bike ride from Toronto to Stratford took 3 h 50 min.

▶When figuring elapsed time that is confined to either the A.M. hours or the P.M. hours, simply add or subtract the times.

a. Find the time that is 3 h 20 min *before* noon.

noon = 12 h

$$\begin{array}{r} {}^{11}\;{}^{60}\\ \cancel{12}\;\text{h}\\ -\;\;3\;\text{h}\;\;\;20\;\text{min}\\ \hline 8\;\text{h}\;\;\;40\;\text{min} \end{array}$$ ← Regroup if necessary.

The time is 8:40 A.M.

b. Find the time that is 2 h 35 min *after* 1:45 P.M.

1:45 = 1 h 45 min

$$\begin{array}{r} 1\;\text{h}\;\;\;45\;\text{min}\\ +\;2\;\text{h}\;\;\;35\;\text{min}\\ \hline 3\;\text{h}\;\;\;80\;\text{min} = 4\;\text{h}\;20\;\text{min} \end{array}$$ ← Regroup if necessary.

The time is 4:20 P.M.

CLASSWORK

Tell how much time has elapsed.

1. from 6:02 P.M. to 9:17 P.M.

2. from 4:13 A.M. to 12:09 P.M.

3. from 10:30 P.M. to 12:30 A.M.

Tell what time it is.

4. 35 minutes before 6:15 P.M.

5. 20 minutes past midnight

Write how much time has elapsed.

1. from 5:07 P.M.
to 6:20 P.M.

2. from 9:37 A.M.
to 11:51 A.M.

3. from 1:39 P.M.
to 5:17 P.M.

4. from 9:30 A.M.
to 1:30 P.M.

5. from 12:05 P.M.
to 8:15 P.M.

6. from 6:53 A.M.
to 11:21 A.M.

7. from 7:32 A.M.
to noon

8. from 8:56 P.M.
to 1:13 A.M.

9. from 10:02 P.M.
to 10:02 A.M.

★**10.** from 7:00 A.M.
to 6:00 A.M.

★**11.** from 10:30 P.M.
to 8:30 P.M.

★**12.** from 11:25 P.M.
to 6:00 P.M.

Write what time it is.

13. 3 hours after 7:43 P.M.

14. 4 hours before 11:08 A.M.

15. 1 h 30 min after 10:30 A.M.

16. 47 minutes before midnight

17. 6 h 35 min before 11:05 P.M.

18. 11 h 59 min after noon

19. 4 h 20 min after 9:00 P.M.

20. 8 hours before 7:00 A.M.

★**21.** 14 hours after 2:13 A.M.

★**22.** 20 hours before 7:30 P.M.

APPLICATION

Use the railroad schedule at the right to solve.

23. How much time elapses between leaving
Ottawa and arriving at Chelmsford?

24. Which city does the train reach 58
minutes after leaving Azilda?

25. On one trip the train reached Thunder
Bay at 11:59 A.M. How many minutes
early was it?

★**26.** The Goldsby family drove from Prince
Albert to Saskatoon in 3 hours 15
minutes. They continued driving to
Regina, which took 4 hours 50 minutes
more. They reached Regina at 6:20 P.M.
At what time did they leave Prince Albert?

Station	Arrive	Leave
Ottawa	—	**11:20**
Sudbury	7:00	8:00
Azilda	8:10	8:12
Chelmsford	8:17	8:19
Levack	8:35	8:38
Cartier	9:10	9:14
Thunder Bay	**12:08**	**12:21**
Ignace	**3:25**	—

Boldface times are P.M.

Problem Solving

SKILLS AND STRATEGIES REVIEW Canada

Read and solve each problem.

1. Lenore is a member of an equestrian team. In a recent competition at the Calgary Rodeo, her horse was able to jump over a hurdle that was 125 cm high. The hurdle was raised 56 cm, but her horse failed to clear it. Finally, the hurdle was lowered 28 cm, and the horse successfully jumped over it. How high was the hurdle that the horse finally cleared?

2. Lenore estimated that she needed 8.25 m of wire to install a light in the stable where she keeps her horse. When the light was installed, she found that she had overestimated by 0.060 m. How much wire did she actually need?

Lenore's horse weighs 474 kg. Lenore weighs 48 kg. The horse, the saddle, and the other equipment weigh 506 kg.

3. What is the total weight of Lenore, the horse, the saddle, and the other equipment?

4. What is the total weight of the saddle and the other equipment?

5. Lenore spends $55 per month to keep her horse in a stable. The horse's food costs $21.75 per week, and the average yearly veterinarian's fees are $300. How much does Lenore spend on the horse in one year?

6. It costs $75 to enter a horse in the jumping contest. If an entry drops out, only $35 of the fee is refunded. There were 27 horses entered, but 4 dropped out. How much money did the rodeo earn from the jumping contest?

7. In an equestrian jumping contest, each score is determined by adding the number of obstacles missed to the time it takes to complete the course. Lenore completed the course in 46.4 s and missed 3 obstacles. Bobby finished in 45.2 s with 4 misses. Kathy finished in 44.6 s with 5 misses. Who won the contest with the lowest score?

8. The director of the rodeo called in a carpenter to build a set of stalls. The building is in the shape of a rectangle. He is going to divide it into stalls by using 6 wooden partitions. Each partition requires 22.5 m of board. How many meters of board must the carpenter order to make the stalls?

Solve. Use the graph for problems 9–12.

**AVERAGE MONTHLY TEMPERATURES
IN VANCOUVER, BRITISH COLUMBIA**

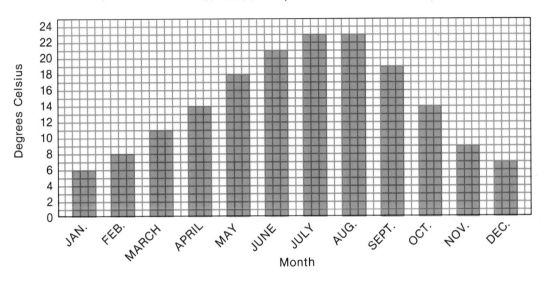

9. From January to June, between which two months is the increase in temperature the smallest?

10. From July to December, between which months is the decrease the same?

11. What is the difference in average temperature between April and June?

12. Which months have the same average temperature?

13. A bus traveled from Buffalo, N.Y., to Toronto, arriving at 12:40 P.M. The bus stopped at the border for 30 min to clear customs. If the actual traveling time was 2 h 15 min, what time did the bus leave Buffalo?

14. The ferry that crosses the Bay of Fundy can carry 32,200 kg. Five cars have boarded so far. Their total weight is 13,640 kg. Ten more cars are waiting to board. If the average weight of each of these cars is 2,600 kg, how many of them can safely board the ferry?

═══ SOMETHING EXTRA ═══

You Find Out

Canada has 10 provinces and 2 territories. For each, find out the name and population of its capital city. Also find out the total population of each province and territory.

1. Which province has the largest population? the smallest population?

2. Which capital city has the largest population? the smallest population?

CHAPTER REVIEW

Choose millimeter (mm), centimeter (cm), meter (m), or kilometer (km) to measure each. pages 118–119

1. length of a sleeve

2. height of a moose

3. distance from Hudson Bay to Lake Superior

4. thickness of a pancake

Choose the best estimate for each weight. pages 122–123

5. a sofa
   - a. 30 g
   - b. 30 kg
   - c. 3,000 kg

6. a shoelace
   - a. 0.5 mg
   - b. 5 kg
   - c. 5 g

7. a station wagon
   - a. 900 g
   - b. 900 kg
   - c. 900 t

8. a library card
   - a. 600 mg
   - b. 6 kg
   - c. 600 kg

Choose milliliter (mL), liter (L), or kiloliter (kL) to measure each amount. pages 124–125

9. cider in a jug

10. soup in a mug

11. water in a duck pond

12. cough syrup in a spoon

Complete. pages 120–121, 126–127, 130–131

13. 8 kg = ___ g

14. 10 L = ___ mL

15. 3,000 m = 3 ___

16. 50 dm = ___ m

17. 2 hg = ___ kg

18. 1.7 cm = ___ mm

19. 0.4 g = ___ mg

20. 3,600 mm = ___ m

21. 200 daL = 2 ___

22. 100 s = ___ min ___ s

23. 2 yr = ___ d

24. 2 wk = ___ h

Add or subtract. pages 130–131

25.
```
  7 min   20 s
− 5 min   11 s
```

26.
```
  3 yr   11 mo
+ 7 yr    3 mo
```

27.
```
  7 wk   3 d   12 h
+ 3 wk   4 d   13 h
```

28.
```
  15 h
− 12 h   24 min
```

Tell how much time has elapsed. pages 132–133

29. from 6:30 A.M. to noon

30. from 11:20 A.M. to 1:10 P.M.

Tell what time it is. pages 132–133

31. 6 h 20 min after 1:00 A.M.

32. 3 h 10 min before 4:05 P.M.

Solve. pages 128–129, 134–135

33. How many 1-liter bottles are needed to hold 2,500 mL of water?

34. Ari drove 950 km to Toronto. He drove 175 km a day for the first 3 days and 180 km a day for the next 2 days. How far was Ari from Toronto after 5 days?

Choose millimeter (mm), centimeter (cm), meter (m), or kilometer (km) to measure.

1. distance from Hawaii to Japan

2. height of a car

Choose the best estimate for each weight.

3. a polar bear

   a. 45 g

   b. 450 kg

   c. 45 t

4. an egg

   a. 150 g

   b. 1.5 kg

   c. 150 kg

5. a honey bee

   a. 100 mg

   b. 1 kg

   c. 100 kg

Choose milliliter (mL), liter (L), or kiloliter (kL) to measure each.

6. water in a fish tank

7. a raindrop

Complete.

8. 6 L = ___ mL

9. 600 g = ___ kg

10. 5 kL = ___ L

11. 200 cg = ___ g

12. 35 dm = ___ m

13. 2.1 mm = ___ cm

14. 11 min 30 s = ___ s

15. 427 d = ___ wk

16. 5 h = ___ min

Add or subtract.

17.   8 d   17 h
     + 6 d   13 h

18.   5 wk
     − 2 wk   3 d

19.   14 min   18 s
     − 10 min   50 s

Find each time.

20. the elapsed time between 5:45 A.M. and 11:00 A.M.

21. the elapsed time between 1:40 P.M. and midnight

22. 3 h 10 min before 2:00 P.M.

23. 11 h after 6:37 A.M.

Solve.

24. Albert weighs 44 kg. Jerry weighs 43,995 g. How much more does Albert weigh?

25. Randi's alarm clock woke her at 7:20 A.M. If she went to sleep at 10:38 P.M., how long did she sleep?

The Kendalls arrived home from their vacation at 2:00 P.M. on March 16. This was 150 h 42 min after they had left home. What was the date and time when they left for vacation?

WORLD TIME ZONES

The universal time (UT) system divides the world into 24 time zones. The starting point is the *prime meridian,* the line of longitude (0°) that passes through Greenwich, England.

WORLD TIME ZONES

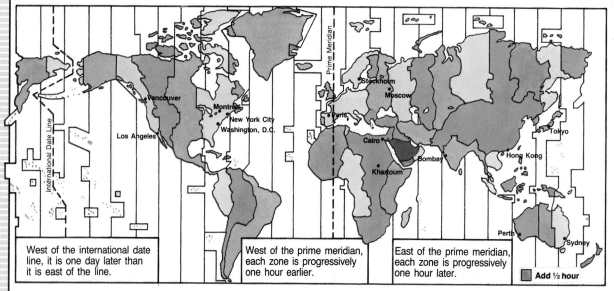

West of the international date line, it is one day later than it is east of the line.

West of the prime meridian, each zone is progressively one hour earlier.

East of the prime meridian, each zone is progressively one hour later.

■ Add ½ hour

This map can be used to find the time in any place in the world. Find the time in each place when it is 2 A.M. Sunday in Greenwich, England.

New York City

Think New York is 5 zones west of prime meridian. 5 hours earlier

It is 9 P.M. Saturday in New York.

Bombay, India

Think Bombay is 5 zones east of prime meridian. 5 hours later
Green color - Add $\frac{1}{2}$ hour.

It is 7:30 A.M. Sunday in Bombay.

Find the time in each place when it is noon on Sunday in Greenwich, England.

1. Khartoum, Sudan **2.** Washington, D.C. **3.** Montreal, Canada **4.** Vancouver, Canada

5. Paris, France **6.** Sydney, Australia **7.** Los Angeles **8.** Hong Kong

Complete this airline schedule.
Call a travel agency or airline office for the amount of air time between a large city near you and each city in the schedule. Use the time zone map to find the arrival time in each city.

Place of Departure	Departure Time	Air Time of Flight	Destination	Arrival Time
_____	7 A.M.	_____	Tokyo, Japan	_____
_____	11 A.M.	_____	Stockholm, Sweden	_____
_____	12 Noon	_____	Moscow, USSR	_____
_____	3 P.M.	_____	Cairo, Egypt	_____
_____	5 P.M.	_____	Perth, Australia	_____

PRECISION OF MEASUREMENT

Steve and Pam are building a boat model. They need to measure accurately so that all the pieces fit together.

Steve measured the plank below in centimeters. It is 4 cm long.

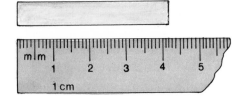

Pam measured the same plank in millimeters. It is 42 mm long.

Whose measurement is more precise?

▶The smaller the unit is, the more precise the measurement. Millimeter is a smaller unit than centimeter, so 42 mm is more precise than 4 cm.

Pam's measurement is more precise.

Which measurement is more precise—7.8 cm or 78 mm?

7.8 cm is precise to the nearest 0.1 cm.

Since 0.1 cm = 1 mm, 7.8 cm and 78 mm have the same precision.

Which measurement is more precise—8 cm or 8.0 cm?

8 cm is precise to the nearest cm.

8.0 cm is precise to the nearest 0.1 cm.

So 8.0 cm is a more precise measurement than 8 cm.

For each pair, tell which measurement is more precise.

1. 12 cm or 121 mm

2. 633 mm or 63 cm

3. 2 m or 201 cm

4. 81 cm or 813 mm

5. 68.7 mm or 6.9 cm

6. 5.1 m or 512 mm

7. 13 cm or 13.0 cm

8. 1,100 mm or 1.1 m

9. 12.8 cm or 128 mm

COMPUTER PROGRAMS AND FLOWCHARTS

Computer instructions can be shown by a flowchart and then developed into a **program.** A program is a set of instructions written in a special computer language.

These BASIC statements and commands are used in programming.

▶NEW clears the computer memory for a new program.

▶PRINT tells the computer to print values or exactly what is inside quotation marks.

▶LET assigns a value to a variable.

▶GOTO tells the computer to branch to another line of the program.

▶IF . . . THEN is used for making decisions. When the expression after IF is true, the computer will follow the instructions after THEN. When the IF part is false, the computer goes to the next line of the program.

▶REM is a remark for the programmer that is ignored by the computer.

▶INPUT tells the computer to wait for 1 or more numbers. Each number is named by a variable.

▶END signals the computer to stop the program.

▶RUN tells the computer to execute the program.

The flowchart and BASIC program below will convert meters to centimeters.

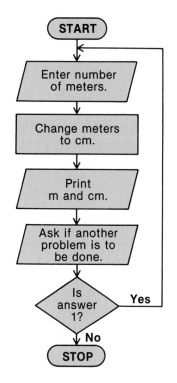

PROGRAM

```
10 REM PROGRAM TO CONVERT M TO CM
20 PRINT "ENTER THE NUMBER OF
   METERS."
30 INPUT M
40 LET C = M * 100
50 PRINT M; " M = ";C;"CM'
60 PRINT "DO YOU HAVE ANOTHER PROBLEM?
70 TYPE 1 FOR YES, TYPE 2 FOR NO."
80 INPUT A
90 IF A = 1 THEN GOTO 20
100 END
```

```
RUN
ENTER THE NUMBER OF METERS.
? 6.2
6.2 M = 620 CM
DO YOU HAVE ANOTHER PROBLEM?
TYPE 1 FOR YES. TYPE 2 FOR NO.
? 1
ENTER THE NUMBER OF METERS.
? 3
3 M = 300 CM
DO YOU HAVE ANOTHER PROBLEM?
TYPE 1 FOR YES. TYPE 2 FOR NO.
? 2
```

Use the program and its output to answer each question.

1. Matt runs the program and enters 7.3 for M and 2 for A. Write the computer output. What does the computer do when it reaches line 90? Will Matt get a chance for another program?

2. Sally runs the same program. She enters 18.1 for M and 1 for A. What will be printed at line 50? What does the computer do when it reaches line 90?

3. Change lines 10, 40, and 50 in the program to change meters to kilometers.

Write an IF . . . THEN statement.

4. If G is equal to 7, have the computer go to line 50.

Write a program for the flowchart. Then describe what the program does.

5.

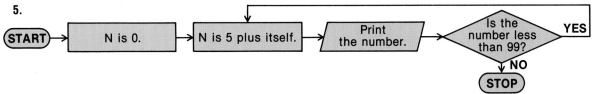

Write the program.

★ 6. Ask for a batting average. If it is over .300, then have the computer print a message like "That's major league!"

AT THE COMPUTER

Run the program on page 140 to find each missing number.

1. 7.256 m = _____ cm
2. 180 m = _____ cm
3. 93.5 m = _____ cm

Rewrite the program on page 140 to convert grams to kilograms. Run the program to find each missing number.

4. 758 g = _____ kg
5. 2,030 g = _____ kg
6. 76.1 g = _____ kg

Run the following programs. Write the output.

7. the program you wrote for **5**

★ 8. the program you wrote for ★ **6**

Choose the correct answers. Write A, B, C, or D.

1. Compare. 6,421.8 ⬤ 6,422

   A >   **C** =

   B <   **D** not given

2. Compare. 0.0050 ⬤ 0.005

   A >   **C** =

   B <   **D** not given

3. Order from least to greatest.
8.39, 8.03, 8.039

   A 8.03, 8.39,   **C** 8.39, 8.039,
      8.039   8.03

   B 8.039, 8.03, **D** not given
      8.39

4. 71.683 + 5.019 + 26.171

   A 92.873   **C** 102.873

   B 102.863   **D** not given

5. 7 − 6.0012

   A 0.9988   **C** 0.9998

   B 1.9988   **D** not given

6. 4.302 × 100

   A 4,302   **C** 0.4302

   B 43.02   **D** not given

7. 6.2)$\overline{18.91}$

   A 30.5   **C** 3.05

   B 3.15   **D** not given

8. $170.493 \div 10^3$

   A 17.0493   **C** 0.170493

   B 1.70493   **D** not given

9. What is the scientific notation for 789,000?

   A 7.89×10^5 **C** 7.89×10^3

   B 7.89×10^4 **D** not given

10. Complete. 7 cm = _____ mm

   A 7   **C** 700

   B 70   **D** not given

11. Complete. 1.64 kL = 1,640 _____

   A mL   **C** cL

   B L   **D** not given

12. What time is it 6 h after 11:15 A.M.?

   A 5:15 A.M.   **C** 6:15 A.M.

   B 6:15 P.M.   **D** not given

13. What time is it 30 min before 6:20 P.M.?

   A 5:50 P.M.   **C** 5:30 P.M.

   B 6:50 P.M.   **D** not given

Solve.

14. Craig had $100. If he spent $65 on a jacket and 0.4 that amount on a shirt, how much money did he have left?

   A $26   **C** $9

   B $35   **D** not given

15. The Wilsons drove 334.8 km on Saturday and Sunday. If they traveled 0.6 that distance on Saturday, how many kilometers did they drive on Sunday?

   A 200.88 km   **C** 134.08 km

   B 133.92 km   **D** not given

Theme: People & Animals

Order of Operations

Angora rabbits are raised for their fur. Each rabbit produces enough fur in one year to make 8 pairs of gloves or 2 sweaters. Marilyn Clark combed enough fur from her rabbits to make 720 pairs of gloves and 210 sweaters. How many rabbits does she own?

the number of rabbits needed to make 720 pairs of gloves	+	the number of rabbits needed to make 210 sweaters	=	the number of rabbits Marilyn owns

$$720 \div 8 \quad + \quad 210 \div 2 \text{ is an } \textbf{expression.}$$

The expression tells how many rabbits Marilyn owns.

▶When an expression has more than one operation, the order in which you perform the operations is important.

To find the value of an expression, follow the order of operations below.

1. Do all operations in parentheses and all operations above or below a division bar.
2. Do all work with exponents.
3. Do all multiplication and division from left to right.
4. Do all addition and subtraction from left to right.

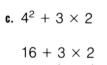

$$720 \div 8 + 210 \div 2 \quad \text{no parentheses}$$
$$90 \quad + \quad 105 \quad \text{no division bars, no exponents}$$
$$195$$

Marilyn owns 195 rabbits.

More Examples

a. $(8 - 3) \times 5 + 17$

$5 \quad \times 5 + 17$

$25 + 17$

42

b. $5 \times 4 + \dfrac{18 \div 2}{8 - 5}$

$5 \times 4 + \dfrac{9}{3}$

$20 + 3$

23

c. $4^2 + 3 \times 2$

$16 + 3 \times 2$

$16 + 6$

22

CLASSWORK

Find the value of each expression.

1. $8 + 3 \times 2$

2. $19 - 36 \div 9$

3. $8 \times 3 + 2 \times 5$

4. $(6 + 4) \times (8 - 3) + 12$

5. $\dfrac{17 - 2}{5} + 6$

6. $5 + \dfrac{6 \times 4}{3} \times 2$

Find the value of each expression.

1. $9 + 8 - 16$ **2.** $8 \times 4 \div 2$ **3.** $5 + 3 \times 12$

4. $62 \div 2 - 8$ **5.** $8 + 35 \div 7$ **6.** $14 + 3 + 2 \times 5$

7. $8 + (9 \div 3) - 4$ **8.** $26 - (3 + 18) \div 7$ **9.** $26 - 3 + 21 \div 7$

10. $(65 + 15) \div 10 + 2$ **11.** $40 - 50 \div 5$ **12.** $17 \times (5 \times 2)$

13. $(15 - 3) \times (9 - 5)$ **14.** $(8 + 5) \times (45 \div 9)$ **15.** $18 - 9 \div 3 \times 6$

16. $(34 + 11) \div 15 + 10$ **17.** $32 + (15 \div 5) - 3$ **18.** $(45 \div 5) + 3 - (4 \div 2)$

19. $\frac{15 + 9}{8} - 2$ **20.** $\frac{5 \times 6}{10} + \frac{2 \times 9}{3}$ **21.** $3 \times 2 - \frac{(12 - 4)}{2}$

22. $\frac{6 \times 3}{2 \times 1} \div 3$ **23.** $(15 + 12) \div 3^2$ **24.** $8^2 - \frac{8 \times 3}{12}$

Write *true* or *false*.

25. $(43 - 9) \times 4 + 5 = 43 - 9 \times 4 + 5$ **26.** $8 \times 10 - 8 + 9 = (8 \times 10) - 8 + 9$

27. $5 \times (14 - 8) + 12 = 5 \times 14 - (8 + 12)$ **28.** $96 \div 12 \div 4 = 96 \div (12 \div 4)$

Use parentheses to make each sentence true.

★**29.** $8 + 3 \times 4 + 5 = 49$ ★**30.** $4 \times 9 + 6 \div 2 = 30$

★**31.** $8 - 3 \div 5 \times 4 = 4$ ★**32.** $3 + 9 \div 3 + 2 \times 5 = 14$

APPLICATION

LOGICAL THINKING

Use 2, 4, 6, or 8 to make each statement true.

1. $\square \times \square + (\square + \square) = 8$ **2.** $\square \times \square - (\square + \square) = 24$

3. $\square \times (\square + \square) - \square = 28$ **4.** $\square \times \square - (\square - \square) = 64$

Replace each ● with +, −, ×, or ÷ to make each statement true.

5. $8 ● 3 ● 4 ● 5 = 20$ **6.** $8 ● 3 ● 4 ● 5 = 33$

7. $8 ● 3 ● 4 ● 5 = 11$ **8.** $8 ● 3 ● 4 ● 5 = 15$

Variables and Expressions

People in many places are trying to make safe nesting beaches for sea turtles. A sea turtle visits a nesting beach from 3 to 7 times each season, leaving about 100 eggs each time. How many eggs does a sea turtle produce in one season?

Let v represent the number of visits.
$100 \times v$ = the number of eggs
Another way to write $100 \times v$ is $100v$.

The letter v is called a **variable.** A variable is a letter used to represent a number. The value of an expression changes as the variable is replaced with different numbers.

▶To **evaluate** an expression, substitute a number for the variable.

$$100 \times v$$

Replace v with each number from 3 to 7.	

$$100 \times 3 = 300$$
$$100 \times 4 = 400$$
$$100 \times 5 = 500$$
$$100 \times 6 = 600$$
$$100 \times 7 = 700$$

The sea turtle produces 300 to 700 eggs in one season.

More Examples

a. Evaluate $a + 5$.
   Let $a = 7$.

   $7 + 5$

   12

b. Evaluate $\frac{r}{12}$.
   Let $r = 84$.

   $\frac{84}{12}$

   $84 \div 12$

   7

c. Evaluate $3b - 2$.
   Let $b = 11$.

   $3 \times 11 - 2$

   $33 - 2$

   31

CLASSWORK

Evaluate each expression. Let $a = 5$ and $b = 6$.

1. $a + 9$

2. $13 + a$

3. $3b$

4. $\frac{42}{b}$

5. $12 - a$

6. $5b + 8$

7. $5b - 9$

8. $b - 4$

9. $a + b$

10. $3a + b$

11. $b - a$

12. $2 \times (a + 4)$

13. $a \times b$

14. $2a + b$

15. $\frac{3b}{2}$

PRACTICE

Evaluate each expression. Let $n = 5$.

1. $3n$
2. $3 + n$
3. $\frac{25}{n}$
4. $18 - n$
5. $n - 3$

6. $2n + 3$
7. $8n - 10$
8. $\frac{35}{n} - 5$
9. $3 \times (n + 2)$
10. $\frac{n}{5} - 1$

Evaluate each expression. Let $a = 3$, $b = 5$, and $c = 8$.

11. $a + 13$
12. $4b$
13. $\frac{c}{4} + 10$
14. $a + b$
15. $3b + 5$

16. $b \times c$
17. $a + 6b$
18. $30 \div b$
19. $70 - 8c$
20. $2a + 3b$

★ 21. $\frac{5a + b}{4}$
★ 22. $\frac{bc - 10}{3}$
★ 23. $\frac{10b - 5a}{7}$
★ 24. $\frac{8a}{6} \times (c - b)$
★ 25. $ab - c$

Find each missing output.

	Input	Output
	n	$3n + 8$
	5	23
26.	13	
27.	20	

	Input	Output
	y	$7y - 12$
	7	37
28.	10	
29.	50	

	Input	Output
	t	$8t + 9$
30.	0	
31.	10	
32.	100	

	Input	Output
	d	$0.1 \times d$
33.	37	
34.	150	
35.	3,300	

	Input	Output
	e	$\frac{e}{2}$
36.	8	
37.	24	
38.	100	

	Input	Output
	f	$6 \times (f + 3)$
★ 39.	3.1	
★ 40.	5.3	
★ 41.	0.8	

APPLICATION

42. Volunteers collect the turtle eggs and bury them in new nests arranged in rows and columns. If the expression $24r$ stands for the number of nests in r rows, how many nests are there in 12 rows?

43. For the past 9 years, Carla Burke has been caring for sea turtles near her island home. The expression $t \div 9$ represents the average number of turtles she cares for each year. Evaluate this expression for $t = 675$ turtles.

147

Writing Expressions

Homing pigeons provided the first "air mail" service. Today, hobbyists like Glenn train their birds for races.

On Sunday, Glenn released 6 more birds than he did on Saturday. Write an expression to show how many birds were released on Sunday.

Use a variable to write the expression.

Let b represent the number of birds released on Saturday.

Then $b + 6$ represents the number released on Sunday.

Suppose Glenn released 8 birds on Saturday. To find how many birds he released on Sunday, evaluate the expression $b + 6$ for $b = 8$.

$$b + 6$$
$$8 + 6 = 14 \longleftarrow \text{ Substitute 8 for } b \text{ to find the value of } b + 6.$$

Glenn released 14 birds on Sunday.

More Examples

a. the sum of a number n and 9 $\qquad n + 9$

b. 8 less than a number y $\qquad y - 8$

c. the product of 8 and a number s $\qquad 8s$

d. 5 more than 3 times a number p $\qquad 3p + 5$

e. a number n divided by 6 $\qquad n \div 6$, or $\frac{n}{6}$

f. the quotient when 15 is divided by a number d $\qquad 15 \div d$, or $\frac{15}{d}$

CLASSWORK

Write an expression for each. Use n as the variable.

1. the sum of a number and 3

2. 10 times a number

3. 5 less than twice a number

4. a number divided by 15

5. a number decreased by 12

6. 8 less than a number divided by 6

Write an expression for each. Use b as a variable.

1. the sum of a number and 3
2. 9 less than a number
3. 7 times a number
4. 8 more than 7 times a number
5. 5 less than 7 times a number
6. the quotient of a number and 11
7. 18 more than twice a number
8. 21 less than 3 times a number
⋆9. 3 times the sum of a number and 5
⋆10. twice a number divided by 3 times the same number

Match.

11. 8 more than a number a
   a. $a - 8$

12. 8 times a number a
   b. $\frac{a}{12}$

13. 8 less than a number a
   c. $12a - 8$

14. 3 more than twice a number a
   d. $a + 8$

15. a number a divided by 12
   e. $12a + 5$

16. 12 divided by a number a
   f. $\frac{12}{2a}$

17. 5 more than 12 times a number a
   g. $8a$

18. 8 less than 12 times a number a
   h. $\frac{2a}{12}$

19. twice a number a divided by 12
   i. $2a + 3$

20. 12 divided by twice a number a
   j. $\frac{12}{a}$

APPLICATION

21. As long ago as 700 B.C., the ancient Greeks used pigeons to carry news of Olympic Game victories. The cubit was a measure of length at that time. Write an expression to represent the distance a pigeon could fly in 5 hours if it flew n cubits in one hour. Evaluate the expression for $n = 10$.

22. A homing pigeon flew 1,000 miles in d days across strange territory to find its way home. Write an expression to represent the number of miles it flew each day of the trip. Evaluate the expression for $d = 2$.

23. Glenn likes to race his homing pigeons. One of his pigeons flew 600 miles one day. Write an expression to represent the pigeon's rate of speed if it traveled for h hours. Evaluate the expression for $h = 10$.

⋆24. This year, Glenn trained 4 more than twice the number of pigeons he trained last year. Last year he trained p pigeons. Write an expression to represent the number of pigeons he trained this year. Evaluate the expression for $p = 15$.

Writing Equations

Studies show that the comfort that house pets give can help patients get well faster.

In this study, 12 patients from Ward Hospital were chosen to participate. The other patients were from Central Hospital. Write an equation to show this.

An **equation** is a number sentence with an equal sign (=).

$$\begin{array}{ccccc} \text{patients from} & + & \text{patients from} & = & \text{total patients} \\ \text{Central} & & \text{Ward} & & \text{in study} \\ n & + & 12 & = & 52 \end{array}$$

↑
Use a variable to represent the number from Central.

The **solution** of an equation is the value of the variable that makes the sentence true.

40 is the solution for $n + 12 = 52$.

$40 + 12 = 52$ ⟵ Substitute 40 for n to check
$52 = 52$ if 40 is a solution.

There were 40 patients from Central Hospital in the study.

More Examples

a. 800 more than a number n equals 1,100. $\qquad n + 800 = 1{,}100$

b. A number y decreased by 30 equals 48. $\qquad y - 30 = 48$

c. The product of 8 and a number p is 240. $\qquad 8p = 240$

d. A number d divided by 15 is 9. $\qquad d \div 15 = 9$, or $\frac{d}{15} = 9$

CLASSWORK

Write an equation for each.

1. A number y increased by 7 equals 32.

2. 8 less than a number x equals 17.

3. 5 times a number t equals 725.

4. A number d divided by 9 is 12.

150

PRACTICE

Write an equation for each.

1. A number n plus 5 is 13.

2. 15 less than a number y is 9.

3. 12 times a number d is 156.

4. The sum of 9 and a number n is 32.

5. Thirty-five divided by a number q is 7.

6. A number d divided by 6 equals 14.

7. Twice a number b equals 40.

8. The product of 6 and a number t is 48.

9. 10 more than twice a number p equals 85.

10. 9 less than 3 times a number r is 39.

★ 11. The sum of a number b and 5, divided by 8 is 13.

★ 12. 8 times the sum of a number n and 6 is 56.

Substitute the given value for the variable in each equation. Then tell if it is the solution.

13. $n + 18 = 25$ Let $n = 7$.   14. $5a = 60$ Let $a = 12$.

15. $9 - x = 5$ Let $x = 7$.   16. $t - 2 = 6$ Let $t = 3$.

17. $2b + 3 = 15$ Let $b = 6$.   18. $3n - 5 = 10$ Let $n = 12$.

19. $\frac{d}{3} + 9 = 15$ Let $d = 12$.   20. $\frac{5n}{4} - 6 = 4$ Let $n = 8$.

21. $\frac{8k \times 3}{6} = 32$ Let $k = 8$.   ★ 22. $\frac{7 + 7p}{5} = \frac{14}{2}$ Let $p = 4$.

APPLICATION

Write an equation for each.

23. Of the 52 patients in the pet study, 20 were men. The number of men plus the number of women (w) equals 52.

24. The number of patients discharged on Monday (m) plus the 8 patients discharged today equals 17.

★ 25. The number of patients who participated in a study is equal to 4 less than twice the number of animals. Let p stand for the number of patients and a for the number of animals.

Mixed Practice

1. $124 + 93 + 1,005$

2. $9,004 - 967$

3. $93 \times 100 \times 5$

4. $4.5 + 45 + 0.45$

5. 43.8×7

6. $17\overline{)952}$

7. $18.016 - 5.32$

8. $1,054 \div 34$

9. $586.2 - 3.819$

10. $15,296 \times 19$

11. $18\overline{)1,023.12}$

12. $0.08\overline{)0.42}$

13. 0.06×0.014

14. 61.3×0.8

15. $46\overline{)370,783}$

Complete.

16. $32 \text{ cm} = \underline{\quad} \text{ mm}$

17. $85 \text{ m} = \underline{\quad} \text{ km}$

18. $7 \text{ cm} = \underline{\quad} \text{ m}$

19. $930 \text{ mg} = \underline{\quad} \text{ kg}$

20. $7.34 \text{ kg} = \underline{\quad} \text{ g}$

21. $1.89 \text{ L} = \underline{\quad} \text{ mL}$

22. $0.06 \text{ kL} = \underline{\quad} \text{ L}$

Addition and Subtraction Equations

Herds of wild ponies live on an island off the coasts of Maryland and Virginia. Dr. Ronald Keiper of the National Park Service found that the ponies were living in 17 herds. If 4 of the herds live on the upper part of the island, how many herds live on the lower part?

Write an equation and solve it.

Let h = the number of herds living on the lower part. Then $4 + h = 17$.

▶To solve an addition equation, subtract the same number from both sides of the equation.

$4 + h = 17$	Use the inverse of adding 4 to solve.
$4 + h - 4 = 17 - 4$	Subtract 4 from both sides.
$h = 13$	Solution
Check $4 + 13 = 17$	To check, replace h with 13 in the original equation.

Of the 17 herds of ponies on the island, 13 herds live on the lower part.

▶To solve a subtraction equation, add the same number to both sides of the equation.

$d - 5 = 18$	Use the inverse of subtracting 5 to solve.
$d - 5 + 5 = 18 + 5$	Add 5 to both sides.
$d = 23$	Solution
Check $23 - 5 = 18$	To check, replace d with 23 in the original equation.

▶Adding or subtracting the same number on *both* sides of an equation keeps the equation balanced.

More Examples

a.
$$x + 9 = 28$$
$$x + 9 - 9 = 28 - 9$$
$$x = 19$$
Check $19 + 9 = 28$

b.
$$32 = a - 13$$
$$32 + 13 = a - 13 + 13$$
$$45 = a$$
Check $32 = 45 - 13$

CLASSWORK

Tell what to do to both sides of each equation to solve.

1. $4 + q = 19$
2. $s - 12 = 35$
3. $a + 35 = 45$
4. $21 = j - 23$

Solve and check.

5. $n + 8 = 15$
6. $m - 9 = 26$
7. $13 + x = 43$
8. $42 = y - 18$

Write what to do to both sides of each equation to solve.

1. $5 + y = 7$ **2.** $n + 13 = 40$ **3.** $x - 19 = 81$ **4.** $45 = b - 10$

5. $r - 3 = 3$ **6.** $30 + t = 52$ **7.** $12 = a - 36$ **8.** $85 = 32 + d$

Solve and check.

9. $x + 9 = 23$ **10.** $4 + y = 12$ **11.** $m - 7 = 13$ **12.** $n - 8 = 5$

13. $a + 10 = 26$ **14.** $n - 13 = 32$ **15.** $19 + r = 40$ **16.** $x - 30 = 21$

17. $p + 9 = 38$ **18.** $7 + c = 7$ **19.** $k - 10 = 0$ **20.** $y - 25 = 35$

21. $23 + t = 52$ **22.** $j - 11 = 46$ **23.** $l + 37 = 114$ **24.** $s - 59 = 53$

25. $91 + x = 132$ **26.** $q - 103 = 89$ **27.** $d + 210 = 375$ **28.** $w - 115 = 180$

29. $143 = j + 29$ **30.** $200 = x - 97$ **31.** $174 = 126 + w$ **32.** $321 = n - 321$

★ **33.** $y + 3 + 1 = 9$ ★ **34.** $r - 2 - 1 = 8$ ★ **35.** $t + 12 - 10 = 38$ ★ **36.** $a - 7 + 11 = 30$

APPLICATION

Write an equation for each problem. Then solve.

37. In one herd of 26 ponies, there are 8 mares and their foals. How many foals are in the herd?

★ **38.** Dr. Keiper observed one herd of 23 ponies. In this herd there were 1 stallion, 15 foals, and some mares. How many mares were there?

CALCULATOR

Use a calculator to solve equations.

Example $x + 3 - 4 = 9$

Press ⑨ ⊞ ④ ⊟ ③ ⊜ [*10.*]

Check $10 + 3 - 4 = 9$

Why does this work? Explain.

Solve each equation, using a calculator.

1. $y + 7 - 5 + 9 - 6 = 18$

2. $r + 8 + 3 - 5 + 7 - 2 = 30$

3. $x + 10 - 13 - 3 - 5 + 7 + 9 = 23$

Multiplication and Division Equations

This 4-pound capuchin monkey helps the young woman do many things. The monkey weighs twice as much as the book. How much does the book weigh?

Write an equation and solve it.

Let b = the weight of the book.
Then $2 \times b = 4$

    or $2b = 4$

▶To solve a multiplication equation, divide both sides of the equation by the same nonzero number.

Think $2b \div 2 = b$

$2b = 4$	Use the inverse of multiplying by 2 to solve.
$\frac{2b}{2} = \frac{4}{2}$	Divide both sides of the equation by 2.
$b = 2$	Solution

The book weighs 2 pounds.   **Check** $2 \times 2 = 4$ Replace b with 2 in the original equation.

▶To solve a division equation, multiply both sides of the equation by the same nonzero number.

$\frac{m}{3} = 8$	Use the inverse of dividing by 3 to solve. **Think** $\frac{m}{3} = m \div 3$
$\frac{m}{3} \times 3 = 8 \times 3$	Multiply both sides of the equation by 3.
$m = 24$	Solution

   Check $\frac{24}{3} = 8$ Replace m with 24 in the original equation.

▶Multiplying or dividing by the same number on both sides of an equation keeps the equation balanced.

More Examples

a. $y \times 5 = 35$
   $y \times 5 \div 5 = 35 \div 5$
         $y = 7$
Check $7 \times 5 = 35$

b. $k \div 9 = 4$
   $k \div 9 \times 9 = 4 \times 9$
         $k = 36$
Check $36 \div 9 = 4$

CLASSWORK

Tell what to do to both sides of each equation to solve. Then solve and check.

1. $3a = 12$ **2.** $\frac{b}{4} = 8$ **3.** $72 = 9 \times n$ **4.** $13 = d \div 6$

PRACTICE

Write what to do to both sides of each equation to solve.

1. $5b = 30$

2. $48 = 16x$

3. $y \div 5 = 7$

4. $\frac{n}{19} = 1$

5. $15y = 75$

6. $\frac{m}{8} = 60$

7. $100y = 500$

8. $70 = g \div 30$

Solve and check.

9. $5a = 15$

10. $7y = 42$

11. $\frac{x}{2} = 4$

12. $9s = 9$

13. $\frac{r}{9} = 5$

14. $6j = 96$

15. $m \div 8 = 21$

16. $72 = 12n$

17. $b \div 8 = 8$

18. $54 = t \times 9$

19. $11z = 77$

20. $\frac{e}{21} = 6$

21. $14 = k \div 6$

22. $12m = 12$

23. $14 = \frac{d}{5}$

24. $f \times 13 = 52$

★ **25.** $(9 + 6) \times b = 60$

★ **26.** $\frac{c}{(8 - 3)} = 10$

★ **27.** $120 \div y = 3$

★ **28.** $500 \div x = 5$

Use a calculator to solve each equation.

29. $6c = 2,100$

30. $\frac{d}{19} = 15$

31. $36q = 324$

32. $y \div 24 = 110$

APPLICATION

Write an equation for each. Then solve.

33. The stack of books weighs five times as much as the monkey. If the books weigh 30 lb, how much does the monkey weigh?

34. One capuchin monkey can complete 8 tasks in 24 min. On the average, how long does it take the monkey to complete each task?

★ **35.** It takes a monkey 2 min 45 s to turn on all the lights in an apartment. If it takes him 15 s per light, how many lights are in the apartment?

★ **36.** How many trips will it take a 6-lb monkey to move a 24-lb stack of books if it can carry half its weight on each trip?

=== MENTAL ARITHMETIC ===

Use the rules for multiplying and dividing by powers of 10 to solve each equation.

1. $10a = 360$

2. $100x = 420$

3. $\frac{x}{10} = 9$

4. $\frac{y}{1,000} = 51$

5. $1,000b = 6,439$

155

Graphing Ordered Pairs

Aquariums are used by marine scientists to study fish and some mammals. People visit aquariums for the pleasure of seeing the many exhibits and shows.

> ADMISSION
> $2.00 PER PERSON

The cost for a family to visit the aquarium depends on the number of family members.

A table can be used to show the costs. To find the values in a table, follow the rule. To find the cost, the rule is: multiply the number of family members by $2.

number in a family	1	2	3	4	5
cost of admission in dollars	2	4	6	8	10

Pairs of numbers can be used to show the cost.

(1,2), (2,4), (3,6), (4,8), and (5,10) are called **ordered pairs.**

The first number in each pair gives the number of people. The second number gives the cost.

An ordered pair can be shown as a point on a graph.

▶In an ordered pair (x, y) the first number x tells how many units to move right. The second number y tells how many units to move up.

To graph point A (1,2), start at 0.

Move 1 unit to the right and 2 units up.

Point B is 3 units to the right of 0 and 4 units up. So B is the graph of the ordered pair (3,4).

CLASSWORK

Write the ordered pair for each point on the graph.

1. T **2.** U **3.** W **4.** P

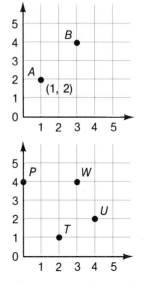

PRACTICE

Write the ordered pair for each point.

1. *A*   2. *C*   3. *S*

4. *U*   5. *V*   6. *R*

7. *T*   8. *P*   9. *W*

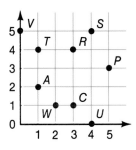

Using graph paper, copy the graph at the right. Then complete it by graphing each point.

10. $N(3,2)$ 11. $B(5,4)$ 12. $D(1,6)$

13. $A(5,0)$ 14. $G(0,3)$ 15. $H(2,5)$

16. $J(5,2)$ 17. $M(2,4)$ 18. $R(4,2)$

19. $F(4,1)$ 20. $C(6,3)$ 21. $K(3,5)$

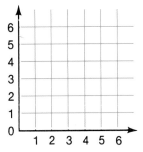

Follow the rule to find each missing number.

Rule: $y = x + 4$

	x	y
22.	0	
23.	2	
24.	4	

Rule: $y = 2x$

	x	y
25.	0	
26.	4	
27.	6	

Rule: $y = x - 1$

	x	y
28.	8	
29.	5	
30.	2	

APPLICATION

31. Using graph paper, copy the graph at the right. Then graph the ordered pairs that show the costs of admission from the table on page 156.

★ 32. Janice Carter works with dolphins at the aquarium. She spends 2 hours each morning and 2 hours each afternoon in the dolphin tank. Make a table of values to show how many total hours she works with the dolphins after 0, 1, 2, 3, 4, and 5 days. Write a rule for the table. Then draw a graph that shows the ordered pairs in the table.

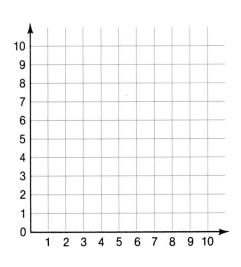

Problem Solving

MAKING AND USING DRAWINGS

Sometimes making a drawing helps you to understand how the facts in a problem are related.

1. Richard Martinez is a mounted policeman in Wingdale. His station, the school, and the bank are all along a straight road. The school is 2.6 km from the station. The bank is 1.7 km from the station. The station is between the bank and the school. How far does Officer Martinez ride from the school to the bank?

What is the question?

How far is it from the school to the bank?

What are the facts?

The station, school, and bank are on the same road.
Distance from station to school: 2.6 km
Distance from station to bank: 1.7 km
The station is between the bank and the school.

Make a plan. Carry it out.

Draw a diagram to show how the station, school, and bank are related. First, use the fact that the station is between the bank and the school. Then label the distances.

Use the information in the drawing. ⟶ 1.7 km + 2.6 km = 4.3 km

Officer Martinez rides 4.3 km from the school to the bank.

Add in reverse order to check. 2.6 + 1.7 = 4.3

The answer is correct.

For some problems, a drawing is given. The information you need to solve the problem is contained in the drawing.

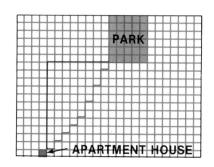

2. Mrs. Lee and Mr. Winston live in the same apartment building. Both walk their dogs to the park each morning. Mrs. Lee takes a straight route, while Mr. Winston takes a zig-zag route, as shown in the drawing. Whose dog goes for a longer walk?

Use the drawing. Count the number of city blocks walked in each route. Find the solution.

Make a drawing to illustrate each of the following situations. Then solve each problem.

1. A dogsled is racing on a triangular course. The first leg of the course is 7 km long, the second is 10 km long, and the third is 7 km long. There is a green flag at the first turn, a blue flag at the second, and a red flag at the finish. Between which two flags is the sled when it has completed $\frac{1}{2}$ the course?

2. Maria trains homing pigeons. Three pigeons fly away from her house. The first pigeon flies 3 km, and the second one flies 1.4 km in the opposite direction. The third pigeon flies in the same direction as the first pigeon but 0.5 km farther. How far apart are the second and third pigeons?

The Animal Adventure Park tour boat follows the 10-kilometer route shown in the drawing. The boat is now at Reptile World.

Use the drawing to solve each problem.

3. How far has the boat traveled from the start of the tour?

★ 4. How far is it from Reptile World to African Safari?

★ 5. How far must the boat now travel to finish the tour?

CREATE YOUR OWN PROBLEM

1. Use the facts in this drawing to create a problem about the sheepdog.

2. Create a problem that requires a drawing about fish in the sea. Make the drawing, and then solve the problem.

Divisibility

In Peru, llamas carry heavy loads for people. A llama can carry up to 45 kilograms.

Can a 90-kilogram load be divided equally between 2 llamas? among 5? among 10?

$$\begin{array}{r} 45 \\ 2\overline{)90} \end{array} \qquad \begin{array}{r} 18 \\ 5\overline{)90} \end{array} \qquad \begin{array}{r} 9 \\ 10\overline{)90} \end{array}$$

When 90 is divided by 2, 5, and 10, there is no remainder.

So 90 is **divisible** by 2, 5, and 10.

The 90-kilogram load can be divided equally among the llamas.

To test for divisibility without dividing, use the rules below.

A number is divisible by	if
2	the last digit is 0, 2, 4, 6, or 8.
5	the last digit is 0 or 5.
10	the last digit is 0.
3	the sum of the digits is divisible by 3.
9	the sum of the digits is divisible by 9.

More Examples

a. Is 162 divisible by 2, 5, and 10?

The last digit is 2.
So 162 is divisible by 2,
but not by 5 or 10.

b. Is 162 divisible by 3 and 9?

Add the digits: $1 + 6 + 2 = 9$.
9 is divisible by 3 and 9.
So 162 is divisible by 3 and 9.

CLASSWORK

Tell if each number is divisible by 2, 5, 10, 3, or 9.

1. 75   **2.** 138   **3.** 210   **4.** 234   **5.** 366   **6.** 157

PRACTICE

Tell if each number is divisible by 2, 5, or 10.

1. 45	**2.** 38	**3.** 60	**4.** 49
5. 105	**6.** 500	**7.** 750	**8.** 692
9. 327	**10.** 423	**11.** 144	**12.** 990
13. 1,462	**14.** 3,870	**15.** 5,455	**16.** 7,060

Tell if each number is divisible by 3 or 9.

17. 87	**18.** 54	**19.** 63	**20.** 93
21. 102	**22.** 178	**23.** 264	**24.** 477
25. 512	**26.** 600	**27.** 735	**28.** 891
29. 1,527	**30.** 3,861	**31.** 6,234	**32.** 8,100

Decide whether each number is divisible by *both* 2 and 3. Write *yes* or *no*.

33. 96	**34.** 102	**35.** 327	**36.** 786
37. 4,332	**38.** 1,020	**39.** 2,188	**40.** 9,999

Answer each question.

★ **41.** If a number is divisible by 2 and 3, is it also divisible by 6?

★ **42.** What is the least 4-digit number that is divisible by 3? Is it divisible by 6? by 9?

APPLICATION

43. Llamas can travel 24 to 32 km a day with a full load. On a 1-day pack trip, which of the possible distances can be divided into 2 equal parts? 3 equal parts? 5 equal parts?

★ **44.** A herder wants to sell 528 llamas. Can he sell them all in groups of 2? 3? 5? 6? 9? 10?

Mixed Practice

1. 37.4 × 20

2. 1.8 × 3.5

3. 29.7 × 1.583

4. 0.008 × 0.07

5. 81.6 ÷ 12

6. 33.8 ÷ 4

7. 96.88 ÷ 1.28

8. 0.09 ÷ 0.003

9. 351 × 100

10. 3,968 ÷ 10

11. 52 × 10,000

12. 18 ÷ 100

13.   3 d 14 h
  + 8 d 13 h

14.   3 min 20 s
  − 1 min 30 s

15.   15 h
  − 10 h 26 min

Complete.

16. 3 L = ___ mL

17. 4,200 g = ___ kg

18. 315 cm = ___ m

19. 12 km = ___ m

Factors

During a race in Alaska, dogsled teams run both day and night. Each 24-hour day is divided into equal periods of running and resting. How many hours do the dogs run each day?

2 equal periods $\longrightarrow$ $2\overline{)24}^{\,12}$ $2 \times 12 = 24$

2 and 12 are **factors** of 24.

The dogs run 12 hours each day.

▶**Factors** are numbers that multiply to give a product.

$1 \times 24 = 24$ $2 \times 12 = 24$ $3 \times 8 = 24$ $4 \times 6 = 24$

The factors of 24 are 1, 2, 3, 4, 6, 8, 12, and 24.

▶A number is divisible by each of its factors.

$24 \div 1 = 24$ $24 \div 2 = 12$ $24 \div 3 = 8$ $24 \div 4 = 6$

$24 \div 6 = 4$ $24 \div 8 = 3$ $24 \div 12 = 2$ $24 \div 24 = 1$

▶**Common factors** of two or more numbers are factors that are the same for each.

factors of 12: 1, 2, 3, 4, 6, 12

factors of 30: 1, 2, 3, 5, 6, 10, 15, 30

The common factors of 12 and 30 are 1, 2, 3, and 6.

The **greatest common factor (GCF)** of 12 and 30 is 6.

CLASSWORK

Find all the factors of each.

1. 16   **2.** 25   **3.** 36   **4.** 20   **5.** 50   **6.** 21

Find the common factors of each. Then find the GCF.

7. 10, 25   **8.** 6, 18   **9.** 8, 20   **10.** 8, 24, 56   **11.** 24, 32, 48

PRACTICE

Find all the factors of each.

1. 15 **2.** 35 **3.** 81 **4.** 38 **5.** 22 **6.** 49

7. 11 **8.** 72 **9.** 63 **10.** 32 **11.** 79 **12.** 120

Find the common factors of each. Then find the GCF.

13. 8, 28 **14.** 4, 26 **15.** 15, 36 **16.** 5, 15 **17.** 9, 12

18. 8, 10 **19.** 14, 21 **20.** 5, 8 **21.** 15, 50 **22.** 6, 8

23. 12, 32 **24.** 12, 36, 60 **25.** 10, 15, 30 **26.** 14, 35, 56 **27.** 16, 24, 72

Solve.

28. Find a pair of factors of 6 whose sum is 5.

29. Find a pair of factors of 10 whose sum is 7.

30. Find a pair of factors of 24 whose difference is 5.

31. Find 3 factors whose product is 18 and whose sum is 8.

Copy and complete each diagram by writing all the factors of each number inside its circle. Write the common factors where the circles intersect.

32.
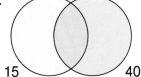
15   40

33.
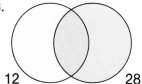
12   28

34.
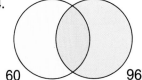
60   96

APPLICATION

35. The average dogsled team will run about 72 miles a day. The dogs run 12 hours a day. How many miles do they run in one hour?

36. Dogsled Teams A and B leave their stations and ride toward each other. The distance between their stations is 36 mi. Team A ran 7.5 mi and Team B ran 6.2 mi. How far apart are they?

★ **37.** During one dogsled race, the dogs had a total of sixteen 3-hour rest periods. If they ran and rested an equal number of hours each day, how many days did the race last?

Primes and Composites

Honeybees help people by pollinating the flowers of fruit and vegetable plants. They also produce honey and wax. To care for her bees, Sarah provides hives.

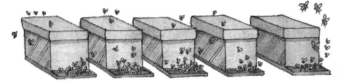

1 × 5, or 5 × 1

Sarah can arrange 5 hives in 1 row. The factors of 5 are 1 and 5. The number 5 is a prime number.

▶A **prime number** is a whole number greater than 1 with only two factors, 1 and itself.

Sarah can arrange 4 hives in 1 row or in 2 rows. The factors of 4 are 1, 2, and 4. The number 4 is a composite number.

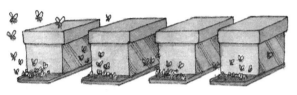

1 × 4, or 4 × 1

2 × 2

▶A **composite number** is a whole number greater than 1 with more than two factors.

Every whole number greater than 1 that is not a prime number is a composite number.

The numbers 0 and 1 are neither prime nor composite.

CLASSWORK

Tell whether each number is prime or composite.

1. 8   **2.** 16   **3.** 11   **4.** 15   **5.** 3   **6.** 29

7. 49   **8.** 24   **9.** 90   **10.** 19   **11.** 21   **12.** 33

PRACTICE

Label each number as prime or composite.

1. 13   **2.** 9   **3.** 17   **4.** 21   **5.** 38   **6.** 45

7. 31   **8.** 7   **9.** 75   **10.** 100   **11.** 50   **12.** 27

Write *true* or *false*.

13. The least prime number is 2.

14. The least composite number is 4.

15. All odd numbers are prime.

16. The only even prime number is 2.

17. All even numbers greater than 2 are composite.

★ **18.** The product of two prime numbers is a prime number.

★ **19.** The sum of any two prime numbers is a composite number.

★ **20.** When a composite number is divided by a composite number, the result is always a prime number.

APPLICATION

21. Find all the prime numbers from 1 to 100, using the **Sieve of Eratosthenes.** Follow these steps.

a. Write all the whole numbers from 1 to 100 in rows of 6.

b. Cross out 1. It is not prime.

c. Circle 2. Cross out all numbers divisible by 2.

d. Circle 3. Cross out all numbers divisible by 3.

e. Circle 5. Cross out all numbers divisible by 5.

f. Circle 7. Cross out all numbers divisible by 7.

When all steps are completed, circle all numbers *not* crossed out.

The numbers circled are prime numbers. The numbers crossed out, except 1, are composite numbers.

22. List all the prime numbers less than 100.

23. Prime numbers that differ by 2 are **twin primes.** The numbers 3 and 5 are twin primes. List in pairs the twin primes less than 100.

===== VISUAL THINKING =====

How can you rearrange the glasses in the top row to make the arrangement in the bottom row by moving only one glass?

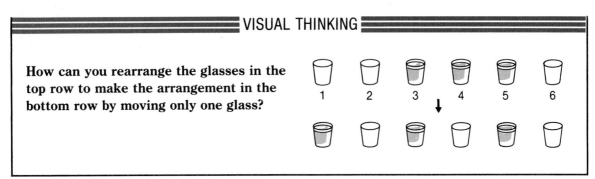

Prime Factorization

▶Every composite number can be written as the product of prime factors. This product is called the **prime factorization** of the number.

Find the prime factorization of 56.
Prime factorization can be found by using a factor tree.

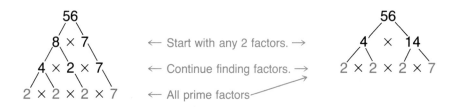

The prime factorization of **56** is $2 \times 2 \times 2 \times 7$.

Use exponents when a factor is repeated. $56 = 2^3 \times 7$

Prime factorization can be found by dividing by prime factors until the quotient is prime.

$$\begin{array}{r} 8 \\ 7\overline{)56} \end{array}$$ Divide 56 by a prime number.

$$\begin{array}{r} 4 \\ 2\overline{)8} \end{array}$$ Continue dividing each quotient by prime factors.

$$\begin{array}{r} 2 \\ 2\overline{)4} \end{array}$$ Quotient is prime.

$56 = 2 \times 2 \times 2 \times 7$

▶Each composite number has only one prime factorization.

CLASSWORK

Copy and complete each factor tree. Then write each prime factorization.

1.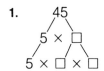

2.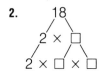

3.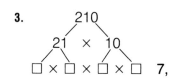

Write the prime factorization of each with and without exponents.

4. 27   **5.** 63   **6.** 44   **7.** 72   **8.** 225   **9.** 130

166

Copy and continue each factor tree. Then write each prime
factorization. Use exponents.

1.

2.

3.

Write the prime factorization of each. Use exponents.

4. 75   **5.** 48   **6.** 68   **7.** 76

8. 99   **9.** 96   **10.** 100   **11.** 120

12. 250   **13.** 336   ★**14.** 963   ★**15.** 1,024

Name the composite number for each prime factorization.

16. $5^2 \times 11$ **17.** $2 \times 3^2 \times 5^2$ **18.** $2^2 \times 7^2 \times 13$ **19.** $3^3 \times 7 \times 11$

Use a calculator to find the missing factors in each.

20.
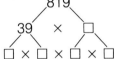

21.
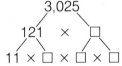

22.
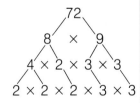

APPLICATION

PRIME FACTORIZATION AND GCF

You can use prime factorization to find the
GCF of two or more numbers.
Find the GCF of 48 and 72. First find the
prime factorization of each number.

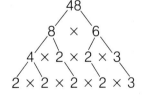

Then find the common prime factors.

The product of the common prime factors
is the GCF.

$48 \quad = 2 \times 2 \times 2 \times 2 \times 3$

$72 \quad = 2 \times 2 \times 2 \times 3 \times 3$

$GCF = 2 \times 2 \times 2 \times 3 = 24$

Use prime factorization to find the GCF.

1. 15, 60   **2.** 25, 75   **3.** 44, 66   **4.** 42, 50, 60

Multiples

Dairy cows are milked in a milking parlor. If 5 cows can be milked in 1 shift, how many cows can be milked in 2, 3, 4, and 5 shifts?

Find the **multiples** of 5 to answer the question.

▶To find the multiples of a number, multiply the number by 0, 1, 2, 3, 4, 5, . . . ⟵ means the list continues indefinitely

0×5	1×5	2×5	3×5	4×5	5×5. . .
0	5	10	15	20	25 . . .

The multiples of 5 are 0, 5, 10, 15, 20, . . .
So 10 cows can be milked in 2 shifts, 15 in 3 shifts, 20 in 4 shifts, and 25 in 5 shifts.

▶A number that is a multiple of two or more numbers is called a **common multiple.**

Find the common multiples of 6 and 8.

Multiples of 6: 0, 6, 12, 18, 24, 30, 36, 42, 48, . . .

Multiples of 8: 0, 8, 16, 24, 32, 40, 48, . . .

The common multiples of 6 and 8 are 0, 24, 48, . . .

▶The **least common multiple (LCM)** of two or more numbers is the least nonzero number that is a multiple of each.

The LCM of 6 and 8 is 24.

You can use prime factorization to find the LCM.

$$18 = 3^2 \times 2 \qquad 24 = 2^3 \times 3$$

Find the prime factorization of each number.

Multiply the highest power of each prime factor. ⟶ LCM = $3^2 \times 2^3 = 9 \times 8 = 72$

The LCM of 18 and 24 is 72.

CLASSWORK

Write the first five multiples of each.

1. 4 **2.** 5 **3.** 7 **4.** 25 **5.** 100

Find the LCM of each.

6. 4, 5 **7.** 4, 12 **8.** 9, 6 **9.** 8, 12 **10.** 3, 5, 6

Write the first five multiples of each.

1. 3   **2.** 10   **3.** 15   **4.** 20   **5.** 8

Find the LCM of each.

6. 3, 4   **7.** 6, 4   **8.** 3, 15   **9.** 8, 5   **10.** 6, 5

11. 9, 12   **12.** 12, 18   **13.** 10, 12   **14.** 15, 20   **15.** 8, 10

16. 20, 8   **17.** 20, 18   **18.** 12, 21   **19.** 6, 14   **20.** 9, 30

21. 2, 3, 4   **22.** 3, 4, 6   **23.** 6, 8, 12   **24.** 5, 15, 20   **25.** 2, 5, 7

Use the given prime factorization to find the LCM for each pair of numbers.

26. $42 = 2 \times 3 \times 7$
$35 = 5 \times 7$

27. $18 = 2 \times 3^2$
$12 = 2^2 \times 3$

28. $60 = 2^2 \times 3 \times 5$
$40 = 2^3 \times 5$

29. $36 = 2^2 \times 3^2$
$24 = 2^3 \times 3$

30. 231, 42   **31.** 16, 20   **32.** 15, 18   **33.** 75, 45

Complete the chart by finding the GCF and the LCM for each pair. Then compare the product of the two numbers to the product of the GCF and the LCM. What do you observe?

	Numbers	GCF	LCM	Product of Numbers	Product of LCM and GCF
34.	6, 10	2	30	6 × 10 = □	2 × 30 = □
35.	4, 8				
36.	10, 12				
37.	9, 15				
38.	6, 5				

APPLICATION

39. One 8-ounce glass of regular milk contains 150 calories. The same size glass of lowfat milk contains 100 calories. What is the least number of glasses of each kind of milk you will have to drink to consume an equal number of calories?

★ **40.** The Holstein Farm Dairy has two milk-loading machines. One loads a case in 18 seconds and one in 24 seconds. If they both start to load at the same time, how many seconds will elapse before they both finish a case together?

Problem Solving

SKILLS AND STRATEGIES REVIEW   Future Dome

Pacificus is a domed, underwater entertainment park of the future. It features sea animals and lies 1,500 m below the surface of the ocean. Oxygen is pumped into the dome of Pacificus.

Solve each problem. If there is not enough information tell what facts are needed.

1. The number of visitors to Pacificus on its opening day was 21,487. Of these, 5,625 were adult men, and 5,687 were adult women. The rest were children. How many children visited Pacificus on that day?

2. Pacificus has a Ride-a-Porpoise Touring Agency. The regular tour lasts 1 hour. Adults pay $5, and children under 12 pay $3. How much does it cost a family to take a regular tour?

3. Cara and Lago leave Pacificus at 10:00 A.M. in their underwater oxygen suits. They reach Mystery Cave at 11:15 A.M. Each suit contains enough oxygen for a 4-hour trip. How long do they have to explore the cave and return to Pacificus?

4. In a narrow passageway, the cave is 27 m high. Several stalactites hang down about 9.7 m. Below, stalagmites stand 10.7 m high. How much room is there for Cara and Lago to swim through?

5. Cara is watching two sea horses play. They hover together in the water for 2 minutes. Then the larger sea horse jumps up 12 cm, drops down 6 cm, jumps up 3 cm, drops down 2 cm, and jumps up 7 cm. The smaller sea horse drops down 11 cm, jumps up 12 cm, jumps up 6 cm, drops down 3 cm, and jumps up 2 cm. How much higher is the larger seahorse?

★ 6. The animals of Pacificus must be fed each day. It costs $15 per day to feed each porpoise. The cost per day to feed each whale is $25. Pacificus has 20 porpoises and 10 whales. How much does it cost to feed the porpoises and whales each day? Which costs more to feed each day?

The graph shows the average daily attendance figures for Pacificus.

7. About how many more women than men visit Pacificus daily?

8. About how many people altogether visit Pacificus daily?

9. About how many adults visit Pacificus daily?

10. What is the difference between the average adult daily attendance and average daily attendance of children?

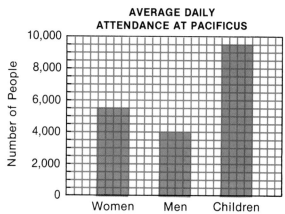

Solve.

11. The dome over Pacificus has 24 sections of glass. Each section contains 45,200 square meters. How much glass is used to make the dome?

12. The 21,000 cubic meters of oxygen inside the dome must be exchanged every hour. A-vents can exchange 2,000 cubic meters per hour. B-vents can exchange 3,000 cubic meters per hour. If 6 A-vents are operating, how many B-vents must also operate to exchange the 21,000 cubic meters of oxygen?

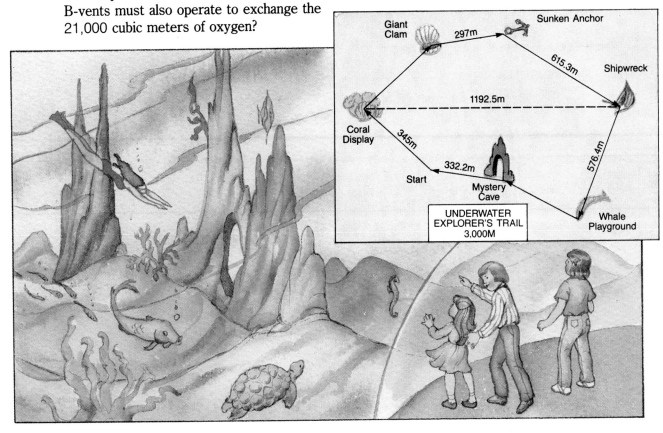

The Underwater Explorers' Trail has several major attractions.

Use the drawing to answer the following questions.

13. How long is the complete trail?

14. How far is it from the Giant Clam to the Whale Playground?

15. The distance from the Coral Display to the Giant Clam is the same as the distance from the Whale Playground to the entrance of the Mystery Cave. How far is it from the Coral Display to the Giant Clam?

16. While swimming the Underwater Explorers' Trail, Cara swam directly from the Coral Display to the Shipwreck. Lago followed the regular route. How much shorter than Lago's route was Cara's?

171

CHAPTER REVIEW

Evaluate. pages 144–145

1. $19 + (8 + 4 \div 2) \times 3$

2. $19 + 8 + 4 \div 2 \times 3$

3. $19 + 8 + (4 \div 2 \times 3)$

Evaluate each expression. Let $a = 4$, $b = 3$, and $c = 7$. pages 146–147

4. $a + 5 - b$

5. $2a - 2b$

6. $a + b + c$

7. $(a + b) + 2c$

Write an expression for each phrase. Use n as the variable. pages 148–149

8. 7 more than a number

9. a number decreased by 5

10. 3 times a number plus 10

11. 14 less than a number divided by 12

Write an equation for each. pages 150–151

12. Nine more than a number x equals 35.

13. A number r divided by 11 equals 12.

Solve and check. pages 152–155

14. $x + 8 = 21$

15. $y - 10 = 17$

16. $18 + m = 35$

17. $r - 83 = 109$

18. $15b = 75$

19. $54 = 9a$

20. $\frac{n}{9} = 14$

21. $y \div 7 = 13$

Follow the rule to find the value of y in each. pages 156–157

22. $y = 2x$, $x = 8$

23. $y = x + 4$, $x = 7$

Tell if each number is divisible by 2, 3, 5, 9, or 10. pages 160–161

24. 963

25. 4,130

26. 590

27. 75,576

Find the GCF and LCM of each. pages 162–163, 168–169

28. 8, 20

29. 9, 16

30. 4, 26

31. 11, 44

32. 2, 4, 8

Tell whether each number is prime or composite. If composite, write the number as the product of prime factors using exponents when possible. pages 164–167

33. 68

34. 225

35. 103

36. 550

37. 270

Solve. pages 158–159, 170–171

38. Mel and his guide dog walked 16 city blocks from home to the supermarket as shown on the drawing on the right. How many blocks will they walk if they take the shortest route home?

39. At a dog show, there are 140 entries. Can the dogs and their trainers parade in groups of 2? of 4? of 6? of 9? of 10?

Mel's Apartment

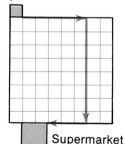

Supermarket

Evaluate.

1. $25 \div 5 + 20 \times 2$

2. $25 \div (5 + 20) \times 2$

3. $18 + 7 - 6 \div 3 \times 4$

4. $18 + b$, if $b = 7$

5. $3a - 5$, if $a = 9$

6. $n \div 7 + 2$, if $n = 63$

Write an expression or equation for each.

7. four times a number n plus eight

8. 17 increased by a number y equals 29.

9. 14 equals the sum of 6 and twice a number r.

Solve and check.

10. $y + 10 = 32$

11. $7m = 84$

12. $x - 7 = 13$

13. $\frac{n}{13} = 9$

Find the GCF and LCM of each.

14. 9, 15

15. 8, 30

16. 21, 63

Tell whether each number is prime or composite. If composite, write as the product of prime factors.

17. 151

18. 57

19. 210

Tell if each number is divisible by 2, 3, 5, 9, or 10.

20. 420

21. 13,485

Follow the rule to find the value of y in each.

22. $y = 3x$, $x = 5$

23. $y = x + 5$, $x = 8$

Solve.

24. A homing pigeon flew a distance of 120 miles in 3 days. If it flew 75 miles in the first 2 days, how many miles did it fly on the last day?

25. Sam and Terry live 12 km apart. They left their homes on horseback and rode toward one another. Sam rode 3.5 km and Terry rode 3.6 km. How far apart are they?

The GCF of two numbers is 7 and the LCM is 210. If one of the numbers is 35, what is the other number?

EXPLORE

CLOCK ARITHMETIC

When you use a 12-hour clock, you are often doing a special kind of arithmetic. You are working in a number system that uses only the numbers on the clock face:
1, 2, 3, 4, 5, 6, 7, 8, 9, 10, 11, 12.

What hour is 5 hours *after* 11:00?

+5 hours

5 hours after 11:00 is 4:00.

What hour is 6 hours *before* 2:00?

– 6 hours

6 hours before 2:00 is 8:00

Using a clock-arithmetic number system, write:

$$11 + 5 = 4$$

$$2 - 6 = 8$$

To add, think of moving the hour hand in a clockwise direction.
To subtract, think of moving the hour hand in a counterclockwise direction.

Use clock arithmetic to add or subtract.

1. $7 + 3 = n$ **2.** $7 + 8 = n$ **3.** $10 + 2 = n$ **4.** $4 + 12 = n$

5. $12 + 6 = n$ **6.** $5 + 9 = n$ **7.** $3 + 11 = n$ **8.** $10 + 9 = n$

9. $9 - 4 = n$ **10.** $4 - 3 = n$ **11.** $5 - 9 = n$ **12.** $3 - 12 = n$

13. $2 - 3 = n$ **14.** $12 - 4 = n$ **15.** $2 - 10 = n$ **16.** $1 - 4 = n$

You can also do clock multiplication.

To multiply 3×5, think $5 + 5 + 5$.

Start at 12.

Move 5 hours clockwise. Do this a total of 3 times.

In this number system, write: $3 \times 5 = 3$

Use clock arithmetic to multiply.

17. $7 \times 4 = n$ **18.** $10 \times 2 = n$ **19.** $5 \times 5 = n$ **20.** $12 \times 3 = n$

21. $3 \times 4 = n$ **22.** $6 \times 3 = n$ **23.** $8 \times 2 = n$ **24.** $1 \times 11 = n$

TRIANGULAR AND SQUARE NUMBERS

The ancient Greeks believed that numbers and geometry were related. They represented whole numbers by dots that formed a triangle or square.

Here are the first four triangular numbers.

```
 •        •           •            •
        •  •        •  •         •  •  •
                  •  •  •      •  •  •  •
                            •  •  •  •  •
 1        3          6           10
```

Here are the first four square numbers.

```
 •       •  •      •  •  •      •  •  •  •
         •  •      •  •  •      •  •  •  •
                   •  •  •      •  •  •  •
                               •  •  •  •
 1        4          9           16
```

Triangular and square numbers are interesting because of their patterns.

1. Draw the next three triangular numbers and name them.

2. Write the sequence of triangular numbers formed so far.

3. Write the sequence formed by the differences between consecutive triangular numbers.

4. Draw the next three square numbers and name them.

You can show that a square number is the sum of two consecutive triangular numbers.

```
    •     • • •           •       • • • •
  • •     • • •         • •       • • • •
• • •     • • •       • • •       • • • •
                                 • • • •
 3  +  6  =  9         6  +  10  =  16
```

5. Show that the square numbers you drew in **4** are each the sum of two consecutive triangular numbers.

MAINTAINING SKILLS

Choose the correct answers. Write A, B, C, or D.

1. What multiplication property is used?
   $(10 \times 4) + (10 \times 3) = 10(3 + 4)$

   A associative   C distributive

   B commutative   D not given

2. Round 1.7854 to the nearest tenth.

   A 1.7   C 2.0

   B 1.8   D not given

3. Estimate. $6.9 - 2.3$

   A 3   C 5

   B 4   D not given

4. 81.2×7.35

   A 596.82   C 5.9682

   B 59.682   D not given

5. $6.37 \div 10^2$

   A 0.00637   C 637

   B 0.637   D not given

6. $24\overline{)86.4}$

   A 36   C 3.6

   B 0.36   D not given

7. Complete. 8.5 mL = _____ L

   A 0.85   C 8,500

   B 0.085   D not given

8.   4 h 35 min
      + 3 h 43 min

   A 7 h 18 min   C 8 h 18 min

   B 8 h 8 min   D not given

9. Complete. 0.75 cm = 0.0075 _____

   A mm   C km

   B m   D not given

10. What is the value of $16 + 32 \div 4 - 1$?

    A 11   C 16

    B 23   D not given

11. Evaluate. $\frac{n}{4} - 4$ Let $n = 20$.

    A 1   C 9

    B 4   D not given

12. Solve. $p - 17 = 39$

    A 22   C 56

    B 46   D not given

13. Solve. $\frac{r}{12} = 30$

    A 2.5   C 350

    B 36   D not given

Solve.

14. In Montreal, Vern took a museum tour that lasted 2 h 10 min. Later he took a bus tour that was 90 min longer. How much time did he spend on both tours?

    A 2 h 50 min   C 5 h 50 min

    B 3 h 40 min   D not given

15. A baseball team buys new bats and gloves for its 12 members. Each bat costs $12.50 and each glove costs $9.85. How much does the team spend altogether?

    A $268.20   C $31.80

    B $150.00   D not given

Theme: The Sea

Fractions

Why is the sky blue? The sky reflects the color of our planet. Since $\frac{7}{10}$ of the earth is covered with water, the sky is blue like the seas of the earth.

The fraction $\frac{7}{10}$ tells what part of the earth is covered with water.

A **fraction** names part of a region or part of a group.

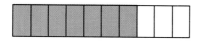

read seven tenths

Fractions name points on the number line.

$$\begin{array}{ccccccccc} \frac{0}{8} & \frac{1}{8} & \frac{2}{8} & \frac{3}{8} & \frac{4}{8} & \frac{5}{8} & \frac{6}{8} & \frac{7}{8} & \frac{8}{8} \end{array}$$

0      $\frac{8}{8}$ names the whole number 1.   1

Fractions express quotients.

$$4 \div 7 = \frac{4}{7} \qquad 9 \div 9 = \frac{9}{9} = 1$$

A **proper fraction** is one in which the numerator is less than the denominator.

$\frac{4}{7}$ and $\frac{7}{10}$ are proper fractions.

An **improper fraction** is one in which the numerator is greater than or equal to the denominator.

$\frac{8}{8}$ and $\frac{9}{3}$ are improper fractions.

CLASSWORK

Write a fraction for the shaded part in each.

1.

2.

Write each as a fraction.

4. $8 \div 15$

5. $7 \div 5$

6. $21\overline{)9}$

7. $6\overline{)6}$

178

Write a fraction for the shaded part of each.

1.

2.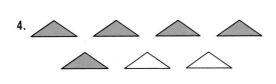

3.

4.

Write each as a fraction.

5. 3 ÷ 18

6. 15 ÷ 27

7. 6 ÷ 10

8. 3 ÷ 7

9. $3\overline{)2}$

10. $6\overline{)5}$

11. $11\overline{)5}$

12. $7\overline{)7}$

Write a fraction for each point labeled A, B, C, or D on the number lines. Then write a fraction for each point named by 1.

13.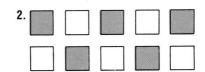

14.

15.

Write a fraction for each.

16. the shells that are *not* tan

17. the shells that are *not* pink

★ **18.** the shells that are *not* pink or black

★ **19.** the shells that are tan or pink

★ **20.** the shells that are pink or tan or black

21. Ryan collected 24 seashells while vacationing in Florida. Five of the shells were conch shells and 19 were clam shells. What fraction of the shells were conch shells? What fraction were clam shells?

★ **22.** Ryan traded shells with his brother Paul. He gave Paul 3 of his clam shells for 1 conch shell. What fraction of Ryan's collection were conch shells after the trade?

Equivalent Fractions

Which sailboat is winning?

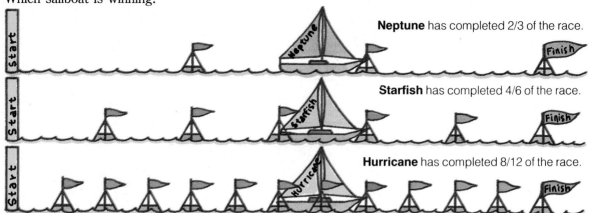

Neptune has completed 2/3 of the race.

Starfish has completed 4/6 of the race.

Hurricane has completed 8/12 of the race.

$\frac{2}{3}$, $\frac{4}{6}$, and $\frac{8}{12}$ name the same number. They are **equivalent fractions.**

No boat is winning. All three boats have completed the same fraction of the race.

▶To find equivalent fractions, multiply or divide the numerator and denominator by the same number, except 0.

$$\frac{1}{2} = \frac{1 \times 3}{2 \times 3} = \frac{3}{6} \qquad\qquad \frac{15}{25} = \frac{15 \div 5}{25 \div 5} = \frac{3}{5}$$

$\frac{1}{2}$ and $\frac{3}{6}$ are equivalent. $\qquad\qquad$ $\frac{15}{25}$ and $\frac{3}{5}$ are equivalent.

More Examples

Find the value for n to make the fractions equivalent.

a. $\frac{3}{4} = \frac{n}{24}$ $\quad$ **Think** $4 \times 6 = 24$

$\frac{3}{4} = \frac{3 \times 6}{4 \times 6} = \frac{18}{24}$

$n = 18$

$\frac{3}{4} = \frac{18}{24}$

b. $\frac{12}{15} = \frac{4}{n}$ $\quad$ **Think** $12 \div 3 = 4$

$\frac{12}{15} = \frac{12 \div 3}{15 \div 3} = \frac{4}{5}$

$n = 5$

$\frac{12}{15} = \frac{4}{5}$

CLASSWORK

Write three equivalent fractions for each.

1. $\frac{1}{3}$ $\qquad$ 2. $\frac{3}{4}$ $\qquad$ 3. $\frac{20}{30}$ $\qquad$ 4. $\frac{36}{45}$ $\qquad$ 5. $\frac{3}{11}$ $\qquad$ 6. $\frac{14}{56}$

Find the value of n in each.

7. $\frac{1}{4} = \frac{1 \times 3}{4 \times n} = \frac{3}{12}$ $\qquad$ 8. $\frac{8}{14} = \frac{8 \div n}{14 \div n} = \frac{4}{7}$ $\qquad$ 9. $\frac{2}{5} = \frac{n}{10}$ $\qquad$ 10. $\frac{20}{36} = \frac{5}{n}$

PRACTICE

Write three equivalent fractions for each.

1. $\frac{1}{4}$ **2.** $\frac{12}{36}$ **3.** $\frac{1}{5}$ **4.** $\frac{5}{9}$ **5.** $\frac{75}{100}$ **6.** $\frac{16}{96}$

Find the value of *n* in each.

7. $\frac{1}{2} = \frac{1 \times n}{2 \times n} = \frac{5}{10}$ **8.** $\frac{3}{8} = \frac{3 \times n}{8 \times n} = \frac{9}{24}$ **9.** $\frac{24}{30} = \frac{24 \div n}{30 \div n} = \frac{4}{5}$

10. $\frac{11}{25} = \frac{n}{50}$ **11.** $\frac{4}{8} = \frac{n}{32}$ **12.** $\frac{32}{48} = \frac{n}{3}$ **13.** $\frac{6}{3} = \frac{n}{18}$ **14.** $\frac{88}{32} = \frac{n}{4}$

15. $\frac{65}{100} = \frac{n}{20}$ **16.** $\frac{16}{7} = \frac{64}{n}$ **17.** $\frac{13}{20} = \frac{26}{n}$ **★18.** $\frac{9}{9} = \frac{n}{10}$ **★19.** $\frac{15}{15} = \frac{20}{n}$

APPLICATION

20. At another race, *Gulfstream* raced against *Neptune, Starfish,* and *Hurricane.* When *Gulfstream* had completed $\frac{10}{24}$ of the race, *Hurricane* had completed $\frac{5}{12}$; *Starfish,* $\frac{2}{6}$; and *Neptune,* $\frac{1}{3}$. Use the number lines to find their positions. Which sailboats are ahead? Which of the fractions are equivalent?

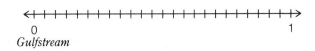
0   1
Gulfstream

0   1
Hurricane

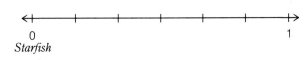
0   1
Starfish

★21. A boat has completed $\frac{3}{8}$ of a race. What fraction of the course must it still sail to complete $\frac{13}{24}$ of the race?

0   1
Neptune

EQUIVALENT FRACTIONS AND CROSS PRODUCTS

If two fractions are equivalent, their cross products are equal. If the cross products are equal, the fractions are equivalent.

$\frac{2}{3} = \frac{8}{12}$ cross products

$2 \times 12 = 3 \times 8$
$24 = 24$

Are $\frac{3}{5}$ and $\frac{7}{10}$ equivalent fractions?

$\frac{3}{5} \bullet \frac{7}{10}$

$3 \times 10 \neq 5 \times 7$ ← The cross products are not equal.
$30 \neq 35$ The fractions are not equivalent.

Use cross products to tell if the fractions are equivalent. Write *yes* or *no*.

1. $\frac{3}{4}, \frac{9}{12}$ **2.** $\frac{6}{11}, \frac{2}{5}$ **3.** $\frac{8}{6}, \frac{20}{15}$ **4.** $\frac{14}{6}, \frac{21}{9}$ **5.** $\frac{5}{8}, \frac{20}{35}$

181

Lowest Terms

Herman Melville wrote about a whale named Moby Dick. He called it the Great White Whale, but Moby Dick was only $\frac{6}{10}$ the size of a blue whale!

▶A fraction is in **lowest terms,** or **simplest form,** when the greatest common factor (GCF) of the numerator and denominator is 1.

To write $\frac{6}{10}$ in lowest terms, first find the GCF of the numerator and denominator.

Factors of 6: 1, 2, 3, 6
Factors of 10: 1, 2, 5, 10
GCF: 2

Then divide the numerator and the denominator by the GCF.

$\frac{6}{10} = \frac{6 \div 2}{10 \div 2} = \frac{3}{5}$ The GCF of 3 and 5 is 1. So $\frac{3}{5}$ is in lowest terms.

$\frac{6}{10}$ in lowest terms is $\frac{3}{5}$.

Moby Dick was $\frac{3}{5}$ the size of the blue whale.

▶Sometimes it is easier to divide the numerator and the denominator by any common factor. Continue to divide until the fraction is in lowest terms.

$\frac{30}{45} = \frac{30 \div 3}{45 \div 3} = \frac{10}{15}$ **and** $\frac{10 \div 5}{15 \div 5} = \frac{2}{3}$ **or** $\frac{30}{45} = \frac{30 \div 15}{45 \div 15} = \frac{2}{3}$

CLASSWORK

Tell if each fraction is in lowest terms. Write *yes* or *no*.

1. $\frac{3}{4}$ 2. $\frac{20}{100}$ 3. $\frac{6}{8}$ 4. $\frac{8}{9}$ 5. $\frac{14}{49}$ 6. $\frac{10}{11}$

Write each fraction in lowest terms.

7. $\frac{10}{30}$ 8. $\frac{6}{8}$ 9. $\frac{9}{15}$ 10. $\frac{8}{32}$ 11. $\frac{15}{35}$ 12. $\frac{12}{120}$

PRACTICE

Tell if each fraction is in lowest terms. Write *yes* or *no.*

1. $\frac{2}{3}$ 2. $\frac{1}{5}$ 3. $\frac{4}{12}$ 4. $\frac{7}{9}$

5. $\frac{3}{15}$ 6. $\frac{9}{20}$ 7. $\frac{35}{63}$ 8. $\frac{50}{125}$

Write each fraction in lowest terms.

9. $\frac{4}{6}$ 10. $\frac{10}{15}$ 11. $\frac{16}{32}$ 12. $\frac{10}{30}$

13. $\frac{25}{30}$ 14. $\frac{10}{40}$ 15. $\frac{6}{24}$ 16. $\frac{12}{16}$

17. $\frac{18}{24}$ 18. $\frac{35}{50}$ 19. $\frac{75}{100}$ 20. $\frac{20}{40}$

21. $\frac{14}{16}$ 22. $\frac{80}{100}$ 23. $\frac{4}{16}$ 24. $\frac{16}{36}$

25. $\frac{25}{45}$ 26. $\frac{40}{75}$ 27. $\frac{16}{44}$ 28. $\frac{22}{55}$

29. $\frac{110}{880}$ 30. $\frac{100}{250}$ ★31. $\frac{78}{195}$ ★32. $\frac{875}{1,000}$

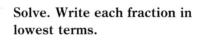

Solve. Write each fraction in lowest terms.

33. What fraction of a year is 30 days?

34. What fraction of a day is 10 hours?

★35. What fraction of a day is 20 minutes?

★36. What fraction of an hour is 45 seconds?

APPLICATION

37. One day, Captain Ahab's chase and struggle with Moby Dick lasted 9 hours. What fraction of a day is that? Write the answer in lowest terms.

★38. The old whaling ship *Portsmouth* was 180 feet long. Whale oil was stored in a 50-foot storage area. What fraction of the ship was not used for storing whale oil? Write the fraction in lowest terms.

Fractions and Mixed Numbers

Luis is collecting samples of seawater for a school science experiment. He has to pour $2\frac{1}{2}$ gallons of water into half-gallon containers. How many containers does he need?

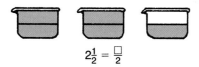

$$2\frac{1}{2} = \frac{\square}{2}$$

$2\frac{1}{2}$ is a **mixed number.** A mixed number can be written as an **improper fraction.** In an improper fraction the numerator is greater than or equal to the denominator.

To write a mixed number as an improper fraction, follow these steps.

Step 1	Step 2
Multiply the whole number by the denominator. Then add the numerator.	Write the sum over the denominator.

$$2\frac{1}{2} \longrightarrow (2 \times 2) + 1 = 5$$

$$2\frac{1}{2} = \frac{5}{2}$$

Luis needs 5 half-gallon containers.

You can write an improper fraction as a mixed number or a whole number.

Step 1	Step 2
First divide the numerator by the denominator.	Write the quotient as the whole number. Write the remainder as the numerator.

$$\frac{21}{9} \rightarrow 9\overline{)21} \quad \begin{array}{r} 2\ R3 \\ \underline{18} \\ 3 \end{array}$$

$2\frac{3}{9}$ ← remainder
   ← divisor $2\frac{3}{9} = 2\frac{1}{3}$

CLASSWORK

Write each as an improper fraction.

1. $1\frac{2}{5}$ 2. $2\frac{1}{4}$ 3. $5\frac{4}{7}$ 4. $10\frac{1}{9}$ 5. $1\frac{2}{3}$ 6. $4\frac{1}{2}$

Write each as a whole number or mixed number in lowest terms.

7. $\frac{10}{4}$ 8. $\frac{22}{7}$ 9. $\frac{27}{3}$ 10. $\frac{13}{5}$ 11. $\frac{34}{8}$ 12. $\frac{45}{9}$

PRACTICE

Write each as an improper fraction.

1. $4\frac{1}{4}$
2. $12\frac{2}{3}$
3. $2\frac{4}{7}$
4. $3\frac{1}{2}$
5. $9\frac{1}{6}$
6. 2

7. $3\frac{2}{5}$
8. $6\frac{1}{4}$
9. $1\frac{3}{6}$
10. $3\frac{3}{4}$
11. $3\frac{5}{6}$
12. $4\frac{7}{12}$

13. $1\frac{7}{9}$
14. $3\frac{15}{16}$
15. $5\frac{3}{8}$
16. $2\frac{3}{5}$
17. $10\frac{2}{9}$
18. $6\frac{4}{15}$

Write each as a whole number or a mixed number in lowest terms.

19. $\frac{17}{3}$
20. $\frac{12}{6}$
21. $\frac{10}{4}$
22. $\frac{7}{3}$
23. $\frac{5}{4}$
24. $\frac{17}{2}$
25. $\frac{15}{4}$

26. $\frac{22}{4}$
27. $\frac{40}{8}$
28. $\frac{33}{16}$
29. $\frac{15}{12}$
★30. $\frac{56}{18}$
★31. $\frac{76}{24}$
★32. $\frac{36}{16}$

Use your calculator to name each as an improper fraction.

33. $15\frac{3}{20}$
34. $27\frac{11}{17}$
35. $35\frac{13}{32}$
36. $86\frac{21}{40}$
37. $142\frac{43}{61}$
38. $205\frac{17}{190}$

Name each point as a mixed number and as an improper fraction in lowest terms.

39. A
40. B
41. C
42. D
43. E
44. F
45. G

APPLICATION

46. To work on his experiment, Luis must pour samples of seawater from beakers into test tubes. If each test tube holds $\frac{1}{5}$ of a beaker of water, how many test tubes does Luis need to hold 4 beakers of water?

★47. Carol Reilly is a scientist working at Seapure Water Corporation. She stores water samples in quart bottles. How many bottles does Carol need to hold $10\frac{1}{2}$ gallons of water?

CALCULATOR

Here is how to enter a mixed number on a calculator.

Enter $30\frac{7}{8}$. [7] [÷] [8] [+] [3] [0] [=] $\boxed{30.875}$

Use a calculator to find the value of each stock in dollars and cents.

Stock	Price Per Share	in Dollars
Seaco Corp.	$77\frac{1}{4}$	
Puraco	$128\frac{5}{8}$	
Clearwater Corp.	$76\frac{3}{8}$	
Seasalt Separators	$19\frac{3}{4}$	

Comparing Fractions

Ann and Paul are painting their boat, the *Blue Marlin*. Ann uses $\frac{3}{4}$ gallon of paint for the port side. Paul uses $\frac{4}{5}$ gallon for the starboard. Who uses more paint?

Compare $\frac{3}{4}$ and $\frac{4}{5}$.

Fractions with different denominators are unlike fractions. To compare unlike fractions, follow these steps.

Step 1   Find the least common denominator (LCD) of the fractions.

$\frac{3}{4} \rightarrow$ 4, 8, 12, 16, 20, . . .   **Think**   The least common multiple of the denominators is the **LCD**.

$\frac{4}{5} \rightarrow$ 5, 10, 15, 20, . . .

The LCD of $\frac{3}{4}$ and $\frac{4}{5}$ is 20.

Step 2   Write the equivalent fractions.

$\frac{3}{4} = \frac{3 \times 5}{4 \times 5} = \frac{15}{20}$

$\frac{4}{5} = \frac{4 \times 4}{5 \times 4} = \frac{16}{20}$

Step 3   Compare the numerators.

$\frac{15}{20}$ ⬤ $\frac{16}{20}$

$15 < 16$, **so** $\frac{15}{20} < \frac{16}{20}$ **and** $\frac{3}{4} < \frac{4}{5}$.

Paul uses more paint, because $\frac{4}{5}$ gallon is more than $\frac{3}{4}$ gallon.

More Examples

a. Compare $3\frac{3}{8}$ and $3\frac{1}{6}$.
Since the whole numbers are the same, compare the fractions.

Think   The LCD of $\frac{3}{8}$ and $\frac{1}{6}$ is 24.

$\frac{3}{8} = \frac{3 \times 3}{8 \times 3} = \frac{9}{24}$

$\frac{1}{6} = \frac{1 \times 4}{6 \times 4} = \frac{4}{24}$

$\frac{9}{24} > \frac{4}{24}$,   so $3\frac{9}{24} > 3\frac{4}{24}$ and $3\frac{3}{8} > 3\frac{1}{6}$.

b. Compare $\frac{5}{6}$, $\frac{4}{5}$, and $\frac{7}{10}$.

Think   The LCD of $\frac{5}{6}$, $\frac{4}{5}$, and $\frac{7}{10}$ is 30.

$\frac{5}{6} = \frac{5 \times 5}{6 \times 5} = \frac{25}{30}$

$\frac{4}{5} = \frac{4 \times 6}{5 \times 6} = \frac{24}{30}$

$\frac{7}{10} = \frac{7 \times 3}{10 \times 3} = \frac{21}{30}$

$\frac{21}{30} < \frac{24}{30} < \frac{25}{30}$,   so $\frac{7}{10} < \frac{4}{5} < \frac{5}{6}$.

CLASSWORK

Compare. Use >, <, or = for each ⬤.

1. $\frac{1}{2}$ ⬤ $\frac{3}{10}$

2. $\frac{1}{4}$ ⬤ $\frac{2}{6}$

3. $\frac{2}{3}$ ⬤ $\frac{5}{8}$

4. $2\frac{1}{6}$ ⬤ $2\frac{2}{9}$

5. $\frac{2}{5}$ ⬤ $\frac{3}{8}$

6. $\frac{2}{3}$ ⬤ $\frac{5}{9}$

7. $\frac{2}{3}$ ⬤ $\frac{3}{4}$

8. $1\frac{1}{4}$ ⬤ $1\frac{3}{16}$

9. $\frac{1}{2}$ ⬤ $\frac{5}{10}$

10. $8\frac{3}{4}$ ⬤ $8\frac{7}{24}$

Compare. Use >, <, or = for each ●.

1. $\frac{2}{5}$ ● $\frac{4}{15}$ 2. $\frac{3}{4}$ ● $\frac{7}{8}$ 3. $\frac{3}{5}$ ● $\frac{6}{10}$ 4. $\frac{3}{4}$ ● $\frac{5}{6}$ 5. $\frac{1}{2}$ ● $\frac{4}{9}$

6. $\frac{7}{8}$ ● $\frac{3}{4}$ 7. $\frac{1}{3}$ ● $\frac{2}{5}$ 8. $\frac{2}{3}$ ● $\frac{3}{4}$ 9. $\frac{3}{8}$ ● $\frac{6}{20}$ 10. $\frac{4}{6}$ ● $\frac{2}{3}$

11. $\frac{3}{5}$ ● $\frac{4}{7}$ 12. $\frac{4}{5}$ ● $\frac{7}{9}$ 13. $\frac{7}{10}$ ● $\frac{11}{16}$ 14. $\frac{3}{4}$ ● $\frac{6}{9}$ 15. $\frac{5}{10}$ ● $\frac{5}{6}$

16. $1\frac{1}{10}$ ● $1\frac{3}{5}$ 17. $3\frac{3}{9}$ ● $3\frac{1}{3}$ 18. $6\frac{4}{5}$ ● $6\frac{7}{8}$ 19. $4\frac{1}{2}$ ● $4\frac{7}{9}$ 20. $5\frac{1}{5}$ ● $5\frac{2}{4}$

List in order from least to greatest.

21. $\frac{1}{2}, \frac{1}{3}, \frac{1}{6}$ 22. $\frac{1}{4}, \frac{3}{8}, \frac{1}{16}$ 23. $\frac{2}{3}, \frac{4}{9}, \frac{1}{4}$ 24. $1\frac{3}{4}, 1\frac{5}{6}, 1\frac{3}{8}$ 25. $\frac{4}{5}, \frac{3}{4}, \frac{5}{6}$

Find a fraction between each pair of fractions.

26. $\frac{1}{2}, \frac{6}{8}$ 27. $\frac{1}{3}, \frac{5}{6}$ ★ 28. $\frac{5}{12}, \frac{5}{8}$ ★ 29. $\frac{4}{9}, \frac{1}{2}$ ★ 30. $\frac{3}{4}, \frac{4}{5}$

APPLICATION

31. In a hydroplane boat race, the *Misty* achieved the top speed of $57\frac{7}{10}$ knots per hour. Its rival, the *Quicksilver,* reached a top speed of $57\frac{5}{8}$ knots per hour. Which was the faster boat?

32. The container ship *Empire Comet* carries $\frac{3}{4}$ of its cargo inside its hold below deck and $\frac{6}{24}$ of its cargo on deck. Does it carry more cargo on or below deck?

33. On a voyage of the transatlantic steamship *Ruritania* from New York to Liverpool, England, $\frac{5}{6}$ of the cabins on the port side and $\frac{3}{4}$ of the cabins on the starboard side are occupied. Which side has more passengers?

★ 34. The supertanker *Petroleum Prince* uses $\frac{2}{3}$ of its fuel on a voyage from Rotterdam to Philadelphia. It refills its tank and at the end of the return trip has a fuel reserve of $\frac{2}{7}$ tank. Does the ship use more fuel on the voyage to or from Philadelphia?

▌MENTAL ARITHMETIC▐

To compare fractions when the numerators are the same, compare the denominators. The fraction with the lesser denominator is greater.

   Example   Compare $\frac{1}{5}$ and $\frac{1}{4}$. Since $4 < 5$, $\frac{1}{4} > \frac{1}{5}$.

Order each group of fractions from least to greatest.

1. $\frac{1}{8}, \frac{1}{9}$ 2. $\frac{2}{5}, \frac{2}{3}$ 3. $\frac{1}{12}, \frac{1}{10}$ 4. $\frac{4}{7}, \frac{4}{9}$ 5. $\frac{5}{34}, \frac{5}{33}, \frac{5}{35}$

Problem Solving

GUESS AND TEST

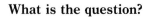

Some problems can be solved by making an intelligent guess at the answer. However, you must test your guess to see if it is correct. If it is not correct, you must make another guess and test it!

1. Harold bought both hooks and weights at the Fish and Tackle Show. He paid $.10 per hook and $.12 per weight. He spent exactly $1. How many of each did he buy?

What is the question?

How many of each did he buy?

What are the facts?

Weights cost $.12 each, and hooks cost $.10 each. Harold spent exactly $1.

Make a plan.

Make some guesses and test each one. Keep a record of your guesses. Try to make each guess better than the one before.

Carry out the plan.

First Guess		Second Guess		Third Guess		Fourth Guess	
8 weights	$.96	7 weights	$.84	6 weights	$.72	5 weights	$.60
0 hooks	.00	1 hook	.10	2 hooks	.20	4 hooks	$.40
	$.96		$.94		$.92		$1.00
does not = $1		does not = $1		does not = $1		This is correct!	

Harold bought 5 weights and 4 hooks.

Check the answer. Does it make sense?

$5 \times \$.12 = \$.60$ $4 \times \$.10 = \$.40$ $\$.60 + \$.40 = \$1.00$ The answer is correct.

Use the guess and test method to solve.

2. Michelle bought fish line at the Fish and Tackle Show. She bought $\frac{1}{2}$ as much red line as white. She bought 27 yards of line altogether. How much of the line was red?

Question: How much of the line was red?

Facts: She bought 27 yards altogether. There was $\frac{1}{2}$ as much red line as white.

Use the guess and test method to solve each.

1. Bobbi and Mitch caught 18 fish from the pier. Bobbi caught $\frac{1}{2}$ as many fish as Mitch. How many did Mitch catch?

2. Roger was in a surf-casting contest. He cast his line 4 times at the tube targets shown. He scored a total of 52. What tubes did he hit?

3. Lucy sells painted conch shells. She sold 30 shells today. She sold 8 more blue shells than red shells. How many blue shells did she sell?

4. Luisa bought some supplies to refinish her boat. She selected 3 items from those shown. She spent exactly $21.95. What did she buy?

5. To make repairs on his boat, Gary spent $41.10 on some of the items shown. He bought 2 of 1 item and 1 each of 2 other items. What did he buy?

6. Mr. Raft collects antique ship propellers. Some have 2 blades, and some have 3 blades. He has 35 of these propellers. They have a total of 81 blades. How many of each type of propeller does Mr. Raft have?

7. Nancy went on a long ocean cruise. She sent out a total of 130 letters and postcards. At the time it cost 22¢ to mail a letter and 14¢ to mail a postcard. Nancy spent $26.20 on postage stamps. How many of each kind did she send?

There is a boardwalk game at a seashore resort. Contestants catch one toy fish from each of three buckets in this order: A, B, C. One way to win a prize is to catch fish marked with fractions in increasing value from bucket to bucket.

8. Nancy caught the fish marked with $\frac{1}{2}$ from bucket A. What fish should she try to catch from buckets B and C to win?

★9. Mitch caught the fish marked with $\frac{1}{2}$ from bucket C. Could he possibly be a winner?

CREATE YOUR OWN PROBLEM

Larry and Susan have 250 shells altogether. Write a problem for which the answer is "Larry has 100, and Susan has 150."

Adding and Subtracting Like Fractions

Sheila can draw air from either of her tanks. If one of her tanks has air for $\frac{1}{6}$ hour and the other for $\frac{4}{6}$ hour, how long can she dive?

$$\frac{1}{6} + \frac{4}{6} = n$$

▶ To add like fractions, add the numerators. Use the common denominator. Write the sum in lowest terms.

$$\frac{1}{6} + \frac{4}{6} = \frac{1+4}{6} = \frac{5}{6}$$
The GCF of 5 and 6 is 1. So $\frac{5}{6}$ is in lowest terms.

Sheila can dive for $\frac{5}{6}$ hour.

▶ To subtract like fractions, subtract the numerators. Use the common denominator. Write the difference in lowest terms.

$$\frac{7}{8} - \frac{3}{8} = \frac{7-3}{8} = \frac{4}{8} = \frac{1}{2}$$

More Examples

a.
$$\begin{array}{r} \frac{1}{4} \\ \frac{2}{4} \\ +\ \frac{3}{4} \\ \hline \frac{6}{4} = 1\frac{2}{4} = 1\frac{1}{2} \end{array}$$

b.
$$\begin{array}{r} \frac{15}{16} \\ -\ \frac{9}{16} \\ \hline \frac{6}{16} = \frac{3}{8} \end{array}$$

c.
$$\begin{array}{r} \frac{5}{8} \\ \frac{7}{8} \\ +\ \frac{4}{8} \\ \hline \frac{16}{8} = 2 \end{array}$$

CLASSWORK

Add or subtract. Write each answer in lowest terms.

1.
$$\begin{array}{r} \frac{7}{8} \\ -\ \frac{2}{8} \\ \hline \end{array}$$

2.
$$\begin{array}{r} \frac{5}{9} \\ +\ \frac{2}{9} \\ \hline \end{array}$$

3.
$$\begin{array}{r} \frac{2}{3} \\ +\ \frac{2}{3} \\ \hline \end{array}$$

4.
$$\begin{array}{r} \frac{3}{6} \\ +\ \frac{5}{6} \\ \hline \end{array}$$

5.
$$\begin{array}{r} \frac{11}{15} \\ -\ \frac{6}{15} \\ \hline \end{array}$$

6.
$$\begin{array}{r} \frac{4}{10} \\ +\ \frac{3}{10} \\ \hline \end{array}$$

7. $\frac{12}{10} - \frac{6}{10}$

8. $\frac{5}{6} - \frac{1}{6}$

9. $\frac{7}{12} + \frac{2}{12}$

10. $\frac{11}{16} + \frac{3}{16} + \frac{9}{16}$

PRACTICE

Add or subtract. Write each answer in lowest terms.

1. $\frac{3}{7}$
$+\frac{2}{7}$

2. $\frac{3}{5}$
$+\frac{1}{5}$

3. $\frac{7}{8}$
$-\frac{3}{8}$

4. $\frac{9}{7}$
$-\frac{5}{7}$

5. $\frac{7}{16}$
$-\frac{5}{16}$

6. $\frac{2}{11}$
$+\frac{7}{11}$

7. $\frac{3}{7}$
$+\frac{4}{7}$

8. $\frac{7}{15}$
$+\frac{11}{15}$

9. $\frac{7}{12}$
$-\frac{1}{12}$

10. $\frac{1}{10} + \frac{7}{10}$

11. $\frac{6}{8} - \frac{1}{8}$

12. $\frac{19}{20} - \frac{11}{20}$

13. $\frac{1}{16} + \frac{3}{16} + \frac{4}{16}$

14. $\frac{5}{6} + \frac{4}{6} + \frac{5}{6}$

15. $\frac{3}{4} + \frac{7}{4} + \frac{4}{4}$

16. $\frac{13}{50} + \frac{12}{50} + \frac{23}{50}$

17. $\frac{13}{15} + \frac{11}{15} + \frac{14}{15}$

18. $\frac{1}{8} + \frac{3}{8} + \frac{3}{8}$

19. $\frac{9}{15} + \frac{7}{15} + \frac{3}{15}$

20. $\frac{7}{6} + \frac{9}{6} + \frac{1}{6}$

21. $\frac{12}{8} - \frac{5}{8} - \frac{3}{8}$

Write the next 3 numbers in each sequence.

★ 22. $\frac{1}{8}, \frac{3}{8}, \frac{5}{8}, \square, \square, \square$

★ 23. $\frac{1}{10}, \frac{2}{5}, \frac{7}{10}, \square, \square, \square$

★ 24. $\frac{15}{16}, \frac{3}{4}, \frac{9}{16}, \square, \square, \square$

APPLICATION

25. A scuba diver exploring an old shipwreck brings back an ancient bottle weighing $\frac{3}{7}$ lb and 6 gold coins weighing a total of $\frac{2}{7}$ lb. What is the total weight of the objects brought to the surface by the diver?

26. To find a shipwreck, a diver was in the water $\frac{4}{5}$ h. If it took him $\frac{1}{5}$ h to find the shipwreck, how long did the diving and resurfacing take?

Mixed Practice

1. 52,863
9,521
+ 18,394

2. $673.29
− 198.57

3. 53,219
× 26

4. 52)408,410

5. 3.185 + 92.3

6. 18.45 − 9.063

7. 25 − 6.08

8. 4.3
× 18

9. 0.05 × 0.2

10. 5.2
×0.04

11. 0.2)15.67

12. 85)2.295

Is each number prime or composite?

13. 9

14. 21

15. 23

16. 18

17. 11

18. 19

191

In several seascapes, Roberta used $1\frac{1}{4}$ tubes of yellow paint, $2\frac{1}{4}$ tubes of white paint, and $1\frac{3}{4}$ tubes of blue paint. How many tubes of paint did she use in all?

$$1\frac{1}{4} + 2\frac{1}{4} + 1\frac{3}{4} = n$$

Step 1	**Step 2**	**Step 3**
Add the fractions.	Add the whole numbers.	Write the sum in lowest terms.

$$\begin{array}{r} 1\frac{1}{4} \\ 2\frac{1}{4} \\ + 1\frac{3}{4} \\ \hline \frac{5}{4} \end{array} \qquad \begin{array}{r} 1\frac{1}{4} \\ 2\frac{1}{4} \\ + 1\frac{3}{4} \\ \hline 4\frac{5}{4} \end{array} \qquad \begin{array}{r} 1\frac{1}{4} \\ 2\frac{1}{4} \\ + 1\frac{3}{4} \\ \hline 4\frac{5}{4} = 5\frac{1}{4} \end{array}$$

Roberta used $5\frac{1}{4}$ tubes of paint.

Find $8\frac{5}{9} - 3\frac{2}{9}$.

Step 1	**Step 2**	**Step 3**
Subtract the fractions.	Subtract the whole numbers.	Write the difference in lowest terms.

$$\begin{array}{r} 8\frac{5}{9} \\ - 3\frac{2}{9} \\ \hline \frac{3}{9} \end{array} \qquad \begin{array}{r} 8\frac{5}{9} \\ - 3\frac{2}{9} \\ \hline 5\frac{3}{9} \end{array} \qquad \begin{array}{r} 8\frac{5}{9} \\ - 3\frac{2}{9} \\ \hline 5\frac{3}{9} = 5\frac{1}{3} \end{array}$$

CLASSWORK

Add or subtract. Write each answer in lowest terms.

1. $\begin{array}{r} 6\frac{5}{8} \\ + 4\frac{1}{8} \\ \hline \end{array}$

2. $\begin{array}{r} 5\frac{3}{4} \\ - 3\frac{1}{4} \\ \hline \end{array}$

3. $\begin{array}{r} 8\frac{2}{3} \\ - 4\frac{2}{3} \\ \hline \end{array}$

4. $\begin{array}{r} 9\frac{4}{7} \\ + 5 \\ \hline \end{array}$

5. $\begin{array}{r} 13\frac{7}{12} \\ - 5 \\ \hline \end{array}$

6. $3\frac{11}{12} - 1\frac{7}{12}$

7. $10\frac{5}{7} - 8$

8. $12\frac{2}{3} - 3\frac{2}{3}$

9. $7\frac{2}{9} + 5\frac{6}{9} + 1\frac{4}{9}$

PRACTICE

Add or subtract. Write each answer in lowest terms.

1. $6\frac{1}{5}$
   $+ 2\frac{4}{5}$

2. $7\frac{1}{8}$
   $+ 9\frac{3}{8}$

3. $4\frac{5}{7}$
   $+ 1\frac{3}{7}$

4. $10\frac{5}{12}$
   $+ 4\frac{11}{12}$

5. $9\frac{5}{12}$
   $+ 4\frac{1}{12}$

6. $6\frac{5}{12}$
   $- 4\frac{5}{12}$

7. $18\frac{7}{10}$
   $- 4\frac{3}{10}$

8. $9\frac{7}{8}$
   $- 3\frac{6}{8}$

9. $15\frac{3}{4}$
   $- 9$

10. $15\frac{7}{8}$
    $- 10\frac{5}{8}$

11. $25\frac{17}{20}$
    $- 16\frac{9}{20}$

12. $13\frac{7}{8}$
    $- 6\frac{1}{8}$

13. $13\frac{7}{9}$
    $- 7\frac{3}{9}$

14. $17\frac{6}{7}$
    $- 9\frac{5}{7}$

15. $14\frac{1}{4}$
    $- 6$

16. $5\frac{3}{5}$
    $8\frac{3}{5}$
    $+ 2$

17. $13\frac{11}{15}$
    $6\frac{13}{15}$
    $+ 9\frac{14}{15}$

18. $17\frac{5}{8}$
    $14\frac{5}{8}$
    $+ 9\frac{7}{8}$

19. $15\frac{7}{9}$
    $8\frac{5}{9}$
    $+ 6\frac{7}{9}$

20. $11\frac{7}{9}$
    $4\frac{1}{9}$
    $+ 20\frac{4}{9}$

21. $14\frac{2}{3} - 6\frac{1}{3}$

22. $7\frac{2}{9} + 5\frac{8}{9}$

23. $16\frac{5}{8} - 12\frac{1}{8}$

24. $50\frac{3}{8} - 30\frac{3}{8}$

25. $12\frac{19}{24} - 6\frac{5}{24}$

26. $15 + 19\frac{1}{2}$

27. $3\frac{5}{9} - 1\frac{1}{9}$

28. $(3\frac{1}{2} - 2) + 4\frac{1}{2}$

Compare. Use >, <, or = for each ●.

★**29.** $18\frac{7}{8} - 12\frac{3}{8}$ ● $1\frac{7}{8} + 3\frac{6}{8}$

★**30.** $7\frac{9}{20} + 8\frac{19}{20}$ ● $24\frac{16}{20} - 8\frac{6}{20}$

★**31.** $4\frac{5}{8} - 2\frac{1}{8}$ ● $7\frac{5}{6} - 5\frac{2}{6}$

Follow the rule if given to complete.

Rule: Add $2\frac{3}{8}$ to
the input.

	Input	Output
	$1\frac{1}{8}$	$3\frac{1}{2}$
32.	$2\frac{3}{8}$	
33.	5	
34.	$3\frac{5}{8}$	

Rule: Subtract 6 from
the input.

	Input	Output
	$9\frac{2}{3}$	$3\frac{2}{3}$
35.	$6\frac{7}{8}$	
36.		$4\frac{1}{2}$
37.		$2\frac{3}{4}$

Find the rule.

★**38.**

Input	Output
$4\frac{3}{4}$	8
$2\frac{1}{4}$	$5\frac{1}{2}$
6	$9\frac{1}{4}$
$1\frac{2}{4}$	$4\frac{3}{4}$

APPLICATION

VISUAL THINKING

What fraction of each figure
is yellow; white; blue?

 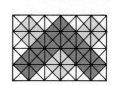 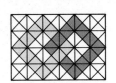

Adding and Subtracting Unlike Fractions

The pea crab is the smallest crab in the world. The measurements shown were recorded by a marine biologist. What is the total length of this pea crab?

Add $\frac{2}{5} + \frac{1}{4} + \frac{2}{5}$ to find the total length.

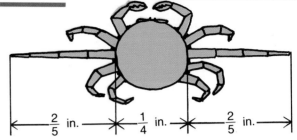

$\frac{2}{5}$ in. $\quad\frac{1}{4}$ in. $\quad\frac{2}{5}$ in.

Step 1

Find the least common denominator. Write the equivalent fractions.

$$\begin{array}{l} \frac{2}{5} = \frac{8}{20} \\ \frac{1}{4} = \frac{5}{20} \\ +\frac{2}{5} = \frac{8}{20} \end{array}$$

Think
The LCD is 20.

The pea crab is $1\frac{1}{20}$ in. long.

Find $\frac{5}{6} - \frac{1}{3}$.

Step 2

Add. Write the sum in lowest terms.

$$\begin{array}{l} \frac{2}{5} = \frac{8}{20} \\ \frac{1}{4} = \frac{5}{20} \\ +\frac{2}{5} = \frac{8}{20} \\ \hline \quad \frac{21}{20} = 1\frac{1}{20} \end{array}$$

Step 1

Find the least common denominator. Write the equivalent fractions.

$$\begin{array}{l} \frac{5}{6} = \frac{5}{6} \\ -\frac{1}{3} = \frac{2}{6} \end{array}$$

Think
The LCD is 6.

Step 2

Subtract. Write the difference in lowest terms.

$$\begin{array}{l} \frac{5}{6} = \frac{5}{6} \\ -\frac{1}{3} = \frac{2}{6} \\ \hline \quad \frac{3}{6} = \frac{1}{2} \end{array}$$

More Examples

a. $\frac{5}{6} + \frac{1}{4} + \frac{1}{2}$ **Think** The LCD is 12.

$$\frac{10}{12} + \frac{3}{12} + \frac{6}{12} = \frac{10 + 3 + 6}{12}$$
$$= \frac{19}{12} = 1\frac{7}{12}$$

b. $\frac{9}{10} - \frac{3}{4}$ **Think** The LCD is 20.

$$\frac{18}{20} - \frac{15}{20} = \frac{18 - 15}{20} = \frac{3}{20}$$

CLASSWORK

Add or subtract. Write each answer in lowest terms.

1. $\begin{array}{r} \frac{11}{16} \\ +\frac{7}{8} \end{array}$ **2.** $\begin{array}{r} \frac{3}{4} \\ -\frac{2}{3} \end{array}$ **3.** $\begin{array}{r} \frac{1}{2} \\ -\frac{1}{6} \end{array}$ **4.** $\begin{array}{r} \frac{3}{8} \\ +\frac{1}{4} \end{array}$ **5.** $\begin{array}{r} \frac{5}{6} \\ -\frac{3}{8} \end{array}$ **6.** $\begin{array}{r} \frac{2}{5} \\ +\frac{1}{10} \end{array}$

Add or subtract. Write each answer in lowest terms.

1. $\dfrac{3}{5}$
$-\dfrac{4}{10}$

2. $\dfrac{5}{9}$
$+\dfrac{1}{3}$

3. $\dfrac{3}{10}$
$-\dfrac{1}{5}$

4. $\dfrac{9}{20}$
$+\dfrac{9}{10}$

5. $\dfrac{7}{12}$
$+\dfrac{1}{4}$

6. $\dfrac{5}{6}$
$-\dfrac{1}{12}$

7. $\dfrac{1}{12}$
$+\dfrac{1}{8}$

8. $\dfrac{3}{4}$
$+\dfrac{1}{5}$

9. $\dfrac{4}{5}$
$-\dfrac{1}{3}$

10. $\dfrac{2}{9}$
$+\dfrac{1}{4}$

11. $\dfrac{3}{4}$
$-\dfrac{5}{12}$

12. $\dfrac{5}{6}$
$-\dfrac{3}{10}$

13. $\dfrac{1}{6}$
$+\dfrac{2}{9}$

14. $\dfrac{4}{5}$
$-\dfrac{1}{2}$

15. $\dfrac{4}{5}$
$-\dfrac{2}{3}$

16. $\dfrac{5}{6}$
$+\dfrac{3}{4}$

17. $\dfrac{9}{10}$
$-\dfrac{4}{15}$

18. $\dfrac{5}{12}$
$+\dfrac{5}{8}$

19. $\dfrac{1}{4}$
$+\dfrac{1}{3}$

20. $\dfrac{5}{6}$
$-\dfrac{3}{4}$

21. $\dfrac{5}{6}$
$-\dfrac{1}{2}$

22. $\dfrac{5}{8}$
$\dfrac{3}{4}$
$+\dfrac{8}{12}$

23. $\dfrac{13}{15}$
$\dfrac{7}{10}$
$+\dfrac{2}{5}$

24. $\dfrac{5}{8}$
$\dfrac{5}{12}$
$+\dfrac{5}{6}$

25. $\dfrac{3}{5} + \dfrac{4}{6} + \dfrac{1}{3}$

26. $\dfrac{4}{5} - \dfrac{1}{4}$

27. $\dfrac{3}{8} + \dfrac{2}{6}$

28. $\dfrac{7}{8} + \dfrac{5}{12} + \dfrac{1}{6}$

29. $\dfrac{17}{20} - \dfrac{3}{8}$

30. $\dfrac{5}{12} + \dfrac{3}{4} + \dfrac{7}{8}$

31. $\dfrac{2}{3} - \dfrac{1}{5}$

32. $\dfrac{17}{25} - \dfrac{3}{10}$

Evaluate each expression if $a = \dfrac{2}{3}$, $b = \dfrac{1}{5}$, $c = \dfrac{5}{6}$, and $d = \dfrac{1}{2}$.

★ 33. $a + c$

★ 34. $a - b$

★ 35. $a + b + d$

★ 36. $d - b$

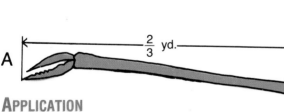

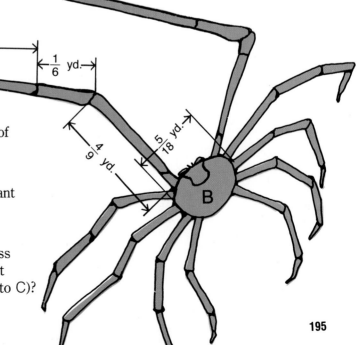

APPLICATION

The illustration shows the measurements of an average giant spider crab of Japan, the largest crab in the world.

37. How long is one claw of an average giant spider crab?

★ 38. One giant spider crab's claw span measured $12\dfrac{3}{4}$ ft. Was that more or less than the claw span of the average giant spider crab (the distance from A to B to C)?

Adding and Subtracting Unlike Mixed Numbers

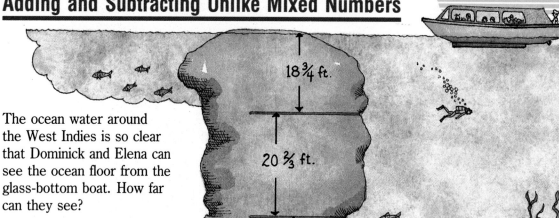

The ocean water around the West Indies is so clear that Dominick and Elena can see the ocean floor from the glass-bottom boat. How far can they see?

Add $18\frac{3}{4} + 20\frac{2}{3} + 7\frac{1}{2}$.

Step 1

Find the least common denominator. Write the equivalent fractions.

$$18\frac{3}{4} = 18\frac{9}{12}$$
$$20\frac{2}{3} = 20\frac{8}{12}$$
$$+\ \ 7\frac{1}{2} = \ \ 7\frac{6}{12}$$

Think
The LCD is 12.

Step 2

Add the fractions. Then add the whole numbers.

$$18\frac{3}{4} = 18\frac{9}{12}$$
$$20\frac{2}{3} = 20\frac{8}{12}$$
$$+\ \ 7\frac{1}{2} = \ \ 7\frac{6}{12}$$
$$\overline{\phantom{+\ \ 7\frac{1}{2} = }\ 45\frac{23}{12}}$$

Step 3

Write the sum in lowest terms.

$$18\frac{9}{12}$$
$$20\frac{8}{12}$$
$$+\ \ 7\frac{6}{12}$$
$$\overline{45\frac{23}{12} = 46\frac{11}{12}}$$

They can see $46\frac{11}{12}$ ft to the ocean floor.

How far must the diver swim to the ocean floor?

Find $46\frac{11}{12} - 18\frac{3}{4}$.

Step 1

Find the least common denominator. Write the equivalent fractions.

$$46\frac{11}{12} = 46\frac{11}{12}$$
$$-\ 18\frac{3}{4} = 18\frac{9}{12}$$

Think
The LCD is 12.

Step 2

Subtract the fractions. Then subtract the whole numbers.

$$46\frac{11}{12} = 46\frac{11}{12}$$
$$-\ 18\frac{3}{4} = 18\frac{9}{12}$$
$$\overline{\phantom{-\ 18\frac{3}{4} = }\ 28\frac{2}{12}}$$

Step 3

Write the difference in lowest terms.

$$46\frac{11}{12}$$
$$-\ 18\frac{9}{12}$$
$$\overline{28\frac{2}{12} = 28\frac{1}{6}}$$

The diver must swim $28\frac{1}{6}$ ft.

CLASSWORK

Add or subtract. Write each answer in lowest terms.

1. $11\frac{1}{6}$
   $+\ 5\frac{4}{9}$

2. $10\frac{9}{10}$
   $-\ 6\frac{2}{5}$

3. $18\frac{1}{3}$
   $+\ 2\frac{4}{5}$

4. $18\frac{5}{6}$
   $-\ 6\frac{1}{3}$

5. $14\frac{2}{5}$
   $2\frac{1}{4}$
   $+\ 3\frac{7}{10}$

PRACTICE

Add or subtract. Write each answer in lowest terms.

1. $2\frac{2}{3}$
    $+\ 4\frac{1}{6}$

2. $7\frac{7}{8}$
    $+\ 3\frac{3}{4}$

3. $4\frac{3}{14}$
    $+\ 10\frac{2}{7}$

4. $10\frac{9}{20}$
    $+\ 8\frac{3}{4}$

5. $5\frac{3}{4}$
    $-\ 2\frac{1}{2}$

6. $7\frac{11}{12}$
    $-\ 3$

7. $12\frac{2}{3}$
    $-\ 8\frac{2}{9}$

8. $7\frac{3}{8}$
    $-\ 2\frac{1}{4}$

9. $12\frac{3}{4}$
    $+\ 19\frac{5}{6}$

10. $7\frac{2}{3}$
    $-\ 3\frac{2}{5}$

11. $37\frac{5}{8}$
    $-\ 16\frac{1}{2}$

12. $35\frac{5}{12}$
    $+\ 16\frac{1}{8}$

13. $21\frac{7}{10}$
    $18\frac{4}{15}$
    $+\ 5\frac{2}{5}$

14. $15\frac{5}{6}$
    $13\frac{3}{8}$
    $+\ 5$

15. $16\frac{2}{3}$
    $5\frac{3}{4}$
    $+\ 10\frac{5}{6}$

16. $60\frac{3}{10} + 35\frac{8}{15}$

17. $25\frac{19}{30} - 9\frac{5}{12}$

18. $54\frac{7}{9} + 10\frac{5}{6}$

19. $12\frac{7}{10} - 7\frac{5}{12}$

20. $18\frac{5}{6} - 9\frac{7}{10}$

21. $17\frac{3}{4} + 11\frac{2}{3} + 8\frac{1}{2}$

22. $26\frac{1}{2} - 14\frac{4}{15}$

23. $15\frac{5}{6} + 12\frac{7}{9}$

Compare. Use >, <, or = for each .

★ 24. $5\frac{1}{2} + 7\frac{3}{4}$ ⬤ $18\frac{5}{8} - 5\frac{3}{24}$

★ 25. $14\frac{4}{5} - 7\frac{1}{3}$ ⬤ $4\frac{7}{10} + 2\frac{5}{6}$

★ 26. $6\frac{7}{8} + 9\frac{1}{2}$ ⬤ $20\frac{3}{4} - 4\frac{3}{16}$

★ 27. $14\frac{5}{6} - 11\frac{1}{3}$ ⬤ $9\frac{7}{8} - 6\frac{3}{8}$

APPLICATION

28. The fish in the diagram on page 196 is $7\frac{1}{2}$ ft from the ocean floor. How far below the surface of the water is the fish?

★ 29. Each year the Catalina Diving Camp has a breath-hold diving contest. Which diver achieved the better record for the final 3 dives of the contest? how much better?

Diver	Minutes
Alberto	$1\frac{1}{3}$, $\frac{1}{2}$, $1\frac{3}{10}$
Marta	$1\frac{3}{5}$, $1\frac{3}{4}$, $\frac{5}{6}$

LOGICAL THINKING

A wise man was asked to divide 17 dollars among 3 students so that J would receive $\frac{1}{2}$, M would receive $\frac{1}{3}$, and V would receive $\frac{1}{9}$. No one else had been able to do this. The wise man took one dollar of his own and added it to the $17, giving him $18. He gave J $9; M received $6; V was given $2. The wise man then took his own dollar back and all left very happy! Why did this work?

Renaming Before Subtracting

The *Mayflower II* is a replica of the original *Mayflower*. In 1957 it crossed the Atlantic Ocean in $7\frac{5}{7}$ weeks. It took the first *Mayflower* 9 weeks to cross in 1620. How much more time did the Pilgrims spend at sea?

$9 - 7\frac{5}{7} = n$

Step 1

Try to subtract.
Rename if you can't.

$$9 = 8\frac{7}{7}$$
$$- 7\frac{5}{7} = 7\frac{5}{7}$$

Think

$\frac{5}{7} > \frac{0}{7}$, so rename.

$9 = 8 + 1$

$= 8 + \frac{7}{7}$

Step 2

Subtract. Write the difference in lowest terms.

$$9 = 8\frac{7}{7}$$
$$- 7\frac{5}{7} = 7\frac{5}{7}$$
$$\overline{1\frac{2}{7}}$$

The Pilgrims spent $1\frac{2}{7}$ weeks longer at sea.

Find $10\frac{1}{4} - 1\frac{5}{12}$.

Step 1

Write the equivalent fractions.

$$10\frac{1}{4} = 10\frac{3}{12}$$
$$- 1\frac{5}{12} = 1\frac{5}{12}$$

Think

The LCD is 12.

Step 2

Rename if you can't subtract.

$$10\frac{3}{12} = 9\frac{15}{12}$$
$$- 1\frac{5}{12} = 1\frac{5}{12}$$

Think

$10\frac{3}{12} = 9 + 1\frac{3}{12}$

$= 9 + \frac{15}{12}$

Step 3

Subtract. Write the difference in lowest terms.

$$9\frac{15}{12}$$
$$- 1\frac{5}{12}$$
$$\overline{8\frac{10}{12}} = 8\frac{5}{6}$$

CLASSWORK

Subtract. Write each answer in lowest terms.

1. 18
   $-\ 7\frac{3}{8}$

2. 9
   $-\ 2\frac{5}{6}$

3. $6\frac{1}{3}$
   $-\ 4\frac{5}{9}$

4. $5\frac{1}{4}$
   $-\ 2\frac{3}{4}$

5. $14\frac{1}{2}$
   $-\ 6\frac{9}{10}$

PRACTICE

Subtract. Write each answer in lowest terms.

1. 13
   $-\ 7\frac{3}{8}$

2. $12\frac{1}{6}$
   $-\ 5\frac{5}{6}$

3. 7
   $-\ 3\frac{5}{8}$

4. $13\frac{2}{9}$
   $-\ 7\frac{8}{9}$

5. $15\frac{1}{12}$
   $-\ 9\frac{11}{12}$

6. 17
   $-\ 6\frac{5}{12}$

7. $14\frac{3}{16}$
   $-\ 9\frac{13}{16}$

8. 10
   $-\ 6\frac{17}{20}$

9. $9\frac{1}{3}$
   $-\ 1\frac{5}{6}$

10. $13\frac{1}{5}$
    $-\ 7\frac{14}{15}$

11. $15\frac{1}{3}$
    $-\ 12\frac{7}{8}$

12. $25\frac{3}{8}$
    $-\ 17\frac{1}{2}$

13. $16\frac{2}{5}$
    $-\ 13\frac{7}{8}$

14. $17\frac{1}{2}$
    $-\ 11\frac{8}{9}$

15. $21\frac{1}{5}$
    $-\ 15\frac{2}{3}$

16. $25\frac{1}{4} - 16\frac{3}{5}$

17. $13\frac{1}{4} - 6\frac{5}{6}$

18. $12\frac{1}{2} - 7\frac{11}{15}$

19. $14\frac{1}{5} - 10\frac{5}{8}$

20. $17\frac{4}{25} - 13\frac{7}{10}$

21. $13\frac{1}{6} - 9\frac{3}{4}$

Complete each chain.

★22. Start ⟶ End

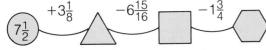

★23. Start ⟶ End

Follow the rule to find each missing number.

Rule: Subtract $5\frac{2}{3}$ from the input.

	Input	Output
	10	$4\frac{1}{3}$
24.	7	
25.	$6\frac{1}{3}$	
26.	$8\frac{1}{6}$	

Rule: Subtract $2\frac{1}{2}$ from the input.

	Input	Output
	9	$6\frac{1}{2}$
27.	5	
28.	$11\frac{2}{5}$	
29.	$7\frac{1}{8}$	

Rule: Subtract $3\frac{4}{5}$ from the input.

	Input	Output
★30.	7	
★31.		$5\frac{2}{3}$
★32.		$6\frac{3}{5}$
★33.		$8\frac{1}{5}$

APPLICATION

34. Vince sells ship models. One weekend he sold 15 models of the *Santa Maria*. He sold $\frac{1}{2}$ as many on Saturday as on Sunday. How many models did he sell on Sunday?

★35. A display shelf for a $6\frac{5}{8}$-inch-long model of the *Mayflower II* is to be cut from an oak board $17\frac{1}{8}$ in. long. If the shelf is to be 5 in. longer than the model, how much oak will be left over?

Estimating with Fractions

About how much deeper was the descent record of 1960 than the record set in 1972?

Estimate the difference between $6\frac{3}{4}$ and $3\frac{1}{8}$.

▶ To estimate with fractions, round each mixed number to the nearest whole number. If the fraction is $\frac{1}{2}$ or greater, round to the next whole number. If the fraction is less than $\frac{1}{2}$, do not change the whole number. Then add or subtract.

1960
The *Trieste* descends $6\frac{3}{4}$ miles —a record that still holds.

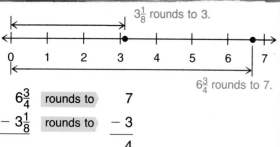

$3\frac{1}{8}$ rounds to 3.

$6\frac{3}{4}$ rounds to 7.

$$
\begin{array}{l}
6\frac{3}{4} \quad \text{rounds to} \quad 7 \\
-3\frac{1}{8} \quad \text{rounds to} \quad -3 \\
\hline
\phantom{-3\frac{1}{8} \quad \text{rounds to} \quad } 4
\end{array}
$$

The *Trieste* descended about 4 miles deeper in 1960 than the *Trieste II* in 1972.

More Examples

a. Estimate $9\frac{1}{5} + 5\frac{5}{8}$.

$$
\begin{array}{l}
9\frac{1}{5} \quad \text{rounds to} \quad 9 \\
+5\frac{5}{8} \quad \text{rounds to} \quad +6 \\
\hline
\phantom{+5\frac{5}{8}} \quad 15
\end{array}
$$

b. Estimate $4\frac{3}{8} - \frac{1}{5}$.

$$
\begin{array}{l}
4\frac{3}{8} \quad \text{rounds to} \quad 4 \\
-\frac{1}{5} \quad \text{rounds to} \quad -0 \\
\hline
\phantom{-\frac{1}{5}} \quad 4
\end{array}
$$

c. Estimate $8\frac{1}{5} + 3\frac{7}{8} + 6\frac{2}{3}$.

$$
\begin{array}{l}
8\frac{1}{5} \quad \text{rounds to} \quad 8 \\
3\frac{7}{8} \quad \text{rounds to} \quad 4 \\
+6\frac{2}{3} \quad \text{rounds to} \quad +7 \\
\hline
\phantom{+6\frac{2}{3}} \quad 19
\end{array}
$$

CLASSWORK

Estimate each sum or difference.

1. $\begin{array}{r} \frac{8}{9} \\ + \frac{2}{3} \\ \hline \end{array}$

2. $\begin{array}{r} 2\frac{1}{3} \\ + 1\frac{1}{2} \\ \hline \end{array}$

3. $\begin{array}{r} 7\frac{5}{8} \\ - 1\frac{1}{5} \\ \hline \end{array}$

4. $\begin{array}{r} 9\frac{11}{12} \\ - 2\frac{1}{2} \\ \hline \end{array}$

5. $\begin{array}{r} 1\frac{3}{8} \\ 2\frac{5}{8} \\ + 3\frac{9}{15} \\ \hline \end{array}$

6. $\frac{9}{15} + \frac{7}{8}$

7. $4\frac{2}{3} - \frac{5}{6}$

8. $14\frac{5}{9} - 5\frac{2}{5}$

9. $10\frac{15}{16} + 9\frac{2}{7}$

PRACTICE

Estimate each sum or difference.

1. $5\frac{3}{5}$
$+ 6\frac{2}{5}$

2. $7\frac{2}{3}$
$- 5\frac{1}{6}$

3. $6\frac{2}{3}$
$+ 4\frac{7}{12}$

4. $5\frac{4}{5}$
$+ 5\frac{1}{6}$

5. $9\frac{1}{4}$
$- 3\frac{1}{12}$

6. $13\frac{5}{6}$
$- 8\frac{1}{2}$

7. $7\frac{1}{12}$
$+ 13\frac{11}{12}$

8. $6\frac{5}{9}$
$+ 8$

9. $1\frac{2}{3}$
$+ \frac{1}{3}$

10. $8\frac{11}{12}$
$- 4\frac{1}{5}$

11. $\frac{4}{5} + \frac{1}{8}$

12. $\frac{2}{3} + \frac{9}{10}$

13. $\frac{7}{12} - \frac{1}{2}$

14. $\frac{4}{5} + \frac{1}{15}$

15. $9\frac{1}{6} - 5\frac{1}{3}$

16. $5\frac{2}{3} + 7\frac{2}{5} + 8\frac{1}{12}$

17. $\frac{7}{8} + 1\frac{6}{7} + 2\frac{2}{9}$

18. $9\frac{3}{7} + 8 + 4\frac{4}{7}$

★ 19. $(\frac{47}{60} - \frac{1}{28}) + (\frac{7}{8} - \frac{2}{19})$

★ 20. $\frac{11}{12} - (\frac{4}{5} + \frac{1}{15})$

Estimate to choose the answer.

★ 21. $5\frac{7}{9} + 7\frac{5}{12}$

  a. $12\frac{5}{36}$

  b. $12\frac{1}{12}$

  c. $13\frac{7}{36}$

★ 22. $27\frac{7}{16} - 14\frac{1}{3}$

  a. $12\frac{7}{48}$

  b. $13\frac{5}{48}$

  c. $14\frac{1}{16}$

★ 23. $\frac{3}{4} + \frac{1}{9} + \frac{1}{8}$

  a. $\frac{71}{72}$

  b. $1\frac{11}{12}$

  c. $3\frac{3}{8}$

★ 24. $5\frac{7}{8} - 1\frac{1}{6} + 3\frac{1}{5}$

  a. $8\frac{23}{24}$

  b. $8\frac{1}{24}$

  c. $9\frac{1}{12}$

APPLICATION

25. The *Trieste* took $4\frac{4}{5}$ hours to descend $6\frac{3}{4}$ miles. The ascent took $3\frac{1}{3}$ hours. About how long was the entire trip?

26. Naomi James of New Zealand holds the women's record for sailing solo across the Atlantic Ocean. In 1980 she made the trip in $25\frac{5}{6}$ days. In 1981 Annick and Martin of France set the 2-women-crew record when they crossed the Atlantic in $21\frac{3}{16}$ days. About how many days less than James did they sail?

MENTAL ARITHMETIC

Here is a quick way to tell if a fraction is greater than $\frac{1}{2}$.

Double the numerator. If the result is greater than the denominator, the fraction is greater than $\frac{1}{2}$.

  Example   Is $\frac{4}{7} > \frac{1}{2}$?   **Think**   Double the numerator is 8. $8 > 7$, so $\frac{4}{7} > \frac{1}{2}$.

Tell if each fraction is greater than $\frac{1}{2}$. Write *yes* or *no*.

1. $\frac{5}{9}$ 2. $\frac{3}{5}$ 3. $\frac{3}{10}$ 4. $\frac{6}{7}$ 5. $\frac{1}{3}$ 6. $\frac{11}{18}$ 7. $\frac{7}{15}$

Problem Solving

SKILLS AND STRATEGIES REVIEW Sea Fare

Solve. Tell if there is not enough information.

1. Mr. Cassidy owns oyster and clam beds that cover $\frac{3}{4}$ acre of bottomland. He uses $\frac{2}{3}$ of the beds for oysters and $\frac{1}{6}$ for clams. The rest is not being used at this time. What part of the acre is used for oysters?

2. Keith works 8 hours a day for Mr. Cassidy. Last Saturday he spent $4\frac{1}{2}$ hours digging oysters. He took 1 hour for lunch and spent $\frac{3}{4}$ hour in the hatchery. The rest of the time he dug for clams. How much time did he spend digging for clams?

3. Mr. Cassidy prepares an algae-control substance for his beds. He mixes chemicals with water according to the table shown at the right. How many cups of chemicals will he use with 10 gallons of water?

Cups of chemicals	$\frac{1}{3}$	$\frac{2}{3}$	1	$1\frac{1}{3}$	. . .
Gallons of water	1	2	3	4	. . .

4. Mr. Cassidy is bagging 50 pounds of oysters for shipping. He has 5-, 10-, and 15-pound bags to fill. How many different ways can he bag the oysters if he must fill at least one bag of each size?

5. Keith is mixing 480 pounds of food for the oyster beds. He blends 1 part calcium, 2 parts iron, and 3 parts charcoal. How many pounds of each item will he use?

Mrs. Locke is a caterer. She is preparing a dinner to be served promptly at 8:00 P.M. The main dish for the dinner is an oyster casserole, served with salad and baked potatoes. Her oyster recipe calls for 40 oysters and requires $1\frac{1}{2}$ hours of cooking time. The potatoes require 45 minutes of cooking time.

6. What time should she put the oyster dish in the oven?

7. How many potatoes should Mrs. Locke prepare?

8. What time should she put the potatoes in the oven?

9. If her dinner is delayed for 45 minutes, what time will it be served?

Mr. Cassidy is preparing an oyster bed in the shape shown. He begins by placing one stake in each corner. Then he places stakes so that there will be 5 stakes on each side.

★10. How many stakes will Mr. Cassidy use altogether?

★11. If the stakes are being placed 3 feet apart, how long will the oyster bed be?

Problem Solving

WHAT IF . . .?

The luxury liner *Princess Patti* is cruising to the Caribbean.
There are 850 passengers on board, including 175 children.
There is a crew of 200. The table shows the number of people
assigned to each of the dining rooms on board.

Dining Room	Adults	Children
A	315	70
B	210	65
C	150	40

1. How many more adults are assigned to Dining Room A
   than to Dining Room C?

2. How many fewer children than adults are assigned to
   Dining Room B?

3. How many people are assigned to Dining Room C?

What if Dining Room C is closed, and both the adults and the
children are divided equally between the other two dining
rooms?

4. How many adults are now in Dining Room A?

5. How many children are now in Dining Room B?

6. How many people are in Dining Room A?

The *Princess Patti* left Miami at 8:00 A.M. and was scheduled
to arrive in Santo Domingo at 6:30 P.M. the same day. The
ship was to stop in the Bahamas for 3 hours on the way.

7. How many hours was the scheduled trip from Miami to
   Santo Domingo?

8. How many hours of actual sailing were scheduled?

9. What time was the ship to arrive in the Bahamas?

What if the ship arrived in the Bahamas at 11:15 A.M.?

10. What time should it leave the Bahamas?

What if the *Princess Patti* is 1 hour and 15 minutes late?

11. When will it arrive in Santo Domingo?

What if the fare was $350 for each adult and $200 for each
child?

12. How much money was collected for fares on this cruise?

Write a fraction for each. pages 178–179

1. △ △ △
   △ △
   Shaded = ☐

2. $7 \div 11$

3. $\xleftarrow{}\underset{0}{|}\!-\!\!-\!\overset{A}{\bullet}\!-\!\overset{B}{\bullet}\!-\!\overset{C}{\bullet}\!-\!\underset{1}{|}\!\!\xrightarrow{}$

   A = ☐ B = ☐ C = ☐

4. denominator: 5
   numerator: 3

Write two equivalent fractions for each. pages 180–181

5. $\frac{4}{9}$

6. $\frac{5}{11}$

7. $\frac{36}{40}$

8. $\frac{85}{90}$

9. $\frac{250}{400}$

Write each fraction as a mixed number or a whole number.
Write each mixed or whole number as a fraction. pages 184–185

10. $\frac{32}{7}$

11. $\frac{14}{2}$

12. $4\frac{3}{8}$

13. $5\frac{5}{7}$

14. $\frac{55}{15}$

15. $10\frac{3}{16}$

16. $15 = \frac{n}{10}$

Compare. Use >, <, or = for each ⬤. pages 186–187

17. $\frac{3}{8}$ ⬤ $\frac{5}{6}$

18. $\frac{2}{3}$ ⬤ $\frac{5}{12}$

19. $2\frac{8}{9}$ ⬤ $2\frac{1}{6}$

20. $\frac{3}{25}$ ⬤ $\frac{6}{50}$

Add or subtract. Write each answer in lowest terms. pages 182–183, 190–197

21. $\frac{3}{5} + \frac{4}{5}$

22. $\frac{22}{16} - \frac{14}{16}$

23. $16\frac{3}{7} - 9\frac{2}{7}$

24. $11\frac{7}{9} + 4\frac{1}{9} + 20\frac{4}{9}$

25. $\frac{2}{9} + \frac{2}{3}$

26. $\frac{4}{5} - \frac{1}{2}$

27. $3\frac{4}{5} - 1\frac{3}{10}$

28. $1\frac{3}{4} + 3\frac{1}{3} + 2\frac{1}{6}$

Subtract. pages 198–199

29. $13\frac{2}{3} - 10\frac{8}{9}$

30. $10\frac{2}{15} - 6\frac{4}{5}$

31. $18\frac{5}{6} - 9\frac{9}{10}$

32. $11\frac{1}{4} - 6\frac{2}{3}$

Estimate each sum or difference. pages 200–201

33. $7\frac{1}{3} + 3\frac{1}{8}$

34. $10\frac{8}{9} - 9\frac{2}{3}$

35. $\frac{2}{3} + 1\frac{1}{4} + 3\frac{4}{5}$

36. $14\frac{7}{16} - 3\frac{3}{8}$

Solve. pages 188–189, 202–203

37. A storm interrupted a sailboat race among three friends. Maria had completed $\frac{7}{9}$ of the race, Joan had completed $\frac{13}{18}$ of the race, and Evan had completed $\frac{5}{6}$ of the race. Order their positions from first to last at the time of the interruption.

38. Mike works $12\frac{1}{2}$ hours at the marina on weekends. He works $2\frac{1}{2}$ more hours on Saturday than on Sunday. How many hours does he work on Saturday?

Write a fraction for the shaded part of each. Then write two equivalent fractions.

1.

2.

3.

Find each value of *n*.

4. $\frac{n}{48} = \frac{5}{12}$

5. $\frac{8}{11} = \frac{48}{n}$

Write each fraction as a whole number or a mixed number. Write each mixed number as a fraction.

6. $\frac{44}{7}$

7. $2\frac{4}{13}$

8. $\frac{122}{12}$

9. $13\frac{3}{4}$

10. $5\frac{5}{9}$

11. $\frac{93}{11}$

Compare. Use >, <, or = for each ⬤.

12. $\frac{4}{9}$ ⬤ $\frac{11}{18}$

13. $1\frac{7}{8}$ ⬤ $1\frac{21}{24}$

14. $4\frac{3}{10}$ ⬤ $4\frac{2}{7}$

Add or subtract. Write each answer in lowest terms.

15. $4\frac{1}{6} + 5\frac{3}{6}$

16. $\frac{14}{15} - \frac{8}{15}$

17. $\frac{7}{18} + \frac{5}{6}$

18. $\frac{3}{5} - \frac{1}{9}$

19. $5\frac{5}{8} + 3\frac{1}{6} + 2\frac{5}{12}$

20. $12\frac{1}{7} - 9\frac{3}{7}$

21. $10\frac{2}{5} - 3\frac{7}{10}$

Estimate each sum or difference.

22. $3\frac{2}{3} + 4\frac{1}{8} + 7\frac{5}{6}$

23. $18\frac{4}{9} - 13\frac{2}{7}$

Solve.

24. Lee and Walt together put in $15\frac{1}{2}$ hours of work a week at the tackle shop. Walt works $3\frac{1}{2}$ hours less than Lee. How many hours does Lee work?

25. It took Bill $8\frac{5}{6}$ hours to paint a side of his boat. Joanne took $5\frac{9}{10}$ hours to paint a side of her boat. How much longer did Bill work?

Brian has 5 gallons of paint for his boat. If he uses $1\frac{1}{4}$ gallons of red, $2\frac{5}{8}$ gallons of blue, and $\frac{5}{6}$ gallon of white, how much paint does he have left?

FRACTION MAZE

Go from START to FINISH using a path between numbers only once. You may go from one number to the next only

- by adding $\frac{3}{4}$ to the preceding number or
- by subtracting $\frac{1}{3}$ from the preceding number.

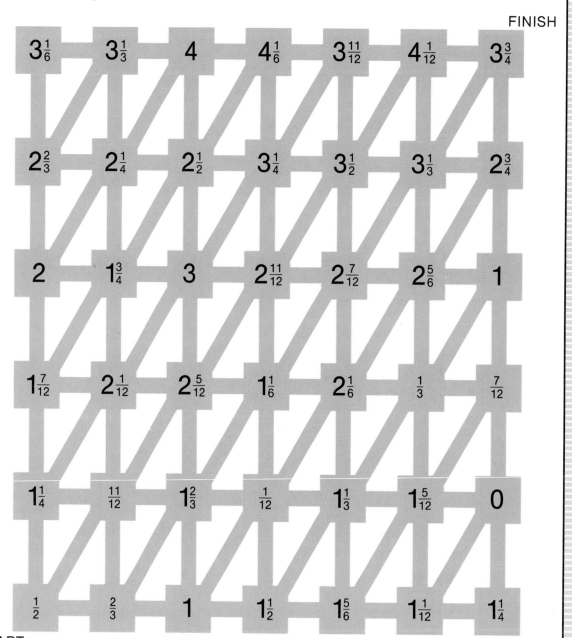

FINISH

START

FRACTION CHAIN

Admiral Cobb's gold chain has 24 links. He
will use the links to pay for his stay at a local
inn. Each link pays for one day. Is it possible
for Admiral Cobb to pay his bill daily without
cutting all 24 links?

Admiral Cobb's solution is started below.
Follow his reasoning for days 1–4.

Day 1 - Cut link 3. Remove the
       link and give it to the
       innkeeper. Keep links 1 and 2.

Day 2 - Give the innkeeper links
       1 and 2. Take back link 3.

Day 3 - Give the innkeeper link 3.

Day 4 - Cut link 7. Give the innkeeper
       links 4–7. Take back links 1
       and 2 and link 3.

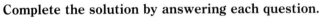

Complete the solution by answering each question.

1. Explain how Admiral Cobb will pay for days 5, 6, and 7.

2. On what day will the admiral make another cut in the chain?
Which link will he cut?

3. Explain how the admiral will pay for days 8–15.

4. What is the least number of cuts possible
to pay for a 24-day stay?

Answer each question. Each link represents $\frac{1}{24}$ of the chain.

5. On what day does Admiral Cobb pay with $\frac{1}{3}$ of the chain?

6. On what day will the innkeeper already have
$\frac{1}{6}$ of the chain and be given $\frac{1}{24}$ more?

7. On what days does the innkeeper give $\frac{1}{24}$ of the
chain in exchange for $\frac{1}{12}$ of the chain?

FACTORS

BASIC contains several useful functions.

The integer function, **INT(X),** gives the greatest whole number that is equal to or smaller than X.

Examples   INT(2.43) = 2   INT(7.98) = 7
                 INT(6/2) = 3   INT(9/2) = 4

INT(X) can be used to determine if a number is a whole number.

```
10 IF N = INT(N) THEN PRINT "WHOLE
   NUMBER"
```

If A/B = INT(*A/B*) then B divides A and B is a factor of A.

```
20 IF A/B = INT(A/B) THEN PRINT B;
   " IS A FACTOR OF ";A
```

This program uses the integer function to find all the factors of a number.

PROGRAM

```
10 REM FACTORS OF A NUMBER

20 PRINT "INPUT A NUMBER"

30 INPUT N

40 PRINT "THE FACTORS OF ";N;"
   ARE: "
```

1 is a factor of every number. ⟶

```
50 LET F = 1

60 PRINT F
```

Try the next number. ⟶

```
70 LET F = F + 1
```

The largest possible factor of N, other than N, is half of N. ⟶

```
80 IF F > N/2 THEN GOTO 110
```

If F divides N evenly, F is a factor. ⟶

```
90 IF N/F = INT(N/F) THEN PRINT F
```

Go back and try the next number. ⟶

```
100 GOTO 70
```

Each number is a factor of itself. ⟶

```
110 PRINT N

120 END
```

Write the output for each program.

1. ```
10 LET X = 6.42
20 PRINT INT(X)
30 END
```

2. ```
10 LET A = 9.99
20 PRINT INT(A)
30 END
```

3. ```
10 LET B = 5
20 PRINT INT(B/3)
30 END
```

4. ```
10 PRINT INT(17/5)
20 PRINT INT(27/3)
30 END
```

★5. ```
10 PRINT INT(7.4 + 2.6)
20 PRINT INT(7.4) + INT(2.6)
30 END
```

★6. ```
10 PRINT 6 * INT(3/2)
20 PRINT INT (6 * (3/2))
30 END
```

Use the program FACTORS OF A NUMBER to find the factors of each number.

7. 12   8. 24   9. 100   10. 37   11. 210

Use the program below to find the quotient and remainder when each number is divided by 7.

```
10 REM DIVIDE BY 7
20 PRINT "INPUT A NUMBER"
30 INPUT N
40 LET Q = INT(N/7)
50 LET R = N - Q * 7
60 PRINT N;"/7 = ";Q;" R";R
70 END
```

12. 824

13. 717

14. 123

15. 1,206

=== AT THE COMPUTER ===

Run the program FACTORS OF A NUMBER to find the factors of each number.

1. 30   2. 36   3. 29   4. 72   5. 1,000

Write a program for each. Then test each program by running it.

6. Count the number of factors for a given number. (Begin with C = 0. Add 1 to C each time a factor is printed. Print the value of C at the end.)

★7. A prime number has only two factors, 1 and the number itself. Determine whether a number is prime by counting its factors.

MAINTAINING SKILLS

Choose the correct answers. Write A, B, C, or D.

1. 50,903 − 6,542

  A 56,441   C 54,461

  B 44,361   D not given

2. What is the average of 15, 43, 27, and 19?

  A 26   C 28

  B 24   D not given

3. 1.83 + 0.051 + 6.64 + 0.39

  A 8.911   C 9.37

  B 8.711   D not given

4. 67.433 ÷ 10^3

  A 0.67433   C 0.067433

  B 67,433   D not given

5. 1.6$\overline{)3.5}$

  A 2.19   C 0.21864

  B 2.1875   D not given

6. Complete. _____ km = 7,451 m

  A 74.51   C 7.451

  B 0.07451   D not given

7. What time is 8 h 42 min after 8:30 A.M.?

  A 4:12 P.M.   C 4:48 P.M.

  B 5:12 P.M.   D not given

8. Which number is divisible by 2 and by 3?

  A 4,172   C 7,431

  B 4,572   D not given

9. Which is the prime factorization of 40?

  A $2^2 \times 5$ C $2^3 \times 5$

  B 2×5^3 D not given

10. What is $8\frac{5}{12}$ as an improper fraction?

  A $\frac{101}{12}$ C $\frac{96}{12}$

  B $\frac{91}{12}$ D not given

11. Compare. $2\frac{6}{16}$ ⬤ $2\frac{3}{8}$

  A >   C =

  B <   D not given

12. $\frac{7}{10} + \frac{1}{8} + \frac{4}{5}$

  A $1\frac{1}{10}$ C $1\frac{3}{5}$

  B $1\frac{3}{8}$ D not given

13. $8\frac{2}{5} - 3\frac{9}{10}$

  A $4\frac{7}{10}$ C $4\frac{1}{2}$

  B $5\frac{1}{2}$ D not given

Make a drawing to help solve 14 and 15.

Kim and Keri live on the same street. They plan to meet at a certain bench by walking toward each other from their houses. The distance between their homes is 27.3 m.

14. How far apart are they after Keri walks 7 m and Kim walks 6.2 m?

  A 14.1 m   C 27.3 m

  B 13.2 m   D not given

15. If each girl is now an equal distance from the bench, how far must each walk to it?

  A 13.25 m   C 7.05 m

  B 14.1 m   D not given

Theme: Museums

Multiplying Fractions

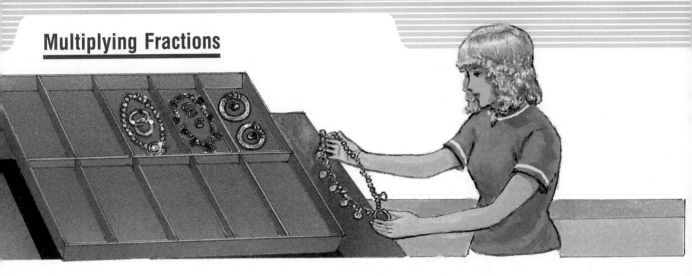

Jane has designed a case for displaying ancient jewelry in a museum. Museum workers are completing the top $\frac{1}{2}$ of the display. They have filled $\frac{3}{5}$ of the top row. What part of the entire case have they filled?

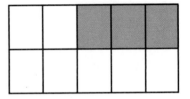

To find $\frac{3}{5}$ of $\frac{1}{2}$, multiply $\frac{3}{5} \times \frac{1}{2}$.

▶To multiply fractions, first multiply the numerators. Then multiply the denominators. Write the answer in lowest terms.

$$\frac{3}{5} \times \frac{1}{2} = \frac{3 \times 1}{5 \times 2} = \frac{3}{10}$$

Museum workers have filled $\frac{3}{10}$ of the entire case.

▶To find the product of a whole number and a fraction, first write the whole number as a fraction. Then multiply.

$$20 \times \frac{1}{4} = \frac{20}{1} \times \frac{1}{4}$$
$$= \frac{20}{4}$$
$$= \frac{5}{1} = 5 \quad \leftarrow \text{ Write the product in lowest terms.}$$

More Examples

a. $\frac{1}{3} \times \frac{3}{4} \times \frac{2}{8} = \frac{6}{96}$
$\phantom{\frac{1}{3} \times \frac{3}{4} \times \frac{2}{8}} = \frac{1}{16}$

b. $\frac{5}{6} \times 8 = \frac{5}{6} \times \frac{8}{1}$
$\phantom{\frac{5}{6} \times 8} = \frac{40}{6}$
$\phantom{\frac{5}{6} \times 8} = \frac{20}{3} = 6\frac{2}{3}$

CLASSWORK

Multiply. Write each answer in lowest terms.

1. $\frac{3}{10} \times \frac{1}{2}$ **2.** $\frac{1}{6} \times \frac{2}{5}$ **3.** $\frac{7}{16} \times 8$ **4.** $\frac{2}{3} \times \frac{4}{5}$ **5.** $\frac{2}{7} \times 21$

6. $\frac{1}{8} \times \frac{4}{5}$ **7.** $20 \times \frac{3}{4}$ **8.** $\frac{1}{6} \times 6$ **9.** $\frac{8}{9} \times \frac{7}{10}$ **10.** $\frac{1}{5} \times \frac{5}{26}$

PRACTICE

Multiply. Write each answer in lowest terms.

1. $\frac{1}{5} \times \frac{1}{2}$

2. $9 \times \frac{5}{8}$

3. $\frac{5}{7} \times 6$

4. $\frac{2}{3} \times \frac{1}{6}$

5. $3 \times \frac{4}{5}$

6. $\frac{5}{12} \times \frac{1}{3}$

7. $\frac{3}{10} \times 5$

8. $\frac{2}{5} \times \frac{5}{8}$

9. $16 \times \frac{3}{8}$

10. $\frac{15}{8} \times \frac{2}{3}$

11. $30 \times \frac{5}{6}$

12. $\frac{3}{4} \times 28$

13. $\frac{2}{25} \times \frac{3}{8}$

14. $\frac{6}{7} \times \frac{1}{4}$

15. $\frac{11}{16} \times \frac{4}{5}$

16. $\frac{7}{10} \times \frac{4}{9}$

17. $\frac{2}{3} \times \frac{7}{12}$

18. $\frac{1}{10} \times \frac{1}{10}$

19. $\frac{1}{4} \times 4$

20. $\frac{4}{7} \times 15$

21. $\frac{5}{6} \times \frac{3}{4}$

22. $\frac{1}{13} \times \frac{2}{3}$

23. $7 \times \frac{4}{5}$

24. $\frac{7}{8} \times 5$

25. $\frac{6}{7} \times \frac{5}{7}$

26. $\frac{3}{10} \times \frac{3}{5}$

27. $\frac{3}{20} \times 9$

28. $\frac{1}{5} \times \frac{7}{8}$

29. $\frac{2}{9} \times 14$

30. $\frac{9}{15} \times \frac{1}{5}$

31. $\frac{1}{2} \times \frac{3}{4} \times \frac{2}{3}$

32. $\frac{5}{8} \times 4 \times \frac{2}{5}$

33. $\frac{3}{10} \times \frac{1}{2} \times 5$

34. $\frac{1}{5} \times \frac{1}{6} \times \frac{1}{3}$

Follow the rule to find each missing number.

Rule: The output is $\frac{1}{4}$ of the input.

Input	Output
16	4
35. 36	
36. 100	
37. $\frac{1}{2}$	
38. 9	

Rule: The output is $\frac{5}{8}$ of the input.

Input	Output
16	10
39. 24	
40. 40	
41. 72	
42. $\frac{4}{5}$	

Rule: The output is $\frac{1}{2}$ more than $\frac{1}{3}$ of the input.

Input	Output
$\frac{1}{2}$	$\frac{2}{3}$
★43. $\frac{1}{3}$	
★44. $\frac{2}{5}$	
★45. $\frac{3}{8}$	
★46. $\frac{1}{10}$	

APPLICATION

47. In the past year, Jane has designed and completed 15 museum cases. Of these, $\frac{2}{5}$ were done for a local museum. How many cases did Jane complete for the local museum?

★48. Jane received $820 for one case. Her profit was $\frac{1}{4}$ of this amount. How much did it cost her to make the case?

=== LOGICAL THINKING ===

Write +, −, or × for each ⬤ to make the sentence true.

1. $\frac{1}{2}$ ⬤ $\frac{1}{2}$ ⬤ $\frac{1}{2}$ ⬤ $\frac{1}{2} = \frac{1}{2}$

2. $\frac{1}{2}$ ⬤ $\frac{1}{2}$ ⬤ $\frac{1}{2}$ ⬤ $\frac{1}{2} = 0$

3. $\frac{1}{2}$ ⬤ $\frac{1}{2}$ ⬤ $\frac{1}{2}$ ⬤ $\frac{1}{2} = 1$

4. $\frac{1}{2}$ ⬤ $\frac{1}{2}$ ⬤ $\frac{1}{2}$ ⬤ $\frac{1}{2} = 1\frac{1}{4}$

Common Factors

While translating this ancient picture writing for a museum, an archaeologist was able to complete $\frac{4}{5}$ of the left-hand column in one week. If each column contains $\frac{1}{2}$ of the writing, what part of the translation was completed at the end of one week?

Multiply $\frac{4}{5} \times \frac{1}{2}$.

Sometimes a shortcut can be used to make multiplication easier. To simplify factors before multiplying, divide a numerator and a denominator by a common factor.

Step 1	Step 2	Step 3
Find a common factor of any numerator and any denominator.	Divide the numerator and the denominator by the common factor.	Multiply the new numerators and denominators.

$\frac{4}{5} \times \frac{1}{2}$ 2 is the GCF of 2 and 4.

$\frac{\overset{2}{\cancel{4}}}{5} \times \frac{1}{\underset{1}{\cancel{2}}}$

$\frac{\overset{2}{\cancel{4}}}{5} \times \frac{1}{\underset{1}{\cancel{2}}} = \frac{2}{5}$

At the end of one week, $\frac{2}{5}$ of the translation was completed.

It is not necessary to divide by the GCF. You can divide by any common factor and continue to simplify factors.

$\frac{18}{19} \times \frac{1}{6}$

$\frac{\overset{9}{\cancel{18}}}{19} \times \frac{1}{\underset{3}{\cancel{6}}}$ Common factor of 6 and 18 is 2.

$\frac{\overset{3}{\cancel{\overset{9}{\cancel{18}}}}}{19} \times \frac{1}{\underset{1}{\cancel{\underset{3}{\cancel{6}}}}} = \frac{3}{19}$ Common factor of 9 and 3 is 3.

Another Example

$\frac{2}{9} \times 54 \times \frac{1}{6}$

$\frac{\underset{1}{\cancel{2}}}{9} \times \overset{6}{\cancel{54}} \times \frac{1}{\underset{3}{\cancel{6}}}$ Common factor of 9 and 54 is 9.   Common factor of 2 and 6 is 2.

$\frac{\underset{1}{\cancel{2}}}{9} \times \frac{\overset{2}{\cancel{\overset{6}{\cancel{54}}}}}{1} \times \frac{1}{\underset{1}{\cancel{\underset{3}{\cancel{6}}}}} = \frac{2}{1} = 2$ Common factor of 6 and 3 is 3.

Multiply. Write each answer in lowest terms.

1. $\frac{2}{3} \times \frac{7}{8}$

2. $\frac{6}{7} \times \frac{14}{15}$

3. $25 \times \frac{2}{5}$

4. $\frac{3}{10} \times 16$

5. $\frac{16}{15} \times \frac{1}{4}$

6. $\frac{3}{4} \times \frac{10}{9}$

7. $\frac{7}{3} \times \frac{9}{20}$

8. $\frac{2}{3} \times \frac{3}{2}$

9. $\frac{1}{10} \times \frac{15}{21}$

10. $\frac{6}{9} \times \frac{3}{4}$

214

PRACTICE

Multiply. Write each answer in lowest terms.

1. $\frac{2}{5} \times \frac{15}{22}$ **2.** $\frac{7}{9} \times \frac{8}{7}$ **3.** $10 \times \frac{7}{20}$

4. $\frac{4}{8} \times 20$ **5.** $\frac{5}{21} \times \frac{14}{25}$ **6.** $\frac{2}{9} \times \frac{21}{30}$

7. $\frac{24}{9} \times \frac{7}{12}$ **8.** $\frac{8}{20} \times \frac{5}{24}$ **9.** $\frac{8}{9} \times 81$

10. $36 \times \frac{5}{10}$ **11.** $\frac{15}{6} \times \frac{3}{20}$ **12.** $\frac{9}{16} \times \frac{8}{21}$

13. $\frac{7}{8} \times \frac{12}{21}$ **14.** $15 \times \frac{7}{12}$ **15.** $81 \times \frac{4}{9}$

16. $18 \times \frac{5}{8}$ **17.** $\frac{3}{10} \times \frac{5}{9}$ **18.** $\frac{5}{24} \times \frac{18}{35}$

19. $\frac{7}{8} \times \frac{5}{14} \times \frac{2}{3}$ **20.** $\frac{2}{12} \times \frac{5}{8} \times 4$ **21.** $\frac{12}{7} \times \frac{7}{10} \times \frac{5}{6}$

22. $\frac{2}{3} \times \frac{3}{5} \times \frac{1}{2}$ **23.** $\frac{8}{9} \times \frac{3}{16} \times 5$ **24.** $\frac{7}{10} \times \frac{25}{60} \times \frac{6}{35}$

Complete. Example: $\frac{1}{6}$ h = <u>10</u> min

        Think   1 h = 60 min $\frac{1}{6} \times 60 = 10$

25. $\frac{3}{10}$ h = __ min   **26.** $\frac{7}{12}$ d = __ h

27. $\frac{7}{6}$ yr = __ mo   **28.** $\frac{3}{5}$ yr = __ d

29. $\frac{1}{3}$ d = __ h   ★**30.** $\frac{1}{4}$ wk = __ h

Evaluate each expression. Let $a = \frac{1}{2}$, $b = \frac{2}{5}$, **and** $c = \frac{5}{8}$.

31. $a \times b \times c$ **32.** $a + b \times c$ ★**33.** $2a + 5b$

APPLICATION

34. An archaeologist has 12 ancient pictures to decode. He has completed $\frac{1}{4}$ of them. How many pictures has he decoded?

★**35.** Nine fifteenths of the archaeologist's pictures were about animals. Of these, $\frac{3}{5}$ were about deer. What part of the pictures were not about deer?

1. $301 + 20 + 5$

2. $500 - 399$

3. 15×631

4. $840 \div 3$

5. $9,500 \div 10$

6. $3.21 + 0.219$

7. $5.6 - 3.001$

8. 0.58×0.65

9. $0.840 \div 0.2$

10. $0.9500 \div 0.01$

11. $\frac{3}{5} + \frac{4}{5}$

12. $2\frac{1}{5} + 3\frac{1}{4}$

13. $\frac{5}{6} - \frac{1}{3}$

14. $9 - 7\frac{3}{8}$

15. $13\frac{2}{3} - 5$

Find the GCF.

16. 6, 8

17. 12, 20

18. 30, 48

19. 2, 15

20. 6, 15, 24

Multiplying Mixed Numbers

Suzanne is playing a math game on this machine at a technology museum. If it takes $2\frac{1}{2}$ minutes to play one game, how much time will 4 games take?

Multiply $4 \times 2\frac{1}{2}$.

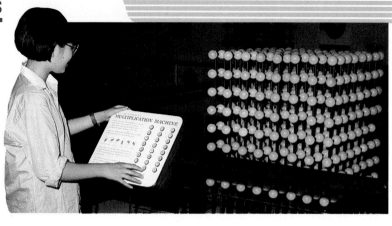

▶To multiply mixed numbers or whole numbers, first write them as improper fractions. Then multiply. Write the answer in lowest terms.

$$4 \times 2\frac{1}{2} = 4 \times \frac{5}{2}$$
$$= \frac{\overset{2}{\cancel{4}}}{1} \times \frac{5}{\underset{1}{\cancel{2}}} \longleftarrow \text{Simplify factors.}$$
$$= 10$$

It will take 10 minutes to play 4 games.

More Examples

a. $4\frac{2}{5} \times 1\frac{4}{11} = \frac{22}{5} \times \frac{15}{11}$

$$= \frac{\overset{2}{\cancel{22}}}{\underset{1}{\cancel{5}}} \times \frac{\overset{3}{\cancel{15}}}{\underset{1}{\cancel{11}}}$$

$$= 6$$

b. $2\frac{1}{4} \times \frac{7}{15} = \frac{9}{4} \times \frac{7}{15}$

$$= \frac{\overset{3}{\cancel{9}}}{4} \times \frac{7}{\underset{5}{\cancel{15}}}$$

$$= \frac{21}{20}, \text{ or } 1\frac{1}{20}$$

c. $2\frac{2}{3} \times 2\frac{7}{10} = \frac{8}{3} \times \frac{27}{10}$

$$= \frac{\overset{4}{\cancel{8}}}{\underset{1}{\cancel{3}}} \times \frac{\overset{9}{\cancel{27}}}{\underset{5}{\cancel{10}}}$$

$$= \frac{36}{5}, \text{ or } 7\frac{1}{5}$$

d. $3\frac{1}{2} \times 8 \times \frac{1}{2} = \frac{7}{2} \times \frac{8}{1} \times \frac{1}{2}$

$$= \frac{7}{\underset{1}{\cancel{2}}} \times \frac{\overset{2}{\cancel{8}}}{1} \times \frac{1}{\underset{1}{\cancel{2}}}$$

$$= 14$$

CLASSWORK

Multiply. Write each answer in lowest terms.

1. $1\frac{1}{9} \times \frac{3}{5}$

2. $6 \times 8\frac{2}{3}$

3. $4\frac{2}{7} \times 14$

4. $3\frac{2}{5} \times 3\frac{3}{4}$

5. $3\frac{1}{8} \times 3\frac{1}{5}$

6. $4\frac{1}{2} \times 2\frac{1}{3}$

7. $6 \times 8\frac{1}{2}$

8. $4\frac{1}{8} \times 1\frac{3}{11}$

9. $3\frac{1}{4} \times \frac{1}{3}$

10. $\frac{5}{6} \times 7\frac{1}{2}$

PRACTICE

Multiply. Write each answer in lowest terms.

1. $\frac{5}{12} \times 3\frac{1}{5}$

2. $\frac{4}{7} \times 10\frac{1}{2}$

3. $\frac{4}{5} \times 2\frac{1}{10}$

4. $\frac{1}{3} \times 2\frac{3}{8}$

5. $\frac{6}{7} \times 3\frac{8}{9}$

6. $2\frac{1}{4} \times \frac{4}{9}$

7. $4\frac{3}{8} \times \frac{8}{25}$

8. $2\frac{7}{10} \times \frac{2}{3}$

9. $5\frac{4}{9} \times \frac{9}{14}$

10. $1\frac{5}{6} \times 9$

11. $6 \times 4\frac{2}{3}$

12. $15 \times 5\frac{1}{3}$

13. $21 \times 6\frac{1}{7}$

14. $4\frac{1}{8} \times 10$

15. $8 \times 2\frac{5}{12}$

16. $4\frac{7}{12} \times 2\frac{2}{11}$

17. $4\frac{1}{8} \times 7\frac{1}{3}$

18. $2\frac{1}{7} \times 3\frac{1}{2}$

19. $3\frac{1}{8} \times 1\frac{1}{15}$

20. $3\frac{3}{4} \times 5\frac{1}{3}$

21. $3\frac{5}{8} \times 2\frac{2}{3}$

22. $7\frac{2}{4} \times 3\frac{2}{15}$

23. $8\frac{1}{3} \times 6\frac{1}{5}$

24. $6\frac{4}{9} \times 10\frac{1}{2}$

25. $4\frac{1}{6} \times 3\frac{1}{3}$

26. $2\frac{1}{4} \times 2\frac{5}{6} \times 4$

27. $1\frac{3}{4} \times \frac{2}{5} \times 1\frac{3}{14}$

28. $3\frac{1}{12} \times 2\frac{1}{2} \times 3\frac{3}{5}$

29. $7\frac{1}{2} \times \frac{4}{15} \times 1\frac{7}{12}$

A stereo record turns at $33\frac{1}{3}$ revolutions per minute (rpm). Find the number of revolutions the record makes during each song. (2:33 means 2 min 33 s, or $2\frac{33}{60}$ min.)

★**30.** "Wabash Cannonball" 2:33

★**31.** "Rock 'n' Roll Is Here to Stay" 2:00

★**32.** "Tomorrow" 2:20

★**33.** "I Want to Hold Your Hand" 2:24

APPLICATION

34. Suzanne and a friend took $3\frac{3}{4}$ min to play a game at the technology museum. How long would it take them to play the game 3 times?

★**35.** One game of Star Mission takes $2\frac{1}{2}$ min and one game of Space Darts takes $3\frac{1}{4}$ min. How long would it take to play both games twice?

═══ MENTAL ARITHMETIC ═══

You can quickly find certain products using the distributive property.

$3\frac{1}{8} \times 24 = (3 + \frac{1}{8}) \times 24 = (3 \times 24) + (\frac{1}{8} \times 24) = 72 + 3 = 75$

Multiply.

1. $2\frac{1}{4} \times 16$

2. $2\frac{1}{6} \times 42$

3. $8\frac{1}{10} \times 50$

4. $7\frac{1}{5} \times 10$

5. $3\frac{1}{4} \times 12$

6. $1\frac{1}{9} \times 63$

7. $5\frac{1}{4} \times 20$

8. $2\frac{1}{8} \times 16$

Dividing Fractions

Two fractions whose product is 1 are **reciprocals**.

$$\frac{2}{3} \times \frac{3}{2} = 1 \qquad 5 \times \frac{1}{5} = \frac{5}{1} \times \frac{1}{5} = 1$$

$\frac{2}{3}$ and $\frac{3}{2}$ are reciprocals. 5 and $\frac{1}{5}$ are reciprocals.

To find the reciprocal of $4\frac{1}{2}$, follow these steps.

- Write $4\frac{1}{2}$ as a fraction. $\quad 4\frac{1}{2} = \frac{9}{2}$
- Exchange the numerator and the denominator. $\quad \frac{9}{2} \diagdown \frac{2}{9}$
- Check by multiplying. $\quad 4\frac{1}{2} \times \frac{2}{9} = \frac{\overset{1}{\cancel{9}}}{\underset{1}{\cancel{2}}} \times \frac{\overset{1}{\cancel{2}}}{\underset{1}{\cancel{9}}} = 1$

Marissa wants to make a copy of this ancient gold necklace. If each link is $\frac{1}{2}$ inch long, how many links are needed for a 12-inch chain?

Find the number of $\frac{1}{2}$'s in 12, or $12 \div \frac{1}{2}$.

▶ To divide fractions, multiply by the reciprocal of the divisor.

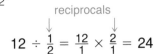

$$12 \div \frac{1}{2} = \frac{12}{1} \times \frac{2}{1} = 24$$

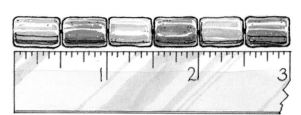

1 in. = 2 links

so 12 in. = 24 links

For a 12-inch chain, 24 links are needed.

More Examples

reciprocals

a. $\frac{9}{10} \div 3 = \frac{\overset{3}{\cancel{9}}}{10} \times \frac{1}{\underset{1}{\cancel{3}}} = \frac{3}{10}$

reciprocals

b. $\frac{3}{4} \div \frac{2}{5} = \frac{3}{4} \times \frac{5}{2} = \frac{15}{8} = 1\frac{7}{8}$

CLASSWORK

Write the reciprocal of each.

1. 3   2. $\frac{3}{4}$ 3. $\frac{10}{3}$ 4. $\frac{5}{6}$ 5. $\frac{1}{7}$ 6. 10

Divide. Write each answer in lowest terms.

7. $\frac{1}{3} \div \frac{4}{9}$ 8. $8 \div \frac{2}{3}$ 9. $\frac{2}{5} \div \frac{7}{10}$ 10. $\frac{3}{4} \div 12$ 11. $\frac{3}{8} \div \frac{1}{6}$

Write the reciprocal of each.

1. $\frac{5}{8}$ 2. 4 3. $\frac{9}{10}$ 4. $\frac{1}{5}$ 5. $\frac{7}{4}$ 6. $\frac{15}{6}$

Divide. Write each answer in lowest terms.

7. $\frac{3}{4} \div \frac{1}{2}$ 8. $\frac{1}{8} \div \frac{1}{4}$ 9. $\frac{9}{16} \div \frac{3}{4}$ 10. $\frac{7}{9} \div 2$ 11. $16 \div \frac{4}{15}$

12. $\frac{6}{7} \div \frac{5}{14}$ 13. $12 \div \frac{6}{25}$ 14. $\frac{7}{10} \div 14$ 15. $20 \div \frac{2}{5}$ 16. $\frac{1}{6} \div \frac{5}{6}$

17. $15 \div \frac{5}{6}$ 18. $\frac{9}{10} \div 2$ 19. $\frac{13}{14} \div \frac{1}{7}$ 20. $\frac{6}{7} \div \frac{3}{4}$ 21. $\frac{3}{8} \div \frac{1}{4}$

22. $\frac{11}{15} \div \frac{1}{3}$ 23. $\frac{2}{3} \div 6$ 24. $\frac{4}{9} \div \frac{4}{9}$ 25. $\frac{5}{8} \div \frac{5}{4}$ 26. $\frac{5}{12} \div \frac{5}{9}$

27. $80 \div \frac{4}{9}$ 28. $\frac{7}{8} \div \frac{9}{16}$ 29. $10 \div 25$ 30. $\frac{7}{15} \div 21$ 31. $\frac{3}{4} \div \frac{1}{12}$

32. $1 \div \frac{4}{5}$ 33. $8 \div 36$ 34. $\frac{7}{15} \div \frac{11}{30}$ 35. $\frac{1}{4} \div 4$ 36. $10 \div \frac{2}{5}$

Find the value of n in each.

37. $\frac{6}{7} \times n = 1$ 38. $n \times \frac{1}{2} = \frac{1}{2}$ 39. $\frac{1}{4} \times n = \frac{3}{8}$ 40. $n \times \frac{1}{9} = 9$

★41. $\frac{1}{6} \times n \times \frac{5}{6} = \frac{5}{12}$ ★42. $n \times \frac{4}{5} \times \frac{5}{12} = 1\frac{1}{3}$ ★43. $\frac{4}{9} \div \frac{4}{9} \times n = \frac{1}{4}$

Follow the rule, if given, to complete.

Rule: Divide the
input by $\frac{2}{3}$.

	Input	Output
44.	$\frac{1}{4}$	
45.	16	
46.	$\frac{5}{7}$	

Rule: Divide the
input by $\frac{3}{5}$.

	Input	Output
47.	$\frac{3}{10}$	
48.	$\frac{6}{5}$	
49.	$\frac{1}{6}$	

Find the rule.

★50.	Input	Output
	$\frac{3}{4}$	1
	$\frac{1}{2}$	$\frac{2}{3}$
	3	4

APPLICATION

51. Marissa is also making a copy of a 15-inch chain to sell in the gift shop. If each link is $\frac{3}{4}$ inch long, how many links must she use to make the chain?

52. If the cost of each link in the 15-inch chain is $8.90, how much will the chain cost? How much would a 21-inch chain of the same kind cost?

Dividing Mixed Numbers

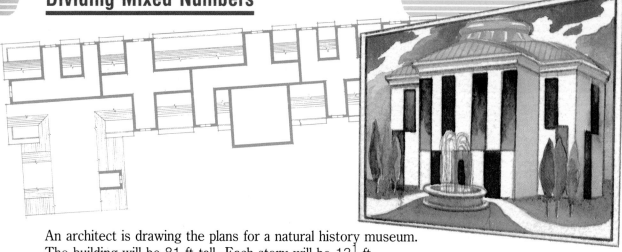

An architect is drawing the plans for a natural history museum. The building will be 81 ft tall. Each story will be $13\frac{1}{2}$ ft high. How many stories will the museum have?

Find $81 \div 13\frac{1}{2}$.

Step 1

Write the mixed number and the whole number as improper fractions.

$81 \div 13\frac{1}{2} = \frac{81}{1} \div \frac{27}{2}$

The building will have 6 stories.

Step 2

Change the divisor to its reciprocal.

$\frac{81}{1} \div \frac{27}{2} = \frac{81}{1} \times \frac{2}{27}$

Step 3

Multiply. Write the answer in lowest terms.

$\overset{3}{\underset{}{\cancel{81}}} \times \frac{2}{\underset{1}{\cancel{27}}} = \frac{6}{1} = 6$

More Examples

a. $24\frac{1}{2} \div 3\frac{1}{2}$

$= \frac{49}{2} \div \frac{7}{2}$

$= \frac{\overset{7}{\cancel{49}}}{\underset{1}{\cancel{2}}} \times \frac{\overset{1}{\cancel{2}}}{\underset{1}{\cancel{7}}}$

$= 7$

b. $7\frac{1}{2} \div 3$

$= \frac{15}{2} \div \frac{3}{1}$

$= \frac{\overset{5}{\cancel{15}}}{2} \times \frac{1}{\underset{1}{\cancel{3}}}$

$= \frac{5}{2} = 2\frac{1}{2}$

c. $\frac{1}{8} \div 1\frac{3}{4}$

$= \frac{1}{8} \div \frac{7}{4}$

$= \frac{1}{\underset{2}{\cancel{8}}} \times \frac{\overset{1}{\cancel{4}}}{7}$

$= \frac{1}{14}$

CLASSWORK

Write the reciprocal of each.

1. $2\frac{2}{3}$
2. $5\frac{3}{5}$
3. $6\frac{2}{3}$
4. $1\frac{2}{3}$
5. $6\frac{6}{7}$
6. $3\frac{3}{10}$

Divide. Write each answer in lowest terms.

7. $\frac{2}{5} \div 3\frac{3}{5}$
8. $3 \div 2\frac{1}{2}$
9. $5\frac{1}{2} \div 1\frac{1}{4}$
10. $8\frac{2}{3} \div 1\frac{2}{3}$
11. $4 \div 6\frac{2}{3}$

PRACTICE

Write the reciprocal of each.

1. $5\frac{1}{3}$
2. $7\frac{1}{2}$
3. $4\frac{3}{8}$
4. $8\frac{3}{11}$
5. $2\frac{2}{5}$
6. $1\frac{1}{7}$

Divide. Write each answer in lowest terms.

7. $\frac{5}{6} \div 2\frac{1}{2}$
8. $4\frac{2}{3} \div 8$
9. $32 \div 3\frac{1}{5}$
10. $\frac{15}{8} \div 2\frac{1}{2}$
11. $8\frac{1}{2} \div 2\frac{3}{4}$

12. $4 \div 3\frac{1}{2}$
13. $\frac{1}{3} \div 6\frac{1}{4}$
14. $2\frac{1}{8} \div 4\frac{1}{8}$
15. $\frac{11}{3} \div 22$
16. $1\frac{3}{10} \div \frac{1}{5}$

17. $3\frac{5}{9} \div \frac{4}{10}$
18. $8\frac{4}{9} \div 2\frac{1}{9}$
19. $11\frac{1}{4} \div 4\frac{1}{2}$
20. $7\frac{1}{3} \div 11$
21. $7\frac{5}{8} \div 7\frac{5}{8}$

22. $3\frac{3}{4} \div 15$
23. $4\frac{1}{3} \div 3\frac{1}{4}$
24. $1\frac{3}{5} \div 2\frac{2}{7}$
25. $2\frac{1}{10} \div \frac{1}{15}$
26. $\frac{12}{5} \div 4\frac{4}{5}$

Follow the order of operations to find the value of each expression.

★ **27.** $\frac{1}{2} + 1\frac{3}{4} \div \frac{5}{8}$
★ **28.** $\frac{5}{6} + \frac{2}{3} \times \frac{3}{4} - \frac{2}{3}$
★ **29.** $\frac{3}{4} \times 1\frac{1}{2} - \frac{1}{4}$

★ **30.** $2\frac{5}{6} \div 2\frac{5}{6} - \frac{3}{4} + \frac{7}{8}$
★ **31.** $2\frac{5}{8} + 3 - 1\frac{1}{2} \times 2\frac{2}{3}$
★ **32.** $12 - 2\frac{3}{4} \div \frac{1}{4} + \frac{5}{12}$

APPLICATION

33. To meet building codes, the architect reduced the height of the museum to 50 ft and the height of each story to $12\frac{1}{2}$ ft. How many stories will the museum have now?

★ **34.** If each story of the building will cost $3\frac{1}{2}$ times the architect's fee of $30,000.00, how much will each story cost?

═══ ESTIMATION ═══

You can estimate the value of expressions involving multiplication and division of mixed numbers.

Example $7\frac{3}{5} \times 8\frac{1}{4} \div 4\frac{1}{3}$ rounds to $8 \times 8 \div 4 = 16$.
The estimate is 16.

Estimate.

1. $3\frac{7}{8} \div 2\frac{1}{4} \times 9\frac{5}{9}$
2. $1\frac{2}{3} \times 1\frac{1}{3} \times 1\frac{1}{8}$
3. $9\frac{5}{8} \div 10\frac{1}{4} \times 4\frac{7}{8}$

4. $20\frac{1}{5} \div 5\frac{1}{3} \times 8\frac{2}{9} \div 15\frac{7}{8}$
5. $9\frac{1}{6} \div 2\frac{2}{3} \times 2\frac{2}{3} \times 11\frac{1}{4}$

Problem Solving

MAKING AND USING TABLES

Tables are useful for presenting and organizing data. Tables help you to examine important information. They can lead you to the solution of a problem.

1. From 1980 through 1986 the Sea Museum kept a record of the weights of their two dolphins—Flynn and Blue. In 1980 Blue weighed 100 kg and Flynn weighed 275 kg. Blue's yearly weight gain was 50 kg. Flynn's yearly weight gain was 75 kg. In what year did Blue weigh $\frac{1}{2}$ as much as Flynn?

Gather the facts that will help to find the year in which Blue weighed $\frac{1}{2}$ as much as Flynn.

In 1980 Blue weighed 100 kg and Flynn weighed 275 kg.

Blue's yearly weight gain = 50 kg

Flynn's yearly weight gain = 75 kg

Make a table showing the dolphins' weight gain through 1986.

DOLPHINS' WEIGHT GAIN (in kilograms)							
Year	1980	1981	1982	1983	1984	1985	1986
Blue	100	150	200	250	300	350	400
Flynn	275	350	425	500	575	650	725

Compare the weights of the two dolphins in each year.

In 1983, Blue weighed $\frac{1}{2}$ as much as Flynn.

Does your answer seem reasonable?

Yes. 250 is $\frac{1}{2}$ of 500.

2. There was a harbor porpoise named Mongo in an adjoining tank. The table below shows Mongo's weight from 1981 until 1986 when he was fully grown. In what year did Mongo reach $\frac{1}{2}$ of his adult weight?

Year	1981	1982	1983	1984	1985	1986
Weight (in kilograms) on January 1	17	35	51	68	90	102

Use the table. Locate Mongo's 1986 weight. Find $\frac{1}{2}$ of the 1986 weight and locate that weight in the table. Answer the question.

Use the table on page 222 to answer the following questions about Mongo.

1. In what year did Mongo weigh 68 kg?

2. What was Mongo's total weight gain between 1981 and 1986?

3. During what year did Mongo gain the most weight?

4. During what year did Mongo gain $\frac{1}{3}$ of his previous weight?

5. Mongo's final weight is how many times his 1981 weight?

★6. What fractional part of his final weight did he gain during 1981?

Solve. Use the table below to answer 7 and 8.

Food	Portion	Calories
Apple	1 medium	80
Fish meal	1 unit	240
Vegetables	4 units	184
Grain mix	1 unit	600
Shrimp meal	6 units	300
Cod-liver meal	2 units	57
Dried algae	1 unit	23

7. Workers at the museum feed Mongo a daily diet that consists of $2\frac{1}{2}$ units of fish meal, $2\frac{1}{4}$ units of grain mix, 6 units of cod-liver meal, and $1\frac{1}{2}$ units of dried algae. How many calories are there in Mongo's daily diet?

8. Mongo receives a special weekend meal. He eats 8 units of vegetables, $3\frac{1}{2}$ units of fish meal, 7 units of shrimp meal, $\frac{1}{2}$ unit of dried algae, and 3 apples. How many calories does he eat in a weekend meal?

9. The workers are emptying a 600-quart tank while they fill a 1,000-quart tank. They empty at the rate of 60 qt per minute and fill at the rate of 40 qt per minute. When will both tanks contain the same number of quarts?

★10. Two new aquariums are being set up. Each one starts with 100 qt of water. The first tank fills at the rate of 20 qt per minute. The second one fills at the rate of 30 qt per minute. When will the first tank contain $\frac{3}{4}$ as much as the second tank?

CREATE YOUR OWN PROBLEM

Write a problem about the Sea Museum. Use the data given in the table.

	DAILY ATTENDANCE						
	Mon.	Tues.	Wed.	Thurs.	Fri.	Sat.	Sun.
Adult	Closed	110	205	100	340	800	800
Child	Closed	85	160	200	210	425	800

Fractions and Decimals

The public library sponsored a special tour of the King Tut exhibit at the Metropolitan Museum of Art. During the first hour that the tickets were on sale, 90 out of the 100 tour tickets were sold.

What part of the tickets were sold during the first hour? Write the answer as a fraction and as a decimal.

$\frac{90}{100} = \frac{9}{10}$ So $\frac{9}{10}$ of the tickets were sold during the first hour.

▶To write a fraction as a decimal, divide the numerator by the denominator.

$\frac{9}{10} = 9 \div 10$
$$\begin{array}{r} 0.9 \\ 10\overline{)9.0} \\ \underline{9\ 0} \\ 0 \end{array}$$

0.9 is the decimal equivalent of $\frac{9}{10}$.

0.9 is a **terminating decimal.** When you divide, the remainder is zero.

Write $\frac{1}{6}$ as a decimal.

$$\begin{array}{r} 0.166\ldots \\ 6\overline{)1.000} \\ \underline{6} \\ 40 \\ \underline{36} \\ 40 \\ \underline{36} \\ 4 \end{array}$$

0.166. . . is a **repeating decimal.** In a repeating decimal, one digit or a group of digits repeats in a pattern.

$\frac{1}{6} = 0.166\ldots = 0.1\overline{6}$ ← The bar is used to show the digits that repeat.

▶To change a mixed number to a decimal, change the fraction part to a decimal. Then add the whole number.

$4\frac{1}{2} = \square$ $\frac{1}{2} \rightarrow \begin{array}{r} 0.5 \\ 2\overline{)1.0} \end{array}$ $4\frac{1}{2} = 4 + 0.5$
$= 4.5$

▶Use the place value of a decimal to write it as a fraction. Then write the fraction in lowest terms.

$0.55 = \frac{55}{100} = \frac{11}{20}$ $0.128 = \frac{128}{1,000} = \frac{16}{125}$

CLASSWORK

Write each fraction or mixed number as a decimal. Write each decimal as a fraction in lowest terms.

1. $\frac{1}{4}$ 2. 0.75   3. $\frac{1}{6}$ 4. 0.8   5. $3\frac{3}{8}$ 6. 0.012

Write each as a decimal. Use a bar for repeating decimals.

1. $\frac{3}{5}$
2. $\frac{1}{4}$
3. $\frac{3}{20}$
4. $\frac{1}{8}$
5. $\frac{5}{9}$
6. $\frac{4}{11}$

7. $\frac{5}{6}$
8. $2\frac{2}{5}$
9. $\frac{7}{25}$
10. $2\frac{2}{9}$
11. $\frac{2}{15}$
12. $\frac{4}{9}$

13. $5\frac{4}{5}$
14. $\frac{19}{25}$
15. $\frac{3}{50}$
16. $3\frac{3}{4}$
17. $5\frac{7}{30}$
★ 18. $4\frac{1}{16}$

Write each as a fraction or a mixed number in lowest terms.

19. 0.3
20. 0.14
21. 3.6
22. 0.45
23. 0.625
★ 24. 4.5625

Compare. Use >, <, or = for each ⬤.

25. $\frac{4}{5}$ ⬤ 0.82
26. $\frac{3}{8}$ ⬤ 0.38
27. $\frac{23}{50}$ ⬤ 0.46
28. $\frac{9}{500}$ ⬤ 0.02

29. $2\frac{4}{15}$ ⬤ 2.26
30. $3\frac{1}{9}$ ⬤ 3.2
★ 31. $\frac{5}{16}$ ⬤ $0.\overline{31}$
★ 32. $\frac{11}{12}$ ⬤ 0.915

List in order from least to greatest.

★ 33. $0.\overline{5}$, 0.5, $0.\overline{05}$
★ 34. 1.2, 1.12, $1.\overline{12}$
★ 35. 0.4343. . ., $0.\overline{4}$, 0.43

APPLICATION

36. The museum sold 0.85 of its available tickets on Saturday and $\frac{7}{8}$ of its tickets on Sunday. On which day were more tickets sold?

37. One hundred tickets were available at the museum. If 0.75 of the tickets sold for $5 each, how much money would the museum receive?

=== CALCULATOR ===

Here is how to use your calculator when working with fractions.

Find $20 \div \frac{1}{8}$ on your calculator.

Press $\boxed{1}$ $\boxed{\div}$ $\boxed{8}$ $\boxed{=}$ $\boxed{M^+}$ $\boxed{CE}$ Then press $\boxed{2}$ $\boxed{0}$ $\boxed{\div}$ $\boxed{RM}$ $\boxed{=}$ ⟶ $\boxed{160.M}$

Use a calculator to solve each.

1. $17 \div \frac{1}{2}$
2. $15 \div \frac{3}{8}$
3. $9 \div \frac{4}{5}$
4. $26 \times \frac{1}{4}$

5. $7 \div \frac{2}{5}$
6. $\frac{3}{4} \times 21$
7. $\frac{1}{2} \div 8$
8. $18 \div \frac{3}{4}$

Expressing Quotients

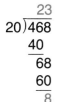

A nautical museum has acquired 468 old coins found in sunken pirate ships. The coins are to be exhibited in special display cases. Each case can hold up to 20 coins. How many cases will be needed to display all the coins?

```
      23
20)468
     40
     ‾‾
     68
     60
     ‾‾
      8
```

The completed division shows that 23 cases will be completely filled and that 8 coins will still remain. One more case will be needed to hold these 8 coins. To display all the coins, 24 cases will be needed. The quotient must be raised by 1.

Suppose the question were: How many cases will be completely filled? The answer would be 23 cases. The remainder is ignored.

▶To give a reasonable answer to a division problem, you may need to raise the quotient or ignore the remainder. In other division problems, you may need to express the remainder in one of three ways.

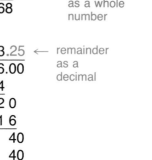

• How many coins are there in the 24th case?

8 coins are in the 24th case.

$$\begin{array}{r} 23 \text{ R8} \\ 20)\overline{468} \end{array}$$ ← remainder as a whole number

• If 8 coins together cost the museum $26, what is the average cost per coin?

The average cost per coin is $3.25.

```
    $ 3.25
8)$26.00
   24
   ‾‾
    2 0
    1 6
    ‾‾‾
      40
      40
      ‾‾
       0
```
← remainder as a decimal

• The museum is open 45 hours every 6-day week. What is the average number of hours the museum is open each day?

The museum is open an average of $7\frac{1}{2}$ h a day.

$$\begin{array}{r} 7\frac{3}{6} = 7\frac{1}{2} \text{ h} \\ 6)\overline{45} \\ 42 \\ \overline{3} \end{array}$$
← remainder as a fraction

CLASSWORK

Divide. Write each quotient in 3 ways.

1. $10 \div 4$

2. $5)\overline{71}$

3. $55 \div 44$

4. $15)\overline{364}$

5. $\frac{430}{11}$

PRACTICE

Divide. Write each quotient in three ways.

1. $2\overline{)75}$
2. $8\overline{)65}$
3. $4\overline{)73}$
4. $6\overline{)58}$
5. $5\overline{)57}$

6. $5\overline{)578}$
7. $4\overline{)199}$
8. $11\overline{)204}$
9. $10\overline{)112}$
10. $12\overline{)554}$

11. $89 \div 25$
12. $909 \div 90$
13. $2,145 \div 52$
14. $5,278 \div 112$
15. $\frac{86}{24}$

16. $\frac{16}{5}$
17. $\frac{25}{2}$
18. $\frac{50}{8}$
19. $\frac{25}{8}$
★ 20. $8,956 \div 360$

APPLICATION

Solve each problem. Use or write each remainder in the most reasonable way.

21. Souvenir coins cost $2.00 each in the museum store. How many coins can Joanna buy with $13.00?

22. Joanna has an album to display her coin collection. Each page holds 30 coins. How many pages will she use to hold 105 new coins?

23. Grades 7 and 8 at Lincoln School are planning a trip to Mystic Seaport Museum. A total of 184 parents, teachers, and students are going on the trip. Each bus holds 54 people. How many buses are needed?

24. It took 2 hours to travel the 125-kilometer distance from Lincoln School to Mystic Seaport. What was the average number of kilometers per hour that the bus traveled?

25. The total cost of the trip, including bus rental and admission to the museum, is $1,794. If the cost is to be shared equally among the 184 people, how much should each person pay?

26. During long voyages, sailors made small carvings in ivory or wood. These carvings are called scrimshaw. Carol has a 67-piece collection of scrimshaw in cases that hold 12 pieces each. How many cases has Carol completely filled so far?

Measuring Length

A science museum plans to exhibit the 150-inch high skeleton of a prehistoric sloth in a room that is 13 feet high. Will the sloth fit?

13 feet = __ inches

To convert units of length, use this table.

> 12 inches (in.) = 1 foot (ft)
> 3 feet (36 in.) = 1 yard (yd)
> 5,280 feet (1,760 yd) = 1 mile (mi)

▶To change to a smaller unit, multiply.

13 ft = __ in.   **Think** 1 ft = 12 in.

13 × 12 = 156

13 ft = 156 in.

Since the room is 156 in. high, the 150-inch skeleton will fit.

▶To change to a larger unit, divide.

80 in. = __ yd   **Think** 1 yd = 36 in.

$80 \div 36 = 2\frac{8}{36} = 2\frac{2}{9}$

80 in. = $2\frac{2}{9}$ yd

▶To add or subtract units of length, it may be necessary to regroup.

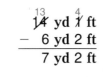

$$\begin{array}{r} 6 \text{ ft} \quad 2 \text{ in.} \\ + 3 \text{ ft } 11 \text{ in.} \\ \hline 9 \text{ ft } 13 \text{ in.} = 10 \text{ ft } 1 \text{ in.} \end{array}$$

Think   13 in. = 12 in. + 1 in.
      = 1 ft 1 in.

$$\begin{array}{r} \overset{13}{\cancel{14}} \text{ yd } \overset{4}{\cancel{1}} \text{ ft} \\ - \quad 6 \text{ yd } 2 \text{ ft} \\ \hline 7 \text{ yd } 2 \text{ ft} \end{array}$$

Think   14 yd = 13 yd 3 ft
      so 14 yd 1 ft = 13 yd 4 ft

CLASSWORK

Complete.

1. 18 in. = __ ft

2. 5 yd 1 ft = __ ft

3. $3\frac{3}{4}$ ft = __ in.

Add or subtract.

4. 3 ft 8 in.
     + 2 ft 7 in.

5. 5 yd
     − 2 yd 2 ft

6. 6 ft 9 in.
     − 5 ft 10 in.

7. 4 yd 17 in.
     + 7 yd 20 in.

Complete.

1. 24 in. = ___ ft
2. 12 ft = ___ yd
3. 180 in. = ___ yd

4. $\frac{1}{2}$ mi = ___ ft
5. 5 ft = ___ in.
6. 18 ft = ___ yd

7. 10 ft = ___ yd
8. 60 in. = ___ yd
9. $4\frac{1}{2}$ ft = ___ in.

10. 27 in. = ___ ft
11. 6 ft 7 in. = ___ in.
12. $2\frac{2}{3}$ yd = ___ ft

13. 7 yd 2 ft = ___ ft
14. $5\frac{5}{6}$ ft = ___ in.
15. $2\frac{1}{2}$ mi = ___ ft

16. 32 ft = ___ yd ___ ft
17. 28 in. = ___ ft
18. 46 in. = ___ ft

★19. 3 mi = ___ in.
★20. 440 yd = ___ mi
★21. $5\frac{1}{2}$ ft = ___ yd ___ in.

Add or subtract.

22.   4 yd 1 ft
    + 6 yd 1 ft

23.   18 ft 10 in.
    − 5 ft 6 in.

24.   7 ft 5 in.
    + 9 ft 10 in.

25.   3 ft 5 in.
    − 1 ft 7 in.

26.   10 yd 1 ft
    − 6 yd 2 ft

27.   9 ft 10 in.
    + 8 ft 9 in.

28.   2 mi 560 yd
    − 1 mi 700 yd

29.   15 ft 11 in.
    + 9 ft 9 in.

30.   7 yd 2 ft 8 in.
    + 5 yd 2 ft 7 in.

31.   8 yd 1 ft 6 in.
    − 5 yd 2 ft 7 in.

★32.   17 yd   3 in.
    − 6 yd 1 ft 5 in.

Compare. Use >, <, or = for each ⬤.

33. 1 ft 3 in. ⬤ 16 in.
34. $3\frac{1}{3}$ yd ⬤ 120 in.
35. $\frac{1}{2}$ mi ⬤ 850 yd

36. 5 ft 4 in. ⬤ 4 ft 16 in.
★37. 6,330 in. ⬤ $\frac{1}{10}$ mi
★38. 16 ft ⬤ 5 yd 10 in.

APPLICATION

39. The museum has just acquired a whale skeleton that is 6 yd long. Can it be carried in a trailer that is 16 ft long?

40. The cost of constructing a display stand for the whale is about $22 per foot. About how much will the museum spend on the stand?

Measuring Weight

The space museum is installing a model of the solar system in its new wing. The nine planets and their satellites will each hang from cords that can hold up to 260 ounces. The heaviest model planet weighs 15 pounds. Can the cord hold the model?

15 lb = ___ oz

To convert units of weight, use this table.

> 16 ounces (oz) = 1 pound (lb)
> 2,000 pounds = 1 ton (T)

▶To change to a smaller unit, multiply.

15 lb = ___ oz   **Think** 1 lb = 16 oz

15 × 16 = 240

15 lb = 240 oz

Since the cord can hold 260 oz, it can hold the 240-oz model.

▶To change to a larger unit, divide.

260 oz = ___ lb   **Think** 1 lb = 16 oz

$260 \div 16 = 16\frac{4}{16} = 16\frac{1}{4}$

260 oz = $16\frac{1}{4}$ lb

▶To add or subtract units of weight, it may be necessary to regroup.

$$\begin{array}{r} 4 \text{ lb } 12 \text{ oz} \\ + 5 \text{ lb } 5 \text{ oz} \\ \hline 9 \text{ lb } 17 \text{ oz} \end{array} = 10 \text{ lb } 1 \text{ oz}$$

Think 17 oz = 1 lb 1 oz

$$\begin{array}{r} \overset{24}{2\!\!\!\!/5} \text{ lb } \overset{17}{1\!\!\!/} \text{ oz} \\ - 8 \text{ lb } 4 \text{ oz} \\ \hline 16 \text{ lb } 13 \text{ oz} \end{array}$$

Think 25 lb = 24 lb 16 oz
so 25 lb 1 oz = 24 lb 17 oz

CLASSWORK

Complete.

1. $5\frac{1}{2}$ lb = ___ oz

2. 3 T = ___ lb

3. 6 oz = ___ lb

4. 20 oz = ___ lb

5. 4 lb 3 oz = ___ oz

6. 2,400 lb = ___ T

Add or subtract.

7. $\begin{array}{r} 5 \text{ lb } 14 \text{ oz} \\ + 6 \text{ lb } 7 \text{ oz} \\ \hline \end{array}$

8. $\begin{array}{r} 14 \text{ lb } 2 \text{ oz} \\ - 6 \text{ lb } 10 \text{ oz} \\ \hline \end{array}$

9. $\begin{array}{r} 7 \text{ T } 900 \text{ lb} \\ + 5 \text{ T } 1,100 \text{ lb} \\ \hline \end{array}$

10. $\begin{array}{r} 3 \text{ lb} \\ - 2 \text{ lb } 10 \text{ oz} \\ \hline \end{array}$

PRACTICE

Complete.

1. 32 oz = ___ lb

2. 4,000 lb = ___ T

3. 4 lb = ___ oz

4. $\frac{1}{2}$ lb = ___ oz

5. $\frac{3}{5}$ T = ___ lb

6. 52 oz = ___ lb ___ oz

7. 6 lb 7 oz = ___ oz

8. $2\frac{5}{8}$ lb = ___ oz

9. 3,500 lb = ___ T ___ lb

10. $10\frac{3}{4}$ lb = ___ oz

11. 40 oz = ___ lb

12. 4,200 lb = ___ T

13. 4 lb 6 oz = ___ oz

14. 36 oz = ___ lb

15. 69 oz = ___ lb

16. $\frac{5}{8}$ T = ___ lb

17. 4,500 lb = ___ T

★ 18. 18 oz = ___ lb

Add or subtract.

19.   5 lb 7 oz
     + 3 lb 5 oz

20.   19 lb 13 oz
     − 11 lb 7 oz

21.   3 lb 12 oz
     + 5 lb 10 oz

22.   8 lb 5 oz
     − 4 lb 12 oz

23.   4 T 1,500 lb
     + 3 T   800 lb

24.   7 T   800 lb
     − 3 T 1,200 lb

25.   15 lb
     − 6 lb 13 oz

26.   8 lb 11 oz
     + 9 lb 5 oz

27.   5 T   700 lb
     + 8 T 1,400 lb

28.   10 T 300 lb
     − 6 T 700 lb

★ 29.   15 lb 12 oz
     12 lb 13 oz
     + 7 lb 14 oz

★ 30.   1 T 1,800 lb
     7 T 1,500 lb
     + 9 T 1,400 lb

APPLICATION

31. A chain in the museum will hold a hanging object that weighs up to 5,000 lb. Will it hold an object weighing $2\frac{3}{4}$ T?

32. Ari is studying a large painting that has a series of vertical stripes. Each stripe is $\frac{3}{4}$ yd longer than the one to its left. If the shortest stripe is 1 yd long, how long is the sixth stripe?

VISUAL THINKING

Suppose one row is added to the bottom of each design. What will be the color pattern of each added row?

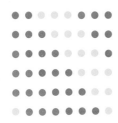

231

Measuring Capacity

Mary is fascinated by a display of early settlers' recipes in a colonial museum. She is copying this recipe for Indian pudding in the style of today's cookbooks. How many cups of milk should she write?

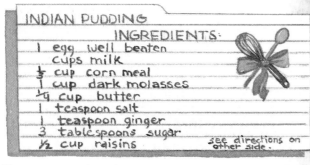

INDIAN PUDDING
INGREDIENTS:
1 egg well beaten
__ cups milk
⅓ cup corn meal
1 cup dark molasses
¼ cup butter
1 teaspoon salt
1 teaspoon ginger
3 tablespoons sugar
½ cup raisins

see directions on other side.

To convert units of capacity, use this chart.

8 fluid ounces (fl oz) = 1 cup (c)
2 cups = 1 pint (pt)
2 pints = 1 quart (qt)
4 quarts = 1 gallon (gal)

▶To change to a smaller unit, multiply.

2 pt = ___ c   **Think** 1 pt = 2 c

$2 \times 2 = 4$

2 pt = 4 c

▶To change to a larger unit, divide.

6 qt = ___ gal   **Think** 1 gal = 4 qt

$6 \div 4 = 1\frac{2}{4} = 1\frac{1}{2}$

6 qt = $1\frac{1}{2}$ gal

Mary should write 4 cups of milk in the recipe.

▶To add or subtract units of capacity, it may be necessary to regroup.

$$\begin{array}{r} 2 \text{ qt } 1 \text{ pt} \\ + 1 \text{ qt } 1 \text{ pt} \\ \hline 3 \text{ qt } 2 \text{ pt} = 4 \text{ qt} \end{array}$$ **Think** 2 pt = 1 qt

$$\begin{array}{r} \overset{2}{\cancel{3}} \text{ gal } \overset{5}{\cancel{1}} \text{ qt} \\ - 1 \text{ gal } 3 \text{ qt} \\ \hline 1 \text{ gal } 2 \text{ qt} \end{array}$$ **Think** 3 gal = 2 gal 4 qt so 3 gal 1 qt = 2 gal 5 qt

CLASSWORK

Complete.

1. 6 pt = ___ qt

2. 2 gal = ___ qt

3. $2\frac{1}{2}$ c = ___ fl oz

4. 5 gal = ___ pt

5. 15 c = ___ pt

6. 28 oz = ___ c

Add or subtract.

7. $\begin{array}{r} 5 \text{ gal } 3 \text{ qt} \\ + 7 \text{ gal } 2 \text{ qt} \end{array}$

8. $\begin{array}{r} 3 \text{ c } 2 \text{ fl oz} \\ - 2 \text{ c } 7 \text{ fl oz} \end{array}$

9. $\begin{array}{r} 2 \text{ c } 1 \text{ fl oz} \\ - 1 \text{ c } 6 \text{ fl oz} \end{array}$

PRACTICE

Complete.

1. 3 pt = ___ c

2. 12 qt = ___ gal

3. 10 pt = ___ qt

4. $3\frac{3}{4}$ gal = ___ qt

5. 35 pt = ___ gal

6. 35 c = ___ qt

7. $10\frac{1}{2}$ qt = ___ gal

8. 50 fl oz = ___ c

9. $12\frac{1}{2}$ c = ___ qt

10. $5\frac{1}{2}$ pt = ___ fl oz

11. 28 oz = ___ pt

12. $6\frac{1}{4}$ qt = ___ c

13. 7 qt = ___ pt

14. 18 c = ___ qt

15. 1 qt = ___ fl oz

16. $6\frac{1}{2}$ pt = ___ qt

★17. $4\frac{1}{2}$ gal = ___ fl oz

★18. $4\frac{3}{8}$ gal = ___ qt ___ pt

Add or subtract.

19.   1 c 2 fl oz
    + 2 c 5 fl oz

20.   4 qt 3 c
    − 2 qt 1 c

21.   1 gal 5 pt
    + 2 gal 4 pt

22.   5 gal 2 qt
    − 4 gal 3 qt

23.   5 c 6 fl oz
    + 9 c 7 fl oz

24.   4 qt 1 c
    − 2 qt 3 c

★25.   7 gal 4 pt 12 fl oz
     + 5 gal 3 pt 4 fl oz

★26.   5 qt
     − 4 qt 2 c 6 fl oz

APPLICATION

27. Mary tried a recipe that called for 2 c 3 fl oz of milk. How many ounces of milk did she need?

28. Using the list of ingredients at the right, how much flour and sugar would you need to make twice the recipe? 3 times the recipe? $\frac{1}{2}$ of the recipe? $\frac{1}{4}$ of the recipe?

CARROT MUFFINS
$2\frac{3}{4}$ c flour
1 c sugar
$\frac{1}{2}$ c grated carrots
2 eggs
1 tsp vanilla
1 tbsp baking powder

Mixed Practice

1.   6,248
    24.1
  + 31.4

2. 8 − 0.333

3. 4.6 × 3.22

4. 9.009 ÷ 0.9

5. 3,191 + 46

6. 3 − 0.001

7. 3,694 − 999

8. 36 × 342

9. 94,130 ÷ 10

10. 4.65 × 10^2

11. 0.793 ÷ 10^3

12. $n + 9 = 25$

13. $n - 25 = 62$

14. $9n = 72$

15. $n ÷ 12 = 12$

Write the prime factorization.

16. 12

17. 48

18. 88

19. 51

20. 108

Problem Solving

SKILLS AND STRATEGIES REVIEW Science Museum

Solve.

Mort and Dolores work as volunteers at the Jefferson Science Museum.

1. The instruments in the weather station at the museum showed that the temperature rose 2 degrees between 9:00 A.M. and 1:00 P.M. It rose 3 degrees between 1:00 P.M. and 3:00 P.M. If the temperature was 68°F at 1:00 P.M., what temperature did Dolores record at 9:00 A.M.?

The next day, Mort was asked to keep a record of the hourly temperatures from 8:00 A.M. to 4:00 P.M. At 8:00 A.M. the thermometer read 54°F. At 9:00 A.M. it read 58°F. It continued to climb 4 degrees per hour until 1:00 P.M. It then fell 3 degrees per hour until 4:00 P.M.

2. What was the highest temperature Mort recorded?

3. At what time was the highest temperature recorded?

4. What was the temperature at 4:00 P.M.?

5. Dolores was assigned to a special lunar exhibit. There were two scales in the room. When Dolores stood on the earth scale, she weighed 126 pounds. On the moon she would weigh $\frac{1}{6}$ of her earth weight. How many pounds did Dolores weigh on the lunar scale?

6. Dolores weighed the lunar rock collection on the earth scale. It showed $31\frac{1}{2}$ pounds. If lunar weight is $\frac{1}{6}$ of earth weight, what would be the weight of the rocks on the lunar scale?

7. At the exhibit on magnetism, Mort threw 3 discs at the magnetic board shown. All 3 discs landed on the board, and he scored 37. On what numbers might Mort's discs have landed?

★ 8. Dolores said, "I scored 38 with my three discs." How might she have done this?

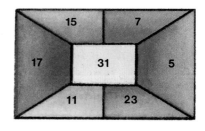

In the computer room there is a mechanical frog in a glass cage. The frog is placed 36 inches from the door of the cage. Each time a button is pressed, the frog jumps half the remaining distance to the door.

9. How far from the door is the frog after the first jump?

10. How far from the door is the frog after the third jump?

11. How far has the frog traveled after the fourth jump?

★ 12. After how many jumps does the frog reach the door?

Mort is making shelves for the museum supply room. He has a 9-foot board. Each shelf is to be $2\frac{1}{4}$ feet long.

13. How many shelves can he get from the board?

14. How many cuts must he make?

15. One wall of the supply room is lined with storage units. Three units cost a total of $460. Two of them cost the same amount. Each of these costs $\frac{1}{2}$ as much as the third unit. What is the cost of each unit?

★ 16. Each storage unit is 34 inches long. The wall is $9\frac{1}{2}$ feet long. The units are centered on the wall. If there are 2 inches of space between units, how many inches of space are at each end of the wall?

Mort and Dolores often work in the auditorium and the energy room.

17. There are 950 seats in the museum auditorium. On Saturday, 432 children attended a lecture. How many more adults than children were in the auditorium?

★ 18. There are 3 pendulums swinging in the energy room. The first pendulum swings back and forth every 5 seconds. The second pendulum swings back and forth every 3 seconds. The third pendulum swings back and forth every 2 seconds. If they are all started at the same time, how often will they have the same starting point?

CHAPTER REVIEW

Multiply. Write each answer in lowest terms. pages 212–217

1. $\frac{7}{12} \times \frac{3}{4}$　　2. $\frac{3}{8} \times \frac{16}{9}$　　3. $\frac{5}{8}$ of 6　　4. $6 \times \frac{1}{18}$　　5. $\frac{8}{9} \times 36$

6. $2\frac{1}{2} \times 3$　　7. $4 \times 1\frac{1}{2}$　　8. $3\frac{1}{2} \times \frac{4}{7}$　　9. $4\frac{1}{5} \times 1\frac{3}{5}$　　10. $2\frac{1}{2} \times 3\frac{1}{2}$

Write the reciprocal of each. pages 218–221

11. $\frac{3}{4}$　　12. $\frac{6}{5}$　　13. 3　　14. $5\frac{1}{2}$　　15. $9\frac{1}{8}$　　16. $10\frac{1}{3}$

Divide. Write each answer in lowest terms. pages 218–221

17. $\frac{3}{4} \div \frac{2}{5}$　　18. $2 \div 10$　　19. $5 \div \frac{1}{25}$　　20. $\frac{3}{6} \div \frac{1}{2}$　　21. $\frac{1}{2} \div \frac{8}{9}$

22. $\frac{49}{16} \div \frac{7}{8}$　　23. $\frac{9}{11} \div 3$　　24. $10 \div 2\frac{2}{5}$　　25. $2\frac{1}{2} \div \frac{1}{2}$　　26. $6\frac{1}{5} \div 3\frac{1}{3}$

Write each fraction or mixed number as a decimal.
Write each decimal as a fraction in lowest terms. pages 224–225

27. $\frac{3}{5}$　　28. $\frac{3}{4}$　　29. $\frac{4}{11}$　　30. $\frac{1}{6}$　　31. $2\frac{7}{8}$　　32. $3\frac{7}{9}$

33. 0.72　　34. 0.625　　35. 0.16　　36. 0.009　　37. 0.3125

Divide. Write each quotient in three ways. pages 226–227

38. $3\overline{)46}$　　39. $\frac{15}{8}$　　40. $75 \div 10$　　41. $\frac{128}{12}$　　42. $18\overline{)398}$

Complete. pages 228–233

43. 48 in. = ____ ft　　　　44. 72 in. = ____ yd　　　　45. 48 oz = ____ lb

46. 4 c = ____ pt　　　　47. 16 qt = ____ gal　　　　48. 5,000 lb = ____ T

Add or subtract. pages 228–233

49. $\begin{array}{r} 4 \text{ ft } 10 \text{ in.} \\ + 2 \text{ ft } 11 \text{ in.} \\ \hline \end{array}$　　50. $\begin{array}{r} 8 \text{ gal } 3 \text{ qt} \\ + 7 \text{ gal } 6 \text{ qt} \\ \hline \end{array}$　　51. $\begin{array}{r} 16 \text{ lb } 12 \text{ oz} \\ - 15 \text{ lb } 13 \text{ oz} \\ \hline \end{array}$　　52. $\begin{array}{r} 7 \text{ T} \\ - 3 \text{ T } 1{,}500 \text{ lb} \\ \hline \end{array}$

Solve. pages 222–223, 234–235

53. How many cartons are needed to hold 749 books if each carton can hold 25 books?

54. A painting is a series of squares inside one another. The largest square is 100 in. on a side. The side of each succeeding square is $\frac{1}{2}$ the length of the side of the preceding square. What is the length of the side of the fifth square? Make a table.

Find each product or quotient in lowest terms.

1. $\frac{3}{4} \times \frac{8}{9}$

2. $\frac{1}{5} \times 40$

3. $1\frac{1}{2} \times 2\frac{2}{3}$

4. $8\frac{1}{2} \times 10$

5. $3 \div 1\frac{1}{2}$

6. $4 \div \frac{1}{4}$

7. $1\frac{3}{5} \div 10\frac{1}{5}$

8. $1\frac{2}{3} \div \frac{3}{8}$

Write each decimal as a fraction in lowest terms.
Write each fraction as a decimal.

9. 0.125

10. $\frac{3}{16}$

11. 0.24

12. $\frac{5}{11}$

Divide. Write each quotient in three ways.

13. $147 \div 8$

14. $12\overline{)2,475}$

Complete.

15. 36 in. = ___ ft

16. 396 in. = ___ yd

17. 7,000 lb = ___ T

18. 24 pt = ___ gal

19. $5\frac{1}{2}$ lb = ___ oz

20. 83 oz = ___ lb ___ oz

Add or subtract.

21. $\begin{array}{r} 10 \text{ lb } 13 \text{ oz} \\ + \ 8 \text{ lb } \ 5 \text{ oz} \\ \hline \end{array}$

22. $\begin{array}{r} 5 \text{ pt } \ 8 \text{ c} \\ - \ 3 \text{ pt } 10 \text{ c} \\ \hline \end{array}$

23. $\begin{array}{r} 10 \text{ yd } 28 \text{ in.} \\ - \ 9 \text{ yd } 35 \text{ in.} \\ \hline \end{array}$

Solve.

24. Hannah wants to triple a colonial recipe for cheese sauce. The recipe calls for $\frac{3}{4}$ c grated cheese. How many cups of cheese does she need?

25. Stephen visited the museum one day each week for four weeks. Each week his visit lasted $1\frac{1}{2}$ times as long as his preceding visit. The first week Stephen spent 80 min at the museum. How long was his visit during the fourth week? Make a table.

Electric pole *A* is $5\frac{1}{3}$ yd high. Electric pole *B* is $\frac{3}{4}$ the height of electric pole *C*, which is $\frac{1}{4}$ higher than electric pole *A*. What is the height of electric pole *B*?

EXPLORE

GRAVITY ON OTHER PLANETS AND ON THE MOON

If you weigh . . .

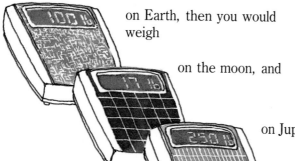

on Earth, then you would weigh

on the moon, and

on Jupiter.

Your **weight** depends on **gravity**.

Gravity is a force that causes bodies to fall back to earth.

Scientists use gravity on earth as a standard to measure gravitational force on other planets and on the moon.

GRAVITATIONAL FORCES					
Earth	**Moon**	**Venus**	**Mars**	**Jupiter**	**Saturn**
1	$\frac{1}{6}$	$\frac{9}{10}$	$\frac{2}{5}$	$2\frac{1}{2}$	$1\frac{1}{10}$

To find how much a 100-lb person would weigh on the moon, multiply his or her Earth weight by the moon's gravitational force.

$$100 \times \frac{1}{6} = \frac{100}{6} = 16\frac{2}{3}$$

$16\frac{2}{3}$ lb   rounds to   17 lb

Solve.

1. Tim weighs 110 lb. Make a table showing his weight on Earth and the amount he would weigh if he were on the moon or on the planets listed above.

2. Suppose you can throw a ball 30 yd. With less gravity you could throw the ball farther. About how far could you throw the ball on the moon? on Venus? on Jupiter? (Divide by the gravitational force.)

3. Use an almanac or an encyclopedia to complete the chart.

Event	Olympic Record	Year Established
High Jump: Men		
Women		
Long Jump: Men		
Women		
Pole Vault		

Imagine that the same events were run on Mars and on Jupiter. What would the records be there? Make a table to show your results. Round distances to the nearest foot to make computation easier.

238 CHAPTER RESOURCE

REPEATED IMAGES

The cover of *SEE* magazine has a picture of a girl holding an even smaller *SEE* magazine. If each repeated image is $\frac{1}{3}$ the size of the preceding one, how much smaller than the original magazine cover will the fifth repeated image be?

Use a table to help answer the question.

Original = 1

REPEATED IMAGES				
1st	2nd	3rd	4th	5th
$\frac{1}{3}$	$\frac{1}{9}$	$\frac{1}{27}$	$\frac{1}{81}$	$\frac{1}{243}$

Each image is $\frac{1}{3}$ the size of the preceding image.

The fifth image will be $\frac{1}{243}$ the size of the original.

Solve.

1. Suppose the smallest image the printing press can print clearly is $\frac{1}{16}$ in. If *SEE*'s cover is 9 in. by 12 in., how many repeated images should you see? What are the dimensions of the last readable image?

2. The letters in the word *SEE* are 3 in. high. If they are readable down to $\frac{1}{9}$ in., on how many repeated covers will the letters be readable?

3. On a poster advertising this issue of *SEE* magazine, the magazine is 36 in. by 48 in. What are the dimensions of the first repeated image? the second? the fifth?

4. On a poster twice the size of the original poster, in which repeated image would the magazine be $2\frac{2}{3}$ in. by $3\frac{5}{9}$ in.?

CUMULATIVE REVIEW

Choose the correct answers. Write A, B, C, or D.

1. Round 32,845 to the nearest thousand.

    A 30,000   **C** 33,000

    B 32,000   **D** not given

9. Compare. 13.198 ⬤ 13.5

    A >   **C** =

    B <   **D** not given

2. Complete. $(7 + \square) + 4 = 7 + (3 + 4)$

    A 3   **C** 10

    B 7   **D** not given

10. 0.08×0.165

    A 0.132   **C** 0.0132

    B 13.2   **D** not given

3. $40,926 - 23,934$

    A 16,992   **C** 17,092

    B 23,012   **D** not given

11. $74.038 \div 100$

    A 7,403.8   **C** 74,038

    B 7.4038   **D** not given

4. Estimate.   4,027
          $\times$ 885

    A 32,000   **C** 300,000

    B 4,000,000   **D** not given

12. What is 653 in scientific notation?

    A 6.53×10^2 **C** 6.53×10^3

    B 65.3×10^2 **D** not given

5. What is the value of 5^4?

    A 20   **C** 25

    B 1,024   **D** not given

13. About how tall is a desk?

    A 74.3 cm   **C** 0.06 km

    B 3.5 m   **D** not given

6. $26,503 \div 17$

    A 159   **C** 1,559

    B 1,627 R14   **D** not given

14. Complete. 60.5 cm = ___ m

    A 60.5   **C** 0.605

    B 0.0605   **D** not given

7. What is the value of 3 in 702.0351?

    A 3 tenths   **C** 3 hundredths

    B 3 tens   **D** not given

15.   3 d   5 h
     + 2 d 20 h

    A 6 d 1 h   **C** 6 h

    B 5 d 1 h   **D** not given

8. $13.05 + 5.6 + 0.008$

    A 18.658   **C** 18.73

    B 13.69   **D** not given

16. What time is it 7 h 12 min before 5:05 P.M.?

    A 9:53 A.M.   **C** 12:17 P.M.

    B 12:17 A.M.   **D** not given

CUMULATIVE REVIEW

Choose the correct answers. Write A, B, C, or D.

17. Complete. 146 kg = ___ g

    A 146,000   C 14.65

    B 1.465   D not given

18. $6 \div 2 \times 4 - 9 \div 3$

    A 1   C 9

    B 3   D not given

19. Solve. $\frac{b}{7} = 21$

    A $b = 3$ C $b = \frac{1}{3}$

    B $b = 147$ D not given

20. What is the GCF of 35 and 14?

    A 5   C 1

    B 7   D not given

21. What is the prime factorization of 2,700?

    A $2^2 \times 3^3 \times 5^2$ C $4 \times 3^2 \times 5^2$

    B $2^2 \times 3^2 \times 5 \times 7$ D not given

22. Give the value of n. $\frac{3}{8} = \frac{15}{n}$

    A 120   C 40

    B 24   D not given

23. What is $\frac{32}{72}$ in lowest terms?

    A $\frac{4}{9}$ C $\frac{8}{18}$

    B $\frac{1}{2}$ D not given

24. $15\frac{5}{6} + 3\frac{4}{6}$

    A $18\frac{1}{2}$ C $12\frac{1}{6}$

    B $19\frac{1}{2}$ D not given

25. $8\frac{3}{7} + 5\frac{2}{3}$

    A $14\frac{1}{21}$ C $3\frac{5}{21}$

    B $13\frac{2}{21}$ D not given

26. $29\frac{2}{5} - 24\frac{9}{10}$

    A $5\frac{1}{2}$ C $4\frac{3}{5}$

    B $4\frac{1}{2}$ D not given

27. $8\frac{1}{3} \times \frac{15}{25}$

    A 3   C $\frac{17}{25}$

    B 5   D not given

28. $\frac{9}{13} \div \frac{18}{26}$

    A $\frac{81}{169}$ C 1

    B $\frac{9}{13}$ D not given

29. What is the decimal for $\frac{3}{8}$?

    A 0.375   C 0.165

    B 0.25   D not given

30. Complete. 28 oz = ___ lb

    A $1\frac{1}{2}$ C $2\frac{3}{16}$

    B $1\frac{3}{4}$ D not given

CUMULATIVE REVIEW

Choose the correct answers. Write A, B, C, or D.

Use the information below to solve 31 and 32.

Patti delivers newspapers every day. She usually delivers 25 newspapers daily, Monday through Saturday. Last week she delivered a total of 178 newspapers. Four of her customers were away from Thursday through Saturday and didn't want newspapers on those days. This week, one customer who usually receives a paper every day will be away.

31. How many newspapers did Patti deliver on Sunday of last week?

    A 21   C 25

    B 40   D not given

32. How many papers will Patti deliver this week?

    A 168   C 183

    B 178   D not given

Solve.

33. On a 3-day field trip, the hiking club was able to travel a total of 24.6 km. If the club continued at the same rate for 5 more days, how far would they have traveled altogether?

    A 41 km   C 32.8 km

    B 65.6 km   D not given

34. If Lisa Maria joined the group at the beginning of the fifth day, how far would she have hiked by the end of the trip?

    A 41 km   C 32.8 km

    B 24.6 km   D not given

Make a drawing to help solve.

35. Two mail carriers left the post office at the same time and traveled in opposite directions. After 1 hour they were 3.5 km apart. If one walked 1.26 km, how far did the other walk?

    A 2.24 km   C 11.1 km

    B 4.76 km   D not given

36. During the second hour each walked 0.5 the distance that they walked the first hour. How far apart were they after 2 hours?

    A 1.75 km   C 5.25 km

    B 4.62 km   D not given

37. A mail carrier leaves the post office and travels along his route 7.2 km north, then 5.4 km east, 9.8 km south, and 5.4 km west, where he makes his last delivery. How many kilometers and in what direction will he go to return to the post office?

    A 2.6 km north   C 5.25 km north

    B 9.05 km west   D not given

Solve.

38. Bryan has 56 black, white, and yellow stones in his aquarium. There are twice as many black stones as white stones, and twice as many white stones as yellow stones. How many yellow stones are there?

    A 32   C 8

    B 16   D not given

39. Bryan removes 2 stones at a time. Each is a different color. What is the greatest number of times he can do this?

    A 24   C 12

    B 22   D not given

Geometric Ideas

This design was made on a microcomputer, using the Logo language. The design suggests points, segments, and angles.

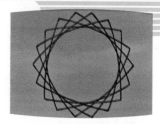

A **point** may be described as an exact location in space.

- write   P
- read   point P

A **line** may be described as a collection of points along a straight path. It has no endpoints.

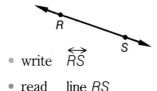

- write $\overleftrightarrow{RS}$
- read   line RS

A **ray** is part of a line. It has one endpoint. It extends endlessly in one direction.

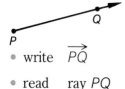

- write $\overrightarrow{PQ}$
- read   ray PQ

A **line segment** is part of a line. A segment has two endpoints.

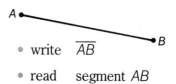

- write $\overline{AB}$
- read   segment AB

An **angle** is formed by two rays that have a common endpoint. The endpoint is called the **vertex** of the angle.

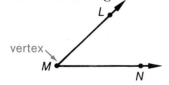

- write   ∠LMN or ∠NML
- read   angle LMN or angle NML

A **plane** may be described as a flat surface that extends endlessly in all directions.

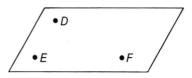

- write   plane DEF
- read   plane DEF

CLASSWORK

Use the figure on the right to complete 1–3.

1. Copy and complete the chart.

Points	
Lines	
Segments	
Angles	

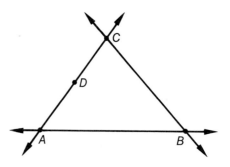

2. Name two rays that have D as an endpoint.

3. Are there any lines in the Logo design above? Why?

244

PRACTICE

Copy and complete the chart for the figure on the right.

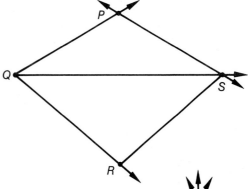

1.	Points	
2.	Lines	
3.	Segments	
4.	Rays	
5.	Angles	

Use the figure on the right to answer 6–17.

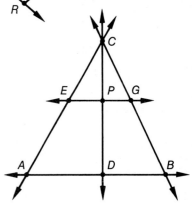

6. Name all the points.

7. Name the rays that have P as an endpoint.

8. Name the ray that has B as an endpoint and passes through D.

9. Name all the segments on $\overleftrightarrow{DC}$.

10. Name the segments that have E as an endpoint.

11. Name three angles that have a vertex at C.

Name each segment.

12. $\overline{AD} + \overline{DB} = $ ___

13. $\overline{CE} + \overline{EA} = $ ___

Answer *yes* or *no* for each and explain.

★ 14. Are $\overline{AB}$ and $\overleftrightarrow{AB}$ the same?

★ 15. Are $\overleftrightarrow{EP}$ and $\overleftrightarrow{PG}$ the same line?

★ 16. Are $\overrightarrow{DP}$ and $\overrightarrow{DC}$ the same ray?

★ 17. Are $\overrightarrow{GE}$ and $\overrightarrow{EG}$ the same ray?

APPLICATION

18. Draw a line. Mark 5 points on it: A, B, C, D, E. How many segments on $\overleftrightarrow{AE}$ can you name? List them.

19. Name the points, line segments, and angles in the Logo drawing at the right.

★ 20. On a sheet of paper, draw a design using segments, angles, and points. Create questions about the design for your classmates to answer.

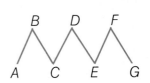

245

Angles

Some art students learn to draw the human figure by studying the angles formed by a wooden model.

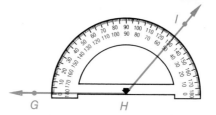

►Angles are measured in **degrees**. Use a **protractor** to find the measure of an angle.

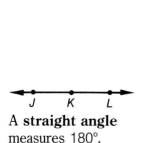

The measure of ∠RST is 45 degrees.
- write m∠RST = 45°

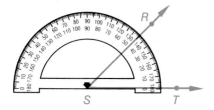

The measure of ∠GHI is 130 degrees.
- write m∠GHI = 130°

Angles are classified according to their measures.

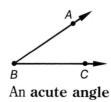

D
symbol for right angle

A **straight angle** measures 180°.

A **right angle** measures 90°.

An **acute angle** measures less than 90°.

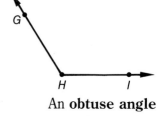

An **obtuse angle** measures greater than 90° and less than 180°.

Use a protractor to draw an angle. Follow the steps to draw ∠ABC with m∠ABC = 50°.

- Draw $\overrightarrow{BC}$.

- Place the arrow of the protractor on B and line up a zero mark with $\overrightarrow{BC}$.

- Mark point A at the 50° mark.

- Draw $\overrightarrow{BA}$.

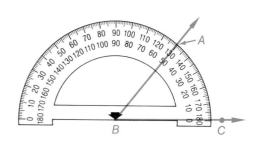

CLASSWORK

Measure each angle. Then classify each as right, acute, obtuse, or straight.

1.

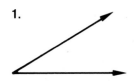

2.

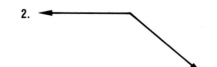

3.

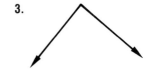

246

Measure each angle. Then classify each as right, acute, obtuse, or straight.

1. ∠EAF   **2.** ∠DAF
3. ∠DAE   **4.** ∠CAE
5. ∠BAE   **6.** ∠CAD
7. ∠BAD   **8.** ∠BAF

Use a protractor to draw each angle.

9. ∠ABC 40°   **10.** ∠GHI 160°   **11.** ∠DEF 25°   **12.** ∠QRS 115°

Classify the angle formed by the hands of a clock at each time.

13. 2:00   **14.** 3:00   **15.** 5:00   **16.** 5:15   **17.** 9:10

★**18.** Through how many degrees does the hour hand move in one hour?

★**19.** Through how many degrees does the hour hand move as the time changes from 12:00 to 1:30?

APPLICATION

20. What types of angles are marked on the wooden model on page 246?

21. Draw a sketch in which the arms of a model form a straight angle; a right angle.

COMPLEMENTARY AND SUPPLEMENTARY ANGLES

If the sum of the measures of two angles is 90°, the angles are **complementary angles.**

If the sum of the measures of two angles is 180°, the angles are **supplementary angles.**

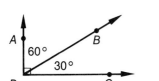

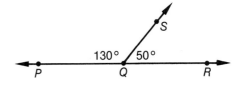

60° + 30° = 90°

130° + 50° = 180°

∠ADB is the **complement** of ∠BDC.

∠PQS is the **supplement** of ∠SQR.

Find the complement of each angle.

1. 50°   **2.** 45°   **3.** 20°   **4.** 62°   **5.** 70°

Find the supplement of each angle.

6. 50°   **7.** 45°   **8.** 100°   **9.** 65°   **10.** 120°

Lines

This modern painting by Kenneth Noland has many parallel lines but no intersecting lines.

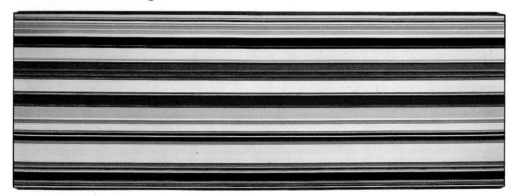

▶ Two lines that meet at a point are called **intersecting lines.**

$\overleftrightarrow{LM}$ intersects $\overleftrightarrow{AB}$ at C.

▶ Two lines in the same plane that do not intersect are called **parallel lines.**

$\overleftrightarrow{PQ}$ is parallel to $\overleftrightarrow{RS}$.

- write $\overleftrightarrow{PQ} \parallel \overleftrightarrow{RS}$

$\overleftrightarrow{IJ}$ intersects both $\overleftrightarrow{PQ}$ and $\overrightarrow{RS}$.

$\overleftrightarrow{IJ}$ is called a **transversal.** When parallel lines are intersected by a transversal, pairs of equal angles are formed.

▶ Two lines that intersect to form right angles are called **perpendicular lines.**

- write $\overleftrightarrow{EF} \perp \overleftrightarrow{GH}$

- read $\overleftrightarrow{EF}$ is perpendicular to $\overleftrightarrow{GH}$.

$\angle EJH$, $\angle EJG$, $\angle HJF$, and $\angle GJF$ are right angles.

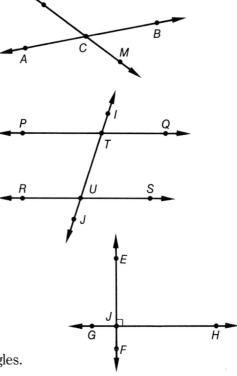

CLASSWORK

Use the figure on the right. Write *true* or *false* for 1–4.

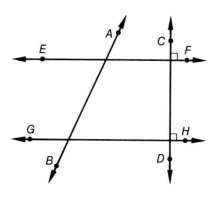

1. $\overleftrightarrow{EF} \parallel \overleftrightarrow{GH}$
2. $\overleftrightarrow{AB} \parallel \overleftrightarrow{CD}$
3. $\overleftrightarrow{CD} \perp \overleftrightarrow{GH}$
4. $\overleftrightarrow{CD} \perp \overleftrightarrow{EF}$

5. How many right angles are formed?

6. Name a line that intersects $\overleftrightarrow{GH}$ but is not perpendicular to it.

248

PRACTICE

In the figure on the right $\overleftrightarrow{RS} \parallel \overleftrightarrow{QT}$. Study the lines and angles to answer the questions. Write *true* or *false* for 1–10.

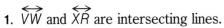

1. $\overleftrightarrow{VW}$ and $\overleftrightarrow{XR}$ are intersecting lines.

2. $\overleftrightarrow{RS}$ intersects $\overleftrightarrow{QT}$.

3. $\overleftrightarrow{XR} \perp \overleftrightarrow{ST}$

4. $\overleftrightarrow{XR} \parallel \overleftrightarrow{VW}$

5. $\overleftrightarrow{RS} \perp \overleftrightarrow{VW}$

6. $\overleftrightarrow{XR}$ intersects $\overleftrightarrow{VW}$ at X.

7. $\overleftrightarrow{RX}$ intersects $\overleftrightarrow{QT}$ at R.

8. $\angle QXS = \angle RSW$

9. $\angle VXT = \angle QXU$

10. $\angle RSX$ is a right angle.

11. Name all the lines that intersect at point S.

★ 12. Is $\angle WSY$ the complement of $\angle YSR$? Explain.

★ 13. Is $\angle VXQ$ the supplement of $\angle QXU$? Explain.

★ 14. Suppose $\overleftrightarrow{AB}$ is drawn through point U, parallel to $\overleftrightarrow{QT}$. What is the relationship between $\overleftrightarrow{AB}$ and $\overleftrightarrow{RS}$? between $\overleftrightarrow{AB}$ and $\overleftrightarrow{VW}$?

APPLICATION

15. Draw a pair of intersecting lines. Use a protractor to measure the angles formed. What can you say about the angles in the drawing?

★ 16. Make a drawing that does not have any pairs of parallel or perpendicular lines. What can you say about the angles in the drawing?

LOGICAL THINKING

Only one line can be drawn connecting any two points.

1. Draw 3 points. Make sure all 3 points do not lie on the same line. How many lines can be drawn connecting the 3 points? connecting 4 points? connecting 5 points? For each drawing, be sure no 3 points lie on the same line.

2. Make a table showing the results of your drawings. Is there a pattern? Can you predict the number of lines that can be drawn connecting 6 points?

Polygons

Monica painted a six-sided figure to decorate the pottery plate she made. The figure is a polygon.

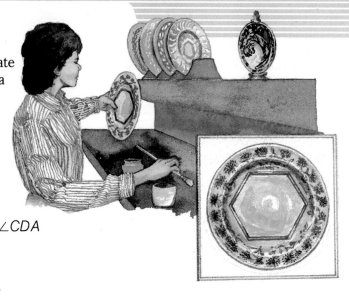

►A **polygon** is a closed plane figure with sides that are line segments.

Polygon *ABCD* has:
  4 sides: $\overline{AB}$, $\overline{BC}$, $\overline{CD}$, and $\overline{DA}$
  4 vertices: *A*, *B*, *C*, and *D*
  4 angles: ∠*DAB*, ∠*ABC*, ∠*BCD*, and ∠*CDA*

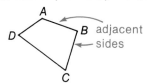

B adjacent sides

Polygons are classified according to the number of sides.

Polygon	Number of Sides, Angles, and Vertices
triangle	3
quadrilateral	4
pentagon	5
hexagon	6

Polygon	Number of Sides, Angles, and Vertices
heptagon	7
octagon	8
nonagon	9
decagon	10

►In a **regular polygon,** all sides have the same length and all angles have the same measure.

regular quadrilateral   regular pentagon   regular octagon

CLASSWORK

Classify each polygon. Then list the sides and vertices.

1. 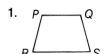 P Q R S

2. A B F C E D

3. R S T

4. U V Y W X

5. Which polygons above are regular polygons?

PRACTICE

Classify each polygon. Then list the sides and vertices.

1.

2.

3.

4.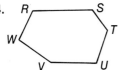

5.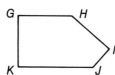

6.

Match.

7. regular quadrilateral

8. heptagon

9. regular hexagon

10. quadrilateral

11. regular triangle

12. hexagon

a.

b.

c.

d.

e.

f.

Write _true_ or _false_.

13. All pentagons have 5 vertices.

14. Some quadrilaterals have right angles.

15. All quadrilaterals are regular.

★ 16. If *ABCDE* is a pentagon, then $\overline{AB}$ and $\overline{CD}$ are adjacent sides.

★ 17. If *PQRS* is a quadrilateral, then $\overline{PQ}$ can be parallel to $\overline{RS}$.

APPLICATION

18. What type of polygon did Monica paint on the plate on page 250?

19. Designers use polygons for patterns in fabrics, floors, pottery, and other materials. Using polygons, draw a design for a fabric or floor.

Mixed Practice

1. $86.125 + 0.6543$

2. $492 - 9.38$

3. $\begin{array}{r} 54.1 \\ -\ 8.725 \\ \hline \end{array}$

4. 0.72×81.91

5. $\begin{array}{r} 1.632 \\ \times\ \ 0.5 \\ \hline \end{array}$

6. 0.02×0.004

7. $1.5\overline{)108.9}$

8. $0.04\overline{)0.268}$

9. $\frac{2}{3} + \frac{5}{6}$

10. $11\frac{3}{8} - 5\frac{1}{3}$

11. $15\frac{3}{4} - 6\frac{1}{5}$

12. $9 - 3\frac{5}{12}$

13. $3\frac{1}{3} \times 4\frac{4}{5}$

14. $\frac{2}{3} \times \frac{9}{14}$

15. $5 \div 2\frac{1}{3}$

List the factors.

16. 8

17. 24

18. 12

19. 15

20. 36

Congruent Figures

Many triangles in this Navajo sand painting are congruent. Figures are **congruent** if they have the same size and shape.

Two segments are congruent if they have the same length.

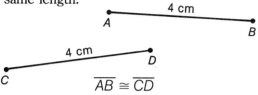

$\overline{AB} \cong \overline{CD}$

↑means   is congruent to

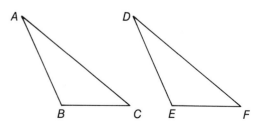

Two angles are congruent if they have the same measure.

$\angle DEF \cong \angle GHI$

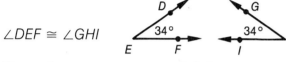

Two polygons are congruent if their corresponding sides and angles are congruent.

Quadrilateral $ABCD \cong$ quadrilateral $PQRS$.

When a tracing of $PQRS$ is placed over $ABCD$, the sides and angles will match.

The parts that match are called **corresponding parts.**

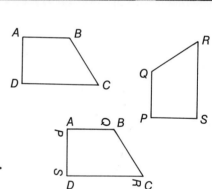

▶Corresponding parts of congruent figures are congruent.

$ABCD \cong PQRS$

corresponding sides		**corresponding angles**	
$\overline{AB} \cong \overline{PQ}$	$\overline{BC} \cong \overline{QR}$	$\angle BAD \cong \angle QPS$	$\angle ABC \cong \angle PQR$
$\overline{AD} \cong \overline{PS}$	$\overline{DC} \cong \overline{SR}$	$\angle ADC \cong \angle PSR$	$\angle BCD \cong \angle QRS$

If $\overline{AB}$ is 3 cm long, then $\overline{PQ}$ is 3 cm long.

If $m\angle ADC = 90°$, then $m\angle PSR = 90°$.

CLASSWORK

Triangles *ABC* and *DEF* are congruent. Complete.

1. $\overline{AB} \cong$ _____

2. $\overline{BC} \cong$ _____

3. $\overline{DF} \cong$ _____

4. $\angle B \cong$ _____

5. $\angle D \cong$ _____

6. $\angle C \cong$ _____

7. If $m\angle B = 110°$, then $m\angle E =$ _____.

8. If $\overline{DF}$ is 35 mm, then $\overline{AC}$ is _____ mm.

Write which pair of figures is congruent in each. Use tracing paper to check.

1.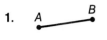

2.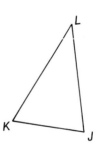

3.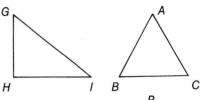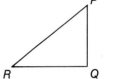

Complete. Quadrilaterals *ABCD* and *TUVW* are congruent.

4. $\overline{AB} \cong$ _____

5. $\angle A \cong$ _____

6. $\overline{BC} \cong$ _____

7. $\angle T \cong$ _____

8. $\overline{UV} \cong$ _____

9. $\angle C \cong$ _____

10. $\overline{DA} \cong$ _____

11. $\angle D \cong$ _____

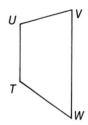

Triangles *JKL* and *PQR* are congruent. Complete.

12. If m$\angle K$ = 75°, what is m$\angle Q$?

13. If m$\angle P$ = 66°, what is m$\angle J$?

14. Which side of triangle *PQR* corresponds to $\overline{JK}$?

15. If $\overline{KL}$ is 3 cm, how long is $\overline{QR}$?

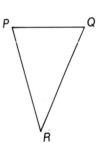

Write *true* or *false*.

16. If triangles *ABC* and *DEF* are congruent and triangle *ABC* has 1 right angle, then triangle *DEF* has 1 right angle.

17. If $\angle GHI \cong \angle PQR$ and $\angle GHI$ is acute, then $\angle PQR$ is acute.

★ 18. If *ABCD* is a square and *PQRS* is a square, then *ABCD* $\cong$ *PQRS*.

★ 19. *DEFG* and *LMNO* are squares. If $\overline{DE}$ = 4 cm and $\overline{LM}$ = 4 cm, then *DEFG* $\cong$ *LMNO*.

APPLICATION

20. How many pairs of congruent triangles do you see in the Navajo sand painting on page 252?

21. This design is made up of quadrilaterals. Are they the same shape? Are they the same size? Are the quadrilaterals congruent?

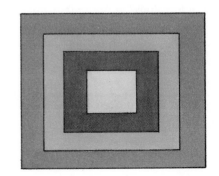

Symmetry

Kaleidoscopes use mirrors to produce symmetric designs.

▶ A figure is **symmetric** about a line if the parts of the figure on opposite sides of the line are congruent.

If this figure is folded along the **line of symmetry,** the parts will match. The figure on one side of the line is the mirror image of the figure on the other side.

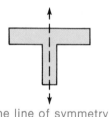

line of symmetry

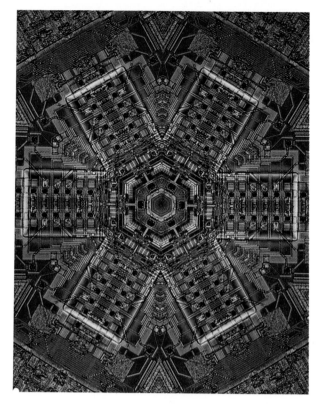

A figure can have one line of symmetry, many lines of symmetry, or no lines of symmetry.

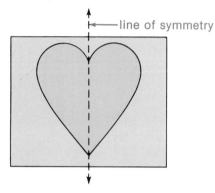

one line of symmetry   four lines of symmetry   no lines of symmetry

If you flip a figure over a line to a new position, the line acts as a line of symmetry.

Each triangle is the mirror image, or **reflection,** of the other.

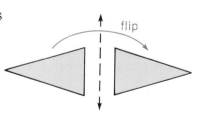

flip

CLASSWORK

Tell if each dotted line is a line of symmetry.

1. 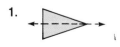   2.   3. 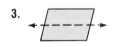   4.

PRACTICE

Is each dotted line a line of symmetry? Write *yes* or *no*.

1.

2.

3.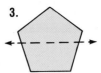

4.

Each figure has one or more lines of symmetry. Trace each figure. Then draw the lines of symmetry.

5.

6.

7.

8.

Trace each figure. Draw the mirror image of each.

9.

10.

11.

APPLICATION

12. Use two mirrors taped together to make a kaleidoscope. Draw a line segment about 10 cm long. Stand the mirrors on the segment as shown. Move the mirrors toward one another until you see a triangle. Continue moving the mirrors toward each other. What other polygons do you see?

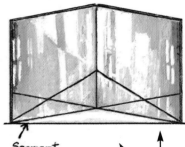

Segment

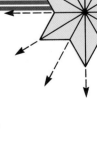

═══ VISUAL THINKING ═══

The six-pointed star has 6 lines of symmetry. How many lines of symmetry does each of these figures have?

1.

2.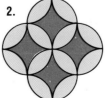

3.

4.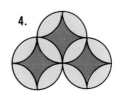

Problem Solving

PATTERNS

THINK
PLAN
SOLVE
LOOK
BACK

The ability to recognize a pattern is a critical problem-solving skill. Sometimes the pattern leads to the answer. Sometimes the pattern *is* the answer.

1. This modern painting is hanging on a museum wall. It is made up of six sections. Describe the missing section.

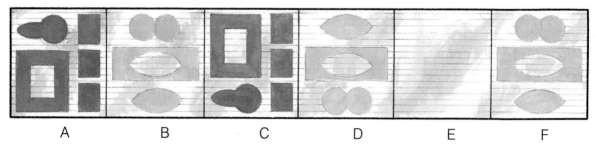

A   B   C   D   E   F

What does the missing section look like?

There are six sections with several shapes in each. Each section is either blue or yellow.

Look for a pattern.

There are really two patterns. One uses shapes. The other uses colors. Sections B, D, and F use the same shapes, with the top and bottom shapes reversed. These sections are yellow. Sections A and C also use the same shapes, with the top and bottom shapes on the left side reversed. These sections are blue.

The missing section, E, is blue. It uses the same shapes as A and C. The shapes are positioned as in section A.

Does the pattern fit with the sections shown?

Notice that section E is the same as section A and section F is the same as section B. The pattern is repeating.

2. Here is part of a design in which squares and rectangles form a certain pattern. Row 5 is not completed. Continue the pattern to describe row 5.

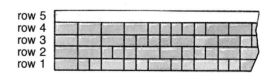

row 5
row 4
row 3
row 2
row 1

Look for the pattern.

row 1: 1 rectangle, 2 squares, 1 rectangle, 2 squares, . . .

Continue the listing for rows 2–4.

Complete the solution by describing row 5.

256

Find the missing numbers or figures to satisfy each pattern.

1.

1		2		3
	5		4	
6		7		8
			9	

2.
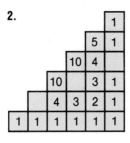

3.
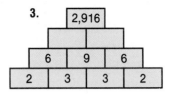

4.
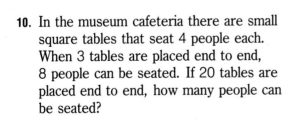

5.
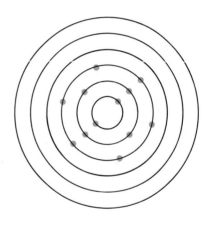

6. 1, 1, 2, 3, 5, 8, ____, 21

7. 3, 4, 7, 11, 18, ____, ____, 76

8. 17, $10\frac{1}{2}$, $6\frac{1}{2}$, 4, ____, $1\frac{1}{2}$, 1

Use patterns to solve.

9. A fountain in the museum courtyard is designed in a series of circles, as shown. The first circle has 2 fountainheads. The next circle has 4 fountainheads. The third circle has 6 fountainheads, and so on. There are 6 circles in the fountain. If the pattern continues, how many fountainheads are in the sixth circle? How many are there in all? Make a sketch of a possible arrangement for the completed fountain.

10. In the museum cafeteria there are small square tables that seat 4 people each. When 3 tables are placed end to end, 8 people can be seated. If 20 tables are placed end to end, how many people can be seated?

★ 11. The museum displays a collection of precious stones in a showcase. The top row of the showcase has 10 stones. The next 3 rows have 13, 11, and 14 stones. The pattern continues to the bottom row, which has 16 stones. How many rows are there in the showcase?

CREATE YOUR OWN PROBLEM

Draw a design that illustrates this pattern. 1, 2, 4, 8, 16, . . .

Triangles

Triangles can be classified according to their sides.

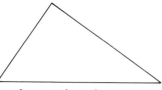

scalene triangle
no congruent sides

isosceles triangle
two congruent sides

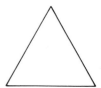

equilateral triangle
three congruent sides

Triangles can be classified according to their angles.

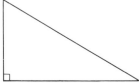

right triangle
one right angle

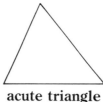

acute triangle
all acute angles

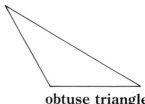

obtuse triangle
one obtuse angle

▶The sum of the measures of the angles of any triangle is 180°.

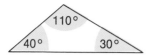

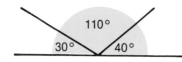

$$30° + 40° + 110° = 180°$$

If you know the measures of two angles of a triangle, you can find the measure of the third angle.

Find m∠A in △ABC.

read   triangle *ABC*

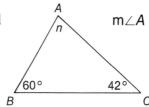

$$m\angle A + m\angle B + m\angle C = 180°$$
$$n + 60° + 42° = 180°$$
$$n + 102° = 180°$$
$$n = 78°$$
$$m\angle A = 78°$$

CLASSWORK

Measure the sides and the angles to classify each triangle in two ways.

1.
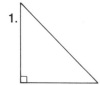

2.

3.

PRACTICE

Measure the sides and the angles to classify each triangle in two ways.

1.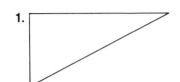

2.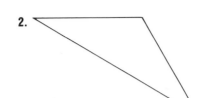

3.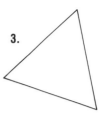

Find the measure of the third angle of each triangle.

4. 35°, 45°

5. 25°, 120°

6. 30°, 90°

7. 65°, 105°

8. 114°, 29°

9. 100°, 21°

10. 57°, 63°

11. 60°, 60°

Write *true* or *false*.

12. All equilateral triangles are acute.

13. All isosceles triangles are equilateral.

14. Some right triangles are scalene.

15. Some isosceles triangles are obtuse.

★16. All equilateral triangles are congruent.

★17. Some obtuse triangles contain one right angle.

APPLICATION

18. Use the figure at the right to identify and name at least one of each type of triangle.

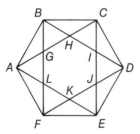

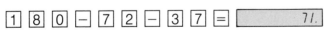

CALCULATOR

The measures of two angles of a triangle are 72° and 37°. You can easily find the measure of the third angle of the triangle on your calculator.

Enter 180. Then subtract the given measures.

| 1 | 8 | 0 | − | 7 | 2 | − | 3 | 7 | = | | *71.* |

The third angle measures 71°.

Use a calculator to find the measure of the third angle of each triangle.

1. 22°, 67°

2. 55°, 106°

3. 31°, 72°

4. 17.5°, 72.5°

Quadrilaterals

This modern German painting has many **quadrilaterals.**

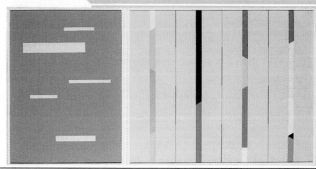

A quadrilateral is a polygon with four sides.

There are some special quadrilaterals.

Quadrilateral		Properties
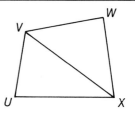 trapezoid		exactly one pair of opposite sides parallel
parallelogram		each pair of opposite sides parallel each pair of opposite sides and opposite angles congruent
rhombus		a parallelogram with all sides congruent
rectangle		a parallelogram with four right angles
square		a rectangle with all sides congruent

$\overline{VX}$ is a **diagonal** of quadrilateral $UVWX$.
$\overline{VX}$ divides the quadrilateral into two triangles.
The sum of the angles in each triangle is 180°.
$$2 \times 180° = 360°$$

▶The sum of the measures of the angles of a quadrilateral is 360°.

CLASSWORK

Classify each quadrilateral. Then name the congruent sides and the parallel sides.

1.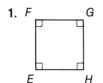

2.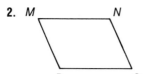

3.

4.

PRACTICE

Classify each quadrilateral. Then name the congruent sides and the parallel sides.

1.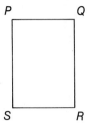

2.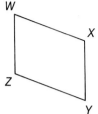

3.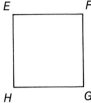

4.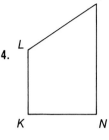

Write *true* or *false*.

5. Every rectangle is a square.

6. Every square is a rectangle.

7. Every trapezoid is a quadrilateral.

8. Every quadrilateral is a trapezoid.

9. Every rhombus is a parallelogram.

10. Every parallelogram is a rhombus.

 Find the measure of the fourth angle of each quadrilateral.

11. 65°, 44°, 108°

12. 90°, 90°, 90°

13. 80°, 39°, 127°

14. 45°, 135°, 45°

Use what you know about parallelograms to find the missing measures.

15.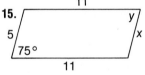

16.

★ 17.

★ 18.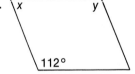

APPLICATION

19. Classify the quadrilaterals in the painting on page 260.

LOGICAL THINKING

Suppose all parallelograms are either red or blue, all triangles are green, all rectangles are red, and all trapezoids are yellow. What color must the squares be?

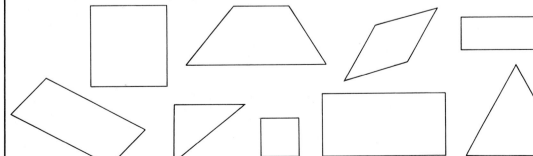

Circles

This Indian beadwork forms a decorative circle on a canvas tepee.

The diagram below shows a **circle** with **center** C. A circle is a closed plane figure. Every point on the circle is the same distance from the center. A **compass** can be used to draw a circle.

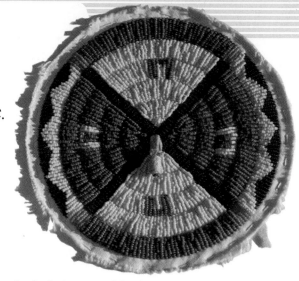

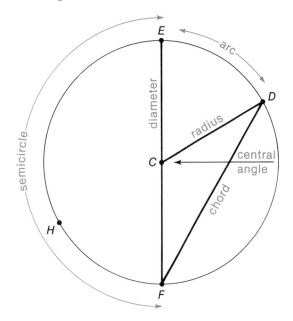

- A circle is named by its center.
- An **arc** is a part of a circle.
- A **radius** is a line segment joining the center to any point on the circle.
- A **chord** is a segment with endpoints on the circle.
- A **diameter** is a chord that passes through the center of the circle. The length of a diameter is twice the length of a radius.
- A **semicircle** is one half of a circle.
- A **central angle** is an angle with its vertex at the center of the circle.

Circle: C Arc: $\overset{\frown}{ED}$ Radius: $\overline{CD}$ Chord: $\overline{DF}$
Diameter: $\overline{EF}$ Semicircle: $\overset{\frown}{EHF}$ Central angle: $\angle DCF$

▶All radii in the same circle are congruent. In circle C above, $\overline{CE} \cong \overline{CD} \cong \overline{CF}$.

CLASSWORK

Use the diagram for 1–7.

1. Name the circle.

2. Name three radii.

3. Name two chords.

4. Name a diameter.

5. Name four arcs.

6. Name two central angles.

7. Name two semicircles.

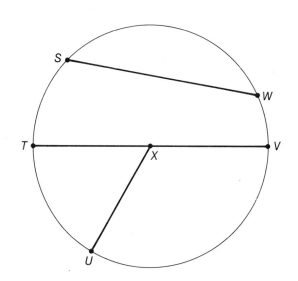

PRACTICE

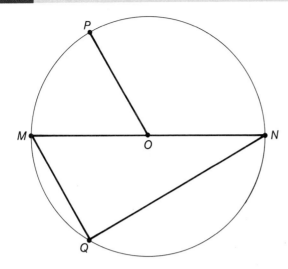

Use the diagram for 1–9.

1. Name the circle.

2. Name three radii.

3. Name a diameter.

4. Name three chords.

5. Name four arcs.

6. Name two central angles.

7. Name two semicircles.

8. If $\overline{OM}$ is 5 cm long, how long is $\overline{MN}$?

9. If $\overline{MN}$ is 14 cm long, how long is $\overline{OP}$?

Write *true* or *false*.

10. All diameters are chords.

11. All chords are diameters.

12. Some radii are chords.

13. All central angles are acute.

★**14.** If $\overline{OP}$ is a radius of circle O, and B is a point on circle O, then $\overline{PB}$ must be a diameter.

APPLICATION

15. Use a compass. Draw a circle with a radius of 5 cm. Draw another circle with a radius of 5 cm. Are the two circles congruent? Are all circles with a radius of 5 cm congruent?

★**16.** Draw 2 circles intersecting at 1 point; at 2 points; at no points. Can you draw 2 circles intersecting at only 3 points?

Mixed Practice

1. $\frac{3}{8} \times \frac{5}{7}$

2. $\frac{12}{21} \times \frac{7}{40}$

3. $6 \times 1\frac{2}{3} \times 2\frac{1}{10}$

4. $3\frac{1}{5} \times 4\frac{3}{8}$

5. $\frac{2}{3} \div \frac{1}{6}$

6. $\frac{5}{8} \div 20$

7. $10 \div 1\frac{2}{9}$

8. $18\frac{1}{2} \div 1\frac{1}{2} \times \frac{1}{4}$

9. $4\frac{1}{2} + 8\frac{1}{3}$

10. $2\frac{1}{4} - \frac{3}{8}$

11. $10 - 5\frac{1}{6}$

12. $\quad$ 4 yd 2 ft
$\underline{+\ 7\ \text{yd 2 ft}}$

13. $\quad$ 5 lb 14 oz
$\underline{+\ 6\ \text{lb 11 oz}}$

14. $\quad$ 7 gal 1 qt
$\underline{-\ 2\ \text{gal 3 qt}}$

15. $\quad$ 27 ft
$\underline{-\ 10\ \text{ft 9 in.}}$

Compare. Use >, <, or =.

16. $\frac{1}{2}$ ⬤ $\frac{2}{3}$

17. $\frac{5}{6}$ ⬤ $\frac{5}{8}$

18. $\frac{3}{4}$ ⬤ $\frac{5}{6}$

19. $1\frac{7}{8}$ ⬤ $1\frac{14}{16}$

Constructing Segments and Angles

You can construct congruent segments and congruent angles, using only a compass and a straightedge.

Construct a segment congruent to a given segment, $\overline{AB}$.

Step 1

Draw any ray longer than $\overline{AB}$. Label the endpoint of the ray C.

Step 2

Place the compass tip on A and draw an arc through B.

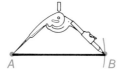

Step 3

Use the same compass opening. Place the tip on C and draw an arc intersecting the ray. Label the point of intersection D.

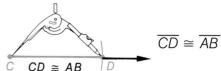

$\overline{CD} \cong \overline{AB}$

Construct an angle congruent to a given angle, $\angle MNO$.

Step 1

Draw any ray, $\overrightarrow{XY}$.

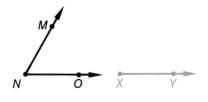

Step 2

Place the compass tip on N and draw an arc intersecting $\overrightarrow{NM}$ and $\overrightarrow{NO}$.

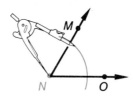

Step 3

Using the same compass opening, place the tip on X, and draw an arc intersecting $\overrightarrow{XY}$ at Q.

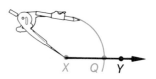

Step 4

Adjust the compass to measure the opening of $\angle MNO$.

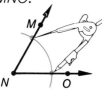

Step 5

Using point Q as center, draw an arc that intersects the first arc at point R.

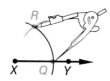

Step 6

Draw $\overrightarrow{XR}$.

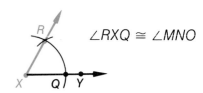

$\angle RXQ \cong \angle MNO$

CLASSWORK

Trace each figure. Then construct a figure congruent to each.

1.

2.
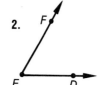

3.

4.
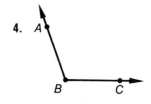

Trace each figure. Then construct a figure congruent to each.

1.

2.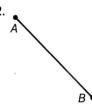

3.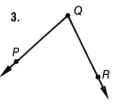

4.

Use a ruler to draw a segment with the given length. Then construct a segment congruent to each.

5. 8 cm   **6.** 5 cm   **7.** 7 cm   **8.** 9 cm   ★**9.** 4.6 cm

Use a protractor to draw an angle with the given measure. Then construct an angle congruent to each.

10. 45°   **11.** 135°   **12.** 90°   **13.** 20°   **14.** 157°

Construct.

★**15.** Draw a segment, $\overline{AB}$. Then construct a segment $\overline{LM}$ so that $\overline{LM}$ is twice the length of $\overline{AB}$.

APPLICATION

16. Ellen Marinas is a motion-picture set designer. She is working on the plans for a scene. Use your compass and straightedge to construct an angle and segment congruent to the angle and segment shown on Ellen's plan.

ESTIMATION

You can use right angles to estimate angle measures.

Think about one third of a right angle

about 30°

Think one right angle plus about one half of a right angle

about 90° + 45°, or about 135°

Estimate the angle measures, using right angles.

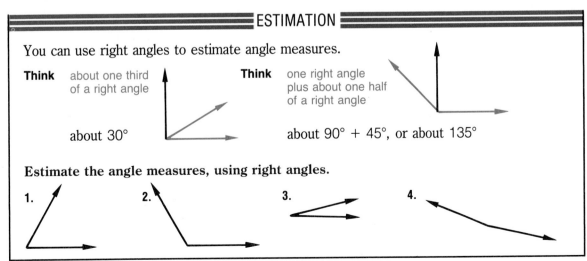

1.   2.   3.   4.

Bisecting Segments and Angles

In drawing plans for this garden, the landscape architect had to bisect segments and angles. To **bisect** means to divide into two congruent parts.

Use a compass and a straightedge to bisect a given segment, $\overline{XY}$.

Step 1

Open the compass to more than half the length of $\overline{XY}$. With the tip on X, draw an arc.

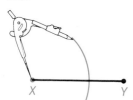

Step 2

Use the same compass opening. With the tip on Y, draw another arc. Label the points of intersection V and W.

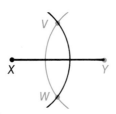

Step 3

Draw $\overleftrightarrow{VW}$. Label point Z at the intersection of $\overleftrightarrow{VW}$ and $\overline{XY}$.

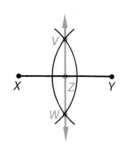

$\overleftrightarrow{VW}$ bisects $\overline{XY}$. $\overline{XZ} \cong \overline{ZY}$. Z is the midpoint of $\overline{XY}$.
$\overleftrightarrow{VW} \perp \overline{XY}$. $\overleftrightarrow{VW}$ is the **perpendicular bisector** of $\overline{XY}$.

Bisect a given angle, $\angle BAC$, using a compass and a straightedge.

Step 1

With the compass tip on A, draw an arc. Label points D and E.

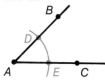

Step 2

Use the same compass opening. Draw arcs with the tip on D and E. Label the point of intersection F.

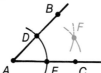

Step 3

Draw $\overrightarrow{AF}$. This ray bisects $\angle BAC$.

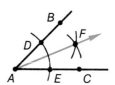

$\overrightarrow{AF}$ is an **angle bisector.**
$\angle BAF \cong \angle FAC$

CLASSWORK

Trace. Then construct the bisector of each figure.

1.

2.

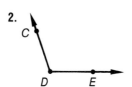

3.

4.

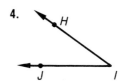

266

Trace. Then construct the bisector of each figure.

1. •L   2. M•   3. •———————•   4. R   S
                        P   Q
      •K   N•   T

Draw a segment 8 centimeters long and an angle of 100°. Then construct each of the following.

5. two 4-cm segments   6. four 2-cm segments   ★7. one 12-cm segment

8. two 50°-angles   9. four 25°-angles   ★10. one 150°-angle

APPLICATION

11. A landscape architect wishes to place a fountain in the center of a rectangular lawn. He draws the diagonals. Show that C is the center by finding the midpoints of each side. Draw lines to connect the midpoints of the opposite sides. Do the lines intersect at C?

★12. The architect is working with a drawing of a triangular flower bed. He bisects each angle of the triangle. At how many points do the angle bisectors intersect? Draw a triangle and construct the three angle bisectors.

═══════ CONSTRUCTING A LINE PERPENDICULAR TO A GIVEN LINE ═══════

Use the bisecting construction to construct a line perpendicular to $\overleftrightarrow{AB}$ at P.

- With the compass tip on P, draw 2 arcs. Label points C and D.
- Bisect $\overline{CD}$. Label points E and F.
- Draw $\overleftrightarrow{EF}$. $\overleftrightarrow{EF} \perp \overleftrightarrow{AB}$ at P.

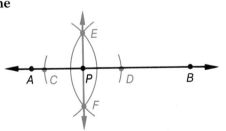

Use this construction to do each of the following.

1. Copy. Construct a right angle with vertex A.

2. Copy. Construct $\overleftrightarrow{PQ}$ perpendicular to $\overleftrightarrow{XY}$ through Q.

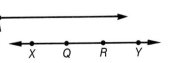

3. Suppose you construct $\overleftrightarrow{SR}$ perpendicular to $\overleftrightarrow{XY}$. What will be the relationship between $\overleftrightarrow{SR}$ and $\overleftrightarrow{PQ}$?

Problem Solving

SKILLS AND STRATEGIES REVIEW   The Art Museum

Solve.

1. Alice Conway is an artist. She prepared a set of four paintings for a new gallery. Together the paintings form a certain pattern. Each painting has a circle, a triangle, a hexagon, and a square. Three of the paintings are shown. Draw the missing painting.

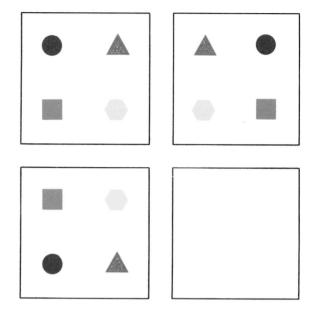

2. Alice is making a frame for another painting. She wants the frame to be in the shape of a square. What should be the measure of each angle?

3. The art museum is hanging three of Miss Conway's paintings in a horizontal arrangement. The paintings are being hung in a straight line. How many ways could the paintings be hung?

4. Miss Conway wants to paint a picture of a full moon with rays coming from the center. The rays are to form equal acute angles. What is the least number of rays she must include in her painting?

5. The gallery purchased three display cases for $520. Two of them were rectangular, and one was circular. The circular one costs $70 more than each of the rectangular ones. How much did each case cost?

6. Paul Yanker is making a set of collages, using rectangular strips of colored cloth. He uses 24 red strips and 56 yellow strips. He uses 3 red strips on each collage. How many yellow strips will he use on each collage if he uses an equal number on each?

7. Claire is working on a collection of collages made of geometric shapes. Pre-cut plastic circles cost $1.25 each, and all polygons cost $.65 each. She spent $71 for 36 shapes. How many circles and polygons did she buy?

8. During her exhibition at the new gallery, Maxine sold three of her paintings for $550 each. She sold a fourth painting for $750. How much money did she make?

9. Barry wants to make wood frames for four paintings. Each painting is a rectangle measuring 48 inches × 60 inches. How many feet of framing strips will he need?

10. Anne begins a mural with 1 square tile. She adds 3 tiles to form a 2 × 2-tile square and then 5 tiles to form a 3 × 3-tile square. She continues in this way until the square mural is completed. Last she adds 17 tiles. What is the size of the mural?

11. In another mural, Anne begins by placing blue tiles in a row. In each succeeding row, she doubles the number of blue tiles. The sixth and final row has 192 blue tiles. How many blue tiles did Anne use in the first row?

Problem Solving

WHAT WOULD YOU DO . . .?

You are responsible for the placement of exhibits for the fine arts show at Ridgewood School. These are the specifications:

Size of exhibit area: 45 yd by 35 yd

Sizes of exhibit spaces: **A.** 3 yd by 4 yd, **B.** 5 yd by 4 yd,
    C. 7 yd by 4 yd, **D.** 10 yd by 4 yd

Number of exhibit spaces: at least 6 spaces
    of each size

Gates: 2 gates, each at least 3 yd wide
    placed on opposite sides of the
    exhibit area; no exhibit can be
    placed within 2 yd of the gates

Aisles: at least 3 yd wide

Answer each question and explain.

1. Could you use guess and test to arrange each exhibit space?

2. Could you alternate each different-size exhibit space until the exhibit area is filled?

3. Could you use the plan from last year and make the necessary changes?

4. Could you find another way?

What would you do?

If you chose to use the plan from last year as a guide, how would you go about setting up your new plan? Use graph paper and the scale:

    1 side of a box on the graph = 1 yd

Draw a length of 45 boxes and a width of 35 boxes. Study the plan from last year. Place the gates so that you will have exhibits on both sides of them. Be sure there are at least 6 exhibit spaces of each size.

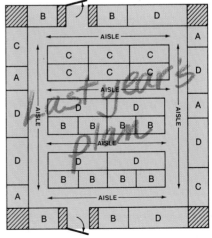

What would you do?

Many people will be coming to this fine arts show. Put one of the gates in a corner so that people will be able to move more freely.

5. How will you arrange the exhibit area now that one gate must be in a corner?

Use the figure to name each. pages 244–249

1. the point of intersection of $\overleftrightarrow{FE}$ and $\overleftrightarrow{DH}$
2. two rays on $\overleftrightarrow{AE}$
3. two segments with endpoint C
4. a line perpendicular to $\overleftrightarrow{AG}$
5. a line parallel to $\overleftrightarrow{AG}$

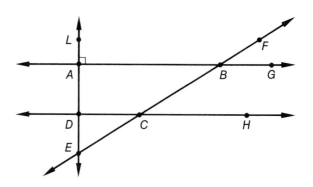

$\triangle ABC \cong \triangle FED$. **Complete.** pages 252–253

6. $\overline{AB} \cong$ _____

7. $\overline{BC} \cong$ _____

8. $\angle A \cong$ _____

9. $\angle B \cong$ _____

Measure the sides and the angles. Then classify each triangle in two ways. pages 258–259

10.

11.

12.

Classify each quadrilateral. pages 260–261

13.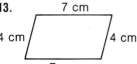

14.

15.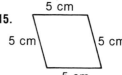

Trace. Then construct a figure congruent to each. pages 264–265

16.

17.

Solve. pages 256–257, 268–269

18. Debra is cutting out circles for a design. Each circle has a radius of 3 cm. How many circles can she fit across on a sheet of paper that is 25 cm wide?

19. Charles is putting his rock collection in a display case. He places 7 rocks in the first row, 11 in the second row, and 15 in the third. If the pattern continues, how many rocks will be in the sixth row?

Use the figure to name each of the following.

1. the point of intersection of $\overleftrightarrow{LP}$ and $\overleftrightarrow{MQ}$

2. two rays on $\overleftrightarrow{LN}$

3. two segments with endpoint P

4. a line perpendicular to $\overleftrightarrow{NR}$

5. a line parallel to $\overleftrightarrow{NR}$

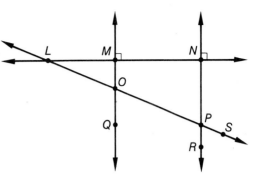

Name each polygon. Give the number of lines of symmetry.

6.

7.

8.

Classify each triangle in two ways. pages 258–259

9.
3 cm 5 cm 4 cm

10.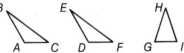
6 cm 6 cm 6 cm

11.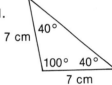
7 cm 40° 100° 40° 7 cm

Name the pair of congruent figures in each.

12.
B E H
A C D F G I

13.
D E M N Q R
G F P O T S

Use the figure at the right to complete 14–17.

14. Name the circle.

15. Name two radii.

16. Name the diameter.

17. Name two chords.

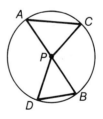

Use a compass and a straightedge.

18. Draw any line segment. Then bisect the segment.

Solve.

19. Sid's vegetable garden is shaped like a rhombus. How many meters of fencing does he need if each side is 3 m long?

20. Find the next three numbers to satisfy the pattern: 1, 3, 7, 15, ——, ——, ——.

In $\triangle ABC$, $m\angle A$ is twice $m\angle B$. $m\angle C$ is 20° more than $m\angle B$, and $m\angle C = 60°$. Find the measures of $\angle A$ and $\angle B$.

COMPASS DESIGNS

You can use your compass to make different designs.

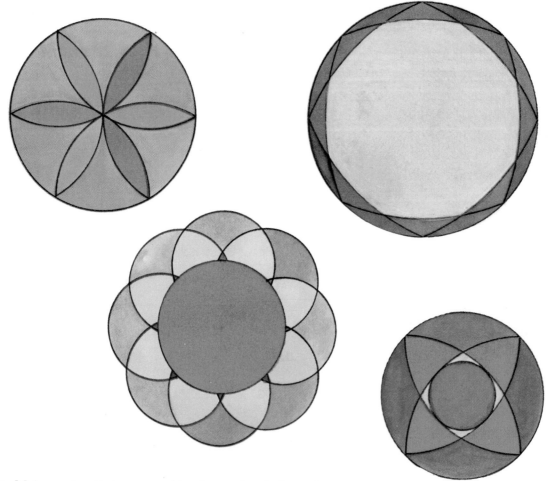

1. Make copies that are equal in size to the designs above.

2. Make larger versions of these designs.

3. Experiment with designs of your own. Color the ones you like best and mount them on construction paper to make a collage.

To construct this design, you need to bisect angles.

4. Make a larger version of this design.

5. Use a compass and a straightedge. Construct a design of your own that requires angle bisection. Color your design.

TESSELLATIONS

Interesting patterns are often used on floors, wall coverings, and fabrics. A **tessellation** is a design in which congruent copies of a figure are arranged to fill the plane in such a way that no figures overlap and there are no gaps.

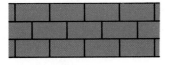 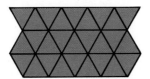 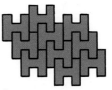 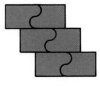

By placing tracing paper over a figure and repeatedly tracing it, you can decide if the figure will tessellate the plane.

Try to make a tessellation for each figure.

1.
parallelogram

2.
trapezoid

3.
quadrilateral

4.
scalene triangle

5.
regular pentagon

6.
regular hexagon

7.
regular heptagon

8. Which of the figures above could not be used for a tessellation?

You can also combine figures to create a tessellation.

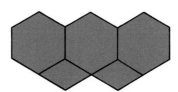

To make an original pattern for a tessellation, start with a parallelogram. Make congruent changes on one or both pairs of sides.

 → → →   →

9. Create one or more tessellations using combinations of figures. Color your tessellations in an interesting way.

10. Create a tessellation, using an original pattern. Show how your pattern was formed. Color your work.

11. Find examples of tessellations in works by the Dutch artist M.C. Escher. Bring the examples to class for discussion.

DIAGONALS OF A POLYGON

FOR and **NEXT** statements are always used together to create a **loop,** or sequence of commands that are repeated.

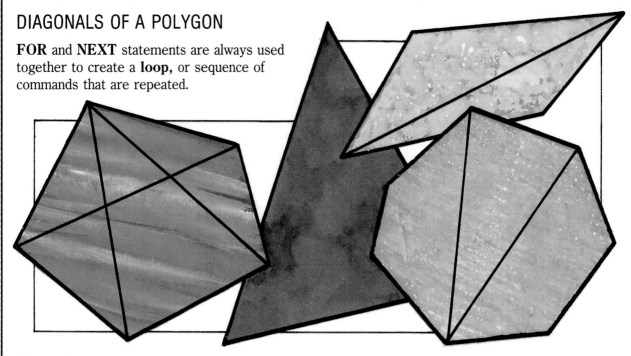

Example   10 FOR X = 1 TO 5   ⟵— X is assigned the value 1.
20 PRINT "HI THERE!"
30 NEXT X   ⟵— X is increased by 1 and the loop is repeated until the value of X becomes *greater* than 5.

Output   HI THERE!
HI THERE!
HI THERE!
HI THERE!
HI THERE!

The program below uses FOR and NEXT statements to find and print the number of diagonals in polygons with 3 sides, 4 sides, . . . , 12 sides. A **diagonal** of a polygon is a segment that joins two nonadjacent vertices.

PROGRAM

Commas cause output to be printed in columns, or "print zones."   ⟶

```
10 REM DIAGONALS OF A POLYGON
20 PRINT "SIDES","DIAGONALS"
30 FOR N = 3 TO 12
```

In an N-sided polygon there are N vertices, and   ⟶
N − 3 diagonals drawn from each vertex. The product of N and N − 3 counts each diagonal twice, so the formula to find the number of diagonals is

$$d = \frac{n \times (n-3)}{2}$$

```
40 LET D = N * (N − 3)/2
50 PRINT N,D
60 NEXT N
70 END
```

Write the output for each program.

1. ```
   10 FOR A = 1 TO 8
   20 PRINT A
   30 NEXT A
   40 END
   ```

2. ```
   10 FOR I = 1 TO 4
   20 PRINT "GOODBYE!"
   30 NEXT I
   40 END
   ```

3. ```
   10 FOR B = 1 TO 6
   20 PRINT B , B * B , B * B * B
   30 NEXT B
   40 END
   ```

4. ```
   10 FOR K = 19 TO 24
   20 PRINT "+-";
   30 NEXT K
   40 END
   ```

★5. ```
    10 FOR S = 1 TO 5
    20 PRINT 10 * S
    30 NEXT S
    40 END
    ```

★6. ```
    10 FOR J = 1 TO 10
    20 PRINT 11-J
    30 NEXT J
    40 END
    ```

Write a program using FOR and NEXT statements to print each of the following.

7. the word MATHEMATICS 25 times

8. the whole numbers from 7 to 19

★9. the even numbers from 0 to 100

★10. the odd numbers from 49 to 67

AT THE COMPUTER

Run each program and check the output.

1. for **7–10** above

Write a program for each. Then run the program and check the output.

2. Display the squares of the numbers from 1 to 30.

3. Print your name 100 times.

★4. Count backward from 100 to 1.

★5. Find the sum of the numbers from 1 to 10.
   (Begin with S = 0. Each time through the loop, add that number to S.)

Choose the correct answers. Write A, B, C, or D.

1. What is the average of 86, 72, 53, 27, and 32?

  A 90   **C** 270

  B 54   **D** not given

2. Round 4.0864 to the nearest hundredth.

  A 4.086   **C** 4.09

  B 4.08   **D** not given

3. $\begin{array}{r} 1.06 \\ \times\ 0.08 \\ \hline \end{array}$

  A 0.848   **C** 8.48

  B 1.48   **D** not given

4. Complete. 6.5 kL = ___ L

  A 6,500   **C** 6.5

  B 0.0065   **D** not given

5. What is the LCM of 18 and 12?

  A 3   **C** 0

  B 36   **D** not given

6. What is $\frac{12}{32}$ in lowest terms?

  A $\frac{3}{8}$ **C** $\frac{1}{4}$

  B $\frac{1}{2}$ **D** not given

7. $9\frac{1}{3} - 8\frac{5}{7}$

  A $1\frac{8}{21}$ **C** $\frac{13}{21}$

  B $1\frac{13}{21}$ **D** not given

8. $\begin{array}{r} 2\ \text{ft}\ 8\ \text{in.} \\ +\ 4\ \text{ft}\ 9\ \text{in.} \\ \hline \end{array}$

  A 6 ft 5 in.   **C** 7 ft 17 in.

  B 7 ft 5 in.   **D** not given

9. $3\frac{3}{5} \div \frac{4}{15}$

  A $13\frac{1}{2}$ **C** $1\frac{11}{25}$

  B $14\frac{1}{2}$ **D** not given

10. What is the measure of $\angle C$ in $\triangle ABC$ if $m\angle A = 65°$ and $m\angle B = 73°$?

  A 52°   **C** 138°

  B 42°   **D** not given

11. What is the name for a polygon with 8 sides?

  A octagon   **C** hexagon

  B pentagon   **D** not given

12. Which is a radius of the circle?

  A $\overset{\frown}{BD}$ **C** $\overline{AC}$

  B $\overline{BD}$ **D** not given

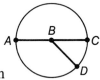

Use the table below to answer 13 and 14.

	Mon.	Tues.	Wed.	Thurs.	Fri.
Sam	3 mg	4 mg	6.2 mg	9.2 mg	13.5 mg
Ned	1.2 mg	2.1 mg	3.1 mg	5.9 mg	9.4 mg

13. Sam and Ned grew crystals for science class. The table shows the weight of the crystals each day for five days. On which day did Ned's crystals weigh 0.5 times as much as Sam's crystals?

  A Wed.   **C** Fri.

  B Mon.   **D** not given

14. How many times larger were Sam's crystals on Friday than they were on Monday?

  A 3   **C** 4.5

  B 10.5   **D** not given

Theme: Communication

Ratios

Most newspapers have a column for readers' letters to the editor. In *The New York Times,* 1 letter out of 21 is published.

A **ratio** is a pair of numbers used to compare two quantities.

The ratio of letters published to letters received is 1 to 21.

Ratios can be written in three ways.

- write   1 to 21, or 1:21, or $\frac{1}{21}$

- read   one to twenty-one

The numbers 1 and 21 are the **terms** of the ratio.

A **rate** is a ratio that compares different kinds of units.

The ratio $\frac{\$.30}{1}$ $\longleftarrow$ cents
$\qquad\qquad\qquad$ $\longleftarrow$ number of newspapers

describes the rate $.30 per newspaper.

Equal ratios make the same comparison or describe the same rate.

▶To find equal ratios, multiply or divide both terms of the ratio by the same nonzero number.

$$\frac{1}{21} = \frac{1 \times 2}{21 \times 2} = \frac{2}{42} \qquad\qquad \frac{16}{24} = \frac{16 \div 8}{24 \div 8} = \frac{2}{3}$$

$\frac{1}{21}$ and $\frac{2}{42}$ are equal ratios. $\qquad$ $\frac{16}{24}$ and $\frac{2}{3}$ are equal ratios.

The ratios $\frac{1}{21}$ and $\frac{2}{3}$ are in lowest terms.

New Tax Takes 6¢ of Your Dollar

To the Editor:
I understand that the new state tax will *ohou llol clhho ollollu cynollo llolclhho oll ohou llol yllo ohou ullouho llolclhh oho c*

Lengthen School Year?

To the Editor:
In our state students are in school 38 out of 52 weeks each year. When Jack Reynolds suggested lengthening the time to *yllo ohou llo clhho ollollu cynollo ullo iho yllo oho ohou ollollu ulloicycuollo ollol lucynoll lo ohou llol clhho ollollu cynollo ullouho yllo ohou llolclhho cynollo oicycuoll*

CLASSWORK

There are 9 newspapers and 11 magazines. Write each ratio in three ways.

1. newspapers to magazines

2. magazines to newspapers

3. newspapers to total publications

4. magazines to total publications

Write each ratio in fraction form.

5. 6 to 7 $\qquad$ **6.** 10:15 $\qquad$ **7.** 12 out of 15 $\qquad$ **8.** 9:11

Write two equal ratios for each.

9. 5:12 $\qquad$ **10.** 6 to 8 $\qquad$ **11.** 18:9 $\qquad$ **12.** 1 out of 4

PRACTICE

Use the drawings to write each ratio in three ways.

1. triangles to squares
2. squares to triangles
3. triangles to all figures
4. all figures to squares

Write a ratio for each.

5. 3 books for $2.00

6. 55 miles per hour

7. 4 columns per page

8. 2 pairs for $25.00

9. 5 lb for $1.89

10. 8 hats to 5 coats

11. 5 tickets for $3.00

12. 45 letters on 1 line

13. 10 students in each group

Write each ratio in fraction form.

14. 3:9

15. 7 out of 35

16. 12 to 30

17. 25:90

18. 18 to 48

19. 15:200

20. 4 out of 72

21. 36:120

Write two equal ratios for each.

22. 5:8

23. 4 to 9

24. 7 out of 11

25. 6:10

26. 30 out of 40

27. 13:26

28. 42 to 16

29. 18:1

APPLICATION

30. At the *Perryville Post,* the ratio of letters published to letters received is 2:16. Write this ratio in lowest terms.

★ 31. Read the opening of the letter to the editor that discusses lengthening the school year. If 2 weeks were added to the school year, what would be the ratio of weeks in school to weeks of the year? Write the ratio in lowest terms.

===== LOGICAL THINKING =====

Use the numbers given to make equal ratios.

1. $\frac{\square}{\square} = \frac{\square}{\square}$ 3, 5, 9, 15

2. $\frac{\square}{\square} = \frac{\square}{\square}$ 1, 4, 16, 64

3. $\frac{\square}{\square} = \frac{\square}{\square}$ 2, 8, 12, 48

4. $\frac{\square}{\square} = \frac{\square}{\square}$ 1, 5, 5, 25

5. $\frac{\square}{\square} = \frac{\square}{\square}$ 20, 30, 40, 60

6. $\frac{\square}{\square} = \frac{\square}{\square}$ 9, 12, 30, 40

Proportions

Television has not replaced radio. In the United States there are 12 radios for every 6 people. This means that there are 2 radios for each person.

The ratio $\frac{12}{6}$ is equal to the ratio $\frac{2}{1}$.   Think $\frac{12}{6} = \frac{12 \div 6}{6 \div 6} = \frac{2}{1}$

A **proportion** is a statement that two ratios are equal.

$\frac{12}{6} = \frac{2}{1}$ is a proportion.

• read   12 is to 6 as 2 is to 1.

▶ In a proportion the cross products of the ratios are equal.

Cross Products

 cross products

$12 \times 1 = 6 \times 2$

$12 = 12$

The cross products are equal, so $\frac{12}{6} = \frac{2}{1}$ is a proportion.

Is $\frac{4}{32} = \frac{2}{16}$ a proportion?	Is $\frac{2}{3} = \frac{8}{9}$ a proportion?
$4 \times 16 \;\bullet\; 2 \times 32$	$2 \times 9 \;\bullet\; 3 \times 8$
$64 = 64$	$18 \neq 24$
The cross products are equal, so the ratios are equal.	The cross products are not equal, so the ratios are *not* equal.
$\frac{4}{32} = \frac{2}{16}$ is a proportion.	$\frac{2}{3} = \frac{8}{9}$ is *not* a proportion.

CLASSWORK

Tell whether or not each is a proportion. Write *yes* or *no*.

1. $\frac{2}{3} = \frac{8}{12}$

2. $\frac{12}{15} = \frac{4}{3}$

3. $\frac{16}{6} = \frac{24}{9}$

4. $\frac{6}{8} = \frac{9}{12}$

5. $\frac{3}{8} = \frac{4}{10}$

Use = or ≠ for each ⬤.

6. $\frac{5}{8} \;\bullet\; \frac{15}{24}$

7. $\frac{3}{5} \;\bullet\; \frac{15}{20}$

8. $\frac{5}{10} \;\bullet\; \frac{9}{18}$

9. $\frac{15}{10} \;\bullet\; \frac{12}{8}$

10. $\frac{5}{6} \;\bullet\; \frac{7}{8}$

PRACTICE

Tell whether or not each is a proportion. Write *yes* or *no*.

1. $\frac{3}{10} = \frac{4}{40}$ 2. $\frac{3}{5} = \frac{1}{2}$ 3. $\frac{14}{16} = \frac{49}{56}$ 4. $\frac{24}{36} = \frac{2}{3}$ 5. $\frac{5}{12} = \frac{25}{72}$

6. $\frac{15}{16} = \frac{120}{128}$ 7. $\frac{2}{9} = \frac{27}{130}$ 8. $\frac{20}{5} = \frac{4}{1}$ 9. $\frac{12}{18} = \frac{56}{84}$ 10. $\frac{21}{75} = \frac{3}{5}$

11. $\frac{3.6}{1.2} = \frac{3}{1}$ 12. $\frac{0.1}{0.1} = \frac{2.4}{2.4}$ ★13. $\frac{1.2}{3.2} = \frac{3}{8}$ ★14. $\frac{0.9}{3} = \frac{5.4}{18}$ ★15. $\frac{1.5}{6.5} = \frac{5}{1.3}$

Use = or ≠ for each ⬤.

16. $\frac{1}{5}$ ⬤ $\frac{4}{20}$ 17. $\frac{3}{4}$ ⬤ $\frac{16}{20}$ 18. $\frac{45}{35}$ ⬤ $\frac{7}{5}$ 19. $\frac{5}{6}$ ⬤ $\frac{30}{34}$ 20. $\frac{3}{5}$ ⬤ $\frac{9}{16}$

21. $\frac{7}{10}$ ⬤ $\frac{28}{40}$ 22. $\frac{6}{9}$ ⬤ $\frac{18}{27}$ 23. $\frac{4}{5}$ ⬤ $\frac{20}{25}$ 24. $\frac{5}{2}$ ⬤ $\frac{50}{22}$ 25. $\frac{11}{3}$ ⬤ $\frac{44}{9}$

26. $\frac{24}{7}$ ⬤ $\frac{96}{28}$ ★27. $\frac{9}{4}$ ⬤ $\frac{108}{56}$ ★28. $\frac{56}{231}$ ⬤ $\frac{8}{33}$ ★29. $\frac{1.5}{4}$ ⬤ $\frac{4.5}{12}$ ★30. $\frac{4.2}{0.6}$ ⬤ $\frac{42}{60}$

APPLICATION

31. During an hour of radio programming, 13 minutes are used for announcements and commercials. Jerry said that was the same as a ratio of 1 to 5. Was he correct?

★32. Jerry conducted a survey of his classmates. He reported that, on the average, each family owned 5 radios. If there were 28 students in the class, each from a different family, what ratio would express the number of radios to students?

═══ CALCULATOR ═══

You can use a calculator to tell whether or not two ratios form a proportion.

Is $\frac{15}{17} = \frac{75}{85}$ a proportion?   **Think** If $\frac{15}{17} = \frac{75}{85}$, then $15 \times 85 = 17 \times 75$, or $\frac{15 \times 85}{17} = 75$.

Press ⬜1 ⬜5 ⬜× ⬜8 ⬜5 ⬜÷ ⬜1 ⬜7 ⬜= ▮ *75.* ▮

Use the method above to tell whether or not these are proportions. Write *yes* or *no* for each.

1. $\frac{21}{18} = \frac{189}{162}$ 2. $\frac{14}{25} = \frac{154}{300}$ 3. $\frac{15}{19} = \frac{180}{228}$ 4. $\frac{35}{43} = \frac{490}{602}$

5. $\frac{17}{39} = \frac{289}{663}$ 6. $\frac{23}{52} = \frac{414}{988}$ 7. $\frac{4.3}{9.6} = \frac{1.075}{2.4}$ 8. $\frac{0.81}{0.73} = \frac{2.025}{0.1825}$

Solving Proportions

When a home telephone number is dialed, the telephone rings once every 5 seconds until it is answered. If the telephone is answered after 30 seconds, how many times was it allowed to ring?

Since the ratio of rings to seconds stays the same, use equal ratios to solve the problem.

Write a proportion.
Let n represent the number of rings in 30 seconds.

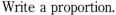

rings $\longrightarrow$
seconds $\longrightarrow$ $\dfrac{1}{5} = \dfrac{n}{30}$

Use cross products to solve the proportion.

$$\dfrac{1}{5} = \dfrac{n}{30}$$
$$1 \times 30 = 5 \times n$$
$$30 = 5n$$
$$\dfrac{30}{5} = \dfrac{5n}{5}$$
$$6 = n$$

The phone rings 6 times in 30 seconds.

▶ Some proportions can be solved by equal ratios.

$$\dfrac{n}{36} = \dfrac{5}{9}$$
$$\dfrac{n}{36} = \dfrac{5 \times 4}{9 \times 4}$$
$$n = 20$$

More Examples

a. $\dfrac{3}{4} = \dfrac{21}{n}$

$3 \times n = 4 \times 21$

$3n = 84$

$\dfrac{3n}{3} = \dfrac{84}{3}$

$n = 28$

b. $\dfrac{n}{12} = \dfrac{5}{15}$

$n \times 15 = 12 \times 5$

$15n = 60$

$\dfrac{15n}{15} = \dfrac{60}{15}$

$n = 4$

c. $\dfrac{6}{n} = \dfrac{2}{0.8}$

$6 \times 0.8 = n \times 2$

$4.8 = 2n$

$\dfrac{4.8}{2} = \dfrac{2n}{2}$

$2.4 = n$

CLASSWORK

Solve each proportion.

1. $\dfrac{n}{9} = \dfrac{18}{27}$

2. $\dfrac{4}{5} = \dfrac{16}{n}$

3. $\dfrac{42}{48} = \dfrac{n}{8}$

4. $\dfrac{7}{35} = \dfrac{8}{n}$

5. $\dfrac{2}{n} = \dfrac{5}{20}$

Solve each proportion.

1. $\frac{3}{4} = \frac{n}{28}$ 2. $\frac{9}{15} = \frac{21}{n}$ 3. $\frac{11}{33} = \frac{n}{18}$ 4. $\frac{6}{24} = \frac{8}{n}$ 5. $\frac{n}{18} = \frac{3}{2}$

6. $\frac{3}{18} = \frac{11}{n}$ 7. $\frac{16}{20} = \frac{36}{n}$ 8. $\frac{n}{35} = \frac{4}{7}$ 9. $\frac{25}{40} = \frac{n}{8}$ 10. $\frac{45}{9} = \frac{20}{n}$

11. $\frac{7}{9} = \frac{n}{54}$ 12. $\frac{4}{100} = \frac{1}{n}$ 13. $\frac{n}{3} = \frac{100}{10}$ 14. $\frac{n}{9} = \frac{32}{144}$ 15. $\frac{7}{n} = \frac{8}{40}$

16. $\frac{n}{3} = \frac{8}{48}$ 17. $\frac{8}{16} = \frac{n}{10}$ 18. $\frac{600}{3,000} = \frac{n}{20}$ 19. $\frac{8}{32} = \frac{n}{20}$ 20. $\frac{10}{n} = \frac{24}{9}$

21. $\frac{n}{3} = \frac{3}{9}$ 22. $\frac{2}{n} = \frac{14}{35}$ 23. $\frac{8}{28} = \frac{n}{0.7}$ 24. $\frac{3}{n} = \frac{14}{2.8}$ 25. $\frac{6}{15} = \frac{2.4}{n}$

26. $\frac{130}{50} = \frac{n}{2.5}$ ★ 27. $\frac{2.4}{n} = \frac{2}{0.3}$ ★ 28. $\frac{n}{5.6} = \frac{0.5}{14}$ ★ 29. $\frac{1.1}{6} = \frac{5.5}{n}$ ★ 30. $\frac{5.2}{n} = \frac{1.3}{1.6}$

Solve.

★ 31. Write a proportion for these cross products: $12 \times n = 8 \times 18$.

★ 32. Each of the cross products of a proportion is 48. One of the ratios is $6:16$. What is the other ratio?

APPLICATION

Write and solve a proportion for each.

33. Some new business phones ring 2 short rings every 5 seconds to let you know that a call is coming from outside the building. How many rings will you count in 35 seconds?

★ 34. Two office phones start ringing at the same time. One rings once every 5 seconds to signal an inside call. The other rings twice every 5 seconds to signal an outside call. How many rings are heard if both phones are answered after 30 seconds?

ESTIMATION

You can use estimation to check the solution to a proportion.

Use cross products to solve.

$$\frac{2}{5} = \frac{n}{21}$$
$$2 \times 21 = 5 \times n$$
$$42 = 5n$$
$$8.4 = n$$

Estimate to check.

$\frac{n}{21} = \frac{2}{5}$

21 is about 5×4, so n should be about $2 \times 4 = 8$. The answer 8.4 makes sense, since it is about 8.

Solve each proportion. Then estimate to be sure the answer makes sense.

1. $\frac{3}{8} = \frac{n}{25}$ 2. $\frac{5}{6} = \frac{32}{n}$ 3. $\frac{3}{2} = \frac{n}{21}$ 4. $\frac{n}{10} = \frac{7}{3}$ 5. $\frac{17}{n} = \frac{3}{4}$

Scale Drawing

A **scale drawing** is an enlarged or reduced drawing of an actual object. The **scale** is the ratio of the distances in the drawing to the actual distances.

Use this scale drawing to find the actual length of the room.

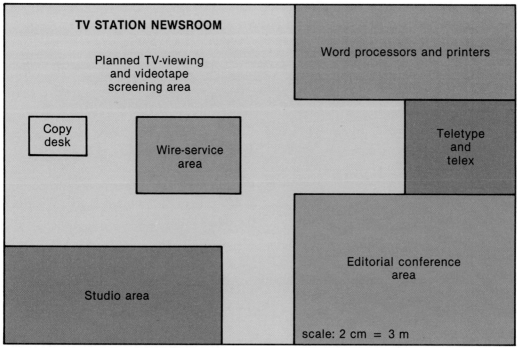

TV STATION NEWSROOM

Planned TV-viewing and videotape screening area

Word processors and printers

Copy desk

Wire-service area

Teletype and telex

Studio area

Editorial conference area

scale: 2 cm = 3 m

The drawing uses a scale of 2 cm:3 m. Every 2 cm on the drawing represents 3 m of the newsroom. To find the actual length of the room, use a proportion.

$$\frac{2}{3} = \frac{14}{n} \quad \leftarrow \text{length on drawing} \\ \leftarrow \text{actual length}$$

$$2 \times n = 3 \times 14$$
$$2n = 42$$
$$n = 21 \quad \text{The newsroom is 21 m long.}$$

Another Example

What is the actual width of the studio area?

$$\frac{2}{3} = \frac{2.5}{n} \quad \leftarrow \text{width on drawing} \\ \leftarrow \text{actual width}$$

$$2 \times n = 3 \times 2.5$$
$$2n = 7.5$$
$$n = 3.75 \quad \text{The actual width of the studio area is 3.75 m.}$$

CLASSWORK

Complete.

1. scale 1 cm:15 m
drawing: 4 cm
actual: _____

2. scale 1 cm:4.5 km
drawing: 6 cm
actual: _____

3. scale 1 cm:1 m
drawing: 7.2 cm
actual: _____

Complete.

1. scale: 1 cm:3 km
   drawing: 6 cm
   actual: _____

2. scale: 1 cm:4.5 km
   drawing: 3 cm
   actual: _____

3. scale: 4 cm:3 m
   drawing: 20 cm
   actual: _____

4. scale: 1 cm:1 m
   drawing: 5.5 cm
   actual: _____

5. scale: 5 mm:10 m
   drawing: 15 mm
   actual: _____

6. scale: 2 cm:5 km
   drawing: 5 cm
   actual: _____

7. scale: 5 cm:120 km
   drawing: 25 cm
   actual: _____

8. scale: 3 cm:35 m
   drawing: 10.5 cm
   actual: _____

9. scale: 2 cm:1 km
   drawing: 17 cm
   actual: _____

Copy and complete the chart below. Use a centimeter ruler to measure each distance on the scale drawing of the newsroom. Then use a proportion to find the actual distances.

		DISTANCE ON DRAWING			ACTUAL DISTANCE	
	Section	Length	Width		Length	Width
10.	Editorial conference					
11.	Teletype and telex					
12.	Word processors and printers					
13.	Wire service					
14.	Copy desk					

APPLICATION

Jack works at the television station. To get from his house in Union to his office in Riverton, he takes Route 17 to Highway 24. Then he takes Route 30 into Riverton.

15. How far does Jack travel along Route 17?

16. How many kilometers does Jack travel from his home to his office?

★ 17. If there were a highway going in a straight line from Union to Riverton, how many fewer kilometers would Jack drive on each one-way trip?

★ 18. Part of Jack's job is to plan a new area to be set up in the newsroom for TV viewing and videotape screening. The area is to be 11.1 m long and 2.25 m wide. What will be its length and width on the drawing?

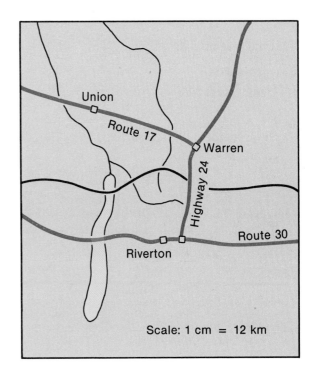

Scale: 1 cm = 12 km

Unit Price

Joyce and her friends publish a magazine called *CompuGames* 3 times a year. They charge $1.25 for a year's subscription. How much does one issue cost?

Find the **unit price** of the magazine.

▶The unit price of an item is a ratio: *price* per *unit of measure*.

To find a unit price, you can use a proportion.

Step 1	Step 2	Step 3

Step 1

Write the rate as a ratio.

$\dfrac{\$1.25}{3}$ ⟵ price ⟵ units

Step 2

Write a proportion. Use 1 for the number of units in the second ratio.

$$\frac{\$1.25}{3} = \frac{n}{1}$$

Step 3

Solve the proportion.

$\$1.25 \times 1 = 3 \times n$
$\$1.25 = 3n$
$\$.416 = n$
$\$.42 = n$ rounded to the nearest cent

One issue of *CompuGames* costs $.42.

▶To find the best buy among items, compare the unit prices.

Which is the better buy—a carton of 5 reams of paper for $48 or a carton of 12 reams for $113.40?

Find the unit price of each.

5 reams for $48

$\dfrac{48}{5} = \dfrac{n}{1}$ ⟵ price ⟵ units

$\$48 \times 1 = 5 \times n$
$\$48 = 5n$
$\$9.60 = n$

12 reams for $113.40

$\dfrac{\$113.40}{12} = \dfrac{n}{1}$

$\$113.40 \times 1 = 12 \times n$
$\$113.40 = 12n$
$\$9.45 = n$

The unit price for 5 reams of paper is $9.60 per ream.
The unit price for 12 reams of paper is $9.45 per ream.
A carton of 12 reams is the better buy.

CLASSWORK

Find the unit price of each.

1. 13 issues for $7.02

2. 12 months for $132

3. 7 cans for $2.45

4. 4 chairs for $99

5. 12 oranges for $4.50

6. 20 hours for $71

PRACTICE

Find each unit price to the nearest cent.

1. 1 dozen donuts for $2.88

2. 52 weeks of *TV-Viewer* for $15.08

3. 4-serving pouch for $1.28

4. 12 granola bars for $4.45

5. 2 qt of juice for $1.89

6. 3 bars of soap for $1.29

7. 4 qt of detergent for $1.99

8. 48 cans for $11.40

9. 2 grapefruit for $.89

10. 3 lb of potatoes for $.98

Complete. Find each unit price to the nearest cent.

★ **11.** 0.25 lb for $1.79
1 lb for _____

★ **12.** 0.45 lb for $2.25
1 lb for _____

★ **13.** 2.5 lb for $1.25
1 oz for _____

APPLICATION

Which is the better buy?

14. rice
  a. 3 lb for $2.79
  b. 2 lb for $1.89

15. crackers
  a. 8 oz for $1.09
  b. 12 oz for $1.59

16. detergent
  a. 24 oz for $2.49
  b. 64 oz for $5.29

17. canned soup
  a. 11 oz for $.31
  b. 18 oz for $.40

18. dishwashing liquid
  a. 32 oz for $2.09
  b. 22 oz for $1.65

19. lunch bags
  a. 25 for $1.00
  b. 48 for $2.40

20. peanut butter
  a. 18 oz for $1.89
  b. 28 oz for $2.69

21. turkey
  a. 8 lb for $6.32
  b. 12 lb for $8.79

22. aluminum foil
  a. 50 ft for $2.79
  b. 75 ft for $3.47

★ **23.** green beans
  a. 2 lb 8 oz for $2.09
  b. 3 lb 12 oz for $3.48

★ **24.** milk
  a. 1 gal for $1.97
  b. 32 oz for $.63

★ **25.** potatoes
  a. 5 lb for $2.59
  b. 9 oz for $.38

ESTIMATION

Estimate the unit price of each item.

4.1 lb for $1.95   **Think**   4 lb for $2.00
                               1 lb for $.50

1. 2.9 lb for $5.85

2. 6 cans for $2.69

3. 3 pairs for $5.75

4. 9 qt for $5.29

5. 8 apples for $.79

6. 7 h for $26.95

7. 4 pears for $.99

8. 11 boxes for $14.75

9. 9 dozen for $40.16

Similar Figures

Mario designed this invitation and had *Copyfast!* make reduced copies, each 15 cm long. Will a copy fit into an envelope that is 16 cm long and 8 cm high?

The invitation and the copy are **similar figures.**

Similar figures have the same shape.

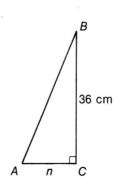

▶ When two figures are similar, the ratios of the lengths of corresponding sides are equal. That is, the corresponding sides are in proportion.

Use this fact to find the height of the copy.

Write the proportion.

original ⟶ $\frac{25}{15} = \frac{15}{n}$ ⟵ copy

The copy is 9 cm high. It will *not* fit into an envelope that is 8 cm high.

Solve the proportion. $25 \times n = 15 \times 15$

$$25n = 225$$
$$n = 9$$

When two triangles are similar, the corresponding angles are congruent and the corresponding sides are in proportion.

$\triangle ABC$ and $\triangle DEF$ are similar.

Find the length of $\overline{AC}$.

$\overline{AC}$ corresponds to $\overline{DF}$. $\overline{BC}$ corresponds to $\overline{EF}$.

Corresponding sides of similar figures are in proportion.

$$\frac{\overline{AC}}{\overline{DF}} = \frac{\overline{BC}}{\overline{EF}}$$

$$\frac{n}{5} = \frac{36}{12}$$
$$12n = 180$$
$$n = 15$$

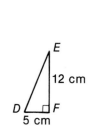

The length of $\overline{AC}$ is 15 cm.

CLASSWORK

ABCD **is similar to** *PQRS*. **Complete.**

1. $\overline{AB}$ corresponds to _____.

2. $\overline{QR}$ corresponds to _____.

3. The length of $\overline{AD}$ is _____.

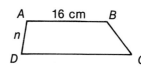

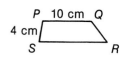

PRACTICE

ABCD is similar to *LMNO*. **Complete.**

1. $\overline{AB}$ corresponds to _____.

2. $\overline{CD}$ corresponds to _____.

3. $\overline{LO}$ corresponds to _____.

4. The length of $\overline{AD}$ is _____.

5. The length of $\overline{NM}$ is _____.

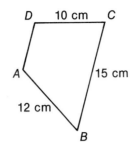

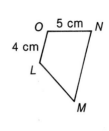

Each pair of figures is similar. Find the length *n* in each.

6.

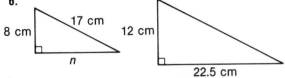

7.

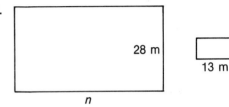

8.

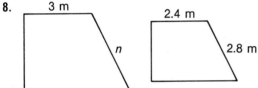

9.

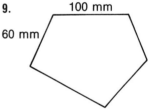

10.

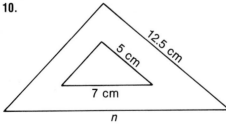

★ 11.

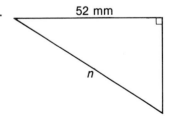

APPLICATION

12. A photograph 10 cm high and 16 cm wide is reduced so that it can be used in a book. The reduced picture must be 8 cm wide. How high will it be?

★ 13. A photocopying machine will reduce the copy to $\frac{9}{10}$ of the original. If a photograph that measures 12 cm × 8 cm is copied at that setting, what space will the new photograph occupy?

289

Problem Solving

SOLVING A SIMPLER PROBLEM

Some problems are complicated because they have large numbers or several parts. To plan a solution, think of a simpler problem, with reduced numbers or fewer parts.

1. A post office in a large city processed 3,103,968 pieces of mail in a week. There are 168 hours in a week. What was the average number of pieces processed each hour?

What was the average number of pieces of mail processed each hour?

3,103,968 pieces per week   168 hours in one week

Solve a simpler problem. Reduce the size of the numbers.

Replace 3,103,968 with 30. Replace 168 with 10. Restate the problem: If 30 pieces of mail are processed in 10 hours, how many are processed each hour?

It is easy to see that the problem can be solved by division. $30 \div 10 = 3$

Now use the same operation to solve the original problem.

$3,103,968 \div 168 = 18,476$

The average number of pieces of mail processed each hour was 18,476.

Does this answer seem reasonable?

Check by multiplying: $18,476 \times 168 = 3,103,968$.

2. There are some games that you can always win if you know the winning strategy. Find the strategy for this game.

Rules

- Two players take turns drawing lines to connect 2 dots that are next to each other.

- No diagonal lines may be drawn.

- A dot may be connected to just 1 other dot.

- The player who draws the last connecting line wins.

Try the game with only 4 dots. The player who goes second is sure to win.

Try 6 dots, and then 8. Do you see a pattern? Should you go first or second to win the original game?

PRACTICE

Use a simpler problem to solve each.

1. On a television screen, an actor appeared to be 12 inches high. The ratio of the height of the image to the actual height of the actor is 4:23. How tall is the actor?

2. Mr. Johnson estimated that he had delivered mail for 84,000 hours during his career. If an average work year has 2,800 hours, for how many years has Mr. Johnson been delivering mail?

3. The director of transportation for a large city wants to put a traffic light at each intersection in the city. There are 769 east-west streets and 184 north-south streets that intersect. How many traffic lights will he need?

4. In a certain city there are 57,800 homes with telephones. Of these, 0.16 use telephones manufactured by Bestphone. Of the homes that use Bestphone, 1 out of 8 have 2 telephones. How many homes have 2 telephones by Bestphone?

5. Ten cities have teams in the Southern Continental Football League. To conduct the annual draft of players, teams in each city must have a direct telephone line to each of the other cities. How many direct lines must be installed by the telephone company to connect the cities?

6. During July, United States Postal Service trucks used 21,875 gallons of regular unleaded gasoline and 15,281 gallons of regular leaded gasoline. The trucks averaged 12.5 miles per gallon. How many miles did the trucks travel in July?

★7. Workers are testing the lights in the 50 offices of a new telecommunications building. All of the office lights are controlled by a master switchboard. The workers begin by turning all the switches on. After one hour they turn the switches off in all the even-numbered offices (2, 4, 6, . . . 50). After another hour they reverse the position of the switches in each office whose number is divisible by 3. (That is, if the switch is on, the workers turn it off; if it is off, they turn it on.) After another hour the workers reverse the position of the switches in each office whose number is divisible by 4. If they continue in this manner, which offices will have their lights on after 50 hours?

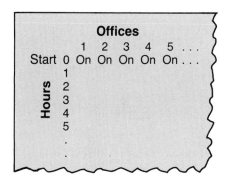

Set up a table like the one at the right. Begin with 10 offices. Which office lights are on after 10 hours? Do you see a pattern in the answers? If not, add more offices and more hours to the table until you find the pattern.

CREATE YOUR OWN PROBLEM

The Rush-It Messenger Company sold their 1976 van for $1,200. The odometer showed 207,000 miles. Write a problem about the van.

Ratios and Percents

Lilah Shea is a reporter for *New Tribune*. She uses a lap-top computer to transmit stories to the main office. A modem sends the computer messages through phone lines to the office computer. On-the-spot stories are now transmitted this way by 35% of *New Tribune* reporters.

A ratio whose second term is 100 is a percent. **Percent** means **per hundred.** The symbol for percent is **%**.

In the example above, 35% means that the ratio of reporters who use lap-top computers to the total number of reporters is 35 to 100, or $\frac{35}{100}$. This means that 35 out of every 100 reporters transmit stories this way.

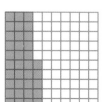
ratio: $\frac{35}{100}$

percent: **35%**

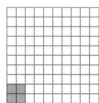
ratio: $\frac{4}{100}$

percent: **4%**

ratio: $\frac{100}{100}$

percent: **100%**

▶ To write a percent as a ratio, divide by 100. $3\% = \frac{3}{100}$

▶ To write a ratio as a percent, find an equal ratio with a second term of 100.

Write $\frac{3}{4}$ as a percent.

$$\frac{3}{4} = \frac{n}{100}$$

$$\frac{3 \times 25}{4 \times 25} = \frac{75}{100}$$

$$\frac{3}{4} = \frac{75}{100} = 75\%$$

Write $\frac{9}{50}$ as a percent.

$$\frac{9}{50} = \frac{n}{100}$$

$$\frac{9 \times 2}{50 \times 2} = \frac{18}{100}$$

$$\frac{9}{50} = \frac{18}{100} = 18\%$$

Write $\frac{6}{200}$ as a percent.

$$\frac{6}{200} = \frac{n}{100}$$

$$\frac{6 \div 2}{200 \div 2} = \frac{3}{100}$$

$$\frac{6}{200} = \frac{3}{100} = 3\%$$

CLASSWORK

Write each percent as a ratio.

1. 15%   **2.** 24%   **3.** 41%   **4.** 125%   **5.** 2%   **6.** 5.25%

Write each ratio as a percent.

7. $\frac{13}{100}$ **8.** 6:100   **9.** $\frac{16.6}{100}$ **10.** $\frac{1}{2}$ **11.** $\frac{4}{5}$ **12.** $\frac{7}{25}$

What percent of each is shaded?

1.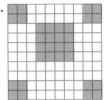
2.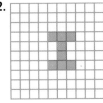
3.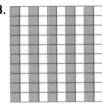
4.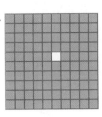

Write each percent as a ratio.

5. 25%   6. 31%   7. 7%   8. 1%   9. 100%   10. 6.5%

Write each ratio as a percent.

11. 9 out of 100   12. 21 out of 100   13. 99 per 100   14. 72:100   15. 1:100

16. $\frac{2}{100}$ 17. $\frac{19}{100}$ 18. $\frac{71}{100}$ 19. $\frac{90}{100}$ 20. $\frac{85}{100}$

21. $\frac{1}{4}$ 22. $\frac{4}{5}$ 23. $\frac{7}{10}$ 24. $\frac{13}{20}$ 25. $\frac{4}{25}$

26. $\frac{1}{2}$ 27. $\frac{1}{5}$ 28. $\frac{3}{10}$ 29. $\frac{7}{20}$ 30. $\frac{21}{25}$

31. $\frac{8}{10}$ 32. $\frac{8}{200}$ 33. $\frac{700}{1,000}$ 34. $\frac{16}{20}$ 35. $\frac{9}{25}$

36. $\frac{10}{500}$ 37. $\frac{950}{1,000}$ ★ 38. $\frac{2}{400}$ ★ 39. $\frac{1}{1,000}$ ★ 40. $\frac{1}{200}$

APPLICATION

41. Just a few years ago, only 2% of the reporters at *New Tribune* used computers. Write this percent as a ratio.

42. Advertisements fill 3 out of every 5 pages of the newspaper. What percent of the newspaper is ads?

VISUAL THINKING

What percent of each is shaded?

1.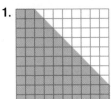
2.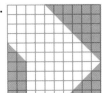
3.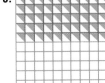

Decimals and Percents

Of every 100 books sold in the United States, 25 are school books.

25% of the books sold are school books.

25% can be written as a decimal.

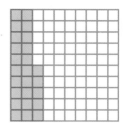

25 hundredths are shaded.

25 hundredths = 0.25

0.25 = 25%

▶To write a percent as a decimal, move the decimal point 2 places to the left.

18.% = 0.18   4.% = 0.04

62.5% = 0.625 $5\frac{1}{2}$% = 5.5% = 0.055

▶To write a decimal as a percent, move the decimal point 2 places to the right.

0.15 = 15%   0.90 = 90%

0.08 = 8%   0.0525 = 5.25%, or $5\frac{1}{4}$%

CLASSWORK

Write each percent as a decimal.

1. 16%   **2.** 35%   **3.** 7%   **4.** 90%   **5.** 14.5%   **6.** $6\frac{3}{4}$%

Write each decimal as a percent.

7. 0.29   **8.** 0.125   **9.** 0.04   **10.** 0.8   **11.** 0.085   **12.** 0.6

PRACTICE

Write each percent as a decimal.

1. 33%	**2.** 1%	**3.** 25%	**4.** 16.2%
5. 20.5%	**6.** 98%	**7.** 13.9%	**8.** 6%
9. $10\frac{1}{2}$%	**10.** 40%	**11.** 4.5%	**12.** $8\frac{1}{4}$%
13. $57\frac{3}{4}$%	**14.** 9.7%	**15.** 1%	**16.** 99.9%

Write each decimal as a percent.

17. 0.84	**18.** 0.7	**19.** 0.03	**20.** 0.35
21. 0.08	**22.** 1.00	**23.** 0.8	**24.** 0.087
25. 0.57	**26.** 0.525	**27.** 0.625	**28.** 0.035

Follow the rule to find each missing number.

Rule: The input and output are equivalent.

	Input decimal	Output percent
29.	0.087	
30.	0.578	
31.		3.5%
32.		7%

	Input percent	Output decimal
33.	19.3%	
34.	66.6%	
35.		0.1925
36.		0.5

Compare. Use >, <, or = for each ⬤.

37. 7.25% ⬤ 0.725

38. 1.5% ⬤ 1.5

39. 0.7 ⬤ 70%

40. 5% ⬤ 0.50

41. 60% ⬤ 0.06

42. 3.5% ⬤ 0.035

APPLICATION

43. *Browsers' Bookstores* report that 30% of their sales are science fiction books. What is the decimal equivalent?

44. Last summer, Terry and Pete ran a paperback-book sale. They sold 95 out of the 100 books they collected. What percent of the books did they sell? What percent did they *not* sell? Write each percent as a decimal.

★ **45.** While flying to California, Martha read 86 pages of a 200-page book. What percent of the book has she not yet finished?

Mixed Practice

1. $3\frac{1}{6} + 2\frac{3}{8}$

2. $\frac{3}{4} + 2\frac{2}{3} + \frac{1}{2}$

3. $23\frac{9}{10} - 12$

4. $6 - 2\frac{3}{7}$

5. $9\frac{1}{3} - 4\frac{3}{5}$

6. $6 \times \frac{5}{6}$

7. $\frac{5}{8} \times \frac{7}{10} \times \frac{4}{7}$

8. $4 \div \frac{2}{5}$

9. $2\frac{1}{3} \div 1\frac{1}{4}$

10. 1.58 + 17.9 + 6

11. 21 × 0.06

12. 16.4 × 0.8

13. $32\overline{)536.96}$

14. $0.4\overline{)29.8}$

15. $1.8\overline{)0.0117}$

Find *n*.

16.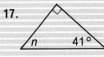

17.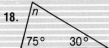

18.

Ratios, Decimals, and Percents

To prepare for a debate, Barbara took a survey of her class at Willow School. Of the students surveyed, 56% felt that the gym should be available on weekends for recreation. Write the percent as a decimal and as a ratio.

▶A percent can be written as a decimal and as a ratio in lowest terms.

$$56\% = 0.56 \qquad 56\% = \frac{56}{100} \div \frac{4}{4} = \frac{14}{25}$$

Of the students surveyed, 0.56, or 14 out of 25, favored opening the gym on weekends.

▶A ratio can be written as a decimal and as a percent. Use one of the following methods.

Use equal ratios.

$$\frac{3}{5} = \frac{3 \times 20}{5 \times 20} = \frac{60}{100}$$
$$\frac{60}{100} = 0.60$$
$$\frac{60}{100} = 60\%$$

Use cross products.

$$\frac{5}{8} = \frac{n}{100}$$
$$5 \times 100 = 8 \times n$$
$$500 = 8n$$
$$62.5 = n$$
$$\frac{62.5}{100} = 62.5\%$$

$$62.5\% = 0.625$$

Use division.

$$\frac{2}{3} = 3\overline{)2.000}$$
$$\begin{array}{r} 0.666 \\ \underline{1\ 8} \\ 20 \\ \underline{18} \\ 20 \\ \underline{18} \\ 2 \end{array}$$

Think
Quotient may be written as a repeating decimal $0.66\overline{6}$ or as $0.66\frac{2}{3}$.

$$\frac{2}{3} = 0.66\overline{6}, \text{ or } 0.66\frac{2}{3}$$
$$0.66\overline{6} = 66.\overline{6}\%, \text{ or } 66\frac{2}{3}\%$$

More Examples

a. $\frac{1}{20} = \frac{1 \times 5}{20 \times 5} = \frac{5}{100}$
$= 0.05 = 5\%$

b. $0.18 = 18\%$
$= \frac{18}{100} = \frac{9}{50}$

c. $72.5\% = 0.725$
$= \frac{725}{1,000} = \frac{29}{40}$

CLASSWORK

Write each ratio as a decimal and as a percent.

1. $\frac{6}{10}$ **2.** $\frac{5}{6}$ **3.** $\frac{1}{8}$ **4.** $\frac{19}{50}$ **5.** $\frac{29}{200}$ **6.** $\frac{17}{20}$

Write each percent as a ratio in lowest terms.

7. 75%   **8.** 80%   **9.** 45%   **10.** 21%   **11.** 24%   **12.** 62.5%

PRACTICE

Write each ratio as a decimal and as a percent.

1. $\frac{28}{100}$ 2. $\frac{12.6}{100}$ 3. $\frac{11}{100}$ 4. $\frac{7}{100}$ 5. $\frac{1}{5}$ 6. $\frac{3}{8}$

7. $\frac{4}{5}$ 8. $\frac{3}{10}$ 9. $\frac{7}{20}$ 10. $\frac{19}{20}$ 11. $\frac{5}{8}$ 12. $\frac{11}{40}$

13. $\frac{3}{25}$ 14. $\frac{195}{1,000}$ 15. $\frac{1}{6}$ 16. $\frac{54}{200}$ 17. $\frac{3}{4}$ 18. $\frac{125}{1,000}$

Write each percent as a ratio in lowest terms.

19. 25% 20. 90% 21. 60% 22. 42% 23. 88% 24. 4%

25. 31% 26. 15% 27. 65% 28. 18% 29. 84% ★ 30. $5\frac{1}{4}$%

Copy and complete.

	Ratio	Decimal	Percent
31.			40%
32.		0.02	
33.	$\frac{17}{1,000}$		
34.		0.19	
35.	$\frac{1}{1}$		

	Ratio	Decimal	Percent
36.			34%
37.		0.08	
38.			7.7%
39.	$\frac{7}{8}$		
40.		0.121	

APPLICATION

41. During the debate, Barbara used 8 minutes to present her opinion, 3 minutes to rebut the opposing opinion, and 5 minutes to summarize. What percent of the time did she spend summarizing?

★ 42. During an hour-long debate, two candidates each answered 8 questions. Each answer took 3 minutes. Each candidate was also given 2 minutes for a closing statement. What percent of the hour was each candidate speaking?

========= CALCULATOR =========

Use a calculator to change each ratio to a percent. Round each percent to the nearest tenth.

Example $\frac{15}{89}$ Press 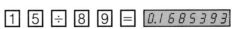 ≈ 16.9%

1. $\frac{13}{29}$ 2. $\frac{214}{534}$ 3. $\frac{327}{814}$ 4. $\frac{358}{1,167}$ 5. $\frac{28}{1,353}$ 6. $\frac{108}{2,000}$

More Percents

The graph shows how a leading automobile company plans to spend its advertising dollars for the coming year. Write the percent of dollars spent in farm journals as a decimal and as a ratio in lowest terms.

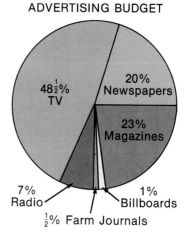

AUTO COMPANY'S
ADVERTISING BUDGET

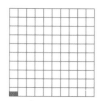

$\frac{1}{2}$% of the amount spent on advertising is spent on ads in farm journals.

$\frac{1}{2}$% = 0.5% = 0.005

$\frac{1}{2}$%

$0.005 = \frac{5}{1,000} = \frac{1}{200}$

The company spends $\frac{1}{2}$%, or 0.005, or $\frac{1}{200}$, of its advertising dollars for ads in farm journals.

Last year the company spent 150% of the amount budgeted for radio advertising. They spent more than the entire amount budgeted. Write the percent as a decimal and as a ratio in lowest terms.

$150\% = 1.50$ $150\% = \frac{150}{100} = \frac{3}{2}$

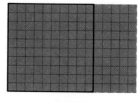

150%

▶To work with percents less than 1 or greater than 100, follow the same rules used for percents between 1 and 100.

More Examples

a. 3 cases out of 10,000

$\frac{3}{10,000} = 0.0003$

$0.0003 = 0.03\%$

b. $2 earned for every $1 saved

$\frac{2}{1} = 2.00 = 200\%$

c. interest rate drop of $\frac{3}{4}$%

$\frac{3}{4} \rightarrow 4\overline{)3.00}$ (quotient 0.75)

$\frac{3}{4}\% = 0.75\%$

$0.75\% = 0.0075$

CLASSWORK

Write each percent as a decimal.

1. 112%   2. 0.8%   3. $\frac{1}{4}$%   4. 250%   5. $\frac{1}{5}$%   6. $\frac{4}{10}$%

Write each decimal or ratio as a percent.

7. 0.2   8. 0.05   9. 0.125   10. 2.3   11. 5.25   12. 3.0

13. $\frac{150}{100}$ 14. $\frac{0.3}{100}$ 15. $\frac{6.5}{100}$ 16. $\frac{4}{1}$ 17. $\frac{5}{4}$ 18. $\frac{18}{10}$

PRACTICE

Write each percent as a decimal.

1. 170% **2.** 0.3% **3.** $\frac{3}{4}$% **4.** 400% **5.** $\frac{4}{5}$% **6.** $\frac{1}{10}$%

7. 0.6% increase in costs   **8.** 200% decline in accidents

9. $\frac{1}{2}$% rise in interest rates   **10.** 125% increase in profits

11. bank interest of $5\frac{1}{4}$%   **12.** finance charge of $18\frac{1}{2}$%

Write each decimal as a percent.

13. 0.4 **14.** 0.125 **15.** 0.09 **16.** 4.5 **17.** 6.25 **18.** 5.0

Write each ratio as a percent.

19. $\frac{125}{100}$ **20.** $\frac{0.6}{100}$ **21.** $\frac{2.75}{100}$ **22.** $\frac{3}{1}$ **23.** $\frac{15}{10}$ **24.** $\frac{4}{3}$

Copy and complete.

	Ratio	Decimal	Percent
25.	$\frac{17}{10}$		
26.		0.008	
27.			370%
28.	$\frac{3}{500}$		
29.			500%

	Ratio	Decimal	Percent
30.		1.07	
31.	$\frac{33}{20}$		
32.			143.1%
33.		1.6	
★34.	$\frac{1}{600}$		

APPLICATION

35. A major food producer used its advertising dollars as follows: 4.7% in newspapers, 7.5% in magazines, 87.2% on television, and 0.6% on radio. Write each of these percents as a ratio and as a decimal.

★36. A major oil company spent 1.3 times as much for advertisements on TV as it did for radio ads. Express this as a percent. For every $100 spent on radio ads, how much did the company spend on TV ads?

NATURE'S BOUNTY
FROM US TO YOU

Problem Solving

SKILLS AND STRATEGIES REVIEW

Use the following information to solve 1–4.

A pigeon flies 36 miles in 3 hours; a courier can walk 2 miles in 30 minutes. An airplane flies 600 miles in $1\frac{1}{2}$ hours; a telephone transmits almost instantaneously. A train travels 80 miles in 80 minutes.

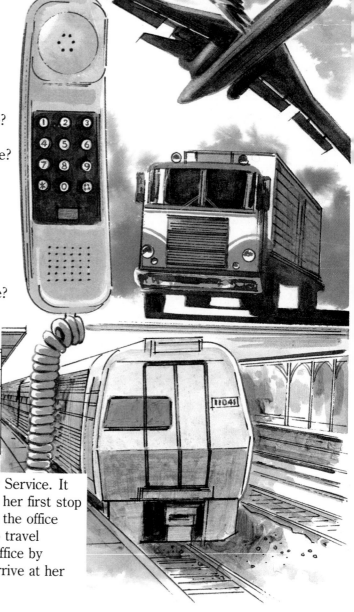

1. Which is the fastest way to deliver a message?

2. Which is the slowest way to deliver a message?

3. List the types of communication described, from fastest to slowest.

4. City Messenger Center handled 645 outgoing messages yesterday. The ratio of incoming to outgoing messages was 2:3. How many incoming messages did they handle?

Use the table below to solve 5.

Stop	Time Spent Waiting
A	20 minutes
B	25 minutes
C	12 minutes
D	20 minutes
E	18 minutes

5. Jan picks up packages for the Speedy Delivery Service. It takes her 15 minutes to get from the office to her first stop (Stop A). It takes her 35 minutes to return to the office from her final stop (Stop E) and 20 minutes to travel between each stop. She must be back in the office by exactly 5:00 P.M. What is the latest she can arrive at her first stop?

Solve.

6. The new satellite has 105 channels for messages. Three channels are turned on the first day, 7 more are turned on the second day, 11 more the third day, and so on. The number of channels turned on each day increases by four. If this pattern continues, in how many days will all 105 channels be turned on?

The drawing below represents a network of small streams. Janet put a message into a bottle and dropped it into the stream at point *A*.

7. How many different paths can the bottle take if it floats downstream to Lucy at point *D*?

8. Suppose Janet's friend Bernie lives at point *F*. How many different paths can the bottle take to float downstream to Bernie?

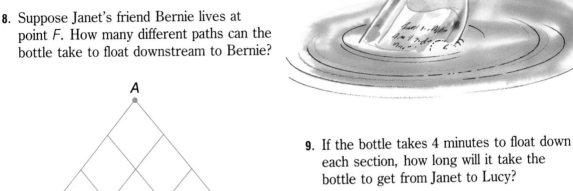

9. If the bottle takes 4 minutes to float down each section, how long will it take the bottle to get from Janet to Lucy?

★ 10. Show all the different places where the bottle could be after floating for 16 minutes.

CHAPTER REVIEW

Use the drawings in A, B, C, and D to write ratios in three ways. pages 278–279

1. A to B
2. C to A
3. B to D
4. C to D
5. A to all
6. A and B to D
7. A to B and D

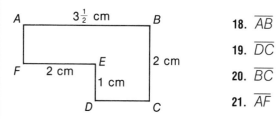

A ▢ ▢ ▢ ▢ ▢   B △ △ △

C ○○○○○○○○○   D ▭ ▭

Use = or ≠ for each ●. pages 280–281

8. $\frac{3}{10}$ ● $\frac{4}{40}$

9. $\frac{7}{8}$ ● $\frac{49}{56}$

10. $\frac{13}{5}$ ● $\frac{90}{35}$

11. $\frac{14}{35}$ ● $\frac{2}{9}$

12. $\frac{5}{3}$ ● $\frac{10}{6}$

Solve each proportion. pages 282–283

13. $\frac{3}{13} = \frac{n}{91}$

14. $\frac{8}{5} = \frac{136}{a}$

15. $\frac{17}{w} = \frac{51}{57}$

16. $\frac{b}{16} = \frac{60}{64}$

17. $\frac{3}{4.2} = \frac{5}{v}$

Use the scale drawing to give the actual length of each side. pages 284–285

A —— $3\frac{1}{2}$ cm —— B
F —— 2 cm —— E, 2 cm, 1 cm
D —— C

scale: 1 cm = 100 m

18. $\overline{AB}$
19. $\overline{DC}$
20. $\overline{BC}$
21. $\overline{AF}$

Which is the better buy? pages 286–287

22. **a.** 2 lb for $.97
    b. 5 lb for $2.34

23. **a.** 8 oz for $1.39
    b. 1 lb 4 oz for $2.50

△ABC is similar to △RST. Find each length. pages 288–289

24. $\overline{RT}$
25. $\overline{ST}$

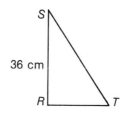

B, 12 cm, 14.4 cm, A, 8 cm, C
S, 36 cm, R, T

Write each ratio as a decimal and as a percent, and write each percent as a decimal. pages 292–299

26. $\frac{5}{8}$
27. $\frac{1}{4}$
28. $\frac{3}{20}$
29. 58.7%
30. $\frac{3}{4}$%
31. 230%

Solve. pages 290–291, 300–301

32. Fred's Furniture Mart spent $780 of its $2,000 advertising budget on a magazine ad. What percent of its budget is that?

33. Lorraine made a reduced photocopy of a poster that was 52 cm wide by 70 cm high. If the copy was 28 cm high, how wide was it?

CHAPTER TEST

Write a ratio for each.

1. 7 chairs, 9 people
    chairs : people

2. 5 wins, 3 losses
    wins : games played

Tell whether or not each is a proportion. Write *yes* or *no*.

3. $\frac{7}{9} = \frac{28}{36}$

4. $\frac{10}{30} = \frac{6}{15}$

5. $\frac{135}{3} = \frac{270}{9}$

Solve each proportion.

6. $\frac{6}{11} = \frac{n}{99}$

7. $\frac{10}{x} = \frac{5}{10}$

8. $\frac{28}{16} = \frac{7}{y}$

9. $\frac{3}{45} = \frac{n}{15}$

Use the scale drawing to find the actual dimension of each.

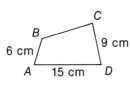
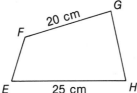

Scale: 1 cm = 0.8 m

10. $\overline{AB}$

11. $\overline{DF}$

12. $\overline{CB}$

Find the unit price of each. Round to the nearest cent.

13. 3 cans for $2.34

14. 6 lemons for $.99

15. 8 bars for $3.00

These two figures are similar. Find the missing measures.

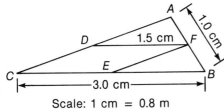

16. $\overline{EF}$ = _____

17. $\overline{BC}$ = _____

Write each ratio as a decimal and as a percent, and write each percent as a decimal.

18. $\frac{21}{100}$

19. $\frac{137}{100}$

20. $\frac{1}{125}$

21. 79%

22. 2.4%

23. 0.5%

Solve.

24. One executive travels by airplane on 3 out of every 4 business trips. Last year she made 36 business trips. On how many trips did she travel by airplane?

25. In a poll a newspaper found that, out of 1,000 readers polled, 550 read more than one paper daily. What percent of the total does that represent?

The ratio of boys to girls working on a school newspaper is 2 : 3. If there are 30 workers altogether, how many are boys?

PROPORTION PROJECT

When artists and painters mix and blend paints, they use proportions in order to get the colors they want.

For this project, you will need:
* poster paint—red, blue, yellow, and white
* 4 sticks
* waxed paper
* 1 paintbrush

Open the jars of poster paint and put a stick in each jar. Mix the paint in each jar.

YELLOW   **RED**   **WHITE**   **BLUE**

Suppose you want to blend red paint and yellow paint in the proportion 1 to 1. Put a dot of red paint on the paper. Put a yellow dot next to it. Use the paintbrush to blend the colors. What color do you get?

Experiment with these proportions. Be sure to clean the brush each time you use it. Name the colors you produce.

1. 2:1 blue to red

2. 1:2 blue to red

3. 1:1 yellow to blue

4. 3:1 yellow to blue

5. 1:3 white to red

6. 2:1 white to blue

7. 1:3 red to yellow

8. 2:3 yellow to red

Use proportions to create colors that could have these names. Write the proportions and exchange them with a classmate. Can he or she make the same color?

9. rusty orange

10. olive green

11. lemon yellow

12. eggplant purple

RATES

You can use proportions to solve problems involving rates.

Blank cassette tapes are selling at a rate of 3 for $4.79. How much will it cost to buy 5 tapes?

3 for $4.79

Use a proportion to find the cost.

Think The ratios of tapes to cost must be equal.

Let n = the cost of 5 tapes.

number of tapes ⟶ $\dfrac{3}{\$4.79} = \dfrac{5}{n}$ ⟵ cost

Use cross products to solve.

$3 \times n = 5 \times \$4.79$

$3n = \$23.95$

$n = \dfrac{\$23.95}{3}$

$n = \$7.983$

The store rounds parts of a cent upward, so 5 tapes will cost $7.99.

The store sold 140 tapes in 2.5 hours. At this rate, how many tapes will they sell in 6 hours?

Think The ratios of tapes to hours must be equal.

tapes sold ⟶ $\dfrac{140}{2.5} = \dfrac{n}{6}$ ⟵ hours

$140 \times 6 = 2.5 \times n$

$840 = 2.5n$

$336 = n$

At this rate the store will sell 336 tapes in 6 hours.

Use a proportion to find each cost.

1. 8 for $3.49
   How much for 20?

2. 6 for $4.95
   How much for 15?

3. 5 for $12.50
   How much for 3?

4. 5 for $11.75
   How much for 3?

5. 6 for $14.50
   How much for 4?

6. 4 for $26.80
   How much for 9?

Solve.

7. Mr. Robbins drives 156 kilometers in 2.6 hours. At this rate, how far will he drive in 6 hours?

8. Mrs. Torres can drive 247 kilometers in 3.8 hours. To the nearest tenth of an hour, how long will it take to drive 120 kilometers?

MAINTAINING SKILLS

Choose the correct answers. Write A, B, C, or D.

1. Complete. $0.147 \text{ kL} = \underline{\hspace{1cm}} \text{ L}$

   A 14.7   C 1,470

   B 147   D not given

2. 234 is divisible by which numbers?

   A 2, 3, and 5   C 3, 5, and 10

   B 2, 5, and 9   D not given

3. What is the LCM of 6 and 8?

   A 24   C 2

   B 48   D not given

4. What is $\frac{12}{30}$ in lowest terms?

   A $\frac{4}{10}$ C $\frac{6}{5}$

   B $\frac{2}{5}$ D not given

5. $16\frac{2}{7} - 5\frac{4}{5}$

   A $11\frac{18}{35}$ C $10\frac{17}{35}$

   B $11\frac{17}{35}$ D not given

6. $12\frac{1}{4} \times 3\frac{3}{7}$

   A 21   C 42

   B 28   D not given

7. What kind of lines are $\overleftrightarrow{AB}$ and $\overleftrightarrow{EF}$?

   A perpendicular   C parallel

   B intersecting   D not given

8. Classify the figure.

   A acute triangle   C obtuse triangle

   B right triangle   D not given

9. Which is a proportion?

   A $\frac{3}{4} = \frac{9}{16}$ C $\frac{14}{2} = \frac{96}{4}$

   B $\frac{7}{9} = \frac{63}{81}$ D not given

10. Solve. $\frac{3}{100} = \frac{n}{1,200}$

    A $n = 36$ C $n = 12$

    B $n = 300$ D not given

11. What is the ratio for 53%?

    A $5\frac{3}{10}$ C $\frac{5}{10}$

    B $\frac{53}{100}$ D not given

12. What is the unit price of 7 cans for $2.45?

    A $17.15   C $1.70

    B $.35   D not given

Solve.

13. The top level of a pyramid has 3 sections. The next level has 6 sections and the next has 12 sections. If this pattern continues, how many levels are there if the lowest level has 96 sections?

    A 6   C 3

    B 4   D not given

14. Complete the pattern. 5, 6, 8, 11, 15, \underline{\hspace{1cm}}

    A 20   C 17

    B 18   D not given

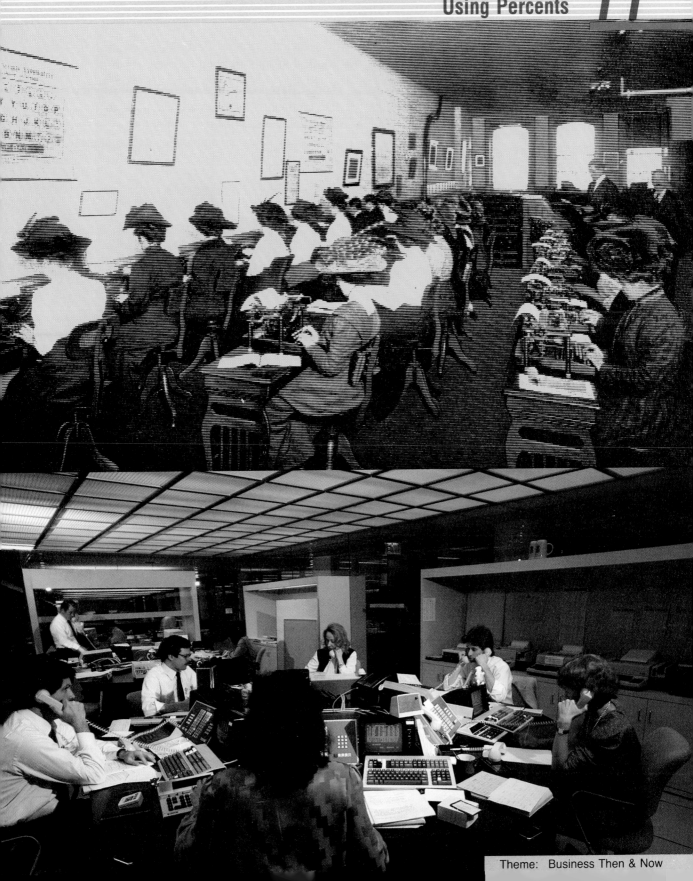

Percent of a Number Using Proportion

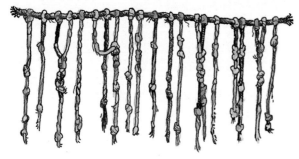

The ancient Incas of Peru used a system of knotted strings to keep records.

Today, businesses like the Lakeland Agency use computers to keep accounts. Of their 80 employees, 45% use computers. How many Lakeland employees use computers?

Find 45% of 80.

▶ To find a percent of a number, you can use a proportion.

Follow these steps.

Step 1   Write a proportion.

$$\overset{\lceil\text{part}\rceil}{\frac{n}{80}} = \frac{45}{100} \quad \text{Let } n = \text{the number of employees}$$
$$\underset{\lfloor\text{whole}\rfloor}{} \quad\quad\quad \text{that use a computer.}$$

Step 2   Use cross products to solve the proportion.

$$\frac{n}{80} = \frac{45}{100}$$
$$100 \times n = 80 \times 45$$
$$100n = 3{,}600$$
$$n = 36$$

Of the 80 employees at the Lakeland Agency, 36 use computers.

More Examples

a. 120% of $75

$$\frac{120}{100} = \frac{n}{75}$$
$$\$9{,}000 = 100n$$
$$\$90 = n$$

b. 5.6% of 30

$$\frac{5.6}{100} = \frac{n}{30}$$
$$168 = 100n$$
$$1.68 = n$$

c. $8\frac{1}{2}$% of 400

$$\frac{8.5}{100} = \frac{n}{400}$$
$$3{,}400 = 100n$$
$$34 = n$$

CLASSWORK

Find the percent of each number.

1. 30% of 390

2. 75% of $400

3. 200% of 37

4. 18% of $72

5. 5.9% of $70

6. 10% of 800

7. 5% of $500

8. $\frac{1}{2}$% of 50

Find the percent of each number.

1. 30% of 120
2. 6% of 4,500
3. 40% of 80
4. 80% of 40

5. 10% of 116.3
6. 80% of 33.5
7. 50% of $118.40
8. 8% of 5,600

9. 25% of $8,000
10. 35% of 2,700
11. 45% of 9,000
12. 75% of 7,600

13. 120% of 45
14. 1% of 85
15. 300% of 95
16. 0.5% of 1,800

★17. 142% of 30
★18. 0.2% of 130
★19. $\frac{1}{2}$% of 90
★20. $6\frac{3}{10}$% of 80

Solve.

21. What number is 10% of 540?
22. What number is 200% of 45?

23. 75% of 160 is what number?
24. 120% of 300 is what number?

25. What is 12% of 75?
26. What is 4% of 18?

APPLICATION

27. American Liberty Insurance Company currently employs 8,100 people at its several locations. Of these employees, 12% use computers. How many American Liberty employees is that?

28. Of the 8,100 American Liberty employees, 24% work part-time. How many of the employees work part-time?

★29. The company plans to offer computer training to 30% of all employees who are *not* currently using a computer. How many employees will they train?

★30. Erica earns $2,500 a month as an employee of American Liberty Insurance Company. She was offered a promotion and an 8% raise. What will her new monthly income be?

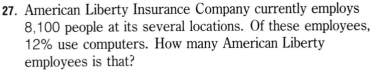

LOGICAL THINKING

1. Does *A*% of *B* always equal *B*% of *A*?

Test your answer by finding each.

2. 5% of 30
   30% of 5

3. 60% of 80
   80% of 60

4. 42% of 34
   34% of 42

5. Do the answers for **2-4** support your answer for **1**?

6. Do you think that *A*% of *B* = *B*% of *A* for any *A* or *B*? Why?

Percent of a Number Using Decimals

The first mail-order business began in 1872. Today, many companies do business through the mail.

SPEED E Mail Order	Name _Ramón Santiago_						
	Street Address _22 Clover Street_						
	City _Glenville_						
	State _Pennsylvania_				Zip _17329_		

CATALOG NUMBER					QUANTITY	DESCRIPTION	PRICE
9	7	2	1	5	1	Solar Calculator	$13.00

How much sales tax must Ramon pay?

The order form shows that Ramon bought a calculator for $13.00.

The sales tax in his state is 6%.

Find 6% of $13.00.

Often it is easier to use a decimal than a proportion when finding percents.

▶To find a percent of a number, change the percent to a decimal and multiply.

$$6\% \times \$13.00 = 0.06 \times \$13.00$$

$$\begin{array}{r} \$13.00 \\ \times \quad 0.06 \\ \hline \$.7800 \end{array}$$

Ramon must pay $.78 tax.

More Examples

a. 150% of 90

$1.50 \times 90 = n$

$135 = n$

b. 9.3% of 200

$0.093 \times 200 = n$

$18.6 = n$

c. $3\frac{1}{2}$% of 80 **Think** $3\frac{1}{2}\% = 3.5\%$

$0.035 \times 80 = n$

$2.8 = n$

CLASSWORK

Find the percent of each number. Use decimals.

1. 40% of 90

2. 18% of $72

3. 7% of $24

4. 300% of 75

5. 8.5% of $80

6. $1\frac{1}{2}$% of 110

7. $5\frac{1}{4}$% of $300

8. $\frac{3}{4}$% of 80

PRACTICE

Use a decimal to find the percent of each number.

1. 20% of 90
2. 65% of $850
3. 9% of 345
4. 15% of $68

5. 17% of 80
6. 100% of 87
7. 150% of 92
8. 82% of 45

9. 75% of $97.40
10. 300% of 125
11. 35% of $195
12. 4.5% of $1,600

13. $9\frac{1}{2}$% of $8,000
14. 3.5% of 160,000
15. 0.3% of 500
16. $26\frac{1}{2}$% of 76

17. 0.7% of 900
18. 20% of 4
19. $5\frac{1}{4}$% of $1,000
20. $\frac{1}{2}$% of 350

21. $\frac{3}{4}$% of 12,000
22. $\frac{1}{2}$% of 8,000
23. $5\frac{1}{4}$% of 11,400
24. $5\frac{3}{4}$% of 10,000

25. $\frac{3}{4}$% of $1,800
26. $33\frac{1}{3}$% of 975
★ 27. $1\frac{5}{8}$% of 64
★ 28. $\frac{3}{8}$% of 4,000

NEW TECH!

The Ultimate Fitness Machine

Cat. Number S-5862... $449.

APPLICATION

29. New Tech offers a stereo component set for $985. What is the total cost if you must include 7% sales tax?

30. New Tech is running a sale on a home alarm system that usually sells for $750. Anyone who buys the alarm system this month will save 10%. What is this month's price?

★ 31. What is the total cost of New Tech's fitness machine if the shipping charge is 5% of the price and the sales tax is $6\frac{1}{2}$% of the price of the machine? Round the answer to the nearest cent.

MENTAL ARITHMETIC

Use the rules for multiplying by powers of 10 to find the percent of each number.

Examples 10% of 9 = 0.1 × 9 = 0.9   1% of 9 = 0.01 × 9 = 0.09

1. 10% of 16
2. 1% of 8
3. 10% of 15

4. 100% of 33
5. 10% of 150
6. 1% of $1 000

7. 10% of $5,000
8. 200% of 75
9. 300% of $50

★10. 15% of 40
★11. 15% of 80
★12. 15% of 50

311

Finding the Percent

In the 1800s, people were expected to work 14 hours a day. What percent of the day did they work?

You can use a proportion to solve the problem.

$\frac{n}{100} = \frac{14}{24}$ **Think** 14 hours is $\frac{14}{24}$ of the day.

$n \times 24 = 100 \times 14$

$24n = 1,400$

$n = 58.\overline{3}\%,\ \text{or}\ 58\frac{1}{3}\%$

In the 1800s, people worked $58\frac{1}{3}\%$ of the day.

Today, most businesses have an 8-hour workday. What percent of the day are modern workers at their jobs?

You can use a decimal to solve the problem.

What percent of 24 is 8?

$n \times 24 = 8$

$\frac{n \times 24}{24} = \frac{8}{24}$

$n = \frac{8}{24} = \frac{1}{3}$

$n = 33\frac{1}{3}\%$

Modern workers are at their jobs $33\frac{1}{3}\%$ of the day.

More Examples

a. What percent of 18 is 27?

$n \times 18 = 27$

$\frac{n \times 18}{18} = \frac{27}{18}$

$n = \frac{27}{18} = \frac{3}{2} = 1.5 = 150\%$

27 is 150% of 18.

b. 3 is what percent of 8?

$3 = n \times 8$

$\frac{3}{8} = n$

$0.375 = 37.5\% = n$

3 is 37.5% of 8.

CLASSWORK

Find each percent.

1. What percent of 12 is 9?

2. 11 is what percent of 20?

3. $24 is what percent of $40?

4. 80 is what percent of 20?

Find each percent.

1. What percent of 10 is 7?

2. What percent of $50 is $21?

3. What percent of 20 is 65?

4. What percent of $200 is $14?

5. 9 is what percent of 72?

6. $5 is what percent of $1,000?

7. 65 is what percent of 100?

8. 4,320 is what percent of 9,000?

9. 32 is what percent of 96?

10. $36 is what percent of $450?

11. What percent of 10 is $\frac{1}{2}$?

12. What percent of $35 is $4.20?

13. What percent of 600 is 27?

14. What percent of 540 is 135?

★15. What percent of 75 is 0.375?

★16. What percent of 16 is 0.64?

★17. $2,700 is what percent of $180,000?

★18. $675 is what percent of $90,000?

APPLICATION

19. At Wilcon Jeans Company, 80 of the 200 employees work part-time. What percent of the employees is that?

20. On Tuesday, 35 of the 200 Wilcon employees worked overtime. What percent of the employees is that?

21. In a week, Ramona works 40 hours. What percent of a week does she work?

★22. At the Outlet Store, 45 employees work the early shift, 125 work the middle shift, and 30 work the late shift. What percent of the employees work the late shift?

PERCENT OF INCREASE OR DECREASE

To find the percent of increase or decrease, write a ratio of the amount of increase or decrease to the original amount. Then express the ratio as a percent.

salary increase from $72 to $90

amount of increase = $90 − $72 = $18

percent of increase = $\frac{\text{amount of increase}}{\text{original}}$

$\qquad = \frac{18}{72} = 0.25$

percent of increase = 25%

price decrease from $200 to $175

amount of decrease = $200 − $175 = $25

percent of decrease = $\frac{\text{amount of decrease}}{\text{original}}$

$\qquad = \frac{25}{200} = 0.125$

percent of decrease = 12.5%

Find the percent of increase or decrease to the nearest percent.

1. salary increase from $95 to $100

2. attendance drop from 25 to 23

3. workweek reduction from 40 h to $37\frac{1}{2}$ h

4. 93 games won last year, 85 won this year

Finding the Number When a Percent of It Is Known

Since the 1940s, businesses have known that television commercials are powerful advertisements. In a recent survey, 160 teenagers said that television influences them to buy certain products. How many teenagers were surveyed?

80% of what number is 160?

$$80\% \times n = 160$$
$$0.80n = 160$$
$$n = 160 \div 0.80$$
$$n = 200$$

200 teenagers were surveyed.

Sometimes it is easier to use a ratio than a decimal when working with percents.

50% of what number is 30?

$$50\% \times n = 30$$
$$\frac{50}{100} \times n = 30$$
$$\frac{1}{2}n = 30$$
$$n = 60$$

More Examples

a. 45% of what number is 36?

$$45\% \times n = 36$$
$$0.45n = 36$$
$$n = 36 \div 0.45$$
$$n = 80$$

45% of 80 is 36.

b. 3 is 0.6% of what number?

$$3 = 0.6\% \times n$$
$$3 = 0.006n$$
$$\frac{3}{0.006} = n$$
$$500 = n$$

3 is 0.6% of 500.

CLASSWORK

Find n.

1. 15% of n is 45.

2. 25% of n is 30.

3. 10% of n is 1.

Solve.

4. 105 is 42% of what number?

5. 40% of what number is 18?

6. 50% of $64 is what number?

7. 285 is 125% of what number?

PRACTICE

Find _n_.

1. 12% of _n_ is 3.

2. 20% of _n_ is $17.

3. $48 is 32% of _n_.

4. 6 is 16% of _n_.

5. 28 is 25% of _n_.

6. 125% of _n_ is 200.

7. 15% of _n_ is $75.

8. 125% of _n_ is 20.

9. 5% of _n_ is 15.

Solve.

10. 45 is 4% of what number?

11. $18 is 0.6% of what number?

12. 5% of what number is 0.2?

13. 50% of what number is 160?

14. 27 is 75% of what number?

15. 105 is 150% of what number?

16. 30% of what number is 120?

17. 48% of what number is 8.64?

18. 0.45 is 3% of what number?

★**19.** $1\frac{1}{2}$% of what number is $3?

★**20.** 8 is $\frac{1}{4}$% of what number?

★**21.** 0.3% of what number is 12?

APPLICATION

22. Don Jackson spends $450 each month on newspaper advertising. If this is 75% of his monthly advertising budget, how much does he spend on advertising each month?

23. The Easy Run Sneaker Company spent $2,500 on magazine ads this month. That is 80% of the amount spent on newspaper ads. How much did the company spend this month on newspaper ads?

24. Lucy spent $12.50 for a year's subscription to _Ad-Time_ magazine. This represented a 40% savings of the newsstand price. What would be the yearly cost of buying _Ad-Time_ at the newsstand?

★**25.** In the 1984 Olympic Games, television and radio rights sold for $280 million. This represented 54.5% of the total income from the games. Find the total income. Round your answer to the nearest million.

CALCULATOR

2 is 5% of what number?   **Press** ⎡2⎤ ⎡÷⎤ ⎡.⎤ ⎡0⎤ ⎡5⎤ ⎡=⎤ ⟶ ▨ 40.

Many calculators have a percent key ⎡%⎤. If your calculator has such a key, use the percent key instead of changing the percent to a decimal.

Press ⎡2⎤ ⎡÷⎤ ⎡5⎤ ⎡%⎤ ⟶ ▨ 40.

Find _n_, using your calculator.

1. 27% of _n_ is 54.

2. 14% of _n_ is 7.7.

3. 16.5% of _n_ is 13.86.

Problem Solving

MAKING AND USING GRAPHS

Graphs are an excellent way of presenting information. They help to organize the facts in a problem.

1. Jan starts selling watches on Monday. She sells 10 watches each day. On what day will her total sales reach 50 watches?

On what day will Jan's total sales reach 50?

She starts on Monday.
She sells 10 watches each day.

Make a graph.

Use the horizontal axis for days of the week.
Use the vertical axis for total sales.
List multiples of 10 along the vertical axis.
Graph the information.
Put a dot where Monday and 10 intersect.
Increase the number of total watches sold by 10 for each day that follows. Place the dots.
Connect the dots with a straight line, as shown.
Read 50 on the vertical axis.
The corresponding day is Friday.
Jan's total sales will reach 50 watches on Friday.

Check to be sure you graphed the information carefully and read the graph correctly.

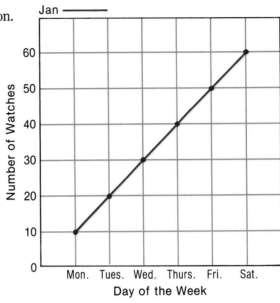

TOTAL SALES

2. Lou starts selling watches on Wednesday. He sells 15 watches each day. On what day will Lou's total sales equal Jan's total? How many watches will each have sold?

Using the graph from problem **1**, a second line is drawn to show Lou's sales.

The point at which the two lines cross represents the day that their total sales will be equal and the total number sold.

Use the graph to answer the two questions.

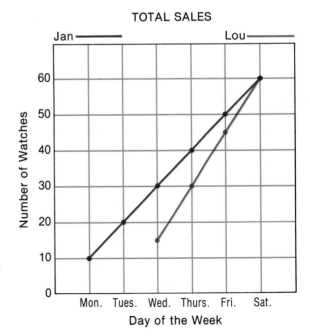

TOTAL SALES

PRACTICE

This graph shows the number of orders received by the Atlas Asphalt Company during one week. Use the graph to answer each question.

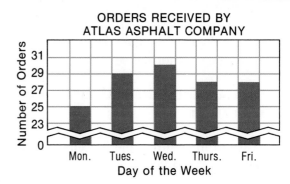

ORDERS RECEIVED BY ATLAS ASPHALT COMPANY

1. How many orders did they receive on Monday?

2. On what day did they receive the greatest number of orders?

3. How many orders did they receive during the week?

4. What was the average number of orders received per day?

5. What percent of the weekly orders was received on Thursday?

⋆ **6.** What was the percent of increase in orders received on Thursday over Monday?

Use the information below to answer 7–10.

The Keystone Auto Dealer sold 10 cars on Monday, 15 on Tuesday, 5 on Wednesday, 10 on Thursday, 30 on Friday, and 35 on Saturday.

7. Make a graph like the ones on page 316 to show the sales for the week.

8. Irene sold 20% of the cars. How many did she sell?

9. What percent of the cars were sold on Monday through Friday?

10. On what day were $33\frac{1}{3}$% of the total sales made?

11. The Benson Messenger Service sent Iris to deliver a package to a client 240 miles away. Iris started out at 12:00 noon traveling at 40 miles per hour. The company sent Mitch to deliver a second package to the same client. Mitch left at 1:00 P.M. and traveled at 50 miles per hour along the same route. At what time will Mitch catch up with Iris?

⋆ **12.** The Royal Fuel Company is delivering oil to Jennifer's house. The truck contains 800 gallons of oil. Jennifer's oil tank has 100 gallons left in it. The tank holds 500 gallons when full. The oil is transferred at the rate of 100 gallons in 5 minutes. How long will it take for the truck and the tank to contain the same amount of oil? How much oil will be in the tank?

CREATE YOUR OWN PROBLEM

Write a problem that uses the information shown on the graph.

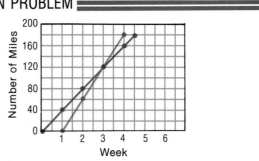

Discounts

Valley Nursery ordered $175 worth of seeds. How much discount did they receive? How much did they pay for the seeds?

The **discount** is the amount that the regular price is reduced.

The **rate of discount** is the percent that the regular price is reduced.

▶To find the discount, use this formula.

discount = regular price × rate of discount

d = $175 × 15%

d = $175 × 0.15

d = $26.25   Valley Nursery received a discount of $26.25.

▶To find the sale price, use this formula.

sale price = regular price − discount

sale price = $175 − $26.25

= $148.75   Valley Nursery paid $148.75 for their seed order.

Another Example

Find the sale price.

regular price: $70   discount: 20%

discount = regular price × rate of discount

d = $70 × 20%

d = $70 × 0.20

d = $14

sale price = regular price − discount

= $70 − $14

= $56

CLASSWORK

Complete. Round each discount to the nearest cent.

	Regular Price	Rate of Discount	Discount	Sale Price
1.	$84	25%		
2.	$40	15%		
3.	$36	15%		
4.	$2.90	8%		

PRACTICE

Find the discount and the sale price for each.

1.   $22.50
33⅓% off

2.  $39.86
15% off

3. $10.50
25% off

4.   $32.00
12½% off

5.  $80.00
15% off

6. $50.00
25% off

7. regular price: $8.40
rate of discount: 15%

8. regular price: $2,715
rate of discount: 30%

9. regular price: $998
rate of discount: 40%

10. regular price: $200
rate of discount: 25%

11. regular price: $187.50
rate of discount: 33⅓%

12. regular price: $7,985
rate of discount: 22%

13. regular price: $195
rate of discount: 20%

14. regular price: $900
rate of discount: 25%

Copy and complete each chart.

	10% DISCOUNT	
	Regular Price	Sale Price
15.	$1,485.00	
16.	$ 308.00	
17.	$ 967.00	

	15% DISCOUNT	
	Regular Price	Sale Price
18.	$4,000.00	
19.	$6,700.00	
20.	$5,800.00	

	8.5% DISCOUNT	
	Regular Price	Sale Price
★ **21.**	$ 250.00	
★ **22.**	$ 840.00	
★ **23.**	$1,020.00	

	13.75% DISCOUNT	
	Regular Price	Sale Price
★ **24.**	$10,500.00	
★ **25.**	$12,700.00	
★ **26.**	$18,200.00	

APPLICATION

27. Valley Nursery placed orders with The Green Thumb Seed Company for the following amounts: $187, $220, and $160. Find the total discount received.

★ **28.** Bob received a **chain discount** of 10 and 10 on a $950 purchase. This means 10% off and then 10% off the new balance. Find the sale price. Is this the same as getting 20% off?

Mixed Practice

1. $1.257 + 13.07$

2. $9.75 - 4.8$

3. $18 - 6.175$

4. 452×0.19

5. $18\overline{)667.08}$

6. $6.7\overline{)57.352}$

7. $1\frac{5}{8} + 2\frac{1}{6}$

8. $18\frac{3}{10} - 13\frac{3}{4}$

9. $27 - 6\frac{7}{8}$

10. $\frac{15}{16} \times 4$

11. $1\frac{1}{3} \times 5\frac{3}{8}$

12. $\frac{8}{15} \div \frac{16}{25}$

13. $4\frac{1}{5} \div \frac{7}{10}$

Name each figure.

14.

15.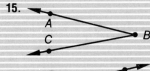

16.

17.

319

Simple Interest

In the early 1800s a New York furniture company introduced the method of buying that revolutionized American business. It was called the **installment plan.**

Buying an item on the installment plan usually means you will pay more for the item. The extra charge for borrowing the money is called **interest.** The original amount of money is called the **principal.** Your money can earn interest for you when it is deposited in a bank.

The amount of interest, paid or earned, is determined by the **rate of interest,** or the percent charged or earned on the money each year.

Sarah is thinking of using an installment plan when she buys this chair. If she takes 2 years to pay, how much will the interest be? How much will Sarah pay for the chair?

Easy Installment Plan 14% 3 Years to pay

▶ To find the amount of interest, use this formula. $I = p \times r \times t$

$$\text{Interest} = \text{principal} \times \text{rate} \times \text{time}$$
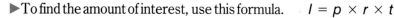
Always express the time in years.

$I = \$500 \times 14\% \times 2$

$I = \$500 \times 0.14 \times 2$

The interest will be \$140.

$I = \$140$

▶ To find the cost of an item, add the interest to the principal.

cost = principal + interest = \$500 + \$140 = \$640
Sarah will pay \$640 if she uses the installment plan.

Another Example

savings account deposit: \$1,200 $I = p \times r \times t$

rate: 12% $I = \$1,200 \times 0.12 \times 0.5$ ←**Think** 6 months = $\frac{1}{2}$ year, or 0.5 year

time: 6 months $I = \$72$

The interest is \$72. The new savings account balance will be \$1,272.

CLASSWORK

Find the interest earned for each.

1. bank deposit: \$350
   rate: 6%
   time: 1 year

2. loan: \$1,000
   rate: 13%
   time: 3 years

3. loan: \$800
   rate: 10.5%
   time: 6 months

PRACTICE

Find the interest earned or paid for each.

1. bank deposit: $500
   rate: 5%
   time: 1 year

2. loan: $1,000
   rate: 12%
   time: 2 years

3. principal: $3,500
   rate: 7%
   time: 3 years

4. loan: $50
   rate: $8\frac{1}{4}$%
   time: 1 year

5. installment purchase:
   $890
   rate: $7\frac{1}{2}$%
   time: 4 years

6. loan: $150
   rate: 6%
   time: 6 months

7. installment purchase:
   $275
   rate: 8%
   time: 6 months

8. installment purchase:
   $2,640
   rate: $8\frac{1}{2}$%
   time: 3 years

★ 9. loan: $1,800
   rate: $9\frac{1}{2}$%
   time: 9 months

Copy and complete the chart.

	Principal	Interest Rate	Time	Interest	New Balance
10.	$2,300	$9\frac{1}{4}$%	1 year		
11.	$10,800	11%	2 years		
12.	$750	8%	6 months		
13.	$1,250	$10\frac{1}{2}$%	6 months		
★ 14.	$1,400	$8\frac{1}{4}$%	15 months		

APPLICATION

15. Mario and June used a 2-year installment plan to buy a
    dining room set priced at $1,849. The interest rate is 14%
    a year. Find the amount of interest and the total cost of
    the dining room set.

★ 16. Find the monthly payments on a car purchase of $8,200
    that is financed for 3 years at 8.8%.

VISUAL THINKING

Write clear directions for
Scott to drive from his home
in Clayton to his new office
in Masonville.

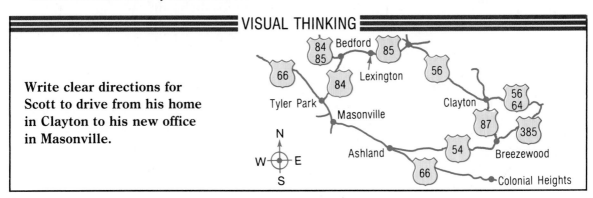

Problem Solving

SKILLS AND STRATEGIES REVIEW

The newest business in the local shopping mall, Computer Universe, is having a grand-opening sale.

1. How many hours per week is Computer Universe open?

2. What percent of their business hours are on Saturday?

3. Computer Universe is awarding door prizes to the first 100 people who make a purchase. They are giving away floppy disks and audio tapes. The disks cost them $1.25 each, and the tapes cost them 85¢ each. The total cost to the store is $99. How many of each kind of prize will they give away?

5. The store manager loaded a program for Mike to try. Part of the display is shown. If this pattern continues, in which column would the number 52 appear?

Computer Universe Store Hours	
Mon. – Wed.	10 AM – 8 PM
Thurs., Fri.	10 AM – 9 PM
Sat.	10 AM – 6 PM

4. The store spent the following amounts on advertising:
   Give-away gifts totaling $99
   150 posters at $1.50 each
   1,000 announcements at 7¢ each
   1,000 postage stamps at 22¢ each
   How much over their budget are they?

A	B	C	D	E
1	10	2	9	3
6	15	7	14	8
11	20	12	19	13
.	.	.	.	.
.	.	.	.	.

6. Logo, a computer language, is used to move a figure, called a turtle, on the screen. Computer Universe is having a Logo demonstration for beginners. The table of commands for the turtle is shown at the right. After you follow the last command, how far is the turtle from its starting point? Make a drawing to show the turtle's path.

```
FORWARD 10 means "Move forward
10 units."
RIGHT 90 means "Turn right 90
degrees."
FORWARD 10 RIGHT 90
FORWARD 20 RIGHT 90
FORWARD 50 RIGHT 90
FORWARD 10 RIGHT 90
FORWARD 20 RIGHT 90
FORWARD 5  RIGHT 90
FORWARD 5  RIGHT 90
FORWARD 15
```

7. Mrs. Carson sold an average of 33 calculators per day for the first 3 days of the sale. She sold 47 on Monday and 18 on Tuesday. How many calculators did she sell on Wednesday?

8. Adam returned a calculator because the [7] key didn't work. He told the manager that he could not do this homework problem, 667 − 374. The manager showed him how to do it on the broken calculator. How can it be done?

Problem Solving

WHAT WOULD YOU DO . . . ?

Fantastic Videos offers a club plan for renting videos. For nonmembers an $80 refundable deposit is required each time you rent. Nonmember rental fees are $2.50 a day during the week and $5.00 a day on weekends. In the coming year, you expect to rent 20 videos on weekends and 5 during the week.

FANTASTIC VIDEO CLUB PLAN

Membership only $75 per year
8 free weekend rentals per year
—Any movie:—
$1.50 per day on weekdays
$2.00 per day on weekends

Answer each question and explain the answer.

1. Do you think it is more economical to be a member or a nonmember?

2. Would you calculate the actual benefits, if any, of membership?

3. Would you shop around to find better club plans?

4. Would you prefer not to have to bring an $80 deposit each time you rented?

What would you do?

Complete the chart below to calculate the benefits of membership.

Membership	Nonmembership
Fee:	Fee:
Free Videos:	Free Videos:
Weekend Rates:	Weekend Rates:
Weekday Rates:	Weekday Rates:
Total:	Total:

How much would you save by becoming a member?

Fantastic Videos developed a new plan for members. Once you have rented 25 videos, a 20% discount is given on each additional video. You have already rented 25 videos.

Answer each question and explain the answer.

5. Could you now rent 3 videos on the weekend for less than $4?

6. How many videos could you rent during the week for less than $10?

What would you do?

7. How many videos do you think you would rent during the week? On weekends? Would you choose to be a member of this club?

CHAPTER REVIEW

Use a proportion to find each. pages 308–309

1. 40% of 150   **2.** 70% of 60   **3.** 75% of $124   **4.** 9% of $4,000

Use a decimal to find each. pages 310–311

5. 300% of 135   **6.** 35% of $225   **7.** 3.5% of 92   **8.** $8\frac{1}{2}$% of 250

Find each percent. pages 312–313

9. What percent of 56 is 35?   **10.** What percent of 40 is 68?

11. What percent of 45 is 18?   **12.** 18.7 is what percent of 85?

13. 336 is what percent of 960?   **14.** $21.78 is what percent of $1,452?

Find *n*. pages 314–315

15. 24% of *n* is 36.   **16.** 0.8% of *n* is 3.   **17.** 130 is 6.5% of *n*.

18. 17% of *n* is $115.60.   **19.** $13\frac{1}{2}$% of *n* is 405.   **20.** 266.4 is $27\frac{3}{4}$% of *n*.

Copy and complete the chart. pages 318–319

	Regular Price	Rate of Discount	Discount	Sale Price
21.	$16.50	20%		
22.	$24.60	$33\frac{1}{3}$%		
23.	$15.00	20%		
24.	$55.00	15%		

Find the interest earned and the new balance for each. pages 320–321

25. $624 at 7% for 5 years   **26.** $800 at 9% for 6 months

27. $750 at $10\frac{1}{2}$% for 3 years   **28.** $1,000 at $8\frac{3}{4}$% for 2 years

Solve. pages 316–317; 322–323

29. Mrs. Cata's company increased the number of employees by 4.8%. If she started with 1,250 employees, how many workers were added?

30. Use the graph at the right. What percent of the computers were sold on Monday and Tuesday?

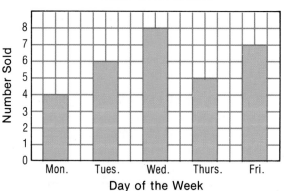

COMPUTER SALES

CHAPTER TEST

Use a proportion or a decimal to find each.

1. 30% of 250

2. 18% of $435

3. 9% of $84

4. 0.4% of 5,000

5. What percent of 96 is 24?

6. What percent of $185 is $74?

7. What percent of 74 is 259?

8. What percent of 184 is 27.6?

9. 32% of n is 304.

10. 14% of n is $80.50.

11. 108.4 is 8% of n.

12. $3\frac{1}{2}$% of n is $26.60.

Copy and complete the chart.

	Original Price	Rate of Discount	Discount
13.		$12\frac{1}{2}$%	$15
14.	$ 65	20%	
15.	$395		$59.25

Find the interest earned and the new balance for each.

16. principal: $450

    rate: $6\frac{1}{2}$%

    time: 4 years

17. principal: $2,800

    rate: 12%

    time: 6 months

18. principal: $3,750

    rate: 14%

    time: 2 years

Solve.

19. Use the graph at the right. What percent of the hours for June did Jerry work during the first week?

20. To purchase a new computer, Lakeland Agency borrowed $7,000 at $13\frac{1}{4}$% for 5 years. How much interest will the agency pay?

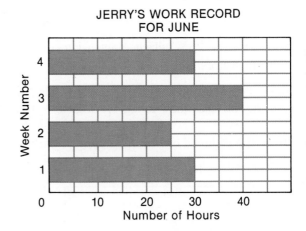

JERRY'S WORK RECORD FOR JUNE

Week Number / Number of Hours

Suppose you borrow $8,000 for 4 years at $12\frac{1}{2}$% interest. If you repay the loan in equal monthly installments, how much would you pay each month?

ENLARGEMENTS AND REDUCTIONS

The colorful rectangle below is the symbol, or logo, for a large manufacturing company. A reduced size of the symbol appears on the company stationery. An enlargement is used for posters and ads. The amount of enlargement or reduction is often given as a percent of the original size.

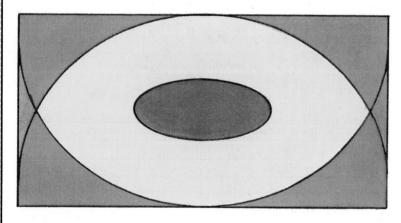

Trace the logo.
Follow the steps to make a copy that is 25% larger than the original.

• Measure the length of the original. ⟶ **4 in.**

• Find 25% of the length. ⟶ **25% × 4**
0.25 × 4 = 1 in.

• Find the length of the enlarged copy. ⟶ **new length = original + enlargement**
= 4 in. + 1 in. = 5 in.

• Use the same method to find the width of the enlarged copy. ⟶ **25% of 2 in.**
0.25 × 2 = 0.5 in.
new width = 2 in. + 0.5 in. = 2.5 in.

Now draw the 25% enlargement using the new length and width measures.

Make a copy of the logo that is 50% smaller than the original. Use the formula   new length = original − reduction.

Draw the reduced or enlarged copy of each logo.

1. 50% enlargement

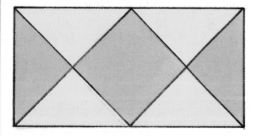

2. 40% reduction

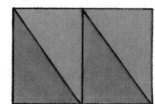

INCOME TAX

The United States federal government and many state governments require an **income tax.** Find your **taxable income** by following the instructions in the government booklets.

There are two kinds of income tax forms. You can either file a detailed report or a short form. People choose the method that is best for them.

Mr. and Mrs. Stewart are filing a joint income tax return using the short form. They compute their taxable income to be $13,590. From the tax table at the right, they find that their income tax due is $1,353.

The Mancinis file their income tax using a detailed form. They use the tax-rate schedule below to find the income tax due on their taxable income of $26,785.

TAX TABLE

If 1040 A, line 19, or 1040EZ, line 7 is—		And you are—			
At least	But less than	Single (and 1040EZ filers)	Married filing jointly	Married filing separately	Head of a household
		Your tax is—			
13,000					
13,000	13,050	1,606	1,265	1,914	1,539
13,050	13,100	1,616	1,273	1,926	1,548
13,100	13,150	1,626	1,281	1,939	1,557
13,150	13,200	1,636	1,289	1,951	1,566
13,200	13,250	1,646	1,297	1,964	1,575
13,250	13,300	1,656	1,305	1,976	1,584
13,300	13,350	1,666	1,313	1,989	1,593
13,350	13,400	1,676	1,321	2,001	1,602
13,400	13,450	1,686	1,329	2,014	1,611
13,450	13,500	1,696	1,337	2,026	1,620
13,500	13,550	1,706	1,345	2,039	1,629
13,550	13,600	1,716	1,353	2,051	1,638
13,600	13,650	1,726	1,361	2,064	1,647
13,650	13,700	1,736	1,369	2,076	1,656
13,700	13,750	1,746	1,377	2,089	1,665
13,750	13,800	1,756	1,385	2,101	1,674

TAX-RATE SCHEDULE

Taxable Income		Income Tax Due	
At least	But less than		On the amount over
$15,000	$18,000	$ 2,000 + 23%	$15,000
$18,200	$23,500	$ 2,737 + 26%	$18,200
$23,500	$28,800	$ 4,115 + 30%	$23,500
$28,800	$34,100	$ 5,705 + 34%	$28,800
$34,100	$41,500	$ 7,507 + 38%	$34,100
$41,500	$55,300	$10,319 + 42%	$41,500

Income tax due = **$4,115 + 30% of amount over $23,500**
= $4,115 + 30% of ($26,785 − $23,500)
= $4,115 + 30% of ($3,285)
= $4,115 + (0.30 × $3,285)
= $4,115 + $985.50
= **$5,100.50 or $5,101** ← rounded to nearest dollar

Use the tax table to find the income tax due on each taxable income for a single person.

1. $13,199   **2.** $13,260   **3.** $13,601   **4.** $13,749.99

Use the tax-rate schedule to find the income tax due on each taxable income. **Round to the nearest dollar if necessary.**

5. $21,650   **6.** $30,390   **7.** $43,775   **8.** $35,200

COMPUTING PROFIT AND LOSS

Computers are often used to prepare financial reports. The program below uses READ and DATA statements to assign values to the variables for income and expenses.

The statement **READ A** assigns the next number in the **DATA** statement to the variable **A**.

Example Together these statements assign the values A = 14 and B = 23.

```
10 READ A ,B
20 DATA 14 ,23
```

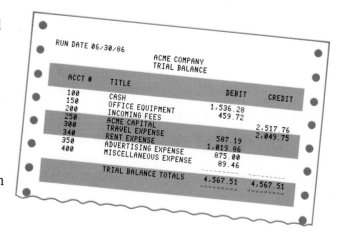

This program uses the income and expenses for two years to compute the profit or loss for each year.

PROGRAM

```
10 REM FINANCIAL REPORT
```

Use spaces inside the quotation marks to center the title. ⟶
```
20 PRINT "        ACME COMPANY"
```

```
30 PRINT"        FINANCIAL REPORT"
```
Print a blank line. ⟶
```
40 PRINT
```

Print headings for each column. ⟶
```
50 PRINT "*****" , "1987" , "1988"
```
```
60 PRINT
```

Store the 1987 income and expenses in I1 and E1. ⟶
```
70 READ I1 , E1
```
Store the 1988 income and expenses in I2 and E2. ⟶
```
80 READ I2 , E2
```

Display the input information. ⟶
```
90 PRINT "INCOME" , I1 , I2
```
```
100 PRINT "EXPENSES" , E1 , E2
```

Compute the profit or loss for each year. ⟶
```
110 LET P1 = I1 - E1
```
```
120 LET P2 = I2 - E2
130 PRINT "PROFIT/LOSS" , P1 , P2
```
Display the profit or loss. ⟶

The values to be read are listed in order. ⟶
```
140 DATA 12463 , 12827 , 14820 , 13425
```
```
150 END
```

Placing DATA statements near the end of a program makes them easy to find and change.

Write READ and DATA statements to assign values for each variable.

1. $K = 19$, $M = 36$

2. $A = 6$, $H = 7$, $Z = 49$

3. $B = 8$, $J = 24$, $S = 80$

4. $R = 10$, $S = 20$, $T = 30$, $U = 40$

Write the output for each program.

5.
```
10 READ W , X
20 READ Y , Z
30 PRINT W/X
40 PRINT Y/Z
50 DATA 10 , 20
60 DATA 25 , 100
70 END
```

6.
```
10 READ A , B
20 LET P = A/B * 100
30 PRINT A;"/";B;"=";P;"%"
40 DATA 1 , 5
50 END
```

7.
```
10 FOR I = 1 TO 3
20 READ P
30 LET D = P/100
40 PRINT P;"% =";D
50 NEXT I
60 DATA 40 , 75 , 100
70 END
```

8.
```
10 READ C , D
20 PRINT "ORIGINAL COST = $";C
30 PRINT "DISCOUNT = ";D * 100;
   "%"
40 LET S = C - C * D
50 PRINT "SALE PRICE = $";S
60 DATA 20 , 0.15
70 END
```

Write a program using READ and DATA statements for each. Make up your own data.

9. Compute the profit (or loss) made by the Computer Club each week of its five-week fund-raising project.

★**10.** Prepare a monthly statement for a savings account showing deposits and withdrawals and the balance after each transaction.

AT THE COMPUTER

Run the FINANCIAL REPORT program with each change to see what happens.

1.
```
70 READ I1 , E1 , I2 , E2
80
```

2.
```
140 DATA 12463 , 12827
145 DATA 14820 , 13425
```

3.
```
140 DATA 12463 , 12827 , 14820 ,
    13425 , 948
```

4.
```
140 DATA 12463 , 12827 , 14820
```

Run each program. Make up your own data and write the output.

5. the fund-raising program you wrote for **9**

★**6.** the savings account program you wrote for ★**10**

MAINTAINING SKILLS

Choose the correct answers. Write A, B, C, or D.

1. What is the GCF of 4 and 16?

   A 16
   B 4
   C 2
   D not given

2. $15 - 4\frac{3}{8}$

   A $10\frac{5}{8}$
   B $11\frac{5}{8}$
   C $11\frac{3}{8}$
   D not given

3. $6\frac{2}{3}$
   $+ 4\frac{7}{9}$

   A $11\frac{4}{9}$
   B 11
   C $10\frac{4}{9}$
   D not given

4. $2\frac{2}{3} \div \frac{16}{21}$

   A $\frac{128}{63}$
   B $\frac{2}{7}$
   C $3\frac{1}{2}$
   D not given

5. Complete. 2 lb 3 oz = ___ oz

   A 27
   B 30
   C 34
   D not given

6. What kind of angle is a 45° angle?

   A obtuse
   B acute
   C right
   D not given

7. What is the diameter?

   A $\overline{DC}$
   B $\overline{AC}$
   C $\overline{BC}$
   D not given

8. Solve. $\frac{16}{10} = \frac{40}{n}$

   A $n = 25$
   B $n = 14$
   C $n = 2.5$
   D not given

9. What percent is the ratio $\frac{4}{5}$?

   A 75%
   B 40%
   C 80%
   D not given

10. What is 125% of 16?

    A 20
    B 25
    C 4
    D not given

11. What is the discount?
    regular price: $35   rate of discount: 25%

    A $26.25
    B $8.75
    C $7.57
    D not given

12. What is 3% of 55?

    A 16.50
    B 0.365
    C 1.65
    D not given

13. 15% of what number is 6?

    A 40
    B 0.9
    C 54
    D not given

Solve.

14. On a billboard a juice bottle is 3 m tall. The ratio of the billboard bottle to the actual bottle is 15:1. How tall is the actual bottle?

    A 7.2 m
    B 0.2 m
    C 45 m
    D not given

15. At Mrs. Parker's office the average number of letters delivered each day is 1,516. How many letters are delivered in 247 days?

    A 374,452
    B 370,212
    C 19,708
    D not given

Theme: Applied Arts in America

Perimeter

Andrew Foster, a landscape architect, has designed this colonial garden for a museum. The outside edge of the garden will be lined with a hedge. What will the total length of the hedge be?

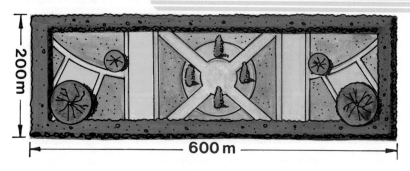

The distance around a polygon is its **perimeter (P)**.

The perimeter of a polygon can be found by adding the lengths of all of its sides.

$P = 600 + 200 + 600 + 200$
$P = 1,600$ m

The length of the hedge, or the perimeter of the garden, will be 1,600 m.

Formulas can be used to find the perimeter of certain polygons.

▶Since a square has four equal sides, its perimeter is four times the length of a side.

$P = 4s$
$P = 4 \times 3$
$P = 12$ m

3 m
3 m

▶Since a rectangle has two pairs of equal sides, its perimeter is twice the length plus twice the width.

$P = 2l + 2w$
$P = (2 \times 5) + (2 \times 3)$
$P = 10 + 6$
$P = 16$ m

3 m
5 m

▶To find the perimeter of any regular polygon, use the formula $P = ns$. In this formula, n is the number of sides and s is the length of each side.

$P = ns$
$P = 6 \times 11$
$P = 66$ cm

11 cm

CLASSWORK

Find the perimeter of each polygon.

1.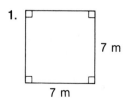

7 m
7 m

2.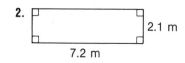

2.1 m
7.2 m

3.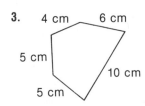

4 cm   6 cm
5 cm
10 cm
5 cm

332

Find the perimeter of each polygon.

1. 4 cm, 9 cm

2. 8 m, 8 m

3. 16 km, 12 km, 15 km

4. 10 cm, 14 cm

5. 13 m, 13 m

6. 8.9 cm, 13.8 cm, 17.3 cm

7. square
$s = 7.3$ cm

8. rectangle
$l = 15$ m
$w = 12$ m

9. rectangle
$l = 5.8$ cm
$w = 1.8$ cm

Find the perimeter of each regular polygon.

10. triangle
$s = 35$ km

11. octagon
$s = 7.2$ mm

12. pentagon
$s = 14.6$ cm

Solve.

13. A regular octagon has a perimeter of 176 cm. Find the length of each side.

★**14.** The perimeter of a rectangle is 80 m. The length is 25 m. Find the width.

APPLICATION

15. A square quilt displayed at the colonial museum measured 425 cm on each side. How much binding had the quilt maker used to bind the edges of the quilt?

16. A museum sculpture garden is 38 m long and 26 m wide. How much fencing is needed to enclose the entire garden?

★**17.** If each step you take is 0.6 m, about how many steps will it take you to walk all the way around the sculpture garden?

LOGICAL THINKING

A garden 50 m wide and 100 m long is to be enclosed with a fence. If fence posts are placed every 10 m, how many posts are needed?

Circumference

The distance around a circle is called its **circumference (C).**

The table below gives the measures of the circumference and the diameter for three circles.

Circle	C	d	$\frac{C}{d}$
P	20.41 cm	6.5 cm	3.14 . . .
R	15.7 cm	5 cm	3.14 . . .
S	88 cm	28 cm	3.14 . . .

Notice that for each circle the quotient $\frac{C}{d}$ is about 3.14.

The Greek letter **pi** (π) stands for the number $\frac{C}{d}$.

π is approximately equal to ($\approx$) 3.14 or $\frac{22}{7}$.

▶ To find the circumference of any circle, multiply $\pi \times$ diameter. Use the formula $C = \pi d$.

Find the circumference of the circle.

$C = \pi d$

$C \approx 3.14 \times 24$

$C \approx 75.36$ cm

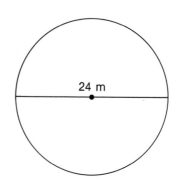
24 m

▶ To find the circumference when the radius is given, use the formula $C = 2\pi r$.

Find the circumference of the circle.

$C = 2\pi r$

$C \approx 2 \times 3.14 \times 9$

$C \approx 56.52$ m

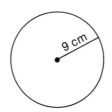
9 cm

Another Example

Find the circumference of a circle with a diameter of 14 cm.

The circumference, rounded to the nearest one, is 44 cm.

$C = \pi d$

$C \approx 3.14 \times 14$

$C \approx 43.96$ cm

CLASSWORK

Find the circumference of each circle. Use 3.14 for π. Round each answer to the nearest one.

1.
24 cm

2.
38 m

3.
3.5 m

4.
6.3 m

5. $d = 7.5$ m

6. $r = 4.3$ cm

7. $d = 5.6$ km

8. $r = 3.7$ cm

Find the circumference of each circle. Use 3.14 for π. Round each answer to the nearest one.

1.
3 m
O

2.
9 m
O

3.
12 cm
O

4.
16 mm
O

5. d = 13 mm

6. r = 2.2 cm

7. d = 100 m

8. r = 35 cm

9. d = 4.5 km

10. d = 1.8 km

11. r = 5.6 m

12. r = 8.4 mm

Use your calculator to find the diameter of each circle. Use 3.14 for π. Round each answer to the nearest one.

13. C = 47.1 km

14. C = 51.339 cm

15. C = 5.966 m

16. C = 628 mm

Find the distance around each figure. Round each answer to the nearest hundredth.

★ 17.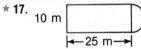
10 m
|← 25 m →|

★ 18.
O
8.2 cm

★ 19.
2 m
2 m

APPLICATION

20. Paul Revere engraved the names of fifteen Sons of Liberty around the rim of the famous Liberty Bowl. To plan for the engraving, he had to know the circumference of the bowl. The diameter is 28 cm. What is the circumference?

21. Jill measured the diameter of a wheel from a colonial wagon. The diameter was 73 cm. About how far will the wagon wheel travel in one complete turn?

★ 22. About how many meters did the colonial wagon wheel travel in 50 revolutions? Round the answer to the nearest meter.

CALCULATOR

With the help of computers, we know the value of π to one million decimal places. The exact value can never be determined, because it is a decimal that never ends and never repeats.

π = 3.1415926535 8979323846 2643383279 . . .

Use a calculator to express each ratio as a decimal. Tell which ratio comes closest to the value of π.

circle A: $\dfrac{C}{d} = \dfrac{22}{7}$

circle B: $\dfrac{C}{d} = \dfrac{333}{106}$

circle C: $\dfrac{C}{d} = \dfrac{355}{113}$

Area

The area of a region is the number of square units needed to cover the region.

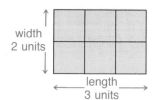

width
2 units

length
3 units

Area = length × width

Area = 2 × 3

Area = 6 square units

Some units of area are the **square centimeter (cm²)**, the **square millimeter (mm²)**, and the **square kilometer (km²)**.

Mary Louisa McCully stitched this sampler in 1840. It measures 54 cm by 45 cm. What is the area of this piece of needlework?

A formula can be used to find the area of a rectangle.

▶ *A = l × w*, or *A = lw*

$A = 54 \times 45$

$A = 2,430 \text{ cm}^2$

The area of the sampler is 2,430 cm².

Since the length and width of a square are equal, this formula can be used to find the area of a square.

▶ Area = side × side

A = s × s, or *A = s²*

Find the area of a square whose side measures 12.5 m.

The area of the square is 156.25 m².

s

s

$A = s^2$

$A = 12.5 \times 12.5$

$A = 156.25 \text{ m}^2$

CLASSWORK

Find the area of each figure.

1.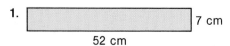
7 cm
52 cm

2.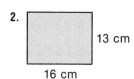
13 cm
16 cm

3.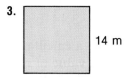
14 m

Find the area of each rectangle or square.

4. $l = 12$ m; $w = 7$ m

5. $s = 15$ cm

6. $s = 9.2$ m

PRACTICE

Find the area of each figure.

1.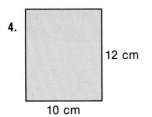
   5 m, 2 m

2. 9 m, 9 m

3.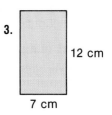
   12 cm, 7 cm

4. 12 cm, 10 cm

5. 9 mm, 27 mm

6.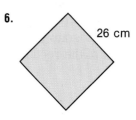
   26 cm

Find the area of each rectangle or square.

7. $l = 10$ m; $w = 6.7$ m

8. $s = 11$ cm

9. $l = 3.4$ m; $w = 2$ m

10. $l = 9.7$ cm; $w = 8.6$ cm

11. $s = 4.9$ km

12. $s = 14.9$ cm

13. $l = 12.4$ cm; $w = 7.3$ cm

14. $l = 7.4$ mm; $w = 6.3$ mm

15. $s = 8.7$ m

Solve.

16. The area of a rectangle is 299 m². Its length is 23 m. Find its width.

★ 17. The perimeter of a square is 40 cm. Find its area.

Find the area of each shaded region.

★ 18. 3 cm, 8 cm, 2 cm, 3 cm

★ 19.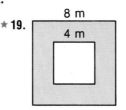
   8 m, 4 m

★ 20.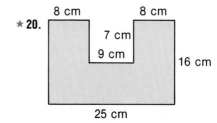
   8 cm, 8 cm, 7 cm, 9 cm, 16 cm, 25 cm

APPLICATION

21. Phyllis is making a panel of stained glass for her front door. What is the area of the stained glass if it is 120 cm long and 20 cm wide?

★ 22. Phyllis was given 32 m of rope to outline an exhibit area at an arts and crafts show. Can she rope off a rectangular area of 48 m²? If so, what are the dimensions of the area? What is the greatest area she can rope off? What are the dimensions of this area?

Area of Parallelograms

To find the area of a parallelogram, find the area of a rectangle with the same base and height.

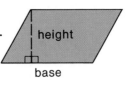

The **height** of a parallelogram is a segment that joins opposite sides and is perpendicular to the base.

Imagine cutting the shaded part of the parallelogram and rearranging the pieces to form a rectangle. The area of the parallelogram is the same as the area of the rectangle.

▶To find the area of a parallelogram, multiply the base times the height. Use this formula.
$A = b \times h$, or $A = bh$

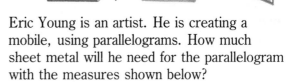

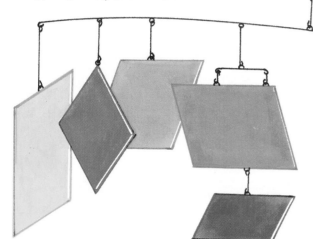

Eric Young is an artist. He is creating a mobile, using parallelograms. How much sheet metal will he need for the parallelogram with the measures shown below?

$A = bh$
$A = 12 \times 9$
$A = 108 \text{ cm}^2$

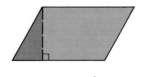

Eric will need 108 cm² of sheet metal.

CLASSWORK

Find the area of each parallelogram.

1. 3 cm, 4 cm

2. 11 m, 14 m

3. 7 km, 9 km

4. 5.3 m, 8.5 m

5. $b = 10$ cm
$h = 3$ cm

6. $b = 5.7$ m
$h = 12.8$ m

7. $b = 22.5$ km
$h = 50.0$ km

8. $b = 11$ cm
$h = 3.2$ cm

PRACTICE

Find the area of each parallelogram.

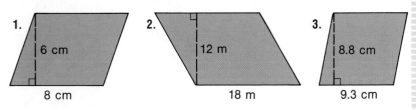

1. 6 cm / 8 cm

2. 12 m / 18 m

3. 8.8 cm / 9.3 cm

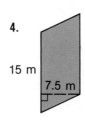 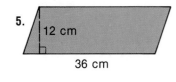 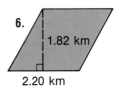

4. 15 m / 7.5 m

5. 12 cm / 36 cm

6. 1.82 km / 2.20 km

7. $b = 13$ cm; $h = 4$ cm
8. $b = 11$ km; $h = 28$ km
9. $b = 14.9$ m; $h = 7$ m
10. $b = 110$ mm; $h = 34.5$ mm

Use your calculator to find the area of each parallelogram.

11. $b = 23.8$ m; $h = 21.1$ m
12. $b = 11.11$ m; $h = 20.02$ m
13. $b = 5.5$ cm; $h = 1.48$ cm
14. $b = 0.96$ km; $h = 0.48$ km

Solve.

15. The area of a parallelogram is 169 square centimeters. The length of the base is 13 centimeters. Find the height.

16. The area of a parallelogram is 1,000 square meters. The height is 25 meters. How long is the base?

★ 17. The base of a parallelogram is 35 centimeters. The height is 2 centimeters more than half the base. Find the area.

APPLICATION

Eric is cutting out shapes for a mobile from a rectangular piece of sheet metal 100 cm long and 50 cm wide.

18. He cuts four parallelograms, each with a base of 15 cm and a height of 17 cm. How much metal does he use?

★ 19. From the remaining metal he cuts six identical squares. Each square has a side 10.5 cm long. How much metal does he have left?

Mixed Practice

1. $4{,}375 + 37{,}098$

2. $9{,}000 - 1{,}286$

3. 437×695

4. $886 \div 40$

5. $2.986 + 0.85$

6. $23 - 12.05$

7. 42.6×3.8

8. $29.76 \div 3.2$

9. $4\frac{1}{8} + 3\frac{1}{2} + 6\frac{1}{4}$

10. $8\frac{3}{7} - 6\frac{5}{7}$

11. $3\frac{5}{6} \times \frac{2}{9}$

12. $3\frac{5}{6} \div \frac{2}{9}$

13. $\begin{array}{r} 4 \text{ yd } 2 \text{ ft} \\ + 6 \text{ yd } 2 \text{ ft} \end{array}$

14. $\begin{array}{r} 12 \text{ h } 27 \text{ min} \\ - 3 \text{ h } 36 \text{ min} \end{array}$

Write each as a percent.

15. $\frac{13}{100}$

16. $\frac{3}{5}$

17. $\frac{3}{10}$

18. 0.84

19. 0.09

20. 6.25

339

Area of Triangles

The first colonists came to America in sailing ships. Today, sails are made for recreational boats.

This triangular sail has a base (*b*) of 4 meters and a height (*h*) of 6 meters. How large is the sail in square meters?

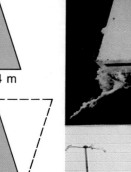

$h = 6$ m

$b = 4$ m

To find a formula for the area of a triangle, think of another triangle congruent to the one given. When the triangles are put together as shown, they form a parallelogram.

6 m

4 m

The area of each triangle is one half the area of the parallelogram.

▶ Area of triangle = $\frac{1}{2}$ × area of parallelogram

Use this formula to find the area of a triangle.

$A = \frac{1}{2} \times b \times h$, or $A = \frac{1}{2}bh$

$A = \frac{1}{2} \times 4 \times 6$

$A = \frac{1}{2} \times 24$

$A = 12$ m²

There are 12 m² of canvas in the sail.

Another Example

Find the area of $\triangle ABC$.

$A = \frac{1}{2} \times 5 \times 7$

$A = \frac{1}{2} \times 35$

$A = 17.5$ m²

The area of $\triangle ABC$ is 17.5 m².

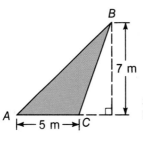

B

7 m

A

5 m

C

Sometimes the height lies outside the triangle.

CLASSWORK

Find the area of each triangle.

1.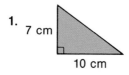
7 cm
10 cm

2. 4 km
3 km

3.
8 m
9 m

4.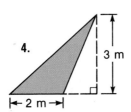
3 m
2 m

5. $b = 7$ dm; $h = 9$ dm

6. $b = 4$ cm; $h = 6.1$ cm

7. $b = 12$ m; $h = 7.4$ m

Find the area of each triangle.

1.
10 m
10 m

2.
27 m
30 m

3.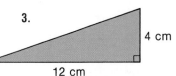
4 cm
12 cm

4.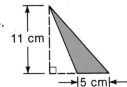
11 cm
5 cm

5.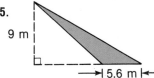
9 m
5.6 m

6.
13 km
15.8 km

7. $b = 9$ m
$h = 16$ m

8. $b = 17$ m
$h = 13$ m

9. $b = 15$ cm
$h = 7$ cm

10. $b = 2.7$ m
$h = 5$ m

★ **11.** Find the area of the shaded figure at the right.

4 cm
4 cm
3 cm
4 cm
4 cm
3 cm

APPLICATION

12. A sail that has an area of 120 m² has a base of 10 m. What is the height of the sail?

★ **13.** A company that makes sails pays $12 a square meter for the first 100 square meters of canvas and $10 a square meter thereafter. What is the cost of the canvas for a triangular sail with a base of 15 m and a height of 26 m?

AREA OF A TRAPEZOID

A trapezoid can be divided into two triangles. To find the area of a trapezoid, find the area of each triangle. Then add the areas.

Area of trapezoid = Area of triangle I + Area of triangle II

$A = \frac{1}{2}bh + \frac{1}{2}bh$

$A = (\frac{1}{2} \times 10 \times 4) + (\frac{1}{2} \times 6 \times 4)$

$A = 20 + 12 = 32$ m²

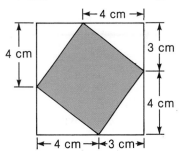
6 m
4 m
II
I
4 m
10 m

Find the area of each trapezoid.

1.
5 cm
2 cm
8 cm

2.
8 m
5 m
10 m

3.
10 cm
4 cm
15 cm

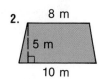
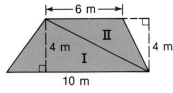

Area of Circles

Here is a way to find the formula for the area of a circle.

Divide the circle into equal parts.

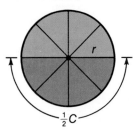

Rearrange the parts to form a figure that looks like a parallelogram.

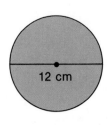

The height is the radius of the circle. The base is half the circumference.

The circle and the parallelogram have the same area.

$A = bh$ ⟵ Use the formula for the area of a parallelogram.

$A = \frac{1}{2}C \times r$ ⟵ Replace b with $\frac{1}{2}C$ and replace h with r.

$A = \frac{1}{2} \times 2\pi r \times r$ ⟵ Replace C with $2\pi r$.

$A = \pi r^2$ ⟵ The result is the formula for the area of a circle.

▶Area of a circle $= \pi \times$ the square of the radius

Find the area of a circle with a diameter of 12 cm.

$A = \pi r^2$

$A \approx 3.14 \times 6^2$ ⟵ If $d = 12$, then $r = 6$.

$A \approx 3.14 \times 36$

$A \approx 113.04$ cm^2

To the nearest one, the area is 113 cm^2.

CLASSWORK

Find the area of each circle. Use 3.14 for π. Round each number to the nearest one.

1.

8 cm

2.

9 cm

3.

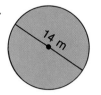

14 m

4.

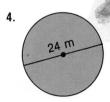

24 m

5. $r = 16$ mm

6. $d = 20$ m

7. $r = 40$ cm

8. $d = 2.6$ m

PRACTICE

Find the area of each circle. Use 3.14 for π. Round each answer to the nearest one.

1.

2.

3.

4.

5. $d = 22$ m

6. $r = 20$ cm

7. $r = 18$ m

8. $d = 24$ cm

9. $d = 15$ m

10. $r = 5.8$ mm

11. $d = 21$ cm

12. $r = 5.2$ m

13. $r = 17$ m

14. $d = 50$ m

15. $d = 38$ cm

16. $r = 3.1$ cm

Find the area of each shaded region. Use 3.14 for π. Round the area of each circle to the nearest one.

17.

★ **18.**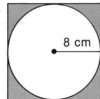

★ **19.**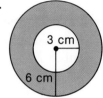

APPLICATION

20. Drums of the Arapaho and other Plains Indians were made from rawhide circles. If the diameter of a rawhide circle was 60 cm, what was its area?

21. A woven circular mat has a diameter of 36 cm. What area can the mat cover?

★ **22.** An Indian tepee had a circular base, or floor. The circumference of the floor was 56.52 m. What was the area of the floor of the tepee?

═══ VISUAL THINKING ═══

Place tracing paper over each figure. Which figures can be traced without lifting your pencil or retracing any segment or arc?

1.

2.

3.

4.

Problem Solving

LOGIC

To solve some problems, more than computation is required. You must organize and examine the various facts and draw conclusions from them.

1. The students in the Arts and Crafts Club painted a design on one wall of the children's playground. They painted the shapes of an isosceles triangle, a square, and a rectangle, using whole-number lengths for the sides. Which shape has the largest perimeter? Use the following clues:

Clue 1—Two sides of the triangle are 7 ft and 6 ft.
Clue 2—One side of the square is 8 ft.
Clue 3—The longest side of the rectangle has the same length as a side of the square.

Examine the information about the figures.

Clue 1 reveals that two sides of the triangle are 7 ft and 6 ft. Since the triangle is isosceles, the third side must be either 7 ft or 6 ft. So the perimeter of the triangle is at most

$7 + 7 + 6 = 20$ ft.

Clue 2 reveals that one side of the square is 8 ft. Since all sides of the square are equal, the perimeter of the square is

$4 \times 8 = 32$ ft.

Clue 3 reveals that the largest side of the rectangle is the same as a side of the square, which is 8 ft. Thus the smaller side of the rectangle can be no more than 7 ft. Its perimeter is at most

$8 + 8 + 7 + 7 = 30$ ft.

So the shape with the largest perimeter is the square.

Does the conclusion agree with the information in the clues?

The perimeter of the square is 32 ft. It is greater than the greatest possible perimeter of the triangle or rectangle.

2. Sometimes conclusions can be reached from a set of statements.

All triangles have 3 sides.
Mike painted a triangle.
Conclusion: The figure Mike painted has 3 sides.

All squares have 4 sides.
Bill painted a 4-sided figure.
Conclusion: No conclusion is possible. Bill could have painted a rectangle.

PRACTICE

Tell whether each pair of statements can be true at the same time. Write *yes* or *no*.

1. The stream dried up.
   Duck decoys are floating in the stream.

2. The bicycle is older than the skates.
   The bicycle was made in 1972.

3. The river is frozen.
   The temperature is 93°F.

4. The blue quilt has a perimeter of 24 ft.
   The blue quilt is rectangular.

Tell whether the conclusion following each given set of statements could be true. Write *yes* or *no*.

5. All islands are surrounded by water.
   Hawaii is an island.
   Conclusion: Hawaii is surrounded by water.

6. Some vases are made of clay.
   Jani bought a vase.
   Conclusion: Jani's vase is made of clay.

7. All bicycles have wheels.
   All carriages have wheels.
   Conclusion: All carriages are bicycles.

8. The Museum of American Folk Art is in New York City.
   New York City is in the United States.
   Conclusion: The Museum of American Folk Art is in the United States.

If possible, write the conclusion that can be reached from each set of statements.

9. Mr. Schulz carves only birds.
   Jamie bought a carving from Mr. Schulz.

10. All squares are rectangles.
    ABCD is a square.

11. All squares are rectangles.
    RSTU is a rectangle.

12. North Carolina is north of South Carolina.
    Columbia is a city in South Carolina.

13. Gary, Arlene, Mitch, and Carol met at a crafts show. Arlene arrived just before Gary. She saw Carol get tickets. Mitch arrived after the other three. In what order did they arrive at the show?

14. Susan made a set of wind chimes using four different geometric shapes. She placed the circle between the square and the rectangle. The square is on the left end. The triangle is on the right end. From left to right, in what order are the shapes?

CREATE YOUR OWN PROBLEM

Write a problem using the information in the picture.

Fran 5ft 4in. Chris 5ft 9in. Paula 5ft 5in.

Space Figures

After visiting Plimouth Plantation, in Plymouth, Massachusetts, Charlie's class decided to make their own model village.

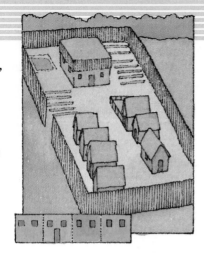

Charlie and Pam used this pattern to make the meeting house. The folded pattern forms a **space figure**.

A space figure is a geometric figure whose points do not all lie in the same plane. **Polyhedrons** are space figures with flat surfaces, called **faces**.

A **prism** is a polyhedron with two parallel and congruent faces, called **bases**. The other faces are parallelograms.

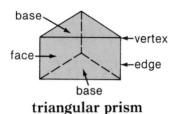
triangular prism

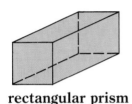
rectangular prism

cube

hexagonal prism

A **pyramid** is a polyhedron with only one base. The base is a polygon. The other faces are triangles. The base is used to name the pyramid.

triangular pyramid

rectangular pyramid

pentagonal pyramid

hexagonal pyramid

These space figures are not polyhedrons. Their surfaces are curved.

cylinder   **cone**   **sphere**

CLASSWORK

Name each figure. Give the number of faces (*F*), edges (*E*), and vertices (*V*).

1.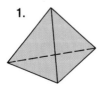
2.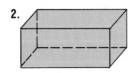
3.
4.

Name each figure. Give the number of faces (*F*), edges (*E*), and vertices (*V*).

1.

2.

3.

4.

Tell if each figure is a polyhedron. Write *yes* or *no*. Name each figure that is *not* a polyhedron.

5.

6.

7.

8.

APPLICATION

The members of Charlie's class used patterns to make all the parts needed for a model village. Choose the pattern that will fold to make each polyhedron.

9. roof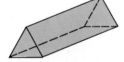

    a.

    b.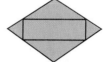

10. chimney

    a.

    b.

11. tower

    a.

    b.

LOGICAL THINKING

Fourteen cubes are glued together as shown. How many of the original faces are not visible from any view (even if you pick up the stack)?

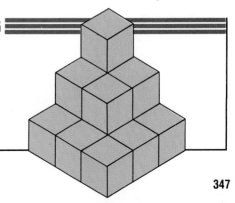

Surface Area of Prisms

All the outer sides of this candlebox have been decorated in the Pennsylvania Dutch style. What is the total area that was painted?

Find the **surface area** of the box. The box is a rectangular prism. The pattern shows its faces.

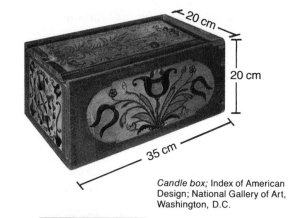

► The surface area of a figure is the sum of the areas of all its faces.

To find the surface area of the box, find the area of each face. Then add.

Candle box; Index of American Design; National Gallery of Art, Washington, D.C.

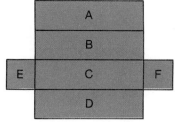

Face	Area
A	35 × 20 = 700 cm²
B	35 × 20 = 700 cm²
C	35 × 20 = 700 cm²
D	35 × 20 = 700 cm²
E	20 × 20 = 400 cm²
F	20 × 20 = 400 cm²

The sum of the areas is 3,600 cm². The surface area of the candlebox is 3,600 cm².

Find the surface area of the triangular prism. Make a pattern to show the faces.

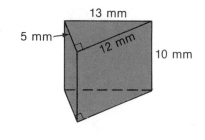

Area A = Area C = $\frac{1}{2}(b \times h)$ = $\frac{1}{2}(5 \times 12)$ = 30 mm²

Area D = $b \times h$ = 5 × 10 = 50 mm²

Area B = $b \times h$ = 13 × 10 = 130 mm²

Area E = $b \times h$ = 12 × 10 = 120 mm²

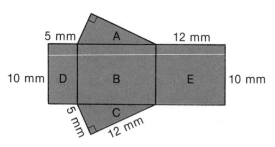

Find the sum.

(2 × 30) + 50 + 130 + 120 = 360 mm²

↑
Faces A and C are congruent.

The surface area is 360 mm².

CLASSWORK

Find the surface area of each prism.

1.
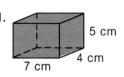

2.
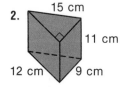

3.
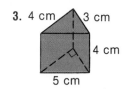

Find the surface area of each prism.

1.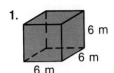
6 m
6 m
6 m

2.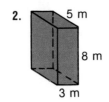
5 m
8 m
3 m

3.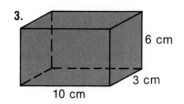
6 cm
3 cm
10 cm

4.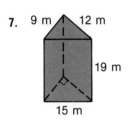
6 cm
9 cm
15 cm

5.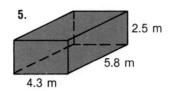
2.5 m
5.8 m
4.3 m

6.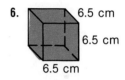
6.5 cm
6.5 cm
6.5 cm

7.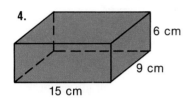
9 m   12 m
19 m
15 m

8.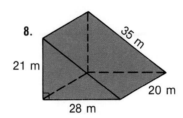
35 m
21 m
20 m
28 m

9.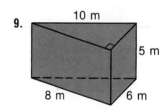
10 m
5 m
8 m   6 m

APPLICATION

10. Carolyn made a sewing box in the shape of a rectangular prism. Its length is 34 cm, its width is 15 cm, and its height is 18 cm. How much fabric does she need to cover all the sides of the box?

11. Juan is building a birdhouse. His plans are shown at the right. How much wood will be used?

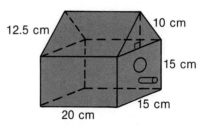
12.5 cm
10 cm
15 cm
15 cm
20 cm

VISUAL THINKING

This pattern can be folded to form a cube.

Which cube would it form?

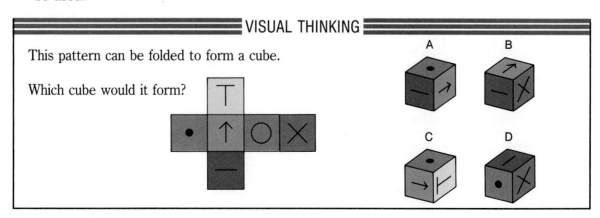

349

Volumes of Prisms

The **volume** of a figure is the number of cubic units needed to fill the figure.

The **cubic centimeter (cm³)** and the **cubic meter (m³)** are units of volume.

Count the number of cubic centimeters in the figure at the right to find its volume.

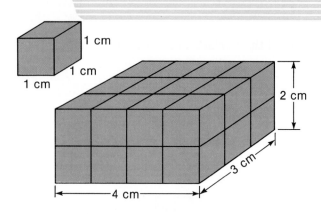

Think 2 layers of 12 cubes = 24 cubes.
The volume is 24 cm³.

The Bishops are building a small ski cabin. They want to buy a wood-burning stove to heat the cabin. To buy the correct stove size, they must know the volume of the space to be heated.

▶The volume of any rectangular prism can be found by using this formula.

Volume = length × width × height

$V = lwh$

$V = 4 \times 8 \times 3$

$V = 96 \text{ m}^3$

The volume of the ski cabin is 96 m³.

▶Since length × width equals the area of the base (B), the formula can be written this way.

Volume = area of base × height

$V = Bh$

$V = 32 \times 3$

$V = 96 \text{ m}^3$

The formula $V = Bh$ can be used to find the volume of any prism.

$V = Bh$ $B = \frac{1}{2} \times 8 \times 3 = 12 \text{ cm}^2$

$\qquad\quad h = 10 \text{ cm}$

$\qquad\quad V = 12 \times 10 = 120$

$\qquad\quad V = 120 \text{ cm}^3$

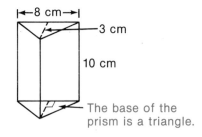

The base of the prism is a triangle.

CLASSWORK

Find the volume of each prism.

1.
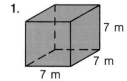
7 m
7 m
7 m

2.
12 cm
4 cm 7 cm

3.
5 cm
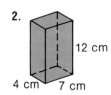
8 cm 12 cm

4.
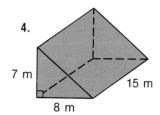
7 m
8 m 15 m

Find the volume of each prism.

1.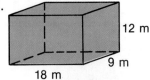
12 m
9 m
18 m

2.
6 cm
8 cm
15 cm

3.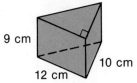
20 m
20 m
5 m

4.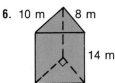
9 cm
10 cm
12 cm

5.
15 m
4 m
6 m

6. 10 m   8 m
14 m

7. rectangular prism
l = 10 cm
w = 12 cm
h = 3 cm

8. rectangular prism
l = 12 cm
w = 11.4 cm
h = 8 cm

9. triangular prism
B = 200 m²
h = 14.4 m

Solve.

10. Which has the greater volume—two 4-centimeter cubes or one 8-centimeter cube?

11. The volume of a rectangular prism is 528 cm³. If the height of the prism is 11 cm, what is the area of the base?

★ **12.** The volume of a rectangular prism is 800 m³. What is the height of the prism if the length is 8 m and the width is 5 m?

★ **13.** The length of a box is twice its height. The width of the box is 10 cm. The height is 7 cm less than the length. What is the volume of the box?

APPLICATION

14. The Bishops are building a rectangular bin for firewood. The dimensions of the bin are 2 m long, 1.4 m wide, and 1.2 m high. What is the volume of the bin?

MENTAL ARITHMETIC

In a cube, l = w = h = edge (e).

Find the volume of each cube.

1. e = 2 m

2. e = 4 cm

3. e = 10 cm

4. e = 20 cm

Surface Area of Cylinders

Margot is a package designer. About how much cardboard is needed to make this cylindrical container for oatmeal?

To find the **surface area** of the cylinder, add the areas of all its surfaces.

To "see" the surfaces, think of cutting apart the cylinder to make a pattern.

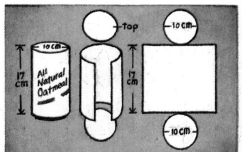

Find the area of each surface.

Area of each circular base

$A = \pi r^2$

$A \approx 3.14 \times 5^2$ ← If $d = 10$, $r = 5$.

$A \approx 3.14 \times 25$

$A \approx 78.5 \text{ cm}^2$

Area of the rectangular surface

$A = bh$

$A = \pi d \times h$

$A \approx 3.14 \times 10 \times 17$

$A \approx 533.8 \text{ cm}^2$

Think The base of the rectangle is equal to the circumference of the circle.

The sum of the areas of the surfaces is $78.5 + 78.5 + 533.8 = 690.8 \text{ cm}^2$.

About 691 cm² of cardboard is needed for the container.

CLASSWORK

Find the surface area of each cylinder. Use π ≈ 3.14.
Round each answer to the nearest one.

1.
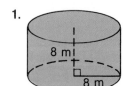
8 m
8 m

2.

7 m
4 m

3.
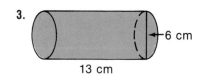
6 cm
13 cm

4.
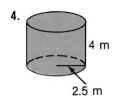
4 m
2.5 m

PRACTICE

Find the surface area of each cylinder. Use π ≈ 3.14. Round each answer to the nearest one.

1.

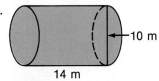

10 cm
8 cm

2.

9 m
20 m

3.

10 m
14 m

4.

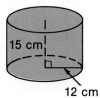

15 cm
12 cm

5.

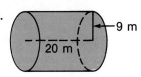

24 m
10 m

6.

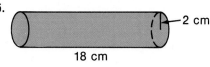

2 cm
18 cm

7. $r = 7$ m
$h = 3$ m

8. $r = 9$ m
$h = 5.6$ m

9. $r = 1.5$ m
$h = 6$ m

10. $d = 6$ cm
$h = 10$ cm

11. $d = 30$ cm
$h = 3.8$ cm

12. $d = 7$ m
$h = 8$ m

13. $r = 5$ mm
$h = 15.2$ mm

14. $d = 3.2$ m
$h = 2.3$ m

15. $d = 13$ cm
$h = 30$ cm

APPLICATION

16. Margot is presenting two packaging designs for a line of canned fruit. Both designs use cylinders with the same height. Can you conclude that both cans require the same amount of sheet metal?

17. Margot is designing a can for a new soup product. The can is to be 11 cm high with a diameter of 8 cm. How much sheet metal is needed to make each can?

★18. Bruce Willis is working on the design for the label of a new brand of vegetables. The vegetables come in cans that are 13 cm high and have a radius of 7 cm. To the nearest tenth, about how much paper does Bruce need for each label?

Mixed Practice

1. 85,006
− 9,797

2. 6,319
× 27

3. 6 × 87,248

4. 23)116,564

5. 87)54,990

6. 5.263 + 981.9

7. 5,024 − 95.83

8. 0.07 × 8.621

9. 0.012 × 5.4

10. 1.9)0.988

11. 5.2 ÷ 0.004

12. $14\frac{4}{5} + 9\frac{1}{12}$

13. $18 - 6\frac{5}{9}$

14. $4\frac{1}{10} - 1\frac{5}{8}$

15. $1\frac{1}{4} \times \frac{5}{8}$

16. $12\frac{1}{8} \div 3\frac{1}{4}$

Solve.

17. What is 12% of 60?

18. 9 is what percent of 12?

19. 18 is 60% of what number?

353

Volume of Cylinders

Priscilla and Jesse are making candles to sell at their school crafts fair. How many cubic centimeters of wax will a can this size hold?

Find the volume of the cylinder.

▶ The volume of a cylinder is equal to the area of the base × the height.

$V = Bh$ B = area of base.

Since the base is a circle, use this formula to find the volume of a cylinder.

$V = \pi r^2 h$

Use the formula to find the volume of the can.

$V = \pi r^2 h$

$V \approx 3.14 \times 5^2 \times 25$

$V \approx 3.14 \times 25 \times 25$

$V \approx 1{,}962.5 \text{ cm}^3$ The can will hold about 1,962.5 cm³ of wax.

Another Example

Find the volume. Use $\pi \approx 3.14$.

$V = \pi r^2 h$

$V \approx 3.14 \times 3^2 \times 15$

   ↑
   If d = 6 m, r = 3 m.

$V \approx 3.14 \times 9 \times 15$

$V \approx 423.9 \text{ m}^3$

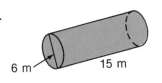

6 m   15 m

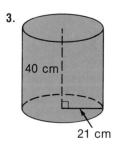

CLASSWORK

Find the volume of each cylinder. Use $\pi \approx 3.14$. Round each answer to the nearest one.

1.

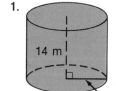

14 m

9 m

2.

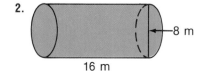

8 m

16 m

3.

40 cm

21 cm

PRACTICE

Find the volume of each cylinder. Use π ≈ 3.14. Round each answer to the nearest one.

1. 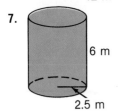 20 m — 6 m

2. 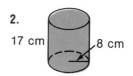 17 cm — 8 cm

3. 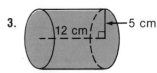 12 cm — 5 cm

4. 14 m — 12 m

5. 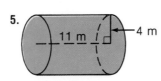 11 m — 4 m

6. 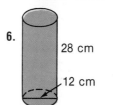 28 cm — 12 cm

7. 6 m — 2.5 m

8. 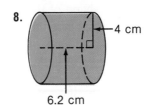 4 cm — 6.2 cm

★9. 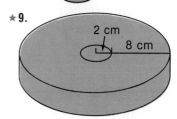 2 cm — 8 cm

10. $r = 4$ cm
 $h = 10$ cm

11. $r = 2$ m
 $h = 6$ m

12. $r = 10$ cm
 $h = 22$ cm

13. $d = 6$ m
 $h = 4.5$ m

14. $d = 18$ cm
 $h = 27$ cm

15. $r = 2.3$ m
 $h = 8$ m

16. $r = 40$ mm
 $h = 150$ mm

17. $d = 15$ cm
 $h = 18$ cm

APPLICATION

18. Jesse is making a candle, using a cylindrical mold that has a radius of 4 centimeters and a height of 30 centimeters. About how much wax will be used?

19. Priscilla used a soup can that has a diameter of 10 cm and a height of 16 cm as a mold for a candle. What is the approximate volume of the soup can?

★20. Jesse is using a cylindrical mold with a diameter of 10 cm and a height of 20 cm. Priscilla is using a mold in the shape of a rectangular prism, with the same height as the cylinder and a square base measuring 10 cm on each side. Who uses more wax? About how much more is used?

★21. Two cans shaped like cylinders are equal in height. The first can has a radius twice as long as the second can. The volume of the second can is 237 cm³. About how much wax will the first can hold?

355

Problem Solving

SKILLS AND STRATEGIES REVIEW Sculptures

Some customary units of measure for area are the square inch and the square foot. Some customary units of measure for volume are the cubic inch and cubic foot. Use these units in solving the problems below.

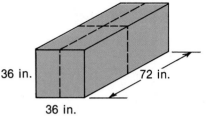

36 in. 36 in. 72 in.

Solve.

1. Suni is making a metal sculpture with pins placed 1.7 inches apart on each face of a triangular prism. How many pins does she use?

2. Mr. Smith is designing a new sculpture in the shape of the rectangular prism in the diagram. He is attaching aluminum stripping to the 6 surfaces as shown by the dotted lines in the drawing. How much aluminum stripping does he need?

3. Mr. Smith's previous sculpture was made of iron pipe $\frac{1}{2}$ inch in diameter. It was in the form of three figures, as shown at the right. The side of the square is 39 inches. The radius of the circle is 21 inches. Each side of the triangle is 32 inches. How many feet of pipe did Mr. Smith use? (Using $\frac{22}{7}$ for π will make the computation easier.)

4. The iron pipe costs $1.86 per foot. How much did Mr. Smith spend on the sculpture?

5. The height of the triangle is $27\frac{1}{2}$ inches. What is the height of the sculpture?

6. What is the area of the region enclosed by the sculpture? (Use $\pi \approx \frac{22}{7}$.)

7. All the pieces of sculpture in the crafts show were sold to customers. Mr. Smith had two pieces of sculpture in the show. What can you conclude?

8. Miss Lowry is making a miniature village and has just finished the outdoor theater. The seats are arranged as shown in three sections. The numbers indicate the number of seats in the rows. If the pattern continues, how many seats are there in all if there are 10 rows in the theater?

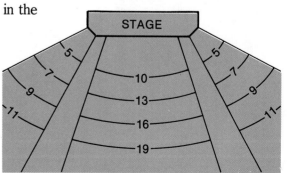

STAGE

5 5
7 7
9 9
11 11
10
13
16
19

Problem Solving

WHAT IF . . . ?

Lena, Angelo, and Joe went to the Morristown Craft Show.
They stopped at the quilt booth. Mrs. Radin was making
patterns for some new quilts.

Solve.

1. Each square of the quilt will contain four strips of color:
   red, blue, yellow, and green. How can Mrs. Radin design a
   square if she wants a yellow section between the red and
   blue sections?

What if Mrs. Radin wants the blue section next to the red,
but not next to the yellow section?

2. How can she design a square?

Lena, Angelo, and Joe walked on to a booth where a person
was making cast-iron doorstops. The doorstops were in the
shape of rectangular prisms, 8 inches × 3 inches × 3 inches.

3. The cast iron weighs 2 ounces per cubic inch. How many
   pounds does one doorstop weigh?

What if the shape of the doorstops is changed to a cylinder
with a 3-inch radius and a height of 8 inches?

4. How much does one doorstop weigh? (Use $\pi \approx 3.14$.)

What if the shape is changed to a right-triangular prism whose
base is a 6-inch × 8-inch × 10-inch right triangle, and whose
height is 12 inches?

5. What is the weight of one doorstop?

At the next booth they were making copper umbrella stands.
Each stand was in the shape of a cylinder.

6. The diameter of one umbrella stand is 8 inches. Its height is
   30 inches. To the nearest tenth, how many inches of
   copper were used for the stand? (Use $\pi \approx 3.14$.)

What if copper costs $.02 per square inch and the
craftsperson wants to make a 50% profit over cost?

★ 7. What should the price of each umbrella stand be?

CHAPTER REVIEW

Find the perimeter and the area of each. pages 332–333, 336–341

1.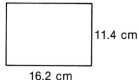
11.4 cm
16.2 cm

2.
4 cm
7 cm

3.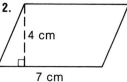
33 cm 50 cm
30 cm
55 cm

Find the circumference and the area of each. Use 3.14 for π.
Round each answer to the nearest one. pages 334–335, 342–343

4.
2 m

5.
16 m

6.
3 cm

7.
10.2 m

Name each figure. pages 346–347

8.

9.

10.

11.

Find the surface area of each. Use 3.14 for π. Round each
answer to the nearest one. pages 348–349, 352–353

12.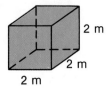
2 m
2 m
2 m

13.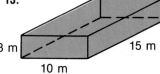
3 m 15 m
10 m

14.
6 cm
4 cm

Find the volume of each. Use 3.14 for π. Round each answer
to the nearest one. pages 350–351, 354–355

15. cube

$l = 5$ m
$h = 5$ m
$w = 5$ m

16. rectangular prism

$l = 7$ m
$w = 2.5$ m
$h = 6$ m

17. cylinder

$r = 8$ cm
$h = 11$ cm

18. cylinder

$d = 12$ cm
$h = 9.5$ cm

Solve. pages 344–345, 356–357

19. What conclusion can you draw from these
2 statements? All cubes have 6 faces.
The gift box has 6 faces.

20. A cylindrical tank has a height of 4 m and
a base with a radius of 2 m. About how
much liquid can the container hold?

Find the perimeter and the area of each.

1.

6.1 cm

6.1 cm

2.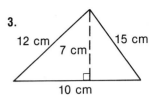

9 m
4 m
16.8 m

3.

12 cm   7 cm   15 cm

10 cm

Find the circumference and the area of each circle.
Use 3.14 for π. Round each answer to the nearest one.

4. $r = 7$ cm

5. $d = 20$ dm

6. $r = 1.5$ cm

7. $d = 2$ m

Name each figure.

8.

9.

10.

11.

Find the surface area of each. Use 3.14 for π. Round each
answer to the nearest one.

12.

6 cm

6 cm

6 cm

13.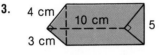

4 cm   10 cm   5 cm

3 cm

14.

5 m

4 m

Find the volume of each. Use 3.14 for π. Round each answer
to the nearest one.

15. cube

$l = 4$ m
$w = 4$ m
$h = 4$ m

16. rectangular prism

$l = 4$ m
$w = 6.5$ m
$h = 2$ m

17. cylinder

$r = 5$ cm
$h = 10$ cm

18. cylinder

$d = 9$ cm
$h = 12$ cm

Solve.

19. Draw a conclusion. All of Manuel's
paintings are landscapes. Mrs. Cole
bought one of Manuel's paintings.

20. The area of a rectangular room is 56 m².
What is the length of the room if the
width is 8 m?

Find the volume of the metal in the hollow pipe.

4 cm   3 cm

30 cm

MAKING A PYRAMID FROM AN ENVELOPE

Follow the directions to make a pyramid. You will need scissors and an envelope. Use either a standard-size or business-size envelope.

Seal the envelope. Draw the diagonals as shown.

Fold and crease along the diagonals. Fold both forward and backward.

Cut out the top triangle. Set it aside to use later.

Fold and crease along the dotted line.

Open the envelope at the fold. Notice the pyramid shapes forming at the sides.

Tuck one of the pyramid shapes inside the other. You now have a triangular pyramid.

Do each of the following, using the pyramid you just made.

1. Use a pencil or a crayon to shade the four surfaces of the pyramid.

2. Open the pyramid, returning it to the shape at the right. Replace the triangle that was cut out. What part of the original envelope is shaded? Consider the entire envelope.

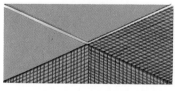

3. Using the information you found in **2**, find the surface area of the pyramid.

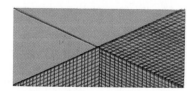

SQUARES AND SQUARE ROOTS

Harriet is making a square mosaic design for a tabletop. The area of the design must be exactly 400 cm². Each colored tile is 1 cm². How many tiles will she need for each row of her design?

The square has an area of 400 cm².

To find how many tiles will fit on a side, Harriet needs to find the **square root** of 400.

The square root of a number n, written $\sqrt{n}$, is a number whose square is n.

The number 400 is a **perfect square**. A perfect square is the square of a whole number.

In a square figure, the area is the square of a side. Each side is the square root of the area.

$A = s^2$ $\qquad\qquad$ $s = \sqrt{A}$

$A = 20^2 = 20 \times 20$ $\qquad$ $s = \sqrt{400}$

$A = 400 \text{ cm}^2$ $\qquad\qquad$ $s = 20 \text{ cm}$

$\sqrt{400} = 20$, since $20 \times 20 = 400$.

Harriet will need 20 mosaic tiles for each row.

Find the square of each.

1. 11 $\qquad$ 2. 13 $\qquad$ 3. 17 $\qquad$ 4. 23 $\qquad$ 5. 32 $\qquad$ 6. 57

Find the square root of each.

7. 16 $\qquad$ 8. 36 $\qquad$ 9. 64 $\qquad$ 10. 144 $\qquad$ 11. 225 $\qquad$ 12. 900

Solve.

13. Harriet is making this square design of red, blue, and green tiles. Each tile is 1 cm². The area of the design is 81 cm². How many tiles of each color does she need?

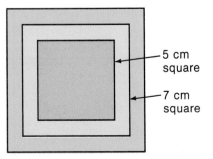

5 cm square

7 cm square

CUMULATIVE REVIEW

Choose the correct answers. Write A, B, C, or D.

1. 6,015 + 406 + 9,634

  A 16,045   **C** 15,045

  B 16,055   **D** not given

2. 34,685 ÷ 57

  A 68 R29   **C** 608 R29

  B 68 R31   **D** not given

3. What is the value of 3 in 0.0035?

  A 3 thousandths   **C** 3 hundreds

  B 3 hundredths   **D** not given

4. 12.045 − 7.148

  A 4.897   **C** 5.103

  B 19.193   **D** not given

5. Estimate. 2,367.53 × 73.9

  A 160,000   **C** 200,000

  B 1,400   **D** not given

6. What is 635 in scientific notation?

  A 63.5×10^3 **C** 635×10^2

  B 6.35×10^2 **D** not given

7. Complete. 3.2 kL = ___ L

  A 32   **C** 3,200

  B 320   **D** not given

8. What is the prime factorization of 56?

  A $2^3 \times 7$ **C** $2^2 \times 14$

  B $2^2 \times 3 \times 5$ **D** not given

9. What is the LCM of 16 and 24?

  A 8   **C** 4

  B 48   **D** not given

10. $15 - 3\frac{4}{7}$

  A $12\frac{4}{7}$ **C** $14\frac{3}{7}$

  B $11\frac{3}{7}$ **D** not given

11. $5\frac{1}{3} \times 1\frac{7}{8}$

  A $5\frac{7}{24}$ **C** 10

  B $7\frac{1}{2}$ **D** not given

12. Complete. 2 ft 7 in. = ___ in.

  A 17   **C** 43

  B 23   **D** not given

13. What kind of angle has a measure of 95°?

  A obtuse   **C** straight

  B acute   **D** not given

14. What is the relationship between $\overleftrightarrow{MN}$ and $\overleftrightarrow{NO}$?

  A parallel   **C** transversal

  B perpendicular   **D** not given

15. What is the name of a polygon with four sides?

  A pentagon   **C** quadrilateral

  B triangle   **D** not given

16. What is $\overline{AC}$?

  A diameter   **C** arc

  B radius   **D** not given

CUMULATIVE REVIEW

Choose the correct answers. Write A, B, C, or D.

17. What is the name of a triangle with no equal sides?

  A isosceles   **C** scalene

  B equilateral   **D** not given

18. Solve for n. $\frac{3}{n} = \frac{15}{35}$

  A 7   **C** 9

  B 5   **D** not given

19. What is the unit price of 25 cans for $7.75?

  A $.31   **C** $193.75

  B $.10   **D** not given

20. What is $\frac{6}{100}$ as a percent?

  A 60%   **C** 3%

  B 6%   **D** not given

21. What is $14\frac{1}{2}$% as a decimal?

  A 14.5   **C** 0.145

  B $1.4\frac{1}{2}$ **D** not given

22. What is $\frac{39}{10}$ as a percent?

  A 3.9%   **C** 390%

  B 39%   **D** not given

23. What is 30% of 180?

  A 54   **C** 72

  B 600   **D** not given

24. 20% of what number is 12?

  A 60   **C** 4.8

  B 2.4   **D** not given

25. What percent of 90 is 30?

  A 15%   **C** $33\frac{1}{3}$%

  B 66%   **D** not given

26. What is the simple interest for $1,200 at 6% for 2 yr?

  A $72   **C** $1,440

  B $144   **D** not given

27. What is the perimeter?

  A 34 cm   **C** 17 cm

  B 57.04 cm^2 **D** not given

28. What is the area?

  A 90 m^2 **C** 35 m^2

  B 48 m^2 **D** not given

29. What is the area of a square with a side of 3.6 m?

  A 14.4 m^2 **C** 12.96 m^2

  B 7.2 m^2 **D** not given

30. What is the area? Round to the nearest one.

  A 154 mm^2 **C** 44 mm^2

  B 22 mm^2 **D** not given

CUMULATIVE REVIEW

Choose the correct answers. Write A, B, C, or D.

Make a drawing to help solve 31 and 32.

31. Two airplanes leave an airport at the same time, traveling in opposite directions. One plane flies at $\frac{1}{3}$ the speed of the other. If the faster plane has a speed of 600 miles per hour, how far apart are the planes after 1 hour?

    A 800 miles   C 600 miles

    B 1,800 miles   D not given

32. How many miles is the slower plane from the airport after $2\frac{1}{2}$ hours?

    A 1,500 miles   C 400 miles

    B 500 miles   D not given

Solve.

33. Carla bought pencils and pens at the school bookstore. Pencils cost $.15 and pens cost $.17 each. How many pencils did she buy if she spent $1.75 in all?

    A 5   C 6

    B 7   D not given

Complete each pattern.

34. 1.5, 1.8, 2.1, ___, 2.7, 3

    A 2.4   C 2.3

    B 2.5   D not given

35. $1\frac{1}{2}$, ___, $\frac{3}{8}$, $\frac{3}{16}$, $\frac{3}{32}$

    A $\frac{3}{5}$ C $\frac{3}{4}$

    B $\frac{2}{4}$ D not given

Solve.

36. There are 20,547 television sets in Miltown. Each of 5,800 families owns 2 sets, and each of 1,700 families owns 3 sets. All the other families own 1 set each. How many families own 1 television set?

    A 3,847   C 5,100

    B 13,047   D not given

37. If each television set is watched an average of 2.25 hours a day, how many hours of television are watched in Miltown each day?

    A 46,230.75   C 23,280.75

    B 25,530.75   D not given

Use the graph to solve 38 and 39.

The graph shows the number of tickets sold for a roller-skating party. The graph is incomplete.

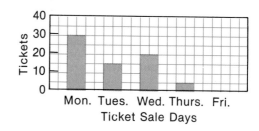

38. On which two days did the sales total 35?

    A Mon. and Tues.   C Wed. and Thurs.

    B Tues. and Wed.   D not given

39. How many tickets were sold on Friday if $300.00 is collected for the 5 days and each ticket costs $2.50?

    A 125   C 50

    B 70   D not given

Theme: Sports

Range and Mode

Statistics is the science of collecting, organizing, and analyzing data or facts.

Teresa is writing a feature story about the girls' basketball team. She collected data on the heights of the players. She made the **frequency table** below to organize the data. The table shows the number of players of each height. The frequency of an item is the number of times it occurs.

Height	Tally	Frequency
5 ft 5 in.	I	1
5 ft 6 in.	II	2
5 ft 7 in.	IIII	4
5 ft 8 in.	I	1
5 ft 9 in.		0
5 ft 10 in.	II	2
5 ft 11 in.		0
6 ft 0 in.	I	1

There are several ways to describe a collection of data.

The **range** is the difference between the greatest number and the least number in the data.

$$\begin{array}{r} \overset{5}{\cancel{6}} \text{ ft} \overset{12}{} \\ - 5 \text{ ft } 5 \text{ in.} \\ \hline 7 \text{ in.} \end{array}$$ ← greatest height ← least height

The range of the heights is 7 in.

The **mode** is the number that occurs most often. Four players are 5 ft 7 in. tall. The mode is 5 ft 7 in.

▶A collection of data may have more than one mode.

Teresa looked at the points scored by individual players during the first two basketball games of the year.

points in game 1: 2, 4, 7, 5, 4, 1, 0, 3 ← One number occurs most frequently. The mode is 4.

points in game 2: 2, 4, 4, 4, 7, 7, 5, 7 ← Two numbers occur most frequently. There are two modes—4 and 7.

CLASSWORK

Make a frequency table for each collection of data. Find the range and the mode or modes for each.

1.

Number of Points Scored					
8	6	4	5	4	5
3	0	6	5	5	8

2.

Ages of Players					
15	17	16	15	15	16
18	14	15	16	16	

PRACTICE

Make a frequency table for each collection of data. Find the range and the mode for each.

1.

Weights of Team Members				
105	112	108	121	115
110	115	100	113	102

2.

Daily High Temperatures (°F)						
78°	81°	84°	90°	80°	80°	87°
85°	84°	70°	73°	79°	79°	84°

3.

Ages of Workers in a Company					
49	42	37	38	22	38
53	37	25	46	37	49

4.

Weekly Salaries of Store Employees					
$250	$310	$280	$210	$320	$250
$350	$250	$225	$250	$350	$310

Find the range and the mode or modes for each collection of data.

5. 2, 10, 10, 20, 5, 15

6. 13, 17, 10, 14, 13, 12, 0, 11, 15, 14

7. 27, 28, 26, 26, 31, 37, 26

8. 1.5, 2.5, 2, 2, 2.5, 2.5, 1.5, 1.5

9. $1.42, $1.25, $2.53, $1.01, $3.13, $1.66, $1.42

10. 5.6, 5.3, 5.6, 5.1, 5.8, 5.6, 5.8, 5.3

11. 984, 986, 975, 886, 961, 975, 962, 944, 875

★**12.** 0.10, 0.01, 0.101, 0.110, 0.011, 0.001, 0.010, 0.110, 0.111

★**13.** The greatest and least numbers in a collection of data are 26.4 and 13.9. Add one more number to the data so that the range is 18.5.

APPLICATION

For 14–19 use the table below, which lists the seating capacities to the nearest thousand.

UNIVERSITY FOOTBALL STADIUMS			
School	Capacity	School	Capacity
Brigham Young U.	66,000	New Mexico State U.	30,000
U. of North Carolina	50,000	Notre Dame U.	59,000
U. of Hawaii	50,000	Ohio State U.	85,000
Iowa State U.	50,000	Stanford U.	85,000
U. of Michigan	102,000	Utah State U.	30,000

14. Make a frequency table.

15. Which stadium has the greatest capacity?

16. What is the range of the capacities?

17. What is the mode of the capacities?

18. If the University of Michigan was not included, would the range be different? If so, what would it be?

19. If Iowa State was not included, would the mode change? If so, how?

Median and Mean

Coach Parker studies batting averages to check the performance of his players. The ranked list below, which shows the averages in order, gives him a better picture.

The mode is a measure of central tendency.

Two other measures of central tendency are the median and the mean.

Team Batting Averages	
Allen	.252
Avalone	.301
Bates	.280
Grey	.325
Kim	.212
Marshall	.199
Post	.343
Rodriguez	.299
Stone	.156

Ranked Batting Averages		
Post	.343	
Grey	.325	
Avalone	.301	
Rodriguez	.299	
Bates	.280	← median
Allen	.252	
Kim	.212	
Marshall	.199	
Stone	.156	

The **median** of a collection of data is the middle number when the data are arranged in order. When there are two middle numbers, the median is the average of the two.

The median of the batting averages is .280.

The **mean** is the sum of all the data divided by the number of data.

To find the mean batting average, divide the sum of the batting averages by the number of batting averages.

$$\frac{.343 + .325 + .301 + .299 + .280 + .252 + .212 + .199 + .156}{9} = \frac{2.367}{9} = .263$$

The mean batting average is .263.

CLASSWORK

Find the median and the mean for each collection of data.

1. Number of runs scored: 5; 4; 6; 7; 0; 4; 9

2. Number of members in some high school bands: 50; 64; 78; 36; 42; 50; 36; 48; 52; 64

3. Number of seats in some school auditoriums: 368; 550; 480; 525; 375; 390; 410; 450; 466

PRACTICE

Find the median and the mean for each collection of data.

1. 10; 14; 25; 19; 12

2. 94; 97; 91; 100; 95; 99

3. 75; 54; 62; 80; 48; 75; 80; 56

4. 21; 24; 18; 33; 17; 25; 31; 20; 18

5. $1.30; $2.25; $3.95; $1.90; $1.50

6. 135; 157; 179; 223; 250; 298; 111; 189

7. 1,160; 1,590; 1,050; 1,840; 1,330; 1,010

8. 14.3 cm; 13.9 cm; 19.0 cm; 16.4 cm; 17.9 cm

9. 12.5; 12.8; 13.7; 13.4; 15.2; 12.2; 12.1; 13.0; 15.9; 13.5

10. 3,105; 4,246; 7,329; 9,688; 11,002

APPLICATION

Use the table at the right to answer 11–18.

11. What is the range of the salaries?

12. How many people are employed?

13. What is the mode of the salaries?

14. Find the total amount paid in salaries for each of the following categories: sales manager, full-time staff, part-time staff.

15. What is the total of all the salaries?

★ **16.** What is the median salary?

★ **17.** What is the mean salary? Round to the nearest dollar.

★ **18.** Would the mean, the median, or the mode be most affected by an unusually high or low number in a collection of data (such as the low salary of $8,000)? Explain your answer.

SILVERDOME SPORTS ARENA SALARIES		
Job	Number Employed	Salary
Director	1	$55,000
Advertising manager	1	$40,000
Sales manager	2	$30,000
Full-time Staff	15	$20,000
Part-time staff	12	$ 8,000

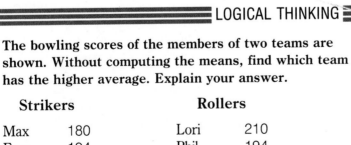

LOGICAL THINKING

The bowling scores of the members of two teams are shown. Without computing the means, find which team has the higher average. Explain your answer.

Strikers		**Rollers**	
Max	180	Lori	210
Fran	194	Phil	194
Glen	187	Jeanne	188
Tracy	194	Tim	200
Annie	196	Sean	186

Graphing Data

Graphs are used to organize and present data in picture form.

In a survey at Jefferson High School, students were asked which sport they preferred. Coach Johnson organized the data from the survey. He made the **bar graph** below. A bar graph is a good way to show comparisons.

Data

Students' Sports Preferences	
Baseball	50
Basketball	80
Hockey	40
Soccer	60
Swimming	40
Track	90

Bar Graph

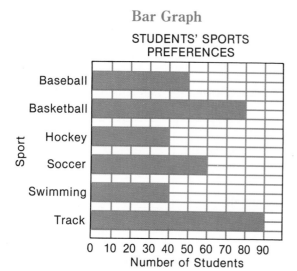

STUDENTS' SPORTS PREFERENCES

To make a bar graph, follow these steps.

- On graph paper draw the horizontal and vertical axes and label them.

- Choose a scale for one axis. Mark equal intervals on that axis from zero to the largest number being graphed.

- Draw a bar for each item. The length of each bar corresponds to the data.

- Give the graph a title.

A bar graph can be horizontal or vertical. A **double-bar graph** compares two related collections of data. This double-bar graph shows the separate responses of boys and girls to the survey.

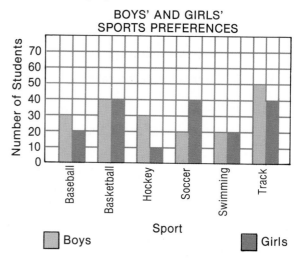

BOYS' AND GIRLS' SPORTS PREFERENCES

CLASSWORK

Use the graphs above to answer each question.

1. Which sports were preferred by more than 50 students?

2. What was the most popular sport among boys?

3. What was the least popular sport among girls?

4. Which sport did more girls prefer than boys?

5. Which sports did more than 30 boys prefer?

370

PRACTICE

Use the bar graph to answer 1–6.

1. Which sport had the greatest attendance?

2. Which sports had attendance under 600?

3. Which two sports had equal attendance?

4. How many people attended basketball games during the month?

5. How many more people attended tennis matches than track meets?

6. The football, soccer, and track events took place outdoors. What was the total attendance at indoor events?

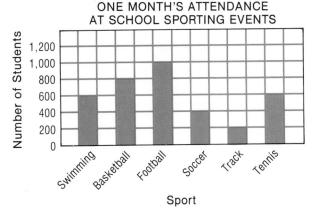

ONE MONTH'S ATTENDANCE AT SCHOOL SPORTING EVENTS

Use the data below to complete the graph.

7. Herman—95 in.
   Wilbur—80 in.
   Orrin—100 in.
   Rafael—74 in.
   Mike—90 in.

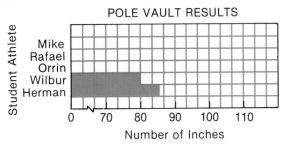

POLE VAULT RESULTS

APPLICATION

Make a bar graph for each collection of sports data from Dade School.

8. Number of points scored during a basketball game:
   Lynn—18; Jean—12; Sara—20; Gina—6; Lee—12; Sue—8

★ 9. Number of students who use gymnastic equipment:
   7th grade: horse—21; balance beam—17; rings—13; uneven bars—8
   8th grade: horse—26; balance beam—19; rings—6; uneven bars—5 (Make a double-bar graph.)

PICTOGRAPHS

Pictographs use symbols to represent the data. Each symbol stands for a certain amount.

Use the pictograph to find the seating capacity of each stadium.

1. Northside
2. Dome
3. National
4. Park

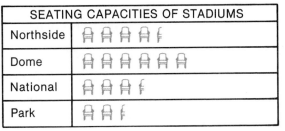

SEATING CAPACITIES OF STADIUMS	
Northside	🪑🪑🪑🪑🪑
Dome	🪑🪑🪑🪑🪑🪑
National	🪑🪑🪑🪑
Park	🪑🪑🪑

Each 🪑 = 10,000 seats

Line Graphs

Felicia has just joined the swim team. At morning practice she is trying to increase the number of laps she can swim. Her progress for the week can be shown clearly on a line graph.

FELICIA'S PRACTICE LAPS				
Mon.	Tues.	Wed.	Thurs.	Fri.
50	100	90	120	150

Line graphs are used to show trends or changes over time.

To make a line graph, follow these steps.

- Use graph paper. Draw the horizontal and vertical axes of the graph and label them.

- Choose a scale for the vertical axis. Mark equal intervals on each axis.

- Locate a point on the graph for each pair of facts. Then connect the points. For this data, one pair is: Mon.,50.

- Give the graph a title.

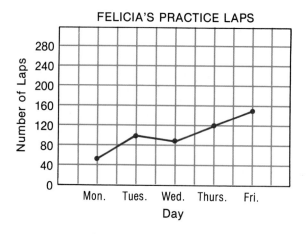

The steeper the line, the greater the change.

A **double-line** graph compares changes in two groups of data. This graph compares Felicia's laps at swimming practice with those of her friend Chen.

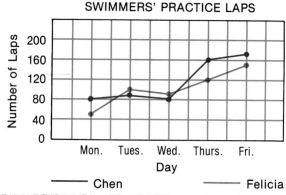

CLASSWORK

Use the graphs above to answer each question.

1. Who swam more laps on Tuesday?

2. On which days did Chen swim more laps than Felicia?

3. On which day was there the greatest difference between the number of laps Felicia and Chen swam?

4. Which swimmer made the best improvement by Friday?

PRACTICE

Use the line graph at the right to answer 1–3.

1. In which two years did the Eagles win the same number of games?

2. Did the team's number of wins increase or decrease between 1982 and 1983?

3. Between which two years did the team have the greatest increase in number of wins?

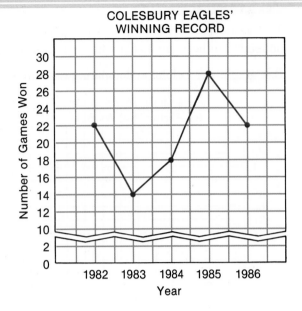

COLESBURY EAGLES'
WINNING RECORD

Use the line graph at the right to answer 4–7.

4. Marc bowled 9 games in one month. Copy and complete the graph for his last five scores, which were 110, 125, 115, 113, and 118.

5. After which game did Marc's scores begin to improve?

6. Between which two games did Marc improve the most?

7. Between which two games was there no change in Marc's scores?

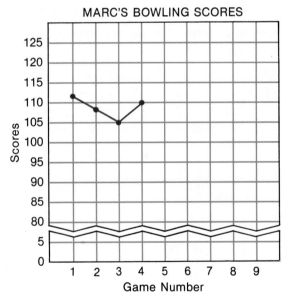

MARC'S BOWLING SCORES

APPLICATION

Make a line graph for each collection of data.

8. Number of strikeouts Leroy pitched in his first five games: game 1—3; game 2—8; game 3—2; game 4—3; game 5—7

9. Total distances Stan rushed in four football games: game 1—160 yd; game 2—220 yd; game 3—190 yd; game 4—150 yd

★10. Rita's scores in figure skating on five days: Monday—5.4; Tuesday—5.6; Wednesday—5.0; Thursday—5.5; Friday—5.6

Comparing Data

The best type of graph to use to display a collection of data depends on the relationship you need to show.

Bar graphs are helpful in comparing quantities.

Line graphs clearly show changes over time.

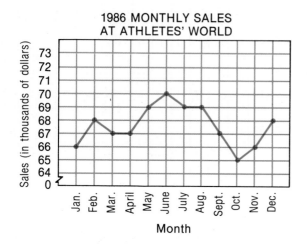

1986 MONTHLY SALES AT ATHLETES' WORLD

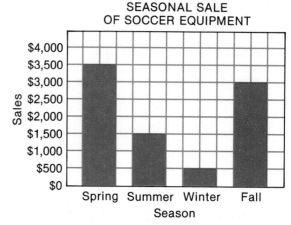

SEASONAL SALE OF SOCCER EQUIPMENT

Circle graphs show the relationship of parts to a whole.

This circle graph shows how the total amount of sales for one day is divided among the five departments at Athlete's World. The percent tells what part of the total each section represents.

What was the amount of the bowling department sales?

Find 5% of $4,000.

$n = 5\% \times \$4,000$

$n = 0.05 \times \$4,000$

$n = \$200$

On Wednesday, sales in the bowling department amounted to $200.

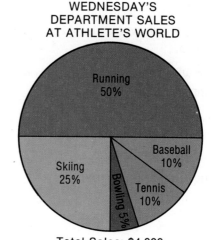

WEDNESDAY'S DEPARTMENT SALES AT ATHLETE'S WORLD

Total Sales: $4,000

CLASSWORK

Use the circle graph above to answer 1–5.

1. Were the combined sales for baseball and tennis greater than or less than the sales for skiing?

Complete the sales chart at the right.

Wednesday's Sales	
Department	**Amount**
2. Skiing	
3. Tennis	
4. Baseball	
5. Running	

374

PRACTICE

The circle graph at the right shows how the sports books in a library are divided according to sport.

Find the number of books for each sport.

1. baseball
2. tennis
3. track
4. swimming
5. gymnastics
6. volleyball

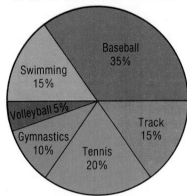

SPORTS BOOKS IN LIBRARY

Total Books: 200

Solve.

★7. The library purchased 50 more books about baseball. What percent of the library's books are now about baseball?

Use the circle graph at the right to answer 8–12.

8. What was the total number of televised sports events?

9. How many football events were televised?

10. How many tennis events were televised?

11. Was the total number of televised events for tennis, bowling, and boxing greater than or less than the number of televised events for baseball?

★12. The network plans to increase the televised sports events to include an additional 20 football games. What percent of televised sports events would then be football games?

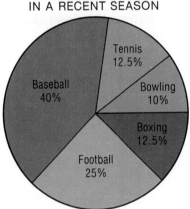

TELEVISED SPORTS EVENTS IN A RECENT SEASON

Total Events: 80

APPLICATION

Make a bar graph or a line graph to show the data in each table.

13.

SEATING CAPACITY OF FOOTBALL STADIUMS	
Stadium	**Capacity (to nearest thousand)**
Memorial Stadium	60,000
Astrodome	50,000
Mile High Stadium	75,000
Three Rivers Stadium	50,000

14.

RYAN'S WEIGHT WHILE IN TRAINING FOR WRESTLING	
Day	**Weight**
1	120 lb
2	122 lb
3	122 lb
4	124 lb
5	123 lb
6	121 lb

Problem Solving

MAKING A LIST

Making an organized list of the data in a problem is another way of clarifying what is actually going on in the problem. Sometimes the list leads to the answer; sometimes the list is the answer.

1. José and León are preparing for a marathon by jogging around a track. They begin together at 7:00 A.M. at the starting line. José completes one lap in 6 minutes. León takes 5 minutes to complete one lap. When will they both be at the starting line together again, and how many laps will each have run at that time?

   José completes one lap in 6 minutes.
   León completes one lap in 5 minutes.

Make a list showing the times that each jogger crosses the starting line.

Lap	1	2	3	4	5	6	7
José	7:00	7:06	7:12	7:18	7:24	7:30	7:36
León	7:00	7:05	7:10	7:15	7:20	7:25	7:30

The list shows that both will be at the starting line again at 7:30 A.M. José will have completed 5 laps, and León will have completed 6 laps.

Does the answer seem reasonable?

Yes. The faster jogger ran more laps.

2. During the baseball playoffs, the Aggies beat the Cougars, 12–3. The Lions lost to the Eagles, 7–5, but beat the Cougars, 4–3. The Cougars beat the Eagles, 5–3. The Aggies beat the Eagles, 6–3, and the Eagles beat the Cougars, 3–0. What was the mean number of runs scored per game by the Eagles? What was the mean number of runs scored per game by the Lions?

To find the mean number of runs, first find the total number of runs scored and the number of games played for each team.

Make an organized list to show the number of runs scored by each team.

Complete the solution.

Solve.

Here are the points scored by periods in the first four basketball games of the season.

Game 1: 17, 23, 16, 18   Game 2: 21, 23, 20, 17
Game 3: 19, 23, 15, 19   Game 4: 31, 23, 20, 23

1. What was the mean score for the first two periods of all four games?

2. What was the mean score for the last two periods of all four games?

3. Find the total score for each game. What was the mean score for the four games?

4. How do you explain that the score was below the mean in three of the four games?

The first 30 fans to enter the stadium are being polled by announcers from three networks. Jack Stone polls every other fan. Cindy Smith polls every third fan, and Janet Puleo polls every fifth fan.

5. How many people are polled by Jack Stone?

6. How many people are polled by Cindy Smith?

7. How many people are polled by exactly 2 announcers?

8. How many people are polled by exactly 3 announcers?

The heights of the starting five players on the Middle School basketball team are 5 ft 5 in., 6 ft, 5 ft 9 in., 5 ft 5 in., and 6 ft 2 in.

9. Make a list of their heights from tallest to shortest.

10. What are the median and the mode of the heights?

11. Danielle, April, Nancy, and Susan are playing a round-robin racquetball match. Each player must play one match with each of the other players. How many matches will be played in the tournament?

★ 12. Jonas Jackson played three baseball games on his birthday. The total number of runs scored by his team in the three games was the same as his age. The product of the numbers of runs scored in the three games is 72. The team never scored more than 6 runs in any one game. No two scores were the same. How many runs did the team score in each game?

═══ CREATE YOUR OWN PROBLEM ═══

Write a problem about hockey using the information given in the list.

Game Number	Shots on Goal	Goals Scored
1	7	1
2	3	3
3	4	0
4	6	0

Experiments and Outcomes

Before the Super Bowl each year, a coin is tossed. The team that wins the toss chooses whether the team will start the game by kicking the ball or by receiving it.

This experiment has two possible **outcomes**—heads or tails. Each outcome is **equally likely** to happen.

An **event** *(E)* is one or more outcomes of an experiment.

Before the toss, the team captain called heads.

There is one **favorable outcome** for this event—that the coin lands with heads up.

The **probability** that the coin lands heads up is 1 out of 2, or $\frac{1}{2}$.

▶ If all the outcomes are equally likely, then use this formula to find the probability of an event, $P(E)$.

$$P(E) = \frac{\text{number of favorable outcomes}}{\text{number of possible outcomes}}$$

so $P(\text{heads})$, or $P(H) = \frac{1}{2}$.

CLASSWORK

Use the spinner for 1–10.

1. List all the possible outcomes for spinning the spinner 1 time.

2. Is each outcome equally likely?

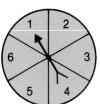

Find the probability of each event.

3. spinning a 5

4. spinning an odd number

5. spinning a 3

6. spinning a number less than 6

7. P(even number)

8. spinning a number greater than 4

9. $P(4)$

10. P(not 4)

PRACTICE

Use the spinner at the right for 1–12.

1. List all the possible outcomes for spinning the spinner 1 time.

2. Is each outcome equally likely?

Find the probability of each event.

3. spinning a 2

4. spinning a 3

5. $P(8)$

6. $P(16)$

7. $P(14)$

8. $P(\text{not } 14)$

9. $P(\text{less than } 12)$

10. $P(\text{greater than } 12)$

★ 11. $P(\text{multiple of } 4)$

★ 12. $P(\text{factor of } 24)$

Without looking, Amy picks one card from those below. Find each probability.

13. $P(F)$

14. $P(B)$

15. $P(O)$

16. $P(L)$

17. $P(\text{not } B)$

18. $P(T)$

19. $P(\text{vowel})$

20. $P(\text{not vowel})$

Pick a marble without looking.

21. List the outcomes for the experiment.

22. List the outcomes for the event that a marble is not red and not yellow.

Find each probability.

23. $P(\text{red})$

24. $P(\text{green})$

25. $P(\text{blue})$

26. $P(\text{yellow})$

27. $P(\text{not yellow})$

28. $P(\text{not blue})$

29. $P(\text{not red})$

30. $P(\text{not yellow})$

APPLICATION

At Camp Winoke a spinner is used each day to determine the sport played.

Spin the spinner once.

31. What is the probability that you will play a sport?

32. What is the probability that you will play football?

33. What is the probability that you will not play tennis?

34. You don't want to play baseball. What is the probability of playing a sport other than baseball?

Probabilities and Relative Frequencies

Hiroko is a market researcher for an advertising company. She asked 100 people what sport they are most likely to watch on television. The results of her survey are shown in the table at the right. What is the probability that a person chosen at random from those surveyed would name soccer?

To find the probability, find the **relative frequency** of the event.

▶ The relative frequency is the ratio

$$\frac{\text{frequency of an event}}{\text{total frequency}}$$

In the survey, the relative frequency of soccer is $\frac{10}{100}$. So, the probability that a person chosen at random from those surveyed would name soccer is $\frac{10}{100}$.

Relative frequency can be used to make predictions. Use the data above to predict how many people would name basketball if 500 were surveyed.

Relative frequency of basketball $= \frac{16}{100}$

Write a proportion. $\frac{16}{100} = \frac{n}{500}$

$8{,}000 = 100n$

$80 = n$

FAVORITE SPORT ON TV

Sport	Frequency
Baseball	26
Basketball	16
Football	28
Ice Hockey	12
Soccer	10
Tennis	4
None	4
Total	100

You can predict that 80 people would name basketball. 80 is an estimate. The results may differ, depending on the sample surveyed.

CLASSWORK

Toss a coin 10 times. Record the results in a frequency table. Combine your results with those of your classmates.

1. What is the relative frequency of tossing heads? of tossing tails?

2. How many heads would you expect in 100 tosses?

3. How many tails would you expect in 250 tosses?

50 students were asked how many hours they spend watching sports on television during the weekend. The table shows the results.

Number of Hours	Frequency
0	3
1	4
2	6
3	12
4	15
5	8
6	0
7	2
Total	50

Find the relative frequency of each number of hours.

1. 1   **2.** 4   **3.** 5

4. 2   **5.** 3   **6.** 7

7. more than 4   **8.** less than 3

Suppose 200 students were surveyed.
Give the frequency that you would expect for each.

9. 4 hours   **10.** 6 hours   **11.** 2 hours   ★**12.** 3 or 5 hours

Use the table at the right.
Find each probability for a toss of the cube.

Top Number on Cube	Frequency
1	4
2	5
3	3
4	5
5	4
6	4
Total	25

13. $P(1)$ **14.** $P(2)$ **15.** $P(3)$

16. $P(4)$ **17.** $P(5)$ **18.** $P(6)$

19. P(an even number)   **20.** P(an odd number)

Suppose the number cube was rolled 75 times.
Give the frequency you would expect for each.

21. 1   **22.** 2   **23.** 3   **24.** 4

25. 5   **26.** 6   ★**27.** a number less than 3   ★**28.** a prime number

APPLICATION

The Nielsen TV rating system monitors 1,200 TV sets to learn what programs people are watching. A rating is given to a TV show based on relative frequency. The relative frequency is given as a percent.

Give the Nielsen rating for each show, based on the 1,200 sets monitored. Use percents.

29. 900 sets tuned to the Super Bowl game   **30.** 72 sets tuned to Monday night wrestling

31. 200 sets tuned to college basketball   **32.** 1,000 sets tuned to the World Series

Mutually Exclusive Events

Hockey coach Ted Schable has this complete collection of pennants for the National Hockey League on his wall. He has another set of these pennants to give to the 21 members of his team. He will distribute them randomly, and each player will receive one.

What is the probability that any one player will receive the pennant of the Stanley cup winner *or* the pennant of the other finalist?

Since a player will receive no more than one pennant, the events cannot occur at the same time.

The events are said to be **mutually exclusive.**

▶ If A and B are mutually exclusive events, then $P(A \text{ or } B) = P(A) + P(B)$.

$P(\text{Stanley cup pennant}) = \frac{1}{21}$

$P(\text{other finalist's pennant}) = \frac{1}{21}$

So the probability of receiving one of these pennants is $\frac{1}{21} + \frac{1}{21} = \frac{2}{21}$.

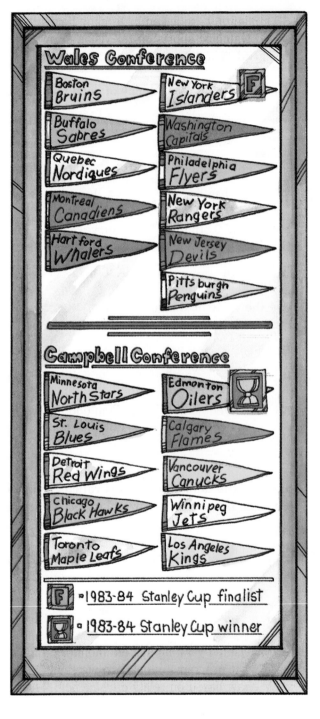

CLASSWORK

Find the probability of a team member receiving each pennant.

1. $P(\text{Boston Bruins})$
2. $P(\text{New York Rangers})$
3. $P(\text{Bruins or Rangers})$
4. $P(\text{Campbell Conference})$
5. $P(\text{Wales Conference})$
6. $P(\text{New York team})$

PRACTICE

Use the spinner. Find each probability in lowest terms.

1. $P(3)$ 2. $P(8)$ 3. $P(3 \text{ or } 8)$

4. $P(2)$ 5. $P(\text{even number})$ 6. $P(2 \text{ or odd number})$

7. $P(6)$ 8. $P(\text{multiple of } 4)$ 9. $P(6 \text{ or multiple of } 4)$

10. $P(\text{number less than } 6)$ 11. $P(\text{number greater than } 2)$ ★ 12. $P(\text{number less than } 6 \text{ and greater than } 2)$

A pennant is chosen without looking. Find each probability in lowest terms.

13. $P(\text{red})$ 14. $P(\text{baseball})$ 15. $P(\text{red or baseball})$

16. $P(\text{hockey})$ 17. $P(\text{hockey or baseball})$ 18. $P(\text{football})$

19. $P(\text{football or baseball})$ 20. $P(\text{blue or red})$ ★ 21. $P(\text{red or blue or green})$

APPLICATION

A class of 15 boys and 20 girls went to the park. There was a baseball game in which 8 boys and 15 girls played. Of the remaining students 2 girls played tennis and 5 boys played basketball. One student is picked at random to help the teacher. Find each probability.

22. $P(\text{a boy or a student who played tennis})$ 23. $P(\text{a student who played basketball or tennis})$

24. $P(\text{a girl or a student who played basketball})$ ★ 25. $P(\text{a student who did not play any sport})$

MATH HISTORY

The 17th-century French mathematician, Blaise Pascal, was a pioneer in the theory of probability. **Pascal's triangle** is shown at the right. Each number in the triangle is the sum of the pair of numbers above it.

```
                    1
                  1   1
second row →  1   2   1
                1   3   3   1
              1   4   6   4   1
            1   5  10  10   5   1
```

The second row of the triangle shows the number of ways in which 2 coins can land if they are tossed.

Number of Heads →	2	1	0
Number of ways →	1	2	1
Probability ──→	$\frac{1}{4}$	$\frac{2}{4}$	$\frac{1}{4}$

- Extend the triangle to the sixth row. How many ways can 6 coins land if tossed? What are the probabilities?

- What other patterns do you see in Pascal's triangle?

Range of Probabilities

The 5 players shown are candidates for captain of the volleyball team. Each is equally likely to be selected. What is the probability that 1 of these players will become captain?

Since these 5 players are the *only* candidates, the event that 1 of them will be selected captain is *certain*. It must occur.

▶ An event that must occur has a probability of 1.

P(selecting 1 of the 5 candidates) $= 1$

What is the probability of selecting 11 for captain? 11 is not a candidate. This event is *impossible*.

▶ An impossible event has a probability of 0.

$P(11) = 0$

▶ The probability of any event is a number from 0 to 1.

The events E and *not E* are called **complementary events.**

$P(25) = \frac{1}{5}$ $P(\text{not } 25) = \frac{4}{5}$

▶ The sum of the probabilities of complementary events is 1.

$P(E) + P(\text{not } E) = 1$

▶ The sum of the probabilities of all the possible outcomes of an experiment is always 1.

CLASSWORK

Pick a card without looking. Find each probability.

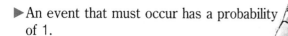

1. $P(1)$
2. $P(5)$
3. $P(\text{not } 5)$
4. $P(3)$
5. $P(\text{less than } 3)$
6. $P(\text{greater than } 3)$
7. $P(8)$
8. $P(\text{not } 8)$

Name the complement of each event.

9. Pick an even number.
10. Pick any number except 2.

PRACTICE

Spin the spinner once.
Find each probability.

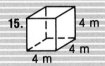

1. $P(3)$ 2. $P(\text{not } 3)$

3. $P(\text{even})$ 4. $P(\text{odd})$

5. $P(7)$ 6. $P(\text{less than } 7)$

7. $P(\text{greater than } 7)$ 8. $P(12)$

9. $P(\text{not } 12)$ 10. $P(\text{not prime})$

11. $P(\text{prime})$ 12. $P(\text{prime}) + P(\text{not prime})$

13. $P(\text{multiple of } 3)$ ★ 14. $P(3 \text{ and odd})$

Write *true* or *false* for each.

15. If $P(A) = \frac{99}{100}$, then A is certain

16. If $P(B) = 0$, then B is impossible

17. $P(C) + P(\text{not } C) = 1$

18. If $P(D) = \frac{3}{10}$, then $P(\text{not } D) = \frac{3}{10}$

19. $P(E)$ may be $= 1\frac{1}{2}$

APPLICATION

A baseball team is moving to a new city. The chart shows all the possible choices and some probabilities for the move.

20. Copy and complete the chart if the probability that Phoenix will be chosen is twice the probability for Boston.

City	Probability
New York	$\frac{20}{100}$
Chicago	$\frac{10}{100}$
Los Angeles	$\frac{15}{100}$
Houston	$\frac{25}{100}$
Phoenix	
Boston	

21. What is the probability that the team will not move to Houston?

22. What is the probability that the team will move to a city in Canada?

★ 23. If New York drops out, will that affect the probabilities of the other cities? Explain what might happen.

1. 27.3
   9.95
   16.87

2. $15.375 + 26.08$

3. $27.1 - 19.93$

4. 1.2×3.84

5. 0.02×0.04

6. $16 \div 3.2$

7. $0.2\overline{)15.8}$

8. $4\frac{3}{5} + 5\frac{1}{6}$

9. $16\frac{1}{10} - 8\frac{3}{8}$

10. $\frac{5}{7} \times 21$

11. $2\frac{1}{7} \times 8\frac{1}{6}$

12. $9 \div 3\frac{1}{2}$

13. $5\frac{1}{2}\%$ of 40

14. $7\frac{1}{4}\%$ of 50

Find the volume of each.

15.

16.

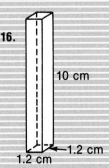

Tree Diagrams and Compound Events

The Melville lacrosse team is purchasing uniforms. Members can choose red or white shorts. They can choose red, white, or striped shirts.

How many possible choices are there for the uniforms?

The **tree diagram** shows all the possible choices, or outcomes.

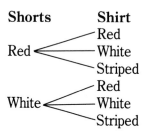

Shorts	Shirt	Outcome
Red	Red	Red, Red
	White	Red, White
	Striped	Red, Striped
White	Red	White, Red
	White	White, White
	Striped	White, Striped

There are 6 possible choices.

You can also multiply to find the answer.

$$\underset{\textbf{choices for shorts}}{2} \times \underset{\textbf{choices for shirts}}{3} = \underset{\textbf{possibilities}}{6}$$

Choosing a uniform is a **compound event**. It is made up of more than 1 event. Here, the events are **independent** of one another. The choice of the shorts does not affect the choice of the shirts.

▶If A and B are independent events, the probability that both will occur, written $P(A,B)$, is

$$P(A,B) = P(A) \times P(B)$$

$P(\textbf{red shorts, striped shirt}) = P(\textbf{red shorts}) \times P(\textbf{striped shirt})$

$$= \frac{1}{2} \times \frac{1}{3} = \frac{1}{6}$$

CLASSWORK

A coin is tossed, and a cube with numbers 1 to 6 is rolled.

1. Draw a tree diagram to show all possible outcomes.

2. List all the outcomes for the event (tails, odd number).

Find each probability.

3. $P(\text{heads}, 3)$

4. $P(\text{tails}, 1)$

5. $P(\text{heads, even number})$

6. $P(\text{tails, not } 4)$

Spin the spinner. Pick a card. Answer exercises 1–9.

1. Draw a tree diagram to show all possible outcomes.

2. List all the outcomes for the event (numbers less than 5, blue).

3. Find the probability of (numbers less than 5, blue) in two ways.

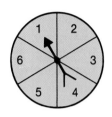

Find each probability.

4. $P(1, \text{red})$

5. $P(2, \text{yellow})$

6. $P(\text{odd}, \text{blue})$

7. $P(6, \text{black})$

8. $P(3, \text{not black})$

9. $P(\text{multiple of } 3, \text{red})$

Pick a marble without looking. Replace it. Pick another marble. Find each probability.

10. $P(\text{red}, \text{blue})$

11. $P(\text{blue}, \text{red})$

12. $P(\text{blue}, \text{green})$

13. $P(\text{blue}, \text{blue})$

14. $P(\text{red}, \text{red})$

15. $P(\text{green}, \text{green})$

★16. $P(\text{blue}, \text{not blue})$

★17. $P(\text{not red}, \text{green})$

★18. $P(\text{green}, \text{not green})$

★19. Suppose you pick a marble and *do not* replace it. You pick another marble. Does the first pick affect the probabilities for the second pick? Are the first and second picks independent events?

APPLICATION

20. Suppose the lacrosse team is also choosing a helmet. Members can choose red or white. Copy and complete the tree diagram on page 386 to show all the possible outcomes. List them.

21. Find the probability of the event (red shorts, white shirt, red helmet); of the event (an outfit of one solid color).

LOGICAL THINKING

A teacher was going to mail three report cards to three students. The teacher addressed three envelopes but did not pay attention to which card was put into which envelope. If all three envelopes were delivered, what is the probability that exactly two students received their own report cards?

Problem Solving

SKILLS AND STRATEGIES REVIEW

Solve.

1. In a weight-lifting contest, the first contestant lifted 200 pounds. Each succeeding contestant lifted 10% more than the person before him. How many pounds did the fourth contestant lift?

2. The chef at Pancake Kitchen can cook 4 pancakes on the griddle at one time. If he cooks the pancakes for 2 minutes on each side, what is the shortest amount of time he needs to cook 6 pancakes?

3. Here are some clues about the points scored by members of the Valhalla College basketball team during the halves of their last five games. Use the clues to make a list that shows the points scored in each half for all 5 games.

Clue 1—In Game 3, they scored a total of 48 points.

Clue 2—They scored 22 points in the second half of Game 1 and Game 4.

Clue 3—Their high score for the season was 36 points in the first half of Game 4.

Clue 4—They scored the same number of points in each half of Game 3, which was 3 points less than they scored in the first half of Game 1.

Clue 5—Fifty points were scored in each of Games 2 and 5.

Clue 6—The ratio of points scored in the first half of the game to the points scored in the second half was 3:2 in both Games 2 and 5.

Use the information below to solve 4 and 5.

Danny, Bobby, and Peter are taking part in a bicycle discovery trip. Bobby bikes 3 mi west, 6 mi north, 1 mi east, 2 mi north, and 8 mi east. Peter bikes 12 mi east, 3 mi north, 4 mi east, 6 mi south, and 10 mi west to end up at the finish line. Danny bikes 6 mi south, 12 mi east, and 9 mi north.

4. How far is Bobby from the end of the course?

5. How long did it take Danny to complete the course?

Solve.

6. In the third quarter of the big game, the score was tied at 21. The punter for the Lions kicked the ball 40 yards. An Eagles player returned the punt 25 yards. A penalty of 15 yards was then called against the Eagles, which put the ball at the 50-yard line. From what line did the punt originate?

7. The Sharks beat the Pythons by 12 points. The total number of points scored was 140. What was the score of the game?

8. The Generals beat the Stars by 4 points. If the Stars had scored twice as many points as they actually did, they would have won by 4 points. How many points did the Generals actually score?

9. A tennis ball is dropped from a height of 100 feet. It rebounds half its height each time it bounces. How far has it traveled when it hits the ground the fourth time?

10. How far does the ball in problem 9 rebound after the fourth bounce?

═══ SOMETHING EXTRA ═══

Strategy Game

This is a game for two people. It is played the way tic-tac-toe is played, but the shape of the game board is different.

Rules
- The first player puts an X in any circle.

- The second player puts an O in any empty circle.

- Players continue to alternate turns. The one who places three marks in a single line is the winner.

- If no one gets three in a line, the game ends in a tie.

Make a copy of the game board and play the game. Think ahead! Plan your moves. Anticipate where your opponent might move, and try to block.

Make a frequency table for each collection of data.
Then find the range, mode, median, and mean for each. pages 366–369

1.

Winning Scores in Football Games				
17	28	7	24	21
28	17	17	7	10

2.

Rainy Days in Each Month					
20	3	11	15	8	11
0	4	15	11	13	6

Make each graph. pages 370–373

3. a bar graph   Number of Students in Sports Clubs:
Soccer—120; Basketball—50; Baseball—90; Football—80

4. a line graph   Mel's Push-ups: Saturday—43;
Sunday—40; Monday—42; Tuesday—47; Wednesday—49

Use the circle graph to answer 5–7. pages 374–375

ACTIVITIES AT TWIN LAKES CAMP

5. Which activity was most popular?

6. There were 150 campers. How many
went rowing?

7. How many campers played either softball
or volleyball?

Softball 25%
Hiking 20%
Rowing 10%
Swimming 30%
Volleyball 15%

Spin the spinner once.
Find each probability. pages 378–379, 382–385

8. $P(6)$

9. $P(7)$

10. $P(\text{odd})$

11. $P(\text{multiple of 3})$

12. $P(9)$

13. $P(\text{not 9})$

14. $P(\text{odd or 4})$

15. $P(\text{even or odd})$

16. $P(\text{prime or 15})$

Pick a card and a marble without looking.
Find each probability. pages 386–387

17. $P(X, \text{green})$

18. $P(E, \text{blue})$

19. $P(\text{not E}, \text{red})$

20. $P(\text{consonant}, \text{blue})$

21. $P(\text{vowel}, \text{not red})$

22. $P(M \text{ or } N, \text{not blue})$

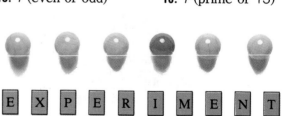

E X P E R I M E N T

Solve. pages 376–377, 388–389

23. In a survey, 115 out of 200 students said
they preferred football to basketball. Give
the frequency you would expect if 800
students were surveyed.

24. You toss a coin and spin a spinner, with
the numbers 1–6. Make a list of all
possible outcomes.

CHAPTER TEST

Find the range, mode, median, and mean for each collection of data.

1. 200, 175, 185, 200, 205, 162, 175

2. 58, 51, 49, 59, 49, 60, 51, 57, 50, 51

Make a bar graph for this collection of data.

3. Types of Pets Owned: Dogs—50; Cats—60; Parakeets—40; Hamsters—30; Goldfish—10; Canaries—10

Use the line graph to answer 4–7.

4. What was the most number of games won by the soccer team in one year?

5. Between which two years did the team improve the most?

6. How many more games did the team win in 1986 than in 1982?

7. In 1985, James School lost 5 soccer games and tied 1. How many games did they play that year?

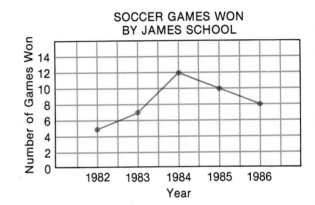

SOCCER GAMES WON
BY JAMES SCHOOL

Choose one card without looking. Find each probability.

8. *P*(green)

9. *P*(white)

10. *P*(not red)

11. *P*(blue or white)

12. *P*(not white)

13. *P*(yellow)

Spin the spinner and pick a disk without looking. Find each probability.

14. *P*(25,S)

15. *P*(20,T)

16. *P*(odd,R)

17. *P*(less than 20,S)

18. *P*(multiple of 10,vowel)

Solve.

19. The Nielsen ratings for one week reported that 480 out of 1,200 families watched the 10:00 P.M. news. Give the rating as a percent.

20. You spin both spinners. Make a list of all possible outcomes.

Five team members shake hands after a game. How many handshakes are exchanged if each member shakes hands with every other member exactly once?

TAKING A POLL

Which spectator sport do you think is most popular in your community? Do you think others agree with your choice? Take a poll!

1. Choose 5 sports. Ask 15 people of various ages which sport they prefer. Also ask which age group they are in. Tally your results in a table like the one below.

FAVORITE SPORT				
Age	Football	Baseball	Hockey	Soccer	Basketball
10–19					
20–29					
30–39					
40–49					
50 and over					

2. Combine your results with those of your classmates. Make a frequency table of the results.

3. Which sport seems to be the most popular?

4. If 1,000 people in your community were surveyed, how many would you expect to prefer each sport?

MISLEADING GRAPHS

The way you present information in a
graph can affect the impression you
make on the reader.

The graph at the right shows attendance at
various sports events in one city. At first
glance, it gives the impression that attendance
at gymnastics events was more than double
that at soccer games. But look carefully at the
scale. Attendance at gymnastics was 11,500,
and attendance at soccer was 10,600—
certainly not a 2:1 ratio!

This is an example of a **misleading graph**.

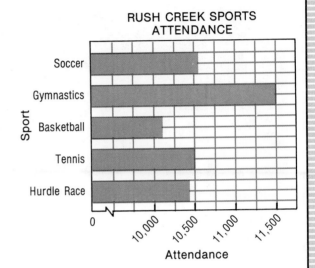

RUSH CREEK SPORTS
ATTENDANCE

Use the bar graph to answer 1 and 2.

1. What has been done to the scale to create
   the misleading impression?

2. What was the attendance at the least
   popular sport? Write this as a percent of
   the attendance at gymnastics.

The line graph suggests a large increase in
the number of families with swimming pools
from 1978 to 1984.

Use the line graph to answer 3–5.

3. What was the actual increase in families
   with swimming pools from 1978 to 1984?

4. Give 2 reasons why the graph is
   misleading.

5. Use the data from the line graph. Draw a
   new line graph with intervals of 4 on the
   vertical scale, starting with 0. Do you think
   your graph gives a truer representation?

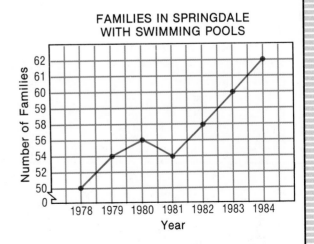

FAMILIES IN SPRINGDALE
WITH SWIMMING POOLS

COMPUTERS IN SPORTS

Joan loves to run and hopes to race in the Olympics someday. The coach uses a computer to analyze her form. Corrections based on her analysis can trim several seconds from her time. With proper training, Joan may become an Olympic medal winner.

Computers are being used more and more in the field of sports.

Baseball was the first sport to use computers for keeping detailed records of players and for analyzing performances. The Oakland A's use a computer to keep track of everything that happens during a game. This includes hits, balls, strikes, runs, errors, and outs. The computer is even used to scout new players for the team.

The strength of an athlete is very important in skiing and ice hockey, which require excellent speed and endurance. Computers can be used to measure this kind of strength. An athlete strains against a device that is hooked to a computer. The computer analyzes the athlete's muscular strengths and weaknesses. The trainer can then use the information to help the athlete overcome many problems.

Computers can show stop-action motion.

The athletes can see every move they made during an event. This close observation helps them to improve their performances and to prevent injuries. It is especially useful in such sports as walking, running, and jogging.

Even the sport of fishing utilizes computers. The computer can analyze fishing conditions, such as water temperature, water depth, and wind direction. Then the computer recommends a specific fishing lure.

Companies that manufacture sports equipment are now using computers to design sneakers, tennis rackets, and golf clubs. This use of computers has resulted in equipment that is much lighter and stronger.

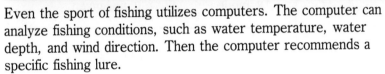

PROJECT

1. Collect newspaper and magazine articles showing computers at work in the sports field. Then make a bulletin-board display featuring those articles.

2. Use the library to find three other ways computers are used in the sports field. Write a report about your findings.

★ 3. Write a computer program to compute a person's batting average.

MAINTAINING SKILLS

Choose the correct answer. Write A, B, C, or D.

1. $\frac{5}{9} \times 63$

   A 35   C 40

   B 45   D not given

2. Name a polygon with eight sides.

   A pentagon   C hexagon

   B octagon   D not given

3. What ratio is equal to $\frac{24}{54}$?

   A $\frac{8}{16}$ C $\frac{12}{37}$

   B $\frac{4}{9}$ D not given

4. What ratio is $66\frac{2}{3}$%?

   A $\frac{1}{3}$ C $\frac{5}{6}$

   B $\frac{3}{8}$ D not given

5. What percent of 40 is 12?

   A 25%   C 30%

   B 70%   D not given

6. What is the interest if principal = $1,200, rate = 3%, and time = $1\frac{1}{2}$ yr?

   A $54   C $1,254

   B $36   D not given

7. What is the area of a circle with a diameter of 42 cm?

   A 132 cm^2 C 9.42 cm^2

   B 66 cm^2 D not given

8. What is the area of a 4.6-meter square?

   A 18.4 m   C 21.4 m^2

   B 9.2 m^2 D not given

9. What is the range for 6.3, 5.02, 19, and 3.5?

   A 8.455   C 5.66

   B 15.5   D not given

10. What is the probability of tossing the number 6 on a cube numbered 1–6?

    A $\frac{1}{6}$ C $\frac{4}{6}$

    B $\frac{1}{5}$ D not given

11. In a collection of data, what is the item with the greatest frequency called?

    A range   C median

    B mode   D not given

12. Toss a coin. What is P(tails)?

    A 1   C $\frac{1}{2}$

    B 0   D not given

Solve.

13. Betty arrived at the party before Artie. She saw Ralph when she walked in. Sally arrived last. In what order did they arrive?

    A R, A, B, S   C R, B, A, S

    B B, A, S, R   D not given

14. Draw a conclusion. *ABCD* is a parallelogram with right angles. It is not a

    A square   C trapezoid

    B rectangle   D not given

Theme: The Desert

Integers

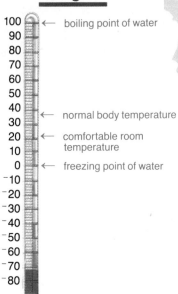

100 ← boiling point of water
90
80
70
60
50
40 ← normal body temperature
30
20 ← comfortable room
10   temperature
0 ← freezing point of water
⁻10
⁻20
⁻30
⁻40
⁻50
⁻60
⁻70
⁻80

July 10, 1913

u cyttaya ꞵttaylaoꞟon llol clꞟlio ollollu cynollo ulloꞟlio ylloo ꞟon llol clꞟlio otlottu cy ulloꞟlio ylla oꞟonclꞟlio ollollu cynollo ulloꞟlio ylla oꞟon llol clꞟlio ollollu cynollo ullo ottq ꞵlottlio yttool clꞟlio ollollu cynollo ulloꞟlio ylla oꞟon llol clꞟlio ollollu cynotto u cyttaon ꞵttaylaoꞟon llol clꞟlio ollollu cynollo ulloꞟlio ylloo ꞟon llol clꞟlio otlottu cy Ʇ₀₎ ylla oꞟou ꞮꞮ ꞏ

January 23, 1971

The Celsius thermometer records
temperatures above and below zero as shown.

Numbers greater than zero are **positive** numbers.

Numbers less than zero are **negative** numbers.

Zero is neither positive nor negative.
⁺57 is read as positive fifty-seven. ⁻62 is read as negative sixty-two.

▶Integers are the numbers
  . . . ⁻3, ⁻2, ⁻1, 0, ⁺1, ⁺2, ⁺3, . . .

The integers from ⁻10 to ⁺10 are shown on the number line
below. Two integers that are the same distance from 0 in
different directions are **opposites.** ⁺3 and ⁻3 are each 3 units
from 0. ⁺3 and ⁻3 are opposites.

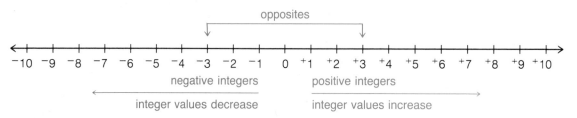

opposites

⁻10 ⁻9 ⁻8 ⁻7 ⁻6 ⁻5 ⁻4 ⁻3 ⁻2 ⁻1 0 ⁺1 ⁺2 ⁺3 ⁺4 ⁺5 ⁺6 ⁺7 ⁺8 ⁺9 ⁺10

negative integers   positive integers

integer values decrease   integer values increase

▶The greater of two integers is the integer that is farther to
  the right on the number line.

⁺4 is to the right of ⁺1.   ⁺2 is to the right of ⁻3.   ⁻4 is to the left of ⁻1.
   ⁺4 > ⁺1   ⁺2 > ⁻3   ⁻4 < ⁻1

CLASSWORK

Write an integer for each. Then write its opposite.

1. a loss of $5   **2.** 10 degrees above zero   **3.** positive 8

Compare. Use >, <, or = for each ●.

4. ⁺7 ● ⁺8   **5.** ⁺5 ● ⁻1   **6.** ⁺1 ● ⁻5   **7.** 0 ● ⁻4   **8.** ⁻8 ● ⁺5

PRACTICE

Write an integer for each. Then write its opposite.

1. a loss of 3 pounds   **2.** a price increase of 6¢   **3.** a gain of 9 pounds

4. 6°C below zero   **5.** negative 30   **6.** positive 90

7. a stock price rise of $4   **8.** 20 meters below sea level   **9.** 15°C above zero

Compare. Use >, <, or = for each ⬤.

10. 0 ⬤ $^+$8   **11.** $^-$1 ⬤ $^-$4   **12.** $^+$3 ⬤ $^+$4   **13.** $^-$3 ⬤ $^+$1

14. $^-$2 ⬤ 0   **15.** $^-$2 ⬤ $^+$2   **16.** 0 ⬤ $^-$6   **17.** $^-$5 ⬤ $^-$3

18. $^-$7 ⬤ $^+$1   **19.** $^-$80 ⬤ $^-$70   **20.** $^+$5 ⬤ $^-$26   **21.** $^-$12 ⬤ $^-$19

Use the number line on page 398. Write the integers in order from least to greatest.

22. $^+$2, $^-$3, 0, $^+$1, $^-$4   **23.** $^-$7, $^-$1, $^+$3, $^-$9, $^+$1, $^-$5

24. $^+$1, $^+$6, $^-$4, $^-$9, $^+$3, $^-$6   **25.** $^-$2, $^+$2, $^-$5, 0, $^+$5, $^-$8

Write the integers that are between the given integers.

★**26.** $^-$2 and $^+$1   ★**27.** $^-$3 and 0   ★**28.** $^+$6 and $^-$2   ★**29.** $^-$5 and $^-$1

APPLICATION

Choose the appropriate temperature for each. Use the Celsius thermometer on page 398.

30. a hot drink

   a. $^-$5°C

   b. $^+$10°C

   c. $^+$75°C

31. your classroom

   a. $^+$22°C

   b. $^+$6°C

   c. $^-$2°C

32. cross-country skiing

   a. $^+$10°C

   b. $^-$3°C

   c. $^+$15°C

Use the table below for 33–36.

33. Which desert had the lowest temperature?

34. List the temperatures in order from least to greatest.

35. In which desert was the temperature the opposite of the temperature in the Gobi?

36. At another time a temperature of 0°C was recorded in the Mojave. Use an integer to represent the change in temperature from that listed in the table.

WINTER TEMPERATURE READINGS IN DESERTS	
Gobi	$^-$12°C
Mojave	$^-$7°C
Painted	$^-$21°C
Sahara	$^+$12°C

399

Adding Integers

A geologist studying rocks in Death Valley National Monument worked part of the day at a site 2 meters above sea level. Later she moved to a site 4 meters higher. How far above or below sea level is the new site?

Write the first location as an integer.
2 meters above sea level $\longrightarrow$ $^+2$

Find $^+2 + {}^+4$.

Use the number line to add integers.

Start at 0.
Move 2 units to the right ($^+2$).
Then move 4 units to the right ($^+4$).

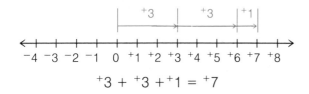

$$^+2 + {}^+4 = {}^+6$$

The geologist's new site is 6 meters above sea level.

Find $^-5 + {}^-3$.

Start at 0.
Move 5 units to the left ($^-5$).
Then move 3 units to the left ($^-3$).

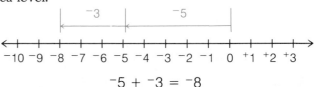

$$^-5 + {}^-3 = {}^-8$$

▶The sum of two positive integers is a positive integer.
  The sum of two negative integers is a negative integer.

More Examples

a. $^+3 + {}^+3 + {}^+1 = n$

b. $^-1 + {}^-4 + {}^-2 = n$

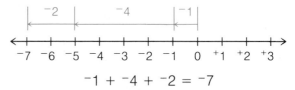

$$^+3 + {}^+3 + {}^+1 = {}^+7$$

$$^-1 + {}^-4 + {}^-2 = {}^-7$$

CLASSWORK

Add. Use a number line if needed.

1. $^+3 + {}^+2$ 2. $^+8 + {}^+1$ 3. $^-6 + {}^-3$ 4. $^-2 + {}^-5$

5. $^+5 + {}^+5$ 6. $^-3 + {}^-2$ 7. $^-7 + {}^-7$ 8. $^+4 + {}^+2$

9. $^-6 + {}^-2$ 10. $^-3 + {}^-7$ 11. $^+6 + {}^+1$ 12. $^-1 + {}^-1$

PRACTICE

Add. Use a number line if needed.

1. $^+4 + {}^+4$
2. $^+1 + {}^+5$
3. $^-3 + {}^-4$
4. $^-5 + {}^-1$

5. $^+6 + {}^+2$
6. $^-2 + {}^-2$
7. $^-8 + {}^-2$
8. $^+5 + {}^+6$

9. $^+9 + {}^+2$
10. $^-2 + {}^-8$
11. $^+7 + {}^+5$
12. $^-3 + {}^-7$

13. $^-5 + {}^-9$
14. $^+12 + {}^+7$
15. $^-8 + {}^-6$
16. $^+15 + {}^+12$

17. $^+6 + {}^+3 + {}^+8$
18. $^-9 + {}^-2 + {}^-4$
19. $0 + {}^-8 + {}^-5$

20. $^+11 + {}^+5 + {}^+3$
21. $^-5 + {}^-6 + {}^-2$
22. $^+10 + 0 + {}^+4$

Compare. Use >, <, or = for each ⬤.

23. $^-3 + {}^-2$ ⬤ $^+3 + {}^+2$
24. $^-3 + {}^-5$ ⬤ $^-2 + {}^-6$
25. $^+4 + {}^+3$ ⬤ $^-5 + {}^-2$

26. $^-8 + {}^-2$ ⬤ $^+6 + {}^+4$
27. $^+3 + {}^+6$ ⬤ $^+6 + {}^+3$
28. $^-5 + 0$ ⬤ $0 + {}^-5$

Evaluate each expression.

29. $^-6 + a$ Let $a = {}^-3$
30. $^+4 + b$ Let $b = {}^+6$
31. $^+15 + n$ Let $n = {}^+7$

APPLICATION

32. Marie does most of her field work in the desert in the morning. One day she began studying rocks at 5:00 A.M., when the temperature was $^+29°C$. When she stopped at 11:00 A.M., the temperature was 9 degrees higher. What was the temperature at 11:00 A.M.?

33. A geologist studied an interesting rock formation at a site 18 m below sea level. He found a similar rock formation at a site 9 m lower. What is the location of the second site?

ABSOLUTE VALUE

The **absolute value** of an integer is the distance that the integer is from 0 on a number line.

$^-5$ is 5 units from 0.
The absolute value of $^-5$ is 5.
Write $|^-5| = 5$.

$^+5$ is 5 units from 0.
The absolute value of $^+5$ is 5.
Write $|^+5| = 5$.

Find each absolute value.

1. $|^-9|$
2. $|^+15|$
3. $|^-6|$
4. $|0|$
5. $|^-24|$
6. $|^+32|$

Adding Positive and Negative Integers

Reservoirs help supply electricity and water to irrigate desert farms. During June the water level in the reservoir that serves Jed Clancer's farm rose 5 feet. During July the level fell 9 feet. What was the total change for June and July?

Think   water rose 5 feet ⟶ ⁺5
water fell 9 feet ⟶ ⁻9

Add ⁺5 + ⁻9 to find the total change.

Use the number line to add.

Start at 0.
Move 5 units to the right (⁺5).
Then move 9 units
to the left (⁻9).

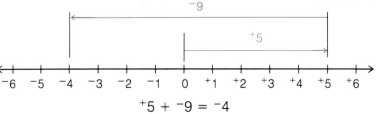

⁺5 + ⁻9 = ⁻4

During June and July the water level in the reservoir decreased 4 feet.

More Examples

a. ⁺6 + ⁻5

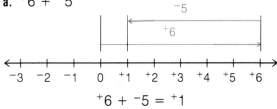

⁺6 + ⁻5 = ⁺1

b. ⁺4 + ⁻4

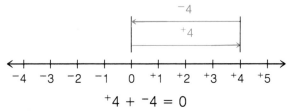

⁺4 + ⁻4 = 0

▶The sum of a positive integer and a negative integer has the same sign as the integer that is farther from zero. The sum of an integer and its opposite is zero.

Opposites are called **additive inverses** because their sum is zero.

⁺2 + ⁻2 = 0
⁻5 + ⁺5 = 0

CLASSWORK

Add. Use a number line if needed.

1. ⁻4 + ⁺2
2. ⁺4 + ⁻2
3. ⁺2 + ⁻5
4. ⁺10 + ⁻10

5. ⁺9 + ⁻7
6. ⁺5 + ⁻4
7. ⁻5 + ⁺4
8. ⁻6 + ⁺8

9. ⁻2 + ⁺5
10. ⁺8 + ⁻8
11. ⁻6 + ⁺4
12. ⁻4 + ⁺6

Add. Use a number line if needed.

1. $^+2 + {}^-3$
2. $^-1 + {}^+6$
3. $^-4 + {}^+3$
4. $^+6 + {}^-2$

5. $^-7 + {}^+2$
6. $^+8 + {}^-6$
7. $^+4 + {}^-9$
8. $^-8 + {}^+10$

9. $^-3 + {}^+9$
10. $^+9 + {}^-3$
11. $^-6 + {}^+1$
12. $^+4 + {}^-5$

13. $^-2 + {}^+2$
14. $^-8 + {}^+4$
15. $^+6 + {}^-7$
16. $^+9 + {}^-9$

17. $^+11 + {}^-8$
18. $^+2 + {}^-9$
19. $^+10 + {}^-6$
20. $^-8 + {}^+13$

Without adding, tell whether each sum is positive or negative.

21. $^+23 + {}^-17$
22. $^+24 + {}^+19$
23. $^-56 + {}^+45$
24. $^-38 + {}^-56$

25. $^-102 + {}^+10$
26. $^+94 + {}^-75$
27. $^+18 + {}^-81$
28. $^+27 + {}^-35$

APPLICATION

In the spring, reservoir levels usually rise as mountain snows melt. During the summer dry periods, water levels drop. The water level in a reservoir is carefully watched. The following data was recorded for October.

Week 1: Water level dropped 3 feet.
Week 2: Water level rose 2 feet.
Week 3: Water level rose 5 feet.
Week 4: Water level dropped 3 feet.

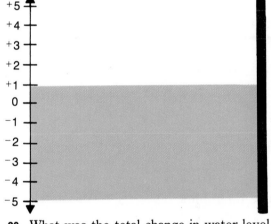

29. What was the total change in water level from October 1 to the end of week 2?

30. During which week was the water level the highest?

31. Using integers, write an equation to show the change in the water level in the reservoir from week 3 to week 4.

Subtracting Integers

Pedro Martinez is a stockbroker. He does research on many stocks before deciding which stocks to buy or sell. One of the companies he is studying manufactures irrigation systems that can be used in desert areas. Last week Aquatech stock sold for $12 per share. This week the stock fell 3 points. What is the price of the stock this week?

You can use subtraction or addition to find the price.

$$^+12 - {}^+3 = {}^+9 \qquad\qquad {}^+12 + {}^-3 = {}^+9$$

This week the price of Aquatech stock is $9 per share. Study these pairs of equations. They suggest a rule for subtracting integers.

Subtraction	Addition	Subtraction	Addition
$^+12 - {}^+3 = {}^+9$	$^+12 + {}^-3 = {}^+9$	$^+7 - {}^+5 = {}^+2$	$^+7 + {}^-5 = {}^+2$
	opposites		opposites

► To subtract an integer, add its opposite.

More Examples

a. $^-4 - {}^-1$

opposites

$$^-4 - {}^-1 = {}^-4 + {}^+1 = {}^-3$$

change to addition

b. $^+5 - {}^+7$

opposites

$$^+5 - {}^+7 = {}^+5 + {}^-7 = {}^-2$$

change to addition

c. $0 - {}^-3$

opposites

$$0 - {}^-3 = 0 + {}^+3 = {}^+3$$

change to addition

CLASSWORK

Find each missing integer.

1. $^+9 - {}^+2 = {}^+9 + \square$

2. $^-6 - {}^+5 = {}^-6 + \square$

3. $^-8 - {}^-3 = {}^-8 + \square$

Subtract.

4. $^-10 - {}^-3$

5. $^-3 - {}^+5$

6. $^+6 - {}^+4$

7. $^+8 - {}^+10$

8. $^-6 - {}^-5$

9. $^-6 - {}^+5$

10. $^+5 - {}^-9$

11. $^-7 - {}^-9$

PRACTICE

Find each missing integer.

1. $^+4 - {}^+6 = {}^+4 + \square$

2. $^-2 - {}^+1 = {}^-2 + \square$

3. $^-3 - {}^+3 = {}^-3 + \square$

4. $^-7 - {}^-4 = {}^-7 + \square$

5. $^-5 - {}^-5 = {}^-5 + \square$

6. $^+9 - {}^+8 = {}^+9 + \square$

Subtract.

7. $^+5 - {}^+7$

8. $^-2 - {}^+3$

9. $^-3 - {}^-4$

10. $^+5 - {}^-1$

11. $^+8 - {}^-8$

12. $^-8 - {}^+8$

13. $^-9 - {}^+4$

14. $^+5 - {}^-3$

15. $^-7 - {}^-2$

16. $^+10 - {}^-4$

17. $^+9 - {}^-5$

18. $^-15 - {}^-14$

19. $0 - {}^-2$

20. $0 - {}^+2$

21. $^-18 - {}^+10$

22. $^+15 - {}^-8$

23. $^-9 - {}^-1$

24. $^+11 - {}^-6$

25. $^-11 - {}^+6$

26. $^-12 - {}^+3$

27. $^-20 - {}^+12$

28. $^+20 - {}^-12$

29. $^-12 - {}^+20$

30. $^+12 - {}^+20$

Evaluate each expression for $n = {}^-5$.

31. $n - {}^+6$

32. $n - {}^-5$

33. $n - {}^+5$

34. $^-4 - n$

35. $^-9 - n$

36. $0 - n$

Replace each $\square$ with the correct sign (+ or −) to make each sentence true.

★ 37. $\square 4 + \square 3 = {}^-1$

★ 38. $\square 6 - \square 2 = {}^+8$

★ 39. $\square 4 - \square 5 = {}^-1$

★ 40. $\square 5 + \square 10 = {}^-5$

APPLICATION

41. On Wednesday, Exacta Corporation stock was selling for $18 per share. This was a $3 rise per share over Tuesday's price. What was the cost of a share of Exacta stock on Tuesday?

★ 42. A share of Janus Corporation stock was selling for $12. The price of the stock rose $4 per share and then fell $6 per share. Using integers, write a number sentence to find the current cost for a share of Janus Corporation stock.

Mixed Practice

1. $\dfrac{3}{8} + \dfrac{7}{8}$

2. $\begin{array}{r} 2\frac{1}{2} \\ + 4\frac{3}{5} \\ \hline \end{array}$

3. $\begin{array}{r} 3\frac{2}{3} \\ - 1\frac{1}{4} \\ \hline \end{array}$

4. $\begin{array}{r} 5\frac{1}{2} \\ - 1\frac{2}{3} \\ \hline \end{array}$

5. $\begin{array}{r} 7 \\ - 3\frac{2}{5} \\ \hline \end{array}$

6. $\dfrac{2}{3} \times \dfrac{6}{7}$

7. $\dfrac{5}{8} \times 6$

8. $1\frac{1}{2} \times 3\frac{5}{6}$

9. $5 \div \dfrac{1}{4}$

10. $2\frac{2}{3} \div 6$

Find the area of each.

11.

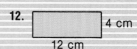
6 cm, 6 cm

12.

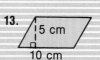
4 cm, 12 cm

13.

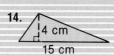
5 cm, 10 cm

14.

4 cm
15 cm

Multiplying Integers

A wind-driven sand dune was steadily moving closer to a desert oasis. Then the wind reversed direction and pushed the dune backwards 5 feet per month. How far and in what direction did the dune move in 3 months?

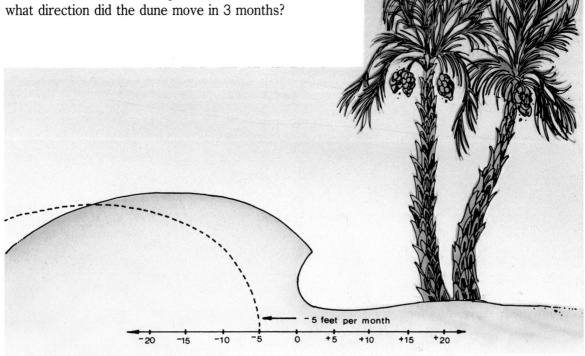

← ⁻5 feet per month

-20 -15 -10 ⁻5   0 +5 +10 +15 +20

A move of 5 feet backwards $\longrightarrow$ ⁻5

Movement in 3 months $\longrightarrow$ ⁻5 + ⁻5 + ⁻5 = ⁺3 · ⁻5 = ⁻15

└ means multiply

The dune moved 15 feet backwards in 3 months.

▶The product of a positive integer and a negative integer is a negative integer.

$$^+4 \cdot {}^-5 = {}^-20 \qquad {}^-2 \cdot {}^+6 = {}^-12$$

▶The product of two positive integers or two negative integers is a positive integer.

$$^+5 \cdot {}^+2 = {}^+10 \qquad {}^-5 \cdot {}^-2 = {}^+10$$

More Examples

a. $^+4 \cdot {}^+3 = {}^+12$ b. $^-6 \cdot {}^+4 = {}^-24$ c. $^+5 \cdot {}^-2 = {}^-10$ d. $^-8 \cdot {}^-3 = {}^+24$

CLASSWORK

Find each product.

1. $^+3 \cdot {}^+4$ 2. $^-5 \cdot {}^+5$ 3. $^-4 \cdot {}^+3$ 4. $^+7 \cdot {}^+6$

5. $^+5 \cdot {}^+2$ 6. $^-2 \cdot {}^+5$ 7. $^-8 \cdot {}^+4$ 8. $^+4 \cdot {}^+8$

Find each product.

1. $^-3 \cdot {}^+5$ 2. $^-7 \cdot {}^-7$ 3. $^-2 \cdot {}^+6$ 4. $^-2 \cdot {}^-8$

5. $^+4 \cdot {}^-1$ 6. $^-3 \cdot {}^-5$ 7. $^+5 \cdot {}^-4$ 8. $^-8 \cdot {}^-6$

9. $^+8 \cdot {}^+9$ 10. $^-2 \cdot {}^-6$ 11. $^+9 \cdot {}^-7$ 12. $^-5 \cdot {}^-8$

13. $^+8 \cdot {}^-8$ 14. $^-6 \cdot {}^-6$ 15. $^-7 \cdot {}^+1$ 16. $^-4 \cdot {}^+5$

17. $^-4 \cdot {}^-4$ 18. $^-12 \cdot {}^-1$ 19. $^+2 \cdot {}^+10$ 20. $^-12 \cdot {}^-4$

21. $^-3 \cdot {}^+2 \cdot {}^-4$ 22. $^-3 \cdot ({}^+5 \cdot {}^-2)$ 23. $^-3 \cdot ({}^-6 \cdot {}^-1)$ 24. $({}^-5 \cdot {}^-1) \cdot (0 \cdot {}^+3)$

Follow the rule to find each missing number.

Rule: Multiply the input by $^+4$.

	Input	Output
	$^+2$	$^+8$
25.	$^-1$	
26.	0	
27.	$^-6$	

Rule: Multiply the input by $^-1$.

	Input	Output
	$^+6$	$^-6$
28.	$^-3$	
29.	$^+4$	
30.	$^-4$	

Rule: Multiply the input by $^-2$ and then add $^+5$.

	Input	Output
★ 31.	$^+2$	
★ 32.	$^-4$	
★ 33.	$^-2$	
★ 34.	$^+6$	

Write the next 3 integers in each sequence.

35. $^+10, {}^+6, {}^+2, {}^-2,$ ___, ___, ___, . . .

36. $^-16, {}^-6, {}^+4, {}^+14,$ ___, ___, ___, . . .

37. $^-5, {}^+10, {}^-20, {}^+40,$ ___, ___, ___, . . .

★ 38. $^-1, {}^+1, {}^-2, {}^+6,$ ___, ___, ___, . . .

APPLICATION

39. The rainfall in a certain desert has been increasing 2 inches per year for 4 years. Write the total change in rainfall as an integer.

★ 40. At noon on a winter day, the temperature in the Sahara was $^+11$°C. If the temperature steadily falls 2 degrees per hour, what will the temperature be at 6:00 P.M.?

MENTAL ARITHMETIC

Use patterns to find the products in each group.

1. $^+3 \cdot {}^+2$
   $^+3 \cdot {}^+1$
   $^+3 \cdot \ \ 0$
   $^+3 \cdot {}^-1$
   $^+3 \cdot {}^-2$
   $^+3 \cdot {}^-3$

2. $^+2 \cdot {}^-3$
   $^+1 \cdot {}^-3$
   $0 \cdot {}^-3$
   $^-1 \cdot {}^-3$
   $^-2 \cdot {}^-3$
   $^-3 \cdot {}^-3$

3. $^+2 \cdot {}^-4$
   $^+1 \cdot {}^-4$
   $0 \cdot {}^-4$
   $^-1 \cdot {}^-4$
   $^-2 \cdot {}^-4$
   $^-3 \cdot {}^-4$

Dividing Integers

A camel stores fat that can be used for energy. If a camel loses 40 pounds of stored fat while in the desert for 5 days, what is the average daily change in weight?

Find $^-40 \div {}^+5$.

You can write a related multiplication sentence to determine the sign of the quotient when dividing integers.

Since $^-8 \cdot {}^+5 = {}^-40$, then $^-40 \div {}^+5 = {}^-8$.

The camel lost an average of 8 pounds each day.

▶ The quotient of a positive integer and a negative integer is negative.

$$^+30 \div {}^-10 = {}^-3$$
$$^-18 \div {}^+9 = {}^-2$$

▶ The quotient of two positive integers or two negative integers is positive.

$$^+15 \div {}^+3 = {}^+5$$
$$^-21 \div {}^-3 = {}^+7$$

More Examples

a. $^+12 \div {}^+6 = {}^+2$ **b.** $^-18 \div {}^-3 = {}^+6$

c. $^+20 \div {}^-4 = {}^-5$ **d.** $^-8 \div {}^+2 = {}^-4$

CLASSWORK

Find each quotient.

1. $^+24 \div {}^-3$ **2.** $^-48 \div {}^-8$ **3.** $^+30 \div {}^+5$ **4.** $^-32 \div {}^+4$

5. $^+54 \div {}^+6$ **6.** $^-35 \div {}^+7$ **7.** $^-42 \div {}^-7$ **8.** $^+16 \div {}^-8$

9. $^-70 \div {}^-10$ **10.** $^+63 \div {}^+9$ **11.** $^+39 \div {}^-13$ **12.** $^-54 \div {}^+9$

13. $^+132 \div {}^-12$ **14.** $^-225 \div {}^-9$ **15.** $^-400 \div {}^-40$ **16.** $^-250 \div {}^-5$

PRACTICE

Find each quotient.

1. $^-28 \div {}^-7$
2. $^-36 \div {}^+6$
3. $^+18 \div {}^-6$
4. $^+21 \div {}^+3$

5. $^-64 \div {}^+8$
6. $^+72 \div {}^-8$
7. $^-48 \div {}^-6$
8. $^+63 \div {}^-7$

9. $\frac{^+20}{^+10}$
10. $\frac{^-81}{^-9}$
11. $\frac{^+56}{^-7}$
12. $\frac{^-49}{^+7}$

13. $\frac{^-96}{^+8}$
14. $\frac{^+64}{^+4}$
15. $\frac{^+100}{^-2}$
16. $\frac{^-100}{^-5}$

Divide.

17. $^-96 \div {}^-8$
18. $^+16 \div {}^-4$
19. $^-18 \div {}^-2$
20. $^-45 \div {}^+5$

21. $^-36 \div {}^+4$
22. $^+10 \div {}^-5$
23. $^-15 \div {}^+3$
24. $^+6 \div {}^-3$

25. $^+12 \div {}^+2$
26. $^+30 \div {}^-3$
27. $^-8 \div {}^+2$
28. $^+18 \div {}^-3$

Evaluate. Use the rules for order of operations.

★ **29.** $^+3 + {}^-3 \cdot {}^+4 - {}^+25 \div {}^+5$

★ **30.** $(^-8 \div {}^+2) - (^-3 \cdot {}^-6)$

★ **31.** $\frac{^-20}{^-5} + (^+6 - {}^-2) + {}^-8$

★ **32.** $(^-4)^2 + (^-2)^3$

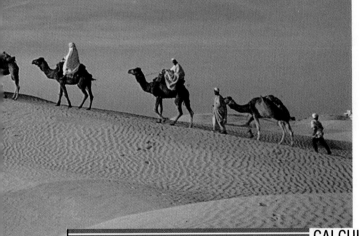

APPLICATION

33. From 8:00 P.M. to midnight, the temperature change in the desert was $^-16$ degrees. What was the average change in temperature per hour?

34. The caravan traveled through the hot desert for 9 days. During that time, one of the camels lost 63 pounds of stored fat. What was the average daily change in the camel's weight?

Problem Solving

ALTERNATE SOLUTIONS

Most problems can be solved by more than one method. Whatever method you use, the answer should always be the same. A good way to check your answer is to solve the problem by an alternate method. Then look back to see that both answers are the same.

1. A camel ride costs $2.00 per person for the first fifteen minutes and $.50 for each additional 10 minutes. Rosa paid $4.00. How long did she ride?

Solution 1
Make a table.

Cost	$2.00	$2.50	$3.00	$3.50	$4.00
Time in minutes	15	25	35	45	55

Rosa rode for 55 minutes.

Solution 2

Work backwards.

$4.00 ⟵ total cost
− 2.00 ⟵ first 15 minutes
$2.00 ⟵ remainder of ride

She rode 10 minutes for each $.50. Divide to find how many $.50's in $2.00.

$$\overset{\textbf{4}}{\underset{\$.50\overline{)\$2.00}}{}} \longleftarrow \text{She took 4 ten-minute rides.}$$

Rosa rode for 55 minutes.

Both methods give the same solution.

Multiply and then add to find the total time she rode.

40 min ⟵ 4 × 10 min
+ 15 min ⟵ first 15 min
55 min

2. Yoki and Lian went out on the desert in their dune buggy. They were out for one hour. A sandstorm came up and they took shelter. They spent 30 more minutes riding their buggy than they did waiting for the sandstorm to stop. How long were they in the shelter?

PRACTICE

Solve each problem by more than one method. Check to see that your answers are the same.

1. Mr. Williamson made a long-distance call to his home. He was charged $2.10 for the first three minutes and $.40 for each additional minute. If the call cost him $6.50, how many minutes did Mr. Williamson talk?

2. While he was at a gasoline station, Mr. Williamson filled up his gas tank and added 1 can of oil. His bill was $14.50. If he spent $10.50 more for the gasoline than for the oil, how much did each item cost?

3. To go from the ranch house to the oasis, you might ride one of three camels: Dusty, Murky, or Zinc. The return trip is made on horseback, and you can ride Belle, King, Prince, or Duke. Mary made the round trip on Monday and rode Dusty and Belle. Juanita made the round trip on Tuesday. What is the probability that she rode the same two animals?

4. A caravan set out from a base camp toward a desert city 166 mi due west. During one week it was forced to head back several times because of bad weather. Here are the distances it covered that week: 32 mi west, 18 mi west, 13 mi east, 29 mi west, 17 mi east, 8 mi west, and 26 mi west. At this rate, how many days will it take to make the journey?

5. Date palms produce an increasing number of dates each year. One tree produced 28 dates during the first year. The next year it produced 35 dates, the third year it produced 42 dates, and the fourth year it produced 49 dates. If the pattern continues, in what year will the tree produce 84 dates?

6. Fifty-four students participated in a poll to select a name for the class mascot, a baby camel. *Lacey* received three times as many votes as *Camelot*. *Gawky* received twice as many votes as *Camelot*. What was the winning name, and how many votes did it receive?

CREATE YOUR OWN PROBLEM

Use this information about the number of visitors to an oasis. Write a problem that can be solved in more than one way. Use at least two methods to solve your problem. Check to see that your answers are the same.

	Number of Visitors
Week 1	16
Week 2	25
Week 3	34
Week 4	43

Addition and Subtraction Equations

Solve equations with integers the same way you solve equations with positive whole numbers. Add or subtract the same integer from both sides of the equation to keep the equation balanced.

Solve for *n*.

$n + {}^+8 = {}^+2$ — Use the inverse of adding ${}^+8$ to solve.

$n + {}^+8 - {}^+8 = {}^+2 - {}^+8$ — Subtract ${}^+8$ from both sides.

$n = {}^+2 + {}^-8$

$n = {}^-6$ — Solution

Check $n + {}^+8 = {}^+2$ — Replace *n* with ${}^-6$ in the original equation.
$\quad\quad {}^-6 + {}^+8 = {}^+2$

More Examples

a. $a + {}^-5 = {}^+2$ — Use the inverse of adding ${}^-5$ to solve.

$a + {}^-5 - {}^-5 = {}^+2 - {}^-5$ — Subtract ${}^-5$ from both sides.

$a = {}^+2 + {}^+5$

$a = {}^+7$ — Solution

Check ${}^+7 + {}^-5 = {}^+2$ — Replace *a* with ${}^+7$ in the original equation.

b. $n - {}^-4 = {}^-9$ — Use the inverse of subtracting ${}^-4$ to solve.

$n - {}^-4 + {}^-4 = {}^-9 + {}^-4$ — Add ${}^-4$ to both sides.

$n = {}^-13$ — Solution

Check ${}^-13 - {}^-4 = {}^-9$ — Replace *n* with ${}^-13$ in the original equation.
$\quad\quad {}^-13 + {}^+4 = {}^-9$

CLASSWORK

Solve and check.

1. $n + {}^-3 = {}^+4$ **2.** $b - {}^+5 = {}^+10$ **3.** $n + {}^+8 = {}^-5$ **4.** $a - {}^-7 = {}^-6$

5. $x + {}^+3 = {}^+2$ **6.** $m - {}^+1 = {}^+2$ **7.** $x + {}^-4 = {}^-7$ **8.** $y - {}^-4 = {}^-3$

Solve and check.

1. $n + {}^+3 = {}^-2$
2. $n - {}^+1 = {}^+2$
3. ${}^-3 = a - {}^-4$
4. $x + {}^-4 = {}^-7$

5. $a - {}^-2 = {}^+6$
6. ${}^-7 = s + {}^+5$
7. $a + {}^-8 = {}^+10$
8. $b - {}^-5 = {}^-8$

9. $b + {}^+6 = {}^-5$
10. $r + {}^-3 = {}^+6$
11. $n - {}^+5 = {}^+2$
12. $n - {}^-7 = {}^+3$

13. $c - {}^+3 = {}^+4$
14. $n - {}^-1 = {}^-8$
15. $x - {}^-7 = {}^+10$
16. ${}^-13 = n + {}^+7$

17. ${}^-9 = x - {}^+3$
18. $a + {}^-9 = {}^+4$
19. ${}^+14 = n - {}^-3$
20. $0 = a - {}^-5$

21. $s - {}^-12 = {}^+42$
22. ${}^+47 = t + {}^+29$
23. ${}^-18 = n - {}^+34$
24. ${}^+36 + c = {}^-5$

25. ${}^+23 = b + {}^-18$
26. ${}^-54 + x = {}^-37$
27. ${}^+43 = s - {}^+27$
28. ${}^+72 + x = {}^+4$

Choose the equation that describes each sentence and solve.

29. A number n increased by ${}^+6$ is ${}^-13$.

   a. $n + {}^-13 = {}^+6$

   b. $n + {}^+6 = {}^-13$

   c. $n = {}^-13 + {}^+6$

30. A number a decreased by ${}^-5$ is ${}^+12$.

   a. $a - {}^-5 = {}^+12$

   b. $a - 12 = {}^-5$

   c. $a + {}^-5 = {}^+12$

31. ${}^-17$ equals a number b plus ${}^+12$.

   a. ${}^+12 + {}^-17 = b$

   b. $b + {}^-17 = {}^+12$

   c. ${}^-17 = b + {}^+12$

32. 5 more than a number y is ${}^-23$.

   a. $5 + {}^-23 = y$

   b. $y + 5 = {}^-23$

   c. $5y = {}^-23$

⋆ 33. A number n plus ${}^+19$ equals the sum of ${}^+8$ and ${}^-12$.

   a. $n + {}^+19 = {}^+8 + {}^-12$

   b. $n = {}^+19 + {}^+8 + {}^-12$

   c. $n + {}^+19 = {}^+8$

⋆ 34. ${}^+7$ less than a number y equals the sum of ${}^+14$ and ${}^-23$.

   a. ${}^-7 = y + {}^+14$

   b. ${}^-7 - y = {}^+14 + {}^-23$

   c. $y - {}^+7 = {}^+14 + {}^-23$

APPLICATION

Write an equation for each. Then solve.

35. On a winter day in the Gobi desert, the temperature at 6:00 A.M. was ${}^-6°C$. At noon the temperature was ${}^+5°C$. What was the change in temperature?

36. On another day the temperature was ${}^+2°C$. If the average winter daytime temperature in the Gobi desert is ${}^-7°C$, by how much must the temperature rise or fall to equal the recorded average?

Multiplication and Division Equations

To solve multiplication or division equations with integers, multiply or divide both sides of the equation by the same integer to keep the sentence balanced.

Solve for n.

$^+2n = {}^-32$ — Use the inverse of multiplying by $^+2$ to solve.

$\dfrac{^+2n}{^+2} = \dfrac{^-32}{^+2}$ — Divide both sides of the equation by $^+2$.

$n = {}^-16$ — Solution

Check $\qquad {}^+2n = {}^-32$ — Replace n with $^-16$ in the original equation.

$^+2 \cdot {}^-16 = {}^-32$

More Examples

a. $^-7a = {}^-28$ — Use the inverse of multiplying by $^-7$ to solve.

$\dfrac{^-7a}{^-7} = \dfrac{^-28}{^-7}$ — Divide both sides of the equation by $^-7$.

$a = {}^+4$ — Solution

Check $^-7 \cdot {}^+4 = {}^-28$ — Replace a with $^+4$ in the original equation.

b. $\dfrac{b}{^-4} = 6$ — Use the inverse of dividing by $^-4$ to solve.

$\dfrac{b}{^-4} \cdot {}^-4 = 6 \cdot {}^-4$ — Multiply both sides by $^-4$.

$b = {}^-24$ — Solution

Check $\dfrac{^-24}{^-4} = 6$ — Replace b with $^-24$ in the original equation.

CLASSWORK

Solve and check.

1. $^+8s = {}^-32$
2. $b \div {}^-4 = {}^-12$
3. $^-9n = {}^+54$
4. $\dfrac{a}{^+7} = {}^-8$

5. $^+8x = {}^-56$
6. $\dfrac{n}{^-2} = {}^-8$
7. $^-6a = {}^+42$
8. $^-y \div {}^+9 = {}^-4$

Solve and check.

1. $^-7b = ^-49$

2. $^+3 = \frac{a}{+11}$

3. $^+4 = n \div ^-5$

4. $8n = ^-32$

5. $^-9n = ^+54$

6. $^-4r = ^-44$

7. $a \div ^+5 = ^-3$

8. $^+6s = ^-18$

9. $n \div ^-5 = ^-12$

10. $^-9b = ^+81$

11. $r \div ^-4 = ^+9$

12. $n \div ^-15 = ^+8$

13. $^+3 = b \div ^+7$

14. $\frac{y}{-10} = ^+8$

15. $^-121 = 11y$

16. $^-4p = ^-32$

17. $\frac{n}{+4} = ^-2$

★ 18. $^-3a + ^-5 = ^+16$

★ 19. $2n - 8 = ^-4$

★ 20. $\frac{a}{-6} + ^-2 = ^+3$

Write an equation for each sentence. Then solve.

21. 7 times a number n is $^-56$.

22. A number y divided by $^+4$ is $^-8$.

23. The product of a number a and $^-3$ is $^+90$.

24. A number b divided by $^+5$ gives a quotient of $^-4$.

APPLICATION

Write an equation for each. Then solve.

25. Cacti can absorb water and store it for use during long dry periods. If a cactus absorbs 42 pints of water and then uses it during a 3-week dry spell, what is the average amount of water used each week?

★ 26. A cactus absorbed 4 pints of water each hour for 3 hours during a rainstorm in the desert. Then it used up 2 pints each day for the first 4 days of a dry spell. How much of the absorbed water does the cactus still have stored?

LOGICAL THINKING

Tell when each is true. Write *always*, *sometimes*, or *never*.

1. The product of two positive integers is greater than the product of two negative integers.

2. If n is a negative number, then n is less than its opposite.

3. If a and b are negative integers, then $a \cdot b$ is negative.

4. If a is a positive integer and b is a negative integer, then $a + b$ is positive.

5. $^-1 \cdot n$ is equal to the opposite of n.

Inequalities

The lowest spot in the Western Hemisphere is in Death Valley, California. It is 86 meters below sea level.

The inequality $n > {}^-86$ expresses the altitude of all other locations in the Western Hemisphere.

▶An **inequality** is a mathematical sentence that uses one of these symbols:

$<$	is less than	$>$	is greater than
$\leq$	is less than or equal to	$\geq$	is greater than or equal to

▶The **solutions** of an inequality are all the values that make the inequality true.

The integer solutions of the inequality $n > {}^-86$ are $^-85$, $^-84$, $^-83$, ...

▶To solve an inequality, use the related equation.

Find the solutions for $n + {}^+3 < {}^+10$.

$n + {}^+3 < {}^+10$

$n + {}^+3 = {}^+10$ ⟵ related equation

$n = {}^+7$

$n < {}^+7$ ⟵ solution: all numbers less than $^+7$

Check Try any integer $< {}^+7$.

${}^+6 + {}^+3 < {}^+10$ ⟵ Replace n with $^+6$ in the original inequality.

${}^+6 < {}^+10$

Another Example

$x - {}^-5 \geq {}^+1$

$x - {}^-5 = {}^+1$ ⟵ related equation

$x = {}^-4$

$x \geq {}^-4$ ⟵ solution: all numbers greater than or equal to $^-4$

Check Try any integer $\geq{}^-4$.

${}^-4 - {}^-5 \geq {}^+1$ ⟵ Replace x with $^-4$ in the original inequality.

${}^-4 + {}^+5 \geq {}^+1$

${}^+1 \geq {}^+1$

CLASSWORK

List the integers that solve each inequality.

1. $x > {}^+3$ **2.** $a < {}^+5$ **3.** $b \geq {}^-4$ **4.** $y < 0$ **5.** $p \leq {}^-2$

Solve each inequality.

6. $x + {}^+2 > {}^+4$ **7.** $y - {}^+3 < {}^+7$ **8.** $j - {}^-1 \geq {}^+5$ **9.** ${}^-10 + z \leq {}^-2$

PRACTICE

List the integers that solve each inequality.

1. $x > {}^+1$
2. $y \le {}^-4$
3. $q < 0$
4. $a < {}^+2$
5. $a \le {}^+2$
6. $z \ge {}^-10$
7. $t \ge {}^-4$
8. $m < {}^+2$
9. $r \le {}^-1$

Solve each inequality.

10. $x + {}^+2 > {}^+3$
11. $y + {}^+2 < {}^-8$
12. $a - {}^+7 \ge {}^-4$
13. $j - {}^+1 \le {}^+4$
14. $t - {}^+3 \le {}^-7$
15. $m + {}^+6 \ge {}^-5$
16. $x + {}^-5 \le {}^+3$
17. $c + {}^+1 < {}^+4$
18. $n + {}^-10 < {}^-10$
19. $y + {}^-10 \ge 0$
20. $x - {}^+10 \le {}^+3$
21. $q + {}^-9 \ge {}^-5$
22. $z - {}^-1 \ge {}^-2$
23. $s - {}^-8 \le {}^+2$
24. $n + {}^+3 \le {}^-8$
25. $r - {}^+3 > {}^+15$
26. $k + {}^-8 \le {}^-20$
27. $d - {}^-18 \ge 0$
28. $x + {}^-18 \le {}^-17$
29. $n - {}^-13 \ge {}^-1$
30. $e + {}^+12 > {}^-12$
31. ${}^+2 + a > {}^+6$
32. ${}^-3 + p \le 0$
33. ${}^-5 + m > {}^-3$
34. $t + {}^+1 < {}^-3$
35. $m - {}^-2 > {}^-4$
36. $n + {}^-1 \ge {}^+1$
37. $r - {}^+2 \le {}^-3$
★38. $x - {}^+4 \le {}^-1 + {}^-3$
★39. $x + {}^-3 \le {}^+6 - {}^-5$

APPLICATION

Write an inequality for each. Then solve.

40. A number n plus positive three is less than positive five.

41. A number a minus negative four is less than or equal to negative six.

42. Five more than a number b is greater than negative two.

★43. When the sum of negative eight and positive five is subtracted from a number n, the result is less than positive 10.

Mixed Practice

1. $\begin{array}{r} 58 \\ \times\ 4 \\ \hline \end{array}$

2. $\begin{array}{r} 72 \\ \times\ 73 \\ \hline \end{array}$

3. 93×100

4. $217 \times 1{,}286$

5. $12\overline{)769}$

6. $52\overline{)1{,}024}$

7. $12{,}849 \div 38$

8. $415.6 + 32$

9. $21 - 8.73$

10. 53.2×0.5

11. $\begin{array}{r} 0.06 \\ \times\ 0.13 \\ \hline \end{array}$

12. $17\overline{)107.78}$

13. $2.4\overline{)164.448}$

14. $0.13\overline{)0.52728}$

Write each in scientific notation.

15. $3{,}000$

16. $40{,}000$

17. $9{,}600$

18. $278{,}000$

19. $23{,}100$

20. $4{,}500{,}000{,}000$

Coordinate Plane

As part of a mathematics project, Cory **graphed** the locations of some Egyptian desert oases. She began by placing tracing paper on a map. Then she drew a horizontal number line, called the **x-axis**, and a vertical number line, called the **y-axis**. The axes intersect at a point called the **origin (o)**. The x-axis and the y-axis are part of the **coordinate plane**.

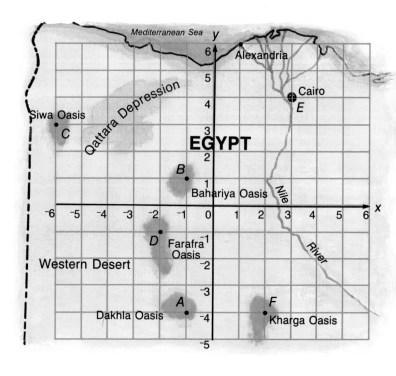

▶ An **ordered pair** is used to locate a point on the coordinate plane.

In an ordered pair (x, y), the first coordinate, x, tells how many units to move left or right of the origin. The second coordinate, y, tells how many units to move up or down from the origin. The coordinates of the origin are (0, 0).

The Dakhlah Oasis is located at point A, 1 unit to the left of the origin and 4 units down from the origin. The ordered pair for point A is (⁻1, ⁻4).

Point C is located at (⁻6, 3). It is 6 units to the left of the origin and 3 units up from the origin.

CLASSWORK

Write the ordered pair for each point on the coordinate plane above.

1. B **2.** D **3.** E **4.** F

Using graph paper, copy the coordinate plane on the right. Then graph each point.

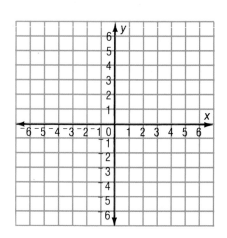

5. P(4, 5) **6.** M(⁻3, 4) **7.** T(2, ⁻4) **8.** N(⁻5, ⁻2)

Write the ordered pair for each point.

1. C   2. F   3. D

4. A   5. B   6. H

7. E   8. G   9. I

10. L   11. J   12. K

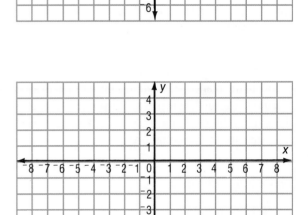

Write the letter of the point named by each ordered pair.

13. (4, 1)   14. (⁻6, 0)   15. (0, 0)

16. (1, ⁻2)   17. (⁻6, ⁻2)   18. (1, 4)

Using graph paper, copy the graph at the right. Then graph each point.

19. A(4, ⁻1)   20. C(0, ⁻4)   21. E(⁻3, 1)

22. F(⁻4, 0)   23. G(3, 4)   24. W(⁻2, ⁻1)

APPLICATION

Use graph paper and draw the x- and y-axis of a coordinate plane. Use it for 25–30.

25. Graph each ordered pair. Connect the points in order.
(⁻5, 4), (2, 4), (2, 1), (⁻5, 1)
What figure is formed?

26. Graph each ordered pair. Connect the points in order.
(5, 0), (11, 0), (9, ⁻3), (3, ⁻3)
What figure is formed?

27. Graph each ordered pair. Connect the points in order.
(⁻12, 0), (⁻10, ⁻5), (⁻9, ⁻3), (⁻8, ⁻5), (⁻6, 0)
What letter of the alphabet is formed?

28. Graph each ordered pair. Connect the points.
(⁻8, 6), (3, 10)
Give the coordinates of another point on the same line.

★ 29. Three vertices of a rectangle are (2, ⁻1), (2, ⁻5), and (⁻4, ⁻5).
Graph the ordered pairs and give the coordinates of the fourth vertex.

★ 30. Graph each ordered pair. Connect the points to make a line segment.
(⁻6, 3), (4, 3)
Give the coordinates of the midpoint of the segment.

Graphing From a Rule

Meteorologists keep records of temperature. The average morning temperature in one desert is 5 degrees warmer than the average evening temperature in the same desert.

$y = x + 5$

This **equation,** or **rule,** shows the relationship between the average morning and evening temperatures.

Use the rule to make a table of values.

The values in the table can be shown as ordered pairs.
(2, 7), (1, 6), (0, 5), and (⁻2, 3) are some **solutions** of the equation $y = x + 5$.

$y = x + 5$

x	y
2	7
1	6
0	5
⁻2	3

You can graph the ordered pairs on a coordinate plane. A straight line can be drawn through the ordered pairs. All points on the line are solutions to $y = x + 5$. The line is the **graph** of the equation.

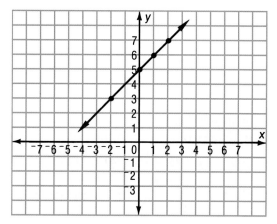

Another Example

Graph the equation $y = 2x$.
Then graph the ordered pairs.

Make a table of values.

x	y
2	4
0	0
⁻1	⁻2
⁻2	⁻4

Solutions:
(2, 4)
(0, 0)
(⁻1, ⁻2)
(⁻2, ⁻4)

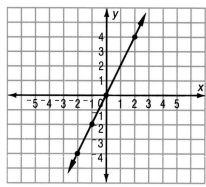

CLASSWORK

Complete each table of values. Then graph each equation.

1. $y = x + 2$

x	y
3	5
1	
0	
⁻1	

2. $y = x - 3$

x	y
3	0
2	
1	
0	

3. $y = x$

x	y
2	2
1	
0	
⁻1	

4. $y = 3x$

x	y
2	6
1	
0	
⁻2	

PRACTICE

Complete each table of values. Then graph each equation.

1. $y = x + 1$

x	y
3	4
1	
0	
-2	

2. $y = x - 1$

x	y
4	3
0	
-1	
-3	

3. $y = {}^-x$

x	y
2	-2
1	
0	
-2	

4. $y = {}^-2x$

x	y
2	-4
1	
0	
-2	

5. $y = x + 4$

x	y
1	5
0	
-1	
-2	

6. $y = \frac{x}{2}$

x	y
6	3
4	
2	
-4	

7. $y = 2x + 1$

x	y
2	5
1	
0	
-2	

8. $y = 3x - 4$

x	y
3	5
2	
1	
0	

Make a table of values. Then graph each equation.

9. $y = x + {}^-4$

10. $y = 2x$

11. $y = {}^-3x$

12. $y = 2x - 3$

13. $y = x - 2$

14. $y = 3x - 1$

★**15.** $x + y = 5$

★**16.** $y - x = 3$

APPLICATION

17. The average winter temperature in the Gobi is usually 4 degrees less than the average winter temperature in the Mojave. Write an equation to show the relationship between the average winter temperatures in the two deserts. Make a table of values and then graph the equation.

18. Using the equation above, find the average temperature in the Gobi when the average temperature in the Mojave is ⁻8 degrees.

VISUAL THINKING

1. Remove 5 sticks and leave 3 squares.

2. Remove 6 sticks and leave 2 squares.

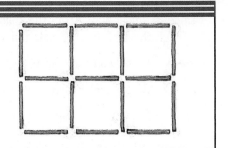

Problem Solving

SKILLS AND STRATEGIES REVIEW

Members of the Explorer's Club take an annual trip. This year they are traveling across the desert to explore desert life.

1. The Carlin family left their home on Tuesday, May 13. They will meet the group and begin the trip across the desert on the last day of May. What day of the week is that?

2. The group left Desert City at 8:30 A.M. They arrived at the signpost at 9:15 A.M. How fast had they traveled?

3. How many miles is it from the hills to the oasis?

4. When you are halfway between the oasis and the caves, how far are you from the hills?

5. Is Desert City closer to the caves or to the oasis? how much closer?

6. Nina dropped $1.00 worth of change in the sand. She picked up 6 of the coins but was still missing 35¢. Which coins did she pick up?

7. While at the oasis the Explorer's Club was entertained by a camel race. The leading racer had received a $1,000 bonus for his first win, a $3,000 bonus for his second win, a $5,000 bonus for this third win, a $7,000 bonus for his fourth win, and so on. Yesterday he had won a race and received a $19,000 bonus. Which winning race was that?

8. There were seven camels entered in the race that the group saw. The first four finishers were Omar, Alexis, Princess, and Lucy. From the following clues, tell the order in which the first four camels finished the race:

   Clue 1—Omar came in third.

   Clue 2—Alexis and Princess did not come in first.

   Clue 3—Princess saw Omar cross the finish line right in front of her.

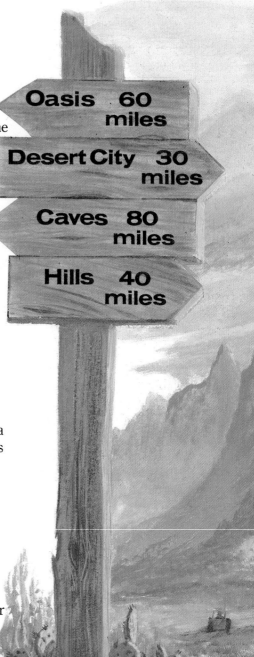

Oasis 60 miles

Desert City 30 miles

Caves 80 miles

Hills 40 miles

As their caravan continued along the road, the children counted the road signs. Some of the signs were rectangular; the others were triangular.

9. If they saw 18 signs and a total of 64 edges, how many of each kind of sign did they see?

10. If each rectangular sign said STOP and each triangular sign said SLOW, how many O's did they see altogether?

11. The Carlins stopped and filled their dune buggy with 22 gallons of gasoline and 2 quarts of oil. Gasoline costs $1.63 per gallon. Oil costs $1.35 per quart. How much change did Mr. Carlin receive?

12. The Explorer's Club looked at a wall drawing inside a desert cave. Part of the drawing is shown.

The pattern continues for three more rows. How many small animal figures are there in the entire drawing?

★ 13. Each dune buggy in the Explorer's Club has an identification flag on the antenna. The flag on the Carlin's antenna is shown. What is the area of the blue portion of the flag?

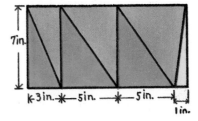

★ 14. The Desert Tourist Bureau offers a full-day tour of the desert, including 5 stops at points of interest. After making a stop at the souvenir shop, the tour stops for lunch at an authentic desert oasis. Before stopping to see drawings in a desert cave, the group stops to view cacti. After lunch the tour stops to watch local people creating sand paintings. This is the final stop. List the desert tour's 5 stops in order.

423

CHAPTER REVIEW

Compare. Use >, <, or = for each ●. pages 398–399

1. 0 ● $^+5$ **2.** $^-5$ ● $^+2$ **3.** $^-3$ ● $^-6$ **4.** $^+1$ ● $^-8$

Write the integers in order from least to greatest. pages 398–399

5. $^+5, 0, ^-3, ^+3, ^-1$ **6.** $^-6, ^-8, ^-1, ^+2, 0$ **7.** $^-7, ^+7, 0, ^+1, ^-8$

Add, subtract, multiply, or divide. pages 400–409

8. $^-5 + ^-2$ **9.** $^-6 + ^+4$ **10.** $^+7 - ^-4$ **11.** $^-3 - ^-5$

12. $^-3 \cdot ^+2$ **13.** $^-8 \cdot ^-3$ **14.** $^+24 \div ^-6$ **15.** $^-27 \div ^-3$

Solve and check. pages 412–415

16. $n + ^+8 = ^-2$ **17.** $a - ^-5 = ^+4$ **18.** $b + ^-5 = ^-9$ **19.** $y - ^+4 = ^-10$

20. $^-6n = ^-24$ **21.** $^-5r = ^+25$ **22.** $\frac{b}{^-4} = ^-5$ **23.** $n - ^-2 = ^+18$

Solve and check. pages 416–417

24. $a + ^+2 > ^+5$ **25.** $n + ^+3 < ^+7$ **26.** $b + ^+9 \leq ^+15$ **27.** $n - ^+16 \leq ^-20$

Write the ordered pair for each point. pages 418–419

28. A **29.** E **30.** D

31. B **32.** F **33.** C

Complete the table of values for each equation. Then graph each. pages 420–421

34. $y = x - 5$

x	y
7	2
5	
3	
0	

35. $y = 4x$

x	y
1	4
0	
$^-1$	
$^-2$	

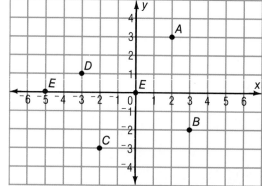

Solve. Pages 410–411, 422–423

36. The temperature one day in the Mojave was $^-7°C$. The temperature on the same day in the Gobi was $^-12°C$. Which desert had the lower temperature?

37. At 6:00 A.M. the temperature was $^-4°C$. By noon the temperature was 7 degrees higher. What was the temperature at noon? Solve, using any method you like.

Compare. Use >, <, or = for each ●.

1. $^-2$ ● $^-5$ 2. $^+3$ ● $^-8$ 3. $^-1$ ● 0 4. $^-5$ ● $^+2$

Add, subtract, multiply, or divide.

5. $^+9 + {^-12}$ 6. $^-8 - {^+3}$ 7. $^-6 + {^-5}$ 8. $^+2 + {^+6}$

9. $^-3 \cdot {^+5}$ 10. $^-8 \cdot {^-2}$ 11. $^+18 \div {^-9}$ 12. $^-32 \div {^-8}$

Solve and check.

13. $n + {^-3} = {^+2}$ 14. $^+5a = {^-20}$ 15. $b - {^+5} = {^+1}$

16. $n \div {^-4} = {^+6}$ 17. $a + {^+3} > {^+5}$ 18. $b + {^-3} \le {^+2}$

Write the ordered pair for each point.

19. A

20. B

21. C

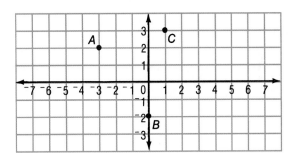

Complete the table of values for each equation. Then graph each.

22. $y = x + {^-2}$

x	y
2	0
1	
0	
-2	

23. $y = 2x - 3$

x	y
3	3
2	
1	
0	

Solve.

24. The temperature was $^-16°C$ on Saturday. It was $^-10°C$ on Sunday. On which day was the temperature lower? Solve, using any method you like.

25. A geologist studied rock formations at a site 5 meters below sea level. Later she moved to a site 9 meters higher. How far above or below sea level was the new site?

Evaluate the expression.

$$(1 - 5)^2 - \left(\frac{3 \cdot {^-4}}{^-2}\right) + (^-1)^3$$

EXPLORE

TRANSLATIONS

Look at triangle *ABC* in the figure at the
right. The coordinates of the vertices are
A(1,1), *B*(4,3), and *C*(4,1). Suppose 3 is
added to the *y*-value of each vertex.

A(1, 1) ⟶ *A'(1, 4)*   *A'* is read as *A* prime.

B(4, 3) ⟶ *B'*(4, 6)

C(4, 1) ⟶ *C'*(4, 4)

If triangle *A'B'C'* is graphed, we see it is
triangle *ABC* moved up 3 units. The new
triangle *A'B'C'* is the **translation image** of
triangle *ABC*. Sometimes a translation is
called a **slide**.

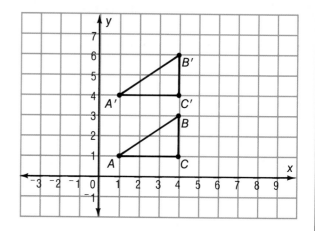

Look at parallelogram *DEFG* with vertices
D(1, 1), *E*(2, 3), *F*(5, 3), and *G*(4, 1).
Translate the figure 6 units to the left. The
new coordinates are *D'*(⁻5, 1), *E'*(⁻4, 3),
F'(⁻1, 3), and *G'*(⁻2, 1). The new
coordinates can be found by subtracting 6
from the *x*-value of each original vertex.

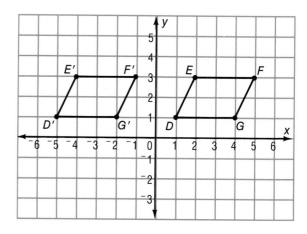

On a coordinate plane, draw triangle *MNO* with vertices
M(2, 2), *N*(2, 5), and *O*(5, 2). Then tell the coordinates
for each of the translations below.
Check by drawing the translation image and labeling the
new vertices.

1. 4 units down

2. 5 units to the right

3. 3 units to the left and 2 units up

4. 2 units to the right and 1 unit down

The coordinates of square *ABCD* are *A*(0, 0), *B*(5, 0),
C(5, 5), and *D*(0, 5). Tell the coordinates for each translation
below.

5. 2 units to the left

6. 4 units to the right and 3 units down

7. 5 units down

8. 1 unit to the left and 2 units up

GRAPHING INEQUALITIES

All the points whose coordinates satisfy the equation $y = x + 2$ are located on the straight line that is the graph of the equation. To locate all the points whose coordinates satisfy the inequality $y < x + 2$, follow these steps.

Step 1 Write the related equation.
$y = x + 2$

Step 2 Make a table of values. Graph the equation, using a dashed line.

x	y
−1	1
0	2
1	3

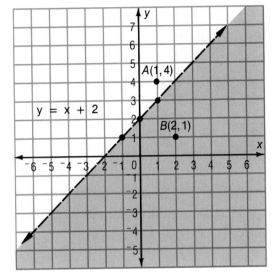

Step 3 Choose any point above the line and any point below the line.

$A(1, 4)$ lies above the line.
$B(2, 1)$ lies below the line.

Step 4 Check each point to see if it satisfies the inequality.

$A(1, 4)$	$B(2, 1)$
$y < x + 2$	$y < x + 2$
$4 \bullet 1 + 2$	$1 \bullet 2 + 2$
$4 > 3$	$1 < 4$

Point B satisfies the inequality.

Step 5 Shade the graph on the side of the line containing the point that satisfies the inequality. $B(2, 1)$ is below the line, so the region below the line is shaded. All points in the shaded region are solutions of the inequality $y < x + 2$.

The line $y = x + 2$ is dashed to indicate that the points on the line are not solutions.

To graph $y \leq x + 2$, a solid line rather than a dashed line is drawn to indicate that the points on the line also satisfy the inequality.

Graph each inequality.

1. $y > x$ **2.** $y < 2x - 1$ **3.** $y \geq x + 1$ **4.** $y \leq x - 2$ **5.** $y \leq 3$

Choose the correct answers. Write A, B, C, or D.

1. What is 7,543,924 to the nearest ten thousand?

  A 8,000,000   C 7,500,000

  B 7,550,000   D not given

2. What addition property is used?
$7 + (2 + 3) = (7 + 2) + 3$

  A Commutative   C Associative

  B Identity   D not given

3. $82,015 - 49,226$

  A 32,789   C 47,211

  B 32,889   D not given

4. Estimate. $76 \times 6,354$

  A 480,000   C 400,000

  B 420,000   D not given

5. What is $7 \times 7 \times 7 \times 7 \times 7$ in exponent form?

  A 5^7 C 35

  B 7^5 D not given

6. $10,981 \div 27$

  A 46 R19   C 406 R19

  B 521   D not given

7. Compare. 0.41 ⬤ 0.409

  A <   C =

  B >   D not given

8. Estimate. $0.436 - 0.27$

  A 0.2   C 0.02

  B 0.1   D not given

9. $4.63 + 3.059 + 3.2$

  A 10.889   C 10.124

  B 35.54   D not given

10. 0.15×0.003

  A 0.45   C 0.045

  B 0.00045   D not given

11. 8.05×10^2

  A 80.5   C 0.805

  B 805   D not given

12. $0.3075 \div 12.3$

  A 0.25   C 0.23

  B 0.023   D not given

13. About how long is a baseball bat?

  A 1 meter   C 1 kilometer

  B 1 centimeter   D not given

14. Complete. 5,260 mL = ___ L

  A 0.526   C 5.26

  B 526   D not given

15. Complete. 612 s = ___ min 12 s

  A 6   C 25

  B 10   D not given

16. What is the value of $8 \div 2 + 4 \times 3$?

  A 16   C 14

  B 24   D not given

Choose the correct answers. Write A, B, C, or D.

17. What is the GCF of 15 and 10?

   A 30   **C** 10

   B 5   **D** not given

24. Complete. 48 in. = ___ ft

   A 4   **C** 2

   B 3   **D** not given

18. What is the LCM of 15 and 10?

   A 30   **C** 10

   B 5   **D** not given

25. What type of angle is a 5° angle?

   A obtuse   **C** scalene

   B right   **D** not given

19. What is $\frac{18}{24}$ in lowest terms?

   A $\frac{9}{12}$ **C** $\frac{2}{3}$

   B $\frac{1}{2}$ **D** not given

26. What is $\overrightarrow{XY}$?

   A line segment   **C** line

   B ray   **D** not given

20. $14\frac{1}{6}$
   $-12\frac{5}{8}$

   A $2\frac{9}{24}$ **C** $1\frac{13}{24}$

   B $2\frac{13}{24}$ **D** not given

27. What type of quadrilateral is *ABCD*?

   A square   **C** parallelogram

   B trapezoid   **D** not given

21. $5\frac{2}{3} \times \frac{9}{15}$

   A $3\frac{2}{5}$ **C** $\frac{5}{17}$

   B $3\frac{3}{5}$ **D** not given

28. Solve. $\frac{n}{5} = \frac{21}{30}$

   A $n = 7.1$ **C** $n = 3$

   B $n = 3.5$ **D** not given

22. What is the decimal for $\frac{1}{8}$?

   A 0.8   **C** 0.2

   B 0.375   **D** not given

29. What is the unit price of 3 for $1.35?

   A $.45   **C** $.35

   B $4.05   **D** not given

23. $\frac{3}{8} \div 1\frac{1}{4}$

   A $\frac{15}{32}$ **C** $3\frac{1}{3}$

   B $\frac{3}{10}$ **D** not given

30. What is the ratio for 28%?

   A $2\frac{8}{10}$ **C** $\frac{7}{250}$

   B $\frac{7}{25}$ **D** not given

Choose the correct answers. Write A, B, C, or D.

31. What is the decimal for $\frac{1}{2}$%?

    A 0.005   **C** 0.2

    B 0.5   **D** not given

32. What is 41% of 126?

    A 51.66   **C** 49.66

    B 3.3   **D** not given

33. What percent of 600 is 24?

    A 40%   **C** 4%

    B 0.04%   **D** not given

34. What is the discount on $80.00 at 20% off?

    A $18.00   **C** $20.00

    B $64.00   **D** not given

35. What is the perimeter?

(parallelogram: 18.6 cm, 10.04 cm, 10.04 cm, 18.6 cm)

    A 57.28 cm   **C** 28.64 cm

    B 186.744 cm   **D** not given

36. What is the area?

(triangle: 10 cm, 19 cm, 13 cm, 23 cm)

    A 230 sq ft   **C** 42 sq ft

    B 115 sq ft   **D** not given

37. What is the volume of a cube that is 10 m × 10 m × 10 m?

    A 100 m^3 **C** 1,000 m^3

    B 30 m^3 **D** not given

38. What is the mode of 8, 3, 4, 3, 6, and 5?

    A 5   **C** 3

    B 4.8   **D** not given

39. What is another name for the average?

    A median   **C** range

    B mode   **D** not given

40. What is P (tossing heads on a coin)?

    A $\frac{1}{2}$ **C** 1

    B 2   **D** not given

41. Compare. $^-7$ ⬤ $^-5$

    A $<$ **C** $=$

    B $>$ **D** not given

42. $^-6 + {}^-3$

    A $^+3$ **C** $^-9$

    B $^-6$ **D** not given

43. What is the product of two negative integers?

    A positive   **C** zero

    B negative   **D** not given

44. $^-75 \div {}^+3$

    A $^-225$ **C** $^+25$

    B $^-25$ **D** not given

Choose the correct answers. Write A, B, C, or D.

Use the poster to solve 45 and 46.

> **FOLK CONCERT**
> Fri. and Sat.
> Sept. 4 and 5
> Surrey Arena
> Time: Cost: Fri. $4.50
> 7:30 P.M.   Sat. $5.50

45. Blake bought 4 tickets for Friday night and spent $3.00 on refreshments. How much did he spend altogether?

A $21.00   C $25.00

B $18.00   D not given

46. How many tickets for Saturday night can Alicia buy with $50.00?

A 8   C 10

B 9   D not given

Solve. If there is not enough information, tell what is needed.

47. Jamel practices piano for 45 min on Monday, 30 min on Tuesday, 55 min on Wednesday, and 40 min on Thursday. How long does he have to practice on Friday to average 45 min a day for these 5 days?

A 55 min   C need total time practiced

B 45 min   D not given

48. Inez jogs in her neighborhood. She starts at home and jogs 12 blocks south. She then runs 10 blocks east and 8 blocks north. She finishes by running 4 more blocks north and then 8 blocks west. How far is she from home when she finishes?

A 8 blocks   C 2 blocks

B 4 blocks   D not given

49. Mr. Walsh arrived at work at 8:50 A.M. He spent 25 min eating breakfast in a restaurant and 40 min traveling from the restaurant to the office. At what time did he arrive at the restaurant?

A 7:55 A.M.   C 7:50 A.M.

B 7:45 A.M.   D not given

50. The drama class is having a car wash to raise money for costumes for the 3 plays this season. Costumes will cost $135.00 for the first play, $93.00 for the second, and $147.00 for the third. At $1.50 each, how many cars must be washed to raise enough money?

A 375   C 562

B 250   D not given

Use the drawing to solve 51 and 52.

6.4 m   3.6 m

|——————— 25 m ———————|

51. Teri and Calvin are on opposite sides of the park, 25 meters apart. How far apart are they after Teri has run 6.4 m toward Calvin and Calvin has walked 3.6 m toward Teri?

A 35 m   C 15 m

B 10 m   D not given

52. If Calvin had run the same distance as Teri did, how far apart would they be?

A 12.2 m   C 37.8 m

B 12.8 m   D not given

Choose the correct answers. Write A, B, C, or D.

53. Robbie and Joseph hit baseballs into the outfield. Altogether, they hit 72 balls. Joseph hit 8 more than Robbie. How many did Robbie hit?

    A 40   C 24

    B 32   D not given

54. Linda caught half as many of the balls as Pam. How many did Linda catch?

    A 24   C 36

    B 48   D not given

Use the table to solve 55 and 56.

DISTANCES TRAVELED BY BIKER'S CLUB					
Day	Mon.	Tues.	Wed.	Thurs.	Fri.
Km	15	10	15	20	5

55. The Biker's Club went on a cross-country trip during one week. The table shows how far the club traveled each day. If Mary joined the group on Wednesday, how far did Mary travel with the club?

    A 15 km   C 40 km

    B 25 km   D not given

56. What distance did the club average each day?

    A 13 km   C 65 km

    B 5 km   D not given

Find the missing numbers in each pattern.

57. 10, 11, 13, 16, ___, 25, 31

    A 21   C 22

    B 18   D not given

58. 20, $12\frac{1}{2}$, $7\frac{1}{2}$, 5, ___

    A $1\frac{1}{2}$ C 2

    B $2\frac{1}{2}$ D not given

59. There are 2,400 families in Cedarville. Of these families, $\frac{1}{6}$ do not own a car, and 25% of the rest own more than 1 car. How many families own more than 1 car?

    A 500   C 400

    B 2,000   D not given

Draw a conclusion from the statements.

60. The sum of the angles of a triangle is 180°. $\triangle ABC$ is an isosceles triangle. $\angle ABC$ and $\angle BCA$ each measure 35°.

    A $\angle BAC$ is acute.   C $\angle BAC = 110°$

    B $\angle BAC$ is 35°.   D not given

Solve.

61. There are 15 pennies in a row with heads facing up. Bart turns every third penny over. Then Kenny starts with the second and turns every other penny over. What is facing up on the 12th penny?

    A heads   C not enough information

    B tails   D not given

pages 2–3

SET 1 Write the expanded form for each number in two ways.

1. 5,632　　　　**2.** 807　　　　**3.** 11,374　　　　**4.** 209,855

5. 24,003　　　**6.** 150,487　　　**7.** 1,920,840　　　**8.** 11,082,371

Write the standard form for each number.

9. ten billion, fifty-three million, nine hundred

10. 100,000 + 40 + 5

11. five hundred thousand, seventy-two

12. 2,000,000 + 80,000 + 700 + 90 + 5

13. nine hundred three million, two hundred forty thousand, sixty-seven

pages 4–5

SET 2 Compare. Write >, <, or = for each ⬤.

1. 53,895 ⬤ 55,495　　**2.** 9,978 ⬤ 9,987　　**3.** 15,301 ⬤ 15,301

4. 721,754 ⬤ 712,754　**5.** 2,151,327 ⬤ 2,153,127　**6.** 60,000,000 ⬤ 59,010,798

7. 372,305 ⬤ 372,350　**8.** 862,084 ⬤ 862,048　**9.** 84,321,843 ⬤ 84,321,843

List in order from least to greatest.

10. 535; 355; 553　　　　　　　**11.** 7,983; 7,893; 7,389

12. 53,482; 53,842; 58,324　　　　**13.** 482,924; 492,249; 492,429

pages 6–7

SET 3 Round each number to the place named.

nearest thousand	**1.** 825	**2.** 1,400	**3.** 1,525
	4. 3,524	**5.** 52,499	**6.** 415,709
nearest ten thousand	**7.** 96,473	**8.** 66,284	**9.** 172,550
	10. 536,425	**11.** 28,989	**12.** 99,888
nearest million	**13.** 4,363,801	**14.** 8,055,643	**15.** 3,736,010
nearest dollar	**16.** $82.61	**17.** $25.51	**18.** $79.42
nearest ten dollars	**19.** $58.16	**20.** $43.25	**21.** $175.10
nearest hundred dollars	**22.** $68.50	**23.** $1,346.00	**24.** $2,250.00

SET 1   Name the properties that are illustrated.
pages 10–11

1. $(10 + 2) + 5 = 10 + (2 + 5)$

2. $13 + 21 = 21 + 13$

3. $35 + 9 = 35 + 0 + 9$

4. $(9 + 7) + 3 = 9 + (7 + 3)$

5. $16 + (7 + 4) = 4 + (16 + 7)$

6. $(3 + 10) + 16 = (10 + 16) + 3$

Use the properties to complete each sentence.

7. $25 + 16 + 5 = \Box$

8. $12 + 19 + 8 = \Box$

9. $351 + 14 + 49 = \Box$

10. $0 + 133 + 17 = \Box$

11. $65 + 237 + 13 = \Box$

12. $127 + 23 + 7 = \Box$

SET 2   Give the estimate and the closer estimate.
pages 12–13

1. 688
  $+ 531$

2. 940
  $- 657$

3. $8,701$
  $- 4,499$

4. $\$2,088$
  $+ 2,493$

5. $6,249$
  $- 350$

6. $23,247$
  $1,863$
  $+ 60,148$

7. $48,326$
  $- 19,850$

8. $\$61,400$
  $7,493$
  $+ 2,540$

9. $840,226$
  $- 336,873$

10. $537,460$
  $+ 30,920$

11. $398,650$
  $+ 205,988$

12. $540,320$
  $+ 395,888$

13. $1,090,009$
  $+ 862,300$

14. $3,285,600$
  $- 909,876$

15. $\$4,650 + \$3,200$

16. $77,188 - 71,881$

17. $466,735 - 248,397$

SET 3   Add. Estimate to be sure each answer makes sense.
pages 14–15

1. 648
  $+ 737$

2. $3,243$
  $+ 977$

3. $\$134.98$
  $+ 24.75$

4. $14,365$
  $+ 8,598$

5. $\$269.53$
  $+ 148.75$

6. 483
  29
  $+ 135$

7. $1,719$
  458
  $+ 336$

8. $18,446$
  993
  $+ 3,255$

9. $\$287.36$
  125.88
  $+ 49.10$

10. $112,530$
  $398,806$
  $+ 234,755$

11. $743 + 526$

12. $2,933 + 6,108$

13. $228,940 + 195,304$

SET 4   Subtract. Add to check.
pages 16–17

1. 838
  $- 459$

2. 356
  $- 165$

3. $\$63.58$
  $- 26.74$

4. $5,508$
  $- 143$

5. $8,745$
  $- 4,580$

6. $31,608$
  $- 7,035$

7. $258,660$
  $- 37,745$

8. $\$508.52$
  $- 443.80$

9. $624,383$
  $- 103,540$

10. $5,041,300$
  $- 3,942,163$

11. $\$55.87 - \$42.99$

12. $8,022 - 7,650$

13. $601,528 - 326,143$

SET 1   Write a related equation to solve.   pages 18–19

1. $a + 8 = 22$ **2.** $18 = h - 11$ **3.** $17 + t = 36$ **4.** $j - 8 = 16$

5. $50 = x + 26$ **6.** $64 - z = 28$ **7.** $41 = 82 - n$ **8.** $26 + q = 41$

9. $19 + v = 66$ **10.** $g - 42 = 24$ **11.** $93 = 80 + c$ **12.** $55 - r = 47$

13. $w = 47 + 37$ **14.** $73 - n = 58$ **15.** $k + 12 = 25$ **16.** $i - 13 = 50$

SET 2   Write *true* or *false*. If true, name the property of multiplication illustrated.   pages 30–33

1. $9 \times 3 = 3 \times 9$ **2.** $7 \times 0 = 7$ **3.** $5 \times (40 + 6) = 5 \times 40 + 6$

4. $79 \times 1 = 79$ **5.** $58 \times 0 = 0$ **6.** $1 \times 6 \times 1 \times 7 = 6 \times 7$

7. $4 \times (3 \times 5) \times 6 = (4 \times 3) \times (5 \times 6)$ **8.** $8 \times 79 = (8 \times 70) + (8 \times 9)$

9. $5 \times (2 \times 3) = 5 \times (3 \times 2)$ **10.** $10 \times (5 \times 8) \times 3 = (10 \times 3) \times (8 \times 3)$

Use a pattern to find each product.

11. $10 \times 55 =$ **12.** $40 \times 4 =$ **13.** $32 \times 6 =$

$100 \times 55 =$ $400 \times 4 =$ $320 \times 6 =$

$100 \times 550 =$ $400 \times 40 =$ $3{,}200 \times 60 =$

SET 3   Estimate.   pages 34–35

1. $\begin{array}{r} 61 \\ \times\, 23 \\ \hline \end{array}$ **2.** $\begin{array}{r} 77 \\ \times\, 82 \\ \hline \end{array}$ **3.** $\begin{array}{r} 154 \\ \times\ \ 36 \\ \hline \end{array}$ **4.** $\begin{array}{r} \$9.41 \\ \times\ \ \ \ 56 \\ \hline \end{array}$ **5.** $\begin{array}{r} 783 \\ \times\, 134 \\ \hline \end{array}$

6. $\begin{array}{r} 183 \\ \times\, 237 \\ \hline \end{array}$ **7.** $\begin{array}{r} 930 \\ \times\ \ 46 \\ \hline \end{array}$ **8.** $\begin{array}{r} \$3{,}505 \\ \times\ \ \ \ 118 \\ \hline \end{array}$ **9.** $\begin{array}{r} 1{,}606 \\ \times\ \ \ 469 \\ \hline \end{array}$ **10.** $\begin{array}{r} 3{,}471 \\ \times\, 2{,}527 \\ \hline \end{array}$

11. 32×38 **12.** 154×91 **13.** 766×845 **14.** $4{,}309 \times 1{,}864$

SET 4   Multiply. Estimate to be sure each answer makes sense.   pages 36–37

1. $\begin{array}{r} 471 \\ \times\ \ \ 8 \\ \hline \end{array}$ **2.** $\begin{array}{r} 218 \\ \times\ \ 56 \\ \hline \end{array}$ **3.** $\begin{array}{r} \$4{,}817 \\ \times\ \ \ \ \ 2 \\ \hline \end{array}$ **4.** $\begin{array}{r} 5{,}469 \\ \times\ \ \ \ 13 \\ \hline \end{array}$ **5.** $\begin{array}{r} 13{,}053 \\ \times\ \ \ \ \ 21 \\ \hline \end{array}$

6. $\begin{array}{r} 353 \\ \times\, 405 \\ \hline \end{array}$ **7.** $\begin{array}{r} \$61.30 \\ \times\ \ \ \ 218 \\ \hline \end{array}$ **8.** $\begin{array}{r} 3{,}288 \\ \times\ \ \ 709 \\ \hline \end{array}$ **9.** $\begin{array}{r} 44{,}731 \\ \times\ \ \ \ 358 \\ \hline \end{array}$ **10.** $\begin{array}{r} 30{,}572 \\ \times\ \ \ \ 706 \\ \hline \end{array}$

11. $4{,}511 \times 5$ **12.** 390×14 **13.** 857×904 **14.** $\$62.40 \times 459$

15. $3{,}708 \times 29$ **16.** 630×111 **17.** $\$875.25 \times 39$ **18.** $\$1{,}030 \times 115$

SET 1 Multiply. Estimate to be sure each answer makes sense.
pages 38–39

1. $5.85
   × 200

2. $3.47
   × 122

3. 209
   × 560

4. 697
   × 209

5. 879
   × 579

6. 353
   × 405

7. 191
   × 847

8. 676
   × 258

9. $61.30
   × 218

10. 4,233
    × 719

11. 3,288
    × 709

12. 2,249
    × 167

13. 13,795
    × 564

14. 30,572
    × 706

15. 44,731
    × 358

16. 857×904

17. 354×869

18. 26.40×459

19. $78,674 \times 212$

SET 2 Write each using exponents.
pages 40–41

1. $5 \times 5 \times 5$

2. $3 \times 3 \times 3 \times 3 \times 3$

3. 6×6

4. $9 \times 9 \times 9 \times 9 \times 9 \times 9$

5. 8

Write each as a product of factors. Then write each in standard form.

6. 3^4

7. 4^6

8. 15^2

9. 5^4

10. 9^3

11. 6^5

12. 1^7

13. 8^4

14. 3^5

15. 10^6

16. 7^3

17. 13^3

18. 3^6

19. 4^5

20. 1^6

21. 13^4

22. 14^4

23. 4^6

SET 3 Find each average.
pages 44–45

1. 10, 11, 8, 11

2. 7, 3, 5, 9, 6

3. 20¢, 25¢, 30¢

4. 59, 69, 58

5. 82, 127, 95, 68

6. $2.02, $4.75, $3.82

7. 41, 37, 33, 31, 45, 29

8. $16.85, $19.23, $12.40, $17.32

9. 303, 485, 127, 360, 290

10. $354, $379, $387, $320, $367, $359

11. 985, 899, 1,005, 1,001, 995, 905

12. 1,385, 1,500, 1,285, 1,458, 2,062

SET 4 Estimate.
pages 46–47

1. $16 \overline{)500}$

2. $32 \overline{)2,450}$

3. $60 \overline{)5,000}$

4. $70 \overline{)4,000}$

5. $80 \overline{)3,000}$

6. $73 \overline{)2,107}$

7. $14 \overline{)5,765}$

8. $31 \overline{)8,207}$

9. $86 \overline{)9,610}$

10. $24 \overline{)74,391}$

11. $93 \overline{)47,203}$

12. $25 \overline{)\$129.78}$

13. $55 \overline{)33,813}$

14. $62 \overline{)529,780}$

15. $28 \overline{)756,041}$

16. $4,703 \div 39$

17. $9,116 \div 28$

18. $84,195 \div 62$

19. $46,804 \div 91$

SET 1 Estimate.

pages 48–49

1. $24\overline{)1{,}512}$ **2.** $32\overline{)1{,}735}$ **3.** $45\overline{)2{,}299}$ **4.** $16\overline{)500}$

5. $67\overline{)25{,}478}$ **6.** $17\overline{)32{,}181}$ **7.** $70\overline{)375{,}194}$ **8.** $35\overline{)\$2{,}500}$

9. $93\overline{)\$180.42}$ **10.** $84\overline{)270{,}125}$ **11.** $56\overline{)100{,}196}$ **12.** $78\overline{)250{,}000}$

13. $39\overline{)84{,}470}$ **14.** $44\overline{)273{,}284}$ **15.** $76\overline{)623{,}171}$ **16.** $16\overline{)156{,}000}$

17. $16\overline{)4{,}600}$ **18.** $16\overline{)5{,}555}$ **19.** $50\overline{)\$2{,}895.80}$ **20.** $85\overline{)1{,}000{,}000}$

SET 2 Divide. Multiply to check.

pages 50–51

1. $91\overline{)79{,}261}$ **2.** $65\overline{)15{,}274}$ **3.** $78\overline{)47{,}999}$

4. $27\overline{)36{,}448}$ **5.** $36\overline{)47{,}124}$ **6.** $336{,}217 \div 43$

7. $\$62{,}548.20 \div 54$ **8.** $112\overline{)178{,}614}$ **9.** $\$92{,}000.00 \div 87$

10. $\$194{,}635 \div 81$ **11.** $389\overline{)1{,}265{,}092}$ **12.** $\$438{,}620.69 \div 917$

SET 3 Divide.

pages 52–53

1. $706\overline{)298{,}980}$ **2.** $321\overline{)237{,}739}$ **3.** $432\overline{)183{,}141}$ **4.** $555\overline{)180{,}627}$

5. $923\overline{)297{,}506}$ **6.** $515\overline{)\$92{,}442.50}$ **7.** $849\overline{)116{,}403}$ **8.** $933\overline{)561{,}667}$

9. $175\overline{)\$56{,}437.50}$ **10.** $290\overline{)178{,}425}$ **11.** $111\overline{)999{,}999}$ **12.** $132\overline{)1{,}263{,}000}$

SET 4 Write a related equation and solve.

pages 54–55

1. $11 \times m = 44$ **2.** $a - 23 = 18$ **3.** $n \div 12 = 12$ **4.** $z - 26 = 13$

5. $\frac{h}{6} = 9$ **6.** $13 \times b = 104$ **7.** $y \div 34 = 5$ **8.** $\frac{m}{10} = 3$

9. $43 \times a = 688$ **10.** $y \div 25 = 29$ **11.** $\frac{a}{9} = 7$ **12.** $b \div 2 = 5$

13. $r \times 10 = 340$ **14.** $(2 + 54) \times y = 504$ **15.** $b - 87 = 29$ **16.** $(32 - 30) \times y = 4$

SET 1 Write each as a decimal.

pages 64–65

1. four and five tenths

2. three and thirty-five hundredths

3. six hundred seventy-one thousandths

4. two and twenty-seven hundredths

5. eight and nine thousandths

6. ninety-one hundredths

7. $\frac{8}{10}$ **8.** $\frac{31}{100}$ **9.** $\frac{803}{1,000}$ **10.** $\frac{91}{1,000}$ **11.** $\frac{47}{100}$ **12.** $\frac{206}{1,000}$

Write each decimal in words. Give the value of the digit 3 in each.

13. 7.3   **14.** 9.93   **15.** 0.283   **16.** 1.073   **17.** 3.62   **18.** 4.312

SET 2 Write each as a decimal.

pages 66-67

1. 8 and 7 hundredths

2. 827 thousandths

3. $9 + 0.7 + 0.001 + 0.0006$

4. 2 and 67 millionths

5. $(3 \times 10) + (4 \times 1) + (8 \times 0.0001)$

6. $(7 \times 10) + (9 \times 0.001) + (1 \times 0.0001)$

7. $(1 \times 100) + (2 \times 10) + (1 \times 1) + (3 \times 0.01) + (8 \times 0.001) + (2 \times 0.00001)$

8. $(3 \times 1,000) + (2 \times 100) + (6 \times 10) + (8 \times 1) + (5 \times 0.1) + (4 \times 0.01)$

9. $(1 \times 10,000) + (1 \times 1,000) + (7 \times 100) + (9 \times 10) + (2 \times 1) + (5 \times 0.01) + (4 \times 0.001)$

Give the value of each underlined digit.

10. 12.0891   **11.** 2.70259   **12.** 0.00357   **13.** 6.867094

14. 0.000451   **15.** 6.904032   **16.** 23.7834   **17.** 9.40157

SET 3 Compare. Use >, <, or = for each ⬤ .

pages 68–69

1. 8.69 ⬤ 8.96   **2.** 9.172 ⬤ 9.0172   **3.** 7.54 ⬤ 7.540

4. 0.0042 ⬤ 0.0402   **5.** 7.0685 ⬤ 7.0586   **6.** 3.5091 ⬤ 3.59

7. 0.0040 ⬤ 0.004   **8.** 37.063 ⬤ 3.7063   **9.** 1.0059 ⬤ 1.00509

Write in order from least to greatest.

10. 5.263, 5.623, 5.671

11. 2.84, 2.48, 2.488

12. 6.12, 6.0102, 6.021, 6.2001

13. 8.4, 8.04, 8.104, 8.004

14. 4.2303, 4.3203, 4.32, 4.2302

15. 1.7, 1.78, 1.7009, 1.8

SET 1 **Round to the place named.** pages 70–71

nearest
hundredth

1. 4.761

2. 18.533

3. 0.8561

nearest
ten-thousandth

4. 13.79519

5. 76.09473

6. 179.53722

nearest dollar

7. $2.07

8. $53.76

9. $80.94

nearest cent

10. $9.758

11. $20.1849

12. $3.5964

SET 2 **Give the estimate and the closer estimate.** pages 74–75

1. 79.63
$+\ 4.79$

2. $\$8.52$
$-\ 1.68$

3. 139.74
$-\ 26.851$

4. 19.05
7.82
$+\ 46.97$

5. 281.48
177.2
$+\ 20.14$

6. 28.1 − 5.62

7. $4.62 + $18.02

8. 83 + 104.25

9. 123.5 − 44.6

10. 2,089.7 + 416.2

11. 7,304.2 − 613.07

SET 3 **Add. Estimate to be sure each answer makes sense.** pages 76–77

1. 9.5
$+\ 7.0$

2. 4.63
$+\ 7.80$

3. $\$54.03$
$+\ 2.11$

4. 77.01
$+\ 12.96$

5. 365.25
$+\ 67.19$

6. 5.59
$+\ 0.82$

7. $\$246.22$
$+\ 16.87$

8. 37.621
$+\ 15.43$

9. 12.276
3.87
$+\ 5.409$

10. 41.735
76.342
$+\ 15.59$

11. $4.63 + $2.85

12. 840.7 + 76.013

13. 8.59 + 26 + 14.5

SET 4 **Subtract. Estimate to be sure each answer makes sense.** pages 78–79

1. 43.8
$-\ 19.3$

2. 308.9
$-\ 41.5$

3. 65.97
$-\ 27.04$

4. $\$538.15$
$-\ 209.06$

5. 183.5
$-\ 97.62$

6. 37.483
$-\ 10.078$

7. 63
$-\ 2.398$

8. 17.903
$-\ 5.0764$

9. 8.9731
$-\ 2.636$

10. 4.40502
$-\ 1.2734$

11. 43 − 24.1

12. 63.93 − 57.02

13. 1.8209 − 0.79

SET 1   Estimate.
pages 90–91

1.   4.12
     × 3.94

2.   73.7
     ×   6.7

3. $2.63
     ×   1.2

4.   50.9
     ×   8.1

5.   8.78
     ×   5.9

6.   1.629
     ×   7.3

7. $205.30
     ×   8.35

8.   4.378
     ×   5.26

9.   39.69
     ×   1.48

10.   976.1
     ×   2.4

11. 2.6 × 7.21

12. $33.05 × 4.5

13. 6.34 × 80.65

14. 405.2 × 85.42

15. 493.71 × 9.176

16. 802.3 × 178.6

SET 2   Multiply. Estimate to be sure each answer makes sense.
pages 92–93

1.   6.2
     × 7.6

2.   7.3
     × 0.2

3.   12.7
     ×   0.5

4. $8.82
     ×   0.5

5.   31.07
     ×   0.13

6.   5.801
     ×   1.09

7.   5.13
     × 7.76

8.   4.19
     × 8.05

9.   6.021
     ×   10.7

10.   2.109
     ×   9.68

11. 3.074 × 0.86

12. 6.15 × 3.27

13. 41.29 × 5.037

SET 3   Multiply.
pages 94–95

1.   0.617
     ×   0.8

2.   0.0812
     ×   0.6

3.   0.0024
     ×   0.8

4.   0.059
     ×   0.05

5.   0.31
     × 0.007

6.   0.043
     ×   0.9

7.   0.639
     × 0.004

8.   0.071
     ×   0.62

9.   0.0047
     ×   0.05

10.   0.0003
     ×   9.8

11. 0.05 × 0.07

12. 0.67 × 0.04

13. 1.5 × 0.02

14. 0.006 × 0.86

SET 4   Multiply or divide using powers of ten.
pages 98–99

1. 50 × 10

2. 50 × 100

3. 50 × 1,000

4. 0.5 × 10

5. 0.5 × 1,000

6. 350 ÷ 10

7. 350 ÷ 100

8. 350 ÷ 1,000

9. 350 ÷ 10,000

10. 3 ÷ 100

11. $3.62 × 10^2$

12. $0.85 × 10^2$

13. $16.53 × 10^3$

14. $0.39 × 10^4$

15. $170 × 10^3$

16. 4,960 ÷ 10

17. $4,960 ÷ 10^2$

18. $4,960 ÷ 10^3$

19. $1.85 ÷ 10^2$

20. $1.85 ÷ 10^4$

21. $0.089 × 10^5$

22. $0.0062 × 10^6$

23. $0.00074 × 10^2$

24. 0.089 ÷ 10

25. $0.089 ÷ 10^3$

SET 1   Divide until the remainder is zero.
pages 100–101
Estimate to be sure each answer makes sense.

1. $6\overline{)18.6}$ 2. $3\overline{)17.628}$ 3. $14\overline{)84.7}$ 4. $18\overline{)120.6}$ 5. $7\overline{)\$36.61}$

6. $5\overline{)207}$ 7. $19\overline{)15.238}$ 8. $24\overline{)97.2}$ 9. $46\overline{)2.668}$ 10. $31\overline{)1,838.3}$

11. $8.3 \div 5$ 12. $2.7 \div 6$ 13. $9.0 \div 12$ 14. $8.5 \div 25$

SET 2   Divide.
pages 102–103

1. $0.9\overline{)3.42}$ 2. $0.07\overline{)14.35}$ 3. $0.3\overline{)25.5}$ 4. $0.17\overline{)0.0459}$

5. $0.002\overline{)1.64}$ 6. $0.56\overline{)4.76}$ 7. $2.1\overline{)2.037}$ 8. $0.093\overline{)0.7533}$

9. $17.4 \div 0.2$ 10. $5.95 \div 0.5$ 11. $5.863 \div 1.3$ 12. $65.25 \div 2.5$

SET 3   Divide. Round each quotient to the place named.
pages 104–105

nearest tenth   1. $6\overline{)9.57}$ 2. $2.4\overline{)35.48}$ 3. $0.67\overline{)0.741}$
                    4. $3.69 \div 0.8$ 5. $1.86 \div 0.29$ 6. $9.5 \div 5$

nearest thousandth 7. $7\overline{)39.02}$ 8. $2.8\overline{)52.98}$ 9. $.16\overline{)3.14}$
                    10. $49.3 \div 6$ 11. $3.5 \div 0.3$ 12. $7 \div 9$

nearest cent   13. $4\overline{)\$12.70}$ 14. $8\overline{)\$35.97}$ 15. $0.4\overline{)\$80.79}$

SET 4   Write each in scientific notation.
pages 106–107

1. 2,600   2. 54,000   3. 85,400

4. 670,000   5. 8,100,000   6. 74,900,000

Write each in standard form.

7. 6.5×10^3 8. 1.5×10^4 9. 8.4×10^6

10. 7.18×10^8 11. 2.768×10^6 12. 6.07×10^9

SET 1 Complete.

pages 118–119

1. 9 m = _____ cm

2. 15,000 mm = _____ m

3. 12 cm = _____ mm

4. 7,000 m = _____ km

5. 800 cm = _____ m

6. 26 km = _____ m

7. 7.5 cm = _____ mm

8. 3 m = _____ mm

9. 400 cm = _____ m

10. 900 mm = _____ cm

11. 18 km = _____ m

12. 5,000 mm = _____ m

SET 2 Complete.

pages 120–121

1. 43 m = _____ dm

2. _____ dm = 10 dam

3. 600 cm = _____ dam

4. 70 hm = _____ m

5. 28 dm = _____ cm

6. _____ m = 890 dm

7. 65 hm = _____ dam

8. 604 cm = _____ dam

9. 9,200 cm = _____ dam

10. 61 hm = _____ km

11. 0.55 km = _____ m

12. 16 cm = _____ dm

13. 37.4 dam = _____ dm

14. 5,400 m = _____ km

15. 85 cm = _____ mm

SET 3 Complete.

pages 122–123

1. 9 kg = _____ g

2. 8 g = _____ mg

3. 6,000 kg = _____ t

4. _____ mg = 9.3 g

5. 180 g = _____ kg

6. _____ kg = 0.9 t

7. 3,800 mg = _____ g

8. 12 kg = _____ g

9. 5 t = _____ kg

10. 82,000 g = _____ kg

11. 6,100 mg = _____ g

12. 4 kg = _____ g

13. 4.5 g = _____ mg

14. 17.2 kg = _____ g

15. 2,084 g = _____ kg

SET 4 Complete. Choose liter (L) or milliliter (mL).

pages 124–125

1. 3,000 mL = _____ L

2. 4,000 L = _____ kL

3. _____ mL = 2 L

4. _____ L = 2.1 kL

5. _____ kL = 1,600 L

6. 8.09 L = _____ mL

7. 25 L = _____ mL

8. 1.9 kL = _____ L

9. 1 mL = _____ L

10. 16 kL = _____ L

11. 1,400 mL = _____ L

12. 18 L = _____ mL

13. 7.4 kL = _____ L

14. 24,300 mL = _____ L

15. 8.05 kL = _____ L

SET 1   Complete. pages 126–127

1. 4.83 m = _____ mm
2. 64.9 hm = _____ dam
3. 7.35 hm = _____ dam
4. 238.5 cm = _____ mm
5. 2.1 kg = _____ g
6. 3,000 mL = _____ L
7. 15 L = _____ hL
8. 52.3 km = _____ m
9. 0.06 kL = _____ L
10. 63.8 cm = _____ dm
11. 560 g = _____ kg
12. 9 mg = _____ dg

SET 2   Add or subtract. pages 130–133

1. 7 yr 6 mo + 4 yr 4 mo
2. 15 h 47 min + 3 h 20 min
3. 9 wk 6 d − 1 wk 4 d
4. 6 min 29 s − 2 min 38 s
5. 8 d 3 h − 7 d 12 h
6. 2 c 90 yr + 3 c 22 yr
7. 9 yr 45 wk + 3 yr 16 wk
8. 35 yr 6 mo − 15 yr 7 mo

Tell how much time has elapsed.

9. from 3:00 P.M. to 7:16 P.M.
10. from 1:34 P.M. to 5:56 P.M.
11. from 7:06 A.M. to 11:04 A.M.
12. from 5:49 A.M. to 2:09 P.M.
13. from 8:25 P.M. to 9:55 P.M.
14. from 11:20 P.M. to 7:55 A.M.

SET 3   Find the value for each expression. pages 144–147

1. $7 + 12 - 2 \times 3$
2. $2 + 4 \div 2 \times 5$
3. $(3 + 5) \div 4 - 2$
4. $5^2 + 4 \times 2$
5. $7 \times 2 + 3 \times 8$
6. $7 + \frac{5 \times 4}{10} \times 2$
7. $(11 - 3) \times 2 + 8$
8. $20 - 64 \div 16$
9. $7 \times 3 + 6 \times 5$
10. $(3^3 \times 2) \div 9 - 4$
11. $(15 - 8) \times 7 + 1$
12. $\frac{16 \times 2}{4} - 5$

Evaluate each expression. Let $a = 6$, $b = 2$, and $c = 4$.

13. $2a + 4$
14. $(a + b) \times c$
15. $2a + 3b$
16. $5 + \frac{a}{b}$
17. $a \times b + c$
18. $\frac{3a + 3b}{2c}$
19. $\frac{4a - 2b}{5}$
20. $ab - c$
21. $25 - 4c$
22. $5c + 2b - 1$
23. $\frac{ab}{c} + a - 4$
24. $7b - \frac{a}{c}$

443

SET 1   Write an expression for each. Use b as the variable.
pages 148–149

1. the sum of 3 and a number

2. 5 more than twice a number

3. the difference between a number and 7

4. twice a number divided by 3

5. the product of 20 and a number

6. 3 less than a number

7. the sum of twice a number and 9

8. 10 divided by twice a number

9. the difference between a number and 40

10. 4 less than 5 times a number

11. 4 more than 8 times a number

12. the difference between a number divided by 3 and 7

13. the sum of 12 times a number and 24

14. the sum of 25 divided by a number and 4

SET 2   Write an equation for each.
pages 150–151

1. 7 less than twice a number n is 3.

2. 3 times the sum of a number and 5 is 48.

3. A number b divided by 12 is 2.

4. One half times a number n plus 4 is 10.

5. 4 less than 5 times a number b is 21.

6. 50 less a number x is 20.

7. A number d divided by 3 is 48.

8. 10 divided by a number g is 2.

9. The sum of 8 times a number and 12 is 60.

10. 5 less than 3 times a number is 25.

11. $\frac{3}{4}$ of a number minus 6 is 30.

12. a number divided by the difference between 6 and 4 is 12.

SET 3   Solve and check.
pages 152–155

1. $x + 9 = 18$

2. $b - 4 = 10$

3. $23 + a = 30$

4. $x - 25 = 5$

5. $75 - a = 33$

6. $99 + a = 135$

7. $b - 96 = 342$

8. $x + 52 = 91$

9. $77 = 7s$

10. $y - 37 = 59$

11. $4b = 28$

12. $\frac{x}{5} = 10$

13. $13 = \frac{39}{r}$

14. $8s = 56$

15. $\frac{y}{2} = 11$

16. $4y = 72$

17. $f + 9 = 24$

18. $k + 10 = 12$

19. $25 = 5y$

20. $\frac{m}{10} = 20$

SET 1   Write the ordered pair for each point.

pages 156–157

1. A **2.** B **3.** C

4. D **5.** E **6.** F

7. G **8.** H **9.** I

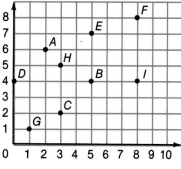

Follow the rule to find each missing number.

Rule: $y = 2x - 3$

	x	y
10.	2	
11.	4	
12.	6	

Rule: $y = 3x + 1$

	x	y
13.	0	
14.	1	
15.	2	

SET 2   Write the number or numbers each is divisible by.
Using the rules for divisibility, test 2, 5, 10, 3 and 9.

pages 160–161

1. 81   **2.** 48   **3.** 72   **4.** 104   **5.** 96

6. 117   **7.** 210   **8.** 315   **9.** 27,072   **10.** 501

11. 63   **12.** 3,135   **13.** 130   **14.** 2,457   **15.** 51

16. 9,651   **17.** 8,045   **18.** 432   **19.** 894   **20.** 687

21. 3,348   **22.** 90   **23.** 378   **24.** 471   **25.** 2,010

SET 3   Find all factors for each.

pages 162–163

1. 12   **2.** 30   **3.** 27   **4.** 51

5. 80   **6.** 100   **7.** 75   **8.** 33

Find the common factors of each. Then find the GCF.

9. 24, 40   **10.** 36, 42   **11.** 32, 80   **12.** 26, 65

13. 11, 121   **14.** 15, 50   **15.** 12, 28, 40   **16.** 48, 18

Label each number as prime or composite. pages 164–165

1. 29 **2.** 39 **3.** 27 **4.** 31 **5.** 51

6. 19 **7.** 23 **8.** 35 **9.** 53 **10.** 63

11. 97 **12.** 109 **13.** 123 **14.** 207 **15.** 153

SET 2 **Write the prime factorization for each. Use exponents.** pages 166–167

1. 48 **2.** 104 **3.** 40 **4.** 117 **5.** 210

6. 315 **7.** 130 **8.** 405 **9.** 75 **10.** 484

11. 150 **12.** 225 **13.** 1,764 **14.** 149 **15.** 900

Name the composite number for each prime factorization.

16. $2^2 \times 3 \times 5$ **17.** $2^3 \times 5^2$ **18.** $3^2 \times 5 \times 7$ **19.** $2 \times 5^2 \times 7$ **20.** $2^2 \times 3^2 \times 5^2$

21. $2^2 \times 5^2$ **22.** $2^3 \times 5^3$ **23.** $2^4 \times 5^4$ **24.** $2^5 \times 5^5$ **25.** $2^6 \times 5^6$

SET 3 **Write the first five multiples of each.** pages 168–169

1. 9 **2.** 6 **3.** 11 **4.** 12 **5.** 30

Find the LCM of each.

6. 10, 12 **7.** 6, 10 **8.** 8, 12 **9.** 4, 10 **10.** 9, 54

Use the given prime factorization to find the LCM of each group of numbers.

11. $15 = 3 \times 5$ **12.** $8 = 2^3$ **13.** $12 = 2^2 \times 3$ **14.** $12 = 2^2 \times 3$
$20 = 2 \times 2 \times 5$ $18 = 2 \times 3^2$ $20 = 2^2 \times 5$ $4 = 2^2$
$10 = 2 \times 5$

13. $14 = 2 \times 7$ **14.** $32 = 2^5$ **15.** $9 = 3 \times 3$ **16.** $42 = 7 \times 3 \times 2$
$16 = 2^4$ $40 = 2^3 \times 5$ $12 = 2 \times 2 \times 3$ $24 = 3 \times 2^3$

17. $10 = 2 \times 5$ **18.** $11 = 11$ **19.** $32 = 2^5$ **20.** $12 = 2^2 \times 3$
$12 = 2^2 \times 3$ $15 = 3 \times 5$ $50 = 2 \times 5^2$ $63 = 3^2 \times 7$

SET 1 Write each as a fraction. pages 178–179

1. $7 \div 12$ **2.** $6 \div 8$ **3.** $11 \div 20$ **4.** $8 \div 35$ **5.** $15 \div 30$

6. $8\overline{)3}$ **7.** $10\overline{)9}$ **8.** $3\overline{)3}$ **9.** $9\overline{)5}$ **10.** $85\overline{)15}$

11. $9\overline{)10}$ **12.** $50\overline{)2}$ **13.** $1\overline{)2}$ **14.** $10\overline{)1}$ **15.** $100\overline{)1}$

SET 2 Find the value of n in each. pages 180–181

1. $\frac{3}{9} = \frac{n}{3}$ **2.** $\frac{8}{16} = \frac{n}{4}$ **3.** $\frac{19}{20} = \frac{n}{100}$ **4.** $\frac{16}{40} = \frac{n}{20}$ **5.** $\frac{3}{10} = \frac{9}{n}$

6. $\frac{3}{16} = \frac{n}{32}$ **7.** $\frac{76}{50} = \frac{n}{25}$ **8.** $\frac{4}{36} = \frac{2}{n}$ **9.** $\frac{6}{35} = \frac{12}{n}$ **10.** $\frac{5}{3} = \frac{n}{12}$

11. $\frac{2}{5} = \frac{n}{15}$ **12.** $\frac{11}{12} = \frac{n}{36}$ **13.** $\frac{22}{22} = \frac{55}{n}$ **14.** $\frac{3}{16} = \frac{n}{64}$ **15.** $\frac{n}{75} = \frac{1}{3}$

16. $\frac{2}{12} = \frac{n}{6}$ **17.** $\frac{n}{14} = \frac{2}{7}$ **18.** $\frac{5}{n} = \frac{20}{60}$ **19.** $\frac{5}{100} = \frac{1}{n}$ **20.** $\frac{25}{n} = \frac{1}{2}$

SET 3 Write each fraction in lowest terms. pages 182–183

1. $\frac{2}{8}$ **2.** $\frac{12}{15}$ **3.** $\frac{16}{18}$ **4.** $\frac{15}{50}$ **5.** $\frac{10}{32}$ **6.** $\frac{15}{60}$

7. $\frac{14}{49}$ **8.** $\frac{9}{45}$ **9.** $\frac{8}{28}$ **10.** $\frac{40}{100}$ **11.** $\frac{33}{77}$ **12.** $\frac{60}{72}$

13. $\frac{10}{90}$ **14.** $\frac{15}{45}$ **15.** $\frac{8}{12}$ **16.** $\frac{13}{65}$ **17.** $\frac{4}{120}$ **18.** $\frac{9}{18}$

SET 4 Write each as a whole number or a mixed number in lowest terms. pages 184–187

1. $\frac{10}{3}$ **2.** $\frac{18}{4}$ **3.** $\frac{36}{6}$ **4.** $\frac{26}{5}$

5. $\frac{45}{10}$ **6.** $\frac{56}{16}$ **7.** $\frac{36}{8}$ **8.** $\frac{20}{7}$

List in order from least to greatest.

9. $\frac{3}{4}, \frac{2}{8}, \frac{1}{16}, \frac{2}{16}$ **10.** $\frac{1}{3}, \frac{1}{4}, \frac{2}{5}, \frac{3}{6}$ **11.** $\frac{5}{12}, \frac{3}{16}, \frac{1}{8}, \frac{1}{2}$

12. $\frac{2}{9}, \frac{1}{3}, \frac{3}{6}, \frac{4}{9}$ **13.** $\frac{15}{12}, \frac{2}{6}, \frac{4}{9}, \frac{2}{4}$ **14.** $\frac{2}{5}, \frac{1}{2}, \frac{1}{8}, \frac{3}{10}$

SET 1   Add or subtract. Write each answer in lowest terms.   pages 190–191

1. $\dfrac{1}{9}$
$+\dfrac{4}{9}$

2. $\dfrac{3}{8}$
$+\dfrac{3}{8}$

3. $\dfrac{8}{10}$
$-\dfrac{7}{10}$

4. $\dfrac{11}{16}$
$-\dfrac{5}{16}$

5. $\dfrac{5}{12}$
$+\dfrac{9}{12}$

6. $\dfrac{6}{7} - \dfrac{3}{7}$

7. $\dfrac{5}{8} + \dfrac{3}{8}$

8. $\dfrac{1}{3} + \dfrac{2}{3} + \dfrac{4}{3}$

9. $\dfrac{5}{10} + \dfrac{4}{10} + \dfrac{7}{10}$

10. $\dfrac{5}{8} - \dfrac{4}{8} + \dfrac{9}{8}$

11. $\dfrac{3}{6} - \dfrac{4}{6} - \dfrac{3}{6} + \dfrac{5}{6}$

12. $\dfrac{4}{8} + \dfrac{5}{8} - \dfrac{7}{8} + \dfrac{3}{8}$

SET 2   Add or subtract. Write each answer in lowest terms.   pages 192–193

1. $4\dfrac{3}{5}$
$-2\dfrac{1}{5}$

2. $3\dfrac{3}{12}$
$+6\dfrac{3}{12}$

3. $11\dfrac{2}{3}$
$-\ 2$

4. $5\dfrac{1}{6}$
$1\dfrac{5}{6}$
$+7\dfrac{1}{6}$

5. $16\dfrac{2}{9}$
4
$+\ 2\dfrac{4}{9}$

6. $9\dfrac{7}{8} - 4$

7. $8\dfrac{6}{7} - 6\dfrac{2}{7}$

8. $7\dfrac{9}{15} + 13\dfrac{1}{15}$

9. $12\dfrac{7}{10} + 5\dfrac{11}{16}$

SET 3   Add or subtract. Write each answer in lowest terms.   pages 194–195

1. $\dfrac{5}{6}$
$-\dfrac{2}{3}$

2. $\dfrac{2}{5}$
$+\dfrac{1}{2}$

3. $\dfrac{1}{3}$
$-\dfrac{1}{8}$

4. $\dfrac{3}{4}$
$+\dfrac{5}{8}$

5. $\dfrac{5}{7}$
$-\dfrac{1}{4}$

6. $\dfrac{9}{10} - \dfrac{1}{3}$

7. $\dfrac{3}{10} + \dfrac{6}{15}$

8. $\dfrac{1}{3} + \dfrac{1}{6} + \dfrac{1}{9}$

9. $\dfrac{3}{4} + \dfrac{5}{6} + \dfrac{5}{12}$

SET 4   Add or subtract. Write each answer in lowest terms.   pages 196–197

1. $18\dfrac{3}{4}$
$-\ 7$

2. $10\dfrac{5}{8}$
$+29\dfrac{1}{2}$

3. $1\dfrac{1}{2}$
$3\dfrac{3}{7}$
$+\ \dfrac{11}{14}$

4. $15\dfrac{1}{6}$
9
$+26\dfrac{3}{8}$

5. $32\dfrac{1}{2}$
$16\dfrac{3}{4}$
$+24\dfrac{5}{6}$

6. $39\dfrac{7}{9} - 17$

7. $8\dfrac{1}{6} + 9\dfrac{3}{10}$

8. $57\dfrac{2}{3} - 20\dfrac{1}{9}$

9. $13\dfrac{3}{16} + 2\dfrac{5}{8} + 7$

SET 1 Subtract. Write each answer in lowest terms. pages 198–199

1. $7\frac{1}{6}$
   $-\ 2\frac{5}{6}$

2. 16
   $-\ 9\frac{3}{4}$

3. $9\frac{3}{7}$
   $-\ 4\frac{5}{7}$

4. $10\frac{3}{14}$
   $-\ 7\frac{3}{7}$

5. $16\frac{1}{3}$
   $-\ 5\frac{5}{12}$

6. 8
   $-\ 3\frac{10}{18}$

7. $12\frac{2}{5}$
   $-\ 4\frac{7}{15}$

8. $26\frac{5}{12}$
   $-\ 15\frac{7}{8}$

9. $21\frac{1}{4}$
   $-\ 14\frac{5}{9}$

10. $28\frac{1}{3}$
    $-\ 11\frac{4}{5}$

11. $18 - 4\frac{7}{16}$

12. $13\frac{1}{4} - 6\frac{7}{12}$

13. $29\frac{1}{6} - 16\frac{3}{5}$

14. $12\frac{2}{5} - 10\frac{4}{7}$

15. $24\frac{3}{8} - 11\frac{4}{5}$

16. $15\frac{3}{4} - 9\frac{5}{6}$

SET 2 Estimate each sum or difference. pages 200–201

1. $9\frac{1}{4}$
   $+\ 4\frac{3}{4}$

2. $7\frac{1}{2}$
   $-\ 2\frac{3}{8}$

3. $6\frac{5}{9}$
   $+\ 6\frac{1}{3}$

4. $10\frac{5}{6}$
   $-\ 3\frac{3}{5}$

5. $6\frac{2}{8}$
   $+\ \frac{9}{16}$

6. $8\frac{2}{7}$
   $-\ 3\frac{3}{4}$

7. $2\frac{7}{12}$
   $+\ 5\frac{1}{15}$

8. $7\frac{5}{6}$
   $-\ 1\frac{1}{3}$

9. $5\frac{5}{11}$
   $+\ 12$

10. 10
    $-\ \frac{13}{16}$

11. $\frac{5}{6} + \frac{6}{7}$

12. $\frac{5}{11} + \frac{7}{8}$

13. $\frac{14}{15} + \frac{1}{3}$

14. $\frac{7}{9} - \frac{3}{5}$

15. $5\frac{5}{8} - 2$

16. $9\frac{4}{5} - 6\frac{1}{3}$

17. $4 + 9\frac{1}{4} + 3\frac{4}{9}$

18. $2\frac{5}{6} + 8\frac{3}{10} + 5\frac{1}{2}$

SET 3 Multiply. Write each answer in lowest terms. pages 212–213

1. $\frac{3}{4} \times 5$

2. $\frac{2}{3} \times \frac{7}{8}$

3. $\frac{5}{7} \times \frac{3}{10}$

4. $\frac{6}{7} \times \frac{4}{9}$

5. $20 \times \frac{3}{5}$

6. $\frac{7}{12} \times \frac{3}{10}$

7. $\frac{12}{13} \times \frac{1}{4}$

8. $\frac{3}{8} \times 14$

9. $\frac{1}{12} \times \frac{4}{5}$

10. $\frac{5}{6} \times \frac{7}{10}$

SET 4 Multiply. Write each answer in lowest terms. pages 214–215

1. $\frac{2}{4} \times \frac{16}{20}$

2. $\frac{5}{8} \times \frac{8}{9}$

3. $\frac{10}{12} \times \frac{2}{5}$

4. $\frac{3}{5} \times \frac{9}{27}$

5. $\frac{5}{24} \times 12$

6. $\frac{10}{4} \times \frac{8}{20}$

7. $18 \times \frac{7}{9}$

8. $\frac{15}{16} \times \frac{6}{30}$

9. $\frac{21}{8} \times \frac{3}{7}$

10. $\frac{18}{30} \times 2$

11. $\frac{4}{10} \times \frac{5}{15}$

12. $\frac{3}{5} \times \frac{5}{9}$

13. $40 \times \frac{2}{12}$

14. $\frac{12}{8} \times \frac{4}{6}$

15. $\frac{2}{9} \times \frac{3}{4}$

SET 1 **Multiply. Write each answer in lowest terms.**

1. $\frac{3}{4} \times 6\frac{1}{3}$

2. $\frac{2}{9} \times 5\frac{5}{6}$

3. $\frac{4}{7} \times 3\frac{1}{2}$

4. $2\frac{2}{3} \times \frac{7}{8}$

5. $3\frac{1}{3} \times \frac{7}{12}$

6. $5\frac{1}{2} \times \frac{1}{10}$

7. $1\frac{7}{10} \times \frac{5}{6}$

8. $3\frac{6}{7} \times \frac{2}{3}$

9. $1\frac{5}{6} \times 10$

10. $10 \times 3\frac{3}{5}$

11. $24 \times 2\frac{7}{8}$

12. $6 \times 2\frac{1}{5}$

13. $3\frac{1}{4} \times 4\frac{1}{2}$

14. $5\frac{5}{6} \times 1\frac{2}{5}$

15. $1\frac{4}{11} \times 7\frac{1}{3}$

16. $\frac{9}{10} \times 14$

17. $3\frac{5}{9} \times 2\frac{1}{2}$

18. $6\frac{1}{2} \times 3\frac{1}{3}$

19. $2\frac{2}{3} \times 9$

20. $7\frac{3}{4} \times 6\frac{1}{2}$

SET 2 **Divide. Write each answer in lowest terms.**
pages 218–219

1. $\frac{2}{15} \div \frac{1}{3}$

2. $\frac{4}{5} \div \frac{3}{4}$

3. $\frac{6}{7} \div 12$

4. $\frac{7}{8} \div \frac{1}{4}$

5. $\frac{1}{4} \div \frac{7}{11}$

6. $\frac{1}{12} \div \frac{4}{9}$

7. $6 \div \frac{1}{12}$

8. $\frac{3}{8} \div \frac{1}{5}$

9. $\frac{1}{2} \div \frac{9}{16}$

10. $\frac{2}{15} \div 2$

11. $15 \div 20$

12. $\frac{1}{4} \div \frac{1}{8}$

13. $\frac{5}{6} \div \frac{2}{3}$

14. $\frac{1}{5} \div \frac{3}{10}$

15. $3 \div \frac{1}{3}$

16. $\frac{5}{9} \div 3$

17. $\frac{20}{21} \div \frac{10}{11}$

18. $\frac{3}{7} \div \frac{5}{9}$

19. $\frac{1}{3} \div \frac{4}{9}$

20. $\frac{6}{7} \div 36$

SET 3 **Divide. Write each answer in lowest terms.**
pages 220–221

1. $4\frac{5}{6} \div \frac{2}{3}$

2. $\frac{12}{7} \div 2\frac{1}{7}$

3. $6 \div 4\frac{4}{5}$

4. $1\frac{5}{9} \div 3\frac{1}{3}$

5. $2\frac{3}{8} \div 2\frac{3}{8}$

6. $16 \div 5\frac{1}{3}$

7. $1\frac{5}{6} \div 2\frac{1}{2}$

8. $\frac{8}{9} \div 16$

9. $4\frac{2}{5} \div \frac{11}{4}$

10. $6\frac{1}{3} \div \frac{5}{9}$

11. $2\frac{1}{3} \div \frac{28}{9}$

12. $25 \div 1\frac{1}{2}$

13. $5\frac{1}{2} \div 3\frac{3}{4}$

14. $1\frac{1}{8} \div 1\frac{1}{4}$

15. $2 \div 3\frac{1}{3}$

16. $9\frac{1}{6} \div 2\frac{1}{3}$

17. $4 \div 1\frac{3}{4}$

18. $7\frac{1}{4} \div 2$

19. $3\frac{1}{3} \div 4\frac{1}{2}$

20. $4\frac{1}{6} \div 4\frac{3}{8}$

21. $4\frac{1}{2} \div 4\frac{1}{2}$

22. $1\frac{1}{2} \div 3\frac{5}{7}$

23. $14 \div 1\frac{1}{6}$

24. $5\frac{1}{3} \div 16$

25. $4\frac{2}{7} \div 1\frac{3}{5}$

SET 1 Write each fraction as a decimal. pages 224–225
Use a bar for repeating decimals.

1. $\frac{2}{5}$

2. $\frac{2}{10}$

3. $\frac{2}{15}$

4. $\frac{2}{12}$

5. $\frac{2}{14}$

6. $1\frac{7}{8}$

7. $\frac{7}{6}$

8. $1\frac{1}{19}$

9. $\frac{23}{11}$

10. $3\frac{3}{14}$

Write each decimal as a fraction in lowest terms.

11. 0.4

12. 0.65

13. 0.256

14. 1.95

15. 0.875

16. 2.34

17. 0.006

18. 0.15

19. 0.0782

20. 3.9

SET 2 Divide. Write each quotient in three ways. pages 226–227

1. $2\overline{)85}$

2. $5\overline{)62}$

3. $4\overline{)55}$

4. $12\overline{)117}$

5. $16\overline{)200}$

6. $54 \div 24$

7. $217 \div 30$

8. $910 \div 42$

9. $1,212 \div 18$

10. $2,462 \div 25$

11. $\frac{13}{4}$

12. $\frac{28}{3}$

13. $\frac{34}{5}$

14. $\frac{61}{8}$

15. $\frac{45}{6}$

16. $20\overline{)225}$

17. $594 \div 16$

18. $\frac{79}{4}$

19. $18\overline{)225}$

20. $354 \div 48$

SET 3 Complete. pages 228–231

1. 144 in. =____ yd 2. $3\frac{1}{2}$ mi =____ ft 3. 14 ft = ____ yd 4. 30 in. = ____ ft 5. $5\frac{1}{3}$ yd =____ ft

6. 48 oz =____ lb 7. $4\frac{1}{2}$ lb =____ oz 8. $\frac{1}{2}$ T =____ lb 9. 6,000 lb =____ T 10. 20 oz = ____ lb

Add or subtract.

11. 7 yd 9 ft
   + 2 yd 4 ft

12. 5 mi 250 yd
   − 3 mi 400 yd

13. 2 lb 13 oz
   + 4 lb 5 oz

14. 6 T 700 lb
   − 1 T 900 lb

15. 9 ft 3 in.
   − 6 ft 9 in.

16. 3 yd 2 ft
   + 8 yd 2 ft

17. 9 qt
   − 1 qt 1 pt

18. 5 pt 1 c
   + 2 pt 1 c

SET 4 Complete. pages 232–233

1. $3\frac{1}{4}$ c =____ oz 2. 9 c =____ pt 3. 5 qt =____ pt 4. 21 qt =____ gal 5. 32 pt =____ gal

6. $5\frac{1}{2}$ gal =____ qt 7. 42 oz =____ c 8. $9\frac{1}{4}$ qt =____ pt 9. 96 oz =____ qt 10. $4\frac{3}{4}$ gal =____ qt

Add or subtract.

11. 5 gal 2 qt 6 oz
   − 1 gal 3 qt 7 oz

12. 1 pt 1 c 7 oz
   + 3 pt 1 c 9 oz

13. 2 gal
   −   1 qt 1 pt

14. 5 gal 3 qt 3 oz
   +   2 qt 5 oz

SET 1 **Use the figure at the right to answer 1–4.** pages 244–249

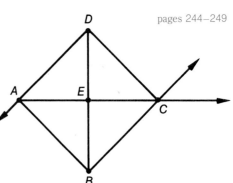

1. Name all the points.

2. Name the rays in the figure.

3. Name all line segments that have *E* as an endpoint.

4. Name three angles that have a vertex at *A*.

Fill in the blanks.

5. If ∠*ABC* is 89°, it is a _____ angle.

6. ∠*ABC* is 40° and ∠*EFG* is 50°. They are _____ angles.

7. ∠*RST* is 180°. ∠*RST* is a _____ angle.

8. ∠*DEF* and ∠*GHI* together equal 180°. They are _____ angles.

9. If $\overleftrightarrow{AB}$ intersects $\overleftrightarrow{RS}$ and forms right angles, then $\overleftrightarrow{AB}$ is _____ to line $\overleftrightarrow{RS}$.

10. If $\overleftrightarrow{CD}$ and $\overleftrightarrow{GH}$ have a common point, they are _____ lines.

11. If $\overleftrightarrow{AB}$ and $\overleftrightarrow{EF}$ have no common point, they are _____ lines.

12. If $\overleftrightarrow{CD}$ and $\overleftrightarrow{GH}$ are parallel and $\overleftrightarrow{RS}$ is a transversal, pairs of _____ angles are formed.

SET 2 **Answer *true* or *false*.** pages 250–255

1. A rectangle is a quadrilateral.

2. A polygon has three or more sides.

3. A hexagon has 7 sides and 7 vertices.

4. A square is a regular quadrilateral.

5. If ∠*ABC* is 45° and ∠*DEF* is 45°, then ∠*ABC* and ∠*DEF* are congruent.

6. If triangle *ABC* and triangle *DEF* have corresponding parts, they are congruent.

Fill in the blanks. △*ABC* ≅ △*DEF*

7. $\overline{AC}$ corresponds to _____.

8. ∠*B* ≅ ∠_____.

9. $\overline{BC}$ is 10 cm in length. $\overline{EF}$ is _____ cm in length.

10. If a figure is symmetric about a line, the opposite parts are _____ images of each other.

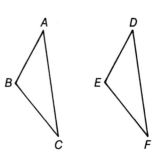

452

pages 258–263

SET 1   **Fill in the blanks.**

1. In △ABC, $\overline{AB}$ = 4 cm, $\overline{AC}$ = 4 cm, and ∠A = 130°.
   △ABC is an _____ _____ triangle.

2. In △DEF, $\overline{DE}$ = 5 cm, $\overline{EF}$ = 6 cm, $\overline{FD}$ = 8 cm, and
   ∠DEF = 90°. △DEF is a _____ _____ triangle.

Find the measure of the third angle of each triangle.

3. 41°, 25°   4. 30°, 125°   5. 70°, 100°   6. 58°, 64°

7. 120°, 23°   8. 48°, 65°   9. 55°, 55°   10. 135°, 32°

Fill in the blanks.

11. $\overline{BC}$ = _____ cm

12. ∠BCD = _____ degrees

13. $\overline{CD}$ = _____ cm

14. ∠ADC = _____ degrees

15. A chord of circle O is _____.

16. A radius of circle O is _____.

17. If ∠AOC = 130°, then ∠COB = _____.

18. If $\overline{AO}$ = 10 cm, then $\overline{AB}$ = _____ cm.

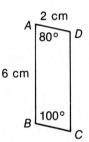

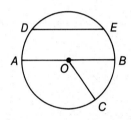

pages 264–267

SET 2   **Answer** *true* **or** *false.*

1. When constructing a segment congruent to a given
   segment, you use a ruler to measure the length.

2. When constructing an angle congruent to a given angle,
   you use a protractor to measure the given angle.

3. An angle bisector divides the given angle into two equal
   angles.

4. The bisector of a line segment is parallel to the given line.

5. The bisector of a line segment forms two right angles with
   the given line.

6. The constructed bisector of a line segment is a
   perpendicular bisector.

SET 1   **Write each ratio as a fraction in lowest terms.**

1. 49:56   **2.** 48 out of 64   **3.** 15 to 80   **4.** 36:72

Write two equal ratios for each.

5. 10:18   **6.** 6 to 11   **7.** 32 to 24   **8.** 11 out of 12

Tell if each is a proportion. Write *yes* or *no*.

9. $\frac{15}{18} = \frac{5}{9}$ **10.** $\frac{8}{20} = \frac{2}{5}$ **11.** $\frac{32}{28} = \frac{18}{14}$ **12.** $\frac{63}{72} = \frac{21}{26}$ **13.** $\frac{4.4}{2.2} = \frac{10.4}{5.2}$

Write = or ≠ for each ⬤.

14. $\frac{90}{72}$ ⬤ $\frac{15}{12}$ **15.** $\frac{26}{18}$ ⬤ $\frac{13}{8}$ **16.** $\frac{65}{106}$ ⬤ $\frac{13}{25}$ **17.** $\frac{5.6}{.8}$ ⬤ $\frac{49}{70}$ **18.** $\frac{1.5}{7.5}$ ⬤ $\frac{18}{90}$

SET 2   **Solve each proportion.**

1. $\frac{n}{14} = \frac{14}{28}$ **2.** $\frac{12}{18} = \frac{20}{n}$ **3.** $\frac{25}{n} = \frac{5}{11}$ **4.** $\frac{7}{35} = \frac{2.5}{n}$ **5.** $\frac{3}{1.7} = \frac{n}{5.1}$

6. $\frac{6.2}{n} = \frac{3.1}{15.5}$ **7.** $\frac{n}{12} = \frac{1.2}{4}$ **8.** $\frac{3.5}{14} = \frac{n}{32}$ **9.** $\frac{0.9}{3.75} = \frac{6}{n}$ **10.** $\frac{15}{16} = \frac{22.5}{n}$

Find the unit price of each to the nearest cent.

11. 3 lb of bananas for $1.00   **12.** 8 packs of gum for $1.19

13. 6 egg rolls for $4.89   **14.** 50 stamps for $11.00

SET 3   **Use the scale to find the actual dimensions of each.**

1. scale: 3 cm = 10 m
drawing: 4.5 cm
actual:

2. scale: 4 cm = 9 km
drawing: 18 cm
actual:

3. scale: 8 cm = 25 km
drawing: 20 cm
actual:

SET 4   *ABCDEF* is similar to *HIJKLM*.

1. $\overline{EF}$ corresponds to _____.

2. $\overline{HM}$ corresponds to _____.

3. The length of $\overline{JK}$ is _____.

4. The length of $\overline{BC}$ is _____.

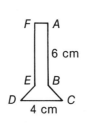
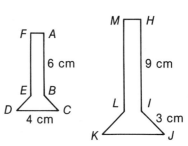

SET 1 Write each percent as a ratio with denominator 100 and each ratio as a percent.

pages 292–293

1. 56%   **2.** 9%   **3.** 81%   **4.** 22.5%   **5.** 8.5%   **6.** 2%

7. $\frac{77}{100}$ **8.** $\frac{6}{100}$ **9.** $\frac{13}{50}$ **10.** $\frac{19}{20}$ **11.** $\frac{14}{25}$

12. $\frac{10}{200}$ **13.** $\frac{650}{1,000}$ **14.** $\frac{25}{500}$ **15.** $\frac{70}{1,000}$ **16.** $\frac{3}{5}$

17. 35%   **18.** 14%   **19.** 1%   **20.** 0.1%   **21.** 0.2%

22. $\frac{2}{1,000}$ **23.** $\frac{2}{100}$ **24.** $\frac{2}{10}$ **25.** $\frac{200}{100}$ **26.** $\frac{4}{5}$

SET 2 Write each percent as a decimal.

pages 294–295

1. 4%   **2.** 38%   **3.** $80\frac{1}{2}$%   **4.** $5\frac{3}{4}$%   **5.** 16.5%   **6.** 7.25%

7. 5.3%   **8.** $33\frac{1}{3}$%   **9.** $8\frac{3}{8}$%   **10.** 42.7%   **11.** $60\frac{3}{5}$%   **12.** $88\frac{2}{3}$%

Write each decimal as a percent.

13. 0.81   **14.** 0.295   **15.** 0.015   **16.** 0.6   **17.** 0.028   **18.** 0.113

19. 0.1   **20.** 0.455   **21.** 0.065   **22.** 0.418   **23.** 0.9225   **24.** 0.6275

25. 0.2   **26.** 0.29   **27.** 0.02   **28.** 0.029   **29.** 0.002   **30.** 0.0029

SET 3 Write each ratio as a decimal and as a percent.

pages 296–299

1. $\frac{5.7}{100}$ **2.** $\frac{12.5}{100}$ **3.** $\frac{4}{100}$ **4.** $\frac{1}{8}$ **5.** $\frac{12}{25}$ **6.** $\frac{68}{200}$

7. $\frac{165}{500}$ **8.** $\frac{185}{100}$ **9.** $\frac{6}{5}$ **10.** $\frac{0.9}{100}$ **11.** $\frac{675}{1,000}$ **12.** $\frac{3.25}{100}$

Write each percent as a decimal and as a ratio in lowest terms.

13. 55%   **14.** 3.2%   **15.** 37.5%   **16.** 0.8%   **17.** 255%   **18.** $\frac{7}{10}$%

19. 0.5%   **20.** $\frac{7}{8}$%   **21.** 450%   **22.** 0.1%   **23.** $1\frac{1}{3}$%   **24.** 0.26%

25. 50%   **26.** 9.4%   **27.** 500%   **28.** 6.5%   **29.** 0.5%   **30.** 0.05%

SET 1 **Find the percent of each number. Use a proportion.**   pages 308–309

1. 15% of 200

2. 56% of 75

3. 95% of 180

4. 35% of 680

5. 30% of $335.50

6. 160% of 65

7. $7\frac{1}{2}$% of 440

8. 6.2% of 500

9. 250% of 18

10. $10\frac{1}{2}$% of 600

11. 40% of 330.5

12. 8% of 650

13. 60% of $85.40

14. 350% of 92

15. 2% of 44

16. $9\frac{1}{2}$% of 1,050

17. 0.5% of 2,800

18. 80% of 540.5

19. 5.5% of 9,000

20. 1% of 8.2

Compare. Use >, <, or = for each ⬤.

21. 20% of 90 ⬤ 90% of 20

22. 40% of 160 ⬤ 60% of 140

23. 70% of 550 ⬤ 80% of 440

24. 25% of 420 ⬤ 50% of 210

SET 2 **Find the percent of each number. Use decimals.**   pages 310–311

1. 6% of 350

2. 85% of $175

3. $1\frac{1}{2}$% of 220

4. 80% of 6

5. 5.8% of 440

6. 0.3% of 2,500

7. 55% of 380

8. 6.5% of $770

9. 25% of $195.40

10. $8\frac{1}{4}$% of 2,000

11. 250% of 630

12. $\frac{3}{4}$% of 140

13. 12% of $90

14. 400% of 18.55

15. 4.25% of 64

16. $\frac{1}{2}$% of 720

17. 0.4% of 575

18. $6\frac{3}{4}$% of 3,300

19. 0.08% of 1,500

20. 8.2% of 110

SET 3 **Find each percent.**   pages 312–313

1. What percent of 1,200 is 144?

2. What percent of 56 is 182?

3. What percent of $300 is $27?

4. What percent of 550 is 341?

5. $127.50 is what percent of $150?

6. $13.25 is what percent of $2,650?

7. $\frac{1}{2}$ is what percent of 25?

8. 50 is what percent of 100?

9. What percent of 2,300 is 86.25?

10. 76.5 is what percent of 900?

11. 25 is what percent of 75?

12. 129 is what percent of 860?

13. 10 is what percent of 25?

14. 20 is what percent of 25?

SET 1   Use a proportion to find *n*.   pages 314–315

1. 35% of *n* is 28.

2. 6% of *n* is 27.

3. 125% of *n* is 110.

4. 8 is 0.4% of *n*.

5. 92 is 5% of *n*.

6. $198 is 55% of *n*.

7. 15% of *n* is $100.

8. 11% of *n* is $40.

9. $55 is 110% of *n*.

Solve for *n* using decimals.

10. 68% of *n* is 238.

11. 275% of *n* is 88.

12. 0.75% of *n* is 24.

13. $125.40 is 6.6% of *n*.

14. 377 is 65% of *n*.

15. $1\frac{1}{2}$% of *n* is 52.5.

16. $385.60 is 15.5% of *n*.

17. $4\frac{1}{2}$% of *n* is 100.

18. $1,000 is 10% of *n*.

SET 2   Complete the chart.   pages 318–319

	Regular Price	Discount Rate	Discount	Sale Price
1.	$ 45.20	15%		
2.	$ 555.00			$ 388.50
3.	$3,870.00	$33\frac{1}{3}$%		
4.	$ 82.40			$ 49.44
5.		$12\frac{1}{2}$%	$ 11.25	
6.			$ 6.58	$ 181.42

SET 3   Find the interest earned for each.   pages 320–321

1. $6,500 at 8% for 3 years

2. $900 at 13% for 1 year

3. $1,200 at $6\frac{1}{2}$% for 6 months

4. $550 at 11% for 9 months

5. $3,800 at $9\frac{1}{2}$% for 2 years

6. $9,500 at 7.7% for 3 years

7. $7,400 at $8\frac{3}{4}$% for 36 months

8. $2,600 at $10\frac{1}{2}$% for 18 months

9. $5,900 at 12.5% for 24 months

10. $10,800 at $9\frac{1}{4}$% for 4 years

SET 1   Find each perimeter.

pages 332–335

1.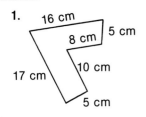

2.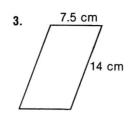

3.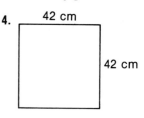

4.

5. an isosceles
triangle
l = 32 mm
s = 17.2 mm

6. a rectangle
l = 22 cm
w = 12 cm

7. a regular
octagon
s = 5.6 m

8. a regular
pentagon
s = 2.8 km

Find the circumference of each circle. Use π = 3.14. Round
each answer to the nearest one.

9.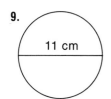

10.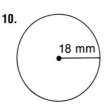

11.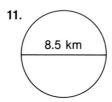

12.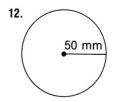

Find the diameter of each circle. Use 3.14 for π.

13. c = 78.5 cm

14. c = 29.83 m

15. c = 5.338 km

16. c = 942 mm

SET 2   Find the area of each square, rectangle, or parallelogram.

pages 336–339

1.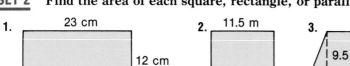

2.

3.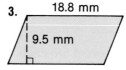

4.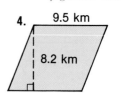

5. l = 31 mm
w = 12 mm

6. s = 15.3 m

7. b = 40.8 mm
h = 21.5 mm

8. s = 18.6 cm

9. b = 15.6 cm
h = 10.5 cm

10. l = 31.9 mm
w = 14.1 mm

11. s = 8.03 km

12. b = 6.85 m
h = 3.14 m

SET 1 Find the area of each triangle.

pages 340–343

1.
8 cm

6 cm

2.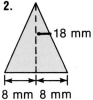
18 mm

8 mm 8 mm

3.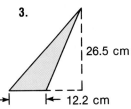
26.5 cm

12.2 cm

4.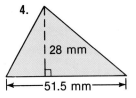
28 mm

51.5 mm

5. $b = 3.5$ m
$h = 6.8$ m

6. $b = 38.8$ mm
$h = 26.5$ mm

7. $b = 17.2$ cm
$h = 21.7$ cm

8. $b = 14.4$ cm
$h = 19.5$ cm

Find the area of each circle. Use $\pi = 3.14$. Round each answer to the nearest one.

9.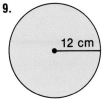
12 cm

10.
7 cm

11.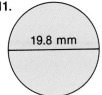
19.8 mm

12.
6.8 m

13. $r = 5.5$ km

14. $d = 40$ cm

15. $d = 64$ mm

16. $r = 14$ m

SET 2 Name each figure. Give the number of faces (*F*), edges (*E*), and vertices (*V*).

pages 346–347

1.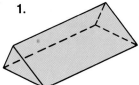

2.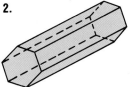

3.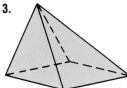

4.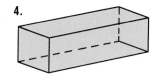

SET 1 Find the surface area of each prism.

1.
24 mm · 10 mm · 6 mm · 26 mm

2.
3.5 m · 3.5 m · 3.5 m · 3.5 m

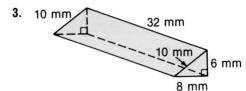

3.
10 mm · 32 mm · 10 mm · 6 mm · 8 mm

4.
3 cm · 15 cm · 15 cm

5.
8.4 m · 4.6 m · 2.1 m

6.
17 m · 8 m · 10 m · 15 m

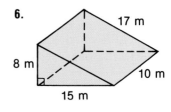

7.
6.2 cm · 4 cm · 11.8 cm

8.
25 mm · 20 mm · 18 mm · 15 mm

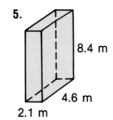

9.
9.3 cm · 9.3 cm · 9.3 cm

SET 2 Find the volume of each prism.

1.
7 m · 6 m · 18 m

2.
8 cm · 12 cm · 22 cm

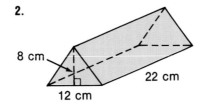

3.
9 mm · 11 mm · 30 mm

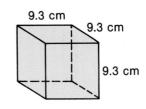

4.
29 cm · 20 cm · 18 cm · 21 cm

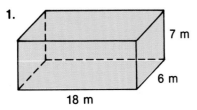

5.
7 m · 7 m · 5 m · 18 m

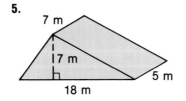

6.
4 cm · 11.5 cm · 6.8 cm

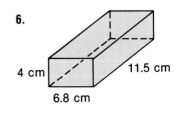

SET 1 Find the surface area of each cylinder. Use π = 3.14. pages 352–353
Round each answer to the nearest one.

1.
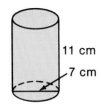
11 cm
7 cm

2.
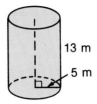
13 m
5 m

3.
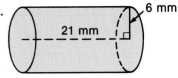
6 mm
21 mm

4.
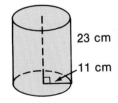
14 m
8 m

5.
11 mm
19 mm

6.
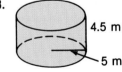
7.4 cm
16 cm

7. r = 5.2 m
   h = 20.5 m

8. d = 4 m
   h = 9.5 m

9. d = 4.5 cm
   h = 9.8 cm

10. r = 14.5 mm
    h = 8 mm

11. d = 2.6 m
    h = 10.5 m

12. r = 6.6 cm
    h = 18 cm

SET 2 Find the volume of each cylinder. Use π = 3.14. pages 354–355
Round answers to the nearest one.

1.
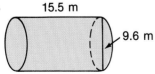
23 cm
11 cm

2.
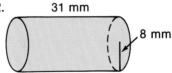
31 mm
8 mm

3.
4.5 m
5 m

4.
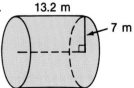
15.5 m
9.6 m

5.
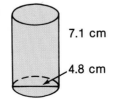
7.1 cm
4.8 cm

6.
13.2 m
7 m

7. r = 2.6 m
   h = 18 m

8. d = 15.6 cm
   h = 28 cm

9. r = 10.8 mm
   h = 35 mm

SET 1 Find the range and the mode for each collection of data.

pages 366–369

1. 18, 25, 6, 10, 24, 17, 12, 21, 10

2. 8.3, 7.9, 6.4, 9.1, 7.9, 7.2, 8.4

3. $1.25, $2.03, $3.00, $1.61, $2.03, $2.74

4. 2,164, 3,000, 2,165, 4,047, 3,000, 3,107

Find the range, median, and mean for each. Round to the nearest tenths.

5. 86 m, 27 m, 52 m, 104 m, 29 m

6. 43, 38, 72, 31, 56, 58, 45, 63

7. 21.5, 16.7, 14.3, 24.2, 20.6

8. 1.2 cm, 2.7 cm, 2.4 cm, 1.7 cm, 3.2 cm

9. 846, 841, 847, 849, 843, 845

10. 114, 116, 112, 123, 110, 119

SET 2 Use the bar graph to answer the problems.

pages 370–371

1. What is the state with the smallest area in sq mi?

2. Which state has an area of about 6,400 sq mi?

3. About how many sq mi is the state of Connecticut?

4. About how many more sq mi does New Jersey have than Connecticut?

5. About how many sq mi is the state of Delaware?

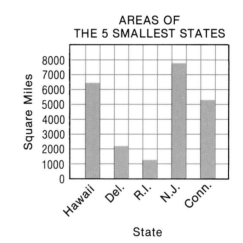

AREAS OF THE 5 SMALLEST STATES

SET 3 Use the line graph to answer the problems.

pages 372–373

1. In what year did Babe Ruth hit the most home runs?

2. When did he hit 54 home runs?

3. How many home runs did Ruth hit in 1926?

4. How many home runs did Ruth hit from 1926–1930?

5. Between what two years did Ruth have the greatest increase in home runs?

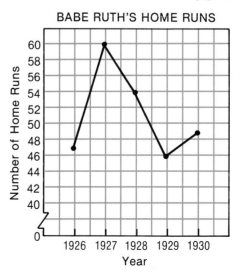

BABE RUTH'S HOME RUNS

SET 1   Use the spinner for 1–15. Find each probability.   pages 378–379

1. spinning a number less than 9

2. spinning a number divisible by 3

3. spinning a number that is not 7

4. spinning a 5

5. spinning an odd number

6. spinning an even number

Spin the spinner once. Find each probability.

7. $P(11)$ 8. $P(1)$ 9. $P(\text{odd})$ 10. $P(\text{even})$

11. $P(\text{less than } 7)$ 12. $P(\text{greater than } 7)$ 13. $P(\text{not } 15)$

14. $P(\text{less than } 1)$ 15. $P(\text{greater than } 1)$

SET 2   Find the relative frequency for each food.   pages 380–381

1. Apple pie   2. Fried chicken

3. Mashed potato   4. Spaghetti

5. Peanut butter and jelly sandwich

6. Steak   7. Other

FAVORITE FOOD OF 100 STUDENTS	
Food	**Frequency**
Apple pie	10
Fried chicken	16
Mashed potato	18
Peanut butter and jelly sandwich	10
Spaghetti	20
Steak	28
Other	2

Suppose 300 students were surveyed. Using the same data, give the frequency you would expect for each food.

8. Apple pie   9. Fried chicken

10. Mashed potato   11. Spaghetti

12. Peanut butter and jelly sandwich

13. Steak   14. Other

SET 1 A pennant is chosen without looking. Find each probability.

pages 382–383

1. *P*(Cincinnati Bengals)

2. *P*(Detroit Lions)

3. *P*(AFC League Champions)

4. *P*(Super Bowl XVIII winners)

5. *P*(NFC team)

6. *P*(AFC team)

7. *P*(Buffalo or Miami)

8. *P*(NFC League Champions)

9. *P*(NFC or AFC League Champions)

10. *P*(Dallas Cowboys)

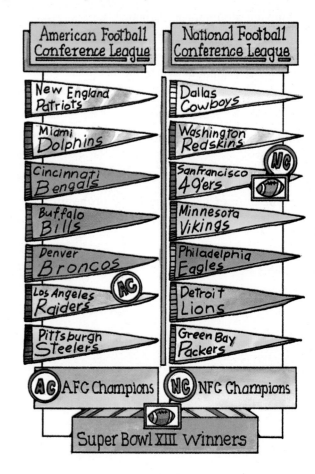

SET 2 Spin the spinner. Toss a coin. Answer the problems.

pages 386–387

1. Draw a tree diagram to show all the possible outcomes.

2. List all the outcomes for the event (heads, even number).

3. List all the outcomes for the event (tails, odd number).

Find each probability.

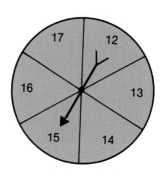

4. *P*(heads, 12)

5. *P*(heads, not 16)

6. *P*(tails, odd number)

7. *P*(tails, number > 13)

8. *P*(tails, number multiple of 4)

9. *P*(heads, even number)

10. *P*(heads, multiple of 5)

11. *P*(tails, not 14)

12. *P*(heads, number < 17)

SET 1 Compare. Use >, <, or = for each ●. pages 398–399

1. $^+1$ ● $^+3$ 2. $^+2$ ● $^-5$ 3. 0 ● $^+5$ 4. $^-7$ ● $^-7$ 5. $^-1$ ● $^+1$

6. $^-9$ ● 0 7. $^-3$ ● $^-4$ 8. $^+6$ ● $^+6$ 9. $^-8$ ● $^+8$ 10. 0 ● $^-3$

11. $^-9$ ● $^-8$ 12. $^+2$ ● $^-30$ 13. $^+6$ ● $^+7$ 14. $^+4$ ● $^-12$ 15. $^-4$ ● $^+12$

16. $^-4$ ● $^-6$ 17. $^+10$ ● 0 18. $^-9$ ● $^+2$ 19. 0 ● $^-15$ 20. $^-16$ ● $^-1$

SET 2 Add. Use a number line if needed. pages 400–403

1. $^+8 + {}^+1$ 2. $^-7 + {}^-3$ 3. $^-3 + {}^-5$ 4. $^+4 + {}^+8$

5. $^-11 + {}^-1$ 6. $^-9 + {}^-3$ 7. $^+4 + {}^+7$ 8. $^-11 + {}^-13$

9. $^+3 + {}^+4 + {}^+6$ 10. $^-8 + {}^-7 + {}^-5$ 11. $^-6 + 0 + {}^-9$

12. $^+5 + {}^+9 + {}^+8$ 13. $^-3 + {}^-5 + {}^-9$ 14. $^-3 + {}^-15 + {}^-10$

15. $^-7 + {}^+2$ 16. $^-4 + {}^+6$ 17. $0 + {}^-3$ 18. $^+8 + {}^-9$

19. $^+4 + {}^-5$ 20. $^-8 + {}^+2$ 21. $^+10 + {}^-1$ 22. $^-9 + {}^+6$

23. $^+8 + {}^-10$ 24. $^+7 + 0$ 25. $^+11 + {}^-3$ 26. $^+1 + {}^-12$

27. $^-7 + {}^+9$ 28. $^-14 + {}^+10$ 29. $^+12 + {}^-9$ 30. $^-6 + {}^+10$

SET 3 Subtract. pages 404–405

1. $^-8 - {}^+2$ 2. $^+4 - {}^-1$ 3. $^-6 - {}^-3$ 4. $^+3 - {}^+9$

5. $^+5 - {}^-6$ 6. $0 - {}^-4$ 7. $^-15 - {}^+12$ 8. $^-14 - {}^-14$

9. $^-9 - {}^-5$ 10. $^-10 - {}^+7$ 11. $^+7 - {}^+5$ 12. $^+13 - {}^-13$

Evaluate each expression if $n = {}^-3$.

13. $^-7 - n$ 14. $^+3 - n$ 15. $n - {}^+9$ 16. $^-3 - n$

17. $^-2 - n$ 18. $n - {}^+5$ 19. $^+1 - n$ 20. $^-7 - n$

SET 4 Find each product. pages 406–407

1. $^+3 \times {}^-2$ 2. $^-5 \times {}^+4$ 3. $^-8 \times {}^-3$ 4. $^+9 \times {}^+1$

5. $^+12 \times {}^-3$ 6. $^-10 \times {}^-4$ 7. $^-7 \times {}^-8$ 8. $^-3 \times {}^+4$

9. $^+5 \times {}^-5$ 10. $^-6 \times {}^+4$ 11. $^-3 \times {}^-7$ 12. $^-9 \times {}^-5$

SET 1 Find each quotient.

pages 408–409

1. $^-45 \div {}^+5$

2. $^+63 \div {}^-9$

3. $^-54 \div {}^-6$

4. $^+32 \div {}^-8$

5. $^-72 \div {}^-9$

6. $^-56 \div {}^+7$

7. $^+20 \div {}^-10$

8. $^-36 \div {}^-4$

9. $\frac{^+60}{^-5}$

10. $\frac{^-49}{^+7}$

11. $\frac{^-18}{^-3}$

12. $\frac{^-52}{^+4}$

SET 2 Solve and check.

pages 412–415

1. $x + {}^+3 = {}^+8$

2. $n - {}^-1 = {}^-3$

3. $^-4 = a + {}^-7$

4. $t - {}^+6 = {}^-8$

5. $^+14 - c = {}^+28$

6. $y + {}^-6 = {}^-14$

7. $^-18 = n + {}^-28$

8. $^+27 + y = {}^+7$

9. $^-51 + x = {}^-43$

10. $^-36 = w + {}^-41$

11. $^+62 + a = {}^+5$

12. $^+53 + y = {}^-1$

Solve and check.

13. $^-6a = {}^-42$

14. $^+4b = {}^-36$

15. $^+8 = \frac{c}{^+5}$

16. $^-7w = {}^+35$

17. $y \div {}^+8 = {}^-3$

18. $n \div {}^-7 = {}^-4$

19. $^+6s = {}^-24$

20. $^-5p = {}^-25$

21. $^-3c = {}^+36$

22. $a \div {}^-11 = {}^+4$

23. $^+6 = b \div {}^+8$

24. $\frac{z}{^-10} = {}^+10$

SET 3 Solve each inequality by writing a related equation.

pages 416–417

1. $x + {}^+3 > {}^+5$

2. $y - {}^+2 < {}^+8$

3. $a - {}^-4 \geq {}^+8$

4. $^-9 + b \leq {}^+5$

5. $c - {}^-1 \geq {}^-4$

6. $s - {}^-10 \leq {}^+1$

7. $r - {}^+6 > {}^+12$

8. $t + {}^-8 \leq {}^+17$

SET 4 Complete each table of values. Then graph each equation.

pages 418–421

1. $y = x + 3$

x	y
3	6
2	
1	
0	

2. $y = x - 2$

x	y
3	1
2	
1	
0	

3. $y = x + {}^-1$

x	y
3	2
2	
1	
0	

4. $y = 2x - 2$

x	y
3	4
2	
1	
0	

466

SET 1   Use the schedule to answer the questions.

pages 8–9

1. When is the restaurant open on Fridays?

2. Does the restaurant ever serve lunch on Mondays?

3. How much earlier does the restaurant open on Fridays than on Thursdays?

4. How much longer is the restaurant open on Thursdays than on Wednesdays?

5. For how many hours is the restaurant open on Tuesday?

Village Restaurant

Lunch — *Fri., Sat., Sun.*
11:30 A.M. – 3:00 P.M.

Dinner — *Daily*
3:00 P.M. – 10:00 P.M.

Late Nights — *Thurs., Fri., Sat.*
10:00 P.M. – 1:00 A.M.

Holiday Weekends
Sun. 11:30 A.M. – 1:00 A.M.
Mon. 11:30 A.M. – 10:00 P.M.

SET 2   Use the table to answer the questions.

pages 20–21

1. Last week, Ms. Kirk, age 66, golfed 9 holes every day. What did she pay to play?

2. Her young nephew golfed with her on Friday and Saturday. How much did it cost for him to play?

3. If they rented a cart on each of the two days, what did they pay for the cart?

4. If they shared the cost of the cart, how much did each pay?

CODY GOLF CLUB

Weekdays $6.00
Weekends $7.50

Senior Citizens
Monday – Friday $5.00

CARTS
9 Holes $6.30
18 Holes $11.50

Call: **555–1111**

SET 3   Solve each problem, if possible. If there are missing facts, tell what is needed. If there are extra facts, tell what they are.

pages 42–43

1. Jupiter has a diameter of about 87,000 miles, 29 times the diameter of Mercury. Earth's diameter is about 7,900 miles, 2.5 times that of Mercury. Jupiter's diameter is about how many times greater than Earth's diameter?

2. Jupiter has 4 times as many moons as Neptune, Pluto, and Earth together. Neptune has 2 moons, and Pluto has 1. How many moons does Jupiter have?

3. Mars is approximately 47 million miles farther from the sun than Earth. About how far is Mars from the sun?

4. Pluto's rotation time is $6\frac{1}{3}$ days. This is approximately 136 hours longer than Neptune's rotation time. What is Neptune's rotation time?

SET 1 **Solve each problem. If there is too much information, tell what is not needed.**

1. The table shows prices of charcoal sticks. To the nearest cent, what is the price per stick in a box of 50?

2. How much more is each stick if bought in a box of 15?

3. The art teacher works from 9:00 A.M. to 2:30 P.M. He orders 3 sticks per student in 5 classes. There are 20 students per class. How many boxes of 50 does he order?

4. What is the least expensive way to purchase 75 sticks?

CHARCOAL STICKS	
Number per Box	Cost per Box
15	$2.25
25	$2.95
50	$4.95

SET 2 **Solve each problem by using a simulation.**

1. Jan decorates a float with a row of balloons in a red, white, blue pattern. She adds a white balloon before each red balloon. What is the pattern now?

2. Next, Jan adds a white balloon after each red and each blue balloon. What is the pattern after she does this?

3. Each pattern of 6 balloons has 1 red one. The float has 18 balloons along each side, 12 balloons along the back, and none in front. How many red balloons are used?

4. The parade starts at the park. Jan drives the float 3 blocks north, 2 blocks east, 4 blocks south, 7 blocks west, and 1 block north. How far is she from the park?

SET 3 **Copy the diagram. Use it to answer the questions.**

1. The driving distance from Walnut Cove to Oak Bay is 796 km. How far is the driving distance from Pine Hill to Oak Bay?

2. The driving distance from Oak Bay to Ashland is twice as far as from Oak Bay to Pine Hill. How far is the distance?

3. Which drive is shorter: Cherry Tree to Hickory, or Cherry Tree to Ashland? How much shorter?

4. Which drive is farther: Pine Hill to Walnut Cove, or Pine Hill to Ashland? How much farther?

5. It took the Lake family 5 days to drive from Hickory to Ashland. What was their average daily distance?

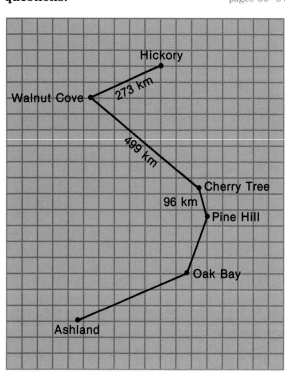

SET 1   Solve each problem.

pages 96–97

1. Skip works for a baking company. He packs 12 cartons of rolls in each shipping box. Each box holds 576 rolls. The number of cartons per box is 4 more than the number of packages per carton. How many rolls are in a package?

2. Skip packs loaves of bread in shipping boxes of 3 different sizes. Each box holds 1.5 times as many loaves as the next smaller size. The largest box holds 45 loaves. How many loaves does the smallest box hold?

3. Skip packs rolls twice as fast as he packs muffins. He packs crackers 2.5 times as fast as he packs rolls. Skip packs 250 boxes of crackers per hour. How many boxes of muffins does he pack in an hour?

4. Skip rides his bike to work. During one week, he rode a total of 13.4 miles, taking a different route each day. Skip rode 2.7 miles on Tuesday. On Wednesday he rode 0.8 mile less than on Tuesday. He rode 1.3 miles more on Thursday than on Wednesday. His riding distance was the same on Monday and Friday. How far did he ride on Monday?

SET 2   Solve each problem.

pages 108–109

1. Working 8 hours a day, Nina wrote a 12-page workbook in 7 days 4 hours. What was her average writing time per page?

2. If Nina is paid $675 for completing the 12-page workbook, what does she earn per hour for her work?

3. Alan's average writing time is 5.5 hours per page. How long would it take him to write a 12-page workbook?

4. Luis wrote a 16-page workbook in 72 hours. How did his average writing time per page compare with Alan's?

5. Vicky earns $9 per hour for proofreading. She earned $126. How many hours of proofreading did she do?

6. Eva receives $171 for proofreading a manuscript. She completes the project in 18 hours. Is she paid more or less than Vicky? How much more or less?

SET 3   Use the table to solve each problem.

pages 128–129

1. Alicia buys 2 packages of lined paper and 3 pencils. How much does she pay?

2. Loi purchases 3 spiral notebooks, 2 pens, and 2 pencils. How much does he pay?

3. Will Betty be able to buy 2 pencils, an eraser, and a pen with $1.00?

4. David buys 3 packages of lined paper, 2 pens, 4 pencils, and a ruler. How much change will he get back from $5.00?

SCHOOL STORE	
Spiral notebook	$.89 each
Lined paper	.79 package
Pencil	.15 each
Eraser	.29 each
Ruler	.39 each
Pen	.49 each

SET 1   John Adams was born on October 30, 1735 and died on July 4, 1826. His son John Quincy Adams was born on July 11, 1767, and died on February 23, 1848.

1. How old was John Quincy Adams when he was inaugurated President in 1825?

2. Who lived longer, John Adams or his son? How much longer?

3. John Adams and Thomas Jefferson died on the same day. In 1797, Jefferson was 53 years old. Who was born first?

4. John Adams was married in 1764, Thomas Jefferson in 1772, and John Quincy Adams in 1797. To the nearest year, what is the average length of time they were married?

SET 2   Make a drawing to solve each problem.

1. Donna's kite reached a height of 120 ft. Ed's kite flew 25 ft lower than Donna's. Bob's kite soared 60 ft higher than Ed's. How much higher did Bob's kite fly than Donna's?

2. Greg decorates a cake with 12 blueberries and 12 raspberries. He alternates the berries around the 4 sides, 5 berries on each short side. If he puts a raspberry in each corner, how many blueberries will be on each long side?

Kim is arranging a table and a lounge chair on one wall of a 12 ft × 12 ft deck. She puts the 2.5-ft-square table in one corner and the 2 ft × 5.5 ft chair in the other corner.

3. If she puts the long side of the lounge chair against the wall, how much space will be left between the furniture?

4. Kim puts the short side of the chair against the wall. Will a 4 ft × 8 ft rug fit lengthwise between the furniture?

SET 3   The graph shows the approximate lengths of underwater tunnels in New York, New York, and Norfolk, Virginia.

1. What is the difference between Norfolk's longest and shortest tunnels?

2. What is the average length of New York's tunnels?

3. If Norfolk's Midtown and Downtown tunnels were connected, would they be as long as the Holland Tunnel?

4. Is the Lincoln Tunnel 3 times as long as the Downtown Tunnel?

5. What is the average length of Norfolk's tunnels?

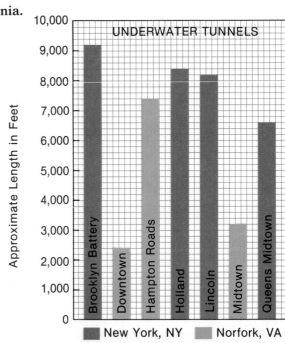

UNDERWATER TUNNELS

Approximate Length in Feet

Brooklyn Battery · Downtown · Hampton Roads · Holland · Lincoln · Midtown · Queens Midtown

■ New York, NY   ■ Norfork, VA

SET 1 Use the guess and test method to solve each problem. pages 188–189

1. Jack and his little brother Rich together picked 16 boxes of strawberries. Jack picked 3 times as many boxes as Rick. How many boxes did Rick pick?

2. Gina, Lynn, and Jerry ate a package of 18 crackers. Gina ate $\frac{1}{2}$ as many as Lynn and $\frac{1}{3}$ as many as Jerry. How many crackers did each eat?

3. The chef made 6 salads. He used 72 olives altogether. He put 2 more green olives than black olives in each salad. How many of each kind of olive did he use?

4. Barbara bought 20 cans of cat food—tuna and beef. The tuna cost 30¢ a can, and the beef cost 39¢ a can. She spent $6.81. How many cans of each did she buy?

5. Find 2 whole numbers whose product is 84 and whose sum is less than 20.

6. Find 2 whole numbers whose sum is 25 and whose product is as great as possible.

SET 2 Solve each problem, if possible. If there are missing facts, tell what is needed. If there are extra facts, tell what they are. pages 202–203

1. At Shenk's Farm Stand, Judi bought 4 bunches of beets. There were 5 or 6 beets in each bunch. The beets cost 79¢ a bunch. How much did she spend?

2. Mick bought 3 heads of lettuce. Romaine lettuce cost $.45 per head, and Boston lettuce cost $.59 per head. How much did he spend on the lettuce?

3. Mrs. Dobson bought 6 lb of grapes at 89¢ a pound. She bought 4 lb of green grapes and 2 lb of red grapes. What did she pay for the grapes?

4. Brent made 12 salads. He put 5 cucumber slices and 4 cherry tomatoes on each. How many pints of cherry tomatoes did he use to make the salads?

SET 3 Use the table to answer the questions. pages 222–223

1. Which animals live from 15–20 years less than an elephant?

2. How many years longer than a whale does an elephant live?

3. An elephant lives how many times longer than a guinea pig?

4. Which animal has about $\frac{1}{5}$ the life span of an elephant?

5. If the animals are ranked from longest to shortest life span, which animal is in the middle?

ANIMAL	LIFE SPAN IN YEARS
Chimpanzee	30
Elephant	47
Guinea Pig	4
Horse	27
Mountain Goat	9
Polar Bear	31
Whale	37

pages 234–235

SET 1   Use the table to solve each problem.

1. Which item has the most calcium in a serving?

2. Which item has the most sodium in a serving?

3. Mr. Alison is on a low-sodium diet—less than 1,100 mg sodium per meal. He has a breakfast of orange juice, corn flakes, milk, 2 slices of toast with 1 pat butter, and coffee. How much sodium will he have?

4. On another day, Mr. Alison has orange juice, 2 slices of bacon, 2 eggs, 2 slices of toast with 1 pat of butter, and coffee. Is he following his diet?

5. Which of Mr. Alison's breakfasts provide more calcium?

6. Make a breakfast menu for yourself and tell how much calcium and sodium are in it.

CALCIUM AND SODIUM IN BREAKFAST FOOD			
Foods	Serving	Calcium	Sodium
Bacon	2 slices	2 mg	325 mg
Butter	1 pat	1 mg	41 mg
Coffee	250 ml	0	0
Corn flakes	25 g	4 mg	251 mg
Egg	1	28 mg	60 mg
Maple syrup	20 ml	35 mg	4 mg
Milk	250 ml	291 mg	120 mg
Orange juice	250 ml	25 mg	4 mg
Pancake	27 g	27 mg	115 mg
Shredded wheat	25 g	11 mg	10 mg
toast, white bread	1 slice	21 mg	170 mg
Tomato Juice	250 ml	17 mg	740 mg

7. One stalk of cooked broccoli, one raw carrot, one raw tomato, and one raw onion contain 6 g of protein. The amount of protein in 3 of the vegetables is the same. They each have $\frac{1}{3}$ as much protein as the fourth vegetable. If broccoli contains the most protein, how much is in each vegetable?

8. A seafood platter contains 6 kinds of fish. Each serving contains the following amounts of iron: bluefish, 0.7 mg; shrimp, 1.6 mg; clams, 3.4 mg; salmon, 0.8 mg; tuna, 1.1 mg; and haddock, 1.2 mg. Kyung Soo ate 3 kinds of fish from the platter, and his iron intake was 6.2 mg. Which fish did he eat?

SET 2   Find the missing elements in each pattern.

pages 256–257

1.

A	b.	D		
a	C	d		
B		E		H

2.

3. 1, 2, 4, 7, 11, ___, ___, 29

5. 28, 14, 20, 10, 16, 8, ___, ___, 13

6. 1, $1\frac{1}{2}$, $2\frac{1}{2}$, 4, 6, $8\frac{1}{2}$, ___, 15

7. 68, 42, 26, 16, 10, ___, ___, 2

4.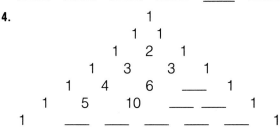

472

SET 1 **Solve each problem.** pages 268–269

1. At a fair, Ida sold 5 knit hats for $9.50 each. She sold a sixth hat for $11.00. How much money did she receive for the hats sold?

2. Ida sold 4 of her hand-knit sweaters for $200. Three of them were pullovers and 1 was a cardigan. The cardigan cost $12 more than each pullover. How much did each sweater cost?

3. Burt used 18 red roses and 45 pink roses to make silk floral arrangements. He put 2 red roses in each arrangement. How many pink roses did he put in each if he used the same number in each arrangement?

4. Brian makes leather goods. He created the following design for a belt. What are the missing elements in his pattern?

$$X = XX - XX = X = XX - ? = ?$$

SET 2 **Solve each problem.** pages 290–291

1. In 1980, the U.S. had a population of 226,545,805. What was the average number of people per state?

2. In the 1970 census, the population of the U.S. was 203,235,298. The 1960 population was 179,323,175. What was the average increase in population each year?

3. An artist drew a picture of Uncle Sam that measured 10 inches high. The picture was reduced for a magazine ad. The ratio of the height of the drawing to the height of the ad was 5:2. What is Uncle Sam's height in the magazine ad?

4. To date, a toy manufacturer has sold over 2,000,000 stuffed dolls. Of the dolls, 3 out of 4 had a pair of blue eyes on them. About how many blue eyes has the manufacturer used?

SET 3 **Solve each problem.** pages 300–301

Brenda grew $1\frac{1}{2}$ inches in a year. Grace grew $1\frac{1}{2}$ inches in 6 months. Paul grew 3 inches in 9 months. In $1\frac{1}{2}$ years, Cyrus grew 3 inches. In 2 years, Lucia grew 5 inches.

1. Who averaged the greatest growth in a year?

2. Who averaged the least growth in a year?

3. List the children from greatest to least in yearly growth.

4. Find the average yearly growth of the 5 people.

5. A veterinarian gave Leon pills to give his dog for 1 week. Leon must give the dog 2 pills 7 times on the first day, 2 pills 6 times on the second day, 2 pills 5 times on the third day, and so on. After the second day, what percent of the pills has the dog taken? Answer to nearer whole percent.

6. Leon and his dog jog together each day. Each day, they jog one-quarter mile farther than the previous day. On Sunday they covered $3\frac{1}{4}$ miles. How far did they jog the previous Sunday?

pages 316–317

SET 1 Use the graph to solve the problems.

1. What was Frank's score on Thursday?

2. How much lower was Frank's score on Friday than on Monday?

3. What was Frank's average daily score for the week?

4. Frank golfed each day with Willie. On Tuesday and Wednesday, Willie's score was 2 strokes less than Frank's on that day. Willie used 3 strokes more on Monday and Thursday. They tied on Friday. Make a bar graph showing Willie's scores.

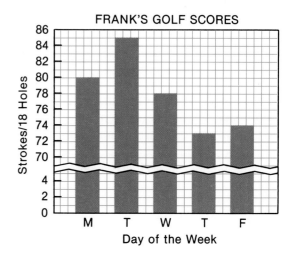

FRANK'S GOLF SCORES

SET 2 Solve each problem.

pages 322–323

1. Gretchen took an average of 12 photos per day during a 4-day trip. She took 12 photos on Thursday, 8 on Friday, and 15 on Saturday. How many did she take on Sunday?

2. Gretchen bought 6 postcards at 20¢ each, writing paper for $1.29, and envelopes for 59¢. How many postage stamps can she buy with her change from $5?

3. Mano's Gift Shop sold 12 yellow, 14 orange, and 39 green visor caps on Saturday. What percent of the caps sold were green?

4. Ms. Mano sold key chains and pins to 21 people. She made $21.45. The key chains sold for $1.10 each, and the pins for 95¢ each. How many of each did Ms. Mano sell?

SET 3 Determine whether the conclusion following each given set of statements is true.

pages 344–345

1. Pine trees bear pine cones.
   The Norway spruce bears pine cones.

2. Pierre speaks only French.
   Debbie spoke to Pierre.

3. Adam, Chris, Eva, and Sara are in line to buy tickets for a movie. Sara is not last. Chris is directly ahead of Sara. Eva is right behind Adam. In what order are they standing in the line?

4. At the movie they each buy peanuts or popcorn at the snack bar. Adam and Sara did not buy the same snack, while Chris and Eva did buy the same snack. Sara and Eva always buy popcorn at the movies. What did each buy?

SET 1 Solve each problem.

pages 356–357

1. How many feet of ribbon are needed to wrap the box in the picture? Add 2 extra feet for tying a bow.

2. What if the box is $\frac{3}{4}$ the size of the one in the picture? Still using 2 feet for the bow, how many feet of ribbon are needed to wrap the box?

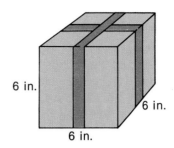

6 in.

6 in.

6 in.

3. Rod wrapped a gift for each of his brothers. Rod wrapped 4 packages. What can you conclude?

4. Sue filled a glass triangular prism with sand. The base is a 3 in. × 4 in. × 5 in. right triangle. What is the volume in cubic inches of the prism?

SET 2 Solve each problem. In each, consider only half-dollars, quarters, dimes, and nickels—no pennies.

pages 376–377

1. The toll at a parkway toll plaza is 40¢. How many different ways can the toll be paid in an exact-change lane?

2. Orlando bought $4.35 worth of groceries. He gave the clerk $5.00. How many different combinations of coins could he receive in change?

3. Zach has 6 coins in his pocket, and their total value is $1.00. What coins does he have?

4. At a movie, Lynn paid for a box of popcorn with 3 coins of one size and 1 different coin. Chris bought the same size box with 3 coins of another size and 1 different size. How much did a box of popcorn cost?

SET 3 Tony's homeroom had car washes to support a foster child. A wash cost $4.00. Use the graph to solve each problem.

pages 388–389

1. On which day did they make the most money? How much did they make?

2. On which day did they wash the fewest cars? How many did they wash?

3. How much money did they earn in the four car washes?

4. What was the average number of cars washed each day?

GRADE 7 CAR WASH	
Apr. 6	■■
Apr. 13	■■■■
Apr. 20	■■■
Apr. 27	■■■■■
■ = 10 cars washed	

5. A can of car soap is mixed with water to wash 10 cars, and the mix cannot be saved. How many cans are used during the month?

Solve each problem by more than one method. pages 410–411
Check that your answers are the same.

1. The ABC Overnight Express Co. will deliver a package on the next day to anywhere in the country for $14.00 up to 1 lb, $25.00 up to 2 lb, and $3.00 for each additional pound up to 10 lb. If Comp-Tech sent a package from San Francisco to Boston and paid $40.00, how much did it weigh?

2. Stephen has a collection of less than 50 marbles. He sold $\frac{1}{3}$ of them to a dealer. He gave half of the remaining marbles to his brother. He traded $\frac{1}{4}$ of the remaining marbles to a friend for some baseball cards. He still has 12 marbles. How many did he have before these activities?

3. An operator-assisted telephone call from New York to Paris costs $6.75 for the first 3 min and $1.20 for each additional minute. It cost Mr. Klein $15.15 to call from New York to a client in Paris. How long was the telephone call?

4. Find the area of the region at the right.

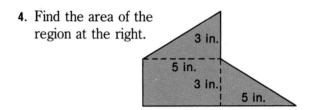

SET 2 **Solve each problem.** pages 422–423

Derek wants to cook chili. Because he does not have all of the recipe's ingredients, he will make substitutions. Use the information below to solve each problem.

CHILI INGREDIENTS

1 onion (small)
1 tablespoon butter
2 pounds ground beef
$\frac{2}{3}$ cup catsup
$\frac{1}{2}$ cup water
$\frac{1}{4}$ cup celery
2 tablespoons lemon juice
1 teaspoon vinegar
$\frac{1}{4}$ teaspoon dry mustard
1 can kidney beans
$\frac{1}{2}$ cup tomato juice
1 teaspoon chili powder

SUBSTITUTIONS

1 cup tomato juice = $\frac{1}{2}$ cup tomato sauce plus $\frac{1}{2}$ cup water

2 tablespoons bottled lemon juice = juice of 1 lemon

1 teaspoon dry mustard = 1 tablespoon prepared mustard

1 small fresh onion = 1 tablespoon instant minced onion

1 clove garlic = $\frac{1}{8}$ teaspoon garlic powder

1. How much instant minced onion should Derek use?

2. How many lemons will he need to squeeze for juice?

3. What amount of prepared mustard should he substitute for dry mustard?

4. Instead of tomato juice, how much tomato sauce and water will he need?

Glossary

absolute value   The distance an integer is from 0 on the number line.
Example: |⁻4| = 4   The absolute value of ⁻4 is 4.

acute angle   An angle with a measure less than 90°.

acute triangle   A triangle with three acute angles.

addends   The numbers that are added.

additive inverses   Two numbers whose sum is zero.
Example: ⁻3 and ⁺3 are additive inverses.
⁻3 + ⁺3 = 0

angle   Two rays with a common endpoint called the vertex.

arc   A part of the circumference of a circle.

area   The number of square units needed to cover a region.

associative property of addition   The way that addends are grouped does not change the sum.
Example: $(a + b) + c = a + (b + c)$

associative property of multiplication   The way that factors are grouped does not change the product.
Example: $(a \times b) \times c = a \times (b \times c)$

average   A number found by dividing the sum of the addends by the number of addends.

base (of a polygon)   base

base (of a space figure)   base

BASIC   A computer language.

binary   A numeration system that uses two as its base.

bisect   To divide into two congruent parts.

central angle   An angle that has its vertex at the center of a circle.

central processing unit (CPU)   The part of a computer where calculations are performed.

chord   A line segment with both endpoints on the circle.

circle   A closed plane figure with all points the same distance from a point called the center.

circumference   The distance around a circle.

common factor   A factor that is the same for two or more numbers.

common multiple   A multiple that is the same for two or more numbers.

commutative property of addition   The order of the addends does not change the sum.
Example: $a + b = b + a$

commutative property of multiplication   The order of the factors does not change the product.
Example: $a \times b = b \times a$

complementary angles   Two angles the sum of whose measures is 90°.
Example: $\angle ABC$ and $\angle CBD$ are complementary angles

composite number   A whole number greater than 1 that has more than two factors.

cone   A space figure with a circular base and one vertex.

congruent figures   Figures that have the same size and shape.

coordinate plane   The plane determined by a horizontal number line, called the *x*-axis, and a vertical number line, called the *y*-axis, intersecting at a point called the origin. Each point of the plane corresponds to an ordered pair of numbers.
Example: (2,1)

corresponding parts   Matching parts of congruent figures.

cross products   Products obtained by multiplying the numerator of one fraction by the denominator of a second fraction, and the denominator of the first fraction by the numerator of the second fraction.
Example: $\frac{1}{2} = \frac{3}{6}$
$1 \times 6 = 2 \times 3$

cube   A space figure with six congruent square faces.

customary system   A measurement system that measures length in inches, feet, yards, and miles; capacity in cups, pints, quarts, and gallons; weight in ounces, pounds, and tons; and temperature in degrees Fahrenheit.

cylinder   A space figure with two parallel bases that are congruent circles.

data   Information that is gathered.

decagon   A polygon with ten sides.

decimal A number with one or more places to the right of a decimal point.

degree A unit for measuring angles.

degree Celsius (°C) A unit for measuring temperature in the metric system.

degree Fahrenheit (°F) A unit for measuring temperature in the customary system.

diagonal A segment joining any two nonadjacent vertices in a polygon.

diameter A line segment that passes through the center of a circle and has both endpoints on the circle.

difference The answer in subtraction.

discount The amount that a regular price is reduced.

distributive property of multiplication over addition If one factor is a sum, multiplying each addend before adding does not change the product.
Example: $a \times (b + c) = (a \times b) + (a \times c)$

dividend The number to be divided.

divisible A number is divisible by another number if the remainder is zero after dividing.

divisor The number by which another number is to be divided.

edge The segment formed where two faces of a space figure meet.
Example:

END The last line in a BASIC computer program.

endpoint A point at the end of a segment or ray.

ENTER The function that instructs a computer to accept and process information. It is also called RETURN.

equal ratios Ratios that describe the same rate or make the same comparison.

equally likely outcomes Outcomes that have the same chance of occurring.

equation A number sentence with an equal (=) sign.

equilateral triangle A triangle with all sides congruent.

equivalent fractions Fractions that name the same number.

estimate To use rounded numbers in computation.

even number A whole number that has a 0, 2, 4, 6, or 8 in ones place.

event One or more outcomes of an experiment.

expanded form A number written as the sum of the values of its digits.

exponent A number that tells how many times the base is used as a factor.

expression A mathematical phrase made up of a variable or combination of variables, and/or numbers, and operations. *Examples:* $5n$; $4x - 7$; $(5 \times 3) + (10 \div 2)$

face A flat surface of a space figure.

factors The numbers that are multiplied to give a product. *Example:* $3 \times 8 = 24$ The factors are 3 and 8.

factor tree A diagram used to find the prime factors of a number.
Example:

flowchart A diagram that shows the steps used to solve a problem.

formula An equation that states a fact or rule.

FOR . . . NEXT Statements in a BASIC computer program that create a loop or a sequence of commands that are repeated.

fraction A number in the form $\frac{a}{b}$. It names part of a region or part of a group. The number below the fraction bar is the denominator. The number above the fraction bar is the numerator.

frequency The number of times a given item occurs in a set of data.

frequency table A listing of data together with the number of times an item occurs.

GOTO A statement in a BASIC computer program that tells the computer to go to another line in the program.

graph A drawing used to present data. Some types are bar graphs, line graphs, and circle graphs.

greatest common factor (GCF) The greatest number that is a factor of each of two or more numbers.

hardware The machinery of a computer system.

height (of a parallelogram) A segment that joins opposite sides and is perpendicular to the base.
Example:

—height

height (of a triangle) A segment drawn perpendicular to the base of a triangle from a vertex of the triangle.
Example:

— height

heptagon A polygon with seven sides.

hexagon A polygon with six sides.

identity property of addition The sum of any number and 0 is that number.
Example: $a + 0 = a$

identity property of multiplication The product of any number and 1 is that number.
Example: $a \times 1 = a$

IF . . . THEN A statement in a BASIC computer program that is used to test a certain condition and then to act on the results.

improper fraction A fraction in which the numerator is greater than or equal to the denominator.

inequality A mathematical sentence that uses one of the symbols $<, \leq, >, \geq,$ or $\neq$.

input The numbers and commands entered in a calculator or computer.

integer The numbers . . . $^-3, ^-2, ^-1, 0, ^+1, ^+2, ...$

interest The charge for borrowing money or the amount paid for the use of money.

intersecting lines Lines that have exactly one point in common.
Example:

$\overleftrightarrow{AB}$ intersects $\overleftrightarrow{CD}$ at point F.

inverse operations Two operations that are opposite in effect. Addition and subtraction are inverse operations. Multiplication and division are inverse operations.

isosceles triangle A triangle with two congruent sides.

least common denominator (LCD) The least common multiple of the denominators of two or more fractions.

least common multiple (LCM) The least nonzero number that is a multiple of each of two or more numbers.

LET A statement in a BASIC computer program that assigns a value to a memory location named by a letter.

like fractions Fractions that have the same denominator.

line A collection of points along a straight path. It has no endpoints.

line of symmetry A line that divides a figure into two congruent parts.

line segment A part of a line having two endpoints.

lowest terms A fraction is in lowest terms, or simplest form, when the GCF of the numerator and the denominator is 1.

mean In a collection of data, the sum of all the data divided by the number of data.

median The middle number or average of the two middle numbers in a collection of data when the data are arranged in order.

memory The part of a computer system that stores all information and instructions.

metric system A measurement system that measures length in millimeters, centimeters, meters, and kilometers; capacity in liters and milliliters; mass in grams and kilograms; and temperature in degrees Celsius.

midpoint A point that divides a segment into two congruent segments.

mixed number A number that has a whole number and a fraction.

mode The number that occurs most often in a collection of data.

multiple The product of a whole number and any other whole number.

mutually exclusive events Events that cannot occur at the same time.

negative integer An integer less than zero.

nonagon A polygon with nine sides.

obtuse angle An angle with a measure greater than 90° but less than 180°.

obtuse triangle A triangle with one obtuse angle.

octagon A polygon with eight sides.

opposite integers   Two integers that are the same distance from zero on the number line.
Example: $^+2$ and $^-2$ are opposite integers.

ordered pair   A pair of numbers used to locate a point in the coordinate plane.

origin   The point of intersection of the *x*-axis and *y*-axis in a coordinate plane.

outcome   A possible result in a probability experiment.

output   The answer given by a computer or a calculator.

parallel lines   Lines in the same plane that never intersect.

parallelogram   A quadrilateral with opposite sides parallel. Each pair of opposite sides and angles is congruent.

pentagon   A polygon with five sides.

percent   A ratio whose second term is 100. Percent means parts per hundred. The symbol % is used for percent.

perimeter   The distance around a polygon.

perpendicular lines   Two lines that intersect to form right angles.

pi (π)   The ratio of the circumference of a circle to its diameter. $\pi \approx 3.14$ or $\frac{22}{7}$.

place value   The value of a digit determined by its position in a number.

plane   A flat surface extending endlessly in all directions.

point   An exact location in space.

polygon   A closed plane figure made up of line segments.

polyhedron   A space figure whose surfaces, or faces, are all flat.

positive integer   An integer greater than zero.

precision of measurement   A property of measurement that depends on the unit of measure used. The smaller the unit of measure, the more precise the measurement.

prime factorization   Writing a number as the product of primes.
Example: $24 = 2 \times 2 \times 2 \times 3$.

prime number   A whole number greater than 1 with only two factors, itself and 1.

PRINT   A command to the computer to show information on the screen.

prism   A space figure with two parallel, congruent faces called bases.

probability   The ratio of favorable outcomes to possible outcomes of an experiment.

product   The answer in multiplication.

program   A list of instructions for the computer.

proper fraction   A fraction in which the numerator is less than the denominator.

proportion   A sentence that states two ratios are equal.
Example: $\frac{3}{6} = \frac{8}{16}$

protractor   An instrument used to measure angles.

pyramid   A space figure whose base is a polygon and whose faces are triangles with a common vertex.

quadrilateral   A polygon with four sides and four angles whose sum is 360°.

quotient   The answer in division.

radius   A line segment with one endpoint on the circle and the other endpoint at the center.

range   The difference between the greatest and the least numbers in a collection of data.

rate   A ratio that compares different kinds of units.

rate of discount   The percent by which a regular price is reduced.

ratio   A pair of numbers that compares two quantities or describes a rate.

ray   A part of a line that has one endpoint and extends endlessly in one direction.

READ   A command in a BASIC computer program that assigns a number in a data statement to a variable.

reciprocals   Two fractions whose product is 1.
Example: $\frac{3}{4} \times \frac{4}{3} = 1$

rectangle   A parallelogram with four right angles.

reflection   The mirror image of a figure.

regular polygon   A polygon with all sides congruent and all angles congruent.

relative frequency   The ratio of the frequency of an event to the total frequency.

relatively prime   Two numbers whose GCF is 1.

REM   A remark for the computer programmer that is ignored by the computer.

remainder   The number that is left over after dividing.

repeating decimal   A decimal in which a digit or a group of digits repeats unendingly in a pattern.

rhombus   A parallelogram with all sides congruent.

right angle   An angle that measures 90°.

right triangle   A triangle with one right angle.

rounding   Expressing a number to the nearest ten, hundred, thousand, and so on.

RUN   An instruction that tells the computer to follow instructions one line at a time.

scale drawing   A drawing made so that actual lengths can be determined from the drawing by using a scale.

scalene triangle   A triangle that has no congruent sides.

scientific notation   A product of two factors. The first factor is a number from 1 to 10. The second factor is a power of 10 in exponent form.

semicircle   A half circle.

similar figures   Figures that have the same shape but not necessarily the same size.

software   A program for a computer.

solution   The value of a variable that makes a number sentence true.

solve   To find all the solutions of an equation.

space figure   A geometric figure whose points are in more than one plane.

sphere   A space figure with all points an equal distance from the center.

square (in geometry)   A rectangle with all sides congruent.

square (in numeration)   To multiply a number by itself. The square of 7 is $7 \times 7 = 7^2 = 49$.

square root   The square root of a, written $\sqrt{a}$, is the number whose square is a.
Example: The square root of 36 is 6, since $6^2 = 36$.

statistics   The science of collecting, organizing, and analyzing data.

straight angle   An angle that measures 180°.

sum   The answer in addition.

supplementary angles   Two angles, the sum of whose measures is 180°.
Example: $\angle ACB$ and $\angle BCD$ are supplementary angles.

surface area   The sum of the areas of the faces of a space figure.

terminating decimal   A decimal that ends or terminates.
Examples: 0.5 and 0.625 are terminating decimals.

tessellation   A design in which congruent copies of a figure are arranged to fill the plane in such a way that no figures overlap and there are no gaps.

transversal   A line that intersects two or more lines.

trapezoid   A quadrilateral with exactly one pair of opposite sides parallel.

tree diagram   A diagram used to find outcomes of an experiment.

triangle   A polygon with three sides.

unlike fractions   Fractions that have different denominators.

unit price   The ratio: price per unit of measure.

variable   A letter used to stand for a number in an expression or equation.

Venn diagram   A special diagram using overlapping circles to show the relationship between groups of objects.

vertex   The point where two rays meet. The point of intersection of two sides of a polygon. The point of intersection of three edges of a space figure.

volume   The number of cubic units needed to fill a space figure.

zero property of multiplication   The product of any number and 0 is 0.
Example: $a \times 0 = 0$

TABLE OF MEASURES

METRIC

LENGTH
1 millimeter (mm) = 0.001 meter (m)
1 centimeter (cm) = 0.01 meter
1 decimeter (dm) = 0.1 meter
1 dekameter (dam) = 10 meters
1 hectometer (hm) = 100 meters
1 kilometer (km) = 1000 meters

MASS/WEIGHT
1 milligram (mg) = 0.001 gram (g)
1 centigram (cg) = 0.01 gram
1 decigram (dg) = 0.1 gram
1 dekagram (dag) = 10 grams
1 hectogram (hg) = 100 grams
1 kilogram (kg) = 1000 grams
1 metric ton (t) = 1000 kilograms

CAPACITY
1 milliliter (mL) = 0.001 liter (L)
1 centiliter (cL) = 0.01 liter
1 deciliter (dL) = 0.1 liter
1 dekaliter (daL) = 10 liters
1 hectoliter (hL) = 100 liters
1 kiloliter (kL) = 1000 liters

AREA
1 square centimeter (cm²) = 100 square millimeters (mm²)
1 square meter (m²) = 10,000 square centimeters
1 hectare (ha) = 10,000 square meters
1 square kilometer (km²) = 1,000,000 square meters

CUSTOMARY

LENGTH
1 foot (ft) = 12 inches (in.)
1 yard (yd) = 36 inches
1 yard = 3 feet
1 mile (mi) = 5280 feet
1 mile = 1760 yards

WEIGHT
1 pound (lb) = 16 ounces (oz)
1 ton (T) = 2000 pounds

CAPACITY
1 cup (c) = 8 fluid ounces (fl oz)
1 pint (pt) = 2 cups
1 quart (qt) = 2 pints
1 quart = 4 cups
1 gallon (gal) = 4 quarts

AREA
1 square foot (ft²) = 144 square inches (in.²)
1 square yard (yd²) = 9 square feet
1 acre = 43,560 square feet
1 square mile (mi²) = 640 acres

TIME
1 minute (min) = 60 seconds (s)
1 hour (h) = 60 minutes
1 day (d) = 24 hours
1 week (wk) = 7 days
1 year (yr) = 12 months (mo)
1 year = 52 weeks
1 year = 365 days
1 century (c) = 100 years

FORMULAS

$P = 2(l + w)$ Perimeter of a rectangle
$P = 4s$ Perimeter of a square
$P = ns$ Perimeter of a regular polygon
n = number of sides
$A = lw$ Area of a rectangle
$A = s^2$ Area of a square
$A = bh$ Area of a parallelogram
$A = \frac{1}{2}bh$ Area of a triangle
$C = \pi d$ Circumference of a circle
$A = \pi r^2$ Area of a circle
$V = lwh$ Volume of a rectangular prism
$V = Bh$ Volume of any prism
B = area of base
$V = \pi r^2 h$ Volme of a cylinder
$I = prt$ Simple interest

SYMBOLS

$=$ is equal to
$\neq$ is not equal to
$>$ is greater than
$<$ is less than
$\geq$ is greater than or equal to
$\leq$ is less than or equal to
$\approx$ is approximately equal to
$\cong$ is congruent to
$\sim$ is similar to
$\ldots$ continues without end
$1.\overline{3}$ repeating decimal 1.333 . .
$\%$ percent
π pi (approximately 3.14)
$°$ degree
$°C$ degree Celsius
$°F$ degree Fahrenheit

$\overleftrightarrow{AB}$ line AB
$\overline{AB}$ line segment AB
$\overrightarrow{AB}$ ray AB
$\angle ABC$ angle ABC
$m\angle ABC$ measure of angle ABC
$\triangle ABC$ triangle ABC
$\overarc{AB}$ arc AB
$\parallel$ is parallel to
$\perp$ is perpendicular to
$2:5$ ratio of 2 to 5
10^2 ten to the second power
$\sqrt{}$ square root
$^+4$ positive 4
$^-4$ negative 4
$|{}^-4|$ absolute value of $^-4$
$(3, {}^-4)$ ordered pair 3, $^-4$
$P(E)$ probability of event E

Index

CREDITS

CHAPTER 1 1: Galen Rowell/High and Wild Photography. 2, 3: Pat Traub. 4: Stewart Green/Tom Stack & Associates. 5: Dan De Wilde for Silver Burdett. 6: *t.* Phil Degginger; *b.l.*, *b.r.* Lee Boltin; *b.m.* Eric Simmons/Stock, Boston. 7: *l.* © Susan McCartney/Photo Researchers, Inc.; *r.* © Dan Hyde/Photo Researchers, Inc., courtesy Mexico Archaeological Museum. 8–12: Gary Undercuffler. 13, 14: E.R. Degginger. 15: Rick Cooley. 16: *t.* Imagery for Silver Burdett; *b.* Dennis Schofield. 17: *t.* The Bettmann Archive. 18–20: Nancy Schill. 21: Christa Kieffer. 22: Rick Cooley. 23: *r.* Rick Cooley. 24: *t.* Malcolm Kirk/Peter Arnold, Inc.; *b.* Gary Undercuffler. 25: *b.* © Michael Philip Manheim/Photo Researchers, Inc. 27: Michal Heron. 28: Bill and Judie Anderson.

CHAPTER 2 29: Group III/Bruce Coleman. 30: Bill Gallery/Stock, Boston. 31: James Sugar/Black Star. 32, 33: Don Dyen. 34: Lane Yerkes. 36: From the MGM release "BREWSTER MCCLOUD: © 1970 Metro-Goldwyn-Mayer Inc. 37: Charles Summers/Tom Stack & Associates. 38, 39: NASA. 40: Deb Troyer. 41: Yerkes Observatory, University of Chicago, Williams Bay, Wisconsin. 42: *t.* NASA. 43: *t.* NASA; *b.* Nancy Schill. 44, 45: Len Ebert. 46, 47: Gary Undercuffler. 48: Imagery for Silver Burdett. 49: No credit. 50, 51: Len Ebert. 52: Lane Yerkes. 53: Len Ebert. 54: NASA. 56, 57: Lane Yerkes. 60: *t.* NASA. 61: Lane Yerkes.

CHAPTER 3 63: Grant Heilman. 64: *t.* Len Ebert; *m.*, *b.* Peter Krempasky. 65: *t.* Peter Krempasky; *b.* Imagery for Silver Burdett. 66: Grace Moore for Silver Burdett. 67: *r.* Jeff Rotman. 68: *t.* Lane Yerkes; *b.* Fred Bavendam/Peter Arnold, Inc. 69: *t.* Cary Wolinsky/Stock, Boston; *b.* Lane Yerkes. 70: Robert Jackson. 71: Peter Krempasky. 72, 73: Floyd Cooper. 74: Len Ebert. 76, 77: Lane Yerkes. 78, 79: Gary Undercuffler. 80: *b.* Nancy Munger. 81: *b.* Charles Varner.

CHAPTER 4 89: Ray Manley/Shostal Associates. 90, 91: Don Dyen. 92: Focus on Sports. 94: Peter Krempasky. 96: *r.* Michael O'Brien/Archive Pictures. 97: Barbara Lanza. 98: Lane Yerkes. 100: *l.* Peter Krempasky; *r.* © Jerry Schad/Photo Researchers, Inc. 101: Dan De Wilde for Silver Burdett. 102: Mary Bausman. 103: Heath Company. 104, 105: Peter Krempasky. 106: NASA. 107: © 1987 DeWitt Jones/Woodfin Camp & Associates. 108: Cameron Davidson/Bruce Coleman. 109: © 1987 Arthur Tress/Woodfin Camp & Associates. 112: Bill and Judie Anderson. 113: Tersch Enterprises. 116: Nancy Schill.

CHAPTER 5 117: Jim Brandenburg/DRK Photos. 118: *m.*, *b.* Gary Undercuffler. 120, 121: Robert Steele. 122: Barbara Lanza. 124: *t.* Peter Krempasky; *m.* Nancy Munger. 126: Calgary Exhibition and Stampede. 127: *l.* © Paolo Koch/Photo Researchers, Inc. 128: *b.* David Madison/Bruce Coleman. 129: *b.* Steve Vidler/Leo de Wys, Inc. 130, 131: Don Dyen. 132: *t.* Shakespeare Festival Theatre, Stratford, Ontario, Canada. 133: Robert Estall/Click, Chicago. 134: Al Messerschmidt/Folio. 138: Kathie Kelleher. 139: Bill and Judie Anderson.

CHAPTER 6 143: Cary Wolinsky/Stock, Boston. 144: A. Lamure/Wilkinson Studio. 144–145: Robin Brickman. 146, 147: John Hamberger. 148: *t.* John Hamberger; *b.* Peter Byron for Silver Burdett. 150: *t.* Lane Yerkes. 152: Mike Price/Photo Researchers. 153: *r.* M.E. Warren/Photo Researchers, Inc. 154, 155: Michael Adams. 156: *t.* Bill and Judie Anderson. 158: *t.* D. De Witt/Click, Chicago. 159: *t.r.* John Hamberger. 160, 161: John Hamberger. 162: *t.* Kathie Kelleher; *b.* Clark Mishler/Alaska Photo. 163: Keith Gunnar/Bruce Coleman. 164: *t.l.*, *b.l.*, *b.r.* Lane Yerkes. *t.r.* Phil Degginger/Bruce Coleman. 165: *t.* Lane Yerkes. 168: *t.* Grant Heilman; *b.* Robin Brickman. 169: John Colwell/Grant Heilman. 171: Barbara Lanza. 175: Norman Owen Tomalin/Bruce Coleman.

CHAPTER 7 177: Robert Overlander/Stock, Boston. 178: *t.* NASA. 180: Rick DelRossi. 182, 183: Don Dyen. 184: *r.* Lawrence Migdale for Silver Burdett. 186: Lane Yerkes. 188: Charles Varner. 189: Bill and Judie Anderson. 190: Jeff Rotman. 192: Laurie Marks. 194: *t.* Rick DelRossi; *b.* E.R. Degginger/Bruce Coleman. 195: Rick DelRossi. 196, 197: Lane Yerkes. 198: *t.* The Granger Collection; *b.* Robert Weinreb/Bruce Coleman. 199: *b.* The Granger Collection. 200: Jim Pearson. 201: Wide World Photos. 203: © Dick Davis/Photo Researchers, Inc. 207: Floyd Cooper. 208: Ronald Seymour/Click, Chicago.

CHAPTER 8 211: © Louis Joyner, Southern Living/Photo Researchers, Inc. 212: Laurie Jordan. 214: *l.* © Brian Brake/Photo Researchers, Inc.; *r.* Jessica Ehlers/Bruce Coleman. 215: © Brian Brake/Photo Researchers, Inc. 216: Museum of Science, Boston, photo for Silver Burdett. 218: *l.* Gary Undercuffler; *r.* Lee Boltin. 220: *l.* No credit; *r.* Bradley Clark. 222: Animals, Animals/Earth Scenes. 223: Zig Leszcynski/Animals, Animals. 224: Lee Boltin. 226: Museo Archeologico Nazionale/Scala/Art Resource. 227: Mystic Seaport, Mystic, Ct.; *inset,* © George E. Jones, III/Photo Researchers, Inc. 228: Dr. Edmund/Royal Ontario Museum, Canada. 228–229: Bradley Clark. 230: Don Patterson. 232: Bradley Clark. 234: Laurie Marks. 235: Lane Yerkes. 238: *t.* Gary Undercuffler; *b.* Focus on Sports. 239: Bradley Clark.

CHAPTER 9 243: © Russ Kinne/Photo Researchers, Inc. 244: *t.* Lou Vaccaro. 246: *t.* Lane Yerkes. 248: *t. Via Blues* by Kenneth Noland/Art Resource. 250: *t.* Bradley Clark. 252: *t.* © 1987 Adam Woolfit/Woodfin Camp & Associates. 253: *b.* Lou Vaccaro. 254: *t.* Manfred Kage/Peter Arnold, Inc. 255: *m.* Lane Yerkes. 256: Paul Anderson. 259: *b.* David Overcash/Bruce Coleman. 260: *Composition 169* by Friedrich Wergemberge-Gildewert, Philadelphia Museum of Art, given by Mr. and Mrs. Henry Clifford. 262: *t.* Nicholas DeVore/Bruce Coleman. 265: *m.* Bradley Clark. 266: *t.* Brian Seed/Click, Chicago. 269: Mou-Sien Tseng. 272: Lou Vaccaro. 274: Ralph Prince.

CHAPTER 10 277: © 1987 Michal Heron/Woodfin Camp & Associates. 280: Dan De Wilde for Silver Burdett. 288: *t.* Laurie Marks. 290: *t.* © 1987 Robert McElroy/Woodfin Camp & Associates; *b.* Dennis Stock/Magnum. 294: *t.* Michal Heron. 299: Samantha Smith. 300: Don Patterson. 301: *t.* Don Patterson. 304: Samantha Smith. 305: *t.* Samantha Smith.

CHAPTER 11 307: *t.* The Granger Collection; *b.* David Forbert/Shostal Associates. 308: *l.* Paul Anderson; *r.* © Richard Hutchings/Photo Researchers, Inc. 309: © Shambroom/Photo Researchers, Inc. 311: Don Patterson. 312: *t.* The Granger Collection; *b.* Spring Industries. 314: Tom Powers. 318: Sally Schaedler. 319: *t.* Gary Undercuffler. 320: Tom Powers. 323: *t.* Gary Undercuffler; *b.* Lawrence Migdale for Silver Burdett. 326: Lou Vaccaro.

CREDITS

1 2 3 4 5 6 7 8 9 10—RRD—93 92 91 90 89 88 87 86

THE DISASTROUS VOYAGE
OF THE SANTA MARGARITA

THE DISASTROUS VOYAGE OF THE SANTA MARGARITA

Richard Woodman

This first world edition published 2008
in Great Britain and in 2009 in the USA by
SEVERN HOUSE PUBLISHERS LTD of
9–15 High Street, Sutton, Surrey, England, SM1 1DF.
Trade paperback edition published
in Great Britain and the USA 2009 by
SEVERN HOUSE PUBLISHERS LTD

British Library Cataloguing in Publication Data

Woodman, Richard, 1944-
  The disastrous voyage of the Santa Margarita
  1. Shipwrecks - Fiction 2. Sea stories
  I. Title
  823.9'14[F]

  ISBN-13: 978-0-7278-6723-0   (cased)
  ISBN-13: 978-1-84751-102-7   (trade paper)

All Severn House titles are printed on acid-free paper.

Typeset by Palimpsest Book Production Ltd.,
Grangemouth, Stirlingshire, Scotland.
Printed and bound in Great Britain by
MPG Books Ltd., Bodmin, Cornwall.

One

El Sobrasaliente

'The Devil! There is always a priest!'

'The señor should mind his tongue.'

The tall figure standing beneath the rustling fronds of the sugar palm spun round to glare open-mouthed at the diminutive figure behind him.

'Devil take you!' the man gasped. 'Where in the name of God did you spring from?' His hand flew to the hilt of a dagger in his waistband, his face drained of colour.

The dwarf drew back, but appeared otherwise unmoved by the tall man's reaction. 'I have been following you, señor,' he answered, his bearded face with its bulging forehead cocked on one side, his wide, thick-lipped mouth in a grin that revealed broken and caried teeth. To the astonished man, this misshapen lump of humanity was a hideous and a terrifying figure. His grip tightened upon the hilt of his stiletto, which caught the light filtering through the palm fronds above.

'For what purpose, you damned and hellish imp?' he asked, partially recovering his nerve, and lowering the blade.

Appearing not to notice this restoration in his quarry's spirits, the dwarf's grin widened into a leer. 'You spoke before like an heretic; now you tremble like one of the faithful caught with his—'

He got no further. The tall man shot out his right hand, grasped his tormentor by the throat and with a single swing thrust the dwarf, with a sickening thump of his head, against the rough bark of the palm tree's bole. Then he lowered his own head to a point that was level with his prisoner's, spitting his words in the dwarf's face.

'What business am I of yours, eh, you dog? Who sent you

to spy upon me?' After a moment to allow the questions to penetrate a mind more concerned with sucking in another breath than comprehending his interrogator, he released the dwarf, who sank to his knees, gasping for air.

Their positions now reversed, the tall man straightened up and stood over his victim, patiently waiting as the wretch struggled to inhale. When the dwarf looked up, the tall man raised his right eyebrow; a mute but eloquent transfiguration of his expression in which the now desperate but perspicacious dwarf perceived a shred of compassion.

'Señor . . . Don Iago . . .' he gasped.

'You know my name, you damned fiend!' Astonished, Don Iago's face hardened again.

'I know what you are called, señor.'

'You are bold, and,' the man added, softening slightly, 'I think lack not courage.'

'You do me some honour and, please believe me, señor, I come as a friend.'

'A friend? You! In this manner? How can *you* come as a friend?'

'To say that there are those that speak against you.'

'How so? Who speaks against me?'

The dwarf shrugged. 'Some that I have heard of.'

'And what do they say?'

'That you are an heretic.'

The tall man sighed. 'How conspicuous in his conduct at the Mass does a man have to be before he is charged with Pharisaic pride?' he said, half to himself. 'Have these whisperers not perceived me at my devotions? Christ knows I have worn my knees to the bone – or is it,' he went on before the dwarf could answer, 'because I have come among them in these heathen clothes?' He plucked at the loose cotton pantaloons, common to the Chinese who manned the junks from Guandong, that he wore under a loose shirt.

'Señor, I . . .'

But the man the dwarf called Don Iago turned away, returning his attention to the great ship offshore, riding to her anchor surrounded by Chinese junks. She lay in deep water off the beach that spread beyond the shade of the palm grove and the tangle of vegetation marking the edge of the forest. For a moment the air was troubled only by the rustling fronds overhead, but then the noise of her loading came across the water again. They could see bales and boxes being hauled aboard from the crowd of junks and sampans that lay moored about her like piglets suckling from a gigantic mother, except that the traffic was the other way. Borne aloft by the great ship's yard and stay tackles, the riches of China were hoisted aboard the capacious hull that, day by day, sank lower in the water. Despite this activity in filling her holds, small gangs of seamen toiled in her upper rigging and Iago knew them to be rattling down, fitting chafing gear, worming and serving, setting up the lanyards in their euphroes and deadeyes as the upper yards were secured preparatory to sailing.

Iago was impressed by the *não*. She was enormous. He knew the Spanish were capable of building such large ships in their colonial shipyards in Havana, on the Caribbean island of Cuba, vessels to rival those built in Spain itself, but the ship at which he was staring had been built here, in the Philippines, on a slip at Cavite less than a mile from where she now lay, loading the produce of China for the passage across the Pacific to Acapulco on the coast of New Spain. He stared upwards in some wonder, for she bore three yards on her fore and mizzen-masts, the uppermost a recent innovation in Spanish ship-fitting. He had heard of such a tall rig with this additional yard and sail – this *juanete* – or topgallant, set above what had, until recently, been the topsail.

But Iago, who had been watching the *não* for some days, was troubled by the dwarf's intrusion and the intelligence he imparted, and could no longer concentrate upon the loading of the *Santa Margarita*.

''Tis not enough,' Iago muttered vehemently, half to himself, 'to have suffered shipwreck and misfortune, but these damned vultures would have a man at the stake for heresy.'

'You condemned a priest to damnation,' ventured the dwarf, standing and rubbing his throat. 'I heard you say so . . .'

Iago returned his attention to the dwarf, ignoring the hostile implication of the freak's remark. 'You look Spanish to me,' he said, regarding the dwarf. 'You are not an Indian.'

'I was born in the islands, señor, not here in Cavite but in Manila.' The dwarf gestured to the eastwards where, on the farther shore of the great bay, the city of Manila lay behind its newly built walls. 'My father was an *hidalgo* who abandoned my mother when he saw what she had born him.'

'A sad and familiar tale,' Iago said softly, wondering what diseases the noble Spaniard had foisted upon the native woman he had impregnated. And this weird yet pitiful scrap of blood, bones and brain was the result. A reflective expression that approached kindness spread across Iago's face so that he looked with more attention at the dwarf. 'What do they call you?' he asked in the same low tone.

'I was christened Ximenez.'

'Ximenez.' Iago reached out his hand and the dwarf quailed, but the large paw was light upon his shoulder. 'I am sorry that I hurt you.'

'It was nothing.'

'You are used to such treatment, eh?'

'I live, señor,' the dwarf said in a low voice as the two men's eyes met, 'closer to the maw of a dog than a woman's mouth, while it pleases God to have me breathe the exhalations of Hell when men fart in my face.'

Iago smiled. 'I admire one who jokes in the face of adversity. And what would you have of me, Ximenez? If you have been following me—'

'For days,' Ximenez broke in, 'and to some purpose, señor.'

Iago ignored the interruption. 'If you have been following me,' he repeated, smiling, 'you will know that I too am a man outside society and closer to you that I am to any woman's mouth.'

Ximenez smiled at the jest. 'A *lady's*, perhaps, señor, but there is a girl in the village that they say you brought with you from China.'

'Ah, you know of her too. And what of her?'

'Do you wish to take her aboard that ship?' Ximenez nodded his head at the great *não*. Above the apparent confusion and industrious clutter about her waist, their eyes were caught by the fluttering pendants at her mastheads and the great red and gold oriflamme of Castile and Aragon lifting at the summit of her high poop. 'For that is where you wish to go, is it not?'

'Perhaps.'

'She is called the *Santa Margarita*, señor.'

'I know.' Iago sighed and turned again to regard the galleon.

'And the woman who came with you?' Ximenez prompted. '*Shall* she go with you?'

'Perhaps.' Don Iago lowered his gaze from the ship and turned back to Ximenez, changing the subject. 'Do you not think, Ximenez, that sailors being so rutting a breed, it is curious to name so great a ship after the patron saint of virgins?'

'I think it curious to name the Son of God *Jesus*, señor.'

'You could burn for that, Ximenez.'

'I thereby place my life and fortune in your hands, Don Iago.' The dwarf made a bow.

Iago laughed. 'You are taking me for more than I am, Ximenez.' Suddenly he squatted down so that their heads were again level. 'The only difference between us, my friend, is that you stand barely higher than a hound, and I may converse with an, er, a . . .'

Ximenez frowned as Iago recalled the Spanish for elephant, *elefante*, and corrected himself. It was not a beast Ximenez knew much about, though he had heard of them in Cathay, or somewhere, but he grasped Iago's meaning. 'If the señor wishes to board the *Santa Margarita* as a *sobrasaliente* he will need a man-servant.'

Iago stood up again and with both hands gestured at his clothes. 'A *sobrasaliente*? Well perhaps, but perhaps not. Do I look like a gentleman that I should need a man to comb my hair? A gentleman's servant would find his master's clothes and I think that impossible . . .'

'I can find you clothes fit for a *sobrasaliente*, Don Iago, and see your hair dressed like an *hidalgo's*.'

'Can you, by Heaven? Do you suppose that I may support my station and have money?'

The dwarf shrugged. 'Of course, señor. In a pouch about your neck.'

'Following me for days . . .'

'My life and fortune in your hands, señor.'

'The Devil! And mine in yours, you damned scoundrel.' But as Ximenez drew back, half cowering, a wry smile crossed Iago's face. Without taking his eyes off the dwarf,

Iago jerked his head at the anchored ship. 'You see the black-robed fathers yonder . . .' Ximenez nodded. 'If their hand is against me . . .'

'Gold, like a fair word, turneth away even the wrath of God, señor, long enough for the *não* to depart these islands.'

'Have you ventured beyond these parts, Ximenez?'

'No, señor.'

'Would you really stand as servant to me?'

'I would.'

'Why?'

'I have no family, señor. No ties. A dwarf has no future here.' He shrugged.

'A better one here where one is known than among strangers. Do you know where the ship goes?'

'Across the great sea to the long coast called Neuva España whence my father came.'

'Do you seek him?'

'I am told he is wealthy and he was married to my mother by a priest in Manila. I am his heir.'

'My gold is more certain than his, Ximenez.'

'One or the other, señor. There is nothing else for Ximenez.'

'You are damnably bold for your size.' Iago cast a look at the ship, watched men moving about on her deck, the dark flutter of habits on her poop and the flash of the setting sun upon a steel morion or a cuirass, then turned abruptly and began to walk inland. 'Come, then. We shall go aboard when you have turned me into a *sobrasaliente*.'

'Don Iago's faith is well placed,' the dwarf said with a smile of success. 'Tomorrow your Ximenez will not be found wanting.'

'*My* Ximenez? Well, well, already I have hangers on. We shall see, you impudent rogue, we shall see.'

And as the tall man swung off down the narrow path through the undergrowth the dwarf hurried contentedly along behind him, his breath forcing a gasping and tuneless whistle through his broken teeth.

Iago woke lathered in sweat with a sudden twist as he evaded the grip of the Spanish pikeman as he had all those years earlier and had done ever since in his ghastly dreams. And, as it always did, the nightmare had shaken him; even awake in its aftermath he felt the vice-like grip of the Spaniard upon his slender child's wrist. He could remember nothing of his boyhood prior to that terrible moment; nothing at all. The images of that morning, a morning in which his life had changed irredeemably, eclipsed all that had preceded it. As he swam into the pre-dawn chill of the day he realized it was the dwarf that had stimulated this latest manifestation of his childhood horror. Ximenez had mentioned his own father. His heartbeat slowed and Iago grasped the fact that this was the dawn of a new day, a score or so of years after the one brought brutally back into his sleeping mind by his dream. He thought of his own father. That Ximenez could entertain the notion of finding his own father struck Iago as at best an irony and at worst an injustice. He himself had never seen his father dead, remembering only the last vague glimpse of a man running out of a door with a drawn sword, a back view of a large man pitched forth to meet his death − for he never returned − with the howl of his wife, Iago's young and fatefully beautiful mother, ringing in his ears.

Now, as Iago lay panting on his palliasse, the perspiration of the dream beaded about the thick hairs upon his broad chest and running from his forehead on to the damp and none-too-clean pillow, he wondered at the veracity of the image. He had recalled it so many times that he had begun to wonder what it owed to its own seminal moment and what to his last, terrified recollection. It was all so vague, so insubstantial, so overlaid with his mother's retelling, sometimes sad, sometimes vitriolic as she imbued her first-born, the progeny of her first marriage, with a sense of his true origin.

It was odd too, he thought lying in his sweat, how he knew of this genesis while at the same time seeing himself − somewhere around the age of ten or twelve when his mother considered he should know that he was not the son of the man he called *padre* − as a little Spaniard; a child of Seville and a familiar of the Guadalquivír along whose reedy banks and muddy flats he had brought a Dutchman's love of boats, an understanding of the tides and the intuitive comprehension of water running towards the ocean. The Spanish called it the Great River, a name adapted from that of the Moors who had driven their keels deep into Andalucía eight hundred years earlier. But his mother told him of greater rivers, of wider meres and vaster marshes than those of the Guadalquivír; those far away in the north under the cloudy skies over Zeeland and the great branches of the Schelde.

'You are the son of Jacob van Salingen, Iago,' she would hiss in his ear when she could trust his discretion, 'and you were yourself baptized Jacob, a Protestant like your father.'

It was a weighty and confusing secret, a mighty burden for a prepubescent youth abducted and adopted in a Catholic country; one that Iago might have unwittingly betrayed had he not possessed that secret image of the large man darting through a door with a drawn sword. But a boy's attachment to his mother is strong and he bore the burden of the responsibility of secrecy with a loyal and unshakeable steadfastness. Perhaps he sensed it was his vulnerable mother's only weapon against a fate that had treated her so callously, or perhaps he recognized a difference between himself and those about him. Besides, he had grown to nurture an instinctive horror of the dark-robed and interfering priests to whom he was supposed to confess his innermost thoughts. Perhaps too he had inherited an aversion to their sacred concern for his welfare, or perhaps he merely imitated his mother's false ingratiation when the man who had carried her away and made her his wife first brought a monk into the little house in Seville.

It was also strange, Iago admitted to himself, that he could recall nothing of the arrival into his life of the Spanish infantry sergeant whom he afterwards called father. His mother never spoke of the horrors of the sack of the town, when the terrible Spanish pikemen finally forced their way into Zierikzee to rape and plunder. He was aware of the obligation of survival and protection that she owed to this presumptuous stepfather and had assumed, or been told by hints and suggestions, that he owed his own existence to the generosity of the man who had rescued both himself and his beautiful and vulnerable mother from the rapacity of a brutal and licentious soldiery to whom the town had been given over after its spirited resistance. In his boyhood and early youth he made no sense of this, a dawning comprehension arriving only with his own tendencies towards immoderate lust; that and the need to fabricate sins to air in the dark depravity of the stuffy confessional where he learned by proxy of the depths to which men sank when moved by the demonic motives that lurked in their essentially evil hearts. Such turmoil deprived Iago of any pretensions to innocence: he felt he had been born in a crucible of mindless violence and, for this disturbing reason, had sought the solitude of the river bank. Here, he could be free.

And with this freedom there came in time the mastery of boats. A proficient oarsman at seven, he could handle a boat under sail at ten and was entrusted with errands by the merchants whose houses flanked the quays along the Guadalquivír, scrambling aboard the ships that worked their weary way upstream from the distant ocean, laden with the fruits of the Indies, their sailors burned black by the sun, their ears pierced by the bright gleam of Indian gold from the land of Eldorado. The shore-going of these exotics was accompanied by drunkenness and whoring; they were surrounded by gipsy dancers, the flash and colour of a seductive wildness and the disturbing music of the guitar. Young Iago, for so he was called, observed their ebullient bravado to be accompanied by a stream of endless, good-natured chaffing. All this excited the boy, who took with alacrity the notes and messages from their resplendent masters standing proud upon their poops. Iago ran and conveyed these important missives to the quiet and splendid merchants in their counting houses along the quays of Seville. Occasionally he would be permitted to accompany one of them, carrying the great man's heavy leather wallet containing the documents pertaining to the ship's voyage, to the Casa de Contratación. Here, at the great door of the splendid trade-house, he would be dismissed with a coin and stand in awe as the *capitáno* disappeared into the cool shadows. Once too, he had performed this office as a *capitáno* went to the Alcázar where he had been summoned to appear in the Cuarto del Almirante. It was from here, the awe-struck Iago learned, that Fernão de Magalhaes was charged with finding the Moluccas by sailing west on behalf of His Most Christian Majesty. That the captain-general did not return alive only added awe to the boy's tenuous connection with these distinguished and brave souls.

Those *capitános* who came to know him well would allow
Iago to climb on to the yards as they ordered their men aloft
to roll the sails into a tight harbour stow. Long before he
could read or write he had become a skilled helper, an adept
who owed more to his Dutch blood than the encouragement of his stepfather. Nevertheless, his adoptive father, seeing
this aptitude in his stepson, insisted he learned all there was
to know about such things, and soon Iago knew much about
ships and could not only tie most of the bends and hitches
required of an able *marinero*, but could box the compass backwards in quarter-points. This feat alone set him apart from
most of the imps who frequented the waterfront in the hope
of pickings from the foolish and impulsive generosity of sailors
newly arrived home.

This recollected sensation of ascendancy now brought a smile
to his face, dispelling the last wraiths of the dream. The past
receded into the night and Iago stirred in the swiftly growing
light of dawn. He stretched luxuriously, fully awake and again
master of himself. Rising, he padded out through the curtain
to where the girl slept. Ximenez had mentioned her too. For
a moment he paused and looked down at her, moved by a
spasm of affection, then he turned aside and went to the door.
The house was a primitive dwelling, more suited to one of
the shipwrights who had fabricated the vast mass of the *Santa
Margarita* on the slipways of Cavite than to a man who had
arrived in the Philippines with a small fortune concealed about
his person. It was this that had dissuaded him from too close
acquaintance with the Gobernador of Manila or any of his
many time-serving and swaggering officials. Iago's inbred
caution sped his exit from the islands. He had been a dissem-
bler all his life, an habitual concealer from necessity rather
than vice, but a man to whom self-revelation was not merely
anathema, but an impolitic folly the consequences of which
might prove fatal. Nor had the manner of his survival been
any different, though his manner of arrival in the Spanish
stronghold of the Philippines was explicable enough. How
he could have betrayed himself so lightly to Ximenez under
the palms the previous night he was at a loss to know, but
the momentary lowering of his guard under the mistaken

assumption that he was alone was a grievous error and the very thought of it brought a sudden apprehensive quickening of his pulse. It was also a measure of his loneliness: occasionally a man must articulate even the most suppressed emotions.

Iago dismissed the excuse of believing himself to be alone as inexcusable, even as it again pleaded for his conduct. Diverting his mind, he wondered for a moment whether sunrise would arrive with a halberdier's guard and an official from the Holy Office intent upon his arrest, or merely a full rice-bowl. Had he the measure of Ximenez? Did the diminutive and crippled human arouse an injudicious pity in him? Was Ximenez perhaps capable of avenging himself on others more fairly made than himself? And was he himself the sacrificial scapegoat of Ximenez's imagination? If so, Iago had been fooled. He considered the matter for a moment; somehow he did not mark the wretched creature for an informer, yet doubt lingered as to the dwarf's trustworthiness. And if he was not to be trusted?

Iago grew suddenly exasperated with himself; he would confront that eventuality when he met it; his sword had a blade as keen as any from Toledo, though its odd shape marked it as a katana from the fabulous islands of Cipangu. In the meantime he needed a shave and, he thought with a contrived but reassuringly wry amusement as he sought the means to accomplish this, if yesterday's encounter had meant anything at all the wretched Ximenez should be here attending upon his person with hot water and a stropped razor. Perhaps in the dwarf's reappearance Iago might place some trust. But if he failed to come, or arrived with a company of halberdiers and a dark-frocked priest – Iago lowered the razor and his eye fell upon the katana in its slings hanging handily above the bed – then God help him.

Iago shaved and broke his fast of rice prepared by the Chinese girl he had brought with him from Cathay. She knelt and served him in silence and swiftly rose with an indrawn breath when Ximenez suddenly appeared in the doorway. The dwarf, decked out in a dark blue doublet of some extravagance but which had clearly been made for him, announced his arrival with a surprisingly discreet cough and a change of attitude.

'Good morning, master.'

Iago, a small beaker of hot coffee at his mouth, stared with astonishment at the dwarf. 'I thought the finery to be for me . . .' he began but fell silent when Ximenez almost impertinently gestured him to silence. Ximenez than stepped back, beckoning to others outside. To Iago's astonishment three short and stocky Filipinos brought in a number of packages, all of which were bound in woven coconut matting, and laid them respectfully on the ground at Iago's feet. After they had withdrawn and Ximenez had followed them outside and paid them for their labour, the dwarf returned to the room. Iago had finished his coffee and was ready for Ximenez's explanation.

'Master,' Ximenez began, producing a knife from the waist of his doublet with a flourish and cutting the sisal bindings of the packages, 'I have provided you with . . .' There was a brief pause and then he lifted or indicated in turn each of his purchases. 'A short cloak of broadcloth; two doublets of velvet, one of crimson, one of blue, both with slashed sleeves; five shirts, two of silk, three of cotton; breeches of black, under-drawers, hose, two pairs of shoes for which I beg my master's indulgence if they do not fit, and, if my master pleases, a fine pair of boots . . .' There were in addition handkerchiefs, ribbons, three ruffs, two pairs of gloves and some lace that Iago thought might have been made in his natal city.

'And for your lady . . .' Ximenez gestured at the Chinese girl who stood coyly watching this extravagant performance in the shadows, 'knowing little of the preferences and peculiarities of women, I have as yet secured only a gown . . .' He drew the rustling grey-blue silk from the final bundle and held it out towards the girl. She came forward and Iago could see the glow of pleasure in her eyes.

'She is pleased, Ximenez,' Iago said.

'Even I can see that, master,' the dwarf said drily and Iago felt in that odd moment a powerful and disturbing sensation as if the three of them were somehow drawn closer together.

'How much did all this cost . . . ?' he began but the dwarf cut him short.

'A little credit, señor,' said Ximenez, reverting for a moment to the style of address that had preceded the formal change in their relationship. 'Let us talk of debts later.'

'And for yourself . . .' Iago gestured at the dwarf's own finery.

'It was the last gift of my mother. She made it for me as the son of an *hidalgo*.' Iago saw the glitter of tears in the dwarf's eyes. 'I have only once worn it before.'

'Then you shall be one again, Ximenez. We shall chance our fortune as equals. I am not so set upon this course that I must have a servant.'

Ximenez shook his head, his ugly face strangely softened. 'I am grateful, señor, but since my mother's death I have lived too long in the ditch like a cur and been whipped too often to appear transfigured. No, I must be your servant and this,' he pointed at his velvet doublet, 'must be thought by the world to be *your* gift.' He brought his head up with a spirited assurance that Iago found touching. 'I fear, master, my attachment to your person, whatever its practical value, will do you little credit when you solicit an appointment aboard the *Santa Margarita*. I am too well known to raise myself other than by my master's indulgence. You will be seen as a fool, master, a newcomer gulled by the plausible monster the midwife allowed to survive.'

'Then we shall have to hide our talents a little, Ximenez.'

'You are not a Spaniard, señor.'

'Was your mother a witch?' Iago responded with a sharp evasion, adding as a half-truth, 'I grew up in Seville and am as Spanish as yourself.'

Ximenez bowed low. 'Of course, master. But I am half Filipino.'

The innuendo was clear and there was a moment's awkward silence and then the girl spoke, diverting Iago's attention.

'Am I now lady of these islands?' she asked in the pidgin that was the lingua franca between Iago and his mistress.

'Yes,' Iago said nodding, his face softening as he turned towards her as she stroked the grey-blue silk.

'And I am in your service, lady,' Ximenez said, adding again to the powerful sense of bonding that Iago felt with a disturbing prescience. Such emotions, he thought with a suppressed shudder, led to love or the stake. Or perhaps both. For a moment the shadow of his dream again crossed his mind and then, as Ximenez held out the under-drawers and the hose, he rose and began to change his apparel. Yet how sure could he be of this timely yet monstrous addition to his slim entourage? The dwarf was clever, cunning even, a perfect agent for the Inquisition, he thought as he felt Ximenez pull the drawstring tight about his waist. And was not this provision of the clothes that Iago sought, almost as if by magical powers, further evidence that Ximenez was working for the priests who constantly surveyed this land like black vultures?

'I have heard, master, that they are wanting officers practised in the arts of the shipman's craft aboard the *Santa Margarita*,' Ximenez remarked with so casual an indifference as he knelt at Iago's feet and offered a shoe. Iago started: the pronouncement was contiguous with his thoughts.

'Master . . . ?' The kneeling dwarf looked up, startled, one hand flat upon the beaten earth floor.

A coldness seized Iago's spirit. He placed his newly shod foot upon the dwarf's fingers, immobilizing him. 'If you prove false, Ximenez,' he said icily, his jerked head indicating the girl quietly tidying the room behind him, 'Ah Fong will kill you. So you must first kill her and then I shall know your intentions.'

The dwarf stared up at him, his eyes full of astonishment and despair. In an intuitive moment Iago saw through the little man's deformity. 'Master, I thought you trusted me.'

'There is much here,' Iago said, his hand waving over the finery spread across the humble room.

'I am a man of resource, master,' Ximenez hissed, a flash of spirit entering him in response to this new humiliation. 'Besides,' he shot back with an ironic shrug, 'it is the señor who is in debt!'

Iago felt a sudden shaming, Ah Fong had stopped what she was doing with a second sharp intake of breath that, Iago knew, signalled disapproval of his actions. He was in grave danger of making an enemy where an instant before he had had an ally, if not a friend. He slid his foot sideways, releasing the dwarf's hand, suddenly squatting in front of Ximenez and taking it up in a firm grip. 'Forgive me, *amigo*, forgive me. I have lived so long on my wits that my trust is not easily given. From this moment on we shall be partners, our parts those of players.'

Ximenez's expression softened. 'My master owes twenty *maravedis*. I had not expected to ask the sum so soon, nor to ask it to clear my name.'

Iago patted the dwarf's hand. 'You shall have it – or its equivalent in gold.'

Ten minutes later the man known as Don Iago Fernandez stepped out into the sunshine accompanied by the dwarf. He wore the blue doublet with slashed sleeves that revealed a white silk shirt, black breeches and hose, with buckled shoes that fitted tolerably well. The only irregularity in his attire was the curious sword that swung upon his hip.

Two

The *Santa Margarita*

From the hired native canoe Don Iago stared up at the vast
bulk of the *Santa Margarita*'s stern looming above him and
marvelled. Close to, the great ship impressed even more than
she did at a distance. Although the timbers wore their coat
of newly applied oil with a soft gloss, there was no other
evidence that the great *não* had not been built in the shipyards of Cadiz or Havana, for she was crafted with all the
skill of the shipwright's art, even to the carvings on her high
poop where, above the windows of the great cabin and the
gallery that ran round the stern, amid a roil of leaves and
palm fronds, a drooping Santa Margarita, her breasts bared by
a torn gown, struggled against the licentious intentions of
what, Iago supposed, were two Roman soldiers. The fashioned woodwork, however, wrought by native craftsmen, had
been modelled on the Spanish soldiery who despoiled their
own women and wore the morion and cuirass of Castile and
Aragon. This unfortunate anachronism was a sharp and painful
reminder of Iago's own mother's situation on that dreadful
morning when the Spanish pikemen burst into their house
in Zierikzee.

For a moment he was chilled by the thought, wondering
if it was an omen, a superstition rising in his mind that the
ship was ill-fated. Then reason reasserted itself. He was a fool
to have his mind corrupted by these rich images. It was
precisely what they were intended to do, one way or another,
terrify and subordinate all sensible men to a state of supine
obedience. He had hardly rid himself of the dark thought
when the real shadow of the ship fell over the canoe as they
rounded her stern. Alongside her hull lay several junks from

which bales and bundles of cargo – some in burlap, others in coconut matting – were being hauled aboard by the yard tackles.

Iago pointed to two manropes hanging down the ship's tumblehome on either side of a battened ladder. As the hired Filipino dug his paddle into the dark water and drove his narrow craft into the shadowed gap, Iago ducked under the slack bights of the junks' mooring lines. A moment later the little canoe rubbed alongside and, grabbing the two manropes made of the straw-coloured hemp for which the islands were famous, he scrambled up the curved strakes of the *Santa Margarita*.

Stepping over the high rail and down upon the deck, Iago was confronted by noise and turmoil. He regarded a confusion of strewn packages, boxes and chests among which scores of seamen and coolies swore and toiled as they sought to secure what seemed at first glance to be an immensity of cargo. Although some of the larger bales were being lowered into the hold through the two small hatchways amidships, it was clear that much was being borne on deck, where a party of swarthy seamen shoved and secured them. These men seemed to be drawn from all quarters of the globe. Dressed only in baggy breeches and headscarves, their naked torsos shone with sweat as they laboured under the hot sun. Forward, Iago's eye was caught by a huddle of female Filipinos, several of whom were washing clothes in wooden tubs; others idled, one plaiting another's hair, while all gossiped cheerfully. They were carelessly and indifferently dressed and clearly the seamen's women. The illusion of disorder, though somewhat modified by the roaring figure of the boatswain whose rattan was freely applied, was in sharp contrast to the *Santa Margarita*'s outward appearance.

Such a scene was not unfamiliar to Iago, though it was some time since he had witnessed this confusion of a large ship loading and preparing for sea. He caught the boatswain's eye and the man stared at him for a moment, before roaring another instruction at an adjacent gang of men. Then, kicking a coolie aside, the man leapt with surprising agility for so large a fellow over an interposing bale to plant himself in front of Iago.

'Señor?' the boatswain said with only a slight interrogative inflection and with the minimal respect to Iago's obvious station. This, too, was a game with which Iago was familiar. He had learned it along the banks of the Guadalquivír as a boy entrusted with an errand to a ship newly berthing alongside the quay.

'Present my compliments to the captain-general,' he said, casually removing his eyes from the large petty officer and affecting a tone of easy disdain. 'Don Iago Fernandez at His Excellency's service.'

The boatswain stood unmoving until Iago, as though just aware of the man's immobility, swung upon him. 'At once!' he commanded with an imperious tone he had long forgotten he possessed. 'Don Iago Fernandez,' he repeated.

For just long enough to make the encounter memorable, the boatswain remained stationary, then he turned away, called a boy and sent him aft with the information, disdaining the errand himself. Without thereafter regarding Iago he resumed his duties in the waist, bellowing even louder to emphasize his own importance in the process of preparing the ship for sea.

Iago followed the boy up the first of two ladders and on the half-deck, clear of the labour of loading, he assumed a pose, his weight on his right leg, his left hand upon the hilt of the katana slung at his waist.

What dogs these Spanish devils are, he thought wryly to himself.

The boy had disappeared through a door under the high poop by which means he could reach the great cabin on the deck below. A few moments later he emerged followed by a richly dressed young man and, throwing a quick and curious glance at Iago the stranger, vanished among the bales, boxes, noise and chaotic movement of the sunlit waist.

'Your name is unknown to us, señor,' the young officer said and Iago favoured him with a deep bow.

'I shall not take offence, señor,' Iago responded. 'I have but recently arrived at Cavite and I am seeking a passage eastwards. I have been a victim of misfortune, señor, and spent time among the Chinese. I am offering my services and am a competent pilot.'

'We have both a pilot-major and a second pilot, señor,' interrupted the other with a pleasantly insolent smile.

'I can pay,' Iago said pointedly. 'I merely wished to indicate my familiarity with,' he gestured expansively forward, 'the business of a ship, should you think I might be useful.'

'You do not seem to understand, señor, the *Santa Margarita* is full. We have little space left for passengers.' The young officer smiled and gave a helpless shrug. 'I am sorry.'

'I see your dilemma,' Iago said quietly, smiling back, 'she is certainly nearing her full lading but,' and he paused for a second to lend emphasis to his intention of insisting, 'I can pay.'

'You would not displace some poor friars.'

'Not willingly but,' it was Iago's turn to shrug, 'accommodation is something one may reach as well as occupy.'

The young man stared at him, saw the pun and grinned. 'You are persistent, señor.'

'Then you will press my suit with the captain-general,' Iago said smiling back and bowing with a finality that, almost against his will, compelled the young officer to retreat into the fastness of the poop. Just as he reached his hand out to open the door, it was flung open and a figure emerged, thrown out in a swirl of black robes. He was followed by two men. One was as tall as the boatswain, though leaner in figure with a clean-shaven, pock-marked face, whose purple and black doublet was echoed in his slashed breeches and dark hose.

From the bow given him by the young officer, who stepped adroitly back from the reeling priest, Iago guessed him to be Juan Martinez de Guillestigui, the captain-general. The other, who appeared to have been responsible for the physical eviction of the priest, was clearly a man of temper. Less gorgeously dressed than his superior, Iago afterwards knew him as Pedro Ruiz de Olalde, the expedition's sergeant-major and Guillestigui's familiar.

'Señor! I protest! In the name of Mother Church!' The priest caught his breath and his balance, outrage stiffening him as all work ceased in the waist and men started with unconcealed curiosity at the scandalous incident on the half-deck above them. At this point the boatswain roared at them and they bent again to their task.

'It is not a matter for Mother Church, padre,' the captain-general announced as Olalde advanced intimidatingly, 'and in invoking her you blaspheme! You have neither the authority nor the skill necessary for the conduct of this or any other vessel and you are insubordinate! Did not our Lord Jesus Christ abjure his flock to render under Caesar those things which are Caesar's? Then remember that here, aboard the *Santa Margarita*, I am like unto Caesar!'

Cowed by this physical and verbal onslaught, the Franciscan friar retreated towards the poop ladder. Those seamen he passed drew aside and crossed themselves. Guillestigui turned away and was then made aware of Iago's presence by the young officer.

He bent his head for a moment, heard what the younger man had to say and then looked up, directly at Iago.

'Who are you and what is your business?'

Iago bowed. 'I am Iago Fernandez, Your Excellency, originally from Seville and hapless from shipwreck upon the China coast where I was compelled to languish before purchasing my liberty. I am but recently come here by way of a junk from Guandong, Excellency, and am anxious to offer my services in order to return to Seville. I am an adept in matters of navigation and might assist your pilot . . .'

Guillestigui turned aside, apparently uninterested, but Iago heard him address the young officer, saying, 'He might be useful; have Lorenzo examine him.' Then the great man vanished below, followed by Olalde. The young officer turned and asked Iago to wait. Then he too disappeared, a few moments later emerging with a heavily bearded, plain-dressed man whose skin was burnt dark by the sun and wind and who was obviously one of the ship's standing officers.

'I am Juan Lorenzo, the pilot-major,' the dark-visaged officer introduced himself with a tired expression. 'I am told you seek a berth aboard this ship?'

Iago introduced himself. 'I am from Seville, Señor Lorenzo, and have been some years at sea. I am a competent pilot and was engaged, in the interest of the House of Gomez of Seville, aboard the trader *Rainha de Portugal* of Lisbon. The brothers Gomez had chartered her on a voyage intended to open trade with his house and Macao—'

'I know the Gomez brothers,' broke in Lorenzo, 'that would be a bold move on their part.'

'Indeed,' added Iago, 'since the two countries were united they saw no reason why, as Spaniards, they might not profit from the Portuguese monopoly.'

'And you,' Lorenzo said, giving Iago a shrewd look, 'must have been placed in a position of some trust.'

Iago inclined his head. 'I was regarded as a confidential servant but was also to learn what I could of the navigation of the Bocca Tigris – in the interests of the House of Gomez.' The two men smiled, understanding each other.

'But you failed to complete the voyage . . .' Lorenzo frowned.

'Yes, señor. The *Rainha de Portugal* struck a reef in the Chinese Seas when she was overwhelmed by bad weather. Although several of us escaped the wreck I am, I am certain, the only survivor. I was fortunate to be picked up by a Chinese fisherman and have spent three years in virtual captivity.'

'In a cage?' asked Lorenzo, who had heard rumours of what the Chinese did to the occasional occidental who fell into their hands.

'Fortunately not.' Iago shook his head, smiling wryly. 'I made myself useful and in due course I found work aboard a large trading junk. That is how I came here.'

'You did not think of going to Macao?'

'I was not master of the junk's trading. Besides I was uncertain as to whether the Portuguese would believe my story, for there is supposed much hostility to us still, especially in Macao. Here I am among Spaniards.'

Lorenzo gave him a rueful look and, lowering his voice, said, 'I hope for your sake that your choice proves wise. Divisions there may be between Portugal and Spain, but perhaps they are preferable to those which divide Castilian from Basque.'

Iago shrugged. 'Like you, Señor Lorenzo, I am a seaman. I can determine latitude, work a traverse and reckon the day's work; I am not ungifted at reading the sea and the sky and know as well as the next man the time to haul in a reef.'

Lorenzo stared at Iago for a moment, then said, 'That popinjay Miguel de Alacanadre, the master-of-camp, said you were able to pay for your passage.'

Iago shrugged. 'Yes, I am able, and would ship as a gentleman
– a *sobrasaliente* – but I thought to make myself useful. I
understand that the ship is new and that you are having diffi-
culties in recruiting a competent crew. I find, however,' he
remarked looking about him, 'the ship seems full.'

A shadow fell over Lorenzo's face. 'Aye, full and overloaded,
which was the chief complaint made by the discalced friar
you saw so rudely put ashore a moment ago. He also objects
to the women . . .' Lorenzo shrugged. 'But you know that a
crew without women is a crew who will make trouble. The
holy friar will be back, of course, along with all the other
useless mouths we are shipping for New Spain, for, in truth,
we have few among the three hundred souls presently named
for embarkation who can call themselves seamen.'

Iago sensed Lorenzo, who had already confided his anxieties as to the state of the *Santa Margarita*'s lading, was seeking
him as an ally. Was he in need of a competent colleague in
face of tyrannical power? It certainly seemed so and Iago
knew only too well the internal tensions arising aboard ship
between the sea-wise professionals and the ambitious hier-
archy who commanded her. From what little he had seen of
Guillestigui and his henchman, Caesar's rule seemed arbitrary
enough.

'Is the captain-general a Basque, then?' he asked quietly.

Lorenzo shot a glance at him, relaxing a little as he realized that Iago had divined his intentions, and nodded.

'Could you then find a berth for me? I am not a Basque,'
he added with a heartening smile.

Lorenzo nodded, seeming relieved of some anxiety. 'I shall
try. Do you wait here a moment.' And with that the pilot-
major disappeared, leaving Iago on the half-deck from where
he watched the rising tide of boxes and bales mount and
overflow the waist.

He was not left long. After a few moments Lorenzo re-
emerged with Miguel de Alacanadre. The two men suppressed
what was clearly a difference of opinion between them.
Alacanadre addressed him: 'The pilot-major has put in a strong
claim for you against which the captain-general has ruled. He
is, however, prepared to admit you as a *sobrasaliente* on payment
of seventy-four maravedis and the sworn undertaking that

you will assist the pilot-major in all things that he demands, standing a watch should he so wish. If you agree, I shall allocate you a place on board; if not I shall require you to leave.'

'I accept,' Iago responded, aware that he had committed himself to a bargain all the advantage of which lay with the captain-general. 'But as a *sobrasaliente* I shall require berths for my two servants,' he added.

'Ah!'

'That is my condition and it goes without saying that a payment of such magnitude is not demanded from a man of mean birth.'

Though he held the gaze of Alacanadre, out of the corner of his eye he saw something like admiration cross the face of Lorenzo. Certainly he had discomfited Guillestigui's chief of staff. The master-of-camp was compelled to hide his irritation with a bow as Don Iago Fernandez, born Jacob van Salingen, joined the *Santa Margarita* shortly before she sailed from Cavite in July 1600.

Used as he was to the life of a dog, Ximenez was unsparing in his condemnation of the conditions he found himself forced to endure in the overcrowded ship. Despite the station of his master, they had been allocated a small area under the half-deck which was curtained off by rough canvas and which, subject constantly to challenges as to its boundaries, never seemed to occupy the same space for two consecutive minutes. When Ximenez complained Iago bade him be silent, explaining that the prevailing confusion would ease once they had put to sea. However, much of Ximenez's anxiety arose from the fact that Don Iago had decided that it would be prudent to pretend that the Chinese girl, Ah Fong, was a boy. Iago knew of the customary prejudice against women which would be aired by any priests making the voyage and he wished to be free from any possible contention that might arise. Moreover, while a degree of tolerance might be extended to the presence of native Filipinos, Ah Fong was Chinese and this might count against her. The matter of her disguise as a boy, Don Iago also asserted, would not prove difficult, citing several cases where Spanish girls had passed for boys. How much easier with a bud-breasted Chinese? Less confident of the shipboard world, Ximenez protested his doubts.

'But, master, how can she make water like a boy? Or shit but on the heads with her arse exposed to any passing glance?' Iago had brushed these apparently insuperable obstacles aside, attesting to Ah Fong's ingenuity. 'I know I am a fool, master,' Ximenez persisted, 'but even a fool knows that a woman is subject to the moon. How shall she disguise her lunar periods?'

'She will manage, Ximenez,' Iago said curtly.

'Happen she is not a girl anyway,' Ximenez muttered, shaking his head and turning away, 'and that you are a pederast . . .'

He got no further. Iago's raised eyebrow, as powerful as the grip Ximenez recalled about his throat, stopped him from further insolence.

'Do not behave like the idiot others take you for, Ximenez, and do not seek to find out the truth, which is as I have told you,' Iago said in a low voice. Then he said: 'If small arses are fancied aboard here, and there will be those who favour them I have no doubt, it will likely be yours that attracts attention.'

'Jesus protect me,' breathed Ximenez, crossing himself vigorously.

'Then hold your tongue and help Ah Fong when she needs it.'

'Of course, master, forgive me.'

'There is nothing to forgive. Your apprehensions on Ah Fong's behalf do you credit. Now stow our gear, stand guard upon it and pray that soon we depart and rid this ship of its parasites.'

Iago went on deck. As a paying gentleman he felt no obligation to assist the final preparations for departure and joined the assorted group of officers upon the poop. One or two of them, he noted, had women with them, trulls like those others forward, although better dressed in tawdry silken finery.

Iago soon struck up a tolerable acquaintanceship with Alacanadre and liked Lorenzo and his mate, Antonio de Olivera, a small, active man. Olivera shared Lorenzo's anxiety as to the over-laden state of the ship and lost no time in remonstrating – to no apparent effect – with the huge *contramaestre*, or boatswain, whom, Iago learned, was a Basque known as Diego de Llerena. To Lorenzo and Olivera were attached a handful of young cadets led by an active young man named Silva. Among the other officers with whom Iago became familiar in those first days were Joanes de Calcagorta, the *Santa Margarita's* gunner, another Basque adherent of the captain-general; Rodrigo de Peralta, like Alacanadre an aide to Guillestigui; and two military officers Capitános Manuel and Ordóñez. Among his fellow passengers was a richly dressed merchant, Don Baldivieso de los Arrocheros, and his wife, Doña Catalina, a good-looking woman who was heavy with child.

At the time most of them were on the poop, a few armed with telescopes, and all watching as another ship, the galleon *San Geronimo*, anchored close to the *Santa Margarita* off Cavite to take aboard a few last consignments from a handful of junks. The *San Geronimo* was to accompany them on the eastern passage across the Pacific and had been loading off Manila, a few miles across the great bay. Several small guns were fired in welcome by Calcagorta from the *Santa Margarita*. The *San Geronimo* responded, saluting the captain-general's standard which was raised at that moment with her own gunfire. Iago watched the pomp, seeking in Guillestigui's face something of the inner man, desirous of determining the quality of this self-styled Caesar. But the captain-general's expression was hidden in the shadow of his morion, and concealed behind the heavy beard he wore. What Iago noticed chiefly about him was the size of the gloved fist that reposed confidently upon the hilt of his long Toledo rapier, and the richness of the rings he wore outside the glove. It seemed an odd thing to wear gloves on so hot an afternoon.

The day before they sailed a large entourage of friars arrived, led by Fray Geronimo de Ocampo, who was accompanied by a handsome youth, Pedro de Guzman. Guzman bore a commission as lieutenant and proved to be the governor's nephew. Another gubernatorial appointee, Capitán Ayllon, accompanied Guzman. Iago also recognized the friar whom Olalde had kicked unceremoniously ashore on the occasion of his first visit to the *Santa Margarita* and whose name, he afterwards learned, was Fray Hernando. With them, though chastely separate, came a handful of nuns. The wimpled, heavily robed figures seemed ungainly under the burning sun and, as though seeking their natural habitat, soon scuttled away into the shadows under the half-deck. These late arrivals only added to the confusion and chaos that reigned between decks as each fought for living space. Even the discalced friars seemed to have accumulated a disproportionate amount of this world's goods for their mendicant status.

The next morning, before the sun had burnt off the mist that lay low over the marshy land which stretched away towards the line of Manila's walls, the last junks were emptied. It was said that no ship had previously loaded so rich a cargo, that among the cases carried below into the after *lazaretto* were chests of gold – certainly several men attested to their extreme weight – and that the Chinese merchants resident in the port, in partnership with the Spanish compradors who mutually arranged the cargo, had vested an immensity of credit in the *Santa Margarita*'s freight. It was also rumoured, and in sincere anxiety by Lorenzo and Olivera, that the ship was overloaded and bore too much weight for her burthen. This fear was contemptuously and publicly dismissed by Pedro Ruiz de Olalde and Diego de Llerena as ridiculous. Those who made it were marked as pusillanimous; was not the *Santa Margarita* a ship of such size that she might embark a cargo that filled her to overflowing as the present one most certainly did by the bales and boxes lashed upon her open deck? Was she not built of the finest hardwoods the Philippines could produce and under the supervision of first-class Spanish shipwrights brought from the east? Were not the hundreds of labouring Filipinos and Chinese providentially cheap and therefore God-given? Had she not been rigged with the hemp derived from the *abaca* palm, found in the archipelago in such profusion that, like the endless supply of timber, it too was ordained by God? And, given their scriptural significance, was it not also a mark of God's favour that their five fine iron anchors had come from Spain, great marks of trust from the distant home-land, symbols of hope, reliability and salvation to be sought only from Christendom itself?

All such rumours, arguments and counter-reasoning Iago

had heard in the days since he had secured his berth and brought his small household aboard. And such was the crowded state of the *Santa Margarita* that opinions had been freely voiced, as if all knew that, for the time being at least and while they were still attached to the shore by the thin thread of expedience, indiscretions might be aired without attracting the unwelcome attentions of their officers. This licence ran throughout the ship, for although Guillestigui had ordered Lorenzo to stop all shore leave for the crew, it did not prevent the sailors from their excessive wenching in those last nights when the officers retired to the great cabin to dine and the little canoes slipped alongside in the darkness and more girls scrambled up the ship's side to slide into the hammocks with their chosen benefactors.

'God's blood,' blasphemed Olalde with a wide grin as he watched one such shadow flit below, 'what must our patron saint be thinking of us now?'

But at last, on the fine sunny morning of 13 July 1600, all activity was stilled by the piercing blast of Diego de Llerena's shrill whistle. The mass of humanity was called to order and assembled to hear the Mass according to station. Falling upon his knees with the devout, Iago watched as the whores emerged and clustered in apparent wonder before the elevated host. Ocampo reminded them that it was the day of the Deposition of St Mildred the Virgin and of another, uncanonized, virgin martyr Margarita, namesake of the ship's eponymous patroness. Under these propitious auspices he warned them against sin, especially that of concubinage which greatly offended God and the very Sainted Margarita herself, after whom the ship was named. The men shuffled awkwardly but this was their only sign of contrition and, after a telling silence, Ocampo signalled the beginning of the voyage by further calling for Santa Margarita herself to intercede on their behalf, and to ask for God's blessing upon their enterprise. Ocampo reminded them of their duty to God, and to the distant King's majesty and, as he was bound to do, to their duty of obedience to Rey Felipe's captain-general, Don Juan Martinez de Guillestigui.

Ocampo raised his right hand, made the sign of the cross and blessed them in the name of the Father, Son and Holy

Ghost. As he lowered his hand, Guillestigui rose to his feet and seemed by his bulk to shoulder aside the spiritual power of Ocampo and assert that of the more immediate and temporal world. The captain-general called out an order. As the congregation broke up, Calcagorta went forward, climbed on to the forecastle and, taking the linstock from a waiting seaman, touched the glowing match to the breech of a gun. As the women trooped giggling below, the single discharge from the unshotted saker, the signal for the beginning of the voyage, made them squeak with a mixture of excitement and fear.

A cable's length away the *San Geronimo*, at the conclusion of her own devotions, dipped her pendant and discharged her own gun in acknowledgement. The twin concussions rolled over the water and were lost amid the swaying tops of the palms and the forest beyond. A short distance further from the *San Geronimo* two other ships did likewise. Then Llerena blew his whistle again and the cries of the mates and leading seamen filled the air as the topmen ascended the rigging and the mass of sailors, even an excited friar or two, bent their backs to the capstan bars and began the tedious task of weighing the anchor. Upon the *Santa Margarita*'s high poop stood the captain-general and his entourage. The sun glanced off their half-armour and ruffled the plumes in their morions. Behind them the red and gold of the great silken ensign, situated on its tall staff set above the empty Virgin's shrine, lifted in the light breeze. As if a benison from God, this blew out of the north-east over the flat swamps and marshes beyond Manila. The men tramped round the capstan until the new iron anchor, transported across half the world from a smithy in distant Seville, drew out of the coral sand at the extremity of its heavy rope cable.

Aboard the *San Geronimo* and the other vessels, men could be seen going aloft and casting loose their own gaskets. After what seemed an age to those, like Iago, waiting on the half-deck, the cry came from the beakhead that the anchor was first a-trip, and then aweigh. Calcagorta again fired the saker as a signal that the captain-general's ship was under way.

'Haul away and sheet home!' bellowed Olivera and the cry was taken up by Llerena. The seamen and hurriedly assembled landsmen tailed on to the halliard falls and as they broke into a chanting rhythm, the heavy topsail and topgallant yards were hauled aloft in readiness.

With the anchor sighted through the clear water as it rose steadily up to the *Santa Margarita*'s beakhead, the yards were braced sharp up and the topsails and topgallant sails let fall and sheeted home. Gathering way through the pellucid sea, they stood to the north close-hauled. Clearing the isthmus that secured Cavite as a bay within a bay, they beat majestically up towards the walls of Manila a few miles away, closing the city until they could see the heads of the curious upon the new ramparts and, in a jutting bastion, the flaunting standards of the governor and the flashing of the sun upon the gold crosses born by crucifers before the Archbishop of Manila. As the ships closed to within cannon shot of the bastion, the first of eleven guns saluted Don Juan Martinez de Guillestigui. As the sound of the last bombard faded, the wind bore down towards them the plaint of a hidden choir and the tolling of the cathedral bells.

In response Lorenzo shouted for the main yards to be hauled aback and the helm put over. The other ships did likewise and the entire squadron hove-to to receive the archbishop's distant and inaudible blessing. A large silk standard was broken out at the mainmasthead, its brilliant red, blue and gold lifting gallantly in the breeze, formal acknowledgement that Guillestigui received the royal mandate and the blessing of Heaven. While this ceremony was in progress a cock, one of a number of mixed fowl confined amidships in wooden basket cages, began to crow. This provoked irreverent sniggering among the crew. Guillestigui smiled beneath the steel curve of his helmet but Lorenzo called the seamen to order.

As the ships began to drift inexorably away, a barge put out from the shore, the sunlight sparkling off the oars as they dipped in perfect unison. At the boat's richly decorated stern a silk ensign trailed in the water and at its bow a small flag showed it bore the person of the captain of the port.

A few moments later this officer, Don Felipe Corço, ascended to the deck, followed by a priest and, borne up behind the cleric at some peril to its dignity, two men with a painted statue of the Virgin Mary. The friars and priests on board, hemmed by the deferential nuns, drew close round this sacred image, and after due ceremony the Blessed Virgin was ensconced high on the poop in her shrine below the great ensign of His Most Catholic Majesty Rey Felipe of Castile and Aragon, of the whole of Spain, of Portugal, Lord of the Indies and the Most Mighty and Sovereign Prince on the face of the earth. To end this valediction, Corço bowed and presented Guillestigui with a new ensign which was hoisted in place of the old. This act finally severed their connection with the shore and Don Felipe Corço shook hands with the captain-general before he descended into his barge. It shoved off from the *não*'s side, the crew lying on their oars as the *Santa Margarita*'s yards were hauled to catch the wind, the great ship swung round and headed south-west. Each firing a salute as they turned, the *Santa Margarita* led her consorts as they in turn swung away from the city and began their long voyage towards Acapulco.

With the wind free and white bow waves growing under their bluff bows and decorated, overhanging beakheads, the fleet of four vessels stood south-west down the vast bay, heading for the narrows and the open sea beyond. Standing on the half-deck, Iago gave a sigh of relief. 'At last,' he breathed to himself.

Three
A Foul Wind

Iago's relief was premature. It was immediately clear to him from his vantage point on the half-deck that much was indeed wrong with the *Santa Margarita*. Her decks remained cluttered with cargo most of which, he guessed, was unofficial trade goods belonging to the ship's senior officers. He knew enough about the regular shipments made from Manila to Acapulco to know there was a limit to the personally enriching private trade in which a ship's officers could indulge. There was also a royal edict that limited the very lading of the ship herself, licensed by the governor and called the *permiso*; it was equally clear, from the gossip about the *não*, that this too had been exceeded. But what most troubled Iago was the dead feeling of the ship beneath his feet, a sensation only an experienced mariner would notice, a combination of lack of buoyancy, of lift to the seas, though these were small and appeared insignificant within the embrace of Manila Bay.

The men most concerned about this were Juan Lorenzo, the pilot-major, and his mate, Antonio de Olivera, both of whom had expressed their anxiety to Iago. In the hours preceding their departure they had discussed the lateness of the season and the necessity for clearing the Embocadero, as they called the Strait of San Bernardino, before the end of August.

'If we do not succeed,' Lorenzo had confided, 'the season of the great storms, *los baguiosas*, will be upon us and we shall have trouble making the Vuelta.'

Iago had agreed. 'I know. It was one such that destroyed the *Rainha de Portugal*,' he said, and he followed Lorenzo's example of crossing himself as the pilot-major uttered a heartfelt prayer that they might not encounter such a wind. The Chinese, Iago recalled, called such a phenomenon *taifun*, meaning 'great wind', and his experience aboard the *Rainha de Portugal* was not one he wished ever to repeat. Now Iago regarded the cluttered deck, full of bales and boxes, which although lashed down greatly impeded the men as they trimmed the yards and, on Olivera's orders, let fall the huge lower sails. Watching their clumsiness, Iago doubted if one in three was an experienced seaman. It was all very well to build ships in the Philippines, he thought – and there was no doubt that the *Santa Margarita* was a well-built and well-found vessel – but little thought had been given to manning a mighty vessel on government service so far from Spain. A number of her crew were, like himself, distressed mariners, men left ashore at Cavite or Manila by the vicissitudes of the seafaring life. A few of these had been shipwrecked, others had overstayed their leave, deserters who had run for a month's lotus eating in the villages that lay in the jungle beyond the Spanish Pale. Such adventurous spirits might be assimilated by the indigent population but all courted hostility, disturbing the relationships forged by the natives. They were often found with their throats slit, or crucified in grim emulation of the images the Filipinos found these haughty invaders worshipped with such ardour and extravagance. The lucky among them returned contritely to their duty and were taken aboard locally built ships, of which the *Santa Margarita* was the latest, largest and most magnificent example.

In addition to these wild characters there were always those seamen left ashore through sickness who, having recovered their health, were shipped out from the hospitals run by the Church authorities. To these had to be added the mixed riff-raff of raw recruits swept up from the waterfront: the wasters, the aimless vagrants, the men of mixed blood, failed tradesmen, reluctant found-out fathers-to-be, reformed drunks and a few Filipinos who, for some dark undiscoverable reason, wished to sail east having heard Heaven knew what half-truths about the lands beyond the sunrise.

And with this polyglot crew came their 'concubines', a euphemism to cover the numerous women recruited through love, lust or cynical promises of future riches for services that were, Iago guessed, best left to the imagination. For now they had been driven below, from where a babel of voices squabbling over space and possessions, complementary bones of contention that would keep arguments going for many weeks, rose to the windswept upper decks. The women, apart from the extra mouths they brought on board, could have their own divisive effect upon a crew picked up from such disparate sources as were those upon whose skill the voyage of the *Santa Margarita* would depend.

Assessing them now, driven by Llerena and his mates with their rattans and rope's ends, Iago did not think them up to much, though he knew that after a week at sea — if the weather was kind to them — a competent crew might be fashioned from such rough material. And in their favour they did at least have the long passage through the relatively sheltered waters of the vast archipelago that made up Rey Felipe the Third's oriental colony. The thought made Iago look ahead, under the roach of the heavy forecourse that lifted and fell with the wind and the sluggish motion of the heavily laden ship.

The Bataan Peninsula swept down from the north, closing Manila Bay from that direction with its dense afforestation. Off its distal point, like a military outwork, lay a hump-backed island he knew to be called Corregidor. The main entrance lay to the south of this island beyond which the southern jaw of the bay met it, rising to a series of jungle-clad peaks. He could see the features of the land with perfect clarity, for the air was dry and the sky clear, save for a bank of low cloud ahead of them, as the *Santa Margarita* and her three consorts forged their steady way to the south-west.

When they had passed the entrance they would swing south and then south-east, almost doubling back and passing south of the main island of Luzon and north of the lesser Mindoro to the south. Then they would weave their way south and east, along Luzon's long, indented coast until they finally doubled its southernmost point. Finally, turning north-east with Samar to starboard, they would pass the channel named for San Bernardino but called by the pilots the Embocadero, before reaching the wide waters of the Pacific Ocean. From there they would begin the Vuelta, the homeward, eastwards passage, reaching up to the higher latitudes and the steady westerly winds discovered by the Augustinian friar Urdaneta in the *San Pedro* thirty-five years earlier.

'It is good, is it not, señor?'

Iago was jerked from his reverie. Beside him stood the dark-robed figure of a friar. 'I am Fray Mateo Marmolejo, señor, and you . . . ?'

Iago fought off his natural revulsion to the inevitable probing endemic to every man who sought to conceal his innate wickedness under a woollen habit.

'I am Iago Fernandez, Father.'

'A *sobrasaliente*,' Marmolejo said knowingly, 'I understand.'

'Fray Mateo is well informed.'

The man shrugged and smiled. 'It is my business to know all the secrets of the human heart; your station is an open matter. What does a gentleman-adventurer seek aboard the *Santa Margarita*, Don Iago?'

Despite an inner resentment at being forced to explain his presence, Iago was wise enough to know that an early openness might save him later interrogation by the importunate Marmolejo or others of his ilk. 'Expedience makes me seek a passage home to Spain, Fray Mateo,' he said in as friendly a manner as he was able. 'I was the sole survivor of the *Rainha de Portugal* of Lisbon.'

'A Portuguese vessel?'

'Yes . . . She was wrecked on her way to Macao.'

'God have mercy,' Marmolejo interjected, crossing himself, forcing Iago to follow suit. 'How many?'

'Upwards of one hundred and twelve souls, Father, though I cannot now recall the correct number.'

'They are known to God,' Marmolejo said, crossing himself again, 'thanks be to Him for His infinite mercy.' The crossing was repeated before the friar resumed his questioning. 'Did you seek service with the Portuguese?'

'I was serving the interests of Sevillian merchants, the House of Gomez, who had chartered the ship. There was much done after the union of the two kingdoms.'

'Ah . . .' Fray Mateo fell silent for a moment, clearly diverted from the thrust of his queries. Iago was minded to move away and end this catechism but could find no pretext. Both men watched a seaman in the waist below coiling down the fag end of a topgallant halliard and then Fray Mateo said conversationally, 'We are blessed by a fair wind. God is good, my son.'

'God is good, Father, but is it wise to attribute every favourable detail to his bounty? Whom do we seek as author of the petty misfortunes that will, inevitably, assail us upon this long and dangerous voyage?'

'Why, to the Devil, of course . . .' Fray Mateo responded sharply, so that Iago regretted his remark, 'and God's will will be done, for He shall triumph.'

'Amen to that,' Iago said in hurried amendment.

'And what do you anticipate will inevitably assail us on our voyage?' Marmolejo asked pointedly.

Iago shrugged and smiled. 'While every seaman must keep his true faith in God, he would not be a seaman if he did not always prepare for the worst, particularly in the way of the weather.'

'Yet that is part of God's creation and therefore of God's ineffable purpose.'

Iago bit off a retort that God must have taken mightily against seamen to so often bend his ineffable purpose to their hardship and destruction. Such a remark would expose him to a charge of blasphemy and was highly incriminating. Instead he remarked: 'And a wise mariner secures his vessel as best he may.'

'And is the *Santa Margarita* not so secured?' Marmolejo asked with such innocence that Iago had to look at him to discover the friar meant no sarcasm.

'Were I her master, I should not so clutter her decks,' Iago answered, gesturing at the state of the waist, then, instantly regretting the confidence, adding, 'I say that between ourselves, Fray Mateo, for I should not like to be thought disloyal . . .'

'But you have your anxieties?'

'In a professional sense, yes.'

Marmolejo waved his own hand towards the cluttered deck with its cargo of boxes and bales, crisscrossed with lashings set tight with a toggle of wood inserted between adjacent strands and twisted to tension the lines. 'This is what troubles you?'

Iago nodded, unwilling to be drawn further by the meddling

cleric then, thinking that his misgivings were deep enough to demand explanation, he expressed them. 'It is not only that they discommode the working of the upper deck,' he said at last, 'but that they raise weights high in the ship. It is always better to keep such things below hatches.'

Marmolejo seemed concerned with this revelation. 'Yes, I comprehend your argument,' he said thoughtfully. 'Much, if not all, is the captain-general's indulgence, that is to say his own or belonging to men of his faction.'

'I did not know there were extreme factions aboard the ship,' Iago said disingenuously.

The friar nodded. 'Alas, my son, tell me when in the affairs of men they are absent?' The question was rhetorical. 'But this is not simply the spiritual against the secular, this is exacerbated by Guillestigui's Basque following. I pray that nothing on this voyage seeks to separate our common humanity.'

'Amen to that,' said Iago with perfect sincerity, lifting his gaze to stare ahead.

Marmolejo sighed. Apparently he had forgotten Iago's warning. Instead of pursuing the matter he merely crossed himself and said, 'Well, my son, all will be well. We are all subject to God's will.'

'Of course, Father, but I see the Devil, or at least the mustering of some of his angels, to the westward.' Iago pointed to the distant horizon.

Beyond the looming bulk of Corregidor and the line of the horizon which glowed like a silver bar against the gathering cloud, the sky had darkened and the mass of boiling cloud was now rolling over the rim of the world.

'I may seem a *sobrasaliente*, Father, but my seaman's instincts warn me that, God or the Devil notwithstanding, that brew is going to punish us for all our sins before nightfall.'

The words were hardly out of Iago's mouth before the sails, which a moment before had been full-bellied and drawing, suddenly fell slack and slatted against the mast as the wind dropped away. The ship's heel eased and a moment later they filled again and the *Santa Margarita*, having faltered momentarily in her stride, picked up speed again.

Iago turned. Behind him Juan Lorenzo was staring ahead, an expression of apprehension on his face.

'Señor Lorenzo!' Iago called to the pilot-major. 'The sky ahead . . .'

'Aye, Don Iago, I see it!' Lorenzo barked an order which brought Diego de Llerena on deck.

'*¡Velas mayores! ¡Palanquins!* Courses! Clew garnets, there! Haul up the courses! Look lively, damn you!' And the waist of the ship came alive as rattans chivvied the reluctant and unfamiliar sailors to the pin-rails while on the poop above Guillestigui, who had not left the deck but had been in conversation with his sergeant-major, Pedro Ruiz de Olalde, moved forward to the rail and looked down, querying the reduction in sail.

'The wind, Excellency,' Lorenzo explained, waving his right arm in the direction of the darkening sky, 'it is about to change.'

'*¡Diablo!*' Guillestigui swore as the wind died away completely, just as the courses were gathered up to the lower yards in their buntlines.

'They would be wise to get the topgallants off the ship too,' Iago said, half to himself and half to Fray Mateo, as a gun was fired to draw the attention of the other vessels to the fact that the captain-general's ship was shortening down. Already the *San Geronimo*'s lower sails were being clewed up.

'That wind,' the friar said, pointing ahead, 'I see it coming and that from the contrary direction.'

Iago too could see the line of white caps that spread rapidly across the darkening sea towards them. 'You have good eyes, Father,' he said wondering whether to intervene and advise Lorenzo to furl the uppermost sails, the topgallants. But the pilot-major, assisted now by the active Olivera, was ordering the helm over and the yards braced sharp up before the *Santa Margarita* was caught flat aback. If she was to be struck by a violent wind she risked dismasting at a stroke.

The accompanying ships in the *flota* were following the captain-general's example and the squadron lay to, yards braced up on the starboard tack, the courses gathered in their bunts, the upper sails flat, drooping lifelessly. As the braces were coiled down, the ship wallowed and Lorenzo ordered the topgallants struck.

'Steady . . .' Iago murmured, as if he were himself at the con and standing close to the men on the whipstaff. He braced himself with such obvious deliberation that instinctively Marmolejo copied him. Iago looked aloft at the topgallants then the topsails. 'For God's sake hurry, master pilot, hurry,' he muttered more to himself than to the nautically ignorant friar beside him. 'What in God's name keeps the men from . . . ?'

Then, as the seamen, having mustered about the fore- and mainmasts, began to start halliards and haul upon buntlines and reefing tackles, below them out from under the break of the half-deck, wandering into the sunshine with an air of curiosity engendered by the activity on deck, strolled Don Baldivieso de los Arrocheros and his pregnant wife.

'Señor,' Iago called down, 'go below and secure your person and that of your wife. This is no place for you at the moment.'

Arrocheros looked up. 'Why . . . ?'

'Do as Don Iago advises, Don Baldivieso,' Marmolejo put in authoritatively, 'we are about to be struck by a squall!'

Making a little cry, Doña Catalina turned away from her husband as the ship was suddenly plunged into the gloom thrown by cloud obscuring the sun. The sea turned dark and then the first breath of contrary wind struck them. It filled the slack sails as they watched the advancing wave-caps and heard the growing noise harping in the rigging. And then it hit them, the wind first, followed by a thin curtain of rain that reduced Corregidor to a purple shadow on the starboard beam as the *Santa Margarita* heeled sharply to the thrust of the squall. The cry of it in the rigging rose to a harsh scream. Beside Iago, Marmolejo, his habit flapping and flogging at his legs, crossed himself with one hand even as the other clung to the rail.

'This is, in truth, a fiendish thing,' the friar called out, choking off the remark and the *Santa Margarita*'s lee rail drove under and Iago spun to call, '¡Juanetes!'

But Lorenzo was already shouting for the topgallant halliards to be let go and Olivera was amidships, wading waist-deep through the sea water cascading over the lee rail while from down below came the noise of breaking crockery, unsecured objects toppling over and the cries of the terrified and uncomprehending passengers among which Iago could hear the squeals of Doña Catalina and the nuns.

'Dear God!' Marmolejo enunciated quite distinctly amid the uproar. Even the starting of the topgallant halliards from their pins did not ease the *Santa Margarita* and she pressed further and further over, driving through the sea with an unimaginable velocity. Looking aloft, Iago could see the problem lay in the angle of heel preventing the topgallant yard parrels sliding easily down their masts. The newness of the gear did not help, but the failure of the sails to drop and lose their energy meant they remained full of wind, exacerbating the peril of their situation.

In the waist Olivera had seen the problem and was shouting to Llerena, and that worthy blew a blast on his whistle to waken the dead, then bellowed for the topmen to get aloft. Still the men in the waist seemed paralysed, stunned into an immobile watching as the ship heeled further and further over. So far over did she lean that water poured over the lee rail into the waist with a roar and the lower yards dipped until the main yardarm touched the surface of the sea. Here it threw up a white plume as it drew along the surface until the ship lifted a little.

'God damn them for idle swine,' Iago growled. He could watch no longer and leapt for the half-deck ladder, ran forward and sprang up, into the weather main rigging. He crossed the deck, climbing the steep angle encumbered by the deck-borne cargo; Olivera was behind him and the resolution of these two men seemed to galvanize a few of the stouter-hearted and more experienced seamen on deck.

Iago heard Olivera shout that he would take the foremast, but he paid little heed as he gasped for breath, inhibited from doing so naturally by the strength of the gale. Once he had begun Iago found going aloft both too easy and dangerous. Such was the *Santa Margarita*'s angle of heel that the slope of the shrouds was so gentle that he could almost run along them despite the fact that it was years since he had been aloft. But he could feel, too, the immense tension in them, for the *Santa Margarita* was overpressed to the very point of disaster, and the huge maincourse, though clewed up in deep festoons of heavy, new canvas, nevertheless flogged in response to the wind driven into it. Such was the violence that it felt as though it must shake the masts, rigging and even the ship herself into a thousand pieces.

Swinging himself over the maintop, Iago grasped the over-taut shaking topmast shrouds and continued his ascent, the great white concavity of the straining maintopsail bellying to leeward, resistant to the half-hearted tug of the reef tackles, its sheets still holding its clews down to the main yard below. It was as stiff as a board, yet it too seemed to tremble and shake. Why, he thought almost inconsequentially as he struggled upwards, had the men on deck not started the sheets?

He looked down, seeing the ship like a half-tide rock, the waist still swept by the sea, the poop and forecastle prominent islands amid the torrent. But Iago was more interested in what lay above him as he climbed over the upper mast doubling. He sought the topgallant shrouds and heaved himself upwards. The uppermost section of the tall mainmast stood before him, bowed and shuddering. About two-thirds of the way up, the heavily beaded maintopgallant parrel had stuck, allowing the sail to lower a little, sufficiently for its bellying bunt to hold the wind and, like a gigantic hand, press the ship further and further over.

It was clear that the new fittings had failed to run: the mast slushing was inadequate, the mast timber too green or too resinous, so that the parrel beads had not revolved and now the tension in the gear held them immobile. Up he went, hand over hand until the jammed parrel was below him. Realizing he had little time, he considered what he should do if he could not dislodge it at once. It struck him that the only solution lay in tearing the sail with his knife but, extending his right leg, bending it and then driving his heel hard downwards on the parrel, he felt it give. Surely to God the slush, so recently applied, must ease his task after he had started the jammed beads. Only yesterday the sailors had been aloft slopping the mixture of oil and grease on the spar; even now, despite the wind, he could smell the stuff and see its gleam on the mast.

He could hear the shouts of men from below, one of them Guillestigui's he thought, but he took no notice. What did they know? He knew only that he must conserve his strength and wait his moment, for the ship's motion, augmented by his height and the vibrating mast, threatened to fling him from his precarious perch.

Carefully he adjusted his position and repeated the downwards kick. The parrel moved a little more; then, with a final thump, he succeeded in spectacular fashion. It ran away, the yard slid downwards and the sail collapsed. Now below him in its folded form it too flapped, adding to the violence that shook the entire mast, but the immense pressure and leverage it had exerted upon the ship was eased. Now, he thought in anticipation, the great ship *must* relinquish her dangerous angle of heel.

But Iago was still obliged to cling on for dear life until those on deck had hauled on the buntlines and gathered the sail up in bunches. He stared forward, gathering his thoughts and allowing his heart to slow. On the foremast Olivera had had no comparable luck. Followed by a lean and athletic seaman, the two men had, at considerable peril to themselves, laid out on the yard. Olivera was in the position of the greater danger, sliding down to leeward, to where the yardarm dipped towards the rush of the black and silver sea; the seaman was climbing into the sky towards the weather yardarm. At Olivera's cry both men, each holding on with one hand, plunged their knives into the new, resistant canvas. There was a second's hiatus and then the foretopgallant tore, first into three wide ribbons and then – as they flogged wildly – into numerous shreds. Horrified, Iago watched the energy transmitted by this disorder whip the foretopgallant yard. Olivera dropped his knife as he clung on, the thin seaman shoved his between his teeth as he too grabbed the yard in fear for his life. Thirty feet away on the maintopgallant shrouds, Iago could now feel the additional tremor of that whipping yard transmitted right through the stays that linked fore and mainmasts.

But while Olivera and his helpmeet had solved their problem by the destruction of the foretopgallant, Iago still had an intact sail to furl. The flogging maintopgallant below him might shake itself to pieces – indeed he half-hoped it would and save him the trouble – but he began to descend and fight his way out along the yard, reaching for the small suspended coil of the outermost gasket. As he leaned over the yard he could see below him the tumblehome of the *Santa Margarita*'s starboard side and the upswung faces of timorous seamen, their mouths open as they stared up at him. They seemed like strangers, inhabiting another world, even another time.

'At what do you stare, you dolts?' he shouted at them. 'Think me a dead man? You will all be dead, you confounded dogs, if you do nothing, for I cannot furl this damned sail alone! Get aloft, you whoresons!'

But if they could not hear his exact words they were already astir; he had shamed them and, led by the cadet Silva, a score were ascending the shrouds even as others finally let fly the topsail sheets and began to haul up the topsails to reef them. After a little while he was joined by the first men arriving on the jerking footrope to assist him. He swore as he almost lost his grip but a moment later was glad of their presence as they fought to gather in the canvas, to suppress it and lash it along the yard. It had become a very personal struggle now. Iago's entire world had shrunk to the trembling spar and the juddering footrope, his life concentrated on the single task of taming and lashing the topgallant sail. It was a war − an epic war for the handful of men engaged − and took all the strength and resolution of which they were collectively capable.

And yet, as they finally prevailed, quelling the swollen bundle of harsh canvas amid torn nails, blood and the turns of the gaskets, he could discern little easing in the ship's angle of heel.

At the point at which Iago and those with him looked up from their completed task, the point at which they managed a grin of congratulation to the man next on the yard, the point at which they rejoined a wider world, released from their private conflict, there was a tremendous explosion and the maintopgallant yard whipped in a spasm that Iago afterwards could only liken to the imagined paroxysm that shattered the body of a hanged man. For a dreadful instant it seemed that all was over, that they had lost their fight, that the ship herself had disappeared and they would all shortly discover what was meant by death and afterlife. Then Iago realized that the maintopsail below them had blown itself out. Relieved of its pressure, the *Santa Margarita*'s heel eased so rapidly that they were almost all flung into the sea below. For a moment each man took hold to save his own life, then it began to dawn upon them that the ship was, at last, recovering something of her equilibrium.

'God be praised!' he heard a man along the yard say, and suppressed an almost hysterical desire to laugh as the fool tried to cross himself before recollecting that it was wiser to hang on to the yard. They began to lay in, sliding down to secure the shredded maintopsail. Half an hour later they were all on deck and, under spritsail, foretopsail, mizzen-topsail and lateen mizzen, the *Santa Margarita* drove as close to windward as she could on the starboard tack. The island of Corregidor was disappearing into the murk astern but the gale still blew with unmitigated fury.

With curiously shaking legs, Iago returned to the break of the half-deck where Marmolejo seemed transfixed, his eyes glowing with a sort of fanatical regard. 'My son, my son, that was well done, well done.'

'It was nothing,' Iago muttered, irritated by the patronizing tone of the friar and the subordination inherent in the minor noun. He leaned on the forward rail, suddenly weary after his exertions, lest he slither to the deck from the odd weakness in his legs.

Lorenzo crossed the deck and smote his shoulder. 'Don Iago, we are indebted . . .' But he was interrupted from the poop.

'Congratulations, Don Iago.' Guillestigui leaned over the poop rail. 'You shall dine with me at the first opportunity.'

Iago straightened up, turning and inclining his head in the captain-general's direction. 'Thank you, Excellency.' The captain-general nodded and addressed Alacanadre; Iago smiled at Lorenzo. 'Antonio de Olivera was the nimbler of us,' he jested and was about to say more to the pilot-major when their attention was diverted to the far side of the half-deck. Ascending the larboard ladder, Fray Geronimo de Ocampo swung himself up, his face uplifted towards the captain-general who stood with Olalde and Miguel de Alacanadre above them all on the poop. What drew their attention to Ocampo's progress were the insubordinate imprecations he uttered against the captain-general and the efforts of Lieutenant Guzman, who sought to restrain the angry cleric.

'Juan Martinez,' Ocampo raged at Guillestigui, 'I warned you of your rapacious greed, a greed I marked long ago in New Spain as your besetting sin. Now you have lost us the ship and destroyed God's purpose in setting us upon this noble voyage . . .'

At first Guillestigui seemed not to have heard this outburst above the roar of the wind but as Ocampo drew closer it became impossible to ignore. Coming rapidly to the top of the poop ladder the captain-general stared down at Ocampo standing at its foot.

'Have a care, Father. Curb your tongue for fear you set a treacherous example. The ship is in less danger than you yourself. Recall you were but an hour or two since preaching obedience to God and myself as captain-general of this *flota*. True we have been through a squall and suffered somewhat, but all is now safe and—'

'This is God's judgement, you *shall* be humbled.'

Beside Iago, Lorenzo stirred. 'What a time for this,' he said in a low voice. 'We shall have to wear ship or run too far towards the shallows under yon point.'

'Come, then,' Iago said, looking to leeward where the land loomed out of the grey murk, 'pass the word. 'Twill be better than this altercation.'

Lorenzo raised his voice and broke the spell. This time the men ran to their stations with a semblance of order and a willingness to try their best that surprised Marmolejo. 'It must be your example,' he said to Iago, but Iago was not listening. He had seen Ximenez emerge into the waist, saw him stare about himself, observed the confused expression on the dwarf's face and then watched the wretched fellow bend over and vomit copiously on to the deck. Fortunately sea water still sloshed about and quickly washed the stinking slime into the scuppers and over the side.

'Ximenez!' Iago called sharply. 'Come here.'

The pallid dwarf dragged himself reluctantly up the ladder to the half-deck. 'Master?'

'How is it below?'

'As if Satan had established himself there, master. Hell itself must be preferable to this . . .' Ximenez heaved again.

'Over the lee side!' Iago commanded, thrusting Ximenez

down the sloping deck, grinning at the dwarf's discomfiture and further amused as the spectacle of seasickness – so contagious among the uninitiated – suddenly infected Marmolejo. As the two turned back inboard wiping their mouths, brothers in misery and adversity, Iago laughed. 'You will not believe me now,' he remarked, 'but it will pass in a day or so.'

The two men, one small, deformed and sumptuously dressed, the other tall, bearded and in his wind-wracked plain habit, stared back bemused.

Under Lorenzo's conning, the *Santa Margarita* turned away from the wind, her yards swinging. Then having brought her high stern to the gale – which caused a drop in the strong apparent wind over the deck and the illusion that all their miseries were at an end – she continued her alteration of course until the rushing air blew in over her larboard bow and her yards were braced sharp up on the larboard tack.

'Now you must spew to starboard,' Iago said to the two wan faces as they gagged and retched again.

As the setting sun, long hidden behind the cloud-bank, drew the day to its close the wind increased. It was clear the *Santa Margarita* was making excessive leeway, and although the high poop kept the ship riding easily, despite the size of the seas that had built up since the onset of the squall, they were making little progress to windward. While they would just weather Corregidor, under so reduced and wounded a rig the *Santa Margarita* was quite incapable of beating clear of the bay. Having almost gained the open sea beyond the narrows, this seemed a twist that proved, or so Fray Mateo Marmolejo averred, that the Devil's tail was kinked.

Having consulted the captain-general, whose permission had to be sought for every manoeuvre of the *flota* despite the fact that Don Juan Martinez Guillestigui was a soldier not a sea-officer, Lorenzo gave orders for the anchor to be readied. The pilot-major had, Olivera told Iago upon enquiring, decided to shelter off Mariveles until the wind moderated. A moderation would not, Olivera thought, be long in coming.

'By tomorrow,' Olivera said, 'if we have bent new sails, we shall resume our passage.'

'I hope you are right,' Marmolejo said, taking himself below. He had voided his belly and sought now the comparative comfort of his hammock. The friar's disappearance was well timed as the *Santa Margarita* drove under the shelter of Cochinos Point. Standing into the adjacent bay at the tip of the Bataan Peninsula, the great *não* approached the village of Mariveles which stood at its head. In sight of the village cooking fires she rounded-to, came head to wind and upright after what seemed to the passengers huddled below an age on her beam ends. As she lost way and the wind began to drive her astern, her best bower anchor was let go from the starboard bow. What was left of the daylight leached out of the torn wrack that drove over their heads as the seamen clambered aloft to furl her remaining sails. It was almost dark as the *San Geronimo* joined them in the anchorage: of the other ships there was no sign.

Upon anchoring, Iago went below. In the meagre light of the glims and lanterns that swung from the deck beams under the half-deck he could see the ship's state was shambolic. The air was stale with vomit and the inhabitants of the space lay about on the haphazard deck cargo in a stupor, relieved only that the ship had ceased her wild antics and anxious that she should not resume them. He could not resist a wry smile at the spectacle of Ximenez prostrate upon a large bale. Only Ah Fong seemed unaffected, though her pretty snub nose wrinkled at the nauseating stink filling the air of the overcrowded space.

'You should have been on deck at my side,' Iago said to her with a grim smile. 'A young man should have been at the side of his master.'

She stared back at him. 'My master would not have me at his side when I see in his eyes he had a mind to have me beneath him,' she laughed.

'Have a care, Ah Fong,' he said with gentle seriousness, 'we must not be caught making two dogs.'

She made a face, a pretty moue, of disappointment. 'I should not want to wait too long,' she said.

Iago pushed the thought aside. After his exertions the thought of submitting to Ah Fong's tender embrace was seductive. 'Wash this poor fellow down, Ah Fong,' he told her, indicating Ximenez's sweat-glazed head.

She shook her head. 'He has the head of a Devil,' she remarked distastefully, 'he is not like other men.'

'No matter. He may do you a service one day. He has a heart like other men and maybe other parts, so be careful.'

'Oh, I have seen his parts, they are like a horse!' She laughed and Iago would have been amused at her candour had not a third party joined them.

'Don Iago . . .'

Iago turned towards Arrocheros. 'Don Iago,' the merchant repeated, his face a mask of horrified anticipation, 'how are we to endure a voyage of such misery?'

Suddenly tired and hungry, Iago responded as politely as his shortening temper allowed. 'It is not, was not, so very bad, señor. Believe me, you will get used to such alarums in due course.'

'Used to such terrors? But it is intolerable!'

'You think so now, Señor Arrocheros, but I do assure you that in a fortnight you will be as seasoned a mariner as myself.'

Arrocheros shook his head in disbelief. 'They tell me you went . . . er, up the masts?'

'I went aloft, yes, to secure the upper sails, the topgallants.' He was too weary to offer a more fulsome explanation. Besides it did not matter. He found his cloak and drew it about his shoulders. Now someone else was calling his name.

'Don Iago!' It was Rodrigo de Peralta.

'Don Rodrigo? What is it?'

'The captain-general asks that you dine with him in an hour.'

Iago nodded wearily. 'In an hour? Certainly. Please thank the captain-general for his courtesy.' Thus disposing of his social obligations, Iago kicked the dwarf. 'Ho! Ximenez! Get off your arse. You have slept long enough. Call me in half an hour with hot water and a razor. I am to dine in state.'

Then Iago lay down and an instant later was fast asleep.

An hour later Ximenez did as he was bid and, feeling a little fresher but with his appetite as yet unassuaged, Iago made his way aft, approaching the great cabin, which extended right across the stern of the *Santa Margarita*. Here he encountered Olivera.

'Do not delay me, señor,' Iago said, 'I am commanded to dine.'

'Aye, Don Iago, I know, as is the pilot-major, but be pleased to let him know the wind is freshening again and that our anchor is dragging.'

Iago cocked an ear. In the half-light of the aftercastle he could feel the thrum of the wind, its transmitted power strangely alive in the ship's timbers. And he could feel something else, something more regular, a small steady vibration that told of the dragging anchor and the tremor its slow movement through the seabed carried upwards to the hull of the *Santa Margarita*.

'Dragging?' he asked and the glare of a glim caught the anxiety in Olivera's eyes.

'Aye and we shall shortly be embayed, for the mouth of the Cañas River lies directly under our lee. You *must* tell the pilot-major!'

'Very well,' Iago responded, fully alarmed, 'I shall pass the word.'

'Thank you, Don Iago.'

Even as Olivera opened his mouth to speak, a gust struck the ship with the force of a cannon shot. Both men felt her snub at her cable, adding to the strain already upon it.

'Do you tell the cabin, Don Iago,' Olivera said, already moving away, 'I must turn up the hands!' Olivera ran forward shouting orders and Iago turned with equal expedition, brushing aside the two sentries at the cabin door, both of whom had been privy to this conversation.

Iago threw open the door on to a colourful and brilliant scene; the candelabra threw a thousand points of light off the glasses, the jewelled costumes of the assembly and the plate upon the table.

'Gentlemen!' he called. 'It is imperative that we make sail before we are cast ashore. The wind has risen and we are in danger of being embayed!'

'*¡Diablo!*' Lorenzo handed his goblet to a servant and, casting a cursory, 'By your leave, Excellency . . .' in Guillestigui's direction, made for the deck.

'It is bad, Don Iago?' the captain-general asked.

'I fear so, Excellency.'

'Perhaps,' remarked Guillestigui, making light of the situation, his tone heavy with irony, 'we shall make a quick passage with such a breeze.' His entourage laughed dutifully.

'Please excuse me, Excellency.' Iago turned away to follow Lorenzo out on deck.

Up in the blustery darkness, with the wind still howling in the rigging, Iago's eyes took a moment to become accustomed to the darkness. Hurrying towards the knot of sea-officers at the break of the half-deck, Iago joined Lorenzo alongside Olivera.

The pilot-major cursed again when he realized the wind's strength and direction. 'Why in the name of the Virgin did you not call me sooner?'

'The wind backed and came up in an instant. It started the anchor from the bottom,' Olivera threw back as he directed the hands forward and aloft, to man the capstan and cast the gaskets off the topsails.

'God grant that we have not left it too late! An extra two men at the helm, for the love of Christ! Where is the gunner?' Lorenzo raised his voice. 'Calcagorta!'

'Señor?'

'A gun for the *San Geronimo*!'

'There is no need!' Iago's words were drowned in the boom of the *San Geronimo*'s saker as she signalled her own warning to the flagship, and they could see a pale parallelogram appear. A moment later all three ghostly topsails were set upon the dark form of their consort's masts. From the waist of their own ship a weird and wailing shanty rose but it was clear from Llerena's howls that the men were having trouble heaving up the cable against the strength of the gale. For five long minutes the men at the capstan strained at their bars, gaining ground with pathetic slowness. Not content with this hiatus, Guillestigui, accompanied by his gentlemen and the senior friar Ocampo, had emerged on to the half-deck with an air of amused, if disturbed, conviviality. They appeared to ridicule the rude sailors at their antics. Several of them still bore goblets.

'Excellency,' Lorenzo almost pleaded, 'this is no place . . .' But Olivera interrupted this remonstrance, calling that the *San Geronimo* was under way. The spectacle of being left behind was too much for Lorenzo.

'Foreyards brace sharp up for the larboard tack! Main and mizzen for the starboard!'

Iago flung himself on the mizzen brace and tailed with the handful of able seamen mustered for the task. With its topsail gone, the main stood naked, though they would brace it and – if and when they cleared the bay – let fall the course. As soon as he was satisfied with the bracing of the yards, Lorenzo ordered the fore- and mizzen-topsails set and sheeted home, immediately shouting: 'Cut the cable!'

From forward came the thump, thump of an axe and then they all felt the ship tremble as the cable parted and, with her head yards braced aback, watched as she fell off the wind and heeled over under the press of the wind in her canvas. When the windward leaches of the foretopsail began to shiver and the sails on the mizzen-mast filled with a crack, Lorenzo bawled: 'Foreyards, sharp up! Starboard tack!'

The *Santa Margarita* leant again to the wind's violence, falling off to leeward and then slowly, ever so slowly to those upon her deck able to judge, began to forge ahead. But they were far from safe. Even with only two topsails full the ship was over-pressed and to those capable of feeling it there was that sluggish submission to the heel which had no countering resistance in it. This and the force of the wind made it imperative to reef both topsails, yet in doing so the *Santa Margarita* would lose way and she had some distance to go before she had worked clear of the river and weathered the eastern point of Mariveles Bay. Once they had fought out into the strait they would be able to ease the helm and run before the storm, all the way back to Cavite, where they could seek shelter to refit the ship; but they had yet to clear the bay without anything carrying away aloft.

Something of the seamen's anxiety must have communicated itself to the onlookers on deck for, as they stood across the bay, one of the friars raised a chant and was quickly joined by others. The words of the psalm could barely be heard above the roar of the wind, the piping of the rigging and the hiss and thunder of the sea, which grew as they drew slowly out of the bay's shelter.

As if initiated into some obscure fraternity, Lorenzo, Olivera and Iago had drawn close together on the half-deck from where they could see the vacillating compass card and line up parts of the straining ship with glimpses of the distant land in order to gauge their progress. Below his breath Olivera was unconsciously swearing; Lorenzo stood rooted to the spot and Iago wondered, if they did have to lay the *Santa Margarita* on the other tack, whether they still had sea-room to wear her, for she would never stay in these conditions.

'Nothing infects the people like the anxiety of the shipmen,' Lorenzo remarked, as if scolding Olivera for some imagined misdemeanour.

'God knows we have cause to be anxious,' retorted Olivera, after which the three men stood in silent encouragement of the helmsmen below them at the whipstaff. After what seemed an interminable time – as the voices of the friars called upon the Trinity of God, the Holy Virgin and Santa Margarita to assist them – the ship drove closer to the point so that the land loomed over them. Even though it lay in their lee, they could smell the rich vegetation of the forest.

And then, quite suddenly and miraculously it seemed to some, the *Santa Margarita* cleared the point and stood out into clear water beyond the headland. For a further ten minutes no man dared break the spell before Lorenzo gave the order to put up the helm and start the weather braces. Slowly the *Santa Margarita* turned to larboard, heading back to the north-east and the refuge of Cavite.

There were cries of praise to God the Father, God the Son and God the Holy Ghost; the Mother of God was invoked, and Blessed St Nicholas, as the patron saint of sailors, was thanked for his intercession. St Clement was remembered and a thin chorus of praise in the reedy voices of the nuns rose to the virtuous and virginal Santa Margarita, whose name-day approached. They had been saved. And not a rope-yarn had broken. That their escape was miraculous was, Father Ocampo asserted in a loud voice in the comparative lull that followed their running before the wind so that all might hear him, 'due entirely to the goodness of Almighty God'.

In the chorus of amens and the multiple crossings of breasts in high- and low-born alike, no one noticed the silent relief of the three sea-officers, Lorenzo, Olivera and the *sobrasaliente* Don Iago Fernandez, whose mouths had run dry.

But Father Ocampo, in the manner of priests, had not finished. He turned and, in his commanding voice, addressed the captain-general.

'Don Juan Martinez, take heed of the escape we have had. Divine Providence has intervened and sent us back, that we may start this voyage again, this time in a spirit of holiness and contrition, sincere in our confessions, clean in our bodies and minds, our ship, which shall be our Ark, made better for her purpose and lightened of the venal load she carries for wicked profit.'

There were those who expected Guillestigui to make a reply, but the captain-general, though he made a remark to Olalde and provoked laughter from those within hearing, turned away and went below to shut himself in the great cabin.

As the bells were struck to mark the watch's halfway point, Iago realized that it wanted two hours to midnight. It seemed like a previous year that they had first drawn the flukes of the anchor from Cavite Bay, rather than the day before. They had it seemed expended a vast amount of energy and, to be sure, had lost several sails. On the other hand they had made no progress in all that eventful time and had succeeded only in leaving one valuable iron anchor to the fishes in Mariveles Bay. That anchor, Iago mused, was irreplaceable: it had been brought all the way from the forges of Seville in distant Spain.

Four
The Curse

Iago woke to find Ximenez standing beside his hammock, hot shaving water and a razor readied for his master. Behind him hovered Ah Fong with his shaving bowl. Iago stretched; he was aware that he had woken in the night that followed his exertions in the *Santa Margarita*'s rigging, somewhere around dawn when her second bower anchor had been let go, its heavy hemp cable had rumbled out through the hawse and the *não* had come to a blessed rest.

'We are again anchored off Cavite, master,' Ximenez explained, 'and Don Felipe Corço has been on board.'

Iago rubbed his eyes and threw his legs out of the bed Ximenez had extemporized for him by throwing a palliasse on top of some boxes. 'Who?' he asked sleepily.

'Felipe Corço, the captain of the port.'

'Oh yes, of course. What does he want?'

'It is more what the captain-general and pilot-major require,' Ximenez said, lathering vigorously, 'though it is Fray Ocampo who makes the most noise with his supplications.'

'And what,' asked Iago erratically as he submitted to having his jaw scraped, 'does the reverend father require from the captain of the port?'

'He has charged Don Felipe to find us more sailors.'

'Huh! I thought every stew from here to Manila had been turned over for *marineros*,' Iago said, his reply punctuated by strenuous exertions of his jaw as he avoided the most painful of Ximenez's ministrations. At last the dwarf had finished and Ah Fong, who had briefly disappeared, now brought Iago some coconut, raisins and rice with which to break his fast. He realized he was ravenously hungry, for the previous evening the promised dinner with Guillestigui had, in the event, never materialized.

'There is much argument,' Ximenez said, cleaning the razor, 'about an anchor.'

'Ah,' replied Iago between mouthfuls, 'indeed.'

'And now the captain of the port has returned to the shore to find us men.'

Later Iago went on deck. It was as though they had never sailed. The upper deck had resumed its chaotic appearance but Iago was able to distinguish a greater and more focused purpose as Llerena, under Olivera's direction, had turned the seamen to, to bend new sails. Also, in the interests of discipline, the women were confined below. Half a cable's length away from them the *San Geronimo* lay at anchor, sails furled; there was no sign of the other vessels. And again, almost in replication of that first day, there was an argument raging in the cabin in which tempers were so hot that they could be heard out in the sunshine of the half-deck.

At the rail, Olivera turned from shouting orders forward, his glance flying to the iron-bound door which led below the poop to the great cabin. Catching his attention, Iago raised an eyebrow in mute enquiry. Olivera shrugged.

'The captain-general has just summoned the pilot-major, apparently Fray Geronimo has just laid further accusations against Don Juan Martinez.'

Recalling the bad blood that clearly existed between the two men, Iago sought its origin. Olivera imparted the gossip: 'Oh, Fray Geronimo de Ocampo was opposed to the appointment of Don Juan Martinez de Guillestigui as captain-general from the beginning. The animosity is mutual and Don Juan wished for the governor to send the reverend father aboard the admiral's ship,' he explained, gesturing to the *San Geronimo*, 'where the fray and the ship's patronym shared a baptismal name, but Ocampo was adamant. He insisted upon joining the captain-general's flag, saying the captain-general was not to be trusted and that he needs must be accompanied by a prince of the Church.' Olivera shook his head. 'No good will come of it.'

'Is Fray Geronimo a prince of the Church, then?' asked Iago.

Olivera shrugged. 'Not exactly, but I believe he is in expectation of a bishopric.'

'The first time I stood upon this deck,' Iago remarked, 'I noted our captain-general had little respect for Mother Church. He ejected Fray Hernando from yonder door with as little ceremony as if he had been an importunate costermonger.'

Olivera's face grew grave. ''Tis said, Don Iago, that the captain-general is an apostate,' he confided in a low voice. 'That is, in part at least, why I am apprehensive about the voyage. As for Hernando,' he added, his tone lightening, 'he is below with half the assembled friars who are all in the pocket of Ocampo. The captain-general may listen, but he will not heed them.'

'Is the pilot-major there too?'

Olivera nodded. 'Oh yes. He too is called to account . . . But now, if you will excuse me, Don Iago . . .'

'Of course, Don Antonio, my apologies.'

Iago took himself to the windward side of the half-deck and began a leisurely pacing. The loss of so important and rare an item as an anchor so early in the voyage was a blow but, anchor or not, they could afford little in the way of delay. The season, late already, was now pressing. Preoccupied with these considerations and distracted periodically by some interesting evolution being carried out aloft as the new sails were stretched along and then bent on the yards, Iago thought the ship herself had proved stout enough and a tribute to those responsible for her design and build. But, as every sea-officer knew, it was the crew who broke before the ship herself failed, unless they had the misfortune to run her on a reef. And even in such a case, it could be argued, the crew had failed first.

But he was not to be allowed the quiet of a speculative reverie for once again the door to the great cabin was opened and, instead of the ejection of a single priest, out came the entire clerisy aboard the *Santa Margarita* amid a torrent of darkly flapping habits. Something of the drama that had culminated in the great cabin could be judged from the stumbling friars, all of whom held their crucifixes as though recently confronted by the Devil himself. And perhaps they had been, for following what looked like a flock of wounded birds, came Guillestigui, the sunshine flashing upon the rings circling his gloved fingers as he gestured at Ocampo. His entire staff followed, flooding the half-deck with brilliant brocade, silks and the sparkle of side arms, for Pedro Ruiz de Olalde, Rodrigo de Peralta and Joanes de Calcagorta bore drawn swords and lunged in playful malice at the discomfited friars. At the rear of this almost frenzied eruption emerged an unhappy Lorenzo.

Ocampo was shouting in Latin while Guillestigui responded in his native Basque. Both Olivera and Iago stared at the spectacle and work ceased throughout the ship, men turning aft from the waist and staring down from aloft; even Llerena lowered his whistle to regard the proceedings on the half-deck. As the principals in this unseemly and unedifying row swore incomprehensibly at each other, others were on the move, and Iago felt himself shoved aside as a group of armed men led by Miguel de Alacanadre rushed up from the waist and, forming a crescent about the now quailing friars, flourished their long Toledo blades in defence of the clerics. They were supported by a resolute group of Spaniards, and some fifteen or sixteen Filipino and Negro servants. Later Iago learned that Alacanadre's party had consisted of Capitán Ayllon, three other minor officers and the combined forces of their serving men and attendants, most of whom he recognized as being his fellow denizens from under the half-deck.

This intrusion outnumbered the captain-general's party and robbed Guillestigui of the initiative, a fact which briefly silenced him and his party. From this reinforcement Ocampo drew sudden courage.

'Now thou see'st how God prevails, Don Juan!' railed the friar. 'Your greed in overloading this ship, named in all piety after the patron of virgins and placed under the protection of the Mother of Christ, is an act of blasphemy as much as a wilful endangering of us all, especially those bent upon God's work and purposed to serve Him in all contrition and humility. Many have warned you about this foolishness but you, in the pride of your conceit, have not listened. You are not fitted for this great enterprise—'

'How dare you, you meddling fool!' snarled Guillestigui, suddenly recovering, aware of the public threat to his authority upon his own deck. 'I am appointed by the governor, Viceroy of the King himself; you yourself yesterday publicly witnessed my standard blessed by the Archbishop of Manila. My authority is absolute over all things temporal and material.' He paused a moment to address the men under Alacanadre and Ayllon. 'And you, you damned fools, put up your weapons lest I hang every mother's son among you for treason against the King and mutiny against my person and authority!'

Treason and mutiny were grave charges. Both carried the penalty of death, the former the additional penalty of attainder. Iago noticed the wavering of the sword blades defending Mother Church, while those borne by Peralta, Olalde and Calcagorta stiffened like dogs' cocks. For a moment all seemed to hang in the balance until two more gentlemen pushed their way through the assembled servants and up the companion ladders from the waist.

'Excellency! Fray Geronimo! I beseech you both to order these blades put up!'

'Capitán Manuel, you would do well to keep out of this matter,' Guillestigui ordered, but Manuel was shouldered aside by his companion, Teniente Guzman.

'Don Juan,' this impetuous young man cried, drawing his sword, 'order your men to disarm, or by Heaven I myself . . .'

As Guzman seemed incapable of moderating his advance on the captain-general, Guillestigui drew his own sword and the two men confronted each other, their blades actually meeting with that dry menace as steel grated upon steel. Both parties drew closer.

'Have a care, you damned imp!' roared Guillestigui, almost beside himself with rage. 'You are only the governor's *nephew*,' he almost spat in the youth's face, 'not the governor himself!'

'Gentlemen, gentlemen . . .' Capitán Gonzalo Manuel tried again to temporize. 'This is a regrettable incident, but I beg you all do not let it cloud the voyage. See how God has saved us from disaster last night and brought us back to Cavite. From here we may make a new beginning to our enterprise. Come, Father Geronimo, take the path of the humility that you and your Order are sworn to . . .'

'God *warned* us yesterday of our wickedness,' Ocampo declaimed, unwilling to let an opportunity go, but then he lowered his voice. 'But you speak good sense, my son, and I only ask, nay in all humility I shall *beg*, Your Excellency, to disencumber the ship of your private trading goods which endanger her, and the women who accompany the crew, whose presence will defile and sicken the men, obstruct them in their duty and are an offence to Almighty God . . .'

'And to our Blessed Santa Margarita,' another added, lest Ocampo should fail in his duty through forgetfulness.

'Both shall remain.' Sure of himself, Guillestigui put up his sword.

'You encourage sin among your men, Don Juan!' Ocampo cried, his voice rising again, baulked by the tall, scarred Basque warrior.

'You, Fray Geronimo, you are consumed by pride! You practice mutiny, you encourage disobedience and you challenge the authority of the King himself! Hell and the Holy Office wait for you.'

'Whilst thou challenge God?' Ocampo cried, staring about him as if a thunderbolt should fall to add emphasis to his assertion. None appeared, though men in the waist crossed themselves and the women drawn on deck by the fracas quailed and drew away into the shadows. It was all Ocampo could take comfort from. 'See how the pious – whose souls you would maliciously imperil with your impiety – fear for their spiritual lives.'

'Enough!' roared Guillestigui. 'You have said enough and shall betake yourself and those who follow you ashore.'

'You have no right to dismiss me, Don Juan, and arrogate to your person far more authority than it is right to do.'

'Then take your poxed case to the governor and take Pedro de Guzman, Capitán Ayllon and their motley following with you! They may stand as your witnesses in whatever court you choose. You may arraign me in my absence but you shall not stand upon my deck one instant more! Go! At once! Now!' And with that Guillestigui put up his sword, spun on his heel and, followed by Peralta, Olalde and Calcagorta, retired into the great cabin, whose door was slammed behind them.

Watching, Iago saw Lorenzo hesitate, then follow declaring himself loyal to the captain-general.

The silence after this abrupt departure was broken by a sudden cry from Ocampo who fell on his knees, hands upstretched towards Heaven holding his crucifix up before him.

His face was contorted with some inner fury that one might have marked as a burning hatred or a zeal for his faith. The intensity of his emotion caused spittle to flicker from his lips in the bright sunshine as he enunciated in a loud and clear voice: 'In the name of God the Father, God the Son and God the Holy Spirit I excommunicate thee, Don Juan Martinez Guillestigui, captain-general of this *flota* embodied here in the ship *Santa Margarita*, and I call upon Santa Margarita, after whose holy martyrdom this ship was piously named, to intercede with Almighty God and spare the souls of those who remain faithful to the teachings of Christ.' He paused before declaiming with a sonorous and chilling gravity: 'But upon the rest I call down God's wrath, that all those who indulge in concubinage, impious practices and thoughtless acts, and imperil the bodies of those entrusted unto them, be cursed now and for all eternity. In the name of the Father, Son and Holy Ghost!'

And such were the power of Ocampo's words and the sincerity of his delivery that the amen which rose from the ship seemed torn from the lips of everyone who heard them. So strong was this response that there were, long afterwards, those who thought they had connived at their own cursing.

The prolonged altercation upon the *Santa Margarita*'s half-deck had attracted the attention of every man and woman on board. But the endurance of its power, at least in the short term, varied from person to person. While Ocampo's curse had struck fear into the hearts of many, planting within them an enduring sense of terror, some had laughed it off. The majority of these were mostly experienced seamen to whom the fulminations of priests, friars and monks were an awkward irrelevance in their harsh lives. Whatever accommodation they had come to regarding the nature of their maker, any sacerdotal presence aboard ship always seemed to bring bad luck and that alone disqualified the clerisy from any serious consideration in the minds of these rude but practical men.

This was true also of the common women on board, most of who were, at least in the eyes of their Spanish overlords, mere 'Indians' and Indian whores at that. Their interest more closely conformed to the preoccupation of survival in this world, rather than any preparation for the next, despite their nominal baptism into the Catholic Church. Moreover, their survival was entirely dependent upon the seamen who had taken them up and befriended them, while many of them perceived their new religion to be a thing that had men in mind. Women, it seemed, played little part in the life of either the Church itself or the life of Jesus Christ. It was not like the spirits they had worshipped in their villages before the tall, bearded ones came among them with their stinks and their darkness.

And while there were some among the Spanish gentlemen who held sceptical opinions, most regarded the pronouncement of Fray Ocampo as self-serving, the railings of a disappointed man, the vicious revenge of a privileged and empowered priest. But the notion that the *Santa Margarita* was overloaded had stuck; the matter was, in fact, indisputable and there was not a man among them, including those most closely associated with the captain-general, that did not know the extent of his venality. It did not help to know that to that of the captain-general they had coupled their own. As a consequence the *Santa Margarita* bore more private cargo than belonged to her senior commander, almost all of it the property of his Basque *cortejo*, or entourage.

Perhaps this unfortunate fact bore upon those responsible for the management of the great ship, deflecting any reflection into a chivvying and a hastening for the *Santa Margarita* to resume her voyage without further delay. Perhaps the spell of Ocampo's curse was in part broken by the reappearance of Lorenzo, who signalled the approach of the barge belonging to the captain of the port. Perhaps too the friar's departure, hastened by the news that Don Felipe brought Fray Ocampo, diverted their minds from the morning's drama.

Lorenzo's face bore the expression of a man upon a mission that he wished he did not have, for he summoned Ayllon and charged him with removing himself, his six under-officers and their sixteen black and Filipino servants, along with Fray Ocampo and his party. He was followed by Olalde, who added the demand that Pedro de Guzman must also leave. In the stir that this caused, Llerena sent the ship's company about their business, which was taking the ropes of Don Felipe's barge, while Olivera advised Iago that he, as the most influential of the passengers, should shepherd the idlers below. Most, it transpired, had already made themselves scarce and Iago found

Arrocheros fussing over a weeping Doña Catalina, who deplored the cursing of the ship's company and the excommunications indiscriminately issued by the vindictive Ocampo.

It was Ximenez, intent upon some errand he had set himself, who brought word of Ocampo's sudden elevation, an elevation that, it was being said, proved the justice of his cause and the goodness of Almighty God.

'The news that Don Felipe brought, master,' he hissed into Iago's bent ear, 'is that he can obtain neither more seamen nor any anchor, but that he brings news that a message was lately sent from Manila to inform Fray Ocampo that a bishopric awaits him.'

'Then perhaps,' remarked Iago with a smile, 'that is why Providence returned us here.'

'They are saying that too, master.'

'Of course they are, Ximenez, of course they are.'

This conversation was broken into by the piercing note of Llerena's whistle summoning all hands to weigh anchor, the second best bower having been used upon their return to Cavite. Going up on deck, Iago found the scene transformed. Having given the order for the anchor to be weighed, Guillestigui was again on deck, standing at the break of the poop in half-armour of morion, cuirass and cuisses, surrounded by his henchmen. On the larboard side of the half-deck the last manifestations of the disembarkation of Ocampo and his party were in progress. Alacanadre and Capitán Manuel were making a plea on behalf of Teniente Guzman, who was asking for a certificate of discharge, detaching himself from direct implication in Ocampo's actions while Ocampo himself, sitting upon a box of his possessions, seemed torn between his providential release to assume the purple and his reluctance to be evicted by edict of the profane and blasphemous Guillestigui.

Ocampo was also surrounded by a group of friars who were to remain, among whom were the three Franciscans, Fray Mateo Marmolejo, Fray Hernando and Fray Agustin. Iago could hear the intense debate, for it was clear Ocampo could not in all conscience leave the spiritual needs of the *Santa Margarita*'s people uncatered for, yet his very curse seemed to doom the faithful who remained to minister to the ship's company. Safe himself, Ocampo sought to appeal to Marmolejo and his fellows, reminding them that if God ordained that the *Santa Margarita* should perish they would be immolated through martyrdom. This was clearly failing to recruit much enthusiasm and only succeeded in attracting Guillestigui's contemptuous dismissal of Ocampo.

'Get you hence, Ocampo, holy martyrs are directed to Christ by God and their consciences, not by your distant abjurations.'

'Damn you, Don Juan!'

'Give these men,' the tall and immobile figure on the poop thundered, 'comfort with thy blessing or prove a false priest!'

The remark was met by an immediate and acquiescent kneeling of Marmolejo and his colleagues and Ocampo knew that he had been cunningly cornered.

'May it please Almighty God that a ship so loaded with evil things and great sins make her voyage according to Thy mighty will!'

And with a smile of triumph at the ambiguity inherent in Ocampo's benediction, Guillestigui joined the fervent chorus: 'Amen!'

This had hardly subsided, however, before the captain-general was insisting that Ocampo leave the *Santa Margarita* immediately. Pointing to Ocampo's private effects of a chest and bed-bundle he said, 'That is one less encumbrance. Now, before I have that chest full of idolatrous claptrap thrown overboard, get down into Don Felipe's barge.'

As Ocampo, mustering all the dignity at his command, rose and threw the frock of his habit over the rail, Iago smothered a smile, for Guillestigui, if not the apostate Olivera thought him, spoke like a Protestant. With one final glare at the captain-general, the wretched priest had gone. Followed by his adherents and watched by the Franciscans left aboard the *não*, Ocampo was pulled away in the boat which flew the standard of Don Felipe Corço.

'That is one less cuckoo in the nest.'

Iago looked round and found Ximenez at his side. 'Aye, but we remain overloaded.'

'How stands the wind?' Guillestigui's voice, invested with new authority, boomed out over the ship.

'Fair, Excellency, from the south-eastward, and we are hove short.'

'Then let us break out the anchor and make sail!'

An hour later, to the boom of a pair of sakers, the *Santa Margarita* stood out clear of Cavite and once again headed again for the island of Corregidor followed by the admiral's ship, the obedient *San Geronimo*.

Although, as a *sobrasaliente*, Don Iago might claim some sort of right to dine at Guillestigui's table, he was not one to insist upon it and that evening the captain-general did not renew the invitation so abruptly curtailed the day before. Iago wondered how Alacanadre, having been among those who had defended Ocampo with a drawn sword, would be regarded by the captain-general. Perhaps even then Guillestigui was consulting his henchmen, or upbraiding the master-of-camp. In one respect Iago remained detached from his Spanish colleagues, despite his formative years having been spent in their midst: he was less impetuous and cooler in his thinking. He would have been more circumspect before drawing a sword, for the act was – for the disguised Jacob van Salingen – an act of irrevocable intent. That Alacanadre had drawn his blade against his commander would be set aside even by Guillestigui, he realized after some reflection, by the fact that it had been in defence of a priest.

The sun set two hours after leaving Cavite, but it was a fine night and it seemed as though the removal of Ocampo, far from inviting God's wrath upon the ship and her company, had instead called forth His blessing. The denizens of the half-deck messed together in what, in a less encumbered vessel, would have been a tolerably clear space in the centre of the tween-deck in which they had erected their makeshift accommodation. Nevertheless they, or more accurately their servants, had drawn together the most substantial chests and made a table round which bales formed a species of seats. Here sat Iago, Don and Doña Arrocheros, a number of the minor officers and soldiers, among them Don Gonzalo Ordóñez and Capitán Gonzalo Manuel. At Don Baldivieso de Arrocheros' insistence the remaining Franciscans were invited to join them, and Iago sat between Ordóñez and his earlier acquaintance, Fray Mateo Marmolejo who introduced him to the others of his Order: Fray Hernando, Fray Agustin (said to have been chaplain to the Bishop of Manila), the bishop's nephew and his cousin.

Arrocheros, who had assumed the dignity of mess president, perhaps because he alone could bring a pretty, if gravid, woman to the extemporized table, had his servants produce wine. Thus fortified all indulged in a forced heartiness that was a product of the events of the previous thirty or so hours.

Nevertheless beneath the swinging oil lamps which threw shadows across the table as the ship worked in the gentle seaway, the meal of roast capon and rice was not without its conviviality, or its revelations. At first no one wished to refer to the departure of Ocampo, but the wine loosened tongues and Arrocheros, a wealthy man who brooked little in the way of interference from others, grew outspoken.

'Perhaps the Reverend Father was correct in this matter of overloading. Certainly our recent experience persuaded me that the ship seemed difficult to handle when in a strong wind. You, Don Iago, would not have gone aloft with such alacrity unless you too entertained some such apprehension. Is that not so?'

Iago felt the attention of the diners focus upon himself. 'The men are inexperienced,' he temporized, 'not used to working a new ship together. It is not unusual . . .'

'But you told me that you thought the ship overloaded and unstable,' pressed Marmolejo.

'That is true,' Iago admitted, 'but I have no desire to cause further anxiety to Doña Catalina,' he added, grasping at a straw. 'Besides, it would be proper to say that her stability is diminished by overloading, not that she is in imminent danger of capsize.'

'But the conditions to induce it are possible?' asked Arrocheros.

'Well . . . yes, that too is true to some extent.'

'I have no desire to sail in an endangered ship, Don Iago,' put in Doña Catalina, her face full of alarm.

'Perhaps then, señora, you should ask your husband to petition the captain-general.'

'He would not listen,' said Fray Hernando, speaking for the first time.

'Why, what manner of man is he?'

'A strong man,' Hernando said, though it was clear several around the table thought any discussion of the character of the captain-general was dangerous. 'A soldier who distinguished himself in the wars against the Indians in New Spain.'

'Gunpowder against arrows, Fray Hernando,' laughed Ordóñez, 'scarcely makes an Alava.'

'Have a care, Don Gonzalo,' advised Marmolejo, 'might is apt to be right, especially within the confines of our little wooden world.'

Ordóñez smiled to himself and then, turning to his neighbour, Iago, muttered, 'Guillestigui is stiff with ambition, which this commission will satisfy if it pays him what he calculates.'

'He seeks to rise high in this world?' Iago asked quietly as the conversation became general and each man turned to his left or right.

'Oh yes, and thinks little of the next. Greed and desire will ensnare him if his sins be discovered.' Ordóñez paused, then went on, 'But how often have you known the wicked perish and the virtuous triumph, eh? Not often, I'm thinking. Would that the priests were right sooner; unfortunately they promise judgement *after* death.'

'Perhaps that is the sublimest justice,' Iago said guardedly, regarding the confiding Ordóñez with some interest, 'and we should not expect that of man to be anything other than corrupt.'

Ordóñez, his face briefly and vividly illuminated by the lanterns, was wrapped in a cynical smile. In the following shadow the grimace stayed in Iago's mind's eye. He responded with casual elegance. 'The world is more corrupted by those who mistake their good fortune for the reward of virtue, Don Iago. Therein lies the true dilemma of mankind.'

In the night that followed, as Iago tossed uncomfortably upon his bedding, he was haunted by Ordóñez's words. Whether or not the world's apparently random inequities constituted humanity's 'true dilemma' seemed indeterminable; that mankind tolerated the manifold abuses that so often contributed to such inequities seemed a more pressing matter.

And this consideration had a bearing upon the material state of the *Santa Margarita*, for she was sluggish in her rolling and, as she cleared Manila Bay and turned south in the light of the dawn, Iago fell into a fitful sleep, dreaming not about the rape of Zierikzee, but of the safety of the great ship.

Five

The Embocadero

In the days that followed there were those among the three hundred souls on board the *Santa Margarita* who jeered at Ocampo's curse. Chief among these was the captain-general, whose Basque following increasingly dominated the ship, and although opinion was divided among the many passengers – and in the case of Don Baldivieso and his wife between spouses – the ship's company largely manifested the indifference of sailors when the weather favoured their ship's passage. Besides, dismissing all thoughts of Ocampo made the resumption of their wicked 'concubinage' easier.

Feelings were otherwise among the priests and the nuns who began to emerge from their prayerful hiding to take the sunlit air. Led by Marmolejo, Hernando and Agustin, and supported by several of the passengers bound to the Church by devotion, they continued to see the conduct of Guillestigui and his officers as the posturings of the vain; a manifestation of secular conceits against which they must maintain a bulwark of prayer. For them the need to plead their cause before God and to invoke Ocampo's dispensation for the success of the voyage was paramount, notwithstanding the fate of Guillestigui himself.

And while the sailors began to enjoy the passage through the islands, pleased that the removal of Ocampo seemed to have improved their prospects, the passengers were increasingly aware of the vast distance they had committed themselves to travelling. Although all of them, except the young born in the Philippines, had come west by sea from New Spain, time had eroded the memory of their earlier voyage. The passage ahead of them had been put out of mind

by the fussy preoccupations of departure, but now many of
the passengers found that even the coasting voyage along the
southern littoral of Luzon to reach the narrows of the
Embocadero seemed an endless and tedious traverse.

The winds were frequently fitful and occasionally contrary;
sometimes the *Santa Margarita* beat back and forth a whole
day in sight of the same prominent feature, a peak like the
Loro de Pico, a hillside, a headland; or they lay becalmed off
a village watching the smoke from its cooking fires rise in a
steady and frustrating column. While the religious, now openly
guyed as 'the Holy Ones', worried about their slow progress,
the seamen – though often called to raise tacks and sheets
and man the braces as the *Santa Margarita* and the *San Geronimo*
beat wearily to the eastward – nevertheless enjoyed what for
them was an easy labour. And while Guillestigui, his staff and
the military officers wined and dined, consuming the fresh
produce with a hearty abandon, Lorenzo and the wiry Olivera
worried as only true sea-officers knew how.

Most of the time the two great ships made fair progress
and the majority on board, pressed closely within the irksome
confines of the ship, spent those first days under way adjusting
to their new life. With the exception of the extreme camps
of the captain-general's exalted cronies and the Holy Ones,
which were each of their nature exclusive, the growth of
factions was subtle and imperceptible. The preoccupations of
daily life, with its myriad demands, inconveniences and down-
right irritations, along with the smooth running of the ship
as she made her steady passage, produced no obvious need
for men and women to take sides. The Holy Ones were an
isolated minority, to be laughed at in the sunny, windless days,
the captain-general's staff no different from Spanish colonial
nobility throughout Rey Felipe's immense imperial dominions. Characteristically, each group kept itself to itself and,
apart from an evening promenade that took the place of the
customary *paseo* ashore, they did not interfere in the management of the ship, leaving such tedious labours to the pilots
and their under-officers.

There was, however, plenty to squabble over in so overcrowded and mismatched a population. During daylight hours
the ship buzzed with the noise of men and women, many

with insufficient to occupy them fully, deprived of sundry necessaries and bound to conform to the rigid disciplines and routines of the ship. These people found the only outlet for their petty frustrations to be a voluble explosion of their woes, real and imagined. The physical fights that sometimes broke out were quickly put down by Llerena and his under-lings, though occasionally, if the altercation involved two of the seamen's women, the pair would be allowed to claw at each other until intervention came from the officers or blood had been drawn. Such dispensations were within Llerena's gift and had a lancing effect on the more ugly moods that developed between decks.

While these arguments flared into spats and rows, there were those few people whose sense of humour or sheer good-natured commonsense soon mollified wounded pride, or settled some silly dispute over who put what where or whose turn it was to assume some duty they shared out in common. In this social confusion, Iago's small household proved itself a model and he himself, along with Don Gonzalo Ordóñez, and Fray Marmolejo of the Holy Ones, became the arbiters of petty squabbles between decks, assuming a magisterial role.

Iago himself was enchanted with the beauty of the passing coastline: green and rolling jungle covered the islets and islands between which the deep blue of a hundred straits opened up invitingly. He was charmed too by the changing light, the nacreous early morning mists which lingered in the narrow valleys, the cool rosy dawns, the brilliance of noon and the blazing sunsets. His seaman's instinct led him to maintain a rigid personal routine, in emulation of the ship's, thus main-taining a diurnal rhythm which minimized all but the most intrusive irritations of his fellow passengers. He took to walking daily in the waist with Ximenez and Ah Fong, initially so that he could enjoy the company of the latter without drawing undue suspicion as to her true status. In this charade the girl and the dwarf masqueraded as equals and he must needs keep both close company; Ximenez proved a witty and agreeable companion while both he and Ah Fong seemed to have struck up a friendship that conversed in a mixture of Spanish, Cantonese and the Portuguese-based pidgin of the

Pearl River. Ah Fong he already knew for a clever woman; now Ximenez demonstrated his own intelligence.

In the seclusion of their private area, secured from prying eyes by the coconut matting and canvas that passed for bulk-heads in that crowded space, quiet conversations were possible, but Iago was scrupulous in maintaining the fiction of Ah Fong's sex and the girl, her small breasts tightly bound, skil-fully dissembled by the judicious use of a bucket. She was also clever in her abuse of the basic cosmetics available to her, her skin losing its soft, feminine glow under applications of soot, while lamp-black rubbed into her hands gave her an appearance identical to the ship's own boys.

The example of his master and the Chinese girl led Ximenez into an easy and pleasant routine. In his less busy moments he blessed his good fortune in stumbling upon the stranger who had come ashore at Cavite only a few weeks earlier. Optimism rode high in the dwarf's heart, for Don Iago treated him like a man, and others aboard, in awe of his taciturn master, adopted a pretence of doing the same. Ximenez knew they were playing him false, but he was content in their acqui-escence. Besides, Ximenez also knew that Don Iago was not what he pretended to be. The secret bound the dwarf to his master closer than the latter ever knew.

Despite these careful arrangements, however, Iago and his two faithful companions were not unaffected by the diffi-culties set before them by the conduct of the captain-general. Once the *Santa Margarita* had cleared the great bight of Manila Bay and stood south and then south-eastwards through the Verde Island Passage, Guillestigui and his senior officers, who had hitherto exercised upon the long poop, had taken to the half-deck and appropriated it for their own use. Here they paced up and down of an evening before dining, the handful of women in their company brought out from the recesses of the aftercastle in out-moded finery to figure the traditional *paseo*. While Guillestigui and his coterie tolerated the occasional use of the half-deck by others, allowing the pregnant Doña Catalina to promenade there with her husband, there was a growing antipathy to anyone else making free of the deck. Iago was himself one of the exceptions.

Thus two-thirds of the *Santa Margarita's* upper deck, cluttered though it was with the officers' private cargo, was effectively banned to some two hundred and sixty people, unless they appeared there for some nautical purpose. This mass of mixed humanity was obliged to make the best of the waist, equally encumbered with cases and bales, not to mention the cages of the fowls and several lactating nanny-goats. Even this limited space was denied them when the ship was manoeuvring, going about at the end of each tack as she closed with the land. Thus the passengers were, for the most part, confined in the inadequate space below decks, a harsh repression to people used to free and daily movement. It took a week or two for the true inconvenience to impinge upon the consciousness of most, who were just recovering from seasickness, and a day or so more for it to assume the status of an injustice, but its enervating effects were inexorable, subtly driving people into a sullen resentment towards the captain-general and his indolent party.

There had been a half-hearted attempt to strike some of the baggage and extra cargo below and it had met with a little success, enough to convince Guillestigui that further animadversion against the overloading and potential instability of the vessel was unjustified. The nature of the *Santa Margarita's* precious lading came as no surprise to Iago, whose time on the Chinese coast had taught him a great deal about the exports made to the Spanish Philippines in exchange for silver – great heaps of silver – from the mines of Zacatecas and Potosí on the far side of the great ocean. Deep in the *Santa Margarita's* hold were cases upon cases of porcelain, lacquerware, jade and ivory carvings, many fashioned according to the demand into images of Christian saints. These curious artefacts would persuade the papacy that perhaps a form of Christianity existed in distant Cathay. Forced in above the stow of the heavy cases containing these products were bales and bales of precious silks, double-wrapped in matting, compressed to fill the space to its uttermost capacity, some even occupying that properly reserved for the consumable stores, such as rice, salted meat and dried pulses. Nor was China the only source of their cargo. Camphor and gemstones came from Borneo; more jewels – chiefly rubies and sapphires – were brought from Siam, together with musk, ebony and elephant ivory. And the ship also bore spices, carried to the Philippines from the Moluccas. Cinnamon and cloves, but chiefly nutmegs in burlap sacks, gave off their subtle aroma and, in sweetening the ship, made tolerable what would otherwise have been a stinking environment for the *Santa Margarita*'s company. All in all it amounted to an immensity of treasure: a Viceroy's dream some called it and, for a man of Guillestigui's stamp, it almost surpassed the most extravagant desire. But, Iago reflected sombrely, a man in the throes of desire is incapable of rational thinking.

It was this realization that displaced Iago's initial astonishment that the anxieties over the *Santa Margarita*'s instability and overloading provoked by the frightening circumstances of their first departure from Cavite had been so easily mollified. It seemed that a mere tidying up of the upper deck once the ship had cleared Manila Bay was sufficient to allay all anxieties, except it seemed those of himself. When one evening he was on the poop watching the *Santa Margarita* settle on her new course after tacking at the head of Tayabas Bay, he again raised the issue with Lorenzo. The pilot-major dismissed it with evident embarrassment.

'The matter no longer concerns me,' he said with a resigned and even fatalistic air, adding, 'and I advise you to forget it yourself. They have.' Lorenzo gestured expansively at a knot of gentry gathered on the half-deck below with their wine glasses and their trollops, but including the gaggle of passengers and crew who crowded in the lower waist and on the forecastle beyond. Lorenzo turned away and Iago raised a wondering eyebrow: he had never before received such curt dismissal from the pilot-major. After a moment, as the ship steadied on to her new course, Lorenzo uttered a few remarks to Olivera then went below. The second pilot caught Iago's eye and, with an imperceptible jerk of his head, walked aft a little, up the long shallow sloping deck to the stern.

'Do not press the matter further, Don Iago,' Olivera said in a guarded tone. 'It is past all redemption now and no one is minded to alter things; they shall stand as they are. There is too much interest vested in our lading, not simply that of the captain-general, but of all your companions under the half-deck.'

'But many of them have been vociferous in their protest.'

'Indeed. While they feared for their lives. Every man would have every other man's goods thrown overboard only so that his own might be saved.' Olivera paused to let the explanation sink in.

'They *all* own cargo?'

'Without exception.'

'I had no idea.'

'You are, if I may say so, Don Iago, an innocent in these matters. Did the Portuguese, whose practices you were employed to observe, not trade in the same way?'

Iago shrugged. 'Perhaps. They were not spared that I should observe their homeward practices. The *Rainha de Portugal* was lost before she reached Macao.'

'It would astonish me if they did not each trade on their own account. D'you see here, in this ship, we have sinned not by exception, but by common greed. The King has decreed that the numbers of galleons trading east from Manila be limited in order that his subjects do not become enriched beyond reason and, of course, their station in life. Prior to your arrival in Cavite, this newly built vessel had her hold measured and divided into so many bales capacity on a standard measurement of a *fardo*. A *fardo* consists of four *piezas* and these are granted as a favour either by the captain-general or the governor – often as remittance to discharge debts or favours to purchase credit – but the remainder may be bought by any citizen of Manila. See Arrocheros there; he has upwards of two thousand *boletas*, or tickets, each entitling him to a *pieza* giving him rights to a considerable portion of the hold. Most, I do not doubt, he has sold on at a profit already, preferring to carry his wealth by letter of credit rather than risk destruction of goods by bilge water, salt and vermin. You have noticed the *gorgojos* that run out of the bread though we are not yet a week at sea?'

Iago laughed at the recollection of the ubiquitous cockroaches. 'Yes, but they are to be found in any ship.'

'Huh,' responded Olivera, 'soon you will have flies, worms, maggots . . .'

'I am not so innocent, Don Olivera, that I have not consumed my portion of a seaman's fare in my time.'

'Well, well, perhaps I misjudge you. If so, forgive me, but that is not the point. The rats devour the silks if they break through the baling, so Don Baldivieso is no fool to sell his *boletas* rather than trade entirely in vulnerable commodities.'

'But there must be some regulation to restrict the rule of human cupidity.'

It was Olivera's turn to laugh with a scoffing exclamation. 'Huh! Oh, indeed! Such regulation as does breed a labyrinthine entwining of interest, preferment and corrupt abuse. Do you not realize, Don Iago, that one attraction of yourself is that you paid to make this voyage and you had no lien on cargo space. Instead, my dear sir, your space was taken by Don Juan Martinez himself and only yesterday I heard him jesting with Olalde that *if we should be so unfortunate* – as if the matter might be an exception and not a rule attaching to any voyage across the Ocean Sea – *to need to jettison cargo, then we might throw all of Don Iago's over the side without loss to our person.* That is exactly what he said, though if you admit that I told you so,' he added drily, 'I shall deny it unto death.'

'Then every gentleman aboard has a right to space?' Iago asked.

'It is worse than that, señor, every man, be he officer, *sobrasaliente*, cleric or discalced friar, has a licensed space. Even the seamen work to secure some small advantage. What chance does regulation stand against such an abundance of folly, I ask you?'

'And you, señor?'

Olivera laughed again. 'Oh, I have an entitlement to space, Don Iago, but like Don Baldivieso, I convert my *boletas* immediately. It is more convenient and,' he added tapping his stomach, 'a letter of credit may be carried in oiled paper against my body until it may be presented in Acapulco or,' and a wistful look came into his eyes, 'perhaps even Seville.'

'Ah yes,' sighed Iago with a sudden warm sentimentality that surprised himself, 'Seville.'

'You know the Casa de Contratación?'

'Oh, certainly.'

'I have never seen it,' Olivera admitted wistfully.

'But you . . .'

'I was born in New Spain, Don Iago, my blood is not pure.'

'No less than most in the King's archipelago, señor, it is not a matter which much impresses me, this obsession with pure Spanish blood.'

'Perhaps that is because you have no need of it, Don Iago.'

'What do you mean?' Iago asked sharply.

'I had heard of a man, a man of some standing, who had arrived from the China coast in a junk. It was said by some – in the manner of waterfront gossip, you understand, Don Iago – that he was not as devoted a Catholic as he should be, that perhaps he had been corrupted by the Chinese idolaters and that he lay with a woman of that country, perhaps even that he was not a Spaniard, but a spy.'

'A spy? Who in God's name for?' Iago felt his face flush and his heart thunder in his breast.

Olivera shrugged. 'The damned English or the ingrate Dutch. Who knows?'

'So,' Iago said as coolly as he could but with mounting passion, 'if that was the sum of waterfront gossip it was well informed, as far as it went. Did it tell you that as a child I played along the banks of the Guadalquivír; that I ran errands for the Casa de Contratación itself? Or that I was known as a boy to most of the ship-masters and seamen of Seville and that I have been chastised, as have all boys, for my inattentions at the Mass? So much for my inconstant faith. As to my lying with a Chinese woman, what would you have me do, Don Olivera, when all my future seemed for a time to be bounded by hedges of bamboo? Take up the practice of Onan and imperil my immortal soul?'

'Then all our souls are forfeit,' Olivera joked. 'But I am not your judge, Don Iago,' he added quickly, seeking to mollify this uncharacteristic outburst. 'On the contrary,' he lowered his voice, 'if I am not mistaken, señor, there may come a time on this voyage – as on any other – when men of understanding and skill may be needed. If we stand apart . . .' Olivera stared directly into Iago's eyes and shrugged his shoulders, 'who knows God's will?'

Angry with himself, Iago was aware that two or three military officers were ascending the poop ladder. An attachment to Olivera seemed both invited and essential and he smiled conciliatingly. 'Not I, señor, but I am persuaded,' he responded swiftly in a low voice, 'that our resolution is often the answer to our prayers.'

'Amen to that,' Olivera muttered with a nod and, turning towards the approaching officers, added, 'and the Devil wears a doublet.' Then raising his voice he said, 'Good evening, Don Rodrigo.'

'What mutiny are you two plotting?' Rodrigo de Peralta asked with a smile.

'Oh,' Olivera replied with a wide grin, 'the usual sort: the murder of the gentry and the taking of the ship to a tropical paradise in which grapes and coconut palms grow in profusion and which is inhabited entirely by concupiscent women.'

'Well, then, I think I shall join your conspiracy,' laughed Peralta light-heartedly. 'But first I come to present the captain-general's compliments and to ask Don Iago to join him at table.' Peralta managed a curt bow to Iago, adding, 'Don Juan apologizes that the matter has been too long delayed.'

Iago bowed in response. 'If the captain-general will allow me a moment to dress my hair and don a doublet, I shall be at His Excellency's command.'

Peralta made a courtly gesture of acquiescence, Iago nodded to Olivera and went forward. Peralta turned and stared aft. The sunset flared scarlet and gold across the western sky, throwing the land into purple shadow.

'The colours of our standard,' he said pointedly. 'Perhaps an omen on our enterprise.' His tone was familiar, inviting confidence. 'What do you make of our friend Don Iago, señor?' he asked after a moment, without looking at Olivera but still staring at the flaming sunset.

Olivera was not fooled. 'A good seaman, Don Rodrigo, and should we need another, a fine sea-officer.'

'And that is all?' Peralta turned and stared directly at Olivera.

Olivera met his gaze. 'That is all I can divine in the man, Don Rodrigo.'

'Hmmm.'

'Do you entertain doubts?' Olivera asked, seizing the initiative.

'Don't you?'

'No. Why should I?'

'I think he is a Portuguese spy.'

'He comes from Seville; and besides, Portugal is now part of His Majesty's dominions . . .'

'That is not quite the point,' Peralta said and, without further explanation, walked forward and descended to the half-deck. Olivera watched him go, then turned west himself and, staring at the sinking sun, crossed himself.

Afterwards Iago was apt to regard the unnerving encounter with Olivera as a blessing, putting him on his guard during the dinner with Guillestigui and his suite. The captain-general asked him some questions as to his background and then the conversation became general. Guillestigui's women sat beside him, and the mistresses of other officers sat at table while the Filipino slaves waited upon them all. Behind his own chair the captain-general kept a large black slave. The man stood motionless throughout the meal. After the women had withdrawn and the gentlemen sat back with their wine, smoking the cigars for which Manila was renowned, Guillestigui commanded Iago: 'Tell us about your shipwreck, Don Iago, and your life among the Chinese.'

'Your Excellency's interest is flattering, but there is little of substance to tell. Chiefly I recall the loneliness . . .'

'They say you took a Chinese wife. Is it true what they say of them?' Olalde remarked, provoking a ripple of salacious laughter.

'It is true that I had a Chinese woman,' Iago riposted, turning to Olalde, 'much as I imagine you lie with a Filipino when the need takes you. As to their anatomy, it is true that many among them have bound, tiny and stinking feet. I did not find that feature attractive, though I believe many Chinese men are aroused by the scent. Such things are incomprehensible to us, but there is much that separates us from the Orientals. As to the rest of their parts, I found them much as most women are fashioned; that is with mouths that alternate sugar and fire. Perhaps that is why the dragon is so revered in China.'

An appreciative snigger ran round the table.

'And the shipwreck?' Guillestigui prompted, apparently satisfied on one score.

Iago shrugged. 'The shipwreck is less easy to jest about,' he said, staring about at them all. 'In short, Your Excellency, it was terrible. We were assailed by a *baguiosa*, or what the Chinese denominate a *taifun*, and, as far as I can divine, no different in violence from the *huracán* I have heard of in the Caribbean. Our vessel, a stoutly built ship of eight hundred tons burthen, might have withstood the onslaught had she been kept to the open sea but at the height of the storm we were cast upon a reef the presence of which we were entirely unaware and over which the seas broke with such extreme and horrifying destructive power that the *Rainha de Portugal* was dashed to pieces within an hour.'

He paused. The memory seemed to overwhelm him and he became the cynosure of their regard as each man conjured up the scene in his own mind's eye.

'Go on, Don Iago,' Guillestigui said encouragingly.

Iago coughed and resumed his account. 'The chaos was indescribable; the rending of the ship's fabric, its fracturing and splitting, the collapse of stout masts, of festoons of rigging, the wind in the sails as they beat themselves to pieces on the deck, the noise, confusion and bloody injury that engulfed us all in a mere matter of minutes defy the powers of speech that I command. All shred of order and discipline vanished in an instant – yet equally there was not one person who flinched, no manifestation of cowardice, for in truth there was no time to think. The most pusillanimous amongst us could have sought no advantage; no man could even save himself, for we were flung like unwanted dolls into a toy box at the whim of the wind and sea. Never, gentlemen, do I wish to see the like again, for the weight of the water that fell upon our decks was like the descent of mountains . . . of rock . . . unmitigated by any . . . any pliant liquid form . . . we were either battered, or swept to our deaths by the score and for those who avoided this onslaught there were the horrors of being trapped below and drowned as in a locked cage.'

Iago paused again. Then someone asked: 'How then did you survive?'

Iago shrugged. 'How so indeed? I was one of perhaps half

a dozen whose station upon the upper deck brought them a few moments of comprehension, though that was scant comfort. On the first waves breaking over the ship, I was forced down upon the deck, flat as any rabbit run over by a cart-wheel, and kept there until I thought that my breast should burst. A moment later I felt the shattered ship rise, then, as it plummeted against the reef in a final jar that destroyed the body of her hull, another wave, a lesser sea than that which went before, carried me straight over the side, through the shattered bulwark. I was sensible of others caught likewise and thought myself doubly unfortunate in that I was in expect-ation of being stove bodily against the rocks on to which our ship had unwittingly driven. Indeed, I saw them rear on either side of me as the sea sank all about me before it was again elevated with a rush that must have borne me clear and into the open sea beyond the reef. That is the only explanation I can deduce – for no other will serve – and remarkably I bore only a few cuts and bruises to mark my singular escape.

'Once I had been thrown or drifted clear I found another man, so bloodied all over that I did not recognize him though I thought that after six months I knew all on board. He called to me that there was something adrift and he pointed so that I caught sight of it and, being a good swimmer and having found such of my wits that I was in those circum-stances likely to recover, I swam towards it. It proved to be a large and substantial grating from the waist. It was hardly damaged and I dragged myself on to it, but when I looked about me, my companion and the saviour of my life had vanished.

'My reaching the grating was but only the beginning, for I was washed so repeatedly off it by the violence of the seas that I thought that I should yet drown until I had the wit to secure my belt to the cross-members. This task, by no means easy to execute, though it seems so here and now, was accomplished after some time and I learned that I had there-after to lie upon the grating otherwise it seemed minded to capsize and drown me underneath where I had secured myself. I do not know how long I struggled but in time I divined the seas ran more regularly and, though they still broke and tossed me about, my platform was steadier. Some other wreckage afforded me a length of rope and, by nightfall, I was at least secure upon my fragile perch.

'I now had hours of darkness to face and a raging thirst.' Iago paused and looked about him. 'I do not know if you have experienced thirst, gentlemen, but I thought that I should rather have drowned.' Then he fell silent, the reminiscence heavy upon his soul, while one or two, including the captain-general, admitted to having experienced the horrors of extreme dehydration.

'But you did not drown . . .' Someone, their curiosity greater than their tact, prodded him again.

Iago stirred, sipped his wine and looked about him as though just arriving in their presence. 'No . . . No, I did not drown . . .' He paused again, adjusted himself in his seat as though gathering up the threads of his story, and cleared his throat. 'No, I was lucky, alone of all that company, almost one hundred and eighty souls who had been gathered to God within a few minutes, I survived.' Iago fell silent again.

'But how?'

'Be quiet,' commanded the captain-general, his deep-set dark eyes glittering in the light of the candles. Iago looked at him and smiled.

'I think I remained upon my grating for only one night, for I recall only seeing one sunset, but a man cannot be certain of such things and the days I spent in China were without reckoning and blur my memory. As to rescue, gentlemen, it came quickly, unexpectedly, and was drawn to the wreck, or downwind of it in the aftermath of the storm, picking up what an impoverished people may find useful. I was included and found myself aboard a large fishing junk which might have been a pirate, for it mounted four dragon-guns. I was given water and then tied up as a devil, I afterwards learned when I had mastered a little of the language. The natives carried me with them through the tail of the storm and in due course they landed me somewhere west of the Pearl River, though exactly where I cannot be certain. There they released me and I was taken to their village headman who pronounced me harmless alone and made me work in the rice fields that lay upon the banks of a small river. Every night I was tied up and left to sleep with the chickens outside the house of the headman. He had a large family and several servant girls, one of which took pity on me and, in due course, took me to her bed – which in truth was more like a cattle byre but it was comfortable enough, dry and warm. The headman, who owned buffaloes and pigs as well as some rice paddies, did not seem to mind as I worked hard. I could see little alternative but to earn his good opinion, nothing could come of demanding anything more. The girl, though a poor and ignorant wench, nevertheless taught me the rudiments of their speech, though, due to the multitude of meanings attaching to the same form, my pronunciation was corrupt and often caused offence. Truly, it is an impenetrable language.

'However, word of my curious appearance – a daily beard, an odd smell and an overlarge nose – soon spread and I was more laughed at than spat upon or beaten. I became something between a pet animal and a favourite hound, and given status accordingly. This is a most important quality, greatly esteemed among the Chinese of that province.

'In due course I accompanied the headman, whose name was Cheng, to a small town called, I think, Sandy Headland. Here I was eventually sold to Cheng's younger brother, who by virtue of his greater wealth had acquired higher status and owned two or three fishing junks. I think that the older Cheng owed his brother money that he could never repay and by trading me the debt was waived while his condescension in relinquishing his possession of my person increased the older Cheng's status in his brother's eyes. They knew that I was a seaman and I was put back to sea, working for some two years aboard a large fishing junk. One day the younger Cheng sent for me and said that he wished to invest in a venture trading a quantity of silk that he knew of to sell to the foreign devils in their islands, meaning the Philippines. He had heard that much silver might be made there and asked if I knew of the place. He too sought to raise himself in society but could not join any established merchants on account of his lowly birth and sought an opportunity to aggrandize himself. Thus he saw me as a possible way of advancing his cause. I said that I knew of the islands and could find them for his vessels, a fact that appeared to fill him with so much delight that I too was raised to new status, received a new gown and was promoted to mate of Cheng's largest junk. Having stripped it of fishing gear, cleaned its stinking fish-hold and fitted it with some additional crude pieces of artillery, we loaded a quantity of silk and sailed to the Spanish islands, anchoring off a small village called, I think, Olongapo at the head of a bay . . . I was confined when we reached the shore, my task being considered over . . . But I see that I bore you.'

'No! No!' they all protested. 'Do go on, Don Iago.'

'Well, I shall cut a long story short. I do not think Cheng made much profit that voyage, not as much as he did afterwards when he permitted me to engage in the bargaining process. But on that first venture he had acquired more silver than he had ever seen in his life before. In due course, seeing that I was to be trusted, Cheng suggested that I marry one of his daughters and after a further year I struck a bargain with him, that, having established him as a merchant, I should buy my freedom from him and with that my right to do as I pleased. He did not, I think, guess that I meant to leave him, assuming that my marriage would tie him to Sandy Headland for the remainder of my life and that I should become his partner. Instead, gentlemen, I arrived in Cavite in one of Cheng's new junks and, if I demonstrated an unfamiliarity with the Mass and the ways of my countrymen, it was because I had become almost a Chinaman, such are the ways of Divine providence . . .' He looked at them and saw expressions of sympathy; they had taken his point. 'You know the rest.'

There was a long silence, then Olalde asked, 'And your wife?'

Iago shrugged. 'It was not a union blessed by the Church,' he said simply, and the young men about Guillestigui laughed as young men do about a woman cast aside. Amid the laughter the captain-general leaned forward.

'Tell me, Don Iago, that sword you bear. It is not Chinese, I think. How did you come by it?'

'It is from Cipangu, Excellency, where it is called a katana.'

Guillestigui nodded. 'Yes, I am aware of that. I am also aware that such weapons are not found in the possession of common men but belong to a race of warriors who dwell in those islands.'

'That is true and is how it came into my possession. It was acquired by my master, by what means I do not know, but it troubled him, perhaps because it was foreign, perhaps because he was unworthy of it, or perhaps because he considered it ill-omened, but he presented it to me as a mark of his particular favour.' Iago did not mention the weapon was a wedding gift and that Ah Fong's father had traded the wicked sword blade out of foolish and drunken bravado. 'They say,' he added, 'that the blades are ancient and that they are tried upon the bodies of three condemned felons whom they rope together for the purpose.'

'That seems indeed an ill-omened thing,' Alacanadre said, crossing himself. He was followed by some among the others, though neither Guillestigui nor Olalde were among them and merely grinned at each other.

''Tis assurance that the weapon is properly honed,' he remarked practically.

'I think you to be a man of *good* omen, Don Iago,' the captain-general observed, raising his glass, 'and I drink to your health.'

'You are most kind, Excellency.' Iago raised his own gleaming goblet and held it out for a servant to refill. He then raised it. 'May I, Excellency, wish success upon this your enterprise.'

And the evening ended with a series of convivial toasts.

Twelve days out from Cavite, the *Santa Margarita* approached the Samar Sea prior to entering the San Bernadino Strait. As she and the *San Geronimo* prepared to alter course and make for the Embocadero, the lookout hailed that sails were in sight. Half an hour later they could see from the upper deck two ships approaching on an opposite, westerly course before the steady breeze: they were the inward *flota* bound from Acapulco for Manila.

Despite the signals made by Guillestigui and the guns fired to draw attention to the *Santa Margarita* and the *San Geronimo*, the two ships stood on, ignoring them. Reluctant to lose any of the ground made so painfully to windward, the captain-general ordered the *Santa Margarita* hove-to, and the longboat to be swung out and lowered. He intended it to be sent to intercept the *flota*. Meanwhile, pointing to a deep bight,

Guillestigui ordered Lorenzo to bring both ships to an anchorage off Ticao while they awaited the return of their boat.

'Excellency,' protested Lorenzo, 'I am uncertain of the bottom hereabouts.'

'Then do you look over the side, señor,' riposted Guillestigui sharply, brooking no impediment to his intentions, 'a blind beggar could see it for sand. Even a soldier knows an anchor will hold in sand, damn you for an old fool.'

'Excellency, it is my duty . . .'

'Damn your duty, Lorenzo!' Guillestigui jerked his head in Olalde's direction and the Basque henchman moved towards the pilot-major.

'Do as you are ordered, Don Juan,' Olalde said almost pleasantly, 'or I shall find employment for your entrails as a girth for my horses at Acapulco.'

'I protest, Excellency, I am not to be spoken to . . .'

'Yes, yes, Lorenzo, but pray see that you obey my orders promptly in future.' Guillestigui turned away and Lorenzo scowled at Olalde.

'You have a care, you damned rogue,' he snarled in a low voice as he went forward to call orders to the crew.

'Oh, I shall, Old Fellow,' Olalde grinned, 'and care of you shall be *my* duty.'

A moment later the *Santa Margarita* let her second best bower go from the bow and the heavy hemp cable rumbled out through the hawsehole. But despite further signals and the firing of several guns, the *San Geronimo* did not haul her yards and follow the captain-general's ship into the bay. Instead, her sails filling with a freshening breeze, she shaped her course for the strait and the broad bosom of the Pacific Ocean lying far beyond it.

As the longboat was manned, Peralta, whose duty it was to execute Guillestigui's orders, called up and asked whether the boat should first make for the *San Geronimo* and order the *não* to anchor with the flagship, but the captain-general waved him away in pursuit of the two strange ships.

'They are your quarry, Don Rodrigo,' Guillestigui shouted for all to hear, his usually confident face wearing a worried expression, 'and you must fly if you are to catch them.'

Peralta waved and a moment later, the longboat's sail hoisted and with Silva at its tiller, it left in hot pursuit.

Iago was unable to discover why Guillestigui attached so much importance to making contact with the two ships, nor was he able to discover a reason from anyone else, though Olivera muttered darkly that it had either something to do with letters of credit and the captain-general's commercial interests, or news of the reception Guillestigui was likely to receive from the viceroy in New Spain. The captain-general, Iago was given to understand, had once carried out a military campaign against the escaped slaves who waged a ceaseless *guerrilla* against the colonial authorities. Guillestigui had not merely suppressed them savagely but was alleged to have appropriated to himself a quantity of booty that the Cimarrones had themselves taken in raids on Church property.

'I do not imagine that an Indian mission station possessed more than a crucifix and a pair of candlesticks worth more than a *real*, but Mother Church is a possessive old witch at times, and our illustrious chief has fingers as sticky as those of a brothel-mistress,' Olivera confided with a grin.

And ironically it was theft that caused the happy mood among the people of the *Santa Margarita* to show its first sign of serious fracture. On the morning after anchoring off Ticao, Don Baldivieso de los Arrocheros approached Iago.

'Don Iago, I beg a moment of your time.'

'What is it, señor?'

'A painful necessity compels me to request that you search the effects of your servant, the dwarf Ximenez.'

'Why so? What is the reason?'

'My wife has lost a ring.'

'And you think Ximenez . . . ?

Arrocheros wrung his hands, his face working with impatience. 'I am almost certain of it, Don Iago. Please, I attach no imputation to your own character . . .'

'Upon my soul, I should hope not!' exclaimed Iago, calling for the dwarf.

'Master?'

'Don Baldivieso here thinks that you have stolen a ring from his wife, Ximenez.'

The shock of the accusation struck Ximenez like the blows he knew would follow if the accusation was falsely proved.

His little world constructed out of the good opinion of others tumbled down about his ears. 'Master! It is impossible . . . Why . . . ? I . . . ?'

'Turn out his effects,' Arrocheros demanded, waving his hands with excitement and outrage.

'No, Don Baldivieso. I take Ximenez's word.'

'The word of a dwarf against that of a gentleman?' Arrocheros spluttered.

'Not against your word, Don Baldivieso, but against your accusation. It is a matter of trust, d'you see. If your wife's ring is in the dwarf's baggage it is not because he stole it, but because someone else did, and then put it there.'

'Then it is that Chinese boy of yours. The ring will be found in the dwarf's gear.'

'No, señor, no, no . . . see, let me show you.' Ximenez moved the short distance to his bed-place and, picking up his rolled hammock, lifted and shook it. A gold and jewelled ring fell on to the grubby planking and, rattling on its rim, subsided on the deck.

Arrocheros warmed the silence with his satisfied smile. 'I told you.' He bent, picked it up and slipped it into his pocket.

'You told me nothing more than where we should find your wife's lost ring, not who had stolen it,' Iago said quietly.

'But it is obvious,' scoffed Arrocheros, 'defending your man does you credit, Don Iago, but your loyalty is misplaced!'

Iago ignored him. Calling for Ah Fong he sent the 'boy' for Fray Marmolejo and when the friar came, Iago said, 'I wish you to take the confession of Ximenez and ascertain whether or not he stole this ring, as I am told he did, from Doña Catalina. You may use the thumbscrew, if you wish.'

'Master . . .' wailed Ximenez.

Marmolejo caught the meaning in Iago's steady glance and nodded his head in understanding. 'Come, my son.'

For a moment both Iago and Arrocheros stood watching the friar lead the dwarf away. Then the disaffected merchant rounded upon Iago. 'I do not understand you, Don Iago. The ring, it was stolen . . . why . . . ?'

'Because the dwarf did not steal it.'

'How can you be so sure?'

'What use has a dwarf for a ring aboard a ship bound on a voyage of six months' duration?'

'He can sell it.'

'Don't be preposterous. Who is going to buy a conspicuous ring in the circumstances under which we exist?'

'He may sell it at Acapulco,' Arrocheros persisted, adding mischievously, 'and gain funds to leave you. The dwarf is an ingrate, an opportunist.'

Iago held up his hand. 'It will do you no good. Do you not see, Don Baldivieso, that you and I are victims of a mischief-maker. By incriminating Ximenez we are made enemies. Marmolejo will find nothing but innocence, unless Ximenez confesses to some singular, small and irrelevant sin.'

'Is that how you describe the theft of a ring?' Arrocheros persisted sullenly.

'No,' responded a tired Iago. 'It is how I describe masturbation.'

The boat returned after two days. They had been unable to catch the two inward-bound ships, which had either failed to see them or, as was judged more probable, ignored them. Disappointed, Peralta, who had been entrusted by Guillestigui as his confidential courier, told the cadet Silva to put about and abandon their hopeless pursuit. When the boat's sail came in sight from the *Santa Margarita* the crew were ordered to weigh the anchor. The cable was almost vertical before they realized the anchor was foul. Beyond heaving it short, they could gain no more.

'*¡Diablo!*' hissed a furious Lorenzo, going forward to stare over the beakhead and down into the translucent water. Far below he could see the dark shape of the anchor, one fluke embedded in a mighty coral head. He stumped angrily aft calling for the *marineros* to try again and for the topmen to let fall a backed maintopsail, but an hour's struggle yielded no result beyond further worsening the pilot-major's temper and angering the captain-general, who was already distressed at Peralta's failure to make contact with the inward *flota*. Now any moment's delay was intolerable to Guillestigui.

'Can you not even weigh an anchor, señor?' he snarled sarcastically at Lorenzo. 'Must I be surrounded by incompetents?'

'If Your Excellency insists on anchoring wherever he pleases he can scarce bring charges of incompetence upon the heads of those whose advice he ignores and contradicts.'

'Hold your tongue, señor!'

'I am bound by my oath, Excellency, to do my duty to you,' Lorenzo said awkwardly, aware of the delicacy of his position on the eve of so long a voyage, 'to counsel you in all matters pertaining to the safety of the ship.' But he rammed home his argument: 'Now we must cut the cable and lose a second anchor.'

'It is only one that *I* have lost, señor,' Guillestigui snapped back. 'You would do well to recollect that it was you who lost the first off Mariveles.'

'That is a lie . . .' an outraged Lorenzo began.

Realizing that he had perhaps gone too far, Guillestigui sought to soothe the outraged pilot-major and went on, 'But that is of little consequence now. We have no need of an anchor once in the open ocean and there yet remain three more.'

'But they are of less weight, Excellency,' replied Lorenzo desperately, seizing the olive branch Guillestigui held out.

'Then let us worry about that when we sight the coast of New Spain. Do you cut that cable. There, does it make you feel better that I give the order?'

'Not greatly,' murmured Lorenzo, stumping forward again, and throwing a look of furious despair at Olivera, who stood at the break of the half-deck, ready to make sail. 'God damn all soldiers who seek to become seamen,' he said from the side of his mouth.

'Amen to that,' Olivera said to himself. And they all felt the great ship twitch as the hefted axes finally cut through her cable to release her.

'Let fall there! Sheet home!'

'Larboard braces! Haul! Helm a-larboard!'

The word was called down below to the helmsmen at the whipstaff and after dancing astern for a few yards until her head fell off the wind and she could lay her course, the *Santa Margarita* began to move forward, gathering a bone in her teeth as she pointed her bowsprit at the narrows known to cartographers as the San Bernardino Strait but to her seamen as the Embocadero.

Six
Doña Catalina

Much to the relief of the pilots, they cleared the Embocadero and left the strait astern on the second day of August, the Feast Day of St Stephen the Martyr. The *San Geronimo* had vanished, to the consternation of those aboard the *Santa Margarita* who assumed that she would be lying-to in the offing awaiting the captain-general, so the great ship entered the Pacific Ocean alone.

Iago kept a watch on deck during the hours of daylight, which relieved Lorenzo of some of the burden of his rank, and his and Olivera's friendship grew closer. This partial assimilation into the *Santa Margarita*'s establishment further estranged him from the mass of the passengers, adding to the animosity of Arrocheros, who had not forgiven him for allowing Ximenez to go unbeaten, for Fray Mateo declared Ximenez's conscience clear of theft and affirmed this with some force. While this pleased Iago, the poor dwarf found that their master's hostility had possessed the Arrocheroses' entire household, so that Ximenez was constantly mocked and taunted by their servants while Fray Mateo's reminder that such trials were to be borne with a fortitude that improved the soul brought little comfort to the miserable little man.

'It is not kind of them,' Ah Fong whispered to Iago as she knelt at his feet and served him his rice and meat one evening.

'Nothing about this ship be kind, my dearest one,' he responded in the low mixture of Cantonese and pidgin in which they conversed. 'Ximenez is like the rest of us; he must endure it all in the hope of more good things coming soon.'

'You belong all my hope,' she said simply, taking his empty

bowl and rising with an elegance that was all female and would have instantly betrayed her had anyone perceptive been watching them.

A cough came from outside the screen, the signal Ximenez used to announce his approach. He drew the heavy curtain aside and entered the confined and cluttered space as the *Santa Margarita* gave a lurch to leeward.

'Ha! This will keep those devils on their knees in the scuppers,' Ximenez said with relish and a gleam of triumph in his eyes. 'You know, master, one advantage of being set by God upon short legs is that I am less toppled than more perfect men by this vile vessel's motion.' It was clear that Ximenez had recovered from his seasickness quicker than some of his fellow sufferers.

'I told you so, but you are a noble philosopher, Ximenez,' Iago said with a grin.

'I serve a kind master, though I was in doubt of the fact when sent to Fray Mateo to confess.'

'He told me that you had thought to shock him but that he had heard so many confess that nothing was capable of doing so . . .'

Ximenez shrugged and began tidying the space. 'What more proof do you need that I am not very different from ordinary men?'

'I was never in any doubt but that you were a good deal wiser than most, Ximenez.'

'Even though I lay with dogs?'

'Is that what was supposed to shock the friar?' Iago asked laughing.

The dwarf shrugged again, tucking a doublet away. 'I had hoped to appear a little extraordinary to him, master.'

'I doubt that Fray Mateo found a lie in the confessional extraordinary.'

'I did not take the ring, master,' Ximenez said, suddenly serious, his large eyes bright with emotion.

'I know that, Ximenez.' Iago's tone was reassuring, trusting. 'But that is no matter. Tell me what occurs on deck?'

Ximenez shrugged. 'Nothing, master. The sea is vast and many are again afflicted with the sickness. There being no islands in sight they wail that they are lost . . . Master, are we lost? I can find no reason to understand how we know how we may proceed beyond the compass in its bowl and even that seems doubtful, for it spins so wildly.'

Iago grinned again. 'You must have faith in the good offices of Señor Lorenzo and Señor Olivera, our pilots. They have the cunning that will see us to Acapulco if God wills it and the wind blows a little in our favour.'

Ximenez had completed folding clothes into Iago's trunk and took up a pair of his boots. 'I had not thought to hear you mention God,' he said dropping his voice and regarding the boots with distaste.

'Aboard this ship we should all mention God as often as it occurs to us to do so. Otherwise, Ximenez . . . What troubles you about those boots?'

'The mildew.' Ximenez frowned over his charges, which he regarded with some pride, having found them for his master with some difficulty. 'I blacked them not two days since.'

'Forbear fussing. Mildew will be your constant companion for the next five or six months, my friend, along with all the vermin that you can imagine, of which more will soon appear other than those taking up residence about our persons. We are – as the poor souls on deck are just beginning to comprehend – crossing a mighty ocean.'

'But how . . . ?' Ximenez's face bore so puzzled a frown that Iago laughed. 'Master, I cannot even make out the question the answer to which I would know.'

'See, Ximenez, it is like this: the compass which you perceive, on those furtive visits you make to peer into its mysteries, is capable of holding a steady reference to the north, allowing the ship's head to point its way in any angular direction relative to it. We are also able to distinguish our latitude, that distance upon the globular surface of the earth above or below the equator – the imaginary but mathematical girdle that encircles the earth midway between the poles. When we reach the parallel of latitude that corresponds with that of Acapulco, our destination and the latitude of which is known to us, all we need to do is to sail east. Unfortunately – and herein lies the art and mystery of navigation – no westerly wind blows along that latitude, so we must seek out the great gyre of the world's winds and follow it and thus, in order to locate that exact parallel upon which Acapulco lies, we must sail north, since we are now to the south of it, until we discover a westerly wind. And,' Iago added with a touch of appropriate and significant irony, 'thanks to the merciful providence of God, we may find a wind favourable to our intent some degrees north of the requisite latitude. Therefore, under its benign influence, we shall cross the ocean until we meet the coast of New Spain, after which it is simply a matter of sailing southwards along its shore until we reach Acapulco. Now, are you clearer in your understanding?'

Ximenez nodded thoughtfully. 'I think so, master.'

'What one must bear in mind,' Iago added, 'is that the distances over which we must pass are long, far longer than you can imagine and so long that they may seem endless. They are not, of course, but they are so extensive that we must be careful of food and water and, when they seem endless, hold to our courage. Occasionally though,' Iago added encouragingly, 'we may land upon an island and replenish our casks . . .'

'And you are certain we know the place upon which Acapulco stands?'

'We know the latitude, which is all we need to know, since at the point that this crosses the coast line, there you will find the place we seek.'

Ximenez digested all this. 'I see,' he said uncertainly. 'And do all men except me know this thing, this lati . . . ?'

'Latitude. No, not all, but the pilots do.'

'So what if they die?' Ximenez asked sharply, a real terror in his expression. 'Shall we drift aimlessly . . . lost to all mankind.'

'No!' laughed Iago. 'We shall consult the pilots' rutters, their books of information without which no pilot worth his salt would claim a berth aboard ship, and learn them for ourselves.'

'Would you do that, master? You yourself acquaint yourself with this information lest the pilots die . . . Would you, master, *could* you?'

'You are apprehensive upon the point?' Iago was curious.

Ximenez nodded vigorously. 'I have twice dreamed the pilots drowned, Señor Lorenzo bound to an anchor by . . .'

But here Ximenez's recollection failed him and while he jerked his head aft at the bulkhead beyond which the captain-general held his state, he mentioned no name.

'If it please you, Ximenez, I shall learn this latitude, though why the master should do the servant's bidding, I am unsure.'

Iago knew the voyage was properly embarked upon when the first punishment was meted out. Unsurprisingly it was for sleeping on watch and the guilty sailor was flogged sense-less, seized to a grating in the waist. All hands, including the male passengers, were summoned to learn of the culprit's crime, to hear Llerena charge him and Lorenzo sentence him and, finally, to witness the punishment.

After the wretch had been flogged, then doused with sea water, cut down and dragged below, his blood was sluiced overboard so that Iago, leaning dispiritedly over the rail, watched the rusty stain rapidly disperse in the wash of white water along the hull as the *Santa Margarita* ran on.

'You find such sights unpleasant, Don Iago?'

Iago looked up to find Marmolejo alongside him. 'It always troubles me that punishments rarely seem to fit the crime, Padre. That the man slept on watch is indisputably repre-hensible, but does it merit reduction to a state of raw meat?'

'The punishment is not meant to be merely condign, Don Iago, it is meant to deter.'

'The individual must suffer for the greater good.'

'Exactly.'

Iago straightened up. 'You are a good man, Fray Mateo, but is it not ironic that there are those who utterly escape punishment for their misdemeanours?'

'That is a different matter, Don Iago, theft is—'

'I was not referring to Doña Catalina's ring, Padre, but to sins as yet undetected . . .'

'You refer to the conduct of this ship?'

Iago looked directly at the friar. 'You are a shrewd man too. Yes, but understand I make no accusation directly . . .' He hesitated a moment.

'Go on, my son. I will extend the confidences of the confes-sion if you wish. You have not made any such as far as I know.'

'As you will, Padre,' Iago said, noting the friar's pointed remark, 'but the punishment of a stupid sailor for a crime which by its nature endangers us all reminds me that it is my opinion that this ship is grossly overloaded. Look below you, see how close is the waterline and yet we bear an immensity of goods of all kinds littering this upper deck . . .'

'You refer to the evils of private trade?'

'I refer to the consequences, rather than the act itself. Would it not be an irony – and I can scarcely believe it would be God's will – if you and your brethren and sisters, all of whom have renounced this world's goods, were to perish because of the wilful cupidity of others?'

'What would you have me do?'

'Have you any influence with the captain-general?'

Marmolejo sighed. 'To be truthful, none at all. I fear Ocampo's curse fell upon an apostate.' There was a brief silence, then Marmolejo asked, 'My son, I do not doubt your expertise in these matters, but Lorenzo and Olivera seem to accept the lading of the vessel and, it has to be said, we have yet made good many miles since our departure from Cavite without mishap. Are you not fretting for no reason?'

'Perhaps, and it is true in part to say that we have made progress without mishap, but recall our plight when pressed by a hard gale off Corregidor. Should we meet such a wind out here,' Iago waved his right arm towards the horizon on the beam, 'with so mighty a fetch across this ocean, we may revive our fears. We have far to go, Padre.'

'That I understand.'

'And the season is far advanced.'

'And you fear the winds they say blow in these latitudes towards the fall of the year?'

'I fear them greatly, Fray Mateo, because I have felt the power of a mighty *baguiosa*.'

'Then it is natural that you should be in constant fear of another such experience,' said Marmolejo with that reasonable air of authoritative dismissal that a priest waves away anxiety, seeming to take it upon his own shoulders. 'But it does not follow that you shall. God is good and does not wish for the senseless deaths of those who serve Him.'

Iago looked at the friar. His own anxiety may have been

heightened by his experiences in the *Rainha de Portugal*, but his instinct told him that if the *Santa Margarita* encountered a *baguiosa*, or *taifun*, she would soon be in difficulties. He shook his head. 'I wish I had your faith, Padre.'

'So do I, Don Iago, so do I.'

And, as he went below, Iago encountered two further consequences of the sleepy sailor's punishment, the first from Arrocheros. The merchant rose from his seat upon a bale and confronted Iago. 'Your dog of a dwarf should have been flogged like that,' he said, an unpleasant gleam in his eye.

'I think not,' Iago said dismissively, making to pass the merchant who stood close to him. The ship, lifting to a swell, caused both men to lurch, making bodily contact. 'Excuse me, Don Baldivieso,' Iago said, but Arrocheros stood his ground.

'The dwarf is a thief, Don Iago,' the merchant said unpleasantly, forcing himself upon Iago so that Arrocheros's breath was hot in his face. 'Those whom God curses at birth are cursed forever and manifest their evil by their marked condition.'

'That is a harsh judgement, señor . . .'

'It is but the sins of the fathers, Don Iago. And God's will,' Arrocheros added pointedly.

'Ximenez is not the dog you take him for, señor. As to his truthfulness, I have absolute faith in Fray Mateo. Please stand aside.' Reluctantly Arrocheros gave ground.

Within the flimsy privacy of their accommodation, Iago met the subject of this unpleasant meeting. Ximenez was sitting head in hands as Ah Fong stroked his head. He did not look up as his master arrived and it was Ah Fong who explained the cause of the dwarf's distress.

'He thinks he should be whipped like seaman topside . . .'

'What?' frowned Iago, unsettled by Arrocheros's unmitigated venom and hostility.

'For stealing Missee's ring.'

'For God's sake!' Iago looked down at the wretched dwarf. 'Ximenez . . .'

Ximenez looked up. His cheeks were wet with tears. 'Master, I . . .'

'For the love of God, Ximenez, put that damnable accusation out of your mind.'

'I could not stand to be flogged like that, master.'

'Nobody is going to flog you, Ximenez. Anyway, you have seen men flogged before, in the public plaza at Cavite, surely?'

'No, master. When a public flogging was pronounced I could not watch. Like the dogs whose company I kept at such times, I cannot stand the smell of blood.'

'You have nothing to fear, so long as your conscience is clear.'

'Master, I did not take the ring.'

'I know that.'

For nine days, under the steady press of the trade wind, the great ship ran through the blue Pacific. The steady routine gradually laid its customary balm upon the men and women on board as seasickness was forgotten and all became as able as the *marineros* at keeping their feet on the gently lifting deck. The mood between decks lightened and Iago's fulfilled prophecy that the seasickness would pass further enhanced his standing. One or two of the male passengers now ventured aloft by way of an excursion, and thought better of themselves for so doing. Even the captain-general's party became subdued by the steadiness of the *vendavales* which drove the *Santa Margarita* north and, in giving them every prospect of a swift passage, encouraged the general mood of optimism throughout the ship. So much was the mood of the ship improved that the appearance of the captain-general and his suite upon the deck was generally greeted with vague motions of respect and deference from those occupied or idling on deck at the time.

Upon these occasions Guillestigui, bereft of his half-armour and often free of his doublet and in his silk shirt-sleeves, seemed in high good humour. No trace of evil consequences following Ocampo's curse troubled his fine, haughty features so that he did indeed seem like Caesar himself, and lord of all he surveyed as the great ship drove her way faithfully northwards in search of a favourable westerly breeze.

In his exposition on the navigation of the *Santa Margarita* to Ximenez, Iago had not revealed how far north they had to sail under the steady influence of the trade winds – the *vendavales* – before reaching the prevailing westerly wind that

Andre de Urdaneta had discovered thirty-six years earlier. A change of latitude of twenty-four or five degrees would have been incomprehensible to Ximenez. Not that this mattered unduly, for it was as though the ship herself seemed intent on a fast passage and while Guillestigui, noting with satisfaction the increasing latitude, claimed this was due to her clean bottom, Lorenzo and Olivera disagreed. Their daily observation of the sun's noonday culmination by means of their backstaffs, when compared with the most generous estimations made by log-chip, persuaded them that they were in the mighty grip of a vast oceanic current, the Kuro Shio.

The rapid progress of the *Santa Margarita* persuaded even the most resistant soul that perhaps there was a magic in being at sea, for the morning sunshine soon dispelled the night's damp, the creak of the ship's fabric seemed a friendly background to the buzz of conversation and even the vermin seemed lulled into less aggressive activity. The blue skies were dotted with light, insubstantial clouds, mere puffballs of vapour that seemed utterly benign and marked only the reliable thrust of the trade wind. Such things seemed to augur well, so much so that even the sceptical Iago was lulled. As day followed day, there was no need to start a brace, trim a tack or haul a sheet, let alone reef a sail as the *Santa Margarita* gradually acquired a personality of her own and bore them in her strong-built hull steadily north in search of the great westerly wind that would carry her far to the east and the King of Spain's dominions in the Americas.

But on the morning of the ninth day, Iago woke to a different motion and knew immediately that a change was coming, as he knew it must. On deck it was visible, its first manifestation a heaving groundswell moving in on their starboard quarter from the south-east. He caught Olivera's eye and, without saying a word, both men stared at the sky to windward. The horizon was no longer straight and sharp as a sword blade as it had been for over a week. Now it was shadowed by a band of cloud that stretched across the sky, as yet a mere hint of something uncomfortable, but a hint marked by a slight strengthening of the trade wind. Olivera sniffed.

'There's bad weather coming,' he said.

'Yes. I don't like the groundswell,' Iago observed.

'We'll be shortened down before nightfall,' Olivera added and Iago grunted his agreement. Further comment seemed superfluous.

By noon the sky was overcast, and the wind had shifted and increased as the two men had predicted. Although the wind had drawn further aft, allowing them to square the yards, it was no longer the benign *vendavales*. Now there was an edge of menace in the breeze and in the afternoon it backed again and the watch braced the yards, heaving down the fore- and mainsheets. Although the topgallants had been taken in, the *Santa Margarita* heeled further than she had done for some time. The easy roll and gentle pitch that had marked her northward progress gave way to an uncomfortable lurch to leeward which combined with an increasingly heavy pitch. Slowly at first but with increasing speed, the wind backed further.

The change in motion brought Guillestigui and his suite on deck, but they retreated after staring about them and cracking a few jests. It was more comfortable in the great cabin; the deck could be left to the seafaring men. By mid-afternoon Lorenzo ordered the topsails reefed and at sunset – a lurid ochre-yellow stripe across the western horizon below dark and lowering cloud – the courses were clewed up and both watches sent aloft to secure the heavy sails along their yards before dark.

'We shall not want them for some days,' Lorenzo remarked to no one in particular. Then, raising his voice to the men aloft on the yards, he sang out, 'Make certain you pass those gaskets and hitch them properly. I don't want those sails torn loose when the gale strikes us.'

As the *Santa Margarita* began to butt into the head sea, her bluff bow rising before thumping into the next wave, spray lifted over the weather bow and streamed across the deck with the force of birdshot. The seamen on deck huddled in the shelter of the break of the forecastle, staring aft at the officers exposed on the half-deck.

Iago took it upon himself to go below and warn his fellow passengers to secure all their personal possessions and to stow away all except those items indispensable to their daily comfort.

'The sight of you always presages doom, Don Iago,' Arrocheros said with unpleasant sarcasm, raising his voice to fight the noise of the vessel as she creaked and groaned, and the slam of a heavy wave struck her weather bow, sending a shudder throughout the hull.

'I fear for once you are right, Don Baldivieso,' Iago responded sharply, catching Doña Catalina's eye with a re-assuring smile. She was a comely enough woman, he thought inconsequentially, and would be in fear for the child she was so obviously carrying. He did not carry his dislike for Arrocheros to his wife. On the contrary, he felt sorry for her and he wondered how close to its term the unborn baby was. Further forward, led by Fray Mateo, Fray Hernando and Fray Agustin, marked conspicuously in the gloom by the high white wimples of the nuns, the Holy Ones knelt in prayer. Iago returned to his own quarters. Ah Fong stood as he drew aside the canvas screen and Ximenez looked up from blacking Iago's boots.

'Is a wind coming?' Ah Fong asked.

He nodded and smiled. 'I fear so. We must tuck any loose things away.' He looked at Ximenez. 'I told you not to bother with those . . .'

'A man must do something, master.' Ximenez's anxiety was palpable.

'My advice is to get some sleep,' he said, reaching for his hammock and indicating the dwarf's bedroll. 'You never know when you may be summoned to man the pumps.'

'I am not a seaman,' Ximenez protested.

'We may all be seamen before this gale has blown itself out,' Iago remarked, disguising his own anxiety under a wry response.

Night added its own terrors to the gale as the *Santa Margarita* staggered hove-to under the onslaught of wind and sea. Only a few glims, ensconced in their horn lanterns for fear of fire, illuminated the darkness under the half-deck where most people turned in, hunkered down in their blankets or swinging in the more comfortable hammocks. There was a grim air of endurance that met the encroachment of damp misery, added to at dawn when the cooks were unable to light the galley stove and everyone faced a day of cold food accompanied by a penetrating chill that seemed inseparable from the fusty dampness that now pervaded every nook and cranny of the ship.

But it was not a gale, as Iago had realized with a sickening void in his entrails. The wind headed them and began to streak the sea with spume and whip the wave crests off. By now he knew they were entrapped by a *baguiosa*, a *taifun*, a *huracán*, call it what you will. The wind was rising fast; already a screaming note tore at the *Santa Margarita*'s fabric and he knew, with an intuitive certainty, that within the hour it would have changed its note so that behind the terrible howling he would hear a deeper note, the boom of a great wind that he had heard only once before. He felt the sudden gripe in his belly, the animal, visceral reaction of fear that chilled his blood and made his heart thunder in his breast. In his mind's eye he recalled Ocampo's curse, echoed now in the rising wind. Then the moment passed: Ocampo was a damned priest and had nothing to do with this great storm. Nor did God. The power of this storm lay in the elemental forces that girded the earth which, whether created by God or caused by the eruptions of natural powers whose origins lay beyond their comprehension, now pressed upon the *Santa Margarita* and her frightened company.

And then, as if to confirm nature's dominant power in the world, he heard above the howl and boom of the typhoon the scream of a woman in the first pangs of labour. Doña Catalina de los Arrocheros had been brought to her full term.

Looking up at a sudden movement Iago saw Ah Fong rise from her bed. The fitful light of the glim fell upon her pale face. Reading her expression of concern, Iago said quickly, 'No!'

His admonition and the screams woke Ximenez.

'But the baby . . .' remonstrated Ah Fong.

'There are women enough in this ship to attend to Doña Catalina,' Iago said sharply.

'But . . .'

'No!'

Slowly Ah Fong subsided on to her palliasse. The scream came again, and with it other noises, of Arrocheros calling for help, of the soothing platitudes of a hurrying nun, of cries for water, for cloths, all pierced by the labouring woman's helpless cries. Setting his jaw, Iago rolled himself into his hammock. 'Go to sleep,' he commanded his companions.

But Doña Catalina's distress and the fury of the storm prevented any sleep under the half-deck that night. About half an hour after her first shrieks, the *Santa Margarita* staggered under the impact of a heavy sea. Falling off her course, the next wave crashed aboard, filling the waist and bursting the forward door between the half-deck and the waist so that a sudden cold sluicing of water poured along the deck, driven by the sudden rising of the bow to the breast of a wave. The deluge threw everything into confusion, soaking in an instant all those unfortunate enough to be lying on the deck. This included Doña Catalina who, laid upon a palliasse, had been propped upon cushions and now wallowed like a sow in a sodden sty amid more general cries of discomfort, shock and outrage.

Iago dropped from his hammock to the deck swearing under his breath. As he dragged his boots on Ah Fong loomed alongside.

'Go see if I can help,' she said as, above the general pandemonium, rose the terrified and continuing pleas of Doña Catalina. Lifting the coconut matting, Iago left Ah Fong and Ximenez looking at each other. The *Santa Margarita* shipped another sea and a second rush of water sluiced about them, bearing in its swirl the detritus of human existence.

The Arrocheros's bed-place was as exposed as a market, lit by an assembly of carefully tended glims and lanterns and full of the curious and the would-be helpful. He could see little of the unfortunate woman for the bulk of two nuns kneeling at her drawn-up feet while another solicitously mopped her forehead which alone of her features caught the gleam of the yellow lamplight. Arrocheros himself stood above her supine figure, braced against the motion of the ship, one hand at his mouth in apprehension. Alongside him stood Fray Agustin, intoning a prayer, while Fray Hernando kneeled and told his rosary, his lips moving with intense and silent devotion. The one thing this great ship lacked, Iago realized, was a physician. Her manning in the Philippines deprived her even of a barber-surgeon, for none had been available or willing to undertake the voyage, and those attached to the garrison were forbidden to desert the colours.

As the ship gave a particularly vicious lurch and all those on their feet grabbed for handholds, Arrocheros saw Iago looking on. The hatred for Iago that had disfigured his features earlier had gone; now there was only a desperation that displaced the merchant's pride.

'Don Iago,' he called, moving towards Iago as though glad of the sight of his enemy and the chance Iago's appearance gave him to do something. 'Don Iago, is there nothing that can be done to ease this damnable ship's motion? My wife is having a difficult time, the birth is not easy . . .' Arrocheros's voice fell away. In the imperfect light Iago could see his forehead was as wet as his labouring wife's, his cheeks streaming with parental remorse. The hand which fell upon Iago's arm shook slightly. 'I beg you, señor.'

'I fear that I can do little to ease your wife's situation, Don Baldivieso. I am sorry, but the storm is at its height and we must simply endure.'

But his placating words were lost in a great cry of joy as, with a mighty grunt, Doña Catalina delivered a fine boy into the topsy-turvy world amid a slithering of bloody slime. Those surrounding her gave vent to their feelings. Arrocheros, transformed in an instant into a happy father, ignoring Iago as he did the reeling deck and the dancing lamplight, moved swiftly to his wife's side as one of the sisters wiped the new arrival and the other knelt to tug gently at the umbilical cord. No one, except Iago, felt the *Santa Margarita*'s deck heel and then cant as the ship climbed the advancing face of a great wave. Afterwards Olivera, who had the watch on deck, told them it had come out of the night like a wall of silent menace, the wind falling calm in its mighty lee, until, investigating this phenomenon and fearing that it might mark their entry into the eye of the storm, he saw above him the crest overshoot the summit of this wall of water.

Below, few realized the imminent peril. All those who could see were watching the snipping of the cord and the delivery of the child into its mother's arms. It was at this moment that the wave broke aboard the *Santa Margarita*.

Reaching out her arms, Doña Catalina never received the

infant, for as the sister held it out to her there arose a noise like the end of the world and the entire space of the half-deck filled with water. It swept about all those assembled to witness the culmination of Doña Catalina's labour, bowling them over, knocking the breath out of them and stopping their cries with the stupefying weight of a cold and pitiless death. Almost all of the lights were doused.

After what seemed an age but amounted to less than half a minute, the staggering ship rose to the thrust of the advancing bulk of the enormous wave itself and the water drained away, reducing rapidly to no more than a foot that slopped around and, though they did not know it then, would stay with them for another two days, washing every personal item out of the possession of its rightful owner. Only two well-fitted lanterns, those hung high under the deck beams, gave light on to the hellish scene as the crowd regained its gasping breath, screaming, shouting, cursing or praying. Slowly, it dawned upon them that this was not the hell they all deserved beyond death, but their own little world torn apart by a great wave. A gasping relief, even a smile, flitted across a few stoic faces until the cry went up:

'The baby!'

'Oh God! My baby!'

'Mother of God! Where is the baby?'

'The baby, the baby . . .'

'He has gone!'

'The wave has taken him!'

'Unchristened!'

'Oh merciful Christ! The sea has torn him from my arms!'

'God curse this ship! Where is my baby?'

For a moment Iago was as stunned and confused as the others. Then, as the resourceful Marmolejo cajoled the driest of the extinguished glims into illumination from those still alight, Iago cast about the lee side of the ship to which she leaned and to which the draining water still ran on its way over the side and out of the labouring vessel. He moved rapidly, wading through the flotsam of human existence, shoving aside the boxes and bales that had torn loose from their lashings, pulling sodden blankets and garments aside, tripping over artefacts and items of unknown description underfoot and underwater until he saw what he sought, the pallid gleam of a tiny body tossed along by the retreating stream of sea water.

The pink mite with its bleeding stump of an unabridged navel was shuddering with cold and shock, its crying inaudible above the prevailing wailing of those behind him. He scooped it up, shouting triumphantly. It was the work of a moment to return to the sodden bed-place of Doña Catalina and restore her baby to her trembling arms.

'Where?'

'He was behind those boxes. The sea must have carried him.'

'Oh, Don Iago . . .' Doña Catalina could say no more and Iago fell back, glad that the child had not drowned. Arrocheros wrung his hand with gratitude and he shook his head. 'It was nothing, nothing. Thank the sister here who delivered the child.' Iago saw her face for the first time, a half-breed Mexican face, old but not withered, kindly in the dramatic light of the lanterns. She smiled and crossed herself.

'It is a miracle,' shrieked one of the watching women, and the cry was taken up all about them. As Iago retreated, his back slapped by the men, three or four women catching his hand and kissing it, he saw Ah Fong among the crowd. She was smiling at him and he felt pure joy fill him, even as the *Santa Margarita* was assailed by another green and breaking sea.

Seven

Dies Irae

The miracle did not last long. Although baptized Francisco by Fray Agustin in honour of his own order, Doña Catalina's son died eight days later. By this time the typhoon had passed and the *Santa Margarita* again sailed north in search of a favourable westerly wind. She faltered once in her onward voyage, hove-to briefly while the tiny body was committed to the deep amid the tears and keening of the women. In honour of the moment the captain-general ordered a gun fired over the sea as the main yards were braced to catch the wind and the battered ship gathered way again. Order had once more been restored between her decks.

After the storm and the short, shipboard life of Francisco de los Arrocheros a different mood pervaded the *Santa Margarita*: one of hardening. It was as though the ordeal of the typhoon had stripped a soft layer of shore-borne and civilized living from the passengers, turning them into more feral beings. Henceforth they adopted something more akin to the behaviour and attitudes of the hardened seafarers. The men among them swore more frequently; a few with intellectual pretensions bravely attempted to argue theology with the friars, while the holy men themselves foresaw a glimpse, if not quite of martyrdom, then of spiritual trial. Following Iago's example, a few cast off the pretensions of the shore altogether and laboured about the ship, filling the time and acclimatizing their bodies along with their mental resilience.

While the laity, adrift in this wasteland of endless water, doubted the goodness of Almighty God, the Franciscans saw the severity of His divine purpose and in solemn conclave together swore to bear witness to their faith whatever lay ahead of them in the coming weeks.

Arrocheros and his wife endured their private purgatory; they became withdrawn, oblivious to the curious denizens of the crowded half-deck all about them. They fell to quarrelling as though in the privacy of their house near the rice market just outside the Parian Gate to Intramuros Manila. Doña Catalina maintained the child, a son and heir to Don Baldivieso's wealth, would have thrived in Manila had her husband not nursed selfish ambitions of returning to Mexico. For his part, the merchant countered that there would be nothing for any heir to inherit if they did not return to Panama, where her brother was 'proving as untrustworthy as a Protestant dog'.

As for the sailors, they merely shrugged, thankful that the wave that had swept the vessel had done nothing worse than loosen a few packages in the waist and frighten the passengers. Such moments were necessary to rid those quartered under the half-deck of their pride and make them appreciate the true worth of the seafaring men upon whose skill and fortitude so much rested. The burial of Francisco de los Arrocheros they dismissed with a shake of the head; better a helpless and puking infant the less amidships than one of their own number. Even their women thought the child better off in the hands of God than aboard the *Santa Margarita*, a view also expressed – though for different reasons – by the sisters of mercy by way of consolation to the distraught Doña Catalina.

Why should the blessed Margarita, some cynics asked, martyred for her virginity, not seek the swift reclamation of a young soul rather than inflict the torments and temptations of human life upon its innocence? Who knew? Those who cared, mostly women, keened their sorrow in the darker recesses of the ship, but within a few days of his death, the little Francisco had faded in the memories of all except his father and mother, for the weather began to improve. There had been mutterings amongst the seamen that Ocampo's curse was the cause of their ill-luck. Alongside this attribution others, more commonly the passengers, among whom Arrocheros himself was the most vociferous, said that the time they had wasted off Ticao had placed them in harm's way. Some notice of this discontent reached Guillestigui, who had been chiefly conspicuous by his absence from public view, for he resumed his appearances on deck. When asked by one of his staff the direct and deliberate question of whether he considered Ocampo's curse influential, he stated in a loud voice that he did not give a damn about Ocampo's curse or his own excommunication. This outburst, contrived as it was, deeply troubled the Holy Ones, but it was soon set aside by the majority on board who began again to feel the warmth of the sun and the balm of favourable winds.

'At sea,' Iago consoled Doña Catalina on one of his occasional visits to the woman, 'hardships are never remembered long.'

'That is heartless, Don Iago,' she said sadly.

'It is the way we survive here,' he said gently, drawing aside as her husband approached. There had been a warming in Don Baldivieso's attitude towards Don Iago since the night of the typhoon's climax. Perhaps the extremities to which this voyage seemed to impel them all had warned the canny merchant that it would pay him to be on the right side of a man of Don Iago's obvious resource. At all events he showed no intemperance to find his former enemy in conversation with his wife.

'The weather improves, thank God,' he said, taking his wife's hand.

'And so must our spirits, husband,' Doña Catalina remarked, lowering her eyes and adding, 'We may have other sons.'

As Arrocheros blushed, Iago made to withdraw with a courteous bow. 'I hope that you do and find God's blessing in a family,' he said, returning to his own quarters.

The *Santa Margarita* continued northwards. Happily, the light winds held true and every sail was set so that she bowled along magnificently, a fine white bone in her teeth, her ensign and pendants lifting nobly and her pilots relieved to see the altitude of the sun diminish on their backstaffs, marking the steady increase in their latitude as they sought Urdaneta's steady westerly winds. Those less enlightened, who were unable to appreciate the apparently unchanging scene as evidence of progress, were heartened to sight land one morning.

A large island, its shore rising to a plateau, passed slowly to the westward and, before nightfall a second similar table-land lay like a dead beast against the sunset.

'The Rica de Oro,' Lorenzo affirmed confidently, 'which lie in thirty-four degrees latitude to the north of the equator.' And with this they had to be content, for the islands lay too far to leeward for them to lose time visiting them.

Two days later, 'not far,' as Olivera told them with an air of recondite mystery, 'from the coast of the fabled land of Cipangu', the wind at last came away from the west. The hearts of all on board soared as the *Santa Margarita*'s head was paid off to the eastwards and the yards swung square to the following and favourable wind. The tacks were eased so they hung in slack bights and the sheets hauled aft, tight as iron bars. Through their hempen strength the *Santa Margarita* was thrust along on her true and most desired course to the eastwards, running downwind towards her distant destination of Acapulco.

It was the moment they had all prayed and waited for, a positive mark of the progress of their voyage, and its accomplishment drove Ocampo's curse further into the shadows, or left it astern in the wake of the hurrying ship. Joy was expressed by all. A pipe of wine was ordered out of the hold by the captain-general and sent by him into the half-deck as a mark of his favour, the grace of Almighty God and in repudiation of Ocampo's curse.

Guillestigui ordered his musicians on deck and the royal standard hoisted to the mainmasthead for the day as though the King's benediction ruled these waters and bode well for their passage. Ocampo's curse was flung aside. The sailors made their traditional claim that all debts, all obligations and all such things as curses were left astern in a ship's wake. The cynical Guillestigui and his staff averred that Ocampo was a false and unholy priest and therefore acted not as a man of God, but as a vindictive man of pride. Consequently his curse was invalid. Among the captain-general's suite, only Alacanadre was heard to demur, reminding them all that the young officer had drawn his sword in defence of Ocampo, and in defiance of the captain-general.

True, the Holy Ones were unwilling to favour any condemnation of the newly appointed bishop, but they were nevertheless infected with the prevailing mood of joy as the fair wind blew them bowling eastwards.

But this happy mood barely outlasted the celebratory meal that evening, for the pilot-major's expression was dark when he came below and asked Iago to keep a watch that night.

'I do not like the moon, Don Iago,' he said quietly, 'and there is less wind than of late.'

On deck Iago joined the two pilots, noting the faltering of the westerly wind and the dark roil of clouds gathering ahead of them. Large numbers of seabirds could be seen flying west, into the dying breeze.

'Flying or fleeing?' Olivera asked nobody in particular.

'If the last storm was not,' said Lorenzo to Olivera as the two sea-officers conferred anxiously upon the poop at the change of the watch, 'this is a *baguiosa*.'

As the clouds gathered again in portent of strong winds, Iago found himself that evening pacing the half-deck in the crepuscular hour in the company of Marmolejo, Alacanadre and Ordóñez. Lorenzo had relieved Olivera and had already exchanged a remark with the promenading party to the effect that the weather was likely to deteriorate overnight. Iago, having been assigned the middle watch, had agreed and the conversation had ebbed away, as each man considered what the coming hours might mean. In the aftermath of the previous storm it had taken days to dry the half-deck, clear up the mess and sort out the sundry odds and ends of personal effects after the inundation. The chaos of deprivation and inconvenience had made the theft of Doña Catalina's ring a trivial matter when a necessity like a comb or hairbrush assumed a new and valuable importance. Some such consideration had in part mellowed Arrocheros's attitude to Iago, combined with the latter's rescue of the baby. But now the thought of facing such appallingly disruptive circumstances a second time weighed heavily upon them all and it was Alacanadre who broke their silence, suddenly stopping and holding on to the rail.

'It *is* the curse of Fray Ocampo,' he said, reviving the powerful spectre. 'I am certain of it. God granted us a respite that tried our pride and we were found to be at fault, our pride overweening. Now this has brought this new and endless misfortune upon us,' he said, nodding towards the darkening sky.

'We do not know that it is to be endless,' Marmolejo temporized.

'I know us to be embarked upon a disastrous voyage, Fray Mateo,' Alacanadre said with deep conviction, 'I feel that I shall die and my soul is uneasy . . .'

'If death is to be thy lot, my son, thou canst die with thy soul intact.'

'I do not want to die, Father!' Alacanadre rounded on the friar, full of outrage. 'I have strong reasons to live,' then he faltered, 'but I should not have remained on board once I had drawn my sword against the captain-general.'

'Then why did you not follow Fray de Ocampo ashore? He was your friend, was he not?' Marmolejo asked.

Iago regarded Alacanadre, his curiosity aroused; he too had wondered why the master-of-camp had remained, indeed that Guillestigui had suffered him to remain. Alacanadre hesitated. In the gathering twilight his face was indistinct, his dark hair had partially escaped its ribbon and blew wildly about his head. Just for a moment Iago saw, or thought he saw, a soul in torment, for it was clear that the matter formed an obsessive preoccupation in the mind of Alacanadre. Perhaps the oncoming night persuaded the worried man to confide in his two companions; perhaps he was incapable of holding his tongue and this, like his impetuous defence of his friend Ocampo, was an indiscretion he might later regret. Whatever his motives, Alacanadre revealed that, as a member of the captain-general's personal staff, he was bound by loyalty. 'But also I am His Excellency's agent and have used my position to load aboard this vessel riches to the utter extent of my fortune.'

'Then you fear thine own cupidity, rather than Fray Ocampo's curse, may have angered Fate?' asked Marmolejo in an amused tone.

'Heaven alone knows,' returned Alacanadre, missing the irony in Marmolejo's reference to Fate rather than God. 'But I do know the power of Fray Geronimo . . .' Alacanadre's voice trailed away as he turned his head to stare at the fading horizon to the west.

Iago, moved, despite himself, but equally intrigued by Marmolejo's attitude to this open confession, asked, 'What of Ocampo's power? Was he so very remarkable?'

'Oh yes,' said Marmolejo, resuming their walk at a slow pace, adjusting to the easy roll of the *Santa Margarita* as she lifted to the groundswell and the rising wind. 'He was not given a bishopric for nothing.'

'He was formidable,' added Alacanadre, mysteriously.

'How so?' Iago prompted. 'I admit the power of his curse was impressive, but surely . . .'

'He was a soldier of the Church,' Marmolejo said, the timbre of his voice assuming a proud ring. 'A true Alcantarine . . .'

'You will have to enlighten me, Father. What is an Alcantarine?'

'The founder of the Discalced Franciscans was Fray Peter of Alcántara who led the latter-day Apostles in the conversion and conquest of Mexico for Christ. Fray Geronimo de Ocampo and his younger brother Fray Francisco were followers of Peter of Alcántara; Geronimo came to the Philippines and Francisco remained in New Spain, where, so I am told, he advocates the formation of a military order. In Paraguay, Francisco had General Caceres arrested by armed men for his abuse of Church property . . .' Marmolejo sighed. 'Who knows . . . who knows . . . ?' He appeared to have finished his narrative, then turned to his distressed companion. 'It is all in God's hands, my son,' he concluded, patting Alacanadre's arm. As if at a signal the three men stopped and stared as one to windward, towards the east whence the night was dark and the sky loomed threateningly.

'This is a bitter hour at sea,' Iago observed, 'with the uncertainty of night ahead of us.'

'Then let us go below,' said Marmolejo in a bravely rallying tone. 'The ship has proved herself once and, with Santa Margarita watching over us, shall do so again. Come, banish your dull spirits, Don Miguel, 'tis not worthy of a brave officer to submit to the hobgoblins upon thy shoulders. Take heart, señor, and, as the sailors say, "Brace up!" '

Hearing the tight grunt that this admonition forced from Alacanadre, Iago followed the master-of-camp and the remarkable Fray Mateo Marmolejo below. Here they separated,

Alacanadre going aft, Iago moving towards his own small space when he felt Marmolejo's hand upon his arm.

'A moment if you please, Don Iago.'

'What is it, Father?'

'You are an experienced mariner. Is this weather unseasonal? For I must confess I feel some weight in Don Miguel's foreboding.'

Iago thought for a moment and then admitted, 'Fray Mateo, God knows I am no expert in these eastern seas but the gyre that Urdaneta guessed existed and led him to locate the westerly winds of high latitudes is no different here in the Pacific from that in the Atlantic. Some have conceived it of a river of winds that flow according to atmospheric laws beyond our present understanding. I am persuaded that there may indeed be some divine system of universal similarity, perhaps of unity—'

'The hand of God, my son,' interrupted Marmolejo.

'Doubtless,' Iago said carefully, resuming his exposition, careful in the priest's presence to attribute everything to God. 'And as with the Atlantic and its western waters, there is a season for storms of similar violence to that of the Caribbean hurricane. Thus logic leads to the conclusion that, as one may have a vile year in the Caribbean, so some such similar circumstances may combine to provoke a . . .' He faltered, unable to lay his mind to a word apt enough to convey what he was trying to explain.

'Some convulsion of the heavens, perhaps, that drives these great winds across the open sea?' ventured Marmolejo.

'Exactly that, but what I think this convulsion must produce is not one *huracán*, *taifun* or *baguiosa*, but a number of them.'

'Like the son follows the father in the endless procession of life itself.' Marmolejo completed the train of thought.

'Exactly so.'

'Then God is almighty indeed, Don Iago,' Marmolejo said, his thin hand again gripping Iago's forearm with an intensity that transmitted the fervour of his faith to his dissembling companion. 'And we may yet witness something like the Creation,' he added, the dim lamplight kindling a wondering expectation in the friar's dark eyes.

'Oh,' Iago responded with a short and wry laugh, 'very

likely. The question is not what we shall witness, but whether we shall live to tell the tale.'

'All men must die, my son. Better a death at the mighty hand of God than at the petty hand of man, or a disgusting surrender to disease.'

'I would not take it as a text to preach upon, Father, for thou might be thought a Jonah.'

The typhoon burst upon them shortly after midnight when Iago had relieved the watch. He was not long left alone, both Lorenzo and Olivera joining him, the pilot-major taking command and giving orders to heave the ship to. The *Santa Margarita's* head was brought up as close to the wind as she would comfortably lie without straining the gear and where she might best ride out the heaviest seas. These grew steadily until their toppling crests thundered aboard the labouring hull and began again to tear at the deck cargo of boxes and bales in the waist and the half-deck. Once again sea water streamed below as the ship rolled; every cabin, every curtained space, every palliasse, every hammock, every wardrobe of clothes, every pair of boots, every storeroom, nook and cranny became drenched. There was soon three, four, five feet of water reported in the well and the pumps were manned. Only the women and the gentlemen of the captain-general's suite were exempt from the tedium of the pumps, otherwise every fit man was mustered to take his turn while the most skilled seamen struggled at the whipstaff to keep the ship's head up into the wind, aided by a relieving tackle and a scrap of sail.

By dawn the wind was so strong that the seas had ceased to curl and break; now their entire crests were torn off into their constituent atoms, filling the air so that it was no longer breathable but had the consistency of cold, salty and satur-ated vapour.

'Christ! We are not fish but that we must breathe out our lives under water!' Ordóñez gasped as he toiled alongside Iago on a pump handle.

'It is your Genesis, Fray Mateo,' Iago remarked with respir-atory difficulty to Marmolejo who was next to them.

'What a fool Adam was to leave Eden . . .' Ordóñez added.

'He listened to the woman,' Marmolejo responded, concluding the staccato exchange. They worked on in silence until, an hour later, they were relieved and ventured under the break of the half-deck to regard the primeval scene, exhausted with their exertions. So accustomed had they become to the motion of the *Santa Margarita* that below at the pumps they had no idea of the extent of her rolling. From the partial shelter of the overhang they watched as the masts swayed back and forth against the low grey scud driving across the sky.

'Does God or the Devil drive us now?' Ordóñez asked, shouting against the terrible booming roar of the wind, as they watched the main yardarm dip so far that it touched the water. That the ship returned to the vertical seemed miraculous to Iago, though he kept his own counsel on the matter. But with so much water within her it would not have surprised him had she lolled and lain on her beam ends until the sea finally rolled her over. So far, Iago realized, their toiling at the pumps had stemmed the ingress of water, but for how long could they keep it up?

And with every roll, with every straining wrack, hog and sag of the hull, the seams would flex and open. In time the very caulking would work loose, reducing them to a water-logged hulk which would in due course founder. He turned away and went in search of something to eat and the solace of sleep.

If the *Santa Margarita* herself was undergoing torture it was as nothing to that of her company. The galley had been swept by a sea, its stove extinguished and several of its utensils carried over the side and lost. What remained of the fresh provisions were also either washed overboard or spoiled by the sea. The milking goats, the chickens and all the livestock had been drowned in the typhoon's initial onslaught, even the rats had been seen swimming, and the chill of the water had a bad effect upon the native Filipino seamen and their women. At this time the Bishop of Manila's nephew had fallen heavily against a stanchion and had his belly ripped open. After three hours screaming he had lost consciousness and lay inert, attended by the Sisters of Mercy.

But sleep eluded even the tired Iago. The noise of his fellow sufferers had fallen to a low wailing and occasional whimper. The slosh of water back and forth across the deck reducing everything to a now familiar pulp could barely be heard above the noise of the ship herself. Her great timbers creaked with a volubility of astonishing magnitude, a noise that sounded to their apprehensive ears to express as eloquently as possible the strain of their torture. Beyond the heavy futtocks and the thick, double layer of planking the rush of the sea could be distinguished clearly, augmented from time to time by the shudder of the hull as a wave either slammed against the tumblehome of the *Santa Margarita's* topsides or landed heavily upon her deck. But what now pierced Iago's consciousness was another sensation: part noise, part movement. Now there was a trembling that was quite different from the hull's creaking strain. It seemed to bear some formulaic relationship with the deep and heavy rolling of the ship; now there was a tremulous shuddering that juddered throughout the vessel at a constant level, except perhaps that – from time to time – it worsened. It took his tired brain a few moments to divine its origin, and then he had it: it was the standing rigging, thrummed by the mighty and insistent wind. If their previous ordeal had been caused by a typhoon of ordinary malice, this was one of infinitely greater malevolence.

Iago lay in his hammock as it jerked on its lanyards and listened, remembering an old yarn he had heard as a boy, along the quays of the Guadalquivír when the bronzed seamen had come ashore with their tall tales. It was the story of the end of the world, which would begin by the blowing of a great wind. 'The rush of Almighty God,' he had been assured by an old sailor whose words were borne on breath as foul as the exhalations of Hell itself, 'the rush of Almighty God as He comes with the armed angels of Heaven to reclaim this wicked, wicked world . . .' The old shellback had called this divine gale the 'masterwind' and said that it would be the wrath of God presaging the Day of Wrath. Somehow this vision of the Dies Irae seemed infinitely more terrifying and more real than the imprecations of the black-robed priests, which preyed so often on his imagination. Now, for all his secret antipathy to the Roman Catholic Church, Iago felt this superstition touch his very soul and he felt the clutch of visceral fear in his gut.

With an oath he flung his legs out of the hammock, instantly regretting his intemperate folly. Cold sea water tore at his bare feet as he searched for hose and boots, which he had stuffed into an angle of timbers under the deck beams above to keep them dry. The few lanterns that gave light on to the half-deck showed the huddled figures of his fellow passengers, many eyes bright and unsleepily vigilant where the candlelight was reflected off the swirling water, showing them like the pale ghosts they might soon become. Ah Fong and Ximenez sat close together, like one of the ivory statues they had in their hold; farther off Don Baldivieso and his wife had ceased their quarrelling and lay wrapped together in blankets, propped up against a lashed box so that their heads and chests remained above the sluicing sea water. Their half-lit faces and hollowed eyes were blurred and immobile masks of utter, helpless misery.

'Where are you going?' Arrocheros asked suspiciously, as if Iago's absence further endangered them.

'I shall be required at the pumps or on deck soon,' he said.

'Will this never end until we reach Acapulco, master?' Ximenez asked.

'We shall never reach Acapulco, you misbegotten idiot!' snarled Arrocheros. 'We need our Saviour Himself on board to still the surgings of this storm . . . those Holy Ones are of no use!'

Iago bent and touched Ximenez and Ah Fong. 'Try and sleep,' he said, 'and whatever happens keep close to one another.' Then, drawing his damp cloak about him, he left them. As he felt the extreme motion of the deck beneath his feet the notion of it needing a miracle to survive this battering seemed not unreasonable.

If there had been noise below it was as nothing to the cacophony on deck. Here was chaos itself, not Genesis but the hours before Genesis, for he could not breathe naturally!

As Iago turned his head this way and that he felt the effect of the wind in his lungs, at one moment filling, at the next evacuating them. It struck him that he would be drowned in this wet air, that it was neither water nor air but something from before Creation had separated the elements, before – he thought in a bleak and terrible moment – even God Himself! This was so great a heresy that he leaned back against the heavy door, pulled the skirt of his cloak about his face and with an effort mastered his breathing.

It was then that the miracle occurred. At least that is what he long afterwards swore, for it suited his circumstances. The idea was not divine and came not from God, but from his past among the Chinese seamen where he had heard them talk of the circularity of a *taifun*. Why he had not recalled it earlier he had no idea, though perhaps to that extent its now surfacing in his mind *was* a miracle; who knows? But recollection filled him with a sudden urgency. First he reached up and grasped a rope that disappeared up from its belaying pin into the shrieking and booming darkness of the night. At one moment it was taut as an iron bar, the next so slack that he could almost have taken another turn with it round the pin. This added evidence of the ship's plight galvanized him and, fighting the wind by crawling, handhold to handhold, passing over some strange and softly resistant items and enduring successive soakings as water poured across the deck, he gradually found his way to the break of the poop. Here Lorenzo was lashed to a stanchion with two or three other figures whom in the gloom of the black night Iago could not then identify.

'Don Juan!'

The officers of the watch seemed sunk in apathy or calenture. Bodies whose souls were preparing to depart them, irresolute men upon the abyss of death.

'Don Juan!'

Above them the merest scrap of the lateen mizzen, a small, hard-reefed triangle of canvas as inflexible as a steel cuirass, combined with the high poop and the struggling helmsmen at the whipstaff below to keep the *Santa Margarita* head to sea. Remarkably they were successful, standing to their posts gallantly and keeping the wind close upon the ship's starboard bow.

By every rule of seamanship the pilot-major and his stoic helmsmen had handled the great *não* with consummate skill. Now Lorenzo could do nothing more, indeed he knew of nothing more any man could do. He, like his men at the whipstaff, remained on duty exhausted.

'Don Juan!' Iago shook the arm of the inert figure; Lorenzo stirred.

'Don Iago? Is it you? What is the hour? Not dawn yet?' His weariness was palpable. 'God help us, Don Iago, God help us . . .'

Iago's mouth was dry as he lowered his cloak. He spoke with difficulty against the wind. 'There is something you must know, Don Juan. Something I learned in China about these winds. Something that I had forgotten until now.'

There was a movement behind Lorenzo, other men heard his words and woke to full consciousness. Calcagorta loomed out of the shadows. 'What rotten advice have you for us, Don Iago, that you recall it only now?'

Iago ignored the gunner, staring into Lorenzo's face and shouting, though it sounded like a whisper: 'These storms, these *baguiosas*, are circular. The wind blows round a centre wherein no wind stirs but all is irregular confusion. Hold the ship's head to the wind and it will drive us inexorably into this . . . this . . .' His tired brain could think of no suitable word to express the form of the centre.

But he had expressed the idea and Calcagorta seized it contemptuously. 'And shall we all rise up to Heaven in this arsehole of the wind?' he bellowed, his soldier's mind employing the humour of both the battlefield and the gallows. And yet, it occurred to the weary Iago, the gunner had touched the essence of this storm's central feature.

'Aye, this windy fundament . . .' Iago echoed, as if all was explained to Lorenzo by this apt metaphor.

'I have never yet been sodomized at sea,' yelled Llerena, leaning forward to add to the strange mixture of coarse incredulity and quasi-scientific exposition.

'We *must* get the ship before the wind, Don Juan,' Iago persisted.

'But we could never manage it . . . the high poop . . . the heavy sea . . . we should broach, roll on our beam ends and founder . . .'

Iago shook his head vigorously. 'It is our only chance. Once in the centre we shall be so violently used that our masts may be shaken out.' He pointed to the main shrouds. 'See where the standing rigging is already slack. More of that and we shall roll the masts out of her . . .'

'All the more reason why we cannot venture a broach,' roared Llerena.

'The thing is impossible, Don Iago,' added Lorenzo by way of confirmation.

'There is less danger of a broach than in maintaining our present heading, Don Juan. See how the strength of the wind is such that the sea is flattened. Were it an ordinary gale with a heavy sea breaking I should agree with you, but if we pay her off the wind, though it will lay the ship down, it will not torture the shrouds and stays as it is doing so now!'

'No! Do not listen to him, Don Juan,' Calcagorta shouted. 'He is a spy, a Portuguese spy!'

Iago was incredulous at this accusation and stared at the knot of sodden, wind-whipped officers before him.

'See, he does not deny it,' Calcagorta pressed his advantage.

'Deny it? Of course I deny it, for the love of Christ! Even if I were a spy what reason . . . what purpose would be served by my wishing myself dead?'

For a moment more he stood before them, then seeing irresolution crystallize into resistance to his ideas, he turned away.

'Get the Holy Ones on deck,' Lorenzo said with a sudden firmness. 'We must pray for our deliverance.'

Iago stood for a moment longer staring at the knot of terrified and exhausted men. Then he turned and slithered away from them to leeward, to crouch defeated in the scuppers. He fell among a soft warmth. Recollecting the strange items he had encountered when first coming on deck, he groped about him. He felt his bare hand nipped sharply and, above the roar of the elements heard the soft, defeated squealings of the dying seabirds, swept into this odd corner like dry leaves in a patio.

'*¡Dios!*' he muttered, horrified, yet unable to move as he squashed them beneath his exhausted body. 'Lord God have mercy,' he said and began to utter his own prayer as the crushed birds died spasmodically beneath him.

*   *   *

For six hours the *Santa Margarita* lay thus head to wind. The men fell idle at the pumps, the officers remained upon deck unrelieved but inactive, even the helm was lashed and abandoned. She demonstrated that a ship's strength will, almost invariably, outlast that of her people and in so doing lulled them all into the feeling that nothing further could go wrong and that the prayers of the Holy Ones, assembled under the half-deck and joined by many of the passengers and some of the crew, had saved them from anything worse.

Upon the deck Calcagorta and Llerena grinned at each other and offered congratulations to Lorenzo. 'Now all we have to do is wait, Don Juan, nothing lasts forever at sea . . .'

And the moment was graced by several of the captain-general's suite appearing on deck, for the wind seemed to the optimistic among them to be easing. But Lorenzo was unmollified and shook his head; Olivera joined them and, upon hearing what had occurred, damned them for fools.

'Don Iago may be right. The Chinese have been working these seas since the beginning of the world,' he said vaguely.

'And what in God's name does that mean?' Llerena asked savagely.

'It means,' Olivera said with the hauteur of a senior officer, 'that you do not know everything, Diego de Llerena. Do you check the lashings on what remains of our deck cargo but don't trouble your head about the handling of the ship.'

'God damn you, you ape!' roared a furious Llerena, moving towards Olivera.

'Silence!' commanded Lorenzo, stepping between the two men. 'Get below, Llerena,' he said turning to the boatswain, 'you have stood on deck long enough.'

'And to little account . . .' Olivera added.

'Enough, Antonio,' Lorenzo snapped.

'And what use are two pilots, eh?' said Llerena contemptuously and turning away. 'Come, Joanes,' he said to Calcagorta, 'let us leave these fools to shit the nest.'

And huddled in the lee scuppers, half hidden by the coils of wet rope hanging from the main pin-rails, Iago heard every word.

★   ★   ★

Towards the middle of the forenoon things changed for the worst. For some time the motion of the ship had become increasingly irregular but such was the exhaustion of all on board that no one appreciated this development until the note of the wind changed. Then, about an hour later, the wind abruptly dropped away with a suddenness that was dramatic in its impact upon the ship, for this was accompanied by two extraordinary phenomena.

Above them the cloud-wrack dissolved and a bright sky appeared.

''Tis the sky of Heaven,' one wondering observer remarked as this revelation transformed the grey, spume-streaked sea into the deepest of blues. But herein lay no benign element but one which now ranged against them the most formidable enemy the *Santa Margarita* had yet faced. This was the centre of the typhoon, where the waves, generated from all points of the compass, ranged against each other. Few words can describe this confusion; the onward rush and collision of masses of moving water formed great rearing summits that fell as fast as they rose and into whose intervening valleys the *Santa Margarita* sank like a toy boat, before being raised up again. And this extraordinary convulsion was accompanied by a new noise, a great sucking and whooshing, a thunderous falling of masses of water upon wooden decks, a slopping and slapping sounding like the handclaps of gigantic fists. Nowhere on the face of the earth, and certainly not wherever they had seen bad weather at sea, did the surface of the ocean so resemble the upthrust and falling away described so eloquently by the psalmist. Such testamentary accuracy proved to the ever-vigilant Discalced Franciscans that the Bible contained the great truths of God's revelation.

But the ship could not survive this wracking without damage, and Iago woke from his stupor to see the results of his own prophecy. Indeed it was the catastrophic tremor that woke him. The maintopmast and all above it went first, and in its falling tore down the foretopmast, damaged the main-yard lifts, broke the starboard bulwarks and took overboard most of the deck cargo stowed in the waist. Three seamen were caught in this torrent of goods, parted ropes, torn sails and heavy spars, and were carried overboard to their deaths.

No one lifted a finger to help them and it was some minutes before Olivera, summoning a reluctant and hostile Llerena, could muster seamen with axes to clear away the wreckage and disencumber the *Santa Margarita* of the dangerous spars that now battered her side like the rams of a dedicated enemy. While she lay thus supine her neglected helm chafed through its imperfect lashings and slammed from side to side, shearing a heavy iron bolt and significantly weakening the rudder hangings. This disaster was not known at the time for the ship continued to lurch and roll, to rise and to fall so that it was dangerous to stand, let alone to move about upon the deck. Indeed it proved almost impossible to cut away the raffle of the falling spars, for a man cannot swing an axe when holding on with one hand and when his gut is one moment in his throat and the next in his boots.

Such a task, insuperable at first glance, took an age to achieve and, as always with such work, was left by the timorous to a few intrepid spirits. Among these Iago laboured, incapable of inactivity when something – anything – could be done. Afterwards he confessed to his first moment of relief when he watched some of the deck cargo cascade overboard. But even when the last rope was severed, the lack of wind kept both ship and wreckage in close proximity, so that the hull was further hammered by the spars and it was not until the sun had set and the sky had grown overcast again that the wind finally separated them.

All now descended again into a hell of noise, for the wind came up as they passed out of the typhoon's centre and once again they were driven into another night of misery and the wrath of God. It was only now that, finding the helm stiff and unresponsive, they realized the rudder had been damaged.

Eight
A Public Concubinage

The damage to the rudder was subtle. Mercifully it still seemed to work, though the force exerted by two men at the whipstaff with others tailing on to the relieving tackles, while sufficient to move the great tiller through a portion of its arc, was inadequate to fully control the ship. It seemed that there was a point beyond which the turning of the rudder required too great an effort and that sheer weight would be too much for the gear. Called below to the steering position by the quartermasters to see for himself, Lorenzo soon concluded that some part of the hinging gear which secured the rudder to the sternpost had either carried away or was distorted so as to inhibit the free swinging movement of the rudder.

On Lorenzo's return to the upper deck, Olivera also went below to confirm the pilot-major's findings. After a few minutes he reappeared on the rolling deck.

'Well?' Lorenzo asked, his voice raised above the howl and roaring boom of the wind.

'I agree with you, Don Juan. I think it must be the upper pintle and gudgeon, or we should not be able to move the tiller at all. Something has carried away . . .' He paused to think for a moment. 'Probably the upper iron banding. But we can still steer, it is just that the helm cannot be put sufficiently far over to larboard for the ship to respond rapidly. We can only hold a lesser angle for longer and hope that the ship returns to her required heading. She will be sluggish, of course.'

Lorenzo nodded. 'Devilishly sluggish. I only hope to God that she will return to her proper heading in time to avoid too often being flung back by another sea.' Their eyes met. Lorenzo shrugged and then crossed himself. 'We shall have to take our chance, at least until the weather moderates. There is nothing to be done in these conditions and even if we can get in under the tuck of the stern, I do not know what we can do.'

'Perhaps we should put back, or find an island with a careenage,' Olivera suggested.

Lorenzo shook his head. 'We should be too much at risk in a careenage, besides the matter of resolving our problem would be risky. Better if we must to make for . . .' His voice trailed off. With her upper spars gone the *Santa Margarita* might be run off before the wind but once the typhoon had passed that meant east across the whole expanse of the Pacific. Returning to Cavite was impossible.

'Cipangu?' Olivera suggested. Again their eyes met; both men recalled what had happened to the crew of the *San Felipe* four years earlier. Lorenzo shook his head and swore a blasphemous oath, but Olivera brightened. 'The stock is a mighty timber,' he reasoned. 'The rudder is affected but is not disabled. The restriction can only be because the stock is prevented from rotating about its axis and thus, I submit, the distortion is working against the stock, which will abrade until it works itself clear. That we can move the rudder argues that this abrading contact is not great, that it will free itself without doing much material damage to the stock . . .'

Lorenzo, perceiving the hopeful argument of his colleague, began to nod. 'I hope to Almighty God you are right,' he said, crossing himself again. Olivera followed suit. 'But drowning men grab at a straw, they say,' said Lorenzo in a resigned tone.

'Let me go below and encourage the helmsmen, and let me tell them to report any easing of the whipstaff and tiller.'

'Very well.' Lorenzo nodded, cheered a little by Olivera's optimism.

Iago met the second pilot as he came below on his way to the steering position. Both men clung to a stanchion as the ship rolled and pitched, their voices raised above the terrible noise of the wind that made of the ship's hull a sounding box for the elemental struggle outside, adding its own tone to the creaks and groans of the tortured hull as the *Santa Margarita* laboured through the heavy seas, along with the groans, cries, imprecations and wails of her distressed company. Olivera briefly informed Iago of their predicament. A moment later, as Olivera went on his way, Arrocheros, clinging from handhold to handhold, accosted Iago.

'What misfortune has befallen us now?' the merchant asked.

'The rudder is partially jammed,' Iago explained, 'not enough, mercifully, to disable us . . .'

'Thanks be to God,' said Arrocheros, crossing himself.

'Amen to that,' Iago forced himself to say, following suit. 'It will probably clear itself in time,' he added, 'or so Antonio de Olivera thinks . . .'

'And what about you? Do you agree with him?'

Iago shrugged. 'It is possible,' he said. 'I did not see the ship on the stocks and have, like you, to trust the pilots. Both men are competent . . .'

'If both men are competent,' Arrocheros said, exasperated, 'why are we in such a parlous state?'

'Don Baldivieso, a typhoon is no respecter of men's abilities, it is an indifferent force reminiscent of the first day of Genesis . . .'

'But I heard you say that if we had run before this wind we should not have lost our upper masts . . .'

Iago held up his hand. An edge of exasperation entered his voice as he mastered himself and summoned whatever patience with this man remained to him. 'That is an assertion I made based on a belief which I had no means of proving before we risked the ship in turning her round. We might have rolled over in doing so, Heaven knows we are overloaded and perhaps Don Juan was right to reject my advice. After all, I have no official position aboard this ship.'

Arrocheros sighed heavily and turned away. Watching him go, Iago's eye was caught by the wan gaze of his wife peering from behind a lifted corner of the coconut matting that marked their private domain. Wrapped in a wet blanket, Doña Catalina lay back against one of the ship's massive frames and regarded her husband and, beyond him, stared at Iago. Strands of her dark hair were stuck to her clammy skin and her eyes were shadowed. She seemed to encapsulate the misery of all the passengers mewed up in the confined half-deck. He tried to smile reassuringly at her, giving her a little bow by inclining his head. For a moment she stared back and, he thought, acknowledged his small courtesy with a quick half-smile before raising her eyes to her husband, who now loomed over her. Iago turned away, mindful of his own pitiful household.

They too huddled behind the imperfect shelter of the mat and canvas screen. Ximenez was rolled into a ball and lay on a sodden palliasse. He seemed to be crooning in a low, self-comforting voice, like a child, Iago thought. Ah Fong was asleep in her own hammock. Sensing the presence of his master, Ximenez rolled over and looked up at Iago. For a moment the two stared at each other and then Ximenez shook his head, woke fully and started to his feet. Iago pushed him gently back.

'Try to sleep, Ximenez. There is nothing for you to do.'

'Except to die, master.'

'You are not going to die, Ximenez.'

'You have consulted Almighty God on this matter, have you, master?'

Iago sank down on the deck, pulling his cloak around him. 'I am constantly on my supplicant knees, Ximenez, as you may have noticed. Now hold your tongue before one of the Holy Ones does the same thing with a pair of red-hot tongs.'

Ximenez made a grimace and then rolled over and drew up his knees. Iago stared at the two of them for a moment before himself settling amid the damp blankets to snatch an hour's sleep.

But their troubles were only beginning. Before Iago was disturbed from his fitful slumber and called to keep his watch on deck, Olivera was confronted with the next problem. It was two hours before midnight and a moderation in the wind and sea had eased the plight of the *Santa Margarita* a little. Despite the damage aloft, the battered ship held her heading, though not her proper course, shrugging off the worst of the heavy seas that rolled down to meet her, and helped in part by the remains of the felled rigging trailing away to windward like an impromptu sea anchor. Olivera jammed himself against the windward rail, took a turn of line about himself and stared ahead, measuring the extent of the wrecked rigging and planning how they might make good the ship's sailing deficiencies. He had hardly settled to this task than Llerena approached. In the half-light the acutely sighted Olivera could make out his face as a tortured mixture of fear and perverse pleasure at being the bringer of bad tidings to the pilots.

'You have more trouble,' Llerena said accusingly.

'You mean *we*, you dog,' growled Olivera emphatically, accurately divining the boatswain's motive and the substance of his message. 'You have come to tell me the ship is making water, no doubt.' Llerena nodded with an affirmative grunt, cheated of the impact he hoped his words would have upon the second pilot. 'Then put the entire watch to the pumps and afterwards tell the carpenters to report their findings to me.'

'I have already ascertained these, though it is obvious to anyone who has been to sea before—'

He got no further. In an instant Olivera had a dagger at his throat, drawn from the small of his back with such speed and pointed with such unerring accuracy at the windpipe of the insolent Llerena on that bucking deck that the big man quailed before the second pilot. 'Be careful, Diego de Llerena, be very careful,' Olivera said with slow emphasis. 'The situation of this ship is so grave that if we do not work together we shall assuredly all die separate deaths. Be careful that yours is not among the first!'

Llerena pulled back, and as quick as it had appeared, Olivera's dagger was returned to its sheath, nestling in his belt under the half-cloak he wore on deck. In the gloom the brief altercation had gone almost unnoticed.

'That was a foolish thing to do, Antonio de Olivera, I shall . . .'

'Do not threaten me with your intimacy with the captain-general and your damnable Basque brotherhood. Leave that until we are on dry land. For the time being do as I say, man the pumps and send the carpenters aft.'

For a moment Llerena stood his ground, wondering in his ponderous way whether to obey the second pilot, but the ship staggered into a sea and a sheet of cold water was flung aft, to strike the boatswain across the back of the head and neck. He withdrew and Olivera stood motionless, awaiting the carpenters. They arrived a few minutes later, two men of mixed blood whose bodies sagged with the fatigue of their labours in the hold. Both men were soaking wet and, exposed on deck, shivered in the chilling wind. Olivera knew what they were going to say.

'She has worked badly, Don Antonio . . .' the first explained.

'She is badly wracked and strained, señor . . .' the other added in corroboration. 'I think much of the caulking is disturbed.'

Olivera nodded. 'It is to be expected,' he said.

'But . . .' began the first carpenter, shifting nervously from one foot to the other, unwilling to venture an opinion. The man faltered, a pathetic reminder in such extreme conditions as the storm continued to thunder about them and the ship to pitch, roll and lurch, of the distances that separate men.

'She may settle again, once this,' and here Olivera gestured to the sea raging alongside, 'blows itself out.'

The carpenter avoided the issue. 'There is too much water in the hold, señor, to sound it properly, some of the crates are afloat and there is much damage as they strike each other. It is difficult to get at the ship's side to inspect it.'

For a moment Olivera felt overwhelmed by the disaster that seemed to assail them from all directions and felt an impulse to strike the senior carpenter, as the man himself feared. In part it was the deferred reaction to Llerena's insult; in part a selfish and dishonourable impulse arising from his own fear. Alarmed at his own reaction and suddenly struck with a visceral terror at their predicament, Olivera turned away. Recovering himself, he faced the carpenters again. 'The watch are mustering at the pumps, do what you can. I understand the state of the ship . . .' Only too well, he added silently to himself as the two half-castes went below.

The strained hull might not 'take up' again when the violent motion eased, and she might now leak with a persistence that would challenge their ability to pump her. Olivera took a slight comfort from the notion that at least the ship had plenty of manpower. A landsman was useless at most tasks on board ship, but he could work a pump handle, thank God. Olivera crossed himself. And as if in answer he heard above the roar of the storm the faint thunk, thunk of the pumps as they began to deliver water up on deck from where, after washing about, it finally drained over the side.

When Iago relieved him Olivera told the *sobrasaliente* of the water in the hold, but also of the advantage of having many souls with which to pump.

'I hope that the storerooms are not overwhelmed, for heavy work will increase the desire for food,' said Iago.

'I had not thought of that,' admitted Olivera.

'We are grown weary with this damnably incessant motion,' Iago consoled him.

'That is no excuse . . . besides I nearly struck the carpenter who told me,' Olivera confessed. 'It is not just fatigue that is overpowering us, Don Iago, it is something else.'

'Surely you do not subscribe to the belief in Ocampo's curse?'

'No, but I fear a breakdown in discipline. Fear is infectious. Men dispense with the notion of staying together, of achieving through unity. They care only about themselves. If I am feeling close to striking an innocent man, God knows –' and here Olivera crossed himself again – 'what those men forward will be thinking if matters get much worse.'

The prescience of Olivera's observation, based as it was upon the exposure of his own inner fears and reactions, proved accurate a few days later, helped by a dramatic easing of the weather as the storm blew itself out and the westerly winds reasserted their dominance over the surface of the Pacific. With a forecourse set and little spread on the after spars, the *Santa Margarita* was put before the wind. Unfortunately her progress was slow and this, combined with the constant and demoralizing labour at the pumps, had its effect upon morale. Other facts discomfited them. Reports of spoiled stores, real enough and hushed up by the officers, drifted inevitably forward, and with them went a perceptible slump in the quality of the crew's rations. At this time, thanks to the ingress of the sea throughout the greater part of the passengers' accommodation, the private stores were found to be spoiled or exhausted, so those who regarded themselves among 'the quality' found themselves driven to subsisting on the same fare as the common *marineros*.

Although desultory attempts were made to right the disorder below decks, these were not successful. Many had lost their resilience, others had lost too many of their personal possessions to recover any equanimity. Nor did the damage aloft, or the missing bulwarks and the drowning of three seamen, do anything other than remind them that the *Santa Margarita*, so puissant at her anchor off Cavite, was a mere piece of drifting flotsam amid the great winds and waves of God's mighty ocean. Once again rose the spectre of Ocampo's curse, and this time it was not suppressed, but talked of constantly and openly so that it worked its corrosive effect upon the entire company, a metaphor to use against Guillestigui and those who represented authority. Though no one actively preached mutiny, there were those who considered Guillestigui's contemptuous dismissal of the man appointed to be the *Santa Margarita*'s spiritual leader removed him from legitimate command. Nor did these philosophical considerations occupy the common sailors; it was among the Holy Ones that such things were discussed, in the low and conspiratorial voices that those who lived among the cloisters and the confessional were expert at.

But it was among the common *marineros* that the real discipline of the ship began to crack. Disorder, at first sporadic, even vague, began to manifest itself. The endemic grumbling among the crew worsened, exacerbated by the ceaseless and back-breaking work of pumping. This current of discontent grew and then spread aft like an insidious infection. When word was passed among the passengers that they would have to join the crew at the pumps, there were those who accepted the logic of the order, but also those who queried it. Among the latter Arrocheros was the most vociferous.

'If I am to pump, I expect those popinjays aft to do the same,' he said, pointedly referring to Guillestigui's suite. It was a claim that found favour with Hernando and the other friars and lay brothers who considered the captain–general and his entourage the God-forsaken authors of their predicament.

And then suddenly there broke out among the sailors forward a shocking licence as, finally exhausted, they reeled from the pumps at the end of their shifts, to fall into the arms of their waiting women. In these explicit circumstances some – particularly the youngest – felt the revivification of arousal and quite openly, upon the upper deck in sight of all curious enough to watch, resorted to a defiant intercourse. Once started, this libidinous expression spread rapidly. The improper conduct in turn aroused the Holy Ones to a similar but contrary fury. They assembled in the waist clutching their Bibles, beads, psalters and missals, and began chanting.

Standing at the break of the half-deck, Lorenzo watched as a bedraggled nun beat the bare buttocks of a furiously rutting seaman while the object of his exertions – herself in the throes of a desperate ecstasy – spat over her lover's shoulder into the nun's face. Laughter and horror accompanied this ridiculous exhibition as others joined in.

Though forbidden by bellowed edict from the pilots, similar acts now followed as the majority of the crew defied authority, calling out that they had done their duty and they could do as they pleased in their watch below! And extraordinarily the sun came out, so that a hellish steam rose from the sodden deck, encouraging a greater number to indulge themselves. Word spread rapidly below and the duty watch abandoned the pumps and tumbled up on deck so that the entire waist of the *Santa Margarita* erupted into a violent and wild sea of exposed flesh, lolling bodies and the cries and shrieks of orgasm as the brief, shameless and flagrant orgy erupted forward.

The Holy Ones withdrew below from where their sanctimonious psalms rose, to the uproarious amusement of Guillestigui and his officers who, with their own women, appeared on the poop along with bottles and glasses and an air of licence that suggested the behaviour of the men forward only mirrored what their so-called betters had been doing for several days throughout the height of the storm.

Caught in between, Iago and the pilots, along with Ordóñez and Alacanadre, watched from the half-deck until a bellow from the poop caused them all to pause.

Guillestigui, the captain-general himself, stood bare-headed in his open doublet, his legs wide apart to brace himself against the motion of the *Santa Margarita*. One arm was about his mistress, the other hand brandished a bottle aloft.

'Santa Maria,' muttered a furious Lorenzo turning away from the display of drunken bravado and catching Olivera's eye, 'the man is mad!'

'My lads!' Guillestigui roared. 'Drink with me to the damnation of cursing priests! See, we are safe! The ship rides the sea! Enjoy your revels and then do your duty!'

A kind of distracted cheer rose from the waist as it appeared the entire crew passed the women among them, some two at a time assailing the wretched drabs, some of whom seemed content to be thus used and none of whom openly protested.

'They will not bend to their duty again without we flog them into submission,' Lorenzo murmured. Olivera growled his agreement.

Iago tore his eyes from the antics of the sailors forward, which had aroused uncomfortable longings in himself, and turned to stare at the captain-general. Like all drunks, Guillestigui did not know when to quit and, having drained his bottle flung it from him. The ship lurched as he did so and, instead of flying clear over the rail, it struck the iron-bound mizzen-topsail halliard block and shivered into a hundred shards. Green glass sparkled as it exploded, catching one of the mulatto women belonging to Calcagorta in the eye and lacerating the cheek of the gunner himself. The woman shrieked and fell back while Calcagorta swore, putting his hand up to staunch the blood running down his face. The other women broke away from their men and clustered about their fallen and howling sister, whose agonies were intense. It took a moment or two before Guillestigui realized what had happened and that he was the author of the twin misfortunes. After staring at the woman he ordered word passed for a priest, an order already anticipated by Lorenzo, who had sent Iago hot-foot below for Marmolejo.

Within the contrasting gloom of the half-deck Iago found the Holy Ones on their knees, hands high in supplication, their faces expressing their anxiety in bearing the sins of the fornicators above them. Friars and nuns prayed together, led by Hernando in a wailing prayer amid the scent of incense which had by now been added to the general stink of the unventilated space. Iago shook Marmolejo by the shoulder.

'Forgive me, Padre, but there is a woman hurt upon the

poop. You are required to help, she has a glass splinter in one eye.'

Marmolejo took this information in without a word, then rose, ran aft to the pile of blankets that represented the extent of his worldly possessions and rummaged for a small bag of stiff wet leather. Grabbing it he followed Iago into the waist, where he crossed himself as a few laggards reached their climaxes and lolled back among those whose sexual satiation was now being followed by that from a score of wineskins passing among them. Iago led up the ladder to the half-deck and then indicated the ladder to the poop. The air was riven by the injured woman's screams, now far louder than the dying typhoon. From the deck below Iago could see her body bucking against the restraint being applied by Rodrigo de Peralta and Olalde in an attempt to prevent her from doing worse injury. Then Marmolejo arrived and knelt beside her, his face expressionless as he regarded her wound.

'Hold her shoulders to the deck,' he ordered to Peralta and Olalde, 'and you,' he said to Capitán Manuel, 'get her head between your knees and both hands upon her forehead. She is not to move!'

The officers quickly did as they were bid. All were now sober as they knelt about the woman who still threw her wracked body about. Then Marmolejo bent over her and a moment later, as she let out a scream of intense agony and passed out, lifted his hand with the long sliver of glass firmly grasped between the thumb and forefinger. Laying this on the deck, from where Calcagorta picked it up and tossed it overboard, Marmolejo turned aside to draw a pot of unguent from his bag. Then he smeared the salve over the bloody wreck of the eye and socket, placed a pledget over it and swiftly bound the wound up with a bandage round the woman's head.

'She will not be the beauty she was,' he said, calling for a bucket of sea water in which to wash his hands, 'nor will she see except with her other eye, but she will live.'

Marmolejo looked at Calcagorta's cheek. 'It is nothing,' the gunner said waving Marmolejo's hand away. 'I have suffered worse.'

'I am sure you have,' Marmolejo responded drily. 'But wash it in sea water.'

The unconscious woman was carried away and the gentry followed Guillestigui below. The captain-general was already asleep in a drunken torpor amid the squalor of his disrupted and once luxurious quarters, his mistress across his breast in a like condition.

And so the afternoon of what one minor lay brother praying amid the Holy Ones would euphemistically call a 'public concubinage' drew to an end. The sailors and their women went below as they awoke from their own stupefying excesses. The sun westered astern of them and began to sink towards the horizon, flooding the sky with a portentous and ochreous yellow flush, while the wind came again steadily out of the west and the *Santa Margarita*, her hull sinking lower in the water as her pumps lay idle, her proud rig broken and reduced to a bellying foresail and her rudder grinding at its stock with every movement of the helm, made her lumbering way eastwards.

The young sailor whose libidinous conduct had initiated the first breakdown in discipline aboard the *Santa Margarita* had obeyed primitive and irresistibly reactive impulses. Such conduct, unthinkable in commonplace circumstances, manifested itself in times of stress, notwithstanding all the restraint preached by the Church against such unlicensed and rampant behaviour, nor the sanctions God in his wisdom – at least insofar as this mystery was explained by his priests – had put in place to curb it. Men and women coupled in wanton abandon in times of epidemic disease and soldiers went mad with lust after storming a besieged and resistant city. The laws of war delivered such a place over to the brutal and licentious soldiery partly as an inducement to tempt them to try and carry a breach, but also to enable them to vent their pent-up fears and to render them after their spree of rape and pillage tractable to military discipline.

No one, not even the most spiritual of the Holy Ones, had been unaffected by the spontaneity and excess of the orgy. For many of the nuns, prayer and thanksgiving that they had escaped rape were sufficient to comfort their return to normality. Marmolejo, Hernando and Agustin felt the powerful desire to flagellate themselves and each other, to beat out of their etiolated bodies the slightest inclination to lust. The process went on far into the evening and produced, from the young sailors later returning to a kind of duty after sleeping off their physical and sexual exhaustion, a ridicule and contempt that separated them in their perverse but practical release from the deeply troubled friars. Likewise their trulls fell to sluicing themselves, practising a primitive douching, while the handful of respectable women who lived under the half-deck merely retired into whatever private fastnesses their menfolk could arrange for them. As for those husbands and fathers who blushed for their women and secretly buried their own salacious desires in loud declarations of affected outrage, they congregated amidships and opened bottles and skins of wine in which to drown the impurity of their thoughts. Somewhere in the great cabin below the poop, Guillestigui and his closest colleagues, Basques to a man, merely continued what, intermittently, they had been engaged in since the captain-general had dismissed Fray Ocampo from the ship, a round of eating and drinking, and of unbridled and orgiastic fucking on their own account.

Like other men Iago had felt the sinister prickle of lust, but its reasons – which he so readily comprehended – recalled the effect of such behaviour upon Zierikzee. He had turned away, notwithstanding that he was powerfully and disturbingly troubled by the physical urge that ran through him like a spasm. He caught sight of Ximenez ogling the events taking place under the break of the forecastle. Partly in pursuit of the dwarf, partly in search of refuge away from the visual agent of a massive temptation and partly anxious for the safety of Ah Fong, he followed Ximenez, who seemed intent on some private course of action. Instinctively this certainty alarmed Iago. When he entered the gloom of their private quarters after the sunshine of the deck it took him a moment to see clearly. Ah Fong was pressed against the ship's side, one hand flat across her mouth, the other between her legs, holding the crutch of her pantaloons against her body. Her eyes were wide as she stared at Ximenez, who knelt before her.

'Missee, please . . . please, let me see . . . Just let me see you,' the dwarf pleaded.

Almost paralysed for a second, Iago thought that Ah Fong was laughing, for although her pose was in part defensive, he knew her too well to be entirely convinced by that hand across her mouth. And then she looked up at him, and Iago knew he was right, for when she removed her hand her smile was irresistible.

'So big!' she exclaimed, her free hand pointing, as Ximenez reared round, his codpiece open, his enormous member rigid with excitement and his right hand working it and himself into a frenzy. With the ship disintegrating around them Ah Fong's laughter and Ximenez's abandon acted upon Iago like a wild catalyst. He stepped over the drooling and masturbating dwarf and stood before the slim Chinese girl.

'Ah Fong . . .' His voice was breathless, his own desire eloquent and infectious.

She called him by her pet name for him and willingly tore down her samfoo pyjamas as he reached for her. Standing and pressing her against the ship's side, a bale half supporting his knees as he reached for her buttocks – once so familiar but in recent weeks until now a memory – he pulled himself free. Her own legs rose and he felt her heels rasp on the rear of his thighs. A moment later he had penetrated her with a sweet and terrible satisfaction as behind them Ximenez gave a low groan and fell to a steady whimpering.

Oblivious to all else the three of them climaxed and then sank slowly to the deck. About them the entire ship was falling silent but for the groans of her wounded fabric, the wail of the Holy Ones and the steady thwack of the flagellating friars. When Iago stirred he found Ah Fong staring at him, her dark, almond-shaped eyes still holding a reflection of her amusement. She stretched out a finger to gently scratch his cheek.

'You still like tiger,' she said, her voice husky, 'even though he,' she added giggling again, her head nodding at Ximenez lying behind Iago, 'is brother to the elephant.'

Iago half rolled over to stare at the dwarf. He was on his back, fast asleep and snoring. His right hand still lingered beside his exposed penis which, even in its now relaxed and flaccid state, surprised Iago with its size and girth.

'Don't you ever think of . . .' he began, turning back to Ah Fong.

Ah Fong giggled again and shook her head. 'He would

divide me . . .' she said, putting her hand up to her mouth again and suppressing her indelicate desire to laugh, but finding it so difficult that she rolled away from Iago, drew her legs up and tried to suppress her mirth in convulsions.

Looking at her, Iago felt himself stir again. He touched her back and moved closer, beginning to gently make love to her. Becoming tumescent he started thrusting himself between the tops of her legs.

To the peering face that parted the curtain to their privacy he seemed to be sodomizing his young male servant.

Nine

The Holy Ones

The assembly of the Holy Ones ended at sunset and although the most devoted of the Franciscan brothers continued to beat themselves as one of the lay brothers lit the glims that illuminated their quarters, it was with flagging ardour. In due course they subsided into silent prayer from which Hernando suddenly rose.

'Brethren,' he said, his voice ringing with a certainty that all thought derived from spiritual conviction, 'we are lost entirely if we submit a moment longer to the unholy, impious and blasphemous authority of Don Juan de Guillestigui.'

'Beware, Brother, that you do not court a charge of mutiny,' warned the more cautious Agustin, dragging himself to his knees and then shakily squatting upon his haunches.

Hernando brushed the warning aside. 'If we must die, 'tis better to do so proclaiming God than merely submitting to His overwhelming justice that cannot now be far from our captain-general's proud head.'

'Mutiny and treason will ensure a martyrdom, Fray Hernando, if that is what you seek,' put in Marmolejo, also squatting. 'Whether or not our captain-general enjoys the powers of knife and rope under the King's mandate matters little. He is a man capable of seizing those powers if presented with what he conceives to be the necessity.'

'Would he dare that?'

Marmolejo smiled. In the half-light, which revealed the friars' bloodied torsos like a devotional painting, his gaunt features had the appearance of a saint long past martyrdom. 'Do you doubt it? Why, he would as soon hang you to establish his authority over the others as wring a chicken's neck for his table.'

'I . . . I am ready,' said Hernando, the timbre of piety in his voice as the sweat of it gleamed on his body.

'If it is the will of God,' said Agustin, seriously, 'that you shall be martyred, Fray Hernando, I conceive it my duty to join you, but I beseech you consider the other souls aboard, the souls placed in our care by Fray Ocampo.'

'Are they not beyond redemption?' Hernando asked fiercely. 'Have they not by their wild concupiscence placed themselves at the very gates of Hell?'

'Perhaps,' moderated Marmolejo, 'but it is not for us to judge. Nor would an attempt by us to remove the captain-general . . . us, Brothers,' he chuckled extending his hands as though awaiting the stigmata, 'a handful of unarmed men of God.'

'Fray Mateo is right, Brother,' said Agustin. 'They would cut us down with cold steel – and relish it, I dare say.'

They fell silent for a few moments, then Marmolejo said, 'The captain-general and his fellow *hidalgos* are not men bred to the sea. Their authority will diminish in concert with the fate of this ship. The power of survival and, one may infer, the present salvation of our corporeal selves lies with the pilots, the mates and those very *marineros* who so recently mocked Almighty God!'

'Don Iago Fernandez may be reckoned with those skilled in seamanship,' Agustin added.

'Indeed,' said Marmolejo.

'Joanes de Calcagorta says he is not to be trusted,' offered Hernando.

'Do you trust Joanes de Calcagorta?' Marmolejo asked, adding, 'Besides, danger and the prospect of death gives men a common cause.'

'Do you suggest we might thereby save Guillestigui?' Hernando asked in astonishment.

'It is our bounden duty to save all those who repent, and who but God knows if even our captain-general might not repent himself of his blasphemy and all his other sins which, I hear, are legion.' Marmolejo's comment seemed to clinch the argument for a moment, though it left their predicament unresolved. Then the friar said, 'Perhaps we might consult Don Iago. He is, I am persuaded, a man of honour and therefore to be trusted in most matters touching our expedition. Moreover he – unlike Lorenzo or Olivera – owes no allegiance to the captain-general.'

'I agree,' said Hernando after considering the matter for a moment, and Agustin nodded. Marmolejo looked round and caught the eye of one of the attending lay brothers.

'Fray Sancho,' he said, calling one over, 'be so good as to wait upon Don Iago and ask if he can come hither.'

'Something needs must be done,' Marmolejo said, rising with a grimace of pain and reaching for his habit, 'for some discipline is necessary without further delay to resume the work of pumping the ship.'

His brothers agreed, the summons of Iago marking the end of their self-scourging. 'The inactivity of the pilots amazes me,' Marmolejo said, wincing as the coarse woollen fabric of his habit rasped his scourged skin. 'I cannot believe that they too fell into that morass of foul indulgence.'

'One never knows what wickedness dwells in the hearts of such men, my Brother,' Agustin said, dragging his own heavy wool habit over his lacerated back, heightened by the stinging remonstrance it gave him.

'Brothers!' Sancho was suddenly among them again, his face whey-coloured with shock, his eyes wide. He gasped inarticulately with the horror of what he had witnessed.

'What is it?' Marmolejo asked sharply. 'Come, pull yourself together, Brother . . . What is it?'

'The . . . the man Iago . . . He is . . . he is . . .'

From the cowering reticence of the messenger Marmolejo half-guessed, half-feared what Sancho's news might be. 'He is *what*?' Marmolejo asked, recalling Sancho to reality, disconnecting his troubled mind from the image of Iago and Ah Fong.

'I knew Geronimo de Ocampo's curse was taking effect,' Sancho blurted out, 'but this . . .'

'What in Heaven's name are you talking about?' Agustin said, standing before the shuddering Sancho.

'Talking about? Why, we are forsaken! Lost! I knew it the moment I saw Antonio de Olivera draw his knife on Diego de Llerena . . . God has deserted us! Oh, Christ, have mercy upon us . . .' Sancho fell to his knees, crossing himself with a fervour that seemed ridiculous as he then fell sideways as the *Santa Margarita* lurched sluggishly into a wave. He struggled upright, helped by Marmolejo, who seized his upper right arm.

'What,' the discalced friar asked with steadying deliberation, 'is Don Iago doing that so disturbs you?'

'He is buggering his Chinese boy!'

There was a moment's silence and then Agustin broke it. 'I said that creature was too handsome to be anything other than a catamite.'

'Aye, Brother, and I mistrusted Fernandez from the start,' added Hernando. 'And never,' he added turning to Marmolejo, 'approved of *your* familiarity with him.'

The news was a greater shock for Marmolejo, whose intimacy with the enigmatic Iago troubled his colleagues. There had been tensions roused over such unnatural acts between young men in his days as a seminarian and he had encountered it occasionally between soldiers on campaign, but now – here – aboard the *Santa Margarita*, amid a dissolute ship's company on the vertiginous threshold of Hell itself, it seemed a final betrayal. Don Iago he had marked as a man of parts, not a sodomitical and perverse wanton, but now he knew not what to think.

With a strangled howl Marmolejo shoved past Sancho and ran towards the screen surrounding Iago's bed-place. He flung back the curtains and stared at the three supine bodies beyond the matting.

Blissfully unaware of Sancho's intrusion, Iago withdrew from Ah Fong a few seconds before Marmolejo invaded their privacy. Lying back, eyes closed in ravished abandonment, he was roused by the sharp rustle of the withdrawn canvas. He met the stare of the prurient Marmolejo, whose eyes roved over first Iago, then the snoring dwarf and finally the shapely buttocks of Ah Fong.

'What unholiness dost thou perpetrate?' Marmolejo asked with Mosaic ferocity.

'What is it to you?' Iago responded with equal indignation,

turning over and drawing a blanket over Ah Fong's haunches just as she too roused from her satiation.

"'Tis too late for that,' remonstrated Marmolejo, 'I have seen enough of your pederasty and the rearmost parts of your catamite . . .'

'My catamite . . . ?' a puzzled Iago queried. 'What do you . . .' Then, slowly, he realized Marmolejo's erroneous conclusion.

'What belong this?' Ah Fong began but Iago was now roused to a fury, a fury that contained all his pent-up hatred of Marmolejo's sacerdotal breed. His left hand cut through the air like a sword blade, silencing Ah Fong.

'Perhaps,' he snarled, 'you have seen insufficient of my catamite, Fray Marmolejo.' Turning to Ah Fong, Iago spoke to her quickly in the dialect he had learned in captivity: 'I lose face in front of priest, my Honeyed One, he thinks I am a man of animal appetites and fuck you through your arse. Obey your master, rise now and show him you are a woman of exceptional beauty.'

Ah Fong in her lassitude was nothing loth. She rose in the semi-darkness, a pale, slender faery figure.

'Do you not think she bears a resemblance to a daughter of Eve, Reverend Father?' Iago said in a low and menacing voice, rising with a corner of the blanket in his hand, to stand beside, and then cover, the young woman. Ah Fong took the blanket from him and Iago stepped forward to confront the stupefied friar just as Ximenez woke and with a grunt stared about him in incomprehension. 'I took you for a better man, Marmolejo,' Iago went on, abandoning respect for the friar. 'Not one so ready to falsely accuse me of . . . of what?' he exclaimed. 'Of sodomy?'

'My son, I . . .'

'Do not assume spiritual paternity until you have begged forgiveness!'

But Marmolejo, charged with the virtue of his flagellation, was not used to so vicious a challenge and proved equal to the changing situation. 'Fornication, Don Iago, is a sin,' he argued.

'What! You would condemn a man for lying with his wife?'

'Your *wife*?'

'Do not measure all men by a common standard,

Marmolejo, or you will be led into temptation and be guilty of spiritual pride.'

Marmolejo felt the words like a blow less pleasant than those he had administered upon himself. 'You have no right to speak to me in that manner.'

'Neither have you to me.'

For a moment the two men stared at each other, then Marmolejo lowered the tone of his voice and said, 'I came here for advice and to make common cause with you for the greater safety of this ship.'

But Iago was too aroused to be so easily appeased. 'You came here to discover me a sodomite!'

'No!'

'You meddle! You intrude! It is the business of you priests! The hearts of men are not their own but that you must pry into them and, like the man extracting an oyster from the shell God encased it in, you tear the entire fabric asunder to its utter destruction!'

'Master! Please, recover your temper, I beg you!' cried Ximenez, leaping to his feet, his flaccid member still dangling from his half-untied codpiece.

'Your dwarf is right, Don Iago,' Marmolejo said, recovering and sharing with the dwarf a recognition of the power of the Church over men. 'Have a care. You talk like a Protestant dog and you are playing with fire.'

'Then burn me!'

Ximenez gave a great cry and flung himself at Iago's feet, clasping his legs and staring up at his master as Marmolejo drew back.

'I think, Don Iago,' Marmolejo said breathlessly, 'it is best that we consider ourselves to have equally traded insults. For myself I am sorry that I misjudged you, though what legitimacy you place upon a heathen marriage is something to be taken up later. For the time being will you, when you are composed, come and discuss what can be done about the disordered state of this ship with myself and my Brothers?'

'Go, master, go,' pleaded Ximenez, shaking Iago's legs so that he almost toppled over. Kicking himself free of Ximenez's awkward and supplicating embrace, Iago frowned and then nodded.

'Very well. I shall come in a few moments.'

When Marmolejo had gone, Iago sent Ximenez for some water and took Ah Fong in his arms. 'Thank you for what you did for me there, my dearest one,' he whispered in her ear. 'In tomorrow's daylight, if it pleases the gods to send us sunshine, you shall put on a lady's dress and I shall walk with you as my most honourable wife.'

'I shall ask the house gods of my ancestors to send us no wind and much sunshine, my beloved one,' she answered smiling, selecting a scented joss stick and lighting it from the lantern swinging from the hook in the deck beam. 'I am glad you made a fool of the foreign devil priest.'

Iago laughed, relieved that it had been Marmolejo and not one of his fellows that had come upon them. 'You were wonderful,' he said, 'a soft scabbard . . .'

'For your bright sword.' She finished the intimate remark with another wide smile.

Turning away, Iago said, 'Cover yourself before you excite Ximenez. I must go to talk with these men of God.'

After Ximenez had brought him a beaker of water, Iago joined the friars. It was clear that Marmolejo had just explained the error of his wild assumption, though how or when it had come to their knowledge Iago had no idea.

'Well? You have summoned me and I have come,' Iago began coldly.

'We wish to consult you about the ship, Don Iago,' Hernando began. 'We feel that not all is being done to save her. No one is pumping, she lies deeper in the water, she will founder if . . .'

'Have you raised these anxieties with the captain-general?' Iago asked.

'We wished to seek your advice.'

'Upon what? Whether the ship will sink unless you pray and every other man pumps?'

'Don Iago!' Marmolejo growled a warning. 'Do not trifle . . .'

Iago bit off a retort and expelled his breath. 'I fear, Fathers,' he said in a more conciliatory tone, 'that I am of little influence but I shall see what I can do.' He made to turn away but Agustin called:

'Stay, Don Iago. A moment more if you please.'

'Fray Agustin?'

'If, Don Iago, as may well be the case, there is a necessity to contest Don Juan's captain-generalship . . .'

Iago gave an incredulous laugh and looked at the circle of friars. For the first time he realized they were in a state of heightened emotion. Then he shook his head. 'You purpose mutiny? You? The guardians of all things spiritually conducive to good order?'

'No!' Marmolejo said sharply, holding up his hand. 'No, my Brothers, no! We purpose nothing but the maintenance of the King's discipline and the Church's rule aboard this ship. But neither shall we founder by ill-conceived concubinage and wantonness. This is neither time nor place . . .'

'A man may couple with his wife whenever it pleases him,' Iago said frigidly, stung with the reference to his recent love-making.

'If she is his wife,' put in Hernando, 'as sanctioned by the holy sacrament of marriage.'

'And if she is,' added Agustin, 'why hast thou concealed the fact for so long and deceived us into thinking quite otherwise?'

'Huh! For two reasons, the first of which you presently demonstrate: that you do not recognize a form of marriage other than that of the Church.'

'How can we? Besides God's rule is worldwide and includes Cathay,' Agustin parried.

'You should not have lain with her, Don Iago, until bringing her before a priest.'

'And how, a captive, was I to know whether I should ever again encounter a priest, Fray Agustin? Pray tell me—'

'What,' broke in Marmolejo, 'was the second reason?'

Iago shook his head to clear it. 'The second reason? Oh, I should not have secured a passage with a wife in train. Or so I judged. Perhaps in this I was mistaken, but in the other matter, your own questions prove the truth of my argument.'

'You speak,' Hernando said, his eyes narrowing, 'like a man who would defy the very authority of the Church.'

'Do you threaten me with the Inquisition, Fray Hernando? If so shall I sit down and pray the *Santa Margarita* founders soon and takes you all with me to Hell!'

'Do not,' said Hernando, his face a mask, the words spat at Iago, 'talk lightly of such matters.'

'If the foundering of this ship is a matter to be taken lightly,' Iago responded, 'then I see that you, Fray Hernando, are bent upon martyrdom.'

'Don Iago!' Marmolejo interjected as Iago spun on his heel and walked from their presence.

'You see,' said Hernando, 'the man is intractable. I smell a Protestant . . .'

'You may smell what you like, Fray Hernando,' said Marmolejo quickly, 'but I fear that Fernandez is right in one thing, your martyrdom is nearer than you may wish.'

'The man is an apostate, like the captain-general,' argued Hernando furiously.

'But we failed in our objective, Brothers,' Marmolejo added, shaking his head.

'But God has revealed a sinner,' Hernando persisted. 'His will is absolute and His purpose divine.'

'Aye.' Marmolejo sighed and shook his head. Then he fell to his knees and, crossing himself, fell to praying.

Iago went on deck. He was furious with himself, furious with Marmolejo and furious with Guillestigui, whose stupidity lay – he felt in some indeterminate way – at the heart of their troubles.

The wind had dropped, though a confused sea still ran in which the *Santa Margarita* wallowed with a sluggishness that presaged a waterlogged hold. The full darkness of the night had fallen, though intermittent cloud exposed the stars and a sickle moon sufficient to show the figures upon the deck. Lorenzo and Olivera stood at the break of the half-deck, facing aft and in conversation with Guillestigui, a few of whose suite stood about him. It was clear that this was no casual conversation, but a conference of sorts. Someone among the captain-general's entourage spotted him, for the pale ovals of several faces turned towards him and he sensed rather than heard all conversation cease.

Then someone, Calcagorta Iago thought, made a remark. Iago heard Guillestigui say, 'No, let him come forward, we have need of him.' Then, raising his voice, the captain-general summoned him. 'Don Iago, pray come hither.'

'Excellency?'

'Don Juan Lorenzo and the carpenters have found a leak and believe they can reduce the ingress of water. Even now the carpenters are preparing to work but we must relieve the ship of some of the water she has taken so that they can get at the place, as you will have no trouble comprehending. The men are exhausted, now they have given way to vice and further prostrated themselves but with leadership and example they will return to their duty without I must resort to the cat . . . Do you follow my argument, Don Iago?'

'Yes, Excellency. You wish that I and some others prominent in the ship but not strictly of her again make ourselves useful on the pump handles.'

'Exactly.'

'Then I shall lead the Franciscan brothers, Your Excellency, if you will permit me to.'

'Of course,' Guillestigui said, and even in the darkness Iago saw the gap in his beard where his teeth gleamed with a smile. 'And my officers will muster others. Don Rodrigo, Don Joanes . . .'

But Iago had gone, returning to the friars with an alacrity that surprised himself.

'Well, Fathers,' he said without any ceremony, 'if you will follow me I shall lead you to your penance. We must needs lighten the ship in order that a leak may be stopped. Your energies as well as your prayers are required by the King's captain-general on the pumps.' Iago stared about him as the news sank in. Then, before anyone spoke, he led them below. 'Come; I shall make seamen of you yet.'

Iago led them to the waist where the pump trunks stood amid the wreckage of the deck cargo. Once there he appointed them two to a handle with a reserve intended to spell each man in turn at half-hourly intervals. Already himself in his shirt-sleeves, he watched them divest themselves of their habits in the faint light, hearing the suppressed in-draughts of breath as they tore the rough cloth off their lacerated flesh. A few moments later the pump handles again rose and fell. After a

moment the pulsating stream of water began to run from the
outlet pipe over the deck at their feet.

'You . . . will . . . find,' Iago said, ejecting each word as he
made the downstroke, 'that . . . you . . . will . . . work . . . best
. . . by . . . breathing . . . out . . . as . . . you . . . haul . . . on . . .
the . . . handle . . .' and so they found it. At regular intervals
one of those resting stepped in and relieved one of those
labouring at the tedious task. When he found himself thus
recovering his strength, Iago encouraged them.

'We are fortunate in one respect, Fathers. Since the ship is
so grossly loaded the amount of water in her, although
lowering her freeboard to a dangerous extent, prevents us
taking on an angle of loll which would be the case were the
water to rush to one side in an empty space.'

Grunts of comprehension greeted this news and, as his turn
to resume work approached, Iago went to the side of *Santa
Margarita* and stared over the rail. The waterline lay not far
below the level of the deck, but it was clear that they stood
a chance of overcoming the ingress, particularly if daybreak
brought them relief, which Lorenzo had promised.

Iago tapped Marmolejo on the shoulder and took over his
handle. Dark scabs seamed the older man's otherwise white
back, but these were splitting under the exertion and fresh
bleeding ran into the sweat and showed up in the starlight
as he drew to one side. Iago resumed the task as though he
had had no break. Up and down, back bent then straightened, arms quickly numbed, his thoughts floating in the
gloom.

After catching his breath Marmolejo asked: 'Tell me, Don
Iago, if the leak is – was – under water and the hold is so
cluttered, how was its whereabouts discovered?'

'I don't . . . know . . . for . . . certain,' gasped Iago, continuing
in the same manner, 'but I imagine that it is not far below the
waterline. Perhaps, as the ship rolled, it was exposed . . .'

Those working with him grunted at the explanation. They
moved like slaves, no further words passing between them.
Hour succeeded hour, the rotating reliefs moved silently, like
wraiths, the resting gasped until it was their turn to resume
work. And so they laboured on until the first light of dawn
flushed the eastern horizon and, at last, the ship seemed to

awake to a new normality. Only then did some seamen, contrite and embarrassed, turn out to relieve them.

Before he went below to sleep, Iago ascended to the half-deck. He had been vaguely aware of others about the ship intent upon saving her. He had caught a glimpse of Lorenzo and one of the carpenters, dripping with water, emerging on deck. With the dawn more men came on deck and the sails were properly trimmed. Under the half-deck Iago found the pilot-major. Lorenzo seemed cheered and less doleful than he had become lately.

'We have stopped the leak, Don Iago, or at least considerably reduced it,' he said, clearly pleased with the efforts of himself and the carpenters. Without waiting for any further questions he went on, 'It was a length of spar, probably the maintopmast which had all but beaten in the ship's side and sprung a seam. We have caulked it and reduced the inflow to a mere trickle. You will be glad to know that you are no longer pumping the Pacific through the *Santa Margarita*.'

'I am indeed.'

'Now the pumps are gaining.'

'Then I shall go below and sleep.'

'And I must consider a jury rig,' Lorenzo said nodding and looking about him. Puzzled at the pilot-major's change of mood, Iago dragged himself below. Ah Fong was asleep in the hammock but Ximenez was awake and polishing his master's boots.

'I told you not to . . .' But he got no further. Even before he had stretched himself full length on the wet palliasse he was fast asleep.

It was almost noon when Iago awoke. The first thing he saw was Ah Fong's face and, recollecting that it was no longer necessary to pretend she was a youth, he reached out to her.

'I shall get you food,' she said rising and Iago lay back. The ship seemed easier, riding better but with a slight heel that bespoke progress. 'We are under way,' he whispered and, staring about him, noticed his polished boots. A moment later Ximenez lifted the canvas curtain and came into the space.

'You are awake, master.'

'So it would seem.'

Ximenez lowered himself to bring his mouth close to Iago's ear. 'They are saying much of the stores are spoiled, master, ruined by the sea water.'

'That is very likely. Do you go and get me some hot water that I might shave.'

'And that the captain-general is sending men into parts of the ship to secure comestibles for his party,' went on Ximenez, rising to do Iago's bidding.

'Is that a fact or mere idle gossip?' Iago asked sharply.

'I have seen men in hauberks going below. They are the captain-general's guard and not seamen. They were armed,' added Ximenez thoughtfully.

'Hot water.'

'Yes, master.'

After he had eaten, Iago went on deck where Olivera stood the watch. Above the forecastle rose the stump of the foremast and from its yard the forecourse bellied out, helped by a smaller sail set on the main, and abaft the main the lateen mizzen was drawing. At the root of the bowsprit a gang of men were at work. Ducking to see below the roach of the forecourse, Iago watched the young Silva out at the end of the bowsprit.

'We are setting up a foretopmast stay to raise a jury fore-topmast,' explained Olivera. 'Then we must work on the main.'

'You have done well, Antonio. Happily Don Juan seemed much cheered by our progress this morning.'

Olivera nodded. 'He had a dream in which he lay with his wife. He is convinced it was sent by the Virgin in answer to his prayers.'

'Ahhh.' Iago recollected Ximenez's dream that the pilots were lost, but held his tongue, merely commenting, 'Faith is a wondrous thing.'

'For those who believe.'

The conversation went no further for in the waist below them Marmolejo emerged and, looking up at the rail above him, remarked upon their progress.

'This is encouraging, gentlemen.'

'Indeed it is,' Iago responded.

'And I must speak with you, Don Iago.'

Iago descended to the waist. 'If this is about the captain-general's conduct or about my own—'

'It is about your soul, Don Iago,' Marmolejo interrupted.

'My soul?'

Marmolejo nodded. 'It is imperilled. I shall forget much of what passed between us, but some matters I cannot ignore. You must be married.'

'I am.'

'Not according to the Christian rite.'

'Can this not await the conclusion of our voyage?'

Marmolejo appeared not to have heard him. 'Your wife needs conversion, baptism and a Christian name . . .'

'Fray Mateo . . .'

'Beware, Don Iago. You have enemies. There are those that believe you to be a spy, an apostate – even a Protestant. This is not a matter to prevaricate over, for prevarication will be taken for conduct so suspicious that, at the end of our voyage, it may attract unwelcome attention. Submit to this and all will be well. You will draw the sting of those who wish you ill.'

Iago looked at Marmolejo, seeking meaning beyond the friar's words. The older man met his stare.

'My son . . .' he began, but seemed unable to go further.

Iago's anger of the day before had gone, wrung out of him by his labour at the pumps. 'Are you too under suspicion, for befriending me?'

Marmolejo lowered his eyes. Iago sighed. 'Fray Mateo, you may say what you like to Ah Fong, she will neither understand nor see the virtue in what you intend.'

'That does not matter, Don Iago, as you well know.'

'I know only that she is Chinese and quite unlike us.'

'God created the world, Don Iago, even the likes of her.'

'She will not relinquish her household gods.'

'All you have to do is to persuade her of the paramountcy of the Christian religion. Come, do you make a start today. See,' and here Marmolejo gestured at the men working about the ship, his voice uplifted, 'we are set fair to make a new start. Why, even the sun shines. Perhaps we have suffered enough,' he added, somehow making Iago recall the mortifying self-flagellation Marmolejo and his brethren had inflicted upon themselves. Did they think the wind and sea thus easily mollified?

'Very well, Fray Mateo, I will speak with Ah Fong this evening and tomorrow you may call upon her and add your theological arguments to my own.'

Marmolejo seemed genuinely pleased, his face lightening. He asked, 'What shall her baptismal name be, my son?'

The question caught Iago off guard but he had the answer in a second. 'Why, Margarita, of course,' he responded with a smile.

'Most appropriate,' said Marmolejo sombrely.

That evening Iago drew Ah Fong to one side and persuaded her of the danger they were all in as a result of her sex becoming known. He explained that it was necessary to appease the Holy Ones in order that they themselves remained untroubled. It was a matter of Iago himself maintaining face, a concept Ah Fong grasped instantly, to which end she must accept the Roman Catholic religion. It was, Iago went on, necessary only to admit belief in what Marmolejo would put to her, and she would thereby secure everlasting life. She could, he assured her, continue to pay homage to her household josses, but that should be henceforth in secrecy.

'This is what you wish?' she asked.

'You know it was necessary that you made like a boy to come with me, Ah Fong?' She nodded. 'This is no different, but it requires all your arts and afterwards you will become my wife in the sense that these men understand. Until then you are, in their eyes, merely my concubine.'

Ah Fong considered the matter for a moment and then bent her head in acquiescence. 'It seems no great matter if that is what you wish.'

Iago kissed her and for several irksome days Marmolejo spent hours with his young and beautiful convert while elsewhere in the ship the crew, under the direction of Lorenzo, Olivera and Llerena, swayed up a jury foremast. Finally, even as Ah Fong knelt at Marmolejo's feet with the Holy Ones in a circle about her and was christened Margarita, the great ship bearing a similar name – though much reduced in her rig – began again to make way.

For a few hours much was forgotten as the *Santa Margarita* forged through the deep blue waters of the Pacific and drew behind her a thin line of disturbed white water. Hanging on either quarter flew the long-tailed sea fowl that the sailors called bosun birds. Among those on board some claimed their troubles were over and that it would not now be long ere they saw the coast of New Spain.

'Is it true, Don Iago?' Doña Catalina asked him one morning. She seemed much recovered from the loss of her baby, perhaps, like the Holy Ones, considering she had made sufficient sacrifice to assure them all a safe passage. Perhaps there was a new quickening in her womb.

'We have some way to go yet, señora,' Iago temporized, not having the heart to inform her that their progress was painfully slow.

But Doña Catalina, like the rest of the hopeful souls aboard the *Santa Margarita*, soon forgot their brief optimism, for the following day the weather turned chilly. The wind fell light and a fog drifted in so that once again the ship wallowed in a low swell that made her creak as though in agony. And then they learned that the rations were to be cut.

'This is an outrage,' Arrocheros spluttered. 'They say the captain-general has taken all the stores into his own custody.'

'Then I suggest you petition him, Don Baldivieso,' advised Iago. 'He cannot ignore a merchant of your standing and influence,' he added drily.

'I shall,' Arrocheros said boldly, almost puffing himself up with sudden determination as he turned aft. Iago went on deck; the fog lay thicker than ever, so that the bowsprit, truncated though it was, vanished into the nacreous vapour. He turned away and went below. Ah Fong was entertaining Doña Catalina, who seemed both pleased to make the Chinese woman's acquaintance amid the boredom of the voyage and to wish to assist Ah Fong's understanding of her new religion.

Ah Fong had been christened that morning and the simple ceremony had awakened a protective fervour in Señora de los Arrocheros, who had stood as godmother. Now she seemed anxious to detach the Chinese woman from her traditional gods, claiming their idolatrous nature was an affront to the one true God. Ah Fong – for she could not yet in truth be regarded as Margarita, aware that this formality was essentially a matter of Iago's standing in the ship – deployed all her courtesy in appearing to accommodate Doña Catalina's explanations and expectations. This acquiescence, naturally easy to Ah Fong, irked Iago and his intrusion disrupted the tête-à-tête.

'Has your husband gone to see Don Juan de Guillestigui?' he asked Doña Catalina.

'He has gone to take counsel with Fray Hernando and the brothers,' she said, looking up at him as Ah Fong rose, beckoning to Ximenez to get hot water so that she might make tea.

Iago nodded, taking off his cloak and sitting. 'The fog persists,' he remarked inconsequentially.

'Don Baldivieso says that it should clear soon.'

'Let us hope that your husband is right, señora, and that the wind, when it comes again, remains favourable.'

Ximenez returned with the hot water and a face twisted with excitement but held in check from expressing himself by the presence of the merchant's wife. Iago stared expectantly at the dwarf.

'Come, Ximenez, this ship is like a village. What is whispered at one end is shouted at the other within an hour . . .'

'Master?' Ximenez feigned incomprehension.

'On a ship, Ximenez, the galley is like a village well. All news is to be had there and – unless I am much mistaken – you have just found something out, eh? I am right, am I not?'

'Even a bat could see you are so full of news that you will burst like a bladder full of wine,' added Ah Fong graphically.

'We are given lentils, master, nothing more than lentil soup while the captain-general keeps a fine table. The Holy Ones and – begging your pardon, señora – Don Baldivieso and some of the others intend going aft in a body to complain.'

'I wish them good fortune. Unfortunately I do not see in our captain-general a man whose bowels will be readily wrung by merciful compassion, but . . .' He shrugged.

Iago's remark seemed to horrify Doña Catalina in her new proselytizing role. 'Don Iago!' she admonished.

'Do you find that an extraordinary proposition, señora?' Doña Catalina nodded. 'Then let us hope that I am wrong.'

But Iago was not wrong. A moment later Arrocheros

himself tore aside the canvas and appeared in outraged and tempestuous mood. 'The man's arrogance surpasses belief!' he cried, beside himself with fury. 'He turned us forward like common seamen,' he fulminated, 'despite our respectful eloquence.'

'What exactly did he say?' Iago asked.

'He told us that prime victuals would go first to those who worked the ship, whereupon I asked why it was now necessary to place any of us upon rations, to which he answered sarcastically that I must be a fool not to have realized that most of our foodstuffs was spoiled in the storms.'

'Well, I shall be surprised if he feeds all his seamen.'

'That is exactly what they are saying at the galley stove, master,' interjected Ximenez.

'What can we do?' asked Doña Catalina, her right hand clasping her breast.

'Bear it with fortitude, señora, we have little choice.'

'But, Don Iago!' Doña Catalina looked from Iago to her husband. 'Is there nothing we can do?'

'Señora, one may hunt what rats can be found on board.'

Now Arrocheros was staring at Iago, an expression of horror on his face. It was clear his hopes lay with Iago but his intelligence was asserting itself over his effrontery at the reception he and his fellow petitioners had had at the hands of Guillestigui. Iago saw horror collapse and fear replace it. Arrocheros was a drowning man and, in the manner of drowning men, clutched at the only straw he could see on his limited horizon. 'Don Iago, you . . . you *must* do something . . . You are our only hope! We can pay you!'

And to this appeal his wife added her own tearful pleading. 'Don Iago, I believe you to possess all the skills necessary to bring this ship safely into a haven.'

Iago felt an upwelling of resentment against these people, helpless though they were. 'Señora, I wish that such things were possible, but I am not the wizard some on board take me for.'

Doña Catalina piously crossed herself and, looking immediately at Ah Fong, said sharply, 'Cross yourself, Margarita, lest Don Iago's words attract the Devil.'

Iago stood, almost cracking his head on the beams above.

'Señora, if the Devil has shipped with us,' he said, cocking his ears to the noise of disturbance on deck above, 'there is no hope at all.'

'Don Iago!' Arrocheros said with a sharp intake of breath. 'Now, if you will excuse me . . .'

Iago made to pass Arrocheros, who said in a low voice, 'They say the Devil has many forms.'

Iago stopped and stared at the merchant, catching himself from making a sharp riposte. Instead he ostentatiously crossed himself and in a low voice agreed with the man barring his way. 'By Heaven, Don Baldivieso, you are right. It would not trouble the Devil to take upon himself the form of a discalced friar, a plumed *hidalgo* or even that of a sleek merchant, God help us all . . .' He let the affront sink in. Then he added: 'In fact his stink so assails my nostrils that I seek even the sea fog to clear my head of his mischief.'

The fog that enveloped them produced a curious change in the ship. It was as though the lack of a horizon shrank the entire world to the limits of the *Santa Margarita* herself. A light breeze held, but from the east, too light to disperse the fog or to hasten them on their way, but just enough to keep steerage on the ship and force them north under jury rig. The sea grew flatter, ruffled only by the zephyr, a contrast after the frights and alarms of the typhoons and the strange excesses of the orgy.

In truth the change was caused by the spoliation of the greater part of the *Santa Margarita*'s stores. The circumscribing fog only emphasized their isolation. Once Guillestigui and his party realized the seriousness of what this meant, there was a reassertion of their authority. For weeks, almost since the day they cleared the Embocadero and were borne north on the wide waters of the ocean, Guillestigui and his henchmen had relinquished day-to-day control of the *Santa Margarita* to the pilots. There had been nothing unusual in this, particularly to a man of the captain-general's stamp, for he was a self-indulgent sensualist who, had he but known it, gave the example for the wild indulgences of the ship's crew when they sensed the bonds of command were loosened by extremity. But once the viands on the cabin table failed to gratify Guillestigui's appetites, it occurred to him something was wrong, and thus it was that he sent his Basque guard to ferret through the ship while he himself imposed upon the entire company a reduction in rations.

Perhaps he himself realized the freedom with which he had allowed the pilots to take over was almost an abdication of his own authority. Certainly the vigour with which he now recovered control of the ship would suggest this to be so; but perhaps the fact that the fog obscured from his sight the mighty power of the surrounding sea also tempted him to exert his will. What he could not see he did not worry about, at least superficially. There would be time enough for that later, when he had regained control over their destinies. And his first duty lay in protecting his private faction.

As the days passed, the fog persisted and they made more progress north than east, it grew noticeably colder. Guillestigui appeared on the poop, pacing it for hours in his cloak, glaring forward over the misty decks and staring ahead to where the steeve of the broken bowsprit vanished into the grey vapour. On the half-deck below, Lorenzo, Olivera and their respective watches carried on their wearying routine. The sails needed the occasional trimming, the pumps needed manning every watch change for about half an hour, and those off duty fished over the side with some success to augment their meagre diet.

It was noticed that Guillestigui seemed to have distanced himself from his entourage. His officers still came on deck with him – indeed he was never alone and always had two or three of his gentlemen in attendance – but they kept their distance, usually huddling in their cloaks in one or other of the quarters, leaving the captain-general to pace athwart the ship along the poop rail and glare down at the minions and the passengers forward.

His presence loomed over the ship so that it seemed that even below one knew he was there. In the end it proved provocative, for Hernando and Agustin considered the presumption of pride, allied with the garnering of all the available stores and their parochial duty to the ship's company, to bring the captain-general within the pale of their own spiritual concern. Thus it was that they approached the captain-general by ascending – unbidden – the ladder from the half-deck to the poop. Lorenzo, who had the watch, tried to stop them.

'Stand aside, my son!' commanded Agustin and such was the gleam in his eyes that Lorenzo – in defiance of his good sense – obeyed. But he could not help watching what happened.

As the discalced friars climbed the ladder, Agustin leading, Guillestigui turned at the end of his walk and approached them with a slow and measured tread. The three men confronted one another at the head of the larboard ladder.

'I do not recall summoning you,' Guillestigui said haughtily.

'You did not, my son,' Agustin replied. 'We are here on God's work.'

'You are not welcome, either of you . . .'

'That we are not welcome by you is of no concern to us,' Agustin went on. 'We have come to discuss the plight we are in and to inform you that while we understand the cabin table remains well stocked, the people are on rations so short that it is unlikely that they will be able to subsist until we reach Acapulco. We come to ask – no, to *insist* that you share what remains of our foodstuffs.'

'Insist? You come to me to insist?' Guillestigui seemed amused. 'Why, you men of God may live on a few beans and a dried crust; that is your avocation. It is not for you to insist upon anything.' His tone was reasonable, so reasonable in fact that it fooled Agustin.

'Don Juan Martinez,' he began, 'it cannot be right to have half – no, the greater proportion of the ship's company – driven to starvation.'

'Starvation?' Guillestigui frowned with mock incomprehension. 'See, good Father, how amidships they are hoisting fishes from the sea just as the disciples did on Galilee . . . Now, I am of a mind to tempt you to turn that bounty to good account except that I know that the Devil tempted Christ and it would be sinful of me to do so. Nevertheless, I consider it wise for you to return whence you came and enjoy some fish and set some to dry for the coming days.'

'We cannot live on fish indefinitely, Don Juan, and you know we can only take fish now with the ship moving so slowly . . .'

'You do not comprehend me, Father. I am ordering you to go below.'

'And I am here to plead the case of the people.'

'Damn the people. If the people wish to speak with me let them send a delegation through the pilot-major. They know how things must be done. I will not tolerate any of you meddlesome religious speaking on behalf of the people. Get below while I still command my temper.'

Hernando made to turn away, plucking at Agustin's habit, but the friar was not so easily persuaded. 'I am not to be so turned off the purpose of my embassy . . .'

'Embassy! Embassy? What gibberish do you spout, you insignificant worm? Get off my deck!' Guillestigui half-turned his head. 'Gentlemen!'

The officers, all three of whom had been trying to hear what was being said, now crowded forward. Peralta had his right hand on his sword hilt, the blade started from its scabbard. 'Remove these vermin!' the captain-general ordered, falling back a pace.

But even as Hernando had the soles of the open sandals that gave his order its name on the top step of the ladder, Agustin dropped to his knees, his right hand holding up the crucifix he wore round his neck. 'You shall not touch me, villains!' he cried, and Peralta and the others hesitated.

'Ah,' said Guillestigui stepping forward again, 'there is one for martyrdom, if I am not mistaken.' He held up his hand to touch Peralta's arm. 'Shall we gratify him his desire? Shall we flay the dog of his skin and make a belt and a box of it to hang round his neck that he may beg upon the streets of Acapulco and live off the charity of the people whose cause he so espouses? What do you think, Rodrigo? Shall we skin the—' and here Guillestigui grabbed the collar and hood of Agustin's habit and with a powerful jerk pulled it down over his arms so that the unexpected movement caused the friar to drop his crucifix. It swung on its leather thong against Agustin's pale chest as his arms were pinioned by the habit. Guillestigui, with a second mighty haul, spun the friar round, exposing the upper part of his back. It was disfigured with the dried and scabby whip-marks of his flagellation.

'Ah, see how he has cheated us of this sport, Rodrigo. He

has spoiled his hide. No wonder he has mustered such affrontery, he has been mortifying himself. He is holy beyond the comprehension of mere *men*.' And with a third movement of his sword arm, Guillestigui threw Agustin from him so that the friar sprawled full length on the deck. Guillestigui jerked his head and Peralta and another officer bent and heaved Agustin down the ladder into Hernando's arms.

'You have had little to say, Fray Hernando. Have Christ or the cat got your tongue, eh?'

'God will judge you, Don Juan Martinez, you may be assured of that.'

'And since God is master of this world, Fray Hernando, he will judge those in high office according to their responsibilities.'

'God help you . . .'

'God *keep* you,' riposted Guillestigui. Then, looking up and seeing many of those forward staring aft at the scene on the high poop, he shouted: 'Turn to your duty, men. Do not trouble yourselves with the prating of these religious.'

And, such is the perversity of human nature, there came a thin cheer from those gladdened by the sight of a discomfited friar, notwithstanding the nature of his mission.

Ten

The Pilot-Major

Iago, Ah Fong and Ximenez were settling for sleep, huddling into their blankets for the damp chill of the fog penetrated their quarters, when the canvas screen was torn rudely aside. Pedro Ruiz de Olalde led two armed men into the small space, their heavy leather boots trampling on Ximenez's blankets.

'Hey, you dogs!' the dwarf began remonstrating as he tried to tug the captured bedding from under the heavy boot-sole.

Olalde silenced him with a single swipe of a short switch. Ximenez recoiled with a sharp yelp, his hand going to the weal rising across his cheek and his eyes glaring with cold fury at his tormentor who stood above him, the faint light gleaming on the sergeant-major's half-armour.

'What the hell are you doing?' Iago cried, throwing his legs out of the hammock.

'Stay where you are, *Don* Iago,' Olalde ordered sarcastically. 'I have come for your sword.'

'My sword? What is my sword to you?'

'The captain-general has given instructions to collect all weapons.'

'I am a gentleman, confound it!' protested Iago.

'So you say. I obey orders.'

'You dishonour me!' Iago exclaimed.

Olalde turned and nodding to the two men beside him pointed to the katana hanging under the beam-knee above Ah Fong's bed-place. 'One cannot dishonour that which is devoid of honour,' he said conversationally, bending down and lifting the corner of Ah Fong's bed covering as he awaited the removal of the sword. His insult conveyed two different and distinct meanings and he seemed pleased with his wit.

Ah Fong snatched the bedding from the prying hand. 'I cannot think how you deceived us into thinking this was a boy, *Don* Iago. Was that not a dishonourable thing to do, eh?'

Having helped themselves to the Japanese sword the two men withdrew, leaving Olalde to regard the three of them discomfited in the relaxed moments before sleep. He looked at Iago.

'*¡Buenas noches!* Don Iago, and do not think that I shall not be watching every move you make.' He next shook his head at Ah Fong and smiled. 'A boy, eh? What a fool you made of us.'

Then he turned, deliberately trod upon Ximenez's bed, leaving a boot-print on the blanket, and, just before letting the canvas fall behind him, he emitted a loud fart.

'*¡Tirarse un pedo, asqueroso!*' Ximenez fulminated, holding his nose while his master above him stared at the swinging canvas curtain.

Iago slumped back into his hammock with an oath, wondering what to do. Should he go in pursuit of his sword at once? He had smelt liquor on Olalde's breath and knew that at this hour those about Guillestigui would be awash with wine. If he were to be admitted to the captain-general's presence, he would almost certainly be humiliated. And yet he knew too, that if he did nothing he was already humiliated in the eyes of Ah Fong, for he had lost face in front of her. He looked down at her and she was staring at him.

'I am not going after those men, beloved,' he said. 'They are drunk, the night is cold and Iago is not a fool.'

She nodded, a brief accommodation of his sometimes incomprehensible behaviour. Ximenez spoke. 'Forgive the presumption, master, but to be humbled by men such as those is no dishonour. It is better to make a time of your own choosing to take revenge.'

'You have some experience of such matters, eh?' Iago said, grinning despite his anger.

'Oh yes, master. It is a natural consequence of dwelling so close to the earth.'

'Then let us bide our time and hope . . . Put out the light.'

It grew colder towards dawn. Iago woke to hear the chatter of Ximenez's teeth. 'Are you frozen, Ximenez?' he hissed.

'Like to a corpse, master.'

Iago swung himself out of his hammock, dragged his blanket after him and covered the dwarf.

'Master . . .'

'Shh . . . Do not wake Ah Fong. I am going on deck,' he said in a low voice, dressing. Ah Fong lay curled up, fast asleep. Sometimes, he thought pulling his doublet on, she did look like a boy. She was from a hardy breed, better used to enduring hardship than poor Ximenez.

On deck the pallid light of dawn made the fog glow with a faint luminosity. The decks were sodden and moisture dripped incessantly from the ropes, sails and spars above them, where it condensed in such a profusion of droplets that they fell like a lazy drizzle. Olivera had the watch and nodded to Iago.

They exchanged greetings. '*Buenas días.*'

'*Buenas días.*'

'There is a swell building,' Olivera said, 'and the wind has yet to come away again from the westward in strength . . .'

Iago divined the anxiety in the second pilot's mind. The swell presaged more bad weather, the failure of the westerly wind any release from this interminable northerly drift. Yet the direction of the swell seemed . . .

But no, in this fog and with the ship wallowing under so little sail, it was impossible to be certain where the wind would come from when it freshened.

'My God, but it is chilly . . .' Iago shivered. He had been too long in tropical climes.

'I hear the captain-general's Negroes are near frozen,' Olivera remarked indifferently as though the shuddering blacks were, like the mysterious column of mercury, merely an indication of temperature. A thought struck Iago and he stared at Olivera; it was simple to ascribe the second pilot's indifference to the customary contempt meted out to the black slaves, but Iago thought he detected something else underlying his attitude, something profounder and therefore disquieting. He sought an answer in the older man's eyes and Olivera noticed the inquisition.

'We are going to the Devil, Don Iago,' he said in a low and confidential tone. 'You, me, that girl of yours, the dwarf, the captain-general, his swinish following, the religious, that fornicating rabble that call themselves *marineros*, the whole damnable lot, benighted Negroes included.'

'Come, this is not cheering . . .'

'Do *you* think we can sail the great ocean under this pathetic rig, our rudder suspect, our stores spoiled, our ship divided into more factions than the Christian kingdoms of Europe? Why, we are incapable of laying our course!'

Iago gave a reluctant nod. 'That swine Olalde forced his way into my quarters last night and took away my sword.'

'That curious and murderous weapon from Cipangu?'

'The same.'

'That is monstrous!'

'Oh, I am offended, *mi amigo*, but I knew them to be drunk and only a fool remonstrates with drunks in authority.'

'But you are a gentleman. A *sobrasaliente*.'

'I might as well have been a Negro.'

'The man has . . .' Olivera bit his lip and changed tack. 'He favours his Basque henchmen. Blood is ever thicker than water. I believe they would do murder for one another and call it friendly obligation.'

'Or loyalty.'

'Ties that bind, eh?' Olivera paused, then added, 'Emotion overrules reason: man's perennial curse.'

They fell silent for a moment and then the second pilot said, 'I think that we should put back to the westward. Lorenzo is of like mind and will speak with the captain-general this forenoon.'

'You think it our only chance?'

Olivera nodded. 'Aye, and a slender one at that.'

'But Cipangu lies to the west,' Iago began.

'I know,' Olivera interrupted, 'and the fate of the *San Felipe* is uppermost in my mind, but that was four years ago.'

'A people with a taste for massacres do not change in four years.'

'Perhaps a cut with a sword such as yours is a swifter, pleasanter death than slowly starving among this shit, like a dog in the gutters of Madrid.'

'I do not think of myself,' Iago said in a low voice, 'but of my wife.'

'A woman makes a man hostage to fortune. Even while she accepts his seed she rips the very manhood from his bowels.'

'God ordained it thus.'

Olivera shook his head and with a short laugh said, 'Oh, no, my friend, it was Adam who caused this misery, the damned fool.'

'Whomsoever. It is thus.'

'You will tell me she is with child next.'

'God forbid,' Iago replied fervently.

They fell silent again and then Olivera asked, 'Have you come to relieve me?'

Iago nodded. 'As you wish.'

'Does a man die best tired or alert?'

'Since the when is unknown to us, and the why is obvious, the how can hang uncertain between the two.'

'Faith, Don Iago, you are too sharp. I shall sleep. She keeps before the wind. Anything else is beyond our crippled state.'

Iago grunted. Perhaps he might haul a brace and make it otherwise, but not much. Besides, if they were to run for Cipangu, what did it matter? He fell to pacing the deck, matching the sluggish wallow of the rolling ship. Dawn grew into daylight, lightening the fog so the *Santa Margarita* swam in a damp, cold and tiny world of her own misery. The watch change which should have seen the oncoming men cheered by having broken their fast and the off-going eager to break theirs was a shambling, resentful milling of chilled and miserable men. Here and there the abusive calls of a hungry shrew followed them on deck.

Hunger and cold are dangerous enemies to discipline, Iago mused. He feared the sullen *marineros* more than all the yellow tribes of Cipangu and wondered if they still had their knives. Looking closer he saw that not one single sailor bore a knife at his belt, only empty sheaths. This, he realized, added reason to the black looks cast aft where, he sensed, they were disappointed to see himself – a volunteer – upon the half-deck.

'Is the helm relieved?' he asked, as much to test their mood as to determine whether the whipstaff was properly manned.

'Aye, sir,' a voice responded, 'but there the matter ends, for there is no breakfast.'

'No, I know. I too am hungry. The pilot-major intends addressing the captain-general in an hour or so.'

A murmuring met this information. 'I understand,' someone

concealed from Iago's line of sight called out, 'I understand the captain-general dined well last night.'

'He may well have done but I was not invited. Now boil some water, there is surely some tea.' Iago temporized in face of the ugly mood of the men.

'I would rather drink Chinese piss from thy wife, Don Iago. It would refresh better.'

Iago ignored the coarse slight, though his heart beat faster, for a danger lurked in that mass of discontented men and he knew the direction it would take. 'Tea will console you a little and the Chinese take it to stay the pangs of hunger, pangs with which they are familiar.'

'We are not Chinese. We are Christians . . .'

'Then you must exercise some Christian fortitude,' began Marmolejo, who appeared on deck amongst them. 'We shall fish again, like the disciples on Galilee, and God will reward us if we have faith.'

At the sight of the friar the men broke up and went about their business with a sullen acquiescence.

'Your appearance is most fortuitous, Fray Mateo,' Iago remarked as Marmolejo joined him on the half-deck.

'I heard them baiting you. This all bears an ugly stamp.'

'Aye.'

'There are a score of Negroes freezing half to death in this damp chill.'

'I know. Lorenzo means to speak to the captain-general later.'

'To what purpose?'

Iago shrugged. 'To turn back, to divert our course to Cipangu. Perhaps to land at the first island we encounter.'

'How far may that be?'

'I do not know. I have not been keeping a reckoning. Perhaps two hundred miles.'

'I hear the dogs conspire, Don Iago, I hope you have sent them about their business.'

Both Iago and Marmolejo turned at the interruption. Neither had heard the captain-general come on deck but Iago bowed.

'A passing mood, Excellency. The men are hungry, that is all.'

'We are all hungry,' Guillestigui said, turning to Marmolejo.

'At least you religious can tolerate it. The mariners, I presume, cannot.'

'The mariners, Excellency, have much to do,' Iago said. 'The ship still needs regular pumping and our lack of progress is demoralizing . . .'

'Do you presume to tell me my business, Don Iago?'

'I presume nothing, Excellency.'

'That is well . . .'

'I shall presume, Excellency,' said Marmolejo. 'We must turn back, or make for the nearest land.'

'Must we, Fray Mateo Marmolejo? And when did you acquire expertise in these matters?'

'As any man knows . . .'

'Do you, Fray Mateo, go below and gather up all the Negroes and move them into the warmth under the half-deck. Gather them to you religious and warm them lest they freeze to death.' Guillestigui glared at Marmolejo until the Franciscan bowed his head and went below. Then the captain-general turned to Iago.

'Well, señor, Pedro de Olalde tells me you have a remonstrance for me.'

'You have no right to deprive me of my sword, Excellency.'

'It is not, I think, a gentleman's sword.'

'In Cipangu it is the mark of a knight.'

'But we are not in Cipangu, nor were you when you acquired it.'

'Is Your Excellency implying I am not worthy of wearing it?'

'You understand me perfectly, señor. You are a *marinero* . . .' And there, it seemed, Guillestigui would leave the matter, with Iago gaping after him as he strode away. He passed a seaman who had been coiling a line down on the poop and, having finished, was coming forward. In passing Guillestigui, the man failed to salute the captain-general.

Guillestigui's gauntleted hand shot out and seized the man's arm. 'What is your name?'

'I am Enrique, señor.'

'Is that the way to address His Most Catholic Majesty's captain-general?'

The man pulled himself defiantly away from Guillestigui's grip. 'I am hungry, señor. An empty belly lacks respect.'

With a rasp Guillestigui had drawn his sword.

'Excellency!' Iago cried, fearful at what the captain-general might do, but Guillestigui was beside himself.

'Let me see this empty belly of yours!' he cried and struck at the seaman, who drew back and parried the disembowelling blade with his right arm. Guillestigui took the arm off above the elbow and Enrique fell back, pumping arterial blood over the deck and crying out with the shock of the assault. The incident had occurred so quickly that few saw it, but those who had stared in stunned silence. Turning forward and wiping his sword blade through his gloved left hand, Guillestigui gathered their attention.

'See there! That is what insolence receives! Think well on it and render to Caesar that which is Caesar's!' Catching Iago's eye and gesturing to the twitching Enrique, he said, 'Throw that thing overboard, Don Iago. We must maintain discipline at all costs.'

The captain-general shot his sword into its scabbard. As he turned to leave he was met by Peralta coming on deck, clearly in quest of his master. Peralta stared for a moment at the scene before him, then Iago heard him tell the captain-general, 'Two of them are dead. Quite frozen.'

'*¡Dios!*' exclaimed Guillestigui, and Iago guessed the expression was wrung from the captain-general on account of the fiscal loss of two black slaves. It scarcely mollified his own resentment at the treatment he had just received, or the supposed punishment and outrageous summary execution of the wretched seaman Enrique.

Guillestigui had led Peralta to the rail where they remained deep in conversation and ignoring Enrique as he lay in a spreading pool of blood. Iago went to the man and lifted him a little but it was too late. He recognized the *marinero* as one of those prominent in the orgy. Now Enrique's face was set in a snarling rictus as his body emptied of blood. A moment later Iago heard the death rattle in Enrique's throat and felt life leave him.

Iago was consumed by a sudden, panicky terror: what would become of them? Yet Enrique's unpredictable death seemed a catalyst, for Iago emerged from his shock aware of a subtle change in the very air about them. The breeze was filling in, the fog lifting. He could see the end of the bowsprit extemporized by the cadet Silva, and the lift in the sails seemed to animate the ship. Iago stared at the weft lifting from the stump of the mainmast and called down to the duty mate to alter course a point to the eastward.

Perhaps . . .

Like the proverbial drowning man, Iago grasped at the passing straw.

The change in the weather brought the ship to life, for the wind continued to shift and before the end of his watch the *Santa Margarita*'s head had been brought round a further five points to the eastward. When, in the wake of Enrique's death, Lorenzo sought an audience with the captain-general, he was refused on the grounds – or so Peralta said – that matters would now swiftly mend themselves and they would soon be heading due east. No argument from the pilot-major would remove Peralta's objection, for his master had retreated to the great cabin.

Also below, but forward, under the half-deck, the Negroes thawed out amid the protests of Arrocheros, who complained of sharing the space with them. Here Iago found Marmolejo praying over the bodies of the dead black slaves and the mutilated Enrique as two nuns prepared them for burial. Any intention to bury them formally was wrecked by Guillestigui, who with his officers now occupied the poop fully armed and dressed in half-armour. The captain-general, angry that his original instruction to toss Enrique's body overboard had been ignored, ordered the corpses thrown over the side – unless, he added, their fellow blacks wished to eat them and thus stay their hunger.

That evening, as the sun set in a lurid chaos of cloud, three of the seamen were reported sick with scurvy and another was said to be close to death. 'Let them die in order that we may live,' the captain-general was heard to remark. 'Go and search the seamen's quarters again for any hidden food. No man should eat that cannot work.'

Once again, as night fell, armed men rummaged the ship, finding little but causing great resentment so that Lorenzo again attempted to speak to the captain-general. Choosing a moment when both were on deck, Lorenzo turned aft and shouted, 'A word with you, Excellency, I must speak with you.'

With a sinister rasp Peralta intervened, drawing his sword and crying, 'I told you to be silent!'

Lorenzo did not falter but drew a dagger from his waist and, surprising Peralta, slashed at the foible of his blade, passing him as he did so and confronting Guillestigui.

'Excellency, you must heed me. It is my bounden duty to acquaint you of the dangers—'

But Olalde jumped in front of the captain-general. 'Give me that,' he snarled, indicating the short weapon Lorenzo still held in his right hand.

With a flick of his wrist Lorenzo threw the dagger over the side. 'Stand aside! I am the pilot-major. Damn you! Stand aside!'

'What do you wish to say, Don Juan, eh?' asked Guillestigui with an affected curiosity. 'That we must put back, or cast ourselves upon the hospitality of the natives of Cipangu?'

'Make a landfall, Excellency. That is all I ask, so that we may put the vessel to rights and recruit our strength.'

'And that is your professional advice?'

'That is my professional advice, Excellency.'

'Then, Don Juan,' Guillestigui replied in a voice heavy with sarcasm, 'I shall consider it and I shall give you an answer in the morning.'

And with this Lorenzo had to be content.

But next morning it was found that one of the captain-general's Biscayan soldiers had died in the night. The cause of death was not clear and it was widely rumoured that those aft thought him a victim of witchcraft.

'What other cause might there be?' they asked. 'He was fit and well yesterday.'

Another, a soldier named Diego, who had been sick for several days, demanded that one of the discalced friars hear his confession. Fray Agustin was summoned and upon speaking with the sick man refused to shrive him, saying he was not dying and that a day or two reflecting upon his sins would bring him closer to a state of contrition. Hearing this Olalde was outraged. He ordered Agustin and his brethren to be denied any food for three days, a foolish instruction that revealed those living aft still had access to provisions. As for

Agustin, he replied that he had not eaten for several days anyway and he would return when the man had humbled himself.

'That holy bastard punishes Diego in order to point a finger of accusation at our captain-general,' opined Olalde to Calcagorta.

'May they all rot in Hell-fire,' the gunner responded. 'Come, let us inform the captain-general.'

Meanwhile Lorenzo, who had kept the morning watch and had handed over to Olivera, remained on deck, awaiting the captain-general's pleasure. The wind had fallen a little but they moved slowly through a blue sea under a sky clear of all but the frivolous clouds of fair weather. Despite these apparent auguries of improving conditions, Lorenzo remained introspective and gloomy. Resigned to the ritual humiliation inherent in the captain-general's contempt for the ship's own officers, he waited, sitting on a box among the remaining cargo lashed forward of the binnacle.

After the days of fog, the dry air seemed invigorating and, he thought, he should be uplifted by the morning. He tried to recall the happiness he had felt when he dreamed of again sleeping with his wife, but he could not recover the mood. Instead, staring out over the starboard beam, he reflected upon the misery the high command of a ship was capable of inflicting upon her company if it resided in the wrong hands. And then his eye was caught by a low bank of cloud gathering to the south-east. They had seen the same thing before and it seemed scarcely possible that yet another *baguiosa* was working its way towards them. Lorenzo's heart sank; surely the Lord God Almighty could not inflict . . .

And then something puzzling happened. Lorenzo was tired. He should have been off watch, asleep, and his mind, preparing itself for an interview with Guillestigui, had been distracted by the assembling cloud-bank. He did not therefore understand why, all of a sudden and on an otherwise beautiful morning, the low cloud should disappear as the sea between the *Santa Margarita* and the horizon seemed to rise in a low and growing hump. By the time his exhausted brain had divined its significance it was too late. All he could do was cry out a warning.

The *Santa Margarita* seemed to stagger in her forward motion.

Iago felt it below and knew she had slipped into the trough of a big swell. Instinctively he knew something was wrong, that the sudden drop in the deck below his feet bore no relationship with the easy motion that had for hours preceded it.

'Hold on!' he commanded Ah Fong and Ximenez as they sat sipping the tea that answered for breakfast in their impoverished state. Even down below they could hear the sudden cry of alarm raised on deck. Iago felt fear uncoil in his belly and the hairs on his neck rose like hackles. A second later the whole starboard side of the *Santa Margarita* shuddered as though slamming into something solid. Then in a roar an immense body of water poured thundering across the *Santa Margarita*'s deck, squirting, streaming and cascading below by way of a thousand routes, spraying water overall and instantly covering the deck to a depth of several inches.

The ship rolled to port under the impact and then, as the roaring of the water sluicing across the deck above diminished, she came upright and seemed to lift as though throwing the burden aside. Iago rushed for the upper deck, where he found utter consternation. Residual water still ran back and forth across the rolling deck and, looking out to port, Iago saw the retreating hump of the rogue swell as it caught the sunlight. Then he saw the smashed bulwarks on the port side of the half-deck, and the men craning over the side and crying out: 'Man overboard!'

'Who is it?' he asked, rushing to the ship's side, aware that the deck was rapidly filling with terrified men and the incident had summoned even the captain-general from his fastness in the great cabin.

'It is the pilot-major!' Olivera said, turning to him, his eyes wide and his face white.

'There is no sign of him!'

'He and his chest have vanished!'

'Put up the helm!'

'God has taken him . . .'

'Or the Devil,' roared a voice above them all. 'Stand fast, belay the helm! Don Juan is dead.'

Guillestigui's outburst silenced them, drawing their attention from the sparkling wake inboard to the deck just vacated by the unfortunate Lorenzo. 'What else was that,' boomed Guillestigui, 'but an act of God? Eh? Whence came that monstrous wave?' The captain-general flung his right hand out to starboard. 'See, there are no more of them, just as there were none before it.'

The thought of such a singular manifestation forced upon them by the captain-general's explanation struck them all like a blow. Several fell to their knees and all crossed themselves with a hasty fervour. Even Iago felt the power of the argument and of Guillestigui's almost diabolical presence. The sudden visitation of death sent a cold shiver down his spine and he recalled that cry of alarm that was Lorenzo's final act in life.

Then a voice broke the silence. 'Excellency! The starboard galleries have gone!'

As one they all ran across the deck to crowd the rail on the starboard side, gasping their astonished surprise at the prospect before them. All along the side of the high poop, jagged timbers stood horizontally from the ship's side like the remains of the floor beams in a burned-out keep. A rising murmur ran among them and Iago, recovering from the shock of the event, turned to see Marmolejo, just then coming on deck, disturbed by the shouts of alarm passing below decks.

'What in the name of God?'

'Some curious and heavy sea caught us. Lorenzo has been lost overboard. There is no sign of him. The entire starboard stern gallery has been torn off the ship's side and God knows what other damage has been done. We must sound the wells.'

'Why do we not put the ship about?'

'How can we? Look about you. It is as much as we can do to keep her somewhere close to her course.'

'A boat, then . . .'

'Boat? What boat is left? Besides, there was no sign of him. That monstrous sea has carried him away. We should never find him. He is gone. Drowned.'

'Dear God!' Marmolejo crossed himself and began praying for Lorenzo's soul.

'Juan . . . Juan . . .' Shock still gripped Olivera. The second pilot digested the implication of Lorenzo's loss. 'My God, my God . . . we are indeed undone . . .' He crossed himself and muttered a few words of Latin. 'But he dreamed only recently that he would lie with his wife again,' Olivera remarked, puzzled by what had occurred.

'Aye, my friend,' Iago said gently, placing a hand on Olivera's arm, 'but others dream too. Only the other night Ximenez dreamed this ship would lose her pilot.'

'¡Dios! How prescient. My poor, poor friend . . .' Olivera shook his head and looked down, but not before Iago had spotted the tears welling up. Grief for a friend and colleague; desperation at their plight; perhaps that personal rage a man feels when it seems that the fates have so conspired against him that he can muster nothing further. Iago withdrew his hand as Olivera seemed to shake himself free of his burden and recall himself to his duty with an in-draught of breath. Then he raised his head and pointed at the eastern horizon. 'I do not like the colour of that sky . . .' he muttered, then he looked at Iago, frowning. 'Another *baguiosa*?'

'Perhaps, Antonio,' said Iago, a growing anxiety gnawing at him, 'but for the moment we *must* sound the well, for the love of Jesus!'

'Yes . . . yes, of course.' Olivera shook himself free of his private preoccupations and crossed himself. 'You are a good man, Iago. For the love of Christ stand by me in the coming hours. I shall have need of you.'

'Of course.'

Finally pulling himself together, Olivera said, 'Do you take the deck and I shall go below . . .' Managing a wan smile he went off, muttering. Then he raised his voice and called for the carpenters. Within five minutes he was back, but Iago already knew the worst. The *Santa Margarita* had assumed a slight list. It was clear that the great ship was again taking in water.

'We must man the pumps,' Olivera cried, his voice cracking with desperation. Iago nodded. 'And muster a party aft to plug the holes left by that missing gallery. Good God, is there no end to our troubles?

Eleven
Reductio ad Absurdum

They had scarcely nailed the planks from broken packing cases over the gaping holes in the starboard quarter and stuffed the interstices with cotton piece goods before the wind had risen. The onset of the panic of self-preservation had infected the men and they had worked like fury for six hours, but at the end of that period, as the sky clouded over and once again they were beset by a gale, all hands were exhausted. To the lack of food was now added a lack of water, several of the casks in the hold being found breached and contaminated with salt.

By nightfall, despite a rallying of the after-guard by Guillestigui – who seemed at last to understand the true obligations of leadership – even the pumping had been abandoned by the gentlemen and the ship was given up for lost. During the night, as the wind and sea grew increasingly furious, the only stirrings on board were the chants of plaints of the Holy Ones who cried out for Heaven's mercy, attributing all their woes to the sins of fornication, greed and excess displayed by all on board from the captain-general to the lowliest *marinero*. Most particularly they called upon God to lift the curse of Ocampo in whose efficacy no one on board except perhaps Iago now had any doubt.

The following morning more of the Negroes were found dead. Some said it was of cold, others claimed shock and fear had killed them.

'I am told by one of their number,' said Marmolejo, who had prayed over them, 'that they abandon life when it is impossible to join the spirits of their ancestors. It is a blasphemy, of course,' he added, 'but not one to surprise us among the heathen.'

'Perhaps not,' Iago responded curtly. He was hungry and worried for Ah Fong to whom he had relinquished the hammock. She too lay in that passive acceptance of the inevitable that Marmolejo found so shocking but Iago had seen before in China. All about them the ship staggered and rolled, her fabric creaking so loudly at times that they had to shout to make themselves heard. To this cacophony were added the wails and groans of all those now crowded into the shelter under the half-deck, most of whom lay amid the constant swirl of water and a complete disorder of blankets, disintegrating straw palliasses, pots, beakers, plates, knives, clothing and every conceivable personal effect brought aboard in Cavite by passengers and crew alike.

'*Reductio ad absurdum*,' remarked Marmolejo, gesturing about them and running a dry tongue about his lips.

Iago merely nodded and braced himself against the *Santa Margarita*'s next lurch as the thunder of yet another green sea rolled over the waterlogged and helpless vessel. Water cascaded down through the ever-loosening caulking in the deck above. A corner of the spritsail was all the standing canvas she had set and there was not a man fit or willing to go aloft and salvage the other canvas, which had long since blown itself to ribbons.

'You have stopped crossing yourself, Fray Marmolejo,' an emaciated Iago observed wryly.

'It is sorely testing,' Marmolejo replied.

And so it was, for death was among the ship's company. After the wretched black slaves and the soldier Diego – who died unshriven – others began to fail. Already weak and hungry, several succumbed to latent diseases but it was the *Santa Margarita* herself that killed others, as if the spirit of the saint after whom she had been named claimed vengeance on the sex that had dishonoured her.

As the typhoon raged and swept the helpless ship in its path, she filled slowly. One morning five people were found drowned overnight, having been engulfed in their sleep, their corpses washed back and forth in the foot or so of water that lay upon the deck.

The discovery provoked a bout of energetic pumping which lasted less than half an hour before those who fell exhausted from the handles lay about the upper deck. Then, in one terrible moment, a green sea foamed aboard and swept seventeen over the side and into the boiling ocean. No one heard their shrieks as water stopped their cries and the booming roar of the great wind sounded its vast funerary note above their last sentient minutes.

And then there were the injured; a dozen or so who were swept off their feet and carried along the decks like corks to strike stanchions or gun carriages or the fine heavy carved ornaments that stood at the head of the main companionway. Arms and legs were broken, some snapping like twigs, while others suffered immense contusions which darkened like gangrene. The woman who had lost an eye was one of these, suffering a compound fracture of her left leg. As the days wore on, the pain of unset bones, of fractures and indeed of gangrene itself caused further deaths, so that in between their heartfelt pleas for mercy, the Holy Ones moved among the sick and dying to save them from damnation.

Men retreated to their bed-places, dragging what women were available with them. At first the latter seemed more resilient than the men, more tenacious of life and less convinced that their time had come, but after almost a week of buffeting, when the labouring ship seemed to be falling apart about them, they too relinquished the ghost. Pain either drove them mad, leaving them raving at the tops of their voices, or reduced them to whimpering shadows. The one-eyed woman lasted a week.

Among it all the Holy Ones shone. Hernando, Agustin, Marmolejo and their brethren, along with the handful of nuns, moved with an emaciated dignity. They had no need of flagellation, their bodies were as excoriated by circumstance as they had never been by their whips. They heard the confessions of the dying, administered the last rites and shrove souls with a quiet dedication that defied the hell that the ship had become. Some of those thus assisted gave promises of renewed virtue, bargaining their lives with God. Many guaranteed chastity in return for continuing existence, even aboard the *Santa Margarita*, but most men and women confronted the inevitable end with the crucifix pressed to their lips, believing themselves close to the martyrs.

Few died well. Most were wracked with agony unless their moment came with a wave and the terror of drowning under tons of water, with perhaps a final glimpse of the *Santa Margarita* drawing away. These passed unconfessed, only a retrospective blessing falling upon the heaving sea if their disappearance was noticed and one of the friars stood clinging long enough upon the poop, alongside the battered figure of the Virgin, to make the gesture of the cross and to utter the prayer of committal.

What discipline remained rested entirely in two camps. Aft, within the security of the great cabin, Guillestigui and his henchmen maintained themselves on the remains of the salvaged food and their wine. Under the half-deck, led by Marmolejo and the Holy Ones, and by Iago and Olivera, what remained of the passengers and the ship's company took shelter. They had almost nothing to eat, though every day a party climbed into the hold, finding among the disturbances of the ship's motion a paucity of indigestible matter: some flour, a handful of mildewing raisins, the remains of a cask of salt beef that had been cast up from the bottom of the hold as the stow above broke up, and a few rats.

Despite a lingering attempt to maintain a watch, the *Santa Margarita* was not under command. Having been run off before the wind she was confined within the embracing advance of the typhoon. In time this had inevitably moved slowly past her and one morning they again found themselves within the centre of the typhoon's eye. They lay in a confused and heaving sea which reared up to what appeared to be an immense height from all directions in a weltering confusion of energy, meeting and crashing and falling back so that anything in its way was subjected to vast, unremitting and random blows as tons of water fell.

Having broken down the barriers erected where the lost stern galleries had wounded the ship's side, such seas began to demolish the after part of the *Santa Margarita* as she lay at their mercy. Having taken Lorenzo, they now smashed what remained of his cabin on the starboard side of the upper poop, next to that of Olivera. To the anger of the two pilots, Guillestigui had filled some of this space with cases of private cargo and a heavy sea carried away the glazed lights and much of the framing across the stern, lifting and loosening the crates so that a subsequent sea tore them free and thrust them against the forward bulkhead. Pierced as it was by a door, it was not long before, with a rending of timber, the packing cases burst through and on to the half-deck, almost sweeping Olivera and the cadet Silva off their feet as they dodged out of the way. Finally the cases and the timbers they had dislodged crashed out through the weakened bulwarks, smashing open as they went, their brilliantly coloured silk contents torn and streaming behind them like garish stains upon the sea. This incongruity, even among the destruction and horror of the ship's physical disintegration, caused the young Silva to remark that it seemed that the sea was laughing at them.

'We are being taunted,' he said with the wonderment of youth that could not quite believe that he too might shortly be confronted by his own death.

'The sea knows too much of our hearts are in those boxes and is extracting its own ruthless tribute,' Olivera replied, clinging on to a starboard backstay, his perception heightened by a ravenous hunger and the wild look of an ascetic.

'You are right, Don Antonio. It has come to get them,' Silva shouted, his eyes wide.

'There were forty cases in there and now look – all are gone!' Olivera said.

'Oh, God, Don Antonio,' Silva cried out pointing, 'see what else has been taken!'

For a moment Olivera was at a loss and then, following the cadet's straightened arm, he saw the empty niche: the votive statue of the saviour's Holy Mother had been carried away by the cruel sea. '¡Dios!' he cried, crossing himself. 'First Juan and now this!'

The *Santa Margarita* was subject to this assault for the remainder of the day, mocked not only by the sea but by the circle of cloudless blue sky high above them while all about the horizon, where they could see it beyond the flying, high-flung crests of the waves, the cloud ringed them. Shortly before sunset, or before the dying of that dreadful day – for the sun made no appearance – the fore-part of the ship received as a heavy a blow as had assaulted the poop a few hours earlier.

The crushing weight of water dragged the ship's head down, tore one of Calcagorta's sakers from its lashings and smashed the *Santa Margarita*'s beakhead with a concussive blow that sent shudders throughout the structure of the entire ship. When her bow rose from the roil of white water that swirled about the destroyed forward section, it bore little resemblance to its previous appearance. Falling from the forecastle, the mighty mass of solid water had swept across the waist, tearing the tarpaulin stretched and battened across the square of the hatch, snapping the two chains which had been padlocked across it. Floating the hatch-boards beneath, it swept five men and a single woman over the side as the *Santa Margarita* lolled over to her larboard beam ends.

Under the half-deck bodies and artefacts fell indiscriminately to the low side. On the half-deck above, Olivera and Iago grabbed at ropes to hold on and watched in stupefied helplessness as the hapless individuals went overboard in a cascade of white water. Waving arms above their drowning heads their screams and cries were cut off as they vanished.

The *Santa Margarita* recovered slowly; filled with water she might have lain there until finally overwhelmed, but such was the furious unpredictability of the upsurging sea that she rolled back to starboard. Olivera and Iago stared at each other.

'I thought—' Olivera said, cutting himself short rather than actually mention their shared fear of capsizing.

''Tis a miracle!' they heard someone cry, and looking round saw four of the five men and the woman gasping like landed fish as the water that had washed them back on board slowly drained away through the gun-ports in the waist.

'We are saved!' one shouted, but at this a shriek went up from alongside and, rushing to the rail, Olivera called for help.

'Fetch a line, here, help!'

Iago ran across the deck, scooped what had once been a neat coil of topgallant brace on a pin-rail from the scupper and began to re-coil it, staring over Olivera's shoulder as he did so. A few yards off the ship's side the fifth man lay spread-eagled and clinging to a hatch-board for dear life. A moment later one end of the line snaked out from Iago's adept hands and landed smack across the man's back. Holding on to the iron staple in one corner of the board with one hand, the seaman caught a hitch round its neighbour in the opposite corner. Then, throwing the bight of the line into the low waist, Iago and Olivera tumbled down the ladder and began to haul the hatch-board in, hand over hand. Within a few moments the sodden and wretched man lay on deck, gasping at their feet.

'You should have left me to drown,' he managed at last as Olivera barked orders for the hatch-board to be replaced and for other timber to be found to nail down over the partially open hold.

'And rouse out some canvas to replace the tarpaulin. Where's that lubber Llerena?'

Iago left Olivera to secure the hatch and helped the half-drowned *marinero* to his shaky feet. 'Had you not called for help we should have left you, my friend,' he remarked in a croak, feeling the salt sharp on his parched and cracking lips. 'What is your name?'

'Luis Rodriguez,' the sailor replied, coughing the last of the water from his throat.

'Well, Luis Rodriguez, perhaps you may yet be glad that you were saved.'

'What chance have we, señor, in all honesty?'

'In all honesty, I have no idea, but we are not yet dead.'

'We might as well be. They say drowning is a pleasant way to die.'

'Yes, but I have never quite understood how this is known as a fact.'

'You think it a story, like those of Hell-fire, to give us comfort for the troubles of the world.'

'I think it very likely . . .' And Iago watched as, shaking his head, the philosophical sailor went below. 'Though what comfort you will find there, Luis Rodriguez,' Iago muttered to himself, 'I am equally at a loss to know.'

'Stop talking to yourself, *amigo*,' Olivera said sharply, tugging the corner of a sodden but recently sewn topsail over the half-secured hatch-square. 'Where the Devil is that pig of a boatswain?'

'He may be among the dead,' Iago said, picking up a corner of the sail and feeling the canvas as hard and resistant as a wooden board. Christ, but they were as weak as babies. And now, childlike, those below decks were appearing as if by common consent despite the seas still thundering about them. Here came Arrocheros and his wife, the Holy Ones, Ximenez and Ah Fong, the sailors that had sheltered below along with their women and, out on the half-deck, came Guillestigui and his entourage, most of whom lurched as much with the wine they had swallowed as with the extreme motion of the *Santa Margarita*. It was clear that no one felt safe below, that word had been put about that even the Holy Virgin had deserted them and the ship was lost. As Olivera and Iago, having finally battened and nailed down the hatch, came up from the waist, those remaining alive aboard the *Santa Margarita* stood lined up along the higher, starboard side of the ship.

Oddly, it seemed as though they had found a form of sanctuary, for while the ship lay on her beam ends and the sea beat all about her, the high starboard side was like a reef just above the level of the raging tide. Although the confused sea seemed to have died down, the respite was only temporary and already the sky was clouding over. Within an hour they would have drifted out of the centre of the typhoon and would again be battling winds of hurricane force.

Olivera sensed this brief respite; turning to Iago he called out, 'God damn Llerena! We must right the ship and remove such of the top hamper as we may!' Casting about him Olivera began bawling orders and such was the power of his personality that many men, even in the extremity of their exhaustion, hunger and thirst, rallied to his cry. Others did not, many lying down where they stood, to be kicked and trodden upon by those bold spirits who undertook the dangerous work of cutting away the remaining masts.

One man, more energetic than most and better fed owing to being Guillestigui's steward, ascended the slope of the main shrouds, drew his sword and hacked at the jeer tackle of the main yard. He was halfway through the heavy ropes when the wind rose again. Within a minute it blew a furious gale that tore at his clothes as he clung on with one hand and hacked at the tackle with the other. At the pin-rail below half a dozen men stood poised with axes, ready to cut away the shrouds the instant the steward had eased the weight of the massive main yard aloft. No one had laid a blade against the straining shrouds when, as if anticipating events and entirely of their own accord, they began to strand. It was impossible to ensure they each bore an absolutely equal strain and, in recent weeks, they had been under incalculable loads. First the one bearing the greatest weight gave way, whereupon the shock ran successively from one to another. The heavy ropes parted, their deadeyes fell and, as the last gave way, the mast itself cracked six feet above the deck. Before the courageous steward had severed the main yard from its jeers, he, the yard and the remains of the mainmast went over the side, sweeping a train of heavy tarred hemp in their wake.

As this ripped across the deck waist-high it tore open the belly of the nephew of the Bishop of Manila, dragging his guts after it in a steaming stream. A deadeye struck his cousin Francisco, smashing his femur so that the stump protruded from his upper thigh and sent both men screaming to the wet deck where they rolled in their separate agonies.

As the mainmast fell the strain on the standing rigging fore and aft brought down what remained of the fore and mizzen-masts. The bowsprit, already wounded by the flying saker and the wreckage of the forecastle, snapped off short and fell under foot so that the ship lost her spritsail and in the general mayhem – as the foremast rigging tore at the channels – two of the *Santa Margarita*'s remaining anchors lashed in the forechains were torn away to fall into the sea.

From the moment the steward had begun work to cut away the huge main yard to the ship becoming a derelict wreck had taken less than three minutes. As they digested the state to which they were reduced it became apparent that they were not about to sink. In fact they could take some cheer from the fact that the *Santa Margarita* had slowly returned to an even keel. And with that realization, despite the continuing howling of the typhoon, Marmolejo led them in a prayer of gratitude which culminated in a begging of the Lord God to have mercy upon them. Even Guillestigui, whose appearance seemed much changed, participated with a fervid enthusiasm.

'God have mercy upon us. Christ have mercy upon us . . .'

Olivera, Iago and a handful of men which now, to Iago's

intense gratification, included Ximenez, managed to get a shred of canvas hoisted on the short stump of the mizzen-mast which, adding to the greater height of even her wrecked poop, forced the ship's head round a little and eased her rolling. Although much reduced forward and with little free-board in her forepart, the worst damage was aft and it was here that water still poured into the ship. Bringing her head up a little into the increasingly regular sea caused the *Santa Margarita* to ride more easily. Thus she lay hove-to without recourse to her helm, a hulk peopled by a hungry and despairing company. Slowly her anxious population gave up their tenure of the deck, making their way below again where, amid the chaos of debris, bedding, clothing, jars, pots and cases of cargo, they tried, half-heartedly, to make sense of their several existences.

But though the typhoon was passing slowly over the *Santa Margarita* it had not yet quite finished with her. Returning to their cabins aft, Guillestigui and the other gentry sought some comfort. While one or two already recanted of their promises to God and sought out a bottle, others fell upon their knees, rosaries, psalters and missals in hand. A few, like the captain-general and the foppish young master-of-camp, Miguel de Alacanadre, fell upon their bed-places. Alacanadre's tiny cabin was immediately below that of the late pilot-major Lorenzo on the extreme starboard quarter of the vessel, just off the great cabin and built in point of fact as a privy. Its structure had suffered initially from the tearing off of the stern gallery while the demolition of Lorenzo's quarters had further opened the timbers of the upper transom. Alacanadre had filled this space with his private trade goods among which were a number of glass jars containing aromatic oils of Chinese origin and, more importantly, considerable value. As he lay on his bunk a sea struck the *Santa Margarita*'s starboard quarter, springing the planking and bodily lifting the athwartships beams so that Alacanadre's cabin split open and half its contents fell out of the ship. A second sea, bursting in through the holes thus opened, floated the glass jars and dashed them to pieces against each other and their surroundings. Bathed in escaping oil, Alacanadre was slashed by the fractured glass and lay in his own gore upon his sodden mattress.

It was ironic that this accident to the one member of his entourage who had opposed the eviction of Ocampo from the *Santa Margarita* should bestir the captain-general, but so it was. Hearing the screams of the master-of-camp as he bled profusely, Guillestigui appeared in the damaged doorway of Alacanadre's wrecked cabin. Seeing the result of Alacanadre's trade goods breaking loose Guillestigui spun round, infused with a startling resolution. Later there were those who said the sight of the bloody youth pricked his conscience and that he finally realized the ship lay in mortal danger through being overloaded with his own private cargo. Others thought this was a sign of encroaching madness. Whatever the cause he rushed out into the gloom of the half-deck, half-dressed, his hair loose and a wild look in his eyes. This was a place he had not visited since the ship cleared the Embocadero, the now lethargic inhabitants of which regarded the unseemly invasion of their miserable privacy by the captain-general as untimely. Those recumbent upon the relics of their straw palliasses looked up in astonishment while the rough curtains of the passengers were lifted to discover the source of the noise.

'Wake up, damn you! Clear away the hatches!' He indicated the two hatches that opened into the half-deck and whose enclosed situation both made the ship awkward to load and protected them from being stove in like those exposed in the waist. Looking wildly about him, Guillestigui caught sight of a clutch of wet seamen huddled forward. 'Come you, here!' he beckoned them urgently. 'Clear away these hatches!' He began tearing at the wooden wedges and, such is the nature of mankind that at the sight of the *hidalgo* commander of their failed expedition ineptly doing the work of a common sailor, the *marineros* gathered round. Within fifteen minutes the cases and bales, jars and mat bundles of Guillestigui's private cargo were being brought up on deck, passed forward and out into the waist. From here they were thrown overboard to the number of four hundred, each one tallied over the side by the captain-general's secretary.

It was by now evening and the sun was setting, appearing as a brazen ball through rents in the clouds shredding away to the west as the typhoon passed on and left them in the minor turmoil of a mere gale. By midnight, as the last of the boxes went overboard, the ship seemed to ride easier, the wind and sea were down and, as if by a miracle, chorizo and wine were circulated among the entire company. And far from evoking curses, since these provisions were clear evidence of hoarding by the captain-general and his staff, Guillestigui earned the plaudits of the wretches he thus saved from starvation.

After they had eaten this meagre meal they were rounded up to man the pumps. The carpenters had reported some nineteen palms of water in the hold, amounting to a little over fourteen feet, and while every fit man and several of the women took their turn at the monotonous chore, others caulked and plugged the obvious leaks by lantern light. Not a soul aboard the *Santa Margarita* had a shred of dry clothing on, everything was wet without exception, but a little more food was found among the officers' cargo and was saved from going over the side.

All night they toiled, dragging a sail under the hull to reduce the ingress of water and lifting hope itself from the very bilges of the wallowing hulk.

Twelve

A Day of Miracles

It was remarkable what a revivifying effect a morsel of sausage and a little wine achieved, even to the extent of extracting from some of the less reflective of the ship's company words of praise for the wisdom of the captain-general. Others found no good in Guillestigui's harbouring of provisions, only a cynical manipulation for, without the help of the *marineros*, the *Santa Margarita* would assuredly founder. This opinion was proved right in the coming hours when the limited rations were dispensed by the captain-general's armed guard and it was noted that nothing was given to those of little use. Thus, but for a meagre dole, the Holy Ones were forced to continue their fast and the passengers were limited to half-rations unless they undertook to pump.

Pumping was the main occupation of the mass of the men; others, under the direction of Olivera and the carpenters, sought out leaks and plugged them. In this way, with a sail under the hull, the hatches again secured and most of the damage to the upper works patched up, the *Santa Margarita*'s watertight integrity improved. There remained one problem, for the sea still poured into the stern of the ship and it took some time to locate the leak. It was Olivera who found the source. In the late afternoon he came on deck, his clothes soaked through, his hair streaked down on his head like lank weed, his face grimy and his hands cut.

Iago was on deck, ostensibly keeping what passed for a watch, and loosely supervising a gang of seamen forward who had effected repairs to the stump of the bowsprit and were fishing a broken spar to what remained of the foremast in order to contrive yet another jury rig. Diego de Llerena was the moving spirit behind this labour, fired with an energy that suggested he must make amends for his unexplained absence. For the last few days the boatswain had been below, having been struck on his head when asleep by a heavy cask during the worst of the typhoon. Reduced to a stupor by the severity of the injury, he had remained inert through pain, fear, hunger and despair, but finally revived at the prospect of meat and drink as the weather moderated and the *Santa Margarita* refused to founder. His reappearance on deck galvanized several other men and whether or not conscience played its part in his heroism, he was now to demonstrate the fullness of his recovery.

He was laying out a tackle prior to hoisting the extemporized foremast when the sodden and exhausted Olivera staggered up to the half-deck to consult with Iago and was thus within earshot of the two men.

'I have found the trouble, Don Iago, but it will be the Devil to fix, right in the tuck of the stern. So far it has defied our efforts, the pressure of the sea throwing all our plugs back in our faces.'

'What exactly is the cause?' Iago asked.

'The iron pintle bands, where they run along the strakes and are bolted through the hull, have become loose, the bolts are either strained or drawn . . .'

'So where they are drawn the water is coming in as through a pipe?'

'Exactly so; and where they are strained it is little better.'

Iago considered the matter for a moment then asked: 'Could you drive the strained bolts straight out?'

Olivera nodded. 'Yes, but then we should double the number of holes letting water directly into the ship.'

'Not if you drew plugs into the holes from outside.'

'I thought of that, and the technique of passing a line out through the holes and picking it up with a grapnel over the stern. The problem is that we should not be able to get a sufficiently watertight fit, even with softwood plugs, for the difficulties of tugging a plug that far down and right under the lower transom—'

'But if you drove the plugs in from outside,' Llerena said, interrupting the conversation, 'could you not stop the water?'

Olivera looked at Llerena with distaste. The two were at odds and the pilot disliked the challenge to his argument. 'One would have to dive beneath the ship to accomplish that,' he said shortly.

'I am willing to try, Don Antonio.'

'You?'

'Yes. I can hold my breath and,' Llerena held up a clenched fist, 'I have the hand for it.'

For a moment Olivera considered the proposition and then, burying his distrust of the boatswain, said, 'If you muster half the strength you used to use to beat the Indians I think perhaps you have. You will need a line about you and you had better come below and see what it is we are trying to achieve.'

'That I will be trying to achieve, I think you mean.'

'As you wish,' Olivera said curtly. 'Come,' and leaving Iago staring after the two of them Olivera led the way below.

They began by running a line out through the foremost bolt-hole on each side which Llerena would use as a guide to the spot. Then, as the *Santa Margarita* wallowed and rolled, with the Holy Ones mustered on deck singing psalms and praying that the wind, which showed every sign of getting up again, did not trouble them for the remaining hours of daylight, Llerena went over the side. His shouted instructions and curses as he dived and surfaced under first one quarter and then the other acted as a crude counterpoint to this wailing psalmody.

One seaman, also on a line, went in with him to help, holding the plugs and the hammer, and calling for more hammers as Llerena dropped the first three. It was he who called up instructions and fished in the bucket which was lowered from the deck on a lizard, carrying down the materials and tools, along with the bottle of wine Llerena demanded. After the loss of the three hammers Llerena got into his stride. He learnt how to anticipate the downward wallow of the ship, and how to kick himself clear of the swell of the stern as it widened out above what had once been the proper waterline so that his gasping breathing was manageable. He found that he could match his dives to each part of the task and that, with his back against the guide-rope, he could drive the plugs in sufficiently. Water pressure would do the rest and, while the first seemed impossible, each successive plug went in a little more easily. The sun had set when the last holes demanded attention and the guide ropes had, perforce, to be withdrawn. An argument had been occupying Olivera and several of the captain-general's officers – who hung over the stern consumed with curiosity – as to whether it was not better to leave the rope in place. Since it lessened the leak it might therefore be considered sufficient, but neither Olivera nor Iago would have it, arguing that it might easily be chafed through or fouled and there might be no other opportunity to attend to the matter.

When these impractical and opinionated young men turned to the captain-general himself to arbitrate, Guillestigui having come on deck to see how matters progressed, they were astonished at his reply.

'Leave this matter to the sea-officers,' he growled, and strode forward to curl a derisory lip at the praying Franciscans and harangue the flagging party at the pump handles.

'That is well,' Olivera remarked, his relief at being left free of further advice clear on his lined and grubby face. 'Let him do what he does best.'

It was a poor jest but it made Olivera smile to himself and Iago chuckled

It was already dark when Llerena, who had been surfacing and diving for three long hours, finally came to the surface with a bellow of triumph. He had been heard intermittently rather than seen from the high overhang of the poop, blowing like a grampus and spitting and cursing as the hull of the *Santa Margarita* rose and fell, often pressing him down before he was ready. Now the news of his achievement spread throughout the ship. The parties at the pumps abandoned the agonizing boredom of their task and, by the time Llerena had been towed along to the waist where the freeboard was least and hoisted over the low rail, almost the entire ship's company was on deck to cheer him.

As the cheers subsided the chanting of the Holy Ones' hymns rose and fell to the final, languid amens of Agustin's fine, vibrant baritone.

Guillestigui invited Llerena to the poop where the stern

lanterns had been lit for the first time in many days. There, against the very last of the twilight, illuminated by the glow of the great lamps, the boatswain and the captain-general shared a bottle of wine. Twenty minutes later, still in his wet breeches, Diego de Llerena lay like a dead hog, fast asleep on a rotting, wet palliasse.

Olivera, judging his moment, suggested to the captain-general that it would be wise to cease pumping and determine overnight how much water was now entering the ship. Guillestigui agreed and the hands were stood down, issued a paltry ration of food and sent below to sleep. The pilot and Iago stood the night watches as the *Santa Margarita* lay a-hull, rolling quietly in the trough of the sea with a light breeze reminding her that she could not long remain thus.

At dawn the ship's company was roused and the wells were sounded. In due course the pumping resumed. Those at the pumps groaned at the thought of another day's work, for their muscles ached from their previous endeavours, but word was soon passed that the ship had taken little water during the night, no more, it was asserted, than she might make in any gale and easily managed by intermittent and routine use of the pumps. In one final burst of energy they worked the handles until they sucked air, whereupon their spirits rose and at noon the Discalced Franciscans called them all to a celebration of the Mass.

But even as Hernando gave the benediction the wind was again rising, the sky clouding over and the sea growing increasingly menacing. An effort was again made to get the ship before the wind. An improvised staysail was stretched forward to the spar lashed in place of the bowsprit end. With half her rudder fastenings lost, she was almost impossible to steer but they ran off, achieving a speed of perhaps two knots.

Towards sunset Iago came below to warn those who would listen that they would have to endure a further storm. The space beneath the half-deck had been transformed. While most of the men had pumped and the others had attended Llerena and the plugging of the lost bolt holes, the women had cleared the worst debris from what had become the main accommodation in an attempt to reassert normality. There were exceptions; not everyone had risen to the challenge.

Doña Catalina had finally lost her nerve at the height of the typhoon when Lorenzo had been lost on the eve of the feast day of the Glorious St Francis. Her depression came not from the loss of the pilot-major, to whom she had never spoken, but from the loss of her own child. At first rallying after this private tragedy, despair at the future and – it was rumoured – a blow on the head caused her to fall into a decline. This was marked by an intermittent wailing which rose and fell, subsiding entirely only when she slept, but at times rising to an unnerving scream that joined that of Francisco, the bishop's nephew whose badly broken leg had putrefied and whose pain was so intense that his life was despaired of.

The Discalced Franciscans did what they could and several of the low women attended Doña Catalina, as did Ah Fong, and even Ximenez was active in fetching and carrying. But it was to Iago that Arrocheros turned for help. All trace of hostility between the two men had long since vanished.

'What am I to do, Don Iago?' Arrocheros agonized. 'She is beside herself with grief.'

'Ah Fong says that you should bring her again to child-bed, Don Baldivieso, and I can see the wisdom of her opinion. They do not give much thought to a lost child in China, there being sufficient in a man's seed to beget more.'

Arrocheros frowned, anger flushing his face. 'Do you think that I can do such a thing *here*,' he gestured about him, 'in *these* circumstances, for God's sake? Besides, even if I succeed how long is it before the child quickens and removes her anxieties?'

'Try, Don Baldivieso, try. Or alternatively, you may pray for a miracle.'

'A miracle? Huh, we all have need of a miracle and even when we earn a little respite as of now, hark how the damned wind rises again. Are we likely to have another storm?'

'Very likely,' Iago replied.

'Then what chance have we got . . . and what chance have I of covering my wife.'

'I can think of worse ways of dying, Don Baldivieso.'

Arrocheros seemed about to speak, thought better of it and turned on his heel. Iago was about to take his own advice and seek out Ah Fong when a loud thumping noise came from forward, sending a shudder through the ship. On deck Iago found the inadequate staysail's luff sagging and the sail flogging. Olivera and several seamen were forward where the extension to the bowsprit had broken loose and swung back and forth in a web of ropes, driving its inner end against the ship's side. The damage to the ship was immediate and threatened worse, yet to cut the wild spar loose would be dangerous.

'Get the staysail lowered,' ordered Olivera, but the extemporized halliard had jammed and clearing it took several agonizing minutes while the bowsprit stump battered at the bow. With the scrap of canvas off the ship, the *Santa Margarita* fell into the trough of the sea and began again to roll.

'If we can cast it loose, we can move the tack inboard and steady the ship,' cried Iago.

'Aye, cut that tack-line,' Olivera told a waiting seaman.

'I have no knife, señor,' the *marinero* replied.

'God damn!' roared Olivera in a needless fury, for Iago had cast loose the end of the line from its belaying pin and in a moment the forward corner of the triangular sail had been drawn back on to the forecastle.

'Get some line and splice in a new tack-line,' Iago said and a sailor hurried off, glad to be given a task that did not risk his life, for all knew what had to be attempted next.

'Someone has to go over . . .'

'I know, I know, and since it is always Diego de Llerena who does the impossible.'

A thin cheer greeted the boatswain's bombast as he came forward, his huge frame braced against the roll of the ship.

'Get out of my way, you milksop dogs.'

They drew aside good-naturedly, relieved and smiling. At first Llerena descended a little, one hand clinging to a rope's end and the other wielding an axe, but he failed to cut the complex raffle adrift, almost falling overboard amid the terrifying tangle of trailing lines and scrambling back on deck white and shaken.

'I cannot cheat death more than once,' he grumbled as the broken spar again crashed against the bow with a blow they could feel through the soles of their feet.

'We must do something . . .'

By now the entire ship was alive with renewed anxiety.

Guillestigui had come as far forward as the half-deck rail and Peralta had been sent to the forecastle for news. Hernando and Agustin arrived, peering over the side as knowledgeably as any seaman.

'Surely we must exert ourselves and remove this,' Agustin gestured at the ravelled mess of ropes and timber pounding the bow like a battering ram as the ship pitched and rolled.

'We need a fucking angel, Father,' said a seaman luridly, 'with wings and a bloody great sword like St Michael. That bugger's muddle is the very Devil himself.'

'My sons,' said Agustin, ignoring the crude language, 'when God calls, all must obey.'

He drew the crucifix and rosary from his waist and held it aloft. 'Go and do your duty with Almighty God at your sides!' he cried. 'This,' he drew their attention to his crucifix, 'and our prayers will protect you!' He turned to Hernando and commanded: 'Brother, join me.'

The two friars held their crucifixes up and elevating their eyes to the stormy skies sent up a Latin chant incomprehensible to the group of goggle-eyed seamen gathered on the forecastle. Despite the heavy roll of the ship, they shuffled awkwardly, the Franciscans' voices loud and insistent in their ears.

Olivera caught Iago's eye and shrugged. Both men looked down at what they hoped would have served as a bowsprit wondering how any man could descend those few dangerous feet for long enough to cut the foul ropes and free the *Santa Margarita* from its menace. Iago was just thinking that either he or Olivera would have to do it and that Olivera, as the only official pilot left aboard, was indispensable and therefore the burden would fall upon himself, when something remarkable happened.

The men were moved by a different spirit: their ignorant susceptibility, the chanting of the two Franciscans, their grim reminders of the sacrifice of Jesus Christ held up before them moved them and elevated them beyond reason. Men pressed forward.

'I'll do it!'

'I'll help . . .'

'And I . . .'

Seemingly from nowhere six axes appeared. One was pressed into Olivera's unwilling hand.

The voices of Agustin and Hernando grew louder, more insistent, blotting out fear. Now they were joined by Marmolejo and others so that, as one, the armed men threw their legs over the side and, hanging on with one hand, bent and assayed the task.

'God grant us a miracle!' someone cried and the plea was taken up as those dangling over the side thump-thumped with their axes. Those unable to help fell on their knees, crossing themselves and pleading a grey and indifferent Heaven for a remission. 'Please, God, a miracle! A miracle!'

And that evening God granted them several, for with a great cry the bowsprit fell clear and, although it tore a hole in the forward bulkhead under the forecastle and damaged the beakhead rails, and although three men suffered minor injuries, a passenger named Gonzalo Manuel had the sense to be ready below to stuff palliasses and bundles of wet and abandoned clothing into the gap and prevent sea water from once again pouring into the hull.

Nor was that all, for more miraculous still – and a sure and certain sign that Almighty God had heard their prayers – a shout came up from below that Doña Catalina's baby had been resurrected.

The men on the forecastle, breathing from their labours, could scarce believe their ears, yet confirmation came that it was indeed the case. Agustin, Hernando, Marmolejo and the other religious looked from one to another their eyes shining.

'I see now,' said Marmolejo, 'that we have been put to these extreme trials so that God might shine His face upon us and humble us to His holy will.'

'Amen . . .'

'Amen!'

Even Guillestigui came forward as they trooped below to witness a true and holy wonder.

Under the half-deck they found a transformed Doña Catalina sitting with her back against a futtock. The miserable and suffering face of the past weeks had gone and now she smiled, a renewed soul. Her left breast was exposed and a dark-haired baby suckled greedily against her soft flesh.

Marmolejo crossed himself and, saying nothing, thought of the shepherds gathered at the command of the Archangel Gabriel amid the dung and straw of the stable in Bethlehem. He could scarcely breathe with emotion and bent his head as the hot tears streamed from his eyes.

'It is as though our lost Virgin has been restored . . .' breathed a theologically confused and hungry Agustin.

'And it is miraculous confirmation for those who doubted it that man liveth after death,' added Hernando. 'Truly you are right, Fray Mateo.'

All about them the staring men expressed their awe, muttering half-forgotten prayers, genuflecting as though the nursing mother was indeed the Holy Virgin herself. Iago, standing towards the rear of the jostling and watching crowd as it swayed to the roll of the ship, sought out Arrocheros. The happy father stood beside the futtock, bent over his wife and speaking to her. He straightened up and raised his hand, a mixed expression of bewilderment, wonder and happiness upon his face.

'It is the very same baby,' he said. 'My wife is certain. The look of him . . . The smell of him . . . It is the same, God be thanked and praised!' Arrocheros fell to his knees, weeping and crossing himself; all the assembled company did likewise, Agustin raising his voice in tremulous praise. An hour later, following a hearing of the holy Mass, the child was christened Francisco, the captain-general standing as a godfather.

The comparison with Moses was inescapable. The baby had been found in a corner of the hold, lying in the remains of a broken packing case as it grounded amid the wet silt left by the retreating bilge water. One of the women had heard its whimpering cry and had brought it up into the half-deck where, with a cry of sublime joy, Doña Catalina had instantly recognized it.

Despite the gale that again belaboured the *Santa Margarita*, within her dark, damp and stinking half-deck, men rejoiced and sang praises to Almighty God as though they meant every word. No one noticed a few sad faces among the common women as they mashed a few mildewed beans that had also been found below that evening. God had granted them a miracle as they had prayed. The small handful of men who complained that a resurrected baby was all very well, but they had now to endure yet another storm, were dismissed as blind fools and Doubting Thomases.

'What care we for another gale?' they were firmly told. 'Have we not endured the worst that the Devil can dish up? Moreover, have we not been given a sign of God's good and benevolent intent towards us?'

Thirteen
Watchwords of the Damned

Their relief was short-lived for hardly had the Mass been celebrated and the infant baptized than an ominous banging was heard above the creaking of the ship, the roar of the wind and sea and the noisy agonies of the malodorous and gangrenous Francisco. Somewhere beneath them the broken stump of the bowsprit remained caught and throughout the following night no one slept, every soul lying awake, waiting for the next thump against the hull. Curiously, after daylight shed a grey light over the turbulent sea, no one quite remembered when it had ceased, only that, as Agustin said, 'It pleased God to move it away.'

Throughout the day the *Santa Margarita* rolled with a relentlessness that wearied the most seasoned sailor. No attempt had been made to re-hoist the scrap of sail forward and most lay about in a state of lethargy, devoid of leadership, hungry, thirsty, bruised and battered. Olivera and his adopted assistant, Iago Fernandez, were totally exhausted, as were Llerena and the other petty officers. As for the captain-general and his staff, although in better physical condition than the others, they were as helpless, lacking any notion of what might be done beyond an intermittent manning of the pumps. For most of those aboard the stricken *Santa Margarita*, the hours passed in a daze of being rolled about, of hitting heads and bodies against the ship's beams and futtocks, of stumbling and cursing and crying in pain as bruise superimposed itself upon tender and painful bruise.

In this state of abject misery no food appeared and the scarcity of water was only eased by a torrential rainstorm. While most people capable of reaching the deck stood and collected the water in their mouths, only a few had the sense to catch more in buckets and jars. To the whimpers, groans and intermittent cries of the dying Francisco were added the moans of the scorbutic, for scurvy had for some time affected many, loosening their teeth in bleeding gums and adding their foul exhalations to the stench which lay like a miasma between decks. Only among the household of Don Baldivieso de Arrocheros did the spark of joy remain alive.

In Iago's quarters a grim mood prevailed. Iago himself sat huddled against the ship's straining side, Ah Fong swinging in the hammock above him and Ximenez curled like a dog at his feet.

'I can hold out little hope to you, my friends,' he said thickly, his tongue dry and enlarged. 'We have done all that we can . . .' He broke off, then rallied and added, 'I have failed you both.'

'No, master, no.' Ximenez stirred and looked up, his flesh loose upon his overlarge and shaking head. His large dark eyes were limpid and more dog-looking than ever before. Iago noticed that his gums were bleeding a little and his breath smelled. Ah Fong leaned out of her swaying hammock, extended her hand and sought that of her husband. Hers was the face of a ghost, a pale, drawn shadow that was, in Iago's eyes, possessed of a beauty that terrified him. When she withdrew her hand with a wan smile, he put a finger into his own mouth and on to a canine tooth. It wobbled ominously in the gum. Withdrawing his finger he held it momentarily beneath his nose. It stank.

The *Santa Margarita* lay a-hull at the mercy of the wind and sea for three days and when the wind dropped, it was a fourth before the swell had subsided sufficiently to persuade a single soul to rouse themselves. That evening it fell away to a perfect calm, the sea, though undulating under the influence of the now distant storm, lay like a vast sheet of grey-blue silk and the sun westered in a blaze of glory.

Word went round that the Holy Ones had persuaded Guillestigui to hear the Mass in his cabin and all were summoned to attend. Here, bringing a few crucifixes, rosaries and votive images from their various quarters, passengers and crew – now indistinguishable by their garments or bearing

– heard Agustin and his colleagues celebrate the mystery of the Eucharist and chant the Litany. Those who could joined in, but the cracked voices and reedy efforts were a measure of their suffering and they looked – as they swayed there, propping each other up as they knelt on the wet deck – like a congregation in Purgatory. Prayers of confession, supplication and dedication were again said, and benediction was granted amid the rustling of over a hundred souls crossing themselves. Conspicuous among these were the captain-general and his suite.

Afterwards Miguel de Alacanadre spoke. His worried face bore the open and suppurating wounds of his ordeal among the breaking glass jars; scurvy prevented these from healing. He ordered two trunks of clothing be brought up from the captain-general's private store in the lazarette and these were distributed amongst the most needy.

'The captain-general and myself wish you to accept these with our affection and goodwill,' he said, to a low murmur of approval, after which the crowd slowly and uncertainly dispersed, for no one could walk properly and every movement had become an effort.

The following day the bishop's nephew Francisco died. He was quickly buried, for his gangrenous corpse stank to high Heaven and offended even those whose rotting gums smelled little better. That night three more souls, all *marineros*, gave up the ghost.

'We need more miracles,' Iago remarked slowly as they contemplated a little fermented rice that Ximenez had found and Ah Fong had dressed.

'That child was not a miracle, master,' Ximenez said in a confidential tone, 'though I dare not say this where others might hear . . .' He looked about him fearfully and gave up his explanation when Ah Fong sniggered.

'All people make big mistake,' she said. 'All fools, except my beloved . . .'

'The child was another's,' Iago said.

Ximenez looked astonished. 'Master . . . How did you know?'

'Do you take me for a fool?'

Ximenez frowned, wrestling with the conflict Iago's

certainty introduced. 'But the authority of the Holy Fathers
. . . They cannot lie.'

'Perhaps not, but they can be mistaken. They are only men,
Ximenez.'

Ximenez appeared to consider this proposition for a
moment then he shrugged. 'I forgot. The master is . . .'

'Hold your tongue!' Iago said sharply. 'Do not think that
because we are all near death and the captain-general acts
like a religious benefactor himself there are not those who
would seek amelioration of their plight by *our* discomfiture.'

It was this thought that forced Iago back on deck as much
as the easing in the conditions. He was, as they all were, a
man at the extremity of his resources. His mood was dark
and he sensed a danger that transcended the simple, visceral
fear of what was to become of them. Men changed in extreme
circumstances and there was something profoundly disquieting in the change in Guillestigui and his after-guard.

The calm that drew Iago forth acted upon other men.
Though famished and scorbutic, enough of them rallied upon
the upper deck to attempt something. Motivated by a strong
desire to survive and, despite their sufferings, revived by the
change in the weather, those still capable of standing on
unsteady feet and tailing, albeit feebly on a rope, worked hero-
ically. In the days that followed they made of the derelict
Santa Margarita something approaching a ship. Help came
from surprising places. Guillestigui himself made an appearance and assisted as two heavy beams were taken out of the
waist and, with infinite patience and several failed attempts,
upended to make a jury mainmast. Once this was stayed, they
next drew the stump of the mizzen and inched it forward to
lower it and wedge it in place of the ruined foremast. While
these spars were being set up and rigged, others, under the
direction of the carpenters, fabricated a blade on a fished spar,
extemporizing a rudder which would give them some control
over the ship's head. As men sat cross-legged on the deck and
sewed torn canvas to make sails, Guillestigui consulted Olivera,
who drew Iago into the conversation.

'His Excellency wishes to know where we are, Don Iago,
in order that we may best determine the course to lay once
we have completed our preparations.'

Iago looked directly at the captain-general. 'With respect, Your Excellency, we may not have much choice. We shall only be able to lay a course before the wind . . .'

'We must make for Cipangu, Don Iago. I am certain that you will find it the nearest land.'

'That may be so, Your Excellency, but unfortunately the least distance is not the arbiter, it is the direction of the wind that will determine the possibilities.'

This response was not what Guillestigui wished to hear, but he held his peace. He contented himself with a warning. 'Our food is limited,' he said, tacitly admitting that he still commanded a quantity of provisions, and so for a month they ran off before the wind, which carried them perversely northwards and westwards more often than not. Only occasionally did they find themselves heading east, for it appeared that the run of typhoons had disrupted the westerly flow of the gyre, further evidence for those that were still able to reason that Ocampo's curse and God's displeasure were real. The winds remained light but the cold and fog struck many and although it transpired that the captain-general's harboured store would yield a meagre ration of ship's biscuit, dried and salted meat and a few sardines, both men and women continued dying and every forenoon was occupied by the sad duty of burial. Saddest of all was the death of the baby Francisco. Doña Catalina, her breasts dry, was inconsolable; not even Marmolejo's insistence that the child was with God stopped her tears. Wracked with grief and despair, filled with a sensation that in taking her resurrected child God himself disapproved of her and all her family, she resumed her decline. Don Baldivieso implored the Holy Ones to pray for her.

'I shall endow your order,' he promised, sobbing, 'with half my fortune if we survive,' he pleaded. And so Doña Catalina lay, a candle at her head and feet, her husband and a Franciscan on their knees at prayer beside her.

Death, like scurvy, was a constant among them. Every morning those who did not rise were inspected by one of the Franciscans. One day a pair of corpses would be discovered, another morning would yield four or five, others as many as eight or ten. The *marineros* died by the score, lying on the deck, pissing and vomiting amid the foetid stink of their sad malady, spitting their teeth on the deck like knuckle-bones and dreaming of luscious fruits and cabbages and streams of cascading waters that many of them had seen on the islands of the Pacific. Few died quietly, most seemed bound for Hell itself as the Holy Ones, the Franciscan brothers, their lay members and the handful of wretched nuns moved among them offering spiritual comfort and the crucified Saviour's assurances of everlasting life.

The living themselves had long since resembled skeletons, their bones showing through their skins, their eyes shadowed, their hair falling out along with their teeth. Some managed to supplement their diet by catching the odd rat and even a dolphin – thus discovering a thin source of antiscorbutic susten-ance – while the wise by now never failed to collect what water fell in the form of rain. Nevertheless, it was clear the *Santa Margarita* was truly cursed. Of this no one was any longer in doubt after the death of the Arrocheros baby, and it was now that the Discalced Franciscans passed among their flock warning them to prepare for an inevitable death and promising everlasting life if they died well.

Those unable to face this prospect with the equanimity that the Holy Ones appeared to demand murmured a heart-felt prayer: 'O Lord God,' they muttered, 'take us, we beseech Thee, to some island and let us die there, not aboard this evil ship, even though we shall have nothing but grass to eat and even if the natives of the place kill us with clubs. Anything, O Merciful God, but an end aboard this death-ship.'

And to seal this covenant they abandoned the virgin saint, Margarita, after whom the hated ship had been named, cleaving instead to Santa Anna. And in answer to their intercessions, every Saturday thereafter – or so they reckoned it – their new benefactress sent them a steady shower of rain. This was not a miracle, Marmolejo explained, but a sign that God wished to ease their suffering at this Christmas-tide. Death itself remained ineluctable. But the hopeful continued to pray for the sight of an island.

Just as the Lord gaveth, he also tooketh away. As the year turned so did the weather. Within an hour the calms and light airs abruptly terminated and they were again assailed by a ferocious wind. Olivera mustered what help he could, the scrap of mainsail was doused and the *Santa Margarita* ran off before the wind. The tortuous motion of the ship caused Olivera's anxiety for the weak rudder to increase by the minute, his only consolation that the wind was from the east. He peered over the stern at the jury rudder, willing its bending shaft not to snap and its nailed boards not to fly apart, calling out to a chain of huddled figures that conveyed his commands below to ease the helm when he thought it under too great a strain. After half an hour he could himself stand the strain of it no longer. In such conditions the thing was largely ineffectual and in despair of wasting a fair wind he gave up and called for the hands to lower the foresail.

A few men crawled across the deck and slackened the sheets, but no one on deck could go out along the springing yard to secure the wildly flogging sail except the young cadet Silva who scrambled aloft. It was an immensely courageous but futile attempt. With a billowing crack the wind lifted the sail and tore it from its robands in several tatters and then carried it overboard. Poor Silva vanished with it, borne away from them into the white welter that once more raged along the battered side of the great ship.

'God have mercy upon him!' Olivera cried, crossing himself and sending below for one of the Franciscans to come on deck and say the Office for the Dead.

Again the *Santa Margarita* fell wallowing into the trough of the sea; again she rolled and again her company rolled with her, flung about within the foul confines of her labouring hull. This extreme motion seemed like a final straw; irrespective of their condition men simply died from no apparent cause other than the desperate tedium of being flung about the ship like balls. Bruised at best, often suffering terrible fractures or cuts and lesions which swiftly rotted, the toll went on and on. All ceremony was abandoned, it became each for him- or herself. Souls flew from bodies unshriven. Doña Catalina, weakened by grief and inertia, died after being flung from her bed-place and striking her head. Neither Arrocheros nor Marmolejo who lay beside her could save her.

It seemed that her despairing husband would follow her, for he fell into a fit and spat blood. No one expected him to survive and, like every other inert and dying person, his plight was ignored as he clung to his dead wife, refusing to relinquish her corpse for burial. Even Marmolejo soon abandoned his attempt to reason with the distracted widower and dragged himself away. So weak were even the fittest that none could stand and brace themselves against the motion of the ship, and those who tried to carry out any duty crawled on knees that were soon raw.

As it became clear that nothing further could be done, Guillestigui abandoned all but his close coterie and again withdrew into the great cabin. It was thus clear that his encouragement of the others had only been motivated by self-interest. The moiety of rations from aft ceased and once again the sharp pangs of extreme hunger bit deeper than ever. It grew colder too, and when Olivera determined their latitude he was convinced that they had drifted north of Cipangu and closed the dreadful coast of Tartary. Snow squalls often now replaced the showers and when it did rain the captain-general's guards requisitioned the water that a few active souls had collected, driving these angry and wretched people to hoist sea water up in buckets and drink it. Within hours most were dead or raving in the bitter cold, to die before the pale and yellow sun rose again.

Those still capable of wishing for anything other than a speedy termination to their pain-wracked lives prayed to be cast away upon the Tartar coast where they could drown in the cleansing yet hated waves of the freezing sea.

A fortnight later, however, and as if to prolong their agony, the wind dropped and a torrent of rain fell so that all still alive drank as much as they might and filled every available receptacle. After so dreadful a period of deprivation some suffered terrible pangs from this superfluity while others became drunk with ecstasy. One seaman stood half naked, consuming beaker after beaker of water as it ran down from a broken hand rail. This acted like a conduit to such an extent that he spontaneously urinated into the pump-trough at his feet. Another, seeing a clear stream pouring from the pump-trough, lapped up the other's micturition.

And then, amid a distant swirl of mist, someone spied land. Scraps of canvas were again set but the ship could not be induced to close the half-seen coastline and Olivera ordered the attempt abandoned, crying out that the currents were contrary and no tide could be anticipated to carry them south-westwards as they wished. Instead they remained at the caprice of the wind and drifted away to leeward.

Marmolejo led a deputation aft. Many of the crawling skeletons now had grotesquely swollen joints and were so contused that their filthy skin was blue with bruising. They laid before Guillestigui a remonstrance but there was little the proud captain-general could agree to do beyond let Olivera determine their course. He too looked now little better than his underlings, a wreck of a man infested with the ravages of scurvy and excess, his sword arm in a sling where he had broken his wrist after falling heavily. It was said he had lost his mistress, to whom he was devoted, but none of the religious had given her the last rites. A morbid rumour circulated that he still lay with her corpse, like the crazy Arrocheros; others said that he had had her body hurled from the stern in a fit of rage. No one cared either way, for few engaged in conversation.

'He has thrown her from the stern, along with half his God-forsaken soldiery,' Marmolejo confided in Iago when they met in one of their increasingly rare encounters. And then rallying himself with a supreme effort of will, the Franciscan reminded Iago: 'You are not yet married according to the Christian rite, my son.'

'It would not seem to matter, Fray Mateo, for I do not expect my wife to live long.'

Ah Fong, who had stood the pangs of hunger far better than the Spaniards or the half-bred seamen and their trulls, had grown very weak. Iago feared for her life. She lay quite still and quiet in her hammock, only her eyes evidence of her continuing existence. Ximenez, himself now a wizened and bent figure with the appearance of a tail-less monkey, was touchingly solicitous. He managed to conjure tea and a little boiled rice and oil for her, but even he had little hope.

It was at this time that Guillestigui gathered the fittest of his officers and, having gone to some trouble to array them-selves, appeared in the half-deck which was now the common accommodation of all those left alive who were not of his Basque acquaintance. They came forward, rusty half-armour making that curiously sinister noise of worn and articulated steel. Calcagorta, Olalde, Peralta and some of the guards bore drawn swords and they stood amid the inert bodies, swaying uncertainly and braced by their hands against the low deck beams overhead.

Guillestigui coughed and imperfectly cleared his throat. His voice, when it came, was barely audible above the creaking of the hull but the import of his words soon spread.

'I,' he announced slowly, 'Juan Martinez de Guillestigui, Captain-General of this Expedition commanded by His Most Catholic Majesty Rey Felipe, do withdraw all rights of provisions and water from all those incapable of labouring for the common good and the handling of this our ship *Santa Margarita.*'

Having delivered himself of this ultimatum, the captain-general withdrew. For some time his audience lay stupefied and then, as those who had been closest to the captain-general passed on the import of his words, a murmur of horror ran among them. Few were capable of sensing outrage; most seemed to acquiesce and bow their heads to the inevitable.

'Death sooner than later,' became the watchwords of the damned.

Having taken steps to best secure the survival of his own men and close household, Guillestigui summoned Olivera and Iago.

He sat in a chair, Peralta, Calcagorta, Olalde and the others slumped about him. Iago noticed the numerous empty wine bottles that lay about the deck. There was neither sight nor smell of any dead mistress.

'I wish the ship to return to Manila,' he said curtly.

Olivera was astonished. 'That, Your Excellency, is impossible,' he protested.

'Why?' Guillestigui asked simply.

'*Why?* Excellency, I have explained, as Juan Lorenzo explained, we are many miles from Manila, we only know our position imperfectly, we are to leeward of the archipelago and . . . and . . .' Olivera raised his hands in despair and looked at Iago for support.

The question and its tone had no less surprised Iago. As Olivera had repeated the often rehearsed reasons for their present course, he studied the captain-general. Guillestigui was not immune from their common sufferings. His mouth was black with scurvy and he was in pain from his broken wrist. Perhaps, speculated Iago, his wits had been addled by the loss of his mistress or his relentless consumption of wine which seemed – even now – unremitting. Iago's deductions seemed confirmed when Guillestigui turned to himself and, as if the foregoing remarks had not been uttered, spoke to Iago.

'To you, Don Iago,' Guillestigui said, 'I have only to say that while you and any other of your fellow passengers assist the pilot here to work the ship, I shall issue you with rations. And to you, Señor Olivera, the same applies to members of the crew. This I shall do here at noon every day and if one of my officers discovers any false claim made on behalf of anyone, I shall hold each of you accountable for the irregularity. Do you understand?'

Iago stared at the captain-general. 'Perfectly, Excellency,' he managed with the slightest inclination of a bow.

'And you?' Guillestigui turned to Olivera.

Olivera could not bring himself to say anything and merely nodded.

'Very well,' Guillestigui concluded, 'at noon daily, until we sight land.'

'Until we sight land . . .' muttered Peralta in imitation of Guillestigui, adding, 'and that you must accomplish without further delay.'

Olivera frowned. 'Excellency,' he croaked, 'I have bent my best endeavours in your service. No man has exceeded my activity and zeal . . .'

'Find me land, Olivera,' Guillestigui broke in, his voice low, dismissing the two men, 'I have had a lifetime of fine words and vain promises.'

The company about the captain-general growled menacingly. Olivera and Iago retired. As they left Olalde snarled: 'Land, you dogs. Apply your cunning and find us land.'

Outside the cabin, in the comparative gloom of the half-deck, Olivera staggered and fell against Iago, overwhelmed by what had just happened. So weak were they that both men fell to the deck and only slowly recovered what remained of their wits.

'He is mad! He has sentenced us all to . . .' Olivera could not complete the sentence.

'I know, Antonio. Death sooner than later . . .'

'What is the point of . . . of anything? How can I tell those who cannot have food?'

'You cannot.'

'Is it best to die?'

'By your own hand?' Iago asked. Olivera nodded. 'The Holy Ones will tell you to do so is a mortal sin,' he replied.

'You do not believe it is a mortal sin?'

Iago shrugged. 'I do not know anything, my friend.'

'They say, or some say, you are . . .'

Iago waited, meeting the eyes of Olivera. The pilot smiled, looked away and gave his head the slightest of shakes, as though throwing aside the suspicious thought.

'Thank God you are a seaman, Iago, and you know that there is only one thing a seaman can do in such circumstances.'

'Ah yes,' sighed Iago, 'there is always the consolation of our duty.'

Guillestigui relieved Olivera of one duty, enforcement of his edict. The following forenoon his guards, under Olalde, came forward and administered kicks and blows to the seamen left alive, urging them to get on deck and attend to their duties, chief among which was that of pumping. Although Olalde and his men ignored the remaining male passengers, they did not scruple to wade among the Franciscans and this turn over of the quick and the dead became a daily routine as the *Santa Margarita*, under a few rags of sail, was kept doggedly before the wind. It seemed that at long last they had found the true westerlies of Urdaneta for, having reached a latitude that an incredulous Olivera calculated as forty-four degrees north of the equator, this slowly dropped as they struggled to the south and east.

A steady increase in temperature revived a few hardy souls, but many continued to die from hunger, scurvy and the harsh blows of Olalde's soldiers. These were indiscriminately applied to both men and women whose bodies were disfigured by bruises, fractures and open lesions. No notice was taken of any protest and all who voiced the slightest opposition were beaten. Many, Ximenez among them, fled into the darkest recesses of the ship to avoid the gratuitous cruelty, but even here they were hunted out by men who seemed revived by such licence. Olalde himself took a vicious delight in torturing others and would stand over his victims, applying the sole of his boot with an increasing pressure upon a vivid contusion.

Even Iago was not exempt. Asleep on his watch below, he was woken by the flat of a sword across his back. As he turned to confront his assailant, he saw Olalde turn Ah Fong out of her hammock so that she fell with a cry half on Iago and half upon the deck. There she lay whimpering with fear and pain for even the constraints of the hammock hurt her tender flesh.

Her cry roused Iago to a fury. 'How dare you!' he fumed, struggling to his feet, only to have Olalde kick him back to his knees.

'You can defend that Chinese whore no better than you can find land, you hound's turd!' the sergeant-major said, swiping his gloved hand across Iago's face and knocking two teeth from his jaw.

Iago spat the incisors out. 'You have no right, Olalde . . .'

Olalde laughed. 'You lisp delightfully, my friend, like a winsome catamite.'

'I shall protest to the captain-general!'

'Do so, by all means. But His Excellency is sick and,' Olalde shrugged, 'is not expected to live.' He grinned down at his victim. 'Joanes is convinced you are a spy. Others say you are a Protestant. As for you . . .' He let his eyes wander over Ah Fong so that instinctively Iago drew her towards him.

'You will have to kill me . . .'

'That would not be very difficult,' Olalde said and with a shove of his heel sent both of them sprawling.

Olalde had hardly left them before Marmolejo, his head bleeding from a blow from one of the guards, touched Iago upon the arm.

In a breathless harangue Marmolejo said, 'Don Iago, I beg you, do not delay, let us marry you, at once, call your dwarf, and I shall fetch Hernando or Agustin . . .'

And so, kneeling abjectly amid the squalor of the half-deck, accompanied by the laughter of Don Baldivieso de Arrocheros, the man whom the world knew as Iago Fernandez was married according to the rites of the Roman Catholic Church to the Chinese woman whom Marmolejo had christened Margarita.

Fourteen
The Hand of God

'It is scarcely credible,' Marmolejo remarked feebly, his voice forced through a throat swollen and ulcerated and a mouth almost devoid of teeth, 'but I have calculated that during this terrible voyage we have endured forty storms.'

Iago nodded slowly, taking his eyes off the grey belly of the square sail hoisted above the forecastle. Both men sat on the half-deck, their backs against the rail, soaking up the warm sunshine.

'And,' Marmolejo went painfully on, 'that is precisely the number of souls still left alive of the three hundred who made up our company last July.'

'Do you detect the hand of God in this numerical coincidence, Fray Mateo?'

'Is it possible you doubt it?' Iago shrugged. 'Listen, my son, Olivera tells me that this ship reached a latitude of forty degrees north. Is that not marvellous?'

'I did not think so at the time,' Iago managed with a smile that cracked his lower lip so that it bled. 'And, if I am not mistaken, the latitude was actually forty-one degrees, which wrecks your divine marvel, Padre.'

'Do not mock God, Don Iago, you verge on the blasphemous.'

'How so? I state a fact; the latitude we reached was forty-one, not forty as you seek to assert.'

Marmolejo sighed. He, like the captain-general, had lost the capacity for logical thought, Iago concluded. And perhaps he himself had done the same, for having thus exhausted his brain, he could not recall whether or not Guillestigui was still living.

'Have you seen the captain-general?' he asked uncertainly.

'The captain-general? I heard his confession and we buried him yesterday. He . . . Now what was it? Oh, yes, he urged us to put about for Manila and begged forgiveness for his sins, in particular the sin of placing Sergeant-Major Pedro Ruiz de Olalde in a position of authority.'

Iago nodded, recollecting something of the turmoil of the last few days. When Guillestigui succumbed to a final fit of melancholy, he had called Marmolejo and Olivera, to tell them that his nominated successor was not to be Olalde, but Rodrigo de Peralta, who was to accept the advice of Olivera in all maritime matters.

'Oh yes,' he said. 'I remember now.' They sat in silence for a while and then Iago remarked. 'Odd that a man of such forceful character should fade so quickly.'

'All is written, my son, even our sufferings.'

'And ironic that Baldivieso should live on,' Iago added.

'God's mercy is beyond our understanding.'

'Perhaps.'

'You doubt it? It has pleased Almighty God to spare you and your Chinese wife. He has some purpose for you yet.'

'To be the last to die in this accursed ship? Huh!' Iago made a gurgling noise that was all he could manage by way of a chuckle. Death had become so commonplace that it no longer frightened any of them.

'God has been pleased to make us suffer much that our sufferings in the hereafter may be light.'

'Are those comfortable words, Fray Mateo?'

'Do you not think so?'

'I am past thinking . . .'

'You are not Spanish, are you, Iago?' Iago sat in silence, feeling the warmth of the sun replaced by the chill shadow of the Holy Office.

'I am not past feeling,' he said in a low voice.

'And yet I mark you for a Christian . . . Who are you?'

'Is this the confessional, Fray Mateo?'

'If you wish. It is, at least by my reckoning, Shrove Tuesday and we stand upon the threshold of Lent.'

'I am Iago Fernandez, by adoption and by baptism into the one true faith.'

'But you were not born so.'

'No. I was born Jacob van Salingen in Zierikzee.'

Marmolejo almost started. 'You are a Netherlander then; a Protestant born . . .'

'Whose father was killed in the storming of that town and whose mother was carried off as booty by the victors. My new father accepted me as his own. Thus I was born one thing and became another.'

A shadow fell across them and they looked up. Marmolejo shaded his red eyes. 'Don Gonzalo . . . Will you not join us?'

Ordóñez, who clung to a rope to steady himself, seemed not to notice the two men at his feet, but stared beyond them, over their heads and out over the ship's rail. He murmured something and then, with an effort, raised his right arm and pointed.

'What is that?' asked Iago. He rolled over, drew up his knees, holding on to the rail, raised himself unsteadily to his own feet. On a level with Ordóñez he heard the officer repeat the word: 'Land.'

Iago felt his heart lurch in his breast. 'Where?' he breathed.

'There!' Ordóñez pointed.

Marmolejo, catching the quickening mood, rose beside them with a grunt. 'What is it?'

'Land,' both men said simultaneously.

'Land?'

'God be praised,' murmured Ordóñez, crossing himself.

'Amen. Amen!' said Marmolejo, raising the crucifix at his waist and touching it to his lips. 'Oh, God be praised!'

Iago staggered forward and called down to a pair of sailors idling in the waist. 'Luis! Ricardo! Pass word below that land is in sight!'

The faces of the two men were transfigured. '*¡Dios!* Land!'

And slowly, in the waist and upon the half-deck, the forty souls remaining alive gathered to stare at the land that lay ahead. All crossed themselves repeatedly, most fell to their knees, even the late captain-general's officers. Peralta ordered Guillestigui's banner hoisted on the jury mainmast and called upon Agustin to celebrate a Mass of thanksgiving for their deliverance.

Even as Fray Agustin raised his voice in the Kyrie, Hernando collapsed, dead they afterwards asserted, of a divine ecstasy.

'See. Thirty-nine,' muttered Iago to himself.

Hardly had the last strained and imperfect note of the plea for Fray Hernando's immortal soul faded than Olivera summoned every fit man to assist in closing the land. They had in prospect the island for which so many had prayed. The sight of it, although requested as a place to die, now filled every heart with the hope of life. But its coast remained distant, at least to the landsmen; the seamen saw it as a thing easy to be swept past and left astern, along with all hopes of survival. The rudder was therefore manned, a scrap of sail hoisted aft to better balance the rig and improve the accuracy of their primitive steering.

What followed seemed to Olivera afterwards to be the most terrifying ordeal he had yet experienced. Every anxiety, it seemed, was compounded by another and this chain of fears reduced his nerves. He trembled at the very thought of failing to bring the *Santa Margarita* to an anchor, yet she had only a single anchor left. He contemplated the preliminary feat of navigating through whatever off-lying dangers that were certain to lie about the island, just as it troubled him that he knew nothing of the quality of the holding ground, if indeed there was any holding ground to afford them an anchorage, or whether the ocean swell would make the enterprise utterly foolhardy to the point of impossibility. And then, suppose them to safely pass through a thousand unknown coral-heads, to be safely brought to their anchor off a beach, how would they get ashore? There was not a boat left and he feared they had insufficient energy to construct a raft. He too had noticed his mind had become unable to concentrate. Witness his present anxiety: all he could do was catalogue the things that could possibly go wrong. He could not construct a single solution; his thinking was muddled; he found himself confusing the want of a boat with the needs of the anchor and it was almost five minutes before he realized that his brain had skipped from the thought that the anchor needed a cable bent on to it, to a curious relief that, since they did not have a boat, they would not need a boat's painter, only to worry that if they succeeded in constructing a raft they would need a rope for it anyway. A rising panic caused Olivera's heart to thunder in his breast with such violence that he thought he might follow Hernando into eternity and it was only Iago's approach that steadied him.

'Are you all right, Antonio?' Iago confronted him, his face anxious.

'Me?'

'Yes, you looked as though you were about to faint.'

Olivera frowned, embarrassed. 'I felt a little odd . . .'

'I will try and find you some wine. I have told Llerena to rouse out the best cable and bend it to the remaining bower anchor.'

Olivera nodded, grasping at the lifeline of reality Iago had flung him. 'Yes, yes, that is good, Iago, and then I shall need a lookout forward if we are to bring the ship through whatever reefs lie ahead. Your eyes are better than mine.'

'As you wish.' Iago paused, then asked, 'Do you know where we might be?'

Olivera shook his head. 'I cannot be certain, but,' he paused, 'it is only a hunch. If my latitude is correct and although my last meridian altitude was good, I have fallen behind in my reckoning and am uncertain of the date, I nevertheless think that this is one of the Ladrones . . .'

'The Thieves' Islands.'

'Yes.'

'And the Indians there . . . ?'

'May not be friendly.'

'I will get you some wine.'

'I am obliged to you, Iago.'

But it was soon clear that the unmanageable state of the ship would not allow them to close the island. The men clustered on the forecastle turned aft to stare in despair and disbelief at Olivera. Learning of this turn of events Rodrigo de Peralta remonstrated with Olivera, insisting that they closed the island, that he had no alternative. But the pilot, having fortified himself as Iago had suggested, had found both his charts and a telescope and, having scanned the coastline as it opened on their starboard bow, held one before him.

'Do you hear me, Antonio de Olivera?' Peralta asked formally.

'Aye, I hear you, but I cannot do the impossible.'

'They are in a blackening mood forward,' Peralta warned, his voice low.

'What is that to me? I am not a wizard that I can make the world different. Stand aside.'

Even as the spirits of all on board fell again and Peralta's hand flew to his sword, Olivera strode forward to the half-deck rail and raising his voice called out to those on the forecastle.

'My lads,' he cried, 'I am confident of our position. That island is Buenavista, which some men call Saipan. I know nothing of it. We can hold a course of south and ahead of us lie two more islands, one of which is Çarpana at which the galleons from Acapulco call. God has granted at last that we may be thrown in the very path of rescue. Where we cannot make an abrupt change of course to fetch the land here,' and Olivera threw out his left hand, 'we may the better use it as a mark to land upon Çarpana ahead of us. It is perhaps ten leagues before our prayers will be answered, but I pray you do not despair.' Turning aside Olivera lowered his voice. 'Don Rodrigo,' he addressed Peralta, 'put up your sword and stand shoulder to shoulder with me.'

'I shall do better than that, señor,' and raising his sword Peralta brandished it so that the sunlight caught it. 'I call upon God's blessings for our staunch pilot, Antonio de Olivera!'

And as one they all cheered, after which Peralta ordered a liberal dole of the remaining provisions so that all might be as strong as possible for the exertions that were yet to come.

At the end it was simpler than Olivera had anticipated. He had underestimated the distance between Buenavista and Çarpana, for his chart was inaccurate but, on the afternoon of 9th February 1601, believing it to be the 5th March, they sighted another island and, carrying the breeze, Olivera decided to stand on. The third of the trio of stern lanterns having been torn from its bracket during the last gale, they fabricated a torch from a lump of wax and a number of candles all placed in a large glass carboy, lit it and raised it on the forecastle. To the intense joy of all on board it was answered by a fire ashore.

Neither Olivera nor Iago could leave the deck, such was their concern that further disaster might yet strike them all. At midnight Olivera sent word to Peralta, demanding that all the officers be returned their swords, and that the seamen had back their knives. Peralta agreed but Iago was to be disappointed; Guillestigui, he was told, had had his katana thrown overboard, believing it was fabricated by devils and cast spells.

'I demand a sword,' he said to Calcagorta, who was rearming them against the possibility of the Indians being unfriendly. The gunner hesitated a moment, then shrugged. 'Take mine,' he said, removing sword, scabbard and baldric.

'And you?' queried Iago.

'The captain-general left a fine Toledo rapier.'

Ashore, the first fire was joined by another which quickly blazed into a brilliant, flaring mark.

'They have lit that deliberately,' Olivera said excitedly. 'They mean it for a beacon!'

The drag of the weed upon the ship's bottom slowed their progress. Frustrated, impatient, but sounding their way inshore, they slowly closed the coast, heading towards the great fire in the light of which they could see silhouettes of figures capering. The leadsman's calls indicated a steadily shelving bottom, its tallow arming showing this to be sand.

'I can hear them!' Iago exclaimed from the rail as he cupped a hand to his ear. 'They seem to be shouting a welcome.'

'Let us not forget they are known for their thievery,' remarked Olivera. 'Is that anchor ready?' he called forward.

'Aye, señor,' came Llerena's response.

'Then we are close enough. Down helm . . .'

With a ponderous reluctance the *Santa Margarita* began her turn into the wind and Olivera ordered the anchor let go. Five minutes later the great ship snubbed round to her anchor, her cable slackened as she rode up to it and Llerena declared them: 'Brought up!'

At last they lay still, rolling gently in the low swell that came ashore and maintained a low surf along the white strip of beach that they could see in the starlight. All now came in deck, many leaning upon each other for support and

Marmolejo led them in prayers of thanksgiving for their deliverance.

Daylight revealed a dazzling green shoreline lying due south of them. Coconut palms fringed a cool, dense forest that beckoned with a beauty they could scarcely contemplate without tears starting from their eyes. Beyond the beach, with its smouldering remains of the beacon fire, the land rose to several summits in the middle distance.

And with daylight came their visitors, hundreds of the Chamorro people in scores of their swift proas. They brought with them quantities of coconuts, sweet potatoes, fish and even water which they desired to trade for iron. In her wrecked state the *Santa Margarita* yielded hundreds of bent nails half torn out of the ship by her ordeal and it was a matter of minutes before it was clear to the more perceptive of the mariners that the Chamorros had found they could easily acquire the desired iron without the trouble of trading. Within an hour the battered hulk was surrounded by a crowd of proas, most tied alongside or to each other, empty of their crews who swarmed aboard in quest of booty.

'Dear Christ, they will tear the ship apart,' remarked Olivera.

'They are like the piranha fishes,' observed Alacanadre, his face disfigured with half-healed scabs.

'How long do you think she will hang together, Antonio? This is far from being a safe anchorage. We must evacuate the ship as soon as possible.'

'Peralta and his gang will want us to discharge the cargo, or such of it that remains after these brigands have helped themselves.'

'I would not press that task upon the people until they have fed and rested. See how that fellow is eating coconuts, why he must have consumed a dozen or more . . .'

'I am more troubled by the Indians invading us. Hey . . . !' Olivera spun round, knocking down a Chamorro who had half-drawn the rapier from its scabbard. 'Well, I'll be damned!'

The Chamorro, scrambling to his feet, retreated muttering to himself and Peralta came on deck, equally indignant. 'Is this to be our reward,' he cried, 'to be robbed of even our weapons?'

'Don Rodrigo,' Olivera said wearily, 'I have brought you to this anchorage, I am exhausted and must sleep. The mariners are the same, yet they must pump the ship. You and the gentlemen aft are soldiers and it is for you now to play your part in our defence. Tomorrow perhaps we will begin to land . . .'

'We are not landing, señor, at least we shall land, but only to cut trees for new masts and yards and to obtain fabric for new sails. I am determined to sail this ship back to Manila. You yourself said that this island lies on the route of the east-bound galleons.'

Olivera was incredulous at this speech. It was clear that despite the six months of their ordeal, Peralta had learned nothing.

'Excellency,' he began with all the patience and deference he could muster, 'we must abandon the ship, she is a hulk. By all means land and cut trees, but raise instead of masts a palisade. Make what name you desire from claiming this land for Rey Felipe but do not, I beg you, presume to tell me that this ship is capable of sailing a mile further. If you doubt me take a turn at the pumps and have a look at the fathoms of weed that festoon our wounded hull. As for masts, yards and sails, pooh . . . !' Olivera ran out of words. He was drooping with fatigue and caught Iago's eye. 'Do you talk some sense into these gentlemen, Don Iago,' he said and, turning his back on Peralta he made his way below.

It was entirely natural that all those left alive aboard the *Santa Margarita* after such a disastrous ordeal should assume they could enjoy a little respite from any labour. Most understood the continuing need to pump the ship, but she leaked less as she rolled gently in the swell and although this was not attended to as assiduously as it should have been, any ingress of water into the ship was kept at bay. To the Chamorro people of Çarpana, however, the arrival of the wreck seemed a gift from Heaven. They knew well the value of iron and the *Santa Margarita* was full of it. They knew too the proud and armoured front these dark, bearded and sharp-featured strangers usually maintained with their death-dealing fire-sticks that could mysteriously kill a man at fifty paces and frighten ten others with their noise and flame and smoke. The Chamorros had tasted their cruelty, the lashes they inflicted if they caught one of their people taking what they had need of. And they knew the burning they could administer if a Chamorro who had kissed their curious carved talismans – those little grotesques with a man writhing in agony upon a cross – and who refused to do it again. That was a truly terrible way to die, bound to a tree and burned alive.

It was clear to the Chamorros that these people were very different, though they seemed of the same breed and spoke the same language. And while they wore rusty half-armour and there were a couple in the dull drab of their cruel priests – those who carried the talismans and ordered the burnings – there the similarity ended. These newcomers stank worse than the others. They had few teeth and no flesh; their hair was lank and patchy; their nails bled and they could hardly stand. Indeed, all they seemed to want to do was sleep. They were ravenously hungry too, and they came from the north, but they brought iron, iron for which, it was quite clear, they had little need for, without help, they were all going to die.

Or so the Chamorro people hoped, for although they had swarmed aboard the great ship, which had clearly lost her masts and rigging, and although they had found the taking of iron to be simple, they feared the stink of the ship, and the touch of the Spanish whose flesh was rotting on their very bones. Few of the Chamorro, and fewer of the surviving Spaniards, knew how rapidly a diet of fresh fruit or vegetables would restore them, though a handful would find out soon enough. In the first hours, after that initial, enthusiastic contact, the Chamorro withdrew, leaving the Spanish to sleep. Then next morning a few bold natives paddled their proas alongside the *Santa Margarita* and again began to trade. At about the same hour and on the prompting of Olalde and Calcagorta, Peralta, having posted armed sentries about the ship which dissuaded the Indians from coming aboard and confined them to trading from their boats, called a council in the great cabin. To Olivera's despair the new captain-general held to his intention to re-rig the vessel and prepare her for a return to Cavite or Manila.

Unfortunately, upon a show of hands, this view prevailed. Olivera groaned audibly and, shaking his head in despair, retired to his quarters in high dudgeon. After his heroic exertions he was, Iago recognized, a broken man.

Fifteen
Rodrigo de Peralta

As captain-general, Rodrigo de Peralta could think of no action other than returning to Manila. Despite her condition, the fact that the *Santa Margarita* still floated seemed to him to demonstrate an unexpected but welcome durability. Since Olivera himself had said that the hand of God had guided them through the torments of Hell to place them in the very westward path of the Manila-bound *nãos*, it followed that the sailing conditions were therefore favourable, and while pusillanimous opinion suggested they await rescue at Çarpana, there were a number of factors that dissuaded Peralta from doing so.

He was advised by Llerena and some others among the common *marineros* that they could re-rig the vessel sufficiently to sail her back to the Philippines. These men also said that, while they lay comfortably at anchor for now, at any moment the wind might rise and they would almost certainly be cast ashore; a speedy decision upon which they could act was therefore essential. To these expert counsels Peralta added cogent reasons of his own. The first was a deep suspicion of the Chamorros, whom he neither trusted, nor liked to have to rely upon for anything. The second was that as captain-general he sought an heroic accomplishment, not a hand-held return in another man's ship. He did not wish to be remembered as the leader of a disastrous enterprise. Peralta wanted to rescue what the famed Juan Martinez de Guillestigui had lost.

And so upon the following morning, as the Chamorros, moved by curiosity and their lust for iron, paddled their proas out to lie off the battered *não* and stare at her, Peralta ordered the building of a boat. This was a painful business, for no one had either inclination or energy, but a craft of sorts was improvised from four large, roughly hewn packing cases whose contents – bales of silk – had been ruined by sea water and hungry rats. These were held together by baulks of timber torn from the remains of the stern gallery.

'It does not seem to occur to anyone,' remarked Olivera to Iago, 'that the more they tear the ship apart, the less of her they have to sail anywhere, let alone Manila Bay.'

'We must stay here, Antonio, on this island until a ship comes,' Iago said insistently, ignoring Olivera's conversational remark and staring at the pilot, who, it was clear, had abdicated all responsibility in his exhausted state. For the first time Iago noticed that Olivera's hair was almost all white, the lines on his face were deeply etched and his eyes were shadowed to the point of giving him a haunted, beaten look. Moreover he stood unsteadily on painfully swollen legs. It was as though, having given of his best, poor Olivera's over-worked body had ceased to function properly. Iago was in little better condition himself. He had been up half the night pacing the upper deck, determining what he and his little household should do. God, his own God, had seen the three of them safely thus far, but Iago reasoned that he owed no allegiance to Peralta and his God-forsaken crew. On a contractual basis alone the expedition had failed him – they were scarcely a quarter of the way across the Pacific – and he thought he might recruit a party opposed to the folly of attempting another voyage. The two disaffected mariners leaned on the rail and watched as Llerena tempted a proa full of the boldest Chamorros to come on board and for three iron hoops help them hoist the extemporized boat over the side.

This they did, laughing between themselves and pointing at the debilitated state of the Spaniards who stood around in a generally bewildered condition.

'This is too familiar,' Olivera muttered anxiously, 'they will see our impoverished state.'

Behind them Peralta gave orders and more iron mast hoops were passed down to the boats into which, as well as a pair of seamen and two soldiers armed with arquebuses, the two carpenters clambered with their axes. Then, apparently spontaneously, a Chamorro slid into what passed for the stern and, giggling excitedly, gestured to the shore and called out something to his friends in an adjacent proa.

'Trading iron for trees,' Olivera scoffed, 'and those arquebuses have no powder. Those poor devils are on a fool's errand.'

The boat of boxes shoved off and the sailors plied their simple board-paddles. Olivera and Iago watched in silence, both thinking the same thoughts. Some little distance off shore the low swell broke on a reef. It was impossible to see whether the reef was of coral or rock, but it was a formidable barrier to so primitive and unwieldy a craft and the surf, though making only a low and intermittent noise, would prove impossible to traverse without a break in the reef.

'How the Devil can they tow a tree out with that thing?' Iago asked, presupposing they could discover a gap in the reef. The boat of boxes edged along the surf to the east, surrounded by proas and accompanied by shouts of encouragement and laughter. In the stern of the boat the lone Chamorro seemed to be enjoying himself, engaging in repartee and gesticulations that, to the increasingly distant and utterly helpless observers lining the rails of the *Santa Margarita*, seemed somehow menacing.

Just as the decks of the ship became suddenly crowded with Peralta and the armed gentlemen on the poop, the passengers amidships and the *marineros* crowded into the waist, so the beach was infested by the curious Indians. Hundreds of Chamorro men emerged from the trees armed with spears. They were joined by some women bearing babies and children who scampered up and down in the shallows like excited puppies.

A murmur of appreciation at the appearance of the half-naked women ran through the assembled ship's company like a breeze through dry grass.

Suddenly the Indian in the stern held up his right arm, indicating that the men should paddle the boat to the right and slip through a gap in the reef. Beside Iago, Olivera suddenly straightened, his old body ramrod-stiff with apprehension.

'There is no passage there!' he shouted, so that Peralta, from his higher vantage point, suddenly took greater interest in the fate of his hopes rather than regarding the women.

A second later, as the boat of boxes completed her turn, a swell humped up and half-obscured it. Then they caught a glimpse of it lifted and borne forward on the crest of the wave, but as the swell culminated and rose to a peaked crest, the boat was hidden again, to make only one further appearance before it was shivered into pieces as the breaker thundered over the reef. As it ran on to dissipate itself upon the beach and finally lap the feet of the delighted children, they could see a brief gleam of yellow planks catching the sunlight amid the bobbing heads of the boat's crew. The solitary Indian was seen wading up the beach, throwing his dark hair from his face.

'My God, the soldiers!' someone cried out and all watched anxiously as the drama was played out.

The arquebusiers had been wearing cuirasses and morions and must surely drown but then, to the intense relief of the watchers, what seemed like a spontaneous movement to assist the wretches in the water caused the people on the beach to surge forward. Fifty or sixty men waded into the sea and within a few seconds, to the accompaniment of a thin cheer from the *Santa Margarita*, the six Spaniards were half-dragged, or stumbled up the beach, supported by Chamorros.

'God be praised!' cried Marmolejo and the company crossed itself with a simultaneous rustle of ruined clothing amid cries of ecstatic joy.

Then, just as they reached safety, the situation was transformed.

'My God, treachery!'

Huddled together on the golden sand, the six Spaniards were suddenly surrounded by their rescuers, increased now to some three or four hundred, shouting men. All waved lances or clubs and suddenly they surged forward and clustered round the Spaniards, dragging them to the top of the beach where they were swiftly bound to the palms. As the terrified victims cried for mercy, the Chamorro people began to stone and beat them to death, finishing their task by bringing burning brands and setting them on fire.

Those watching from the *Santa Margarita* were aghast.

Without a boat they had no means of intervening and their general lassitude only added to their feeling of abject impotence. While Marmolejo summoned the Holy Ones to pray for the departing souls even as they ascended to Heaven, Calcagorta fumed at his inability to find powder dry enough to charge one of the sakers and send an iron ball or two crashing into the mass of Chamorros gleefully dancing on the beach and waving and gesticulating at the helpless Spaniards watching from the wreck of their ship.

'They are not fools, these Indians,' Olivera said, turning away. 'They know what a properly fitted-out Spanish *não* should look like. They have seen the westbound ships with their ensigns and standards, their figures of the Virgin and the pomp of cannon fire, the glitter of arms and armour. Who knows what grudges they bear us for our possession of iron, or for any cheating in our dealing with them, real or imagined. We must appear as sacrificial victims brought to them by their own gods . . .'

'You are gloomy, Olivera,' snarled Calcagorta, returning to the half-deck from his futile attempt to ignite the powder in the breech of a saker. 'Save your cavilling for another occasion. Those bloody savages need teaching a lesson and if you are not the man to do it then leave it to Joanes de Calcagorta and Pedro Ruiz de Olalde!'

Olivera said nothing, but watched the gunner join Peralta and his suite on the poop. Then, without looking at Iago, he went below.

'Master?' Iago took his eyes from the retreating pilot and regarded Ximenez at his side.

'What is it?'

'The mistress has cooked some flying fish and dressed a little rice . . .'

'But the rice is rancid.'

'I know, master, but, begging your pardon, your wife is a woman of determined habit and there is some fruit and coconut which she had traded.'

Iago looked at Ximenez, whose survival astonished him. 'I am wondering, Ximenez, if you regret meeting me beneath that other palm grove and whether we shall all end up like those unfortunate men beneath the trees yonder.'

Ximenez shrugged. 'I am certain that if God does not rule this world then the Devil does. Either way the fortunes of poor Ximenez are of little account. I can at least count myself among the fortunate in having experienced this voyage and I still live.'

'I am not certain that I understand your argument, Ximenez,' Iago said almost fondly, placing his hand upon the dwarf's shoulder, 'but I shall not baulk at coconut and papaya.'

'Do not eat too much fruit, master, it induces a looseness difficult to control.'

For five days they were prisoners aboard the ship. By degrees the Chamorros approached again in their proas and by degrees the Spaniards accepted them. There was little they could do to stop the Indians coming on board and the dead are soon forgotten. Every man thought he could negotiate his own salvation by showing cordial friendship to an individual Chamorro and nails and knives bought help with the interminable if intermittent pumping.

This chore remained essential to the saving of the ship and her intended eventual return to the Philippines but the Chamorros did not like pumping, perceiving that they were undertaking labour that brought them no advantage beyond a few nails. It was clear that the strangers should do their own pumping, and if they were too weak then the ship would soon fall into their own hands and they could have as many nails as they wished.

Then, on the sixth day, they found the *Santa Margarita* suddenly striking the reef.

It was a gentle bump at first, so gentle that one could almost dismiss it as a figment of an over-anxious imagination. Iago felt it and his heart missed a beat, so reminiscent was it of the fate of the *Rainha de Portugal*. Then a swell rolled in, lifted the ship and set her down again. This time there could be no doubt about it: they had run aground. When a third time she landed violently, the whole structure of the hull shuddered with the shock. Twice more she lifted and dropped with such force that she was quickly bilged. Thereafter, though the swells rose and fell about her, and the tide flooded and ebbed, she lay impaled upon the reef.

It was not coral, but sharp, crenated limestone, hard as adamantine and as destructive as any explosive device of Calcagorta. Even as this sequence of disastrous events was taking place, Olalde was roaring threats of death to the malefactor who had severed the cable. It was Iago that, pushed beyond the limit of his patience and anxious to bring the matter of their collective future to a resolution, shouted at Olalde to hold his tongue.

'Can you not grasp the fact that the cable was rotten?' he cried. 'Go and look over the bow at the remains hanging from the hawsehole and concentrate your thoughts upon staying alive, not killing . . .'

'What do you know about it, Don Iago,' growled Olalde, pointing at the forecastle. 'Those bastards forrard have compromised us because they are milksops and lack the bowels to take us back to Manila. They have cut that cable thinking to force the hand of the captain-general.' And, he might have added, of Pedro Ruiz de Olalde.

Iago dismissed the notion. He thought it unlikely any of the *marineros* would cut the cable and thus deliberately deprive the ship of her one last anchor even if some among them could not face the prospect of making the long passage back to the Philippines.

'He knows only how to shout and bully,' Iago muttered, 'we have need of cunning here, not bombast.'

'You are right, Don Iago.' Iago looked up to see Arrocheros and Ordóñez standing near him. 'But,' Arrocheros went on, 'I hold you responsible . . .'

'What? For a rotten cable?'

'No, for everything, from Ocampo's curse to this pass to which we have been brought.'

'I think you overstate your case, Don Baldivieso,' said Ordóñez hurriedly, taking the merchant's arm and trying to draw him away as he made exculpatory faces at Iago.

Iago shrugged. Arrocheros's mind was unhinged. He smiled at Ordóñez as Arrocheros called out, 'We shall all die like dogs, Don Iago, and all because of you . . .'

'Aye, he is a spy,' put in Calcagorta from the poop but Marmolejo called them to order.

'What is to become of us if we fight among ourselves? We

must make common cause . . .' he began, but someone forward, a sailor it was thought, cried out:

'What? Like the holy disciples the night Christ was crucified?'

'God help us all, Fray Mateo,' interjected Iago as the Discalced Franciscan passed him by. 'We are assuredly lost now.'

'So thinks the captain-general. You are summoned to a council in the great cabin.'

There was much arguing in the cabin. If Peralta had thought himself secure in his assumption of office as captain-general, it was clear that even within his own Basque faction others sought their own way, if not the role of leader. Calcagorta and Olalde both advised strong measures.

'We can dry some power, I'm sure,' proclaimed Calcagorta, 'and then we may use both sakers and arquebuses.'

'You cannot wipe out the entire population,' Olivera put in wearily.

'Guillestigui would have done,' Olalde growled.

'My sons,' Marmolejo advised, 'we must convert them to Christ and then, in all humility . . .'

'Fuck your humility, Marmolejo!' exclaimed Olalde. 'If we lack cannon we do not lack swords and every mariner has a knife!'

'Do we have the strength to fight a prolonged battle?' Ordóñez asked.

'Not in my opinion,' said the hitherto silent Teniente Pedro de Guzman.

'And every Chamorro male has a lance twice the length of your Toledo blades,' added Olivera lugubriously.

Olalde rounded on the pilot in a fury. 'Then what in the name of Satan do you advise, eh?'

'I have already told the captain-general that we need to build a fort,' Olivera explained in patiently measured tones. 'This will secure us, and from its fastness we may trade with the Indians and await the arrival of a ship from Acapulco, which will not now be long in coming.'

A prolonged silence greeted this statement. Its obvious good sense weighed on the minds of those eager for a more active and immediate outcome.

'I agree,' said Iago at last, despairing of others coming to the pilot's support.

'You,' said Olalde pointedly, 'you would agree with anything Olivera said.'

'That is because he speaks sense.'

'Why, you damned, insolent—'

'Don Pedro,' Peralta said curtly, 'this is a council, not a bear-pit. Don Iago's right to speak—'

'Talk not of rights, Don Rodrigo,' cut in Calcagorta, adding with a voice envenomed with sarcasm, 'there are those of us who believe Don Iago to be a Portuguese spy.'

'And others who think him worse, a Protestant with a Chinese witch for a whore.'

'Damn you, Olalde,' Iago said, 'I would remind you that I am a *sobrasaliente* and paid for my passage.'

'That is what you would wish us to believe,' Calcagorta said.

'My sons, hold your peace. I can vouch for Don Iago,' Marmolejo interjected, moving between Iago and the two men.

'So too can I,' Ordóñez said.

'And I,' added Alacanadre.

'Arrocheros has evidence,' Olalde said menacingly.

'Arrocheros is insane,' scoffed Ordóñez.

'Gentlemen, we have weightier matters to consider!' Peralta sought control of the council.

As they grew silent, Iago said with a stiff bow, 'With your permission, Your Excellency, and since my honour is in question, I have no desire to express any further opinion other than to support the good sense of Don Antonio.'

Peralta nodded and Iago withdrew. Behind him as he left the great cabin, he heard a rising tide of argument above which Rodrigo de Peralta's voice called for silence.

Iago went swiftly to his quarters. Arrocheros was hanging around listlessly, as he had done for days. He did not seem to mind, having little connection with reality. Two Chamorros watched him curiously.

'See these devils, Don Iago?' he said, indicating the Indians. 'They have come to speak to you . . .'

Iago ignored the weak-minded merchant and dived under

the canvas curtain. Inside Ximenez almost stabbed him with his dagger.

'Oh, master, forgive me! I thought you were one of those Indians. Don Baldivieso encourages them, speaks of them as your familiars and calumniates against you.'

Iago put a finger to his lips and said loudly, 'Do you clean my boots, you idle dog!' and then as Ximenez stared at him in astonishment he bent quickly to the dwarf's ear. 'Clean my boots,' he whispered, 'overhaul the best attire for myself and for you and sing loudly while you work.' Then he straightened up and, parting the curtain, almost fell over Arrocheros crouched outside. Iago shoved past him and went in quest of Ah Fong.

He found her trading nails and other knick-knacks for coconuts, some more of the excellent flying fish and a bag of rice. Calling her to him he led her below and here he whispered instructions into her ear while Ximenez sang an obscene song he had heard on the waterfront at Cavite. It told of the adventures of a sailor, a whore and a donkey. When it came to the sailor's name, which in the song was Luis, Ximenez inserted his own. It ruined the scansion but gave him immense pleasure and made him seem the essence of a rollicking tar.

When he had given his instructions to Ah Fong and she had nodded her quick comprehension, Iago left them and went on deck. The Chamorros were already infesting the upper deck, mostly hanging over the after rails and advising others who clung to the *Santa Margarita*'s side and industriously picked bent nails from the wreckage of the stern gallery. It was almost low water and the size of the *Santa Margarita* was obvious as she lay broken-hulled upon the reef, her weathered sides almost devoid of the rich paint she had once borne so proudly, her bottom invisible under its thick growth of weed.

Iago marvelled briefly that they had driven that battered hull through any weather, let alone the forty *baguiosas* of Marmolejo's calculations. Such a contemplation made ridiculous the proposition that they could take the ship back to Manila. But Iago had more pressing matters to consider. Inside the binnacle and untouched by the light-fingered Chamorros,

Lorenzo's telescope lay. Iago took it up and scanned the shore.
A pair of Indians regarded him curiously and then resumed
their work of deconstructing the ship. The ease with which
the iron yielded itself pleased them and, for the moment at
least, seemed to draw the teeth of their savagery.

Perhaps, Iago thought, that as long as the Spaniards
remained on their ship, the Chamorros would tolerate them.
It was ashore, as trespassers, that they would be in danger.
And yet, if they were to preserve their own lives, it was
ashore that they must go. He saw few eminences that would
support a fort, even suppose they were left in peace for
sufficient time to fell the requisite number of palm trees.
Sighing he turned about and looked seaward, almost willing
a be-pendanted *não* to heave in sight and relieve them of
all their anxieties. Should he pray for a miracle? And if he
did, should he pray as a Protestant or a Catholic? After all,
he thought with an edge of gallows humour, he could claim
to be both. In the end all he did was note that the wind
was onshore and rising. Of course the wind would die away
at sunset and come away from off the land during the night,
but suppose the *terral* did not materialize? Suppose the
onshore wind derived from some passing storm and the
breakers rolled in? Inert upon the rocky reef, a few hours
of pounding would see the *Santa Margarita* shivered into a
thousand broken timbers. The sensation of the grounding
had sent his heart racing as it recalled the brief and savage
ordeal of the *Rainha de Portugal*.

God! What a terror that had been! He caught himself
involuntarily crossing himself at the very thought of it. And
then with a resurrection of that grim humour that consoled
him at such moments of self-ridicule, he hoped one of those
accusatory swine below in the great cabin would hear a
report of Don Iago privately crossing himself when he
thought no one was looking. That festering Arrocheros! Of
all the men to be still living when so many had died! What
was that if not proof that life was nothing more than a
lottery?

Iago's reflections were abruptly broken into by the emer-
gence on to the deck of the council. Marmolejo crossed the
deck towards him.

'Don Iago, we are resolved to make the best of it ashore. We must find an interpreter and enter into negotiations.'

'That is something, Fray Marmolejo.'

'I am sorry for what they said about you,' Marmolejo said consolingly.

'Don't be, Father. It would be blasphemy if I said that they do not know what they do, but they are short-sighted fools.'

'That is true. I have succeeded in joining them in prayer and reconciliation.'

'And I have been crossing myself, Father,' Iago said wryly, but Marmolejo missed the irony.

'I am glad to hear it, my son.'

'And by what means do we intend to seek guarantees from these savages?'

'We shall trade them all the iron they can recover from the ship in return for a safe passage ashore and a place where we may build a fort, though we have called it a village.'

'Very clever. And what about water?'

'We shall secure a spring.'

'And food?'

'Fish,' Marmolejo gestured seawards and then swept his arm towards the shore, 'coconuts, papayas and what of God's bounty is provided for these people.'

Iago sighed and nodded. It was the best that could be hoped for. 'Too much fruit seems to loosen the bowels.'

'Aye, Gonzalo Manuel has a bad attack,' Marmolejo observed, 'as does Fray Agustin.'

'And are we to negotiate for passage ashore?' asked Iago.

Marmolejo nodded. 'And we must pray for a successful outcome.'

And two days later, after scurvy had carried off three men despite all they had tried to prevent it and several others had hung their buttocks over the heads to release streams of yellow liquid, the *Santa Margarita* was surrounded by hundreds of proas, some said five hundred of them. The Chamorros had come, or so all on board believed, to convey the Spaniards ashore after an agreement pompously concluded upon the poop by Peralta and his suite and three Chamorros who appeared from their dress and deportment to be men of some standing in Çarpana. This ended with a blessing from the assembled Holy

Ones. The psalms had intrigued the Chamorros, one of whom assiduously crossed himself in imitation of Agustin and Marmolejo, to the amusement of his fellows.

Iago had been right about the wind. A heavier surf was running now and, although they began the disembarkation safely enough in the lee of the ship, the swell dashed itself against the *Santa Margarita*'s weather side with such violence that occasionally she shuddered with the impact. Gathering up bundles of belongings and told off in twos and threes, passengers and crew clambered down into the outrigged proas to be paddled ashore by the Chamorros. In their haste to get clear of the surf several of the craft were overset. While the Chamorros swam merrily ashore, Marmolejo was one of those who fell into the sea and was only pulled from it after a struggle since he was weighed down by his heavy, sodden woollen habit. Ordóñez too fell in. He was wearing armour and drowned before he could be dragged clear of the breakers. His body was carried up to the line of palms and laid out ready to be buried.

As each proa reached the sandy strand it was met by several lance-bearing warriors who closed each group of survivors and conducted them into the vegetation and along narrow footpaths to their villages. Thus broken up into small groups, the Spanish were cheated of their fort and from that moment of fragmentation were reduced to helplessly small factions.

Most were taken and concealed in huts in the village they learned was called Atetito and it was here that Iago and his two followers were brought. Iago had been at some pains to dissociate himself from the Spanish, in particular Peralta and the other so-called gentlemen. He had felt the parturition inevitable after the deprivation of his sword so that the accusations of Olalde and Calcagorta did not surprise him. Neither did he attribute their hostility to the denouncements of the crazy Arrocheros; these had merely provided a pretext, seized avidly by Olalde and his cronies.

Iago had instructed Ximenez to dress himself in his finest and therefore most durable clothes. He had also been told to gather as much negotiable iron as it was possible for him to carry and to fill another small knapsack for Iago to carry. Ah Fong was told to put on the grey silk dress that Ximenez had bought for her in Cavite and which, despite being stained by sea water, transformed her androgynous appearance. She had also dressed her hair and, though somewhat dishevelled, bore the appearance of a person of quality. Moreover, since Iago had noticed the readiness with which the Chamorros traded with both Ah Fong and the two remaining Filipino women, seeing in them not so much their gender as their racial distinction from the Spanish men, he thought that she might prove the key to their survival.

He had urged her to negotiate a separate passage ashore with the fisherman from whom she had bought the flying fish, and this saw them safely to the beach where, although they were met by a group of spearmen, the fisherman had guaranteed that they would be taken to his own hut. They were among the last to leave the *Santa Margarita* and they slept that night in comparative safety – just as the fisherman had promised.

In the following days a series of tragedies unfolded. The first death occurred through natural causes. To the intense sadness of all, Fray Mateo Marmolejo failed to recover from his soaking, but died of a fever two days after landing. His soul was accompanied to Heaven by a requiem Mass that, against the inclinations of their hosts, the few assembled Holy Ones left alive managed to sing. Agustin in particular mourned his Brother, and seemed fatally marked by his death. Eight of the *marineros* also died of wounds, diarrhoea, broken bones or severe contusions acquired in the disembarkation. Agustin busied himself with their last rites and burials, moving among the sick unimpeded by the Chamorro people who, he thought, had encountered priests before.

Indeed, it was clear that the Chamorros had not adopted a policy of slaughtering the Spaniards wholesale. Rather, from time to time it seemed to Iago that the death of a few removed the threat of trouble from the rest, so that the stoning and clubbing of the six men in that first improvised boat that had upset in the surf established the natives as masters of the strangers. Iago was apt to attribute this vague hostility to the folly of the Spanish in trying to force the Chamorros to pump the *Santa Margarita*. He had long seen such behaviour

among those who had adopted him for the arrogance that it
was. Now, such hauteur begged for humiliation and he strove
to detach himself from any charge of it, separating himself
from Peralta and his chief and most influential officers, Olalde
and Calcagorta, who saw no reason for subtle discourse with
the natives of Çarpana. Nevertheless, for some days a kind of
peace reigned. The Chamorro people were not unkind to
them, though they were careful to keep them apart. In general
the natives provided them with food, but they showed a
marked revulsion to those unable to control their bowels.

Chief among these was Captain Gonzalo Manuel,
commander of the captain-general's guards. He had spent
much of the voyage prostrated by seasickness and otherwise
under the influence of Olalde and now he seemed unable to
throw off the diarrhoea brought on by the avid consumption of fruit. Since this had proved a rapid specific against
the scurvy, Manuel's fate was an ironic one. Suddenly one
morning, when walking through Atetito with two Chamorros
after helping them carry a catch of fish back to the village,
Manuel was taken with an uncontrollable spasm. Groaning
and tugging at his belt, he hurried off the track to squat
urgently between two huts and void himself. A moment later
he had left a stinking yellow runnel in the hard, dry earth.

His Chamorro escort wrinkled their noses against the stench
and backed away, while a bare-breasted woman ran from the
adjacent hut, screaming her outrage at the unfortunate man
as he sought to button himself. The noise drew the attention
of a crowd, most of whom were young men and boys who
came running up. The cause of the row was obvious and –
such was the Chamorros' disgust – that the youngsters picked
up stones and circling Manuel, threw them at him. One struck
his head, then another and he instinctively crouched down,
trying to protect his head before another stone hit him in
the lower face. With a cry of pain he fell back and rolled in
his own filth.

More cries of revulsion assailed him as he strove to rise,
only to be met by another barrage of stones. The assault was
remorseless and purposeful; the aim of the throwers was accurate, the force all that they could muster. The stones struck
him repeatedly in such numbers and with such violence that,

in a few moments, Manuel was beaten unconscious. Here he lay while the stones reduced him to a bloody pulp until his body ceased to twitch.

Had the Spanish acquiesced in their fate and lived peaceably among the simple Chamorros until a *não* from Acapulco hove in sight, more might have survived, but it was not in the nature of certain men to possess their souls in patience. As a result their bodies paid the price. Peralta, Olalde and Calcagorta had been insufficiently separated. In the beginning the nature of their close relationship was not understood by the Chamorro chiefs, who thought it better to keep the men who had made the agreement aboard the *Santa Margarita* together, where they might best be supervised.

Neither Olalde nor Calcagorta were men who could accept their fates lying down and Peralta, fearful of losing his illusory powers as captain-general, was obliged to go along with them in their noisy protests and their insistence upon forms of respect quite alien to the Chamorros. Not that the Indians were entirely ignorant of the Spaniards' ways. They had some inkling of what it meant when the great silk banners Peralta had insisted were brought ashore were hoisted by Diego de Llerena to the top of a palm tree. Olalde and Calcagorta, with Llerena's help, had engineered a touching ceremony in which a small residue of gunpowder had been fired in a dried-out arquebus to intimidate the Chamorros and salute the banner presented to the *Santa Margarita* seven months earlier by the episcopate of Manila. Hardly had the ceremony concluded than a Chamorro cut the halliards and the brilliant oriflamme fluttered to the ground.

With a roar of outrage, Olalde rushed forward, his sword drawn. His intention to strike the offending Indian was thwarted by Alacanadre, who stepped in front of him and, catching Olalde unawares, knocked him down and took up Olalde's dropped sword.

'Hold hard, Don Pedro,' Alacanadre cried, 'you will have us all killed . . .'

Olalde staggered to his feet, red with humiliation and fulminating at the disliked Alacanadre's intervention until Peralta called to him to consider the wisdom of the master of camp. But matters were swiftly taken out of their hands, for the

Chamorro whom Olalde had sought to kill had run off and now returned with a swelling crowd. Seeing Alacanadre with a sword they suddenly ran forward and, seizing him, dragged him away, ignoring the protests of Peralta and the others, and restraining them from following. It was only later they learned what had happened to Miguel de Alacanadre.

The colonel had been taken to the other side of Atetito where a shallow pit had been dug, ready perhaps for some such exemplary execution. Having thrown the Spanish officer into the pit he was stoned to death. Then he was left for a day in the sun, attracting the flies, the kites and the gulls who picked first at his eyes and face. He lay exposed for long enough for several of the Spaniards to be escorted past in order to learn his fate. One of these was Diego de Llerena.

The following day the tough *contramaestre* broke away from his conductors with whom he was going down to the beach and ran back to the pit in which Alacanadre's stinking corpse decomposed. Here he began scrabbling at the earth in an attempt to cover Alacanadre's body and prevent its desecration by the carrion-eaters. Finding a piece of wood he tried using this as a spade to better and more quickly effect his objective, but his actions offended the Chamorros. Running after him they attempted to push him into the pit on top of the corpse. But Llerena was less easy to overcome, fighting off his attackers so that he stood defiant on the edge of the pit panting in the stench given off by Alacanadre's body and brandishing the short piece of wood like a club.

Once again a crowd was rapidly summoned; stones were picked up and others went in search of more, for the area had been denuded the day before and Llerena prevented anyone from recovering those heaped against Alacanadre's body. But the inevitable assault began and soon Llerena was the target of another remorseless attack. But Llerena was a Basque, a pelota player of skill, and for several minutes he successfully dodged or struck out of the way a number of stones with his wooden club. Eventually, however, with some two hundred shouting Chamorros surrounding him and perhaps half that number hurling small rocks at him, he began to succumb.

For a moment it seemed as though numbers and the hail

of stones would overwhelm him, but then Llerena showed the immensity of his strength and raw courage, suddenly staggering forward waving his extemporized club. Once among the nearest Chamorros, the others ceased throwing stones for fear of hitting their friends. Llerena, a big and imposing figure, literally waded through the crowd and it drew back, almost letting him go as if in admiration of his bravery. At last he broke out of the ring, limping calmly away, back towards the hut where he was held. Curiously, the Chamorros seemed satisfied and let him go.

The next day his custodians came for him and took him down to the beach. All seemed to have been forgiven and forgotten, for they indicated that he was going fishing and he boarded the proa. A few minutes later, its sail hoisted, it skimmed off across the sparkling blue sea, heading for the blue peaks of a distant island. Diego de Llerena, *contramaestre* of the *Santa Margarita*, had bought his freedom on the neighbouring island of Tinian.

That same day the Chamorro chiefs who had concluded the agreement aboard the *Santa Margarita* came before Peralta and noisily demanded a council. By dint of pidgin, gestures and the uncertain services of a tall Chamorro who knew a few words of Spanish and Fray Agustin who knew something of the Chamorran tongue, they made it known to Peralta that the behaviour of his people was unacceptable.

Rodrigo de Peralta, in a florid and demonstrably arrogant declamation that needed little or no translation, declared the action of the Chamorros to be heathen and outside God's laws. The imprecations that he called down upon Atetito and the other villages where the handful of survivors were being kept fell upon deaf ears. The chiefs came for an earnest of the Spaniards' future conduct. Agustin eventually grasped this simple request and told Peralta.

'Excellency, they desire nothing more nor less than the gold chain you wear as a guarantee of our peaceable behaviour.'

An outraged Peralta put up his hand to clutch the gold chain and pendant that depended upon his breast. 'That is impossible!' he exclaimed. 'Quite impossible! It is my own, my father . . .'

'Excellency, I beseech you, this is not a moment for pride of possession, your life, our lives, depend upon you relinquishing it.'

'But my honour . . .'

'It is your duty, Excellency. You are the captain-general . . .'

'Don't you tell me my duty!'

The debate was terminated by the senior of the Chamorro chiefs. He stepped forward and struck Agustin in the chest. The Franciscan was not expecting the blow and fell backwards. The chief's hand swung in a swift movement and made to seize the pendant on Peralta's breast. But the captain-general turned away and the chief was frustrated. As Peralta stepped away those about him moved forward, two of the guards drawing their swords. Someone called for Calcagorta, who was absent from Peralta's company, but by the time word had reached the gunner, Peralta and those with him had been seized.

Carried bodily down to the beach by two of the largest men, the captain-general struggled in vain. The two Chamorros stumbled out into the shallows with their burden, then lifting the writhing Peralta high above their heads they dashed him against the sharp limestone reef. The blood spurted from Peralta's cuts and, bending, the two Chamorros picked him up again, then dashed him a second time against the rock. After the third time he had been thus cast down one of them removed the gold chain and, leaving Rodrigo de Peralta's broken but still living body to bleed to death and the incoming tide to carry him away, they brought the chain and presented it to the chiefs.

Summoned too late to intervene and frightened by the implacable nature of what he had just witnessed, Joanes de Calcagorta watched from the partial concealment of the palm trees.

Sixteen
Don Baldivieso

Peralta was not the only one killed that afternoon. In fact all of those assembled about him were carried off and murdered, one by one. Some were stoned, others flung violently upon the sharp limestone; all those who witnessed Peralta's defiance of the request of the Chamorro chiefs paid the price for their captain-general's intransigence except for Agustin, who was saved by his habit and his few words of Chamorro. Ironically it was Peralta's most significant accomplishment as Guillestigui's successor but it cost him his life. It also contributed to Calcagorta's anxieties and yet – such is the vanity of human aspiration – in spite of fear and the unravelling of the Spanish cause, the gunner assumed the title of captain-general with the confidence that one who held it had some meaning in the tiny world that was the island of Çarpana.

Although the village of Atetito was small, the segregation of the survivors ensured that it was some time before Iago learned what had occurred. In fact the Chamorro people, having by their murder of Peralta and his guard removed the source of Spanish arrogance, afterwards willingly accorded the dead Spaniards a burial ceremony according to their own rites. It was by being summoned to attend this that Iago discovered what had happened.

The burial of the shattered bodies of Peralta and his fellows was conducted by Agustin and one of the Franciscan lay brothers. Sancho was among the last of the dwindling band of Holy Ones who, by now, were resigned to martyrdom. After the brief committal and interment the Spaniards were conducted back to their various huts. Iago was sensible of the wisdom and the rationale of the Chamorros, but he was disturbed by the absence at the Mass of Calcagorta and the remaining handful of Basques, sensing that they were meditating trouble. Also missing from the obsequies of Peralta and his last companions in arms was Don Baldivieso de los Arrocheros.

Iago was at a loss to know quite what had happened to the deranged merchant. Consequently he charged Ximenez with discovering the whereabouts of these lost souls in the knowledge that the dwarf, closer in stature to the native Chamorros, had in the days he had lived among them established a curious rapport with the indigenous population.

'Ximenez find out more in one day than proper-fella find out in a whole year,' he said to Ah Fong who, in her sensitive and intuitive way, knew that of the three of them it was Iago himself whose life was in the greatest danger. Ah Fong felt this exposure acutely; although she knew she might outlive her beloved husband, she could not exist without him in any of the strange worlds into which he had led her since their betrothal in the far-off province in which she was born.

Not that she resented this; on the contrary, she knew that Iago's lust had saved her from being sent into a brothel, or sold to an old mandarin as an amusing bauble for a senile imperial official. Iago, the long-nosed *fan kwai*, had graced her life with something beyond the grasp of her imagination and, coming from a land and culture where life was cheap, she worshipped her lover in a manner peculiar to herself.

Iago comprehended something of this, but not the depth to which it extended. Yet this curious relationship had made itself manifest to many during the protracted labours of the *Santa Margarita*, exciting most of all an envy in many male bosoms, among them Calcagorta and Don Baldivieso de los Arrocheros. Calcagorta, a man of deep passions and shallow convictions, had regarded Iago's revealed love with a simple, pure jealousy. He not only lusted after women in a general sense, he lusted after a love as specific as that which clearly existed between the *sobrasaliente* Don Iago Fernandez and the beautiful Chinese butterfly who had emerged from the ambiguous chrysalis that had come aboard at Cavite. For this simple reason Calcagorta had embraced the notion of Iago as a Portuguese spy with enthusiasm. A man who dissembled over the sex of his 'servant' was clearly complex enough not to be trusted. Joanes de Calcagorta was a man for whom the simple rule of cause and effect ran no deeper than the combustion in a saker's chamber. In fact, just as his gunner's mind gave no thought to the moral issue of the target at which he aimed, he had no interest in any evidence to support the contention that Iago was a spy. It did not much matter to him whether or not the stranger who had come aboard at the last minute at Cavite was engaged in espionage or not. Indeed since the two kingdoms that shared a peninsula had been united, the assertion was extreme and unlikely. The fact that anti-Lusitanian prejudice had been born in Calcagorta from boyhood stood as one prop to his contention. The other rested upon the fact that Iago had demonstrably practised a deception and lied about the sex of his supposed 'servant'. Such 'facts' allied to envy were sufficient to damn him in Calcagorta's eyes.

For Don Baldivieso matters were incomparably simpler: Iago possessed what he himself had lost and there was no justice in the comparison. Arrocheros had noticed a lack of sincerity in Iago's devotions, instinctively divining a distance between the man's true intellect and his faith. Arrocheros was, after all, a man who made his living from bargaining, of reading a face and making an assumption informed by experience. He was also a devout Catholic whose devotion embraced the sacerdotal fear of nonconformity and feared the workings of the Holy Office. Moreover, devotion to the one true faith required proof of zeal. Such massive considerations rose to the top of a troubled mind. That he was unhinged after the tragic death of his lovely wife only increased these natural – almost instinctual – tendencies. Like an old man whose age appears to confirm wisdom but only actually exposes hitherto hidden qualities, Arrocheros read Iago as a man distinct from the normal.

If this hypothesis needed any further confirmation it lay in the isolation of Iago, his wife and his unspeakably odious dwarf. Arrocheros fastidiously reasoned to himself – and anyone else who would listen – that evidence of apostasy or something worse existed under their very noses. Look how this Iago and his crew of familiars were immune from any interference from the heathen, evil, unchristian Chamorro. These black devils were the Devil's spawn and see: this Iago lay among them like a brother! What more condemnatory evidence did one want to suggest witchcraft and a cogent explanation for all their troubles?

In the hours of boredom and inactivity forced upon the survivors of the wreck of the *Santa Margarita* such notions took avid root. No one except Olivera recalled the stalwart duties undertaken by the *sobrasaliente*, particularly after the pilot-major, Juan Lorenzo, had been washed overboard. And as their numbers reduced, they formed into two camps: those whose natural allegiance led them to cling to that other wreckage, the institutions of Rey Felipe II and his new captain-general, Joanes de Calcagorta; and those who regarded Don Iago Fernandez as the last of the true gentlemen who had shipped out of Cavite aboard the *Santa Margarita*.

As the representatives of the most advanced society in Western Europe, it might be supposed that the Spanish survivors of the wreck of the *Santa Margarita* would have reviewed their situation and seen the benefits attending it. Not only had they found refuge on the very route of east-bound shipping where rescue was only a matter of time, but – had they possessed the wit to perceive it – their treatment at the hands of the Chamorro people was not entirely unkind. Only, as the subtler Iago had realized thanks to his long sojourn at the hands of the alien Chinese, when Spanish behaviour failed to conform to what their hosts required and expected, was punishment meted out. What the Chamorro visited upon their unwelcome guests was not the murder the Spaniards took it for, but execution for unacceptable acts. Such a course of action was not merely a punishment for the transgressor, but a warning to the others. It puzzled the Chamorros that this obvious and condign message did not appear comprehensible to the Spaniards, despite the clear and deliberate escalation of horror in the method of each execution, and the involvement of as many men as ought to have made them realize the entire population supported the action. Help, the Chamorros intended the Spaniards to understand, was conditional upon their absolute obedience to the rules of conduct prevailing in Chamorro society.

Thus those whose islands had been named by the Spanish navigators for the thieves who inhabited them sought to impose their will upon the human flotsam cast up upon their shores. Nor was the severity of that first example of the bludgeoning of the men in the boat of boxes misplaced. On the contrary its immediate and deterrent effect was deemed absolutely necessary by the tribal chiefs. The Chamorro people had been too often the victims of the casual cruelty of the passing Spanish who, landing from their enormous ships with their great hulls, huge sails, fluttering banners and fire-spitting sides, sought to make them kneel and pay respect to the image of a tortured man nailed to a cross. And when one of their hideous and malodourous company, beyond himself with deprivation and inflamed with lust, raped one of their women, they were astonished when a party of steel-clad arquebusiers shot the six men who beat him to death for his crime. From such major violent encounters to the petty cheating that went on in trade transactions, the Chamorro formed a deep pool of grievance and resentment which made it the more remarkable that they gave an inch of room in their huts to the scarecrows arriving at Çarpana in their battered *não*.

Only the oddly habited religious, who tenaciously clung to the distasteful image of the tortured man nailed to his cross and who sought to learn their language and their ways, earned any respect and persuaded the Chamorros that not all Spaniards acted with such high-handed arrogance. But even these hooded and habited strangers insisted upon the destruction of their own gods and the incomprehensible superimposition of the dying martyr as the one true God. Moreover, though this was a further incomprehensible aspect of the strangers' religion, this aspect of the sole True God was but one leg of a three-legged combination they puzzled over called the Holy Trinity.

To the Chamorro, death was extinction in this world, and they could only try and understand if it was this insistence on the veneration of a crucified man that moved the visitors to such contempt of themselves.

The view of the remnant Spaniards clinging to Calcagorta as their captain-general was very different. After their protracted ordeal at sea their arrival at Çarpana was at once a blessing and a curse. It did not seem the safe refuge that it promised, for their vicious reception at the hands of the Chamorros and the ambivalent way in which they had been treated left them profoundly uncertain. This sense was heightened by the weakened state to which they had been reduced, increasing their susceptibility to paranoia. The realization that their lives depended entirely upon the goodwill of the despised 'Indians' deepened their impotence but increased their desire to recover the mastery of their fate.

Some might have argued that the final workings of the tragedy demonstrated the ultimate perversity of man's supposed virtues, for it arose from a collective desire to strive against the perceived hostility of providence. But, just as death is separated from life by the integrity of a fragile membrane or the uncertainty inherent in the perfectly sequential timing of a heartbeat, so too is civilization divided from barbarism by the turn of a word, or a phrase, or the imperatives of blood and discipline.

Other than Iago, Ah Fong and Ximenez, living in the hut of the fisherman who had befriended them, the handful of remaining Spaniards still in Atetito were domiciled in the huts near that of Calcagorta. All were Basques who saw in this specific and tribal reduction a mark of God's favour. Their original leader, Juan Martinez de Guillestigui, had paid the sacrificial price for their survival and there were those who now whispered that this was not unlike the sacrifice of Christ. Such arguments gained credibility from their isolation and fear as much as from the results, both physical and mental, of the privations they had endured. From this part-mystical, part-blasphemous and part-visceral consensus they sought a means of re-empowering themselves.

It was Don Baldivieso de los Arrocheros who provided the catalyst to fuse aspiration with conclusion. Alone among the castaways, Arrocheros seemed impervious to any attempt the Chamorros made to control him. With his abstracted air and torn finery he simply shoved past any warrior intent upon obstructing him and so amused were the Chamorros by his behaviour that, making the gesture by which they indicated insanity, they let him go as a harmless curiosity, evidence of Spanish inferiority, to be ridiculed by the women and children. At first he wandered from Atetito to the other villages and tried lodging with the few Spanish quartered there. At Pago he found Olivera, pale and sick, his legs still swollen and wracked with pain. The old Chamorro woman who had taken Olivera in and looked after him indicated where Arrocheros might sleep and brought him food, only to shoo him away next morning. He went without any outward sign of resentment, shambling back along the path towards Atetito followed by a small barking dog and a handful of children, muttering to himself as he went. In time he settled upon a routine. Every morning he would walk to Pago and see Olivera, merely squatting to stare at the wretched pilot and defying the assiduously tender old woman's curses. Then he would amble to the southern extremity of Atetito where Iago lived.

Iago went often to sea with the fisherman. He had come to admire the skill of the Chamorro at catching fish and quickly learned that his own help was appreciated so that they began to communicate and in doing so established a simple friendship. More personally satisfying to Iago was the discovery that the proa – with its outrigger alternately lifting and kissing the glittering surface of the tropical sea and its triangular sail full of wind – sped faster than he could have imagined possible for any boat. Caught up in this experience, enjoyed daily except when the weather threatened and the surf ran so high that it broke over the wreck of the *Santa Margarita*, Iago paid little attention to the concerned reports given him by Ah Fong or Ximenez at the equally quotidian appearances of Arrocheros.

The madman would sit squatting a little distance outside the hut throughout the heat of the day, simply staring at Ah Fong and Ximenez as they came and went. He appeared to mutter ceaselessly and seemed impervious to the natives' taunts or to the floods of abuse that from time to time a frustrated Ximenez would fling at Arrocheros in an attempt to drive him away. Then finally, and entirely in his own time, Arrocheros would rise and wander off into the undergrowth from where, an hour or two later, he would emerge, heading for the huts of the Basques.

He came here, night after night, to sleep outside the hut in which Agustin was quartered. He would kneel in prayer alongside the last of the Discalced Franciscan brothers, devoutly telling his rosary and praying for the souls of Doña Catalina and the miraculous baby Francisco de los Arrocheros who had risen miraculously from the dead, Christ-like in his innocence.

Such devotion was a mere mask, for it brought him no comfort. Malice festered within Don Baldivieso, stirred by the imbalance of his reason, and it found form in a vast and consuming animus against the man he knew as Don Iago Fernandez. So audibly, eloquently and obviously in his nightly prayers did Arrocheros utter his apparently heartfelt supplications that Don Iago's sins should be forgiven that Agustin grew increasingly intrigued. Arrocheros, in pleading that the Almighty should recognize the great contribution made by Iago Fernandez in the preservation of them all during the *Santa Margarita*'s disastrous voyage, adumbrated a great sin attaching to the hero.

Eventually the Franciscan could no longer hold his tongue and invited Arrocheros to confess. In seeking a state of grace the merchant perjured his soul and bore false witness, though he had gleaned the supposed evidence – or most of it – from long and patient observation. The man they knew as Iago was, Arrocheros assured Agustin, an impostor and a Protestant. He had little absolute proof of these facts but they found resonance in Agustin's mind with certain doubts cast by Fray Mateo Marmolejo when they were discussing the state of Iago's soul and his relationship with the odd Chinese hermaphrodite with whom he lived.

Of this enigmatic figure, whose revelation as a woman had deeply troubled the celibate Franciscans, Arrocheros had concrete information. She was without doubt a witch; he had himself watched her go through a daily ritual, a ritual which set aside the sacrament of her Christian baptism.

'And what is this blasphemous act?' Agustin asked with outward patience and inner turmoil.

'She worships at a shrine of devils. She keeps it hidden, a small thing which opens like a miniature altarpiece revealing in scarlet and yellow and blue and gold the most hideous of devils who . . . who . . .' Arrocheros spluttered in his outrage, his tongue coated with white saliva, and spittle frothing from his mouth.

'Who what, my son?' cajoled Agustin with the patience of the inquisitor.

'Who . . . who . . . who . . .' Arrocheros almost grunted with sexual fervour as he sought to process the images that rushed through his imagination. 'Who fuck . . . fuck . . . fuck with coiling dragons!' he managed at last.

After a pause, during which Arrocheros's violent breathing subsided, Agustin asked, 'And is there anything else you wish to tell me of her?'

Arrocheros nodded. 'She makes curious characters on leaves with soot and then lights them, muttering incantations . . .'

Agustin drew in his breath sharply, his eyes lighting with fervour as he crossed himself. Arrocheros copied him, warming to his subject and watching the Franciscan in the hope of encouragement.

'And there is . . .'

'Go on, my son. These are God's words, not your own.'

'There is the dwarf, Ximenez. He is her familiar.'

'I see. You have evidence?'

Arrocheros nodded. Watching daily, Arrocheros had observed the close relationship that had grown up between Ximenez and Ah Fong, fostered by the long hours of Iago's absence at sea. Not that the slightest impropriety took place between them but in helping the fisherman's wife by tending the fire, cleaning the simple clay pots, washing clothes and attending to the primitive tasks of daily life, they chatted and smiled. Ximenez had never been so happy, no other woman had ever touched him with the kindness of Ah Fong and he would have died for her rather than have her hurt in any way. When one day she cut herself on her leg and the wound turned septic, Ximenez opened the red and throbbing scab and sucked it until he had drained it of pus. This action, reported by Arrocheros, was clear and unambiguous evidence that Ah Fong suckled the subhuman error of God's creation.

To this Arrocheros was able to add one further and damning incident. On two occasions he had followed Ximenez into the brushwood. The dwarf moved fast through the undergrowth and outran his shambling pursuer, who stumbled awkwardly in his boots. When Arrocheros caught up with Ximenez he was kneeling at the rear of a goat.

'And what was he doing?' Agustin asked, prompting Arrocheros for an answer as he fell silent, his eyes wild and his right hand moving beneath his tattered gown.

'*It,*' Arrocheros gasped with heavy emphasis, closing his eyes and expelling his breath in a long sigh.

'You mean . . . ?' The shock of comprehension spread across Agustin's face.

'Yes,' gulped Arrocheros, falling silent and kneeling back on his haunches, his eyes closed and breathing heavily.

Agustin crossed himself but Arrocheros was lost in onanistic ecstasy. He did not say – and perhaps he had not seen – that Ximenez rose from the nanny goat's udder with a small bowl of milk for Ah Fong and the fisherman's wife. His mind had been filled then, as it was filled now, with other visions.

Agustin spent that night on his knees, seeking guidance. The long months of privation, the poor diet, the loss of his fellow Franciscans and so many of the Holy Ones in the aftermath of the wreck, combined with his own preservation as if for some purpose, to confer upon him a sense of spiritual unity with the ineffable.

He rose with the sun and went in search of Calcagorta and found the captain-general lying with one of the last surviving of the sailors' women. 'You sin, Excellency,' he said matter-of-factly after wishing the captain-general good morning.

'It is a common sin, Fray Agustin, to which I am irre-deemably attached,' Calcagorta said sharply. 'You have not come here to save me.'

'No, I have come here to tell you that we shall receive neither God's grace nor rescue until we have purified ourselves of all the evils that surround us.'

The precise meaning of this was obscure to Calcagorta. 'If you mean that trull,' he said, half-turning to indicate the hut and the woman within, but Agustin held up his hand.

'I talk not of peccadilloes, Your Excellency. The having of a wench is, for a man of your vigour, stamp and high office, a pardonable offence in the eyes of God. No, Excellency, I mean that we have laboured under a curse for too long. Fray Geronimo de Ocampo was not wrong, for we have dwelt with the most insidious of associations: a witch, her familiar and a man whose very origins we know nothing of and yet have suspected since we sailed from Cavite.'

'Iago Fernandez,' hissed Calcagorta a slow smile crossing his face. 'Iago Fernandez and his Devil's household. And to think I gave the bastard my sword.'

'Exactly, Excellency,' Agustin said, raising his crucifix to his lips. 'Arrocheros has been watching him.'

Calcagorta frowned, his pleasure seemingly modified by this revelation. 'But he is mad.'

'May not the mad see the divine, Excellency? Does their insanity not enable them to penetrate the cloisters of our closed and circumscribed minds?' He paused as a puzzled Calcagorta digested this difficult argument, adding, 'Since nothing happens without God willing it, is this not the purpose for which He turns their reason?'

'Is it?' Calcagorta asked ingenuously, staring at the friar.

Looking Calcagorta in the eye Agustin said in a low voice, 'That is what I believe.'

After a moment's consideration, Calcagorta nodded.

They came for Iago that evening as he ate his meal of fresh fish, asking him to attend a council meeting.

'Not go,' Ah Fong said quickly, but he smiled at her.

'I must,' he said simply, 'it is in our best interests.'

But as he walked off, the watching Ximenez asked, 'Why did three men come to ask the master to go to a council?'

With one hand flying to her mouth as she watched Iago marched off, Ah Fong shook her head and then, as two of the men seemed to close deliberately behind Iago's back, she drew in her breath sharply, shuddering with premonition.

At the top of the beach and within sight and sound of the wrecked ship upon which the surf pounded remorselessly, they bound Iago to a palm tree. Agustin asked him to confess his faith. Was he a Protestant? He chose not to answer under duress. Was his name truly Iago Fernandez?

'What I am is known only to God who knows all . . .'

Calcagorta swiped his heavy hand across Iago's face so that his ring cut his victim's cheek. Blood ran from the centre of a red weal seared across Iago's cheek and nose.

Agustin stepped forward. 'Leave him to God's counsel until the morning,' he urged and Calcagorta, thinking himself of the ripening thighs of the woman he had had last night and who was rapidly recovering her figure after the emaciating experience of recent weeks, nodded agreement.

'We shall see you in the morning,' he said grimly. Posting guards and followed by Agustin, the new captain-general retired for the night.

Seventeen

Ximenez

The pain of the night was beyond Iago's experience. The weight of his tired body tugged at his bonds, his muscles went into spasm, he was wracked with cramp, thirst, constriction, fear and despair. Why he had not simply confessed his devotion to the Roman Catholic faith he had no idea but he had been taken unawares and unsuspecting. Once he had expressed defiance and then showed intransigence, he had left no room for manoeuvre and knew what his fate was to be. Such thoughts tumbled through his mind until increasing waves of pain occluded them altogether.

In the first, excruciating hours, as daylight leached out of the western sky and the tropical night rolled over him, he knew that Ximenez lurked in the offing, for he heard the dwarf's foul abuse as the attentive guards drove him away. Slowly, however, the pain altered from specific torments to a general, overwhelming agony and he slipped in and out of consciousness as the indifferent constellations marched overhead.

He rallied at first light, his tongue thick in his mouth, his head so exceptionally full that he thought it might simply burst, but then he fainted again. Involuntarily a viscous urine trickled down his leg; later it attracted insects and flies. As he woke to full daylight the bells of hell itself seemed to ring in his ears.

The guards had been relieved at midnight and they remained awake and alert, so that a watchful Ximenez was unable to do anything to help. The faithful dwarf remained within yards of his master throughout the night but at daylight, as the Spaniards stirred in the adjacent huts, he withdrew to await events. After a further hour, during which Ximenez could hear but not see what was happening and therefore remained in ignorant concealment, Calcagorta called a muster of his Basque henchmen. Expecting them to move down to the beach, Ximenez was puzzled by the sound of them all dying away, until with a flash of intuition he realized that they had gone for Ah Fong.

He failed in a frantic attempt to work round the village and reach the fisherman's hut in time to warn her and was almost caught as he dodged the entire party as it returned with its terrified prisoner. By the time Ximenez returned to a position where he could see the tree to which Iago was lashed, they had brought Ah Fong face to face with her tortured husband.

Ximenez's heart thundered in his breast, for he was familiar with cruelty during his life in Manila and Cavite under Spanish colonial rule. The black crow of the priest would lead it, of course. With a pang Ximenez recalled that first encounter with the stranger he had come to admire, and the unguarded imprecation against priests that Don Iago had let fall from his lips.

From his hiding place in the undergrowth he could see Fray Agustin approach Iago, whose body was largely obscured by the ribbed bole of the tall coconut palm. The Franciscan, Ximenez thought, raised the crucifix to Iago's lips and then stepped back while Calcagorta, resplendent in salvaged finery and half-armour, stepped forward from the half-circle of Basques. Two of these stalwarts held Ah Fong who seemed, at this distance, an insubstantial wraith. Ximenez could see Agustin's mouth asking questions and, in a moment of obvious frustration, one of the men was sent to bring water for Iago. No attempt was made to allow him to drink; instead the bowl was thrown in his face, which made the armed men laugh and Ah Fong flinch.

What seemed like an interrogation went on for some time and then Agustin suddenly stepped back. He seemed to relinquish his prisoner just as Ximenez knew the Inquisitors of the Holy Office did when they made over their victims for execution. Calcagorta now made a gesture and the two men holding Ah Fong shoved her forward. Agustin, facing Iago, gestured towards her and then appeared to be waiting for an answer. All present seemed focused for some time upon Iago's face which Ximenez, far behind the tree, could not see. Then the spell broke and Ah Fong was forced on to her knees from behind and Calcagorta waved his arm as though giving an order. A man stepped forward and ripped the now grubby grey silk from Ah Fong's shoulders, exposing her breasts. Ximenez could hear her scream and then watched as she was lugged to her feet and frogmarched to an adjacent palm. Before tying her to the tree, where in order to be seen by Iago she was sideways on to Ximenez, the remainder of her clothing was torn from her slender body.

It was obvious what would happen to her as men shuffled forward, appearing to draw lots by means of straws picked off the ground. At one point Agustin came forward and tried to intervene and Ximenez concluded that Iago – confronted with Ah Fong's victimization – had acquiesced in whatever Agustin asked of him. It was too late to stop the collective move to dishonour the Chinese woman.

As the first man approached, loosening his breeches to the catcalls of his mates, Ximenez drew in his breath.

'No!' he whispered, suppressing the natural cry of the outraged, the tears hot on his cheeks. Falling on to his knees and easing the long knife he kept in his belt, he began to inch forward faster and faster as Ah Fong's cries rent the morning air. As he moved between and in the shadow of the tall trees Ximenez had no idea how many men spent themselves, only that Ah Fong – the most gracious lady he had ever known and the only woman who had treated him as a human being – was being repeatedly violated. In the last seconds of his stealthy approach, nothing of which had been suspected by the distracted Spaniards, Ximenez was aware of the feral smell. Like the dogs whose acquaintance his fellow men had compelled him to make, he suddenly found the stink triggered a reaction. He was on his feet, the knife in his hand, his short, powerful legs covering the few yards out of the shadow of the palms in less time than it took to draw the attention of the lusting crowd. He crashed into the bulk of Pedro Ruiz de Olalde as the sergeant-major reached orgasm. Ximenez thrust the knife deep into the man's pink belly and heaved it upwards, extracting it as Olalde fell back, his eyes an astonished and confused mixture of exquisite sensation. Leaving his tumescence inside Ah Fong and his steaming entrails trailing in the wake of his fall, he fell on to his back.

The queue of men behind him saw the rabid form of the dwarf as Ximenez turned towards Ah Fong.

Crying, 'Forgive me!' he cut her throat to the spine.

The cry of horror that this threw up from the assembled men was the first of a hue and cry that followed Ximenez as he dashed back into the cover of the palm grove, dodging away under the leafy canopy, his sturdy legs rapidly increasing the distance between him and his pursuers. Not all followed, and after half a mile the pursuit ended.

'We shall catch him.'

'That little bastard cannot hide . . .'

'There is nowhere he can go.'

The muttering among the discomfited pursuers, most of whom had not yet taken their pleasure of the Chinese girl, soon ended. Calcagorta stood unsullied alongside an ashen-faced Agustin among those left in the guilty and immobilizing confusion of post-coital satisfaction. All stared at the dis-embowelled corpse of Olalde and the hideous wreckage of what, a moment ago, they had lusted after.

'Who told me that freak was with Olivera?'

'Arrocheros, Excellency,' someone advised.

The captain-general stared at the Franciscan, who stood looking as though he might faint. 'Is it the stink of Olalde's guts, or the shock of a naked woman that disturbs you, Father?' Calcagorta asked sarcastically.

Agustin put a hand to his mouth and turned his head away. He could not say for shame what he knew in that ghastly moment would lie in his mind's eye like a mote and accompany his nightmares for the rest of his life. Then Calcagorta addressed another question to him.

'And what of that other piece of human flotsam?' he asked the Franciscan, indicating Iago who hung in his bonds like an imitation and blasphemous re-enactment of Christ cruci-fied. 'Have you finished with him?'

'Excellency!'

Calcagorta looked up. The men who had chased the dwarf

into the forest were remerging from the shadow of the trees. Inexplicably they had all stopped and several were pointing. Calcagorta turned to see what they were indicating.

Behind them the beach was dark with Chamorro warriors. They were advancing slowly in perfect silence; some wore elaborate feather-plumed headdresses; all bore spears.

'Jesus Christ,' breathed Calcagorta, crossing himself and lugging out his sword. 'To me, men, rally around me or we are all lost!'

Behind him he heard Fray Agustin begin to pray as the men under the trees ran forward. Those still stupefied by the sight of the body of the woman they had just violated turned away from the horror. The Spaniards closed on their captain-general and waited for the Chamorro attack.

Iago had no perfect recollection of that morning beyond a vague memory of sunlight following the agonized hours of the night and something terrible happening after water had been thrown over him. He had a vague recollection around a sudden appearance of Ah Fong, but much of this remained mercifully lost beneath the pressing preoccupation of pain. Only when the noise of the furious fighting began did he stir and rally.

Outnumbered by the Chamorros, Calcagorta's stand was – judged by the odds – a demonstration of the man's raw courage. He and the last of his companions fought furiously for their lives as instinct and their martial training had conditioned them to. All were wounded before they were killed, and though some died quickly others had ends as painful and humiliating as that of Ah Fong.

In the end it was the stink of it all that finally revived Iago, who raised his head at last to regard the carnage strewn about him. The stench, the steam from the body of Olalde and others opened up by Chamorro weapons, the buzz of the flies that this shambles attracted and the sight of the Chamorros picking over the fallen enemy made him think he was dead and this was Hell. He was, he thought, on the edge of the Inferno and the brown and near-naked men who walked among the dead and dying appeared like so many under-devils, Satan's henchmen in quest of souls to burn. Among this extraordinary sight he failed to distinguish the pallid form of Ah Fong as she remained, head lolling to one side, tied to the tree to his right.

Instead his returning consciousness – insofar as it could cope with anything other than an all-consuming pain – became occupied with the crowd which grew around him. He was vaguely aware that this was not the first such gathering, but that it was different from the last. Slowly his reason asserted itself and he recalled that what was missing was a threatening figure and then, as if by some magical process, that figure was shoved forward.

Somehow Iago appreciated that matters were different now. The black-habited man was no longer haranguing him. Instead he was on his knees with two of the under-devils bent over him. And the glitter of armour, the red smiles of lips half-concealed by beards and the swaggering, slashed-silken splendour was absent from this crowd. This assembly was bigger too, indeed it seemed to grow constantly as it washed up to stare at the disembowelled figure of Olalde at Iago's feet.

'Is that Olalde?' he asked at last, but his voice was only a cracked whisper and in the general noise of excitement no one heard him, not even the kneeling Agustin who was confronting his own crucifix which one of the two be-plumed men beside him was holding in his face.

It took some time before the terrified Agustin realized the blasphemous connection the ignorant savages were making between the Saviour of Mankind and the heretic bound to the natural stake God had planted for his execution. To the Franciscan the similarity of Iago to the crucified Christ was far less obvious than to the Chamorros. But in due course he made the intellectual connection, feeling a spark of understanding pride before roundly and vehemently denying the appalling and erroneous comparison.

Shaking his head and expressing his negative horror so violently that spittle flew from his lips, Agustin felt the hands of the Chamorro release him. He fell forward, tears of fright, relief and abject misery seeping from his shut eyes on to the dry earth beneath him. Stepping towards the palm tree, the Chamorros cut Iago's bonds so that he in turn fell forward helplessly like a sack of onions, to lie beside Agustin, their heads scarcely a foot away from each other.

This was how Ximenez and Olivera found them a little later, after the crowd of Indians had dispersed. During the fighting the escaping Ximenez had run to Olivera's village and roused the pilot from his sickbed against the vociferous protests of the old woman. Helping Olivera to his feet, Ximenez explained himself and Olivera – with a mighty effort of that indomitable will that had brought the *Santa Margarita* to her final anchorage – rose to the demands of friendship. Hardly able to walk at first, Olivera made better progress as his circulation revived and he felt the benefit of the exercise.

'Is it not ironic,' he gasped as he tried to hurry after the capering and impatient Ximenez, 'at the moment of Don Iago's extremity, you have done me good.'

'But I killed the master's wife,' wailed Ximenez, dashing the tears from his twisted face. He was beside himself with the urgency of the occasion, furious that Olivera could hobble no faster, but aware that only Olivera could do anything to save Iago's life as well as his own. He had brought the pilot back with him in the vain hope that Olivera could mediate. On their way they had met the fleeing Sancho, the last Franciscan lay brother, and by now the very last of the Holy Ones. Seeing Ximenez approaching, Sancho had stood stock-still in terror for his life at the hands of the dwarf, before falling to his knees and crossing himself repeatedly until reassured by Ximenez that he meant him no harm. Neither Ximenez nor Olivera understood what Sancho meant by his babbling account of the Chamorro attack until Ximenez drew Olivera's attention to the faint noise of shouting coming from the beach ahead of them.

By the time they found the scene of the bloody skirmish only a few of the older men and some women remained on the beach, stripping the dead Spanish and carrying off the bodies of a dozen or so Chamorros. Olivera recoiled in horror at the sight of Ah Fong and Olalde and at first they thought both Agustin and Iago were dead, until the former moved and Sancho rushed to his side.

'Get them water,' Olivera commanded, almost restored to his old, energetic self and adding 'At once,' as the lay brother hesitated.

Agustin came to, staring at the head of Iago, whose eyes opened only when Ximenez moistened his lips. With infinite care the dwarf patiently worked his master up into a sitting position with his back against the tree to which he had so recently been tied. Iago cried out with the agony of returning circulation and the shooting pains that every move caused but at last, as he settled against the palm bole, the waves of pain began to subside.

It was then that he saw Ah Fong.

Arrocheros walked on to the scene of the carnage he had caused to find Ximenez, Agustin and Sancho burying the severed body of the slender Chinese girl. He laughed to see Don Iago Fernandez sitting weeping against the palm tree, and laughed even louder to see the busy dwarf labouring furiously to disguise the stream of tears running down his own face. Had Ximenez not dropped his knife in his retreat from his mercy killing of Ah Fong, he would have plunged it into Don Baldivieso's stomach and disembowelled the merchant as he had the sergeant-major, but Agustin and Sancho restrained him and in due course Arrocheros simply squatted and watched. Kneeling at Iago's side Olivera, who could do little more, occupied himself chafing Iago's limbs. Although still in pain from his legs, he was no longer a prostrated man.

As the three men finished Ah Fong's burial and crossed themselves for the last time over the low mound under which she lay buried, Iago looked up.

'Tell me what has happened.'

The three of them looked from one to another and then at the ground. Olivera shook his head. 'Don Iago . . .' he began but faltered and stared out over the battleground of the bloody beach with its corpses already crisping in the hot sunshine of noontide.

'Ah Fong . . .' a puzzled Iago began, a memory emerging from his pain like a ghost rising from marsh gas, 'what happened to Ah Fong?'

At this plaintive query Ximenez shuffled like a dog across the ground between Ah Fong's grave and his master, burying his head against Iago and almost nuzzling up to him in an animal act of abject submission as his back heaved with mighty sobs.

'Master, oh, master . . . Forgive me, master!' he sobbed.

Iago shook his head with incomprehension. 'What is there to forgive?' he asked falteringly.

'I killed her, master. I, the dwarf Ximenez, spawn of Satan and eater of dog's turds . . . It was I who killed her . . .'

'Why should you kill her?'

'My son,' said Agustin, crawling forward, 'we were trying to save your soul and the soldiers brought the heathen child before you to persuade you to confess and declare your faith.'

'Heathen child?' Iago frowned, his intelligence awakening with the outrage he felt at the friar's words. 'You had her christened . . . Margarita.'

'But my son, she remained a heathen at heart . . .'

But Iago was no longer listening. 'I remember,' he broke in, suddenly moving with the ferocity of the recollection and wincing with the pain of it. Ximenez drew back on his haunches, still crouching like a dog but turning his head towards the priest. 'I remember,' went on Iago, his voice distant. 'You had her raped!' His voice rose with the horror of it.

'No, no! No, it was not I who ordered the men to violate her,' Agustin said, trembling, 'it was Olalde and Calcagorta who did that.'

'But you knew that was what would happen,' said Olivera, himself imagining the scene. 'You deliberately collaborated and encouraged those bastards to goad the men to an outrage.'

'She was a heathen child,' Agustin said unctuously.

'Did you not baptize her?' Olivera asked, pressing Iago's argument.

'She was guilty of apostasy,' Agustin replied.

'What do you mean?'

'Arrocheros saw her praying to her heathen gods. She was no more a Christian than the Indians here.'

'You used her like dog's meat,' Ximenez said with a quiet menace.

Agustin looked at him, as though obliged to recognize the distasteful duty of acknowledging the dwarf's part in this. 'No,' he said with an air of triumphant intellectual superiority, 'it was you who treated her like meat . . .'

He got no further, for with a screech Ximenez sprang at Agustin's throat, his powerful hands closing about the Franciscan's scrawny neck, his thumbs pressed hard on his windpipe as they flailed together in the sandy dust.

It took Sancho and Olivera all their strength to prise Ximenez off Fray Agustin. As they struggled on the ground before him Iago tried to remember what had happened. Nearby the squatting Arrocheros laughed wildly.

A hundred yards away a group of half a dozen curious Chamorros turned away, talking quietly among themselves.

It was ten days later when they found the body of Agustin. Having confessed himself to Sancho he appeared to have expired alone on the beach during that night. No one knew precisely what had killed him, though he died with the marks of Ximenez's thumbs imprinted upon his throat. Some said he had taken his own life, others that death had claimed his spirit naturally. No one knew his age and none of the survivors other than Sancho regretted his passing.

Although there were rumours of other Spaniards who had run or been taken to distant parts of Çarpana, there were now only five men left at Atetito. Iago had asked the fisherman if Olivera could come and live with them and the men had built a second hut to accommodate them all. To do this they had salvaged some timbers cast up along the shore from the *Santa Margarita*, which was now breaking up. Olivera came with the old woman, who still insisted upon looking after him. No one could explain why she had attached herself to him, but she seemed willing to skivvy for them all. Her presence gratified Ximenez once his conscience was eased by Iago's forgiveness.

Iago said little beyond occasionally patting Ximenez upon the shoulder. He was increasingly given to long, withdrawn silences, but he uttered never a word of reproach to the dwarf and seemed content that Ximenez had saved the lovely Ah Fong from a prolonged defilement. It was a subject no one mentioned and Ximenez himself remained uncertain whether Iago truly understood exactly what had happened. In the days that followed they returned to the fisherman's hut and picked up the threads of their lives, the Chamorros apparently tolerating this tiny rump of the crew of the great ship that was falling apart so conveniently upon their doorsteps.

Sancho was a diffident addition to the trio. As one of the Holy Ones, he had had little to do with Iago or Olivera, and his acquaintance with Ximenez during the voyage was distanced by sanctity and contempt. Nevertheless, he mustered a Christian forbearance of his new companions and, out of a genuine compassion, brought Arrocheros back into the fold.

At first he would not come and stuck to squatting outside the little compound but Sancho gently persuaded him first to eat and then to sleep with them so that gradually his mumblings grew less, his laughter less wild and on one memorable evening he leaned forward after they had eaten their meal around the fire and tapped Iago upon the shoulder.

'I understand, Don Iago, that you lost your wife.' Caught by the formality of the delivery and the remark itself, the look of poignant agony that crossed his master's face made Ximenez almost mad with anger. The common embargo on the subject was not to be so rawly exposed by the mad Arrocheros. Ximenez looked quickly at Iago, who stared at Arrocheros with a curious, longing look that Ximenez had never seen before and could not interpret.

'That is correct, Don Baldivieso,' Iago said, after mastering the heavy pressure of emotion that Arrocheros's words conjured up. Looking at the merchant he sensed a change in the lunatic, and nodded. 'She was killed . . .' Iago faltered a moment and then added, 'as was yours, Don Baldivieso.'

'Yes, Don Iago,' Arrocheros said calmly, 'so was mine. It is a misfortune that afflicts some men. A sad business, I dare say . . .' And without explaining to which of the widowings he referred, Arrocheros stared sadly into the fire.

That evening was doubly memorable because it was also the eve of their rescue. Next morning they were about to attend to the day's labours when they were aware of the shouts of a running group of Chamorros. A moment later Iago's fisherman friend burst into their hut, gabbling the words that Iago understood to mean a great ship like the *Santa Margarita*.

The *não* had appeared off the southern coast and word had been passed north to Atetito. With bursting hearts the five survivors struggled south as fast as their legs could carry them, arriving on the shores of a shallow bay beyond which lay a ship as splendid as the *Santa Margarita* had once been. Drawn up upon the golden strand lay one of her boats and a group of Spanish gentlemen in morions and cuirasses, attended by seamen and surrounded by a large crown of Chamorros. At the appearance of the ragged survivors the Chamorros parted and, on the rim of the gathering, the five men stopped short and stared. An unnatural silence fell upon the crowd.

After all their hardships it seemed impossible that this day had come. Even Iago welcomed the sight of the dark, bearded faces and beyond them the flutter of the pendants and ensign of Imperial Spain.

One of the Spanish officers broke away and strode towards them. He wore thigh boots of red Morocco leather, red hose and doublet and breeches of black silk, slashed with dark purple. His blue steel cuirass was alive with Moorish decoration and a high curved morion shadowed his face from the burning sun. With a gentle tinkling of spurs and the faint noise of his sword belt and scabbard that protruded behind him like a peacock's tail he scrunched through the sand towards them.

'I am Don Rivera de Maldonado,' he said, swinging half round and gesturing a gloved hand at the distant *não*, 'commander of the *Santo Tomas*. And you?'

'Antonio de Olivera, surviving pilot of the *Santa Margarita*, bound from Cavite towards Acapulco,' Olivera declaimed, making his bow and introducing the others. 'Don Iago Fernandez, a *sobrasaliente*; Fray Sancho of the Discalced Franciscans; Don Baldivieso de los Arrocheros, a merchant, and this is Ximenez, Don Iago's servant.'

They bowed each in turn, including Ximenez, whose obeisance was greeted with a laugh. 'We are back in civilization,' he remarked to his master as they walked down to the *Santo Tomas*'s boat for passage out to the anchored ship.

'God help us,' replied the man men called Iago Fernandez.

They were regarded as old men aboard the *Santo Tomas*. Well treated and accommodated, they recovered such of their health as God returned to them. They said little about their ordeal to those among the *Santo Tomas*'s company who questioned them. A few rumours were started but these were quashed by Don Rivera de Maldonado, and for an account of the voyage most were willing to listen to the loquacious Sancho.

After they had returned to Manila, they learned how their consort the *San Geronimo*, which had abandoned them in the Embocadero, had had no more luck than the *Santa Margarita*. She too had been caught in the same extraordinary sequence of typhoons but had put back, only to be wrecked on the Philippine coast of Catanduanes. Later still, they heard how, the following year, the remaining survivors had been taken off Çarpana by the *Jesus Maria*, commanded by one Don Pedro de Acuña.

In after years, when Iago Fernandez and Arrocheros had gone into partnership and lived together in a house near the rice-market outside the Parian Gate of Intramuros Manila, they only occasionally referred to the events that had joined their lives, rarely remarking on the differences which had once lain between them, or how one had destroyed the happiness of the other. They absorbed themselves in a lucrative trade in silks, pearls and jade, and when they touched upon the shared ordeal of their younger years it was usually to bemoan the losses of thousands of *reales*' worth of such merchandise that lay amid the limestone reefs of the distant island of Çarpana. Never did they touch upon that which each had truly lost.

If in festive mood, they would speculate on a fantastical voyage they would make in which they would employ the Chamorros to dive and bring up the treasures lying in the sand among the rotting timbers of the *Santa Margarita*. But the reminiscence cut too near to the bone to be pursued; it was an old man's dream and as such, they sometimes wondered if it had ever really happened.

They had given their account of the voyage on oath to Maldonado, who acted as *oidor* and took down their depositions. To the surprise of all, the statement of Arrocheros was the most lucid. In giving it he seemed to have fully recovered his wits and it was as though every event had burned itself indelibly into his mind. In contrast, Olivera and Iago, having been so busy with the survival of the ship at the time, had trouble recollecting the precise sequence of events.

Ximenez was not asked, but he knew that the circumstances of Ah Fong's death and his master's ordeal had cast a long shadow over Iago's memory and it was not in the faithful Ximenez's interests to rummage in that dark repository. For his part the dwarf remembered everything as though it had occurred the previous day, but he kept his own counsel.

Olivera did not reach Manila, but died and was buried at sea, where he belonged. As for Sancho, it was he who having made a short statement to Maldonado, and satisfied the curious among the *Santo Tomas*'s crew, afterwards gave a fuller but less objective account to a fellow member of his order. Fray Juan Pobre faithfully recorded their conversations in a lurid but partial tale in which the evils of the apostate Guillestigui became the consequence of Ocampo's curse and doomed all aboard the *Santa Margarita* except those redeemed by the Grace of Almighty God.

Little more was added by those rescued in 1602 by the *Santo Tomas* other than accounts of the horrors of oppression by the Chamorros of the Ladrones Islands. Sadly, by the time of their rescue little goodwill existed between the two racial groups and few elsewhere were interested in further details of the fate of the *Santa Margarita*.

As his master aged, Ximenez used to vet his papers, seeking out those involuntarily signed 'Jacob van Salingen' with a worrying persistence that suggested Iago sought some way back to his past. It was a thing that was never mentioned and Ximenez remembered on that first encounter how Iago had had trouble recalling the Spanish for elephant. It was at that moment the dwarf knew he was not Spanish. Only after Iago's death did Ximenez raise the matter with Arrocheros, who admitted that he had long suspected his partner was no Spaniard. The revelation ensured that Ximenez transferred his loyalty to his master's associate for the remainder of Arrocheros's life. And for his part Arrocheros, having no other relative living in the Philippines, assigned the dwarf as his heir.

Ximenez survived them all, a richly dressed dwarf who dwelt outside the Parian Gate and dealt in silks, pearls and jade, and died one day on his knees before a small heathen shrine in red and gold and blue in which twined fierce gods and dragons. Those who discovered his body remembered the story of the *Santa Margarita* and said, with absolute certainty, that it had been part of the treasure carried aboard the ill-fated ship. Others thought so cheap a thing could never have been part of what was regarded as a cargo worthy of being a viceroy's dream.

Hearing of the curiosity and of the reports insisting upon the corruption inherent in the images, the Archbishop of Manila ordered the thing to be sought out and destroyed. Afterwards the house was to be exorcized and the body of the dwarf burned.

Author's Note

This novel is an imaginative reconstruction based upon what we know of the ill-fated and disastrous voyage of the *Santa Margarita*. Most of the characters, Guillestigui, Calcagorta, Olalde, the pilots Lorenzo and Olivera, the *contramaestre* Llerena, Arrocheros and others, actually existed and their characters as depicted conform to what was recorded at the time. The circumstances of Ocampo's departure, the curse, the false start to the voyage and the lateness of the season all follow the sparse record, as do the train of events which subjected both the *Santa Margarita* and the *San Geronimo* to an extraordinary sequence of typhoons and storms.

What are here known, as they were known to the Spanish, as the Ladrones Islands, are today called the Northern Marianas. Çarpana, or Zapana, is now known as Rota. It is here that the remains of the great Philippine-built Spanish *não* still lie, having slipped from the reef and settled upon a softer bottom. At the time of writing the wreck is being excavated.